SILENT CITY ON A HILL

SILENT CITY ON A HILL

Picturesque Landscapes of Memory and Boston's Mount Auburn Cemetery

BLANCHE M. G. LINDEN

with new color photography by Richard Cheek

and new black-and-white photography by Carol Betsch

University of Massachusetts Press   Amherst & Boston

in association with

Library of American Landscape History   Amherst

Printed in China

LC 2006103297
ISBN 978-1-55849-571-5

Designed by Jonathan D. Lippincott
Set in Caslon 540
Printed and bound by C&C Offset Printing Co., Ltd.

Library of Congress Cataloging-in-Publication Data
Linden, Blanche M. G., 1946–
Silent city on a hill : picturesque landscapes of memory and Boston's Mount Auburn Cemetery / Blanche M.G. Linden.
p. cm.
"Revised and redesigned edition"—Foreword.
Includes bibliographical references and index.
ISBN-13: 978-1-55849-571-5 (pbk. : alk. paper)
ISBN-10: 1-55849-571-1 (pbk. : alk. paper)
1. Mount Auburn Cemetery (Cambridge, Mass.) 2. Cemeteries—Landscape architecture—Massachusetts—Cambridge. 3. Cambridge (Mass.)—Buildings, structures, etc. I. Library of American Landscape History. II. Title.
F73.61.M8L56 2007
929'.5097444—dc22

2006103297

British Library Cataloguing in Publication data are available.

Illustrations on page 209 reproduced by permission of the Corcoran Gallery of Art, Washington, D.C.
Fig. 10.2: Thomas Cole, *The Departure*, 1837. Gift of William Wilson Corcoran, acc. no. 69.2, oil on canvas, 39½" x 63".
Fig. 10.3: Thomas Cole, *The Return*, 1837. Gift of William Wilson Corcoran, acc. no. 69.3, oil on canvas, 39¾" x 63".

FRONTISPIECE: *Cemetery of Mount Auburn*, engraving by W. H. Bartlett, 1839. From *American Scenery; or, Land, Lake and River Illustrations of Transatlantic Nature* (London: George Virtue, 1840). Courtesy Mount Auburn Cemetery Archives.

In memory of my beloved mentor and friend Dr. Henry David Shapiro (1937–2003) as my monument to him in the spirit of Mount Auburn where students and colleagues contributed to build memorials for notable, exemplary teachers to be emulated by future generations.

CONTENTS

PREFACE

BY ROBIN KARSON

Mount Auburn Cemetery, America's first landscape executed in the Picturesque style, was laid out in 1831 on a hilly, seventy-five-acre parcel four miles west of Boston. The site was acclaimed in its own era and ever since as one of the nineteenth century's most important public places. Today Mount Auburn is a National Historic Landmark, a serene haven for birds and birdwatchers, and the final resting place of many well-known literary figures, politicians, artists, religious leaders, and landscape architects—from Henry Wadsworth Longfellow to Charles Eliot. The story of the founding and early decades of this remarkable place is told in *Silent City on a Hill.*

Blanche M. G. Linden's study of Mount Auburn began three decades ago as a doctoral dissertation at Harvard University, in which her focus was the cemetery's cultural underpinnings and the international sources on which its Picturesque design drew. *Silent City* was published in 1989 to wide acclaim and an award from the American Society of Landscape Architects. As the years passed, the first edition became increasingly rare and, as a result, expensive. The new LALH edition, which is an affordable paperback, corrects, revises, expands, and updates the original text. The revised edition also features color photographs by Richard Cheek and specially commissioned black-and-white photographs by Carol Betsch, a larger format, a new, expansive design, and a foreword by Mount Auburn president William C. Clendaniel, who describes the preservation dilemmas challenging the nondenominational and still active cemetery.

Silent City begins with a discussion of dismal urban burial places that persisted through the Middle Ages and prevailing ideas about death and nature. The narrative progresses to the eighteenth century, when liberal English travelers visited classical sites in Greece and Italy and returned to create gardens such as Stowe and Stourhead, naturalistic layouts that were intended for the cultivation of moral philosophy. Embellished by monuments and shaped by a new, modern style of design—the Picturesque—these landscapes were characterized by a rejection of linearity and guided instead by the concept of *genius loci*, the spirit of the place. The style was soon embraced by the French, and it came to shape landscapes at estates such as Ermenonville (where Rousseau is entombed), Monceau, and Désert de Retz, as well as at the cemetery of Père Lachaise, where a "cult of ancestors" was realized through secularized burial reform.

Even before the new style reached the United States, American civic leaders concerned about the lack of material commemoration in the young republic had begun to create monuments to remind citizens of the important events and political figures associated with the nation's formative years. Coincidentally, a strong demand for burial reform arose, and in both initiatives, the citizens of Boston—the Athens of America—took the lead. U.S. Associate Supreme Court Justice Joseph Story, Mount Auburn's first president, spearheaded an effort to establish the cemetery as a new form of nonprofit corporation, assisted by Dr. Jacob Bigelow, a physician who developed new uses of therapeutic plants and wrote extensively on New England flora, and General Henry A. S. Dearborn, an attorney, politician, military engineer, and leader of the Bunker Hill Monument Association. As founding president of the Massachusetts Horticultural Society, Dearborn also provided Mount Auburn's initial landscape design, drawing on extensive readings about the Picturesque and using aspects of Père Lachaise as his model. The cast of notables supporting these protagonists includes Daniel Webster, Edward Everett, and the Reverend William Ellery Channing, who were in turn encouraged by many other liberal politicians, academics, journalists, and philanthropists who focused their civic spirit and Whiggish ideas on the new cemetery.

Mount Auburn quickly became Boston's chief tourist attraction, not only for the elite, who came by carriage, but also for the working class, who arrived via new streetcar lines. While some proprietors were appalled by the seeming violation of sanctified exclusivity, others delighted in the landscape's use as pleasure grounds. Literature, guidebooks, and personal travelers' accounts spread the cemetery's fame, and Mount Auburn soon inspired other "rural" cemeteries, from Philadelphia to Brooklyn, Baltimore, Pittsburgh, Cincinnati, Louisville, and many small towns. Marveling at the popularity of the new burying grounds, the tastemaker A. J. Downing recommended them as models for public parks, the first of which was set centrally into New York City, designed by Frederick Law Olmsted and Calvert Vaux.

In addition to tracing this complex background, the new edition of *Silent City* examines changes to Mount Auburn's original Picturesque landscape, as rural and forest settings throughout were transformed into focal points that reflected the aesthetics of the "Beautiful." Half of the woodland was thinned to permit some trees to reach specimen size. Lawns were created, first in the old sense, as clearings or sunny spaces for exotic ornamentals, then as groomed greenswards and as settings for gardenesque architectural details. By the 1870s, the taste for monuments and mausoleums was turning from the neoclassical and Egyptian Revival to the more elaborate styles of the Gothic and Victorian. Linden also considers the fencing and curbing manias that came to segment the once pastoral landscape during the last part of the nineteenth century.

The LALH revised edition includes an epilogue in which Linden summarizes the many changes that have occurred at Mount Auburn in the twentieth century. As cemetery president Israel Spelman observed in 1875, "In Mount Auburn, intended as the repository of the dead of successive generations, we should expect to find, as we really do, tombs, monuments, and graves embodying the changing feelings and tastes of different periods." Illuminating the cemetery's richly intertwined layers of history, *Silent City* continues to support enlightened stewardship of them.

Many people were involved in this ambitious publication. I am particularly grateful to the excellent leaders and staff of Mount Auburn Cemetery—President William C. Clendaniel; Janet Heyward, former Vice-President of Interpretive Programs; Margaret Winslow, Curator of Historical Collections; Bree Harvey, Director of Education & Visitor Services; and the Cemetery Trustees, who generously supported work on the revised edition. I am also very grateful to Blanche M. G. Linden for revising her original text and for her passion for Mount Auburn, which sparked new understanding of this important landscape many years ago and has not diminished since.

I thank Paul Wright, retired senior editor of University of Massachusetts Press, for pointing LALH toward this project; Press director Bruce Wilcox for seeing the value in it; and Jack Harrison, for supervising production. I also thank Richard Cheek and Carol Betsch, whose fine photographs capture the spirit of this place and contribute a welcome poetic note. Finally, I am grateful to the many people of LALH whose talent and attention to detail are apparent in this fine volume: Carol Betsch, project manager; Jane Roy Brown, illustration coordinator; Mary Bellino—proofreader, fact-checker, and research savant; Amanda Heller, manuscript editor; Neil Brigham, office assistant; Martin White, indexer; and Jonathan Lippincott, our talented book designer. Thank you all.

Robin Karson
Executive Director, LALH

LALH

Library of American Landscape History produces books and exhibitions about North American landscape history. Our mission is to educate and thereby promote thoughtful stewardship of the land.

FOREWORD

BY WILLIAM C. CLENDANIEL

The publication of a revised and redesigned edition of *Silent City* is a legacy project of Mount Auburn Cemetery's 175th anniversary. This handsome new book, published by the University of Massachusetts Press in association with Library of American Landscape History, is an important event for anyone interested in American landscape history, the history of American cemeteries, or the social history of Boston. As the first North American large-scale designed landscape open to the public, Mount Auburn has significance in American history far beyond its status as the final resting place of many of the nation's intellectual, political, and entrepreneurial elite. Mount Auburn was the first landscaped cemetery in the new nation, and it served as the model for the creation of hundreds of "rural" cemeteries throughout New England and across America. The popularity of those cemeteries, and the resulting writings of such tastemakers as Andrew Jackson Downing, led directly to the creation of our public parks, starting with Central Park in New York City in the late 1850s. It is this significance that led to Mount Auburn's being named a National Historic Landmark in 2003.

Originally published in 1989 with the support of Mount Auburn Cemetery, and then being out of print for several years, *Silent City* is the seminal work on the philosophical and practical reasons why the Cemetery was created. It is an important work of scholarship that describes in depth the many currents of thought that came together in Boston in the third and fourth decades of the nineteenth century and led to Mount Auburn's founding. And it is the only detailed description of the physical and institutional growth of the Cemetery in its first four decades other than Jacob Bigelow's own *A History of the Cemetery of Mount Auburn*, published in 1859.

But *Silent City* also sheds valuable light on other aspects of American history—the early history of artistic patronage; the rise of the great Victorian-era landscaped cemeteries; the strong desire of the young republic to commemorate its heroes; the impulse to integrate European horticultural ideas into the developing continent, including the founding of one of the first in a long line of horticultural societies; and the changing attitudes toward death, burial, and commemoration. *Silent City* also includes wonderful stories of the people of Boston and New England, many of them significant figures in American history. Creating the cultural, academic, and business institutions of the new nation, they were laid to rest in this "new American landscape," and their memorials still intrigue visitors to Mount Auburn today. We are all grateful to the Library of American Landscape History and its director, Robin Karson, for making this new edition possible.

Silent City was originally published shortly after I became Mount Auburn's eleventh president, and for the last eighteen years it has been immensely valuable to me and my colleagues as we have worked to preserve the essential features of this great landscape while at the same time adapting the institution to a changing society. I believe no one can successfully plan for the future without understanding the past, and *Silent City* has provided us with historical knowledge critical to our work. In 1990 Mount Auburn's Trustees and staff began a comprehensive master planning initiative under the leadership of The Halvorson Company, with Elizabeth Vizza as project manager. Finished in 1993 and given an Honor Award by the American Society of Landscape Architects, the Master Plan was greatly aided by the research in *Silent City*. Very much in use today, the plan guides ongoing innovative designs of new interment gardens.

Finally, *Silent City* is of great value to the contemporary visitor to Mount Auburn. Unlike many historic sites, the Cemetery has no single period of significance, no one style that predominates, no single place that tells the whole story. It is an incredibly rich composition, comprising layers of landscape design that were laid down next to and on top of what went before. Mount Auburn has never been a static historic artifact of one particular generation but a growing, evolving institution and landscape. *Silent City* helps visitors decode the current landscape and explains the origins of the complexities of the historic plantings and structures that greet them today. In the new edition, contemporary color photographs by Richard Cheek and black-and-white images by Carol Betsch bring to life the vibrancy of the contemporary Mount Auburn.

Silent City also brings alive the excitement that Victorian visitors felt when they first encountered Mount Auburn. It describes how delegations from cities around the country came to see what Bostonians had created and took Mount Auburn's principles home to create their own rural cemeteries. History repeats itself today as trustees and staff from many of America's historic cemeteries journey to Mount Auburn to look at our innovative interment gardens, preservation strategies, and interpretive programs, as well as how we are gaining financial support from foundations, individuals, corporations, and government agencies to ensure Mount Auburn's preservation for future generations.

At the same time, hundreds of thousands of visitors come from all over the world—to bird-watch, take a contemplative walk, enjoy the diverse and meticulously maintained plantings, examine the monuments, visit the graves of family members or notables, paint, photograph, or conduct research in the archives. *Silent City* provided us with both the intellectual underpinning and historic images with which to help these individuals understand our 175-year history, through the visitors center in Story Chapel, audio tours, and numerous interpretive panels in the landscape showing the enormous changes that have taken place over time.

Eighteen years ago a generation of scholars and general readers alike gained a deeper understanding of one of our nation's most significant and beloved landscapes through reading the first edition of *Silent City*. We hope a new generation will gain the same understanding with this new edition and, with that understanding, will support Mount Auburn and all its progeny so that they may remain intact for future generations.

William C. Clendaniel
President, Mount Auburn Cemetery

Bigelow Chapel (1845), with Victorian-inspired lawn garden and Sphinx Civil War monument (1872). Photograph by Richard Cheek.

Maria Frances Coppenhagen monument, designed by Martin Milmore (1874), with flowering dogwoods. Photograph by Richard Cheek.

LEFT: Detail of Sphinx Civil War monument, designed by Dr. Jacob Bigelow and carved by Martin Milmore (1872).
Photograph by Richard Cheek.

RIGHT: Bulfinch family monument. The urn was originally placed in the Tontine Crescent development designed by Charles Bulfinch in downtown Boston.
Photograph by Richard Cheek.

LEFT: Magoun family monument (ca. 1850).
Photograph by Richard Cheek.

RIGHT: Homer children monument (ca. 1850).
Photograph by Richard Cheek.

James family lot with Sawyer monument in background. Photograph by Richard Cheek.

Auburn Lake. Photograph by Richard Cheek.

Halcyon Lake with Mary Baker Eddy memorial, before landscape restoration. Photograph by Richard Cheek.

Fales and Nichols monuments with view towards Willow Avenue. Photograph by Richard Cheek.

Putnam family lot with Appleton monument in background. Photograph by Richard Cheek.

Bigelow Chapel with Lawrence family lot in foreground. Photograph by Richard Cheek.

Mary Baker Eddy memorial, designed by Edgerton Swartwout (1917), detail with flowering cherry. Photograph by Richard Cheek.

Sprague family monument, detail with Spanish hyacinths. Photograph by Richard Cheek.

Gove children monument, designed by William Freedley (ca. 1850). Photograph by Richard Cheek.

Spruce Knoll, designed by Julie Moir Messervy (1995). Photograph by Richard Cheek.

Halcyon Garden, designed by Reed Hilderbrand Associates (2001). Photograph by Richard Cheek.

SILENT CITY ON A HILL

INTRODUCTION

> If we were able to go back to the elements of states and to examine the oldest monuments of their history, I doubt not that we should discover in them the primal causes of . . . the habits, the ruling passions, and, in short, all that constitutes what is called the national character.
>
> —Alexis de Tocqueville, *Democracy in America* (1832)

Like many of his era, Alexis de Tocqueville, the noted French observer of formative American society and culture, believed in the possibility of reinventing the state in republican terms and in the necessity of building monuments to epitomize and preserve civic virtue. In the new republic, the art of the painter, the sculptor, the architect, and the landscape gardener would augment and perpetuate the work of statecraft. Art, especially if commemorative, would help define the nation's history in secular terms compatible with its political ideals and their preservation. During his travels in America in the fall of 1831 through the spring of 1832, Tocqueville found that many of the young nation's leaders held beliefs similar to his own about the importance of material commemoration, being familiar with French post-Revolutionary debates on the social imperative to foster a "cult of ancestors," a pressing necessity in the wake of their iconoclastic rejection of the old order, the traditions of Church and king.[1] Americans, like the French and some English liberals before them, drew heavily on the new aesthetics and a philosophy that reached back to classical models as antidotes to the forms sanctioned by the establishment they had so recently rejected.[2]

From 1825 on, for six years before Tocqueville's visit, Bostonians had been planning to create a new funerary institution for the display of monuments of the sort that was becoming both fashionable and politically functional in England and France, first in innovative picturesque landscaped gardens and then in "rural" cemeteries. Mount Auburn Cemetery, coincidentally dedicated in the autumn of Tocqueville's visit, was designed to reflect republican taste and ideology, newly defining the nation's short history. Their motivations were both idealistic and practical. In planning America's first "rural" cemetery, the founders helped reform local burial practices at a time when those old ways were under attack as no longer desirable in the center of the burgeoning city. As an innovative, nonsectarian, nonprofit corporation, Mount Auburn embodied characteristics that Tocqueville judged distinctly American, exemplifying urban leaders' ability to organize and work through voluntary "civic associations," independent of but chartered by government, to form institutions to stabilize their society and elevate its level of culture. Bostonians proudly showed off Mount Auburn as their chief attraction, evidence of local and national worth.[3]

This book begins with an inquiry into the intellectual and aesthetic forces contributing to the design of landscapes of memory that preceded Mount Auburn's founding, including the rise through the eighteenth and early nineteenth centuries of a new historical consciousness shaped by a conjunction of larger spiritual and political trends and associated with British and American Whigs, as well as with the enlightened in France trying to stabilize their new cultures in the wake of a revolutionary iconoclasm. It then analyzes the development of America's first "rural" cemetery from its formative period into the 1870s, an era marked by the taste for a "picturesque" landscape embellished by fine architecture and monuments, all reflecting its founders' ambitions to create an exemplary cultural institution as well as an enduring and beautiful place for burial and commemoration of the dead.[4]

In order to understand the revolutionary dimensions of such change, the first chapter, "Common Pits and Grim Graveyards," describes the anachronistic status quo, the squalid conditions in the deliberately urbanized, Church-controlled places of death throughout Western civilization from the fifth century on. Such institutionalization of death had served as an agent of social and political control. Those who died in the Church's good graces were literally and figuratively incorporated into the body of the Church by way of the anonymous cemetery or churchyard. There, one's earthly identity was lost among the masses of the dead in exchange for assurances of salvation. The first major challenge to this old order came in the seventeenth century from Calvinists whose calls for a return to the "purer" forms of early Christianity earned them the epithet "Puritan."[5]

In contrast, religious Dissenters insisted on secularizing burials by refusing to consecrate their "burial grounds" or "graveyards" as sacred space. They removed burials, whenever possible, from proximity to the church, itself simply called a "meetinghouse"; and they avoided "any recurrence of prayers offered to the dead or on their behalf," even shunning use of the cross, placed in Catholic and Anglican churchyards to prompt such prayers. There would be no extreme unction, funeral mass, or prayers for the deceased. When Calvinists rejected "superstitious" funerary practices, they referred to papist rather than to pagan forms.[6] The doctrine of predestination made the uncertainty of one's postmortem fate central to the Calvinist mind, and their burial places epitomized this theological harshness. In colonial New England, the chaos and barrenness of the Puritans' town-center graveyards suggested the fate of the unregenerate. The flat, gray slate stones that began to appear in the 1660s graphically represented in a rich iconography formulaic messages of *memento mori* or *tempus fugit* that urged passersby to acknowledge the inevitability of death, the fleetingness and insignificance of earthly existence, rather than the lives of individuals or the sense of a common history made by shaping their fate through secular works, however good. The bodies of the founders and leaders of the colony and then of the heroes of the Revolution were often lost amid the commonality of the rest of the community of the deceased.[7]

In Western societies into the seventeenth century, concepts of the past had been of a linear sequence of cataclysmic events through which God determined the lives and fates of men and civilizations, leaving little room for acknowledging human agency. The rise of science asserted man's ability to know and change. This evolved in the eighteenth century to an emphasis by liberal thinkers on the cycles of Nature as operative principles driving the course of history as well as serving as metaphors for it. Providence might intervene, but men became empowered to insert themselves into the course of history by making dramatic breaks with tradition and many established laws. This new concept of history, combined with a rediscovery of both Nature and ancient civilizations, subverted Christian orthodoxy and hereditary political systems, providing a vocabulary for redefining the past and man's relationship to it. The quest to reattain a more natural state of society, free from the corruptions of the traditions of Church and State as well as hereditary aristocracy, parallels the revolutionary attempts of Calvinists to simplify Christianity; and, furthered by the rise of other Protestant Dissenters, it became an even more radical break. Historicism enhanced the concept of a return to the "pure" roots of early religions, even the pre-Christian, considered closer to the deity. Liberals picked out and emulated select forms and patterns, often ancient, now to be used in very different ways; or they applied acceptable "lessons" from the distant past to new circumstances. Marking a radical discontinuity with an authoritarian heritage now rejected as corrupt, this historicism aimed to start over by asserting a continuity between the present and remote periods judged to be more natural. The self-conscious, selective mimicry of ancient styles with the intent to *make* history anew produced the flowering of "neoclassical" design, including that used in "picturesque" eighteenth- and early-nineteenth-century landscapes of memory—philosophical gardens and, later, "rural" cemeteries.

Members of new elites on both sides of the Atlantic were drawn to a cyclical view of the fate of civilizations and empires. With regard to the events of 1688 in England, 1776 in America, and 1789 in France, the term "revolution" meant a deliberate return to a previous, purer state, a new beginning with positive connotations, reflecting the belief that men could actively determine the fate of their societies, that they could re-form civilization, rid it of the corruptions of the immediate past, and re-create an idealized natal epoch, an Eden or Arcadia where "natural law" and "natural religion" prevailed. England's Glorious Revolution had rearticulated constitutional liberties lost for centuries. Urging such retrospection, Henry St. John Bolingbroke (1678–1751), once a Tory, then a Deist, and often self-exiled to France, explained in 1735: "From the earliest accounts of the time, our ancestors in Germany were a free people, and had a right to assent or dissent to all laws; that right was exercised and preserved under the Saxon and Norman kings, even to our days; and may an uninterrupted exercise thereof, continue till time shall be no more." English Whigs, opponents of the authoritarian Tory establishment, looked to the Golden Age of Liberty, to King Alfred the Great (849–899 AD) and their Anglo-Saxon ancestors, to Magna Carta and the rule of the secular common law.[8]

The "enlightened" came to believe in the "revolutionary" possibility of reversing the inexorable forces of Nature[9] in cyclical history—birth, decline, and decay—by swinging the pendulum of "Time" back to an Arcadian new beginning or rebirth, thus bypassing the inevitable and expected "Fall" by taking control of their own destinies. The cyclical concept of history ran counter to orthodoxy, premised on the tyranny of political and theological stasis, providing justification in naturalistic terms for the rejection of the establishment by distinct sectarian and political factions and coalitions of new elites—newer nobility, the gentry, professionals, merchants, bankers, and prosperous artisans, an "aristocracy of merit," as Jefferson and others phrased it. Its proponents gained a personal stake and sense of responsibility in discarding their recent past and inventing a new one. Barring such a rebirth, death would be the ultimate revolutionary, for civilizations as for individuals. History would now be interpreted in secular terms, celebrating the founding events and individuals who epitomized civic virtue, asserting natural law as the basis for new republican states. Jefferson even declared that each generation might have its own revolution.

Protestant Dissenters focused on allegories unrelated to scripture, simpler spiritual lessons drawn from the natural world of man's journey through life. The idea of a metaphoric landscape was suggested in John Bunyan's widely read pious tract *Pilgrim's Progress*, first published in 1678. The Baptist preacher presents an account of the arduous travels of Christian, an Everyman, along the long and winding path from the City of Destruction to the Celestial City "upon a mighty hill." Protestants identified with the quest of the traveler through a landscape punctuated, like life, by challenges and hazards—the Hill of Difficulty, the Valley of Humility, the Valley of the Shadow of Death, the Delectable Mounts, the Slough of Despond, Mount Marvel, Mount Innocent, and Mount Charity, as well as the River of Death. *Pilgrim's Progress*, rivaling the Bible as a best-seller well into the nineteenth century, inspired its readers to look for symbols in the material world—and even to design landscapes that epitomized such ideas and values.[10]

The metaphor of travel as an experience of learning and growth found its real-life counterpart as increasing numbers of the elite made the Grand Tour of Italy and Greece in the eighteenth century in search of "picturesque" pastoral scenes punctuated by classical antiquities and other ruins, melancholy monuments to the heights of civilization in a distant past. Visitors flocked to historical sites such as Lake Avernus, site of the grotto of the mythical Cumaean sibyl, where Aeneas supposedly descended into the underworld in search of his father. Travelers were drawn to ancient extramural funerary landscapes, which seemed so much more appealing than their own. English and French tourists came to see the

Fig. I.1. Monument of the sisters Demetria and Pamphile and tombs of Greek Worthies, Ceramicus outside of Athens's Dipylon Gate. From a stereographic photograph by Underwood and Underwood, ca. 1880. Collection of the author (hereafter BMGL).

Fig. I.2. Burials along the road outside of Pompeii. Albumen photograph by Giorgio Sommer, ca. 1875. BMGL.

Ceramicus, the ancient cemetery outside the Athenian gates where Plato met with his students in the Academy. They walked among the extramural burial sites of Rome's Appian Way and Pompeii. Eventually, some even made their way to ancient sites in Egypt, Palmyra, and Baalbec. In England, they sought out Tintern Abbey and other Gothic ruins. Such "picturesque" sites testified to the resurgence of Nature, triumphant after the fall of civilization and its structures, a message that spoke to those critical of their own immediate past. Such experiences were sobering as well as inspirational. (Figs. I.1, I.2.)

The itinerary of Joseph Addison, Whig editor of *The Spectator*, kept him abroad from 1701 from 1703. On returning to England, he proselytized for creation of picturesque landscapes with long vistas and woods framing ancient monuments and architectural fragments, relics of a distant past, scenes like those in pictures painted by Salvador Rosa, Nicolas Poussin, Claude Lorrain, and others seen in their travels, with engraved copies often brought home as souvenirs—hence the term "picturesque." Richard Boyle, third Earl of Burlington, returned from Italy in 1719 determined to re-create such scenes in his own gardens at Chiswick. The French poet Jacques Delille credited travelers' discoveries of ancient artifacts in the naturalistic countryside of Italy with inspiring the modern taste for landscape design drawing on allegorical and historicist themes. Catering to such tastes, designs for a new sort of expansive garden, not constricted and enclosed, wound the visitor's steps along sinuous paths, past structures fabricated to stir philosophical or ancient historic associations, through areas of sunlight in "lawns," into the darkness of dells and grottoes suggestive of death, and emerging to views of distant vistas and panoramas—all thought capable of stirring "sublime" emotions. The putting into landscape forms of a metaphoric journey through life, or the pilgrimage of the soul seeking knowledge of the eternal, influenced even those who did not share Bunyan's evangelical faith, those who preferred to think in the more secular terms of the questing journeys of Aeneas and other classical heroes. The circuit walk or "tour" in naturalistic English gardens was designed to present a sequence of programmed spiritual or philosophical experiences that gave physical form to abstract ideas that resonated deeply for those familiar with Bunyan.[11]

Chapter 2, "The English Garden: Memory, Nature, and Design," traces the philosophical and political currents that presaged invention of the form and formula of the eighteenth-century English landscaped garden. English Nonconformists and Whigs were the first and chief champions of developing their own "picturesque" landscapes imbued with allegory and historicism. Whiggish philosophers celebrated political liberties governed by natural law and reason, using "Liberty" in the Lockean sense of freedom to enjoy property without interference, a concern of those ambitious to enclose their land, to build estates, and to win more power in Parliament free from Tory interference. Their reverence for the "rural" carried associations of retreat from the political corruptions of the court to their own country estates, asserting their personal independence and the natural claim of the landowner to political power. Rejection of the older taste in gardening, a taste for French or Dutch formalism associated with the ecclesiastical and monarchical establishment, became a matter of ideology preached by Addison and other Whigs, resulting in the "modern" style of gardening.[12]

Horace Walpole likened naturalistic gardens to the English Constitution. Theorists suggested that their sinuous paths represented old English liberties. There, Whigs enshrined references to an ancient Saxon history of constitutionalism and a defense of individual liberties championed by King Alfred, values they also represented in classical architecture drawn from the republics of Greece and Rome. Many gardens incorporated references to legendary ancestors predating Alfred, such as Aeneas. Some made material reference to Druids as exemplars of natural law. So wide-ranging was the quest for alternatives to the immediate past that some gardens displayed Egyptian structures, naïvely intended to imply an even older and purer source of law and civilization. All included diversified naturalistic land forms (the "Genius of Place") and plantings which referred not only to natural law but also to the inexorable processes of Nature according to the cyclical view of history. The elevation of "taste" through exposure to all of these elements, so philosophers argued, would improve the moral and ethical character of a new class of citizens able to govern themselves—a "natural aristocracy" who would stabilize civilization in radically new ways.[13]

The taste for the picturesque also had nostalgic motivations. It tried to compensate through deliberately designed irregularities for the disappearance of a truly natural wildness owing to deforestation in much of Britain and France. Historian Arthur O. Lovejoy judged that English garden landscapes conveyed "a sense of the transitoriness of all natural beauty and human glory." Reminders of inexorable change and the cycles of Nature and History, they provided natural sites for placement of commemorative monuments, even for the graves of those who rejected burial by the Church. These gardens were personal meditative places designed to foster solitary indulgence in the "pleasures of melancholy," a philosophical exercise recommended to heighten introspection and retrospection in a way that appealed even more to that era's nascent romantic sensibilities than to the proponents of Reason. They were "Museums" (*mouseion* in Greek), with the classic connotation of "seats of the Muses," places of inspiration. Perhaps these were the first fantasy landscapes—fantasy being defined as "the realm of vivid imagination, reverie, depiction, illusion . . . the natural conjuring of mental invention and association; the visionary world."[14]

Development of a new mindset termed "affective individualism" also informed elements of English gardens, as well as the picturesque funerary landscapes that later drew upon them as models. The historian Lawrence Stone finds that these trends accompanied "massive shifts in world views and value systems" to represent "perhaps the most important change in *mentalité* to have occurred in the Early Modern period, indeed possibly in the last thousand years of Western history." "Affective individualism" refers to a change in values from the "distance, deference, and patriarchy" of the open-lineage family to increasingly emotional relationships between spouses and between parents and children, including new ideas about child-rearing and the remembrance of "loved ones" after death. Stone argues that this rise in sentiment is traceable from the late seventeenth century on, spreading first among the upper classes, gentry, and professionals. For instance, Alexander Pope (1688–1744) commemorated his widowed mother in his gardens at Twickenham west of London, often acclaimed as the "Paradigm of the Picturesque Garden" and an "eloquent expression" of his era's "pictorial and poetic sensibility." That sensibility was based on Whiggish sentimentality and the philosophical and political ideas about "life, liberty, and the pursuit of happiness" propounded in England, then in France, but most successfully in the United States; and it also informed the rise of a more personal commemorative impulse.[15]

Chapter 3, "The French Cult of Ancestors and the Birth of Père Lachaise," traces the adaptation of English garden tastes, rejecting formalism for naturalism, by some of the French elite for their estates. That eventually resulted in the creation of innovative funerary landscapes to permit a display of patriotic commemoration and personal sentiment unprecedented in modern times. French philosophers, Revolutionaries, and reformers praised "the *sublime melancholy* of the English nation." Many adapted elements of Whiggish culture, thought of as alternatives to their old order; but they took the elements of naturalistic landscape design further than the English by applying them to proposals for burial reform, thus fostering a "cult of ancestors" as a means of counteracting the iconoclastic excesses of their revolution. These impulses met in Père Lachaise Cemetery, founded on the outskirts of Paris in 1804, and it, in turn, provided a model for creation of Boston's Mount Auburn.[16] Liberal philosophers, aestheticians, and politicians recommended institutionalizing this ideology through monuments and naturalistic landscapes of memory. They thought of landscape gardening as a liberal art like poetry, painting, sculpture, and architecture, capable, as William Wordsworth put it, of moving "the affections under the control of reason." By melding naturalism with classicism, the landscape or monument designer could impart the lessons of moral philosophy and natural law as surely as any other form of art or literature.[17]

In America in the 1820s, a new party, also called Whigs, arose out of the New England Federalists in opposition to "King Jackson," president and leader of the Democrats. American Whigs shared with their English friends a reverence for "natural law" and aimed to strengthen the liberty won in Independence to create a new nationalism under the Constitution, an "American System," a common culture to foster economic and social stability. They revered George Washington as their equivalent of King Alfred, a defender against invaders and a champion of natural law. On both sides of the Atlantic, Whigs turned from Church orthodoxy to liberal Dissenting Protestant sects, even Deism, looking to Nature and to the commemorative monuments of classical civilizations for ways to symbolize and perpetuate their new ideology. Among many changes brought about by American religious liberals, especially Unitarians, Universalists, and Transcendentalists, was a reevaluation of deathways through burial reform and provisions for enshrining secular memory.

They, too, shared in the trends toward affective individualism and melancholy sentiment. With the growth of romanticism, their urge to commemorate took on private as well as public dimensions. Chapter 4, "An American Sensibility to Melancholy," surveys the early flowering of that sentiment in literature and material culture, including the wish to remember individuals by reforming traditional burial places and creating new alternatives. James Hillhouse spearheaded the creation of New Haven's New Burial Ground (1786, renamed the Grove Street Cemetery in the 1870s) to ensure burials in family lots in perpetuity more than a decade before the French founded Père Lachaise. Sensitivity went hand in hand with sensibility on both sides of the Atlantic, especially among urban elites.

Because of conditions endemic to their urban area, Bostonians responded early to the perceived need for putting public memory in place by building patriotic monuments. Chapter 5, "The Necessity for Monuments: Art and Public Commemoration in the Young Republic," describes the developing impulse to proclaim in material terms a new secular, civic, and national past in early-nineteenth-century America. Many leaders had an affinity for the British Whiggish ideal of returning to an Edenic beginning and shared the belief in the efficacy of monuments to convey lessons of moral philosophy and civic virtue. In the correspondence of their declining years, John Adams and Thomas Jefferson debated the potential uses and hazards of art in a republic. Protestant millennialism contributed symbolic meaning to the Revolution and the new republic, and this spirit too favored erecting monuments to laud the nation's auspicious beginning.[18] By the semicentennial of Independence, marked by the deaths of Adams and Jefferson, the simultaneous passing of two of the remaining founders, Americans began in earnest to create material representations of patriotism, history, and republican values to sustain their governmental "experiment" through future generations. They began to build upon and reinterpret commemorative design precedents from abroad, heeding Wordsworth's call for memory and imagination "to enshrine the spirit of the past / For future restoration." Many believed that monuments and historic places could be imbued with patriotic meaning to live on in the popular imagination. Urban elites, at a time of dramatic changes in old patterns of life as port towns became burgeoning cities, especially felt the need to create a national identity, a "usable past," and lay a local claim to instrumentality in it.[19]

Following the War of 1812, Boston experienced an urban explosion that transformed its size, shape, and character. Population jumped from 33,250 to 43,290 between 1810 and 1820, then to 70,000 in 1830, triple its Revolutionary-era numbers. It was no longer the homogeneous New England town of the seventeenth century or even the stagnating port it had become in the late eighteenth. In 1822 Boston formally became a city, putting aside town government by selectmen for that by mayor, aldermen, and common council.[20] The social shape changed as well. The North End, economically and socially mixed in the late colonial era, was left to the lower and middling classes, while the rising elite moved to new residences developed on Beacon Hill or to nearby country estates in Cambridge, Dorchester, Brookline, and Roxbury. Since the prosperous in these peripheral areas still looked to urban life and institutions, a new metropolitan consciousness developed, expanding the constituency that favored improving the city and its amenities; they were all "Bostonians."

Growth brought prosperity but also anxiety. For many, the nascent industrialization ringing Boston represented not progress for all but unsettling change, the uprooting of the rural from which many of them had come. Other factors predisposed Yankees, heirs of Calvinist forefathers, to thoughts of the better aspects of their lost past and of death, lending a particular timeliness to the taste for nostalgia and melancholy that now permeated Western romanticism. The Commonwealth's legislative General Court hotly debated religious disestablishment in light of escalating sectarian fragmentation, especially the Unitarian controversy factionalizing congregation after congregation, town after town. The Panic of 1819 inaugurated a long depression, the most severe economic crisis in the nation's young history. Countless citizens lost their homes, farms, businesses, and property. Massachusetts lost Maine, which became a separate state in 1820. Economic paralysis persisted through the 1820s, and the psychological, political, legal, and institutional ramifications continued for over a decade. Extremes in the economic cycle fomented chronic insecurity and pessimism, especially among the newly developing elite.

As Harrison Gray Otis wrote in 1823, "Two years ago our sun had sunk never to rise again." Recovery was brief. Echoing John Winthrop's call to make Boston "a City upon a Hill," the philosopher Amos Bronson Alcott more optimistically articulated the region's self-confidence, declaring in 1828: "There is a city in our world upon which the sun of righteousness has risen. There is a sun which beams in its full meridian splendour upon it. Its influences are quickening and invigorating the souls which dwell within it. It is the same from which every pure stream of thought and purpose and performance emanates. It is the city that is set on high. . . . Boston!" By 1830 some Boston boosters determined that the only way to save their city and region was to assume a posture of dogged optimism. Thomas Green Fessenden, editor of the *New England Farmer*, cautioned: "The cry of *decline* is one of the causes of decline. Many hear this cry and hearing no answer to it, take it to be true." He believed that setbacks were temporary and not signs of imminent demise, especially if Yankees would fall back on civic virtue and stewardship of wealth. After all, he asked, "to what portion of the earth is one to go to find more general comfort and natural thrift than in New England?"[21] Bostonians cherished a sense of their own exemplary importance. Many cultural leaders harkened to such rhetoric, believing that through public-spirited efforts they could carry on the principles on which their city, region, and nation had been founded, forestalling the demise of all.

Yet leaders' fears that Boston was not keeping pace with improvements in competing commercial seaboard cities exacerbated their insecurities and motivated them to plan projects for improving their culture and environment. Hastening not to be outdone by southern competitors in upstart Baltimore who had already begun building patriotic monuments, Boston's leaders chartered one of the nation's first voluntary associations to build a giant obelisk-shaped structure on the site of the Battle of Bunker Hill in Charlestown across the Charles River from Boston. (Fig. I.3.) Proclaiming the centrality of Boston's role in the Revolution, the monument was so ambitious in scale that it would take two decades to complete. The cultural elite was troubled by British allegations that Americans lacked a history and civilization of their own and that this presaged dire consequences for the republican experiment. They set out to make their city the "Athens of America," a cultural capital

Fig. I.3. Boston and Bunker Hill, view across the Charles River from the east. This scene of the pastoralism surrounding the "Athens of America" shows the Bunker Hill Monument as complete, although it was still under construction. Engraving by William H. Bartlett, 1839. BMGL.

whose hegemony would be ensured by the creation of literary journals and clubs, institutions to foster knowledge and the arts, all modeled on European precedents but reshaped to meet American needs. Bostonians began to look beyond New York, Philadelphia, and Baltimore to recent urban improvements in London, Liverpool, Edinburgh, and Paris.

Josiah Quincy, Boston's second mayor in 1823, tackled many problems associated with rapid urban growth. He made burial reform a major issue in his crusade to eliminate filth in the crowded city. The debate over allowing crypt burials in churches preoccupied many in the wake of acute public health problems in New York; but burial reform was more than a matter of sanitation. General Henry A. S. Dearborn observed: "We cannot speak confidently with respect to the dangers to health which arise from such practices. It has probably been over-rated, if, indeed, it exists at all." Chapter 6, "Grave Problems: Urban Burial Controversies," explains the dimensions of the controversy over such burials and the first proposals for creation of an extramural cemetery.[22] The public debate echoed the rhetoric of many of the era's other social and political issues, especially the anti-elitism of the mechanic class (artisans, skilled workers, shopkeepers) in resistance to attempts by the elite to invent new forms indicative of social status.

Bostonians wanted to revise their burial practices as much for practical as for aesthetic reasons. Their glutted old graveyards, squeezed in next to buildings and streets, had scant space for more burials and seemed repulsive. A genteel revulsion toward foul smells and the imposition of new standards of public cleanliness led to calls internationally for reforms in the name of public health. Often the new standards were simply a result of increasingly refined taste rather than a real understanding about the consequences of lack of sanitation, but they developed with enough force to impel a number of reforms in the urban environment, backed especially by those aware of the escalating value of urban real estate.[23] Hence, the motivations for burial reform encompassed more than the commemorative impulse, the spread of affective individualism, and the adoption of design precedents from abroad. They were complicated by the texture of social and cultural change experienced by urbanites in Europe in the early nineteenth century, involving pragmatic considerations as well as common ideals and fears premised on medical controversies over disease causation. Mayor Quincy's proposal for one large extramural burial place serving and symbolizing the city contributed to discussion of plans for such a new institution, but the municipality could not implement all that beyond its constricted corporate boundaries.

Burial reform would require voluntary, private initiative; and Bostonians were the most active of American urbanites in forming such associations for various civic purposes. By the 1820s, prosperous merchants, industrialists, bankers, real estate speculators, and new professionals had replaced the old colonial elite, the Tories, many of whom had evacuated with the British after the Revolution. Sons of ministers, farmers, and sea captains, they had recently made their way from towns surrounding the "Metropolis of New England" into prominent positions. The new upper class coalesced through bonds of marriage and kinship as well as institutional affiliations—particularly ties formed at Harvard College. Boston's new elite sought ways to redefine gentility and to create modern traditions in regional as well as national terms, rejecting the anachronistic and helping define an "aristocracy of merit."[24]

One such individual, the young doctor Jacob Bigelow, stepped forward in 1825 to propose to a circle of his influential friends that they found a voluntary association to procure land for a "rural" cemetery. Chapter 7, "The Cemetery Idea and the Founding of Mount Auburn," traces the development of Bigelow's proposal under the auspices of the new Massachusetts Horticultural Society (1829), with General Henry A. S. Dearborn as its first president. A combined cemetery and experimental garden project, it complemented the intentions and ambitions of the society's founders, who sought to develop a better stock of plant materials to strengthen the regional and national economy and to improve their urban and rural environment through diversified plantings and naturalistic landscape design. Bigelow, Dearborn, and their friends were confident that by encouraging "rural" taste they could create a harmony between the city and the countryside—between New England's rural past, its present, and its future. Finally, George Brimmer offered an ideal site for the venture. The old farm straddling the Cambridge–Watertown line had been dubbed "Sweet Auburn" by Harvard students who frequented the place for its natural beauties replete with the Genius of Place that was required as a prerequisite for a picturesque landscape. Echoing this circle of friends, Alexander Everett noted the similarities between Père Lachaise and the proposed "rural" cemetery at Mount Auburn: "While they tend to promote the salubrity of cities, they connect agreeable images with the recollections of the past, and the anticipation of the future; and strip the idea of death of part of the horrors with which superstition and weakness of our nature have unnecessarily invested it." In founding Mount Auburn, Everett's associates were attempting not just to solve the city's burial problems but to develop an American culture, in all senses of the word.[25]

The proposed cemetery was also intended to be an agent of the founders' historical consciousness, to endure for all time, even after a potential cataclysm. One anonymous Bostonian recounted in the *New-England Magazine* that while in a state of "pensive melancholy" on the "lofty hill" at Mount Auburn just before its consecration as a cemetery, surrounded by Nature resurgent, he had a vision of "the city of riches and splendor," the "Queen of the North," engulfed by a "gale of desolation" and deluge, leaving only "one great green wilderness, quickened into luxuriant life by the bright sun, as on the first morning of creation." The writer concluded: "No city shall be eternal but the City of the Dead. . . . In the mighty system of the universe, not a step of the destroyer, Time, but is made subservient to some ulterior purpose of reproduction, and the circle of creation and destruction is eternal."[26] General Dearborn told Bostonians in October 1831: "Even in this country, the moss-grown stone outlasts the most durable habitations of our fathers. It would seem as if man has desired to re-assure himself, in the presence of death, that he is not all frailty, by raising monuments, which long after he is gone, may resist the waste of time." As late as 1861, as if echoing Jefferson, the Bostonian Wilson Flagg still believed that "revolution after revolution is destined to pass over us," leaving only "Mount Auburn: Its Scenes, Its Beauties, and Its Lessons," the title of his book.[27]

Chapter 8, "Cemetery or Garden? Landscape Design and Conflicting Institutional Purposes," traces the development of Mount Auburn's initial picturesque landscape design by Horticultural Society president Dearborn, assisted by Bigelow and other members of the Society's Garden and Cemetery Committee. It explains the reasons for the reincorporation of Mount Auburn in 1835 as an institution independent of the Horticulturists. Over the next two decades, as seen in Chapter 9, "Art and Nature Balanced: Creating a Marble History in the Forest Cemetery," little change was made in the naturalistic landscape Dearborn had shaped beyond the accretion of monuments, markers, tombs, and other "improvements" on family burial lots. Proprietors and contributors to subscription campaigns increasingly displayed their new commemorative consciousness with personal and public import. In Chapter 10, "Embellishing the Picturesque: Structures in the Landscape," we see how the addition of major buildings and monuments in various architectural styles by the cemetery corporation drew inspiration from English landscaped gardens. Founders and proprietors expressed definite ideas about which forms derived from antiquity would be appropriate for their funerary landscape. Issues of shifting tastes as well as cultural priorities both inside the institution and in the nation at large conspired to make even some of these contributions of art and architecture controversial, as a new generation of cemetery trustees and proprietors questioned the initial Whiggish historicist mission of the institution.

Through its first four decades, Mount Auburn attracted national and international recognition. Visitors from abroad made it a major stop on itineraries that included a barge ride on the Erie Canal, gazing at the sublime wonder of Niagara Falls, and inspection of booming frontier cities like Cincinnati—the Grand Tour of the United States. Tourists' rave reviews vindicated Bostonians' pride in their city's cultural accomplishments. Area residents flocked to the cemetery as well, using it as a "pleasure ground," much to the distress of some of the older, original proprietors. Gradually, it seemed to become something other than the morally refreshing "asylum" that its genteel founders intended. Chapter 11, "The Rage for Mount Auburn: Sacred Site or Pleasure Ground?" describes the cemetery's immense popularity and renown, which led to internal debate over whether the place should be protected from indiscriminate public uses or left open for the more democratic purpose of serving as a secular park.

From its founding, Mount Auburn's example had served as catalyst for the "rural" cemetery movement that swept the nation as leaders in city after city, large and small, created similar picturesque cemeteries. By the 1850s these multifunctional landscapes served as urban cultural amenities, providing open green space for tranquil, edifying recreation and for display of fine commemorative sculpture and architecture. The popularity of such naturalistic landscapes inspired the first proposals for public parks for urbanites and even for the first designed suburbs that adapted similar landscape elements for other uses. The famed arbiter of horticultural taste, Andrew Jackson Downing, cited Mount Auburn in advocating that his friend President Millard Filmore convert Washington's Mall into such a landscape: "A national park like this, laid out and planted in a thorough manner, would *exercise as much influence on public taste* as Mount Auburn Cemetery near Boston has done. Though only twenty years have elapsed since that spot was laid out, the lesson there taught has been so largely influential that at the present moment the United States, while they have no public parks, are acknowledged to possess the finest rural cemeteries in the world." Although the Mall would not immediately be laid out in that fashion, Downing used similar arguments in crusading for public funding for creation of New York's Central Park.[28]

Meanwhile, other changes had been set in motion in Mount Auburn's landscape. Chapter 12, "Transformation to the 'Garden' or 'Sculptured' Cemetery," surveys the accretion of a diverse array of funerary artifacts that eroded the landscape's initial picturesqueness as proprietors exercised their rights to erect lot enclosures, monuments, stones, and tombs displaying increasingly eclectic tastes. In doing so they drew on the talents of architects, sculptors, carvers, monument dealers, and foundries, creating a new local growth industry. The trustees also began to resculpt the terrain and to remove about half of the existing forest growth, permitting the introduction in newly opened spaces of ornamental shrubs and diverse trees able to grow to specimen shape. Sunny clearings or "lawns" allowed growth of turf and "exotic" flowers, not only native wildflowers. With the trustees' permission, Bigelow supervised the redesign of many parts of the grounds, creating new spaces for burials by filling in wetlands and lowering some of the hills while smoothing "steep acclivities." By the 1870s, few referred to Mount Auburn as a "rural" or "forest" cemetery.

The public "rage" for Mount Auburn waned after the Civil War, although "Decoration Day" annually drew in thousands for patriotic celebrations until major monuments to the war on Boston Common and in other public spaces in the metropolitan region superseded the centrality of the cemetery for such communal commemoration. Beyond the schism that had threatened the Union, a great disjuncture in mentalities coincided with the Civil War era, not necessarily a matter of cause and effect. The idealistic vision of the founders seemed passé. While historian Garry Wills has deemed Mount Auburn "one of the principal cultural institutions of the nineteenth century," he might have specified the antebellum era. Wills writes that Edward Everett informed and epitomized the spirit of that era as "America's first truly professional Hellenist," a founding supporter of Mount Auburn, as well as mentor to Emerson, to so many others at Harvard, and to Boston's intellectual community. Everett rose to national political prominence and expressed in his long 1863 speech at the dedication of the Gettysburg Federal Cemetery the ideology of commemoration and the "culture of death" that had informed Mount Auburn's founding. Grim reality had shattered that culture. Wills contrasts Everett's two-hour oration with Abraham Lincoln's terse, eloquent, and far more famous Gettysburg Address, finding there a major shift in mentality from the old to the new epitomized by the two men and their speeches. Everett's burial on a central hillside at Mount Auburn in 1865 was just another conspicuous marker of the passing of an era.[29]

By the century's last quarter, only a few of the aging clung to the founders' grand ambitions for Mount Auburn as an institution representative of the "Athens of America." The historical consciousness that premised its creation was ephemeral, limited to those of a class and a generation celebrating their primacy in shaping the national heyday of development. Newer generations shared different experiences, priorities, and tastes. Reverence for old interpretations of the past gave way to the belief in progress, especially after the nation emerged intact from the crucible of the Civil War. Americans put behind them cataclysmic and cyclical concepts of history. Faith in science and technology informed a new optimism about the limitless possibilities of change, replacing the older belief that the founders' idealism could stabilize the republic into an uncertain future. Significantly, in Edward Bellamy's utopian novel *Looking Backward* (1888), Julian West passes his last day in the nineteenth century visiting Mount Auburn on Decoration Day with his betrothed, Edith Bartlett, before waking from an extended mesmerized sleep in Boston in the year 2000.[30]

Perhaps that change in mentality represents one of the generational revolutions in thought Jefferson had predicted. Mount Auburn's new proprietors and the heirs of the original ones wanted only a pleasant personal place in which to bury and commemorate their dead, and Mount Auburn was no longer their sole or primary option. Ironically, when Americans put their past under grass or sculpted it in stone, they rendered it no longer "usable" in the Whiggish sense for those with different priorities and mindsets. The "culture of death" was no longer the same. Melancholy did not appeal to an era freeing itself from the brief efflorescence of Victorian sentimentality. For a time, Mount Auburn and other cemeteries fashioned after its example lost their original purpose as historical institutions, although they endured for personal commemoration and burials.

Still, Mount Auburn occupies a position of pivotal significance in the history of landscape design, marking the transition from the aesthetics of eighteenth-century English gardens to the picturesque in America. It contains rich material evidence for the historian intent on discovering how Americans tried to define a relatively new past in both public and private terms. Studying its development and transformation over 175 years reveals changing tastes and mentalities—ever-evolving notions about Death, Nature, and the commemoration of community and family. The narrative of this book necessarily ends in the 1870s, except for a brief epilogue surveying twentieth-century developments, leaving other crucial chapters in Mount Auburn's transformation from "garden" cemetery to arboretum and its more recent contributions to the historic landscape preservation movement for another volume.

Mount Auburn is much more than the prototypical historic designed landscape and the accretion of artifacts and notables interred there, exemplary of different eras—more than the sum of its parts. Changing American deathways and styles of commemoration have been accommodated through the decades. As it approaches its bicentennial of dedicated stewardship, constantly planned renewal, and adaptations to cultural changes, Mount Auburn remains vibrant in a constant renaissance, its beauties repeatedly renewed through the seasons while it still serves actively as a place for burials and for preserving memory. A new "rage" now draws public recognition and enjoyment of its intricacies while it flourishes as an educational institution for design students, horticulturists, ornithologists, and preservationists. Mount Auburn's designation as a National Historic Landmark in 2003, for its "exceptional value or quality in illustrating and interpreting the heritage of the United States," one of fewer than 2,500 sites so honored, very few of them landscapes, attests to all that.

1

COMMON PITS AND GRIM GRAVEYARDS

If Beauty *could the beautiful defend*
From Death's dominion, then fair Absalom
Had not been brought to such a shameful end:
But fair and foul unto the Grave must come.

—Michael Wigglesworth, "A Song of Emptiness, To Fill Up the Empty Pages Following, Vanity of Vanities" (1657)

ACCEPTANCE OF THE INEVITABILITY, THE ugliness, and the finality of death was institutionalized in the old order dating from the fifth century and persisting into the eighteenth throughout Western civilization, extending into New England as in Old England. Historical consciousness throughout this period was minimal, limited to tales of the divine right of kings, heroes defending a sacred cause, and saints interceding for the living. Secular memory was suspect, and there was little material commemoration. Details of the achievements of notables were reduced to myths transmitted through oral tradition. Although the advent of humanism and the rediscovery of classical civilizations in the fifteenth century were harbingers of change to come, medieval traditions were firmly entrenched. The lessons, rituals, and places of death remained ecclesiastical monopolies.[1]

No cemetery could exist apart from the Church, literally and figuratively. Burials *ad sanctos*, in consecrated ground within a town, either in or adjacent to a church, became the rule, in contrast to the Roman Law of the Twelves Tablets and the Theodosian Code, which had consigned the dead to uninhabited areas outside the city walls. Older Gallo-Roman, barbarian, Celtic, and Merovingian cemeteries in open fields were either abandoned or consecrated for continued use. Churchmen refused to let Christian Saxons keep their old rural burial places. In Carolingian Germany, forcibly converted to Christianity, ecclesiastics decreed the abandonment of pagan cemeteries. In the vicinity of old Roman cities, however, Christian martyrs had been buried alongside pagans in "suburban" locations, and their graves became cult objects. Ecclesiastics often built churches atop the sites to accommodate pilgrims at masses held over the martyrs' bones but also to control the growing cult of saints. The churches of Saint-Marcel, Saint-Germain, Saint-Martin, and Sainte-Geneviève in Paris, as well as Saint-Seurin in Bordeaux and Saint-Victor in Marseilles, were built over Merovingian burial places beyond the town walls. Many such sites remained extramural until the eleventh century but eventually became centers of population growth encouraged by Church leaders in order to extend religious control throughout the area.[2]

Denying burial in consecrated ground was an ecclesiastical punishment. Medieval man did not think in terms of having an individual grave in a fixed place *in aeternum*. He cared only that the Church accept his body, to dispose of it as it pleased but within sacred ground so that he might be included in the regular prayers for the collective dead. Extramural burial sites unaffiliated with the Church were only for suicides, the excommunicated, the executed, and some of their family members. Often the bodies of such pariahs were merely left exposed to the elements, to beasts of prey, and to the jaded glances of travelers, or discarded in refuse dumps, seldom with even a covering of earth in a shallow grave. In times of dire necessity, victims of plague were dumped in hastily dug pits beyond the town walls, protected neither spiritually by the relics of a saint nor physically from predators by cemetery walls.

The words *ecclesia* and *cimeterium* became nearly synonymous, although use of the latter latinized Greek word remained limited to clerical, scholarly language until the seventeenth century. Terms for burial space adjacent to a church or chapel were purely architectural—*aître* (atrium), *charnier* (charnel house), or "ossuary" (the covered cloister or gallery in which bones were stacked after removal from the common grave). The word "cemetery" did not enter English usage until the nineteenth century. But it was devoid of association with the Church and its architecture, referring solely to a landscape.

In instituting this system and insisting on urbanization of burials, the Church deliberately overturned many heathen, rural burial practices. The process was difficult to establish in areas where Germanic, Romanic, Celtic, and Slavic peoples had a rich, pantheistic folklore which persisted, mixing paganism with Christian beliefs long after conversion. In Celtic religion, wells, rivers, ponds, and sacred trees, especially the oak, were assigned patron gods and goddesses; these served as objects of veneration and marked choice sites for burials. In Teutonic belief, certain trees were capable of capturing the spirits of the dead. To demonstrate the superiority of Christianity, around 723 the Anglo-Saxon missionary Saint Boniface cut down the sacred oak reputed to contain the spirit of Donar, the Teutonic god who whispered messages from its branches. In many pre-Christian northern European belief systems, conceptions of the afterlife resembled the Greek Elysium, a pastoral or gardenlike setting, and may have had common roots in ancient Indo-European tradition. Undoing these deeply entrenched pagan practices and beliefs drawn from ancient "natural" religions required the full force of Church law. Early efforts included the prohibition by Ambrose, fourth-century bishop of Milan, later canonized, of the practice of consuming bread and wine at the graves of saints, as had formerly been the custom over the burial places of pagan heroes.

While most Western Christians considered rapid dissolution of the body desirable as well as inevitable, they did not dispose of the righteous dead by exposure to wild animals and birds of prey as other cultures did. One aim of burial was to prevent the packs of wolves that roamed the countryside from drawing sustenance from the corpses, increasing in numbers and endangering the living. The wolf population grew dramatically after epidemics and famines. In cold winters, wolves were so bold as to enter towns and disinter bodies from common pits in churchyards, especially those on the urban periphery such as Saint-Germain-des-Près, then surrounded by fields southwest of the center of Paris, the Ile-de-la-Cité. The ubiquitous European wolf had a greater impact on landscape and town design than has been acknowledged. It was to keep out such animals as well as men with criminal intentions that a French edict in 1695 required that all cemeteries be enclosed by solid walls with locked gates. City walls on the Continent were defensive, those in England often only administrative. In England, in contrast to France and Germany, great medieval cathedrals as well as simple parish churches were often built at the edge of town rather than in the center. Thus, some churchyards were truly rural. One Frenchman enviously observed in 1779 that in Britain, wolves had been eliminated six centuries before, while they still ravaged French cities, even entering fortified gates to kill children, although by that time they had been largely confined to eastern European forests. A single explanation such as the absence of wolves, however, does not suffice to account for the prevalence of rural churchyards in England as opposed to the Continent. Nevertheless, wolves must be acknowledged as one factor that influenced differences in the built environments of death.[3] (Fig. 1.1.)

If cultural patterns alone were enough to explain the distinctions between English and French deathways, then Puritan towns in New England would have fol-

Fig. 1.1. Engraving of English country churchyard from *Gentleman's Magazine and Historical Chronicle*, ca. 1810. BMGL.

lowed the freer spatial arrangement of English towns. Instead, the close clustering of houses near burial grounds, part of the central commons, in Massachusetts towns not only epitomized ideals of community but also served a defensive purpose. Although Puritans separated their burial grounds from their meetinghouses, deliberately rejecting the "papist superstition" of burial *ad sanctos*, they located their graves in town centers to keep corpses out of easy reach of roaming wolves, which were a problem in the New World as well as the Old. Since wolves preyed upon stray cattle, many towns constructed palisades to protect livestock kept in town, frequently grazing in the graveyard. Even fences did not keep wolves from the dead. One Watertown, Massachusetts, resident recalled in the 1840s, "It was the custom of our ancestors, in many localities, to fill up the grave after internment with stones that the remains might be protected from wolves." Bounties on wolf heads and pelts eliminated most of the beasts by the mid-eighteenth century.[4]

Traditional Symbolism in Funerary Plantings

A few isolated trees appeared in churchyards, and these retained their old funerary significance, which varied from one religion to another. The flame-shaped evergreen cypress (*Cupressus sempervirens*) was favored in southern Europe and Muslim countries. Ancient Greek belief held that Apollo turned Cyparissus into a cypress, making the tree symbolic of death and immortality. In France it appeared only on the graves of the elite. The walnut was the funerary tree in Poitou, France; the rowan, said to be sacred to Druids, in Wales; and elms in northern Europe. Rose bushes had been used in English burial grounds since the Roman occupation. In southern Europe, rosemary, grown to hedge height, was "the most highly esteemed of all flowers for the dead." The evergreen emits a strong, pleasant odor which counteracted the stench of the burial place. For that reason, it was considered "effective in retarding putrefaction," a quality favored by the elite who could merit or afford private tombs to separate their remains from those of the vulgar masses, and who from the fifteenth century on aspired to postmortem preservation.[5]

Along with rank weeds and grasses, the most common vegetation in English, Scottish, and Irish churchyards was the "unlucky" yew, "planted in almost every church-yard throughout the kingdom." Some renowned large yews of the 1700s reputedly dated from the fourth and fifth centuries. According to lore, souls spent time in purgatory perched in yew branches, and yew roots could find and quiet the mouths of the dead. Like ivy, the yew, being evergreen, had symbolized immortality since pagan times. But trees, especially those with superstitious associations, in burial places had to be perceived as in the benefit of the Church to be permitted at all in Christian burial places. Ecclesiastics tolerated them, either ignoring the lore or co-opting it. Some English parishes grew a few trees in churchyards to provide lumber for church repairs. Yews served as a source of pliable wood for longbows for the militia. In the tenth century, priests dedicated holy yews to various saints and, lacking palm fronds, used their branches in Palm Sunday ceremonies. Churchmen rationalized the practice by declaring the yew an unattractive plant that would not seduce the faithful back to pantheism, for few would choose to sit "Beneath a gloomy Yews unhealthy Shade / Whose noxious Covert's shunn'd by Bird and Beast." The yew was thus one of the few plants considered "safe" for graveyards, as it would not be taken to symbolize a sacred Nature.[6]

Churchmen shunned graveyard plantings just as they rejected the image of heaven as a garden. It was precisely the superstitious valuation of various plants persisting from paganism that prompted Counter-Reformation leaders formally to ban plants in cemeteries in the period after the Council of Trent in 1563. Extending the council's work in defining sacraments and dogma, especially those related to death such as extreme unction, purgatory, and veneration of relics, Charles Borromeo, later canonized, declared in 1577 the formal ban on planting trees, shrubs, vines, flowers, and grasses in cemeteries. Local post-Tridentine councils extended the Catholic fight against vestiges of paganism and rustic folk practices with similar bans. The Church's attempt to combat pantheistic folk practices of ancient origin did not always succeed, however. The bishop of Rennes in Brittany, a French region with a strong Celtic heritage, banned yews in cemeteries as heathen relics—peasants supposedly made "evil use of them"—as well as impediments to gravedigging and circulation of air. Priests who tried to carry out the order for their uprooting encountered violent resistance.[7]

Urban Burials

From the ninth century on, ecclesiastics refused permission for prosperous landowners to be buried *in agris suis* (in their own fields) or *in quaedam solitaria loca* (in any solitary location) even if the propertied elite paid for the privilege or created private, sacred ground by acquiring a martyr's relic and erecting a chapel. Burial for the faithful could take place only *in locum publicum et ecclesiasticum*, in an urban location owned by the Church. As late as the seventeenth century in England, wrote a Calvinist historian, "no corpse could be carried away from home for burial; and, if such burial took place, the body was required to be exhumed and returned to its own parish cemetery for final interment." In 1682, the bishop of Rennes ruled that none of the faithful in his diocese could be buried away from the parish church without specific provision in an approved will. Elsewhere, only heretics such as Waldensians and Hussites managed to avoid the Church-controlled burial system and found their own graveyards.[8]

Urbanization of burial places involved more than Church control. Medieval Christians considered nature evil, the tainted vestiges of Eden lost in Adam's Fall or the wilderness outside the sacred walled Garden into which God thrust Man in punishment for original sin. Even the tamed nature of the walled garden seemed inappropriate to the burial place and the lessons about death that it objectified. By refusing to permit burials in rural locations, the Church also made sanctioned burial places material manifestations of theological doctrine. Like the unruly urban graveyard, death was incomprehensible chaos to be accepted with resignation on faith alone.

Despite the medieval institutionalization of the cult of the dead, cemeteries remained primarily functional places for disposal of corpses. Only the relics of saints, kings, knights, some nobles, and leading ecclesiastics were preserved and enshrined with posterity in mind. Now and then, aristocrats could purchase postmortem commemoration by patronage of the Church. The *very* elite might be entombed in the church sanctuary or a crypt below, while members of lesser nobility and confraternities had vaults in the nave or the churchyard. Earthen burial was for the masses. Most bodies were consigned to the common grave, whether small or more often large, for only as long as it took flesh to decompose. After a few years, as a matter of course, bones were removed to an ossuary for drying and then to the charnel house, located under or adjacent to the church. In most cases, the bones would be mixed indiscriminately with other anonymous remains. As early as the thirteenth century, even small-town churches in France "sat on beds of human bones" which had accumulated over the years.[9]

Small churchyards in town centers enforced the fearful anticipation of death with the hortatory message of *memento mori* (Remember that you must die) ever visible. Many remained focal points at night owing to the "lantern of the dead," the flame lit atop a small tower commonly placed in the burial area. The inevitable cross glimpsed over high walls or atop a locked lych-gate was meant to solicit a prayer for the souls of the dead from passersby. The wills of those who lacked the status to be buried on the east side of the church, nearest the altar, requested burial to the south or west so that their graves would be often passed by those attending services, who might be inclined to pray for them. So often was this location chosen "that it was difficult to prevent other por-

Fig. 1.2. Ruins of Melrose Abbey, Roxburghshire, Scotland, ca. 1891. The abbey, which was destroyed in 1544 and 1569, is shown here from the southwest, where graves were placed to elicit prayers from those entering the church. From a stereographic photograph by G. W. Pierce. From the 1860s into the 1920s, such images, called stereographs, became popular. They were meant to be viewed in stereoscopes, either hand-held or parlor furniture models, to get a three-dimensional effect. Before photographs could be published by presses or were pasted into books, stereographs provided photographic images for public mass-viewing. BMGL.

tions of the churchyard from becoming actually disused."[10] (Fig. 1.2.)

Paris had to develop a system to ease the gross overuse and crowding of its *cimetières* decades before reformers began to scrutinize London's churchyards. The Saint-Innocents, the oldest operative Parisian cemetery, was the first to attract attention. When founded in the tenth century, the Saint-Innocents or des Champeaux (Little Fields) was located next to the small Merovingian church of Saint-Germain-l'Auxerrois northeast of the town walls. In 1186, King Philippe Auguste enlarged the urban enclosure to encompass the trapezoidal cemetery and built other high walls around it, secured at night by a locked gate. Reputedly the most conspicuous, notorious, and fearsome of all European burial places, it was, by the seventeenth century, a walled wilderness in the heart of the city's market quarter. Cloisters built in the fourteenth century surrounded a barren earthen area measuring about two hundred by four hundred feet. One wall bore a mural of thirty panels depicting the *danse macabre* of skeletal Death confronting the living of all social stations, an image suggestive of purgatory at best. By the mid-eighteenth century, the Innocents served twenty-two parishes and received dead from the Hôtel-Dieu (hospital) and epidemic victims. In eight centuries it had buried over 2 million Parisians, most in trenches or *fosses communes* up to thirty feet deep and twenty feet square. They remained open, covered by crude planks, until filled to capacity and above with bodies in shrouds. Only then did sextons cover the anonymous pit with a thin layer of dirt, but just for a brief time. Soil in parts of the Innocents was mounded eight feet above street level when pits were newly filled. The standard two years' burial was usually too short to permit complete decomposition of bodies before bones were removed so the pits could be reused. Still, tales persisted that the earth there had the power to consume flesh in one to nine days. Generous use of powdered lye, a caustic chemical, and quicklime, to minimize soil acidity and odors, sped up the process. (Figs. 1.3, 1.4, 1.5.)

Practices at the Innocents were not unique in Paris or elsewhere in Europe. Only about 5 to 7 percent of the dead escaped the fate of the common trench. Smaller pits contained only about 150 bodies. Newer and smaller Parisian cemeteries such as Sainte-Marguerite, created in 1634, had trenches up to twelve feet deep. This was the rule rather than the exception in most Catholic countries. Burial of the great mass of people was simply a matter of disposal, at best in hallowed ground. Even the bodies of notables—the likes of Molière (1622–1673) and Jean de La Fontaine (1621–1695) in France and Mozart (1756–1791) in Vienna—were consigned to common pits. Madame de Pompadour (1721–1764), once the influential mistress of Louis XV, escaped the fate of mingling with

Fig. 1.3. The Saint-Innocents Church and Cemetery (*Cimetière des Champeaux*), Paris. Engraving, ca. 1780. BMGL.

Fig. 1.4. The Saint-Innocents Church and Cemetery, Paris. Engraving, ca. 1780. BMGL.

Fig. 1.5. The Saint-Innocents Cemetery and Ossuary, Paris. Engraving by Bernier, 1786. BMGL.

the masses in the Innocents by stipulating in her will that she was to be buried in a leaden coffin near the central cross of the churchyard, but even that permanent receptacle was exhumed, reburied, dug up again, and lost. Only an elite minority could purchase the privilege of a family tomb or perhaps a small memorial tablet to counteract temporarily the anonymity of the system and to proclaim memory at the burial place.

Through the centuries, complaints by the common people about treatment of the dead per se were few or went unrecorded and unheeded. One Frenchman reflected his countrymen's resignation in 1683, writing, "Among our people it makes no difference whether we are buried in a cemetery or in a place where asses are flayed." A 1701 translation of the French poem "The Temple of Death" describes a typically barren burial place crowded with gaping pits and graves, where "Poisons are all the Plants the Soil will bear, / And Winter is the only Season there." French cemeteries remained but "a Collection of Ruins of many Ages, and the Rubbish of Twenty Generations." Louis-Sébastien Mercier (1740–1824), author of bourgeois dramas and follower of Rousseau, observed, "He who wishes to be mourned after death should not die in Paris." Indeed, the number of wills stipulating a desired place of burial declined throughout the eighteenth century, indicating not so much a disregard for location as an indifference grounded in the lack of options and resignation to the dreadfulness of any choice that might be made.[11]

By the mid-eighteenth century, escalating urbanization and the rise of a bourgeoisie had accentuated perceptions of and complaints about the social inequities of the funerary system. Ambitions for postmortem remembrance arose among the newly prosperous, who found it increasingly painful to bury their dead anonymously with the masses or to anticipate with the requisite selfless humility their own burial under such conditions. Many who were concerned with issues impinging on self-interest and individuality questioned Church sanctions and traditions, whether or not they converted to Protestantism. The "affective individualism" that historians identify as having transformed familial relationships escalated, with ramifications for attitudes toward burial in that era.[12]

Complaints stemming from newly sensitized tastes and increasingly sentimental family relationships among the bourgeoisie and lesser nobility became empassioned. In the words of the architect Pierre Patte (1723–1814), cemeteries were "veritable refuse dumps." As he gazed in the 1790s into the gaping common pits containing the remains of fathers, brothers, spouses, children, kin, and friends, the public prosecutor Nicher-Cérisy, otherwise a cold-blooded revolutionary, wondered how his supposedly enlightened generation could tolerate such a profanation of Man. His perspective would be echoed again and again by reformers in decades to follow. Marchant de Beaumont complained that "the remains of the vulgar masses went incessantly to stuff the vast common pits—putrid miasmas struck neighborhoods with epidemics as if to punish the living for lack of respect for the dead." The old cemeteries were "narrow, hideous, fetid places where the sun hardly shone." The remains of the poor were buried "by the hundreds in large, deep pits kept open for months on end. Thousands of bones torn from the earth before being reduced to dust added to the horror of these awful places, where the poor hardly dared place a foot during the burial of their dead ones; the middle class had no greater advantages." The bourgeoisie considered cemeteries even more offensive than slaughterhouses, prisons, insane asylums, and hospitals where the terminally ill went to die. All of those institutions were ripe for reform by removal from the centers of urban life. The French began to ponder ways to accomplish that in Paris.[13]

Charges of public health dangers combined with aesthetic complaints to hasten reform. Even a few Church officials, newly sensitized to stench and squalor and urged on by prosperous parishioners, called for burial reform. New sensitivities to foul smells from rotting corpses increased the momentum. Foul odors could no longer be rationalized as sacred or simply ignored; they became suspect as evil in the mundane sense of engendering disease, if not in a supernatural sense as well. At the Clamart cemetery in Paris, adjacent to the royal botanical gardens, investigations in 1713 by Marc-René D'Argenson, lieutenant-general of the Paris police, responded to complaints of polluted air. This led to the discovery of two pits, one containing over thirteen thousand and the other over eighteen thousand bodies, each intended for only ten thousand. D'Argenson demanded that quicklime be added to these trenches and that they be mounded over with four hundred cartloads of dirt. He issued new regulations limiting the size of mass burials. Thereafter, each pit could be no larger than ten feet deep, nine feet wide, and forty-eight feet long and hold a maximum of five hundred bodies deposited in no more than seven orderly layers; but no regulatory agency existed, and the order proved unenforceable.[14]

Responding to increasing criticism by those of influence, the Parlement of Paris charged physicians in 1734 to investigate the sanitary conditions in cemeteries. The resulting report, however, called only for better maintenance. Continued criticism of burial places, paralleling demands for secularization if not complete disestablishment of Church control, escalated through the late eighteenth century. Both France and England gave close attention to theories and proposals set forth in the other country. Even before the Revolution, French secular authorities were determined to have a say in burial practices administered for all by the Church. After an inquisition from 1763 to 1765, a report from the king's procurator general to the Parlement of Paris declared the capital's burial grounds glutted. Parlement ordered them closed in 1765, but with no effect. Years passed until, on March 10, 1776, King Louis XVI confirmed the order but exempted the Innocents, the worst of the lot. The royal decree authorized municipalities to purchase land outside city limits to create new cemeteries. Each parish, according to the plan, could have a walled enclosure of consecrated ground with common pits, but small areas of private grave space would also be made available. The grounds would still be devoid of monuments or plantings, landscape amenities that were, after all, unprecedented; nor would they be readily accessible to visitors (though with use of cemeteries distant from the home and parish of the deceased, mourners often ceased to accompany the body beyond the church).

When civil decrees, to say nothing of sentiment and taste, proved ineffective in changing the Church-run burial system, funerary reformers resorted increasingly to arguments about the public health dangers of urban cemeteries. Félix Vicq-d'Azyr (1748–1794), head of the Société Royale de Médecine, superintendent for epidemics, and the queen's physician, took this approach in the 1778 publication of his *Essay on Burial Places and Dangers*, borrowing ideas from an Italian treatise which

Fig. 1.6. Passageway in the ossuaries added to the Paris Catacombs, old limestone quarries southwest of the city limits. Engraving by Frederick Nash, ca. 1820. BMGL.

postulated that noxious effluvia from mass graves might engender disease. Vicq-d'Azyr's theories had an international impact for decades, far beyond the question of burial reform in French cities.[15]

Without cooperation from ecclesiastical authorities, however, no action could be taken in Paris or in any other cities controlled by the Roman Catholic or Anglican churches. Theories, studies, complaints, and even decrees with the force of law were of no avail until 1780, when the basements of several houses bordering on the Innocents caved in under the weight of two thousand cadavers in an adjacent grave fifty feet deep. The incident precipitated a decisive report on the ill effects of the burial system by Cadet de Vaux, Inspecteur Général des Objets de Salubrité, read before the Royal Academy of Science in 1783. Finally, in turn, the Council of State, on November 9, 1785, ordered the cemetery to be destroyed and replaced by a public market. But more than a civil decree would be necessary to dismantle the Innocents. Under intense pressure in 1786, Monseigneur Leclerc de Juigné, archbishop of Paris, reluctantly lent the Church's authority to the move, ordering the cemetery's final suppression.

Under the supervision of the Royal Society of Medicine, the earth of the Innocents was broken to a depth of five feet and sifted to yield as many bones as possible. These were transported to subterranean limestone quarries west of the city, consecrated as an ossuary. The Church renamed them the Catacombs in reference to the secret labyrinth under Rome used by early Christians for burial as well as worship. The architect Héricart de Thury supervised the artistic arrangement of the bones in corridors and rooms carved out of the quarries. The spectacle created by moving the contents of the Innocents to the Catacombs at Montrouge on the southeastern urban periphery continued, even by torchlight, for two years, serving as a mild prelude to the public spectacles of death witnessed in the next decade under the Reign of Terror. (Fig. 1.6.)

English Churchyards and Dissenters' Solutions

English Calvinists rejected the objects and symbols of the churchyard as superstitious relics intended to make the common man "enter into a bondage of fear with reference to spirits of evil, which he would be taught to conceive of as roaming in malicious throngs invisibly through space, on mischief to men intent." Soliciting prayers at the cemetery from passersby was akin to the corruption of selling indulgences, Calvinists charged, "falsely pretending to the people that they had delivered their dear friends from purgatory and neutralizing all civil and ecclesiastical discipline."[16]

Their criticisms were not unfounded. The Church did indeed conceive of the churchyard as a means of imposing social control. After passing the cemetery, men were meant to proceed on, sobered by the inevitability of their own demise and their dependence on the Church as the sole source of salvation. Locating burial grounds in the midst of the town, however, did not prevent them from becoming barren, unsightly places. The need to use and reuse almost every inch of the small, constricted space allotted precluded planting trees and shrubs. Accounts of trees with funerary significance appearing in graveyards before the eighteenth century are misleading. Engravings of burial grounds in English rural villages reveal the same wilderness in microcosm that existed in burial grounds in the heart of London, Paris, and other European cities. Many Protestants, rejecting the authority of the Catholic Church, particularly as dictated by the Counter-Reformation, turned back to older folkways not explicitly banned in the Bible. In turn, the Church excluded Protestants from burial in the hallowed ground of Roman Catholic or Anglican cemeteries. In 1598, Bishop Henri de Sponde advised the Huguenots of Bordeaux to "search, if you will, in other cemeteries than those [of the Catholic Church] to which you no longer have any right, either by nature or by humanity, . . . or by religion."[17]

The emergence of new notions about death as well as the reform of practices and places associated with it relate directly to the rise of Protestantism, Calvinism in particular. Seeds of John Calvin's theology were planted in France, flowered in Switzerland, and took root most successfully in England and its colonies. The Calvinist rejection of papist culture necessitated the creation of new and alternative cultural forms. Places of "Publique Buriall" were to be secular and civil, the funeral liturgy abolished; "in the burial of the dead," Calvin prescribed, "we must use some honest shew." He personally, but unsuccessfully, demanded that his own grave site not be marked so that followers would not treat his remains as relics.[18]

Codification of Calvin's notions about burial and other subjects appeared in *A Directory for the Publique Worship of God, Throughout the Three Kingdoms of England, Scotland, and Ireland*, approved by Parliament as law in 1644:

> When any person departeth this live, let the dead body, upon the day of Buriall, be decently attended from the house to the place appointed for Publique Buriall, and there immediately interred without Ceremony.
>
> And because the customs of kneeling down, and praying by, or toward the dead Corps, and any other such usages, in the place where it lies, before it be carried to Buriall, are Superstitious: that for that, praying, reading and singing both in going to the Grave . . . have been grossly abused, are no way benificiall to the dead, and have proved many ways hurtfull to the living, therefore let all such things be laid aside.
>
> Howbeit, we judge it very convenient, that the Christian friends which accompany the body to the place appointed for publique Buriall, do apply themselves to meditations, and conferences suitable to the occasion. And, that the minister as upon other occasions, so at this time, if he be present, may put them in remembrance of their duty.
>
> That this shall not extend to deny any civill respects or differences at the Burial, suitable to the rank and condition of the party deceased while he was living.

The Westminster Assembly of Divines (1644) radically revised English Church doctrine and practices through the Westminster Confession (1646). Denouncing the Anglican episcopacy in favor of congregationalism, the "Enforcers of Conscience" created a new national church, excluding the priests, rituals, and places of the Anglican Church and the "Bondage of Canon Law."[19]

Among other changes, the Calvinists imposed "Publique Buriall" on all of Britain for a time. They established "burying grounds" or "graveyards" without proximity to meetinghouses, which were themselves unconsecrated structures no longer called "churches." They eschewed the terms "churchyard" and "cemetery," associated with Church control. Believers in the doctrine of predestination, they considered presumptuous the expectation that all the dead were destined for "the resurrection to eternal life." Such matters were beyond man's ability to influence through good works in life or prayers thereafter.

The institutionalization of secular, nonsacred burial places was most successful in England and its colonies, even after the overthrow of Cromwell's Commonwealth and restoration of the Catholic-leaning Stuart monarchy in 1660, which reestablished Anglican control. The Church could again arbitrarily refuse burial in consecrated ground to the excommunicated, the unbaptized, suicides, lunatics, and those found guilty of capital crimes. After the Act of Uniformity (1662) under Charles II reimposed Anglican rule, Puritans, Quakers, Presbyterians, and other Independents, forced into formal "nonconformity" as Dissenters, suffered the same postmortem fate. They, for their part, were equally loath to associate the remains of their dead with the "popish" or to pay burial fees to Church of England coffers.

In 1665, Dissenters petitioned the Corporation of the City of London for land north of the Moorgate for their own burial ground. They received approval to create a small graveyard at Bunhill Fields, a block-square site used for burying the dead outside Church auspices since Elizabethan times. Edward Seymour, Duke of Somerset, first used the place, said to be the site of an ancient

Fig. 1.7. Tomb of Dr. Isaac Watts, Bunhill Fields Burial Ground, London, ca. 1860. From a stereographic photograph by William Miller. BMGL.

Fig. 1.8. John Bunyan's new tomb with effigy, 1862, in Bunhill Fields, erected by the public subscription campaign led by the Earl of Shaftesbury, ca. 1865. Bunhill Fields was closed to further burials in 1854 but kept intact by the Bunhill Fields Preservation Committtee in 1865, and an Act of Parliament in 1867, leading to its 1869 dedication as a London park. Photograph by Dundall Downes in *The Pilgrim's Progress*, 1865.

Saxon tumulus, for burial in 1547, reinterring there a thousand cartloads of bones from the charnel house of Saint Paul's Cathedral. Henceforth, the grounds, dubbed "Bone Hill," were used as a common cemetery during the plague of 1665 and the Great Fire of 1666. Use was haphazard until Nonconformists received permission to enclose the site with a brick wall and gate.[20] There, across the City Road from John Wesley's house, Puritans, Baptists, Methodists, Presbyterians, Quakers, Swedenborgians, Independents, and other Nonconformists established a new cult of tombs, erecting monuments to religious, intellectual, and political leaders. Called the Dissenters' Westminster Abbey or Campo Santo by virtue of the number of notable burials, this repository juxtaposed the cenotaph of Isaac Watts with the graves of Daniel Defoe; Susannah Wesley, mother of the leaders of Methodism; George Fox, founder of the Society of Friends; and many of Cromwell's associates. William Blake's grave is also there, its precise location unmarked and forgotten. The sarcophagus of John Bunyan, who died in 1688, served as a focal point, revered much like the relics of a saint placed to sanctify a Catholic church and churchyard, the very forms rejected by the Nonconformists. One observer wrote in 1819, "So numerous have been and still are the dying requests of his idolaters to be buried as near as possible" to the grave of the author of the popular *Pilgrim's Progress* "that it is not now possible to obtain a grave near him, the whole surrounding earth being entirely preoccupied by dead bodies." Clearly there was no policy of routinely vacating old graves to make way for new burials as had been the case in Church cemeteries.[21] (Figs. 1.7, 1.8.)

Dissenters considered Bunhill Fields common for all of London and nondenominational in that anyone who could not or would not be buried under High Church auspices could find a place there for a price. Freeholds for rare available space were sold in perpetuity until the land ran out in 1832. The sale of graves in perpetuity was innovative and signaled new motivations in Calvinist theology to keep the body intact in its original place of "rest" so that it could be identified. Bunhill Fields also provided facilities for the less eminent in a central trench in which coffins were stacked, later covered by a paved walk. For all its social novelty, Bunhill Fields offered nothing innovative in terms of landscape design. The narrow spaces between crowded stones were rank with weeds or packed with barren earth as in any Anglican churchyard. One visitor wrote that in the 1840s it was "choke-full of graves in a state of neglect, and so far as disorderly arrangement and want of care were concerned, made a painful impression." By 1852, when the last of the dead were interred, the grounds held about 124,000 bodies. Over six thousand vaults and tombs were sunk seven or more feet underground. Like older churchyards, it had few plantings. Still, it had signaled radical Protestants' nascent impulse to create a new kind of burial place, including the use of gravestones for commemorative purposes independent of Church or State.[22]

The small cemeteries that had been used for many centuries posed problems of crowding and filth in London as in Paris. In 1671, John Evelyn described English churchyards as "filled up with Earth &c to the very top of the Walls, & many above the walls, so as the Churches seem'd to be built in pits." Worse yet, as one eighteenth-century epitaph described a London churchyard:

> *Here nauseous weeds each pile surround,*
> *And things obscene bestrew the ground;*
> *Sculls, bones, in moulding fragment lie,*
> *All dreadful emblems of mortality.*

Even newer London churchyards such as Saint Margaret's and Tothill Fields (1640) had become typically unpleasant by the nineteenth century.[23]

The utility of small urban churchyards was extended by an efficient system for recycling space and disposing of exhumed bones. As late as 1819 one Englishman observed, "Many tons of human bones every year are sent from London to the north, where they are crushed in mills contrived for the purpose and used as manure." Demand for such fertilizer was even greater than could be met by the periodic emptying of urban graves. According to one Lincolnshire resident: "The eagerness of English agriculturists to obtain this manure [human bones] and the cupidity of foreigners in supplying it, is such as to induce the latter to rob the tombs of their forefathers. Bones of all descriptions are imported, and pieces of half-decayed coffin attire are found among them." The extent of the sale of human remains to English fertilizer mills is unknown, as are the international dimensions of the trade. Use of human remains for fertilizer was considered such a sordid business that few records of the practice remain, but it was known even in America. One Bostonian observed in 1832, "In some places, so little is the respect for the dead, that the mouldering bodies have been bartered to nourish vegetation." The practice continued for decades, as Mrs. Basil Holmes, investigating the disappearance of old London churchyards, reported in 1896.[24]

That practice did not ease the crowding, nor did the existence of over a hundred parish churchyards, each very small, scattered throughout London. Many hundreds of others, some dating back to the Romans and Saxons, had been built over by churches, schools, businesses, houses, and streets over the centuries—even more so with the advent of railroad construction. By 1840, the churchyard of St. Martin-in-the-Fields, only two hundred feet square, still contained an estimated seventy thousand burials. One Englishman observed in 1845: "Many a time have I shudderingly passed by the old graveyards of London. I have one of them now in my mind's eye—it is situated in one of the most densely populated portions of the metropolis, between Fleet Street and Holborn, surrounded by high, dark dwellings, whose smokey walls frown upon the small patch of mortality. Not a blade of grass cheers that lonely charnel-house, but its black, uneven surface lies bare to the sun whenever that luminary can pierce the mass of fog and mist which envelopes the overgrown city." The few gravestones, he reported, "which lie here and there, bearing frail records of scarcely more enduring love, are broken and defaced. . . . One miserable, stunted tree, with blackened trunk and leafless boughs, remains—a horrible libel upon vegetation."[25] Such urban horrors impelled a literary nostalgia for the simplicity of the English country churchyard long before the burial reform movement resulted in new legislation.[26]

Tradition and Reform in New England

Even in colonial Massachusetts towns surrounded by rural land, burial grounds were small plots within central commons sandwiched among the living. Overcrowding became a particular problem in Boston. As early as the 1730s, the town's three original burial places—the first, now King's Chapel (1630); the second, Copp's Hill (1660); and the third, Old Granary (1660)—had so little space left that the dead often had to be buried four deep or in small common trenches. A fourth graveyard was opened on the distant south end of the Boston Common in 1756. Tradition holds that it was the first used for blacks (most of them slaves), "strangers" who died while visiting Boston, and Catholics. There, too, during the Revolution, the British buried their common soldiers, if not in mass graves where they fell. Since it was farthest from the market center of the town, Bostonians considered it the least desirable site, reflecting an unwillingness to consider the possibility of creating more commodious burial places in more remote locations. A tradition of burial close to home persisted.

New England graveyards indicate the same urge to secularize burials that was evident among English Calvinists until Cromwell's fall in 1660 and in the Dissenters' Bunhill Fields (1665). The symbolic importance of structuring burial space outside the sphere of the Church was not lost on the English authorities. After the Catholic King James II revoked the Massachusetts Bay Company charter and established administrative control through the Dominion of New England, his hated governor, Sir Edmund Andros, dug up part of Boston's first burying ground in May 1688, displacing the graves of the colony's founding fathers so as to plant the Anglican King's Chapel there. He had multiple motives. First and foremost, his small group of Anglicans needed their own church. Bostonians begrudged their use of the Old South Meeting House, and Andros wanted to sanctify the ground where he had buried his wife, Marie, the previous February. But there were larger, symbolic reasons as well. Conversion of the originally secular burial ground to a churchyard amounted to the forcible imposition of royal political and religious control over the Puritan Commonwealth. For Tories, the act may have served as ritual retaliation against the Puritan Cromwell's destruction of High Church property in England three decades before. But Bostonians resented the loss of their political autonomy and the "very grievous" introduction of "idolatrous" papist forms such as the closing of schools and shops on Christmas even more than the violation of the graves of John Winthrop, Isaac Johnson, and many of the town's first settlers, whose precise locations in many cases had been long forgotten.[27]

Indeed, seventeenth-century New England ministers preached a Puritan rationale for continuing to disregard the dead. Increase Mather (1639–1723) declared that "to praise the dead is to praise corruptible flesh . . . to praise memory is to worship the dead." Only Providence could determine who were the "Saints," the "saved," an inscrutable mystery to man. Ministers counseled congregants to look upon their burial grounds and recognize the common fate of all men. William Cooper (1693–1743) urged, "Look into the grave, and see a dead body, that has been buried there but a month or two, all covered with darkness and corruption, and say whether it is suitable for one to have high thoughts of himself." Gazing into gaping graves, which became unavoidable as urban life closed in upon the poorly kept burying grounds, was meant to mortify pride, to quash individualism and the ambition to realize worldly goals.[28]

Burial landscapes were not structured for public access, let alone meditation on the example of those who lived in the past. No paths guided visitors' steps among the graves. Tombs were tightly clustered, occupying virtually every bit of space. New Englanders treated their graveyards as commons, not unlike other functional parcels of land reserved to serve communal needs. (Fig. 1.9.) Most burial grounds doubled as pastures for grazing cattle on their well-fertilized grasses, more desirable than the grass of the central common, while their enclosures kept the cattle from straying. In 1703, the town of Boston gave George Ripley responsibility for watering the bulls kept "by night in the burry-

Fig. 1.9. "Old Burial Hill," Plymouth, Massachusetts. From a stereographic photograph by William S. Robbins, ca. 1860. BMGL.

ing place" later called the Granary. Likewise, in 1713, James Williams persuaded the selectmen "to Lett unto him the grass of Ye South burying place" for forty shillings. For the privilege, he agreed to pay for any damage "wch may happen to the graves by reason of his cows going there." In 1718, William Young paid only fifteen shillings "for his Cow^{s} grazeing in the Old Burying place the Last Summer." In 1758, John Ramstead spent three pounds, six shillings, and eightpence for the "Herbage" in the south (Granary) graveyard. Similar practices existed even in rural towns around Boston. In 1654, the selectmen of Roxbury, then a separate town, recorded that after "a voat consarning the burying place Mr John Alcok was granted liberty to fed the burying place he keping the sayd burying place in good and sufficyent fenc and a gate with a locke and two kieas." A century later, Roxbury town fathers again voted to "Lett as Usual the Herbage" in the graveyard. The practice was not questioned until the early nineteenth century, when new notions developed about what activities should be acceptable in a town and concerns arose about issues of sanitation involved in keeping animals in overused burial grounds.[29]

It was not yet common to place markers over every burial site, although scholars have yet to determine who merited a marker in Puritan New England. Was it simply a matter of the deceased's having family or friends with sufficient means to commission the gravestone, or ready availability of local carvers to make one? Some stones, indicating only the name of the first burial or that of the patriarch, were placed over family tombs, inconspicuous, vertical brick and masonry shafts belowground. A few others mark multiple burials of children who died during epidemics. Well into the eighteenth century, the iconography of these stones objectified the persistence of the medieval dualism of good and evil, despite Church sanctions, although scholars have interpreted the ubiquitous death's-head as a "spirit portrait" or sign representing the soul of the deceased. The thin, flat stones, usually of gray slate with engraved letters often painted black, emphasized the message of *momento mori*, the reminder that each individual must die, the grim lesson of Calvinistic predestination. Commemoration of individual lives and mundane accomplishments had no place in New England graveyards.[30] (Figs. 1.10, 1.11.)

With the exception of London's Bunhill Fields and New England graveyards, the secularization of burial grounds was still rare. An impulse toward reform was growing, however, and it involved far more than religious practices. It drew upon trends in taste and sentiment that were beginning to permeate the culture by way of new classes of literate artisans, merchants, and professionals in France as well as in Old and New England. A new international consensus was developing. When Wordsworth (1770–1850) repeated in his "Essay upon Epitaphs" (1810) the usual complaints about "the unsightly manner in which our monuments are crowded

Fig. 1.10. Death's-head on Mrs. Hannah Goodkin stone, 1688, Cambridge (Massachusetts) Burial Ground. Photograph by BMGL, 1978.

Fig. 1.11. Dual stone with "spirit portraits," 1752 and 1744, Concord (Massachusetts) hillside burial ground. Photograph by BMGL, 1978.

together in the busy, noisy, unclean and almost grassless church-yard of a large town," he went further than most previous critics by offering a vision of a new sort of place that would reintegrate Death with Nature, a funerary setting that would serve as a landscape of secular memory, both personal and communal. The first models for such places appeared with the development of eighteenth-century English landscaped gardens, then with the adoption of that trend by the French, and finally with radical funerary reform in the wake of the French Revolution.[31]

2

THE ENGLISH GARDEN

Memory, Nature, and Design

God Almightie first planted a garden.

—Francis Bacon, *Of Gardens* (1625)

Gardening is more antique and nearer God's work than poetry.

—Charles Bridgeman (1725)

History in general is a Romance that is believed, and . . . Romance is a History that it not believed.

—Horace Walpole, letter to Robert Henry (1783)

Nature was a less fearsome concept for the English in the seventeenth and eighteenth centuries than for many other Europeans, and rural places were seen as attractive retreats by those who espoused the new religious, philosophical, and political leanings and rejected the old order. Their taste for idealized Nature had revolutionary implications, involving first the effort to find appropriate sites for contemplation of the Divine outside Church auspices and later the desire of the literate elite for places that epitomized the new conceptions of "natural law," history, and the relationship between civic virtue and culture. The new commemorative sensibility found expression in neoclassical forms in picturesque settings, as in the formulaic English "landscaped garden," later emulated on the Continent and in America.

Out of these changing sensibilities and tastes arose the commemorative impulse, the new desire for memorialization. Philippe Ariès attributes it to an alteration in the "collective unconscous." Lawrence Stone finds that for the rising elite in the sixteenth century, "the art of dying was replaced by the art of living." Reflections once put off until the approach of death were "spread out over the whole space of a lifetime," imbuing every day with "a melancholy sense of the brevity of life." By the eighteenth century, at least for liberal intellectuals, the fear of death was "replaced by the idea of mortality in general" and thus "lost its intensity." Melancholy, no longer pathological, was considered virtuous, and granted the value formerly associated with dying a "good death." Naturalistic landscapes designed to stir the sentiment of melancholy appealed to this new mentality. They came to be perceived as appropriate places for commemorative structures.[1]

Once it became a matter for contemplation, death could no longer remain banal, an inevitability to be accepted on faith alone. Even the Calvinists, who had emphasized logic rather than simple faith or revelation, came to value sentiment as a means of achieving the correct state of mind in which to follow the paths of virtue. As early as the 1630s they decided that the ideal place for contemplation of death was amid Nature, precisely the sort of thinking that post-Tridentine Catholics decried as pantheistic. The Puritan poet John Milton (1608–1674) rejected the old notion that melancholy was a symptom of sickness. In *Il Penseroso* (ca. 1635), he praises the meditative mood of the person "who by day courts the dark shadows in the close coverts of a wood by the brook." Milton postulates a proto-romantic landscape, advising the pensive man to retreat:

> *To arched walks of twilight groves,*
> *And shadows brown, that Sylvan loves,*
> *Of pine or monumental oak,*
> *Where the rude axe with heaved stroke*
> *Was never heard the nymphs to daunt,*
> *Or fright them from their hallowed haunt.*[2]

Milton envisioned a garden as the re-creation of Eden. Such a landscape was capable of bewitching the observer with the "cherub of Contemplation" or personified "Sleep." The spirits of this wooded wilderness were benign, no longer the demons of Christian tradition. In contrast to the "loathed Melancholy" despised by the active men of the world in Milton's *L'Allegro* (1632), such a natural landscape fostered "divinest Melancholy," with its implications of holiness, wisdom, and beauty. The realization of Milton's vision came into vogue in secularized terms in the late seventeenth century, just as sites of wooded wilderness were in fact becoming scarce with the denuding of the English countryside for timber.

The fashionable melancholy of Cromwell's Commonwealth endured among Dissenters thereafter. Despite persistent use of a grim iconography of death and stern warnings about man's postmortem fate, Puritanism in both Old and New England contained the seeds of a more benign, less medieval view of death. Puritans constantly scrutinized their daily lives, their souls, and their environment for evidence of the design of Providence for themselves and their communities. They urged each individual to confront his or her mortality. The cult of the melancholy in literature and landscape had its origins in this aspect of radical Protestantism.

At the same time, the growing desire for status—and for commemoration—inspired the royalist physician Sir Thomas Browne (1605–1682) to warn his readers in *Hydriotaphia: Urne-Buriall; or, A Discourse of the Sepulchrall Urnes Lately Found in Norfolk* (1658) of the futility of wishing "to extend our memories by monuments." The identity of ancients who were interred with such intentions had long been forgotten, wrote Browne: "The iniquity of oblivion blindly deals with the memory of men without distinction to merit of perpetuity. The greater part must be content to be as though they had not been: to be found in the register of God, not in the record of man." Thus, "in vain do individuals hope for immortality, or any patent from oblivion. There is nothing strictly immortal but immortality." Browne's tract failed to slow the growing commemorative impulse, whose flame was fanned by other, more influential intellectual and cultural forces.[3]

Even some Anglican authors lauded a "religious melancholy or pious sadness." John Evelyn (1620–1706), a royalist, learned to celebrate the taste for the rural from his self-imposed exile, first in France and Italy upon the outbreak of Cromwell's Civil War, then on an estate in Deptford, southeast of London, where, in 1653, he began developing its gardens until the Restoration in 1660 brought his return to prominence. In England by then nature itself was in ruins, and therefore prompted the same nostalgia and melancholy as other symbols of the past. Among their many acts of iconoclasm, Cromwell's Puritans had cut down the old trees in ancestral parks. Nature destroyed, however, seemed even more sublime than Nature primeval. Evelyn's *Silva; or, A Discourse of Forest-Trees* (1664), the first book published by the Royal Society (1660), lists "forests in England, many of which are without trees," and contemplates ways of reforesting His Majesty's largely denuded realm, though only the very wealthy could afford the luxury of preserving woods and planting trees for their aesthetic value alone.[4]

Evelyn's suggestions for a landscape appropriate for burials are informed by a classical taste. *Silva* recounts the history of "divine, as well as civil uses" of groves consecrated as by the ancients "to the Gentile Deities and Heroes." Oak groves or "Arboreus Temples" provided sublime sites for worship. Plato, Evelyn notes, planted trees over burial sites "to obumbrate the departed," and the "Saviour chose a garden as a place of Sepulchre." Thus, "for many weighty causes, there are no places more fit to bury our dead than in our gardens and groves, or airy fields, *sub dio*, where our beds may be decked and carpeted with verdant and fragrant flowers, trees, and perennial plants, the most natural and instructive hieroglyphics of our expected resurrection and immortality."[5]

To build up the nation's depleted timber resources, Evelyn recommended planting in gardens and cemeteries profitable trees, both useful and ornamental, from around the world. Burying the dead in forests would preserve land for growing trees. Evelyn liked the "architectonial qualities" of trees, among the most stable elements in a landscape. In his essay "The Sacredness and Use of Standing Groves" he not only points to the emotional benefits to be derived from a wooded setting but also suggests that trees in a burial place would have didactic as well as practical uses. Although English landscape gardeners did not immediately heed his advice about creating "natural philosophers' gardens," by the next century the English were developing timber reserves on private estates while at the same time creating places of melancholy contemplation.[6]

After the plague of 1665 and the Great Fire of London in 1666, Evelyn crusaded unsuccessfully for establishing extramural cemeteries modeled after the Ceramicus outside Athens or the burial places along Rome's Appian Way. His suggestions for wooded cemeteries were far different aesthetically from the picturesque landscapes later developed in English gardens. He proposed creating a "universal cemetery to all the parishes" of London on a mile-long linear strip of land north of the city walls. There, visitors could stroll through "ample walks of trees, the walls adorned with monuments, inscriptions and titles, apt for contemplation and the memory of the defunct." Despite his reference to it as a "funeral grove," the description suggests a huge open-air nave under an arched canopy of trees, its walls displaying funerary tablets like those in churches.[7] Sir Christopher Wren (1632–1723), who with Evelyn planned London's reconstruction after the Great Fire, proposed similar cemeteries for display of monuments designed by architects and sculptors. Wren hoped to do away with churchyards and church crypts, which might endanger the health of the city's residents. Both Evelyn and Wren proposed burial grounds that would not differentiate according to parish or sect but would serve all of London. They shared as well the growing desire, even among Anglicans, for more widespread commemoration than was possible under the Church-controlled burial system.[8]

The taste for melancholy, or pleasure from subtle sadness, cultivated in a naturalistic setting developed as a variation on and an outgrowth of the Calvinist theology of election. The Dissenting (Baptist) minister George Cokayne (1665–1722), a friend of John Bunyan, urged his congregation in 1691 "to walk amongst the Tombs while we are here; that Death might not be a surprise." Samuel Clarke (1675–1729), philosopher, rationalist, and author of *A Discourse Concerning the Unchangeable Obligations of Natural Religion* (1706), considered the "most overt proof of Election a longing for death and a delight in musing upon it." The Nonconformist hymn writer Isaac Watts (1674–1748) counseled melancholy meditation in *Reliquiae Iuveniles* (1742) and recommended the burial ground as an ideal setting.[9] It was at this time that the word "sentimental" achieved currency. According to the historian John Draper, a sentimentalist was nothing more than "a Calvinist who believes himself saved" and "finds signs of personal grace through meditation."[10] Louis Cazamian also observes that in England "midnight thoughts, the obsession of the grave, the effusions of intimate grief and the pleasure of shedding tears, are directly connected through their innermost origins with the renascence of the Puritan spirit, which is favored by the rise of the middle class."[11] England's so-called Graveyard School of poets and the associated cult of the melancholy were natural outgrowths of these trends in Protestantism that were rapidly evolving beyond the Calvinists and the liberal sects into philosophies shared by those who retained loose Catholic and Anglican affiliations, Freemasons and Deists, and Whigs, the political opposition to the old order.[12]

As religious orthodoxy declined, a void remained to be filled by reason and recognition of "natural" rather than divine law. Sacred space was secularized and reshaped in more natural forms. Poets and theorists supplanted ministers in prescribing places for spiritual reflection. They favored naturalistic landscapes containing ruins and monuments. Philosophers and designers shared ideas on how material commemorative forms could make better citizens.[13] Allegorical figures and mythological events drawn from classical literature were used to teach moral and philosophical lessons about the relationship of the self to the universe, of man to Nature.

The word "taste"—meaning perception or appreciation of quality, especially in reference to landscapes—

came into use in England in the early eighteenth century. Milton and Addison used the word in reference to a discerning sense of the appropriate, harmonious, beautiful, and excellent. Taste would, they believed, be a catalyst for the good. Hence, both the word and the concept took on ideological and spiritual connotations. And the taste that was forming at the turn of the eighteenth century would soon be exemplified by "the picturesque."

Inventing "the Picturesque"

Numerous sources in art, literature, and philosophy encouraged the growing interest in melancholy and in naturalistic places to foster meditation. As early as 1675, Evelyn wrote his friend Browne of his intention "to show how the air and genius of gardens operate upon the human spirits towards virtue and sanctity . . . [h]ow caves, grots, mounts, and irregular ornaments of gardens do contribute to contemplative and philosophical enthusiasm; how *elysium, antrum, nemus, paradysus, hortus, locus*, etc., signify all of them *rem sacrum et divinam*; for these expedients do influence the soul and spirits of men and prepare them to converse with good angels." Evelyn adapted Robert Burton's theories from *The Anatomy of Melancholy* (1621), which held that a pensive state of mind could be induced by a stroll "amongst orchards, gardens, bowers, mounts, and arbours, artificial wilderness, green thickets, arches, groves, lawns, rivulets, fountains, and such like pleasant places." By the eighteenth century these notions would coalesce into the "picturesque" style of landscape design.[14]

The term "picturesque," applied to a naturalistic landscape, refers to design elements derived from the paintings of Claude Lorrain, a Frenchman who lived in Rome from 1625 until his death in 1682. He and others after him depicted scenes featuring ancient Roman monuments in the Italian countryside. The British elite snapped up these images, purchased in sepia drawings and etchings on their sojourns in Italy in the eighteenth century. Lorrain's contemporary, Nicolas Poussin (1594–1665), diverging from the imagery of the French baroque, depicted the theme of death in a pastoral setting in his *Et in Arcadia Ego* (1636), showing shepherds contemplating an ancient sarcophagus. The painting marked "a radical break with the mediaeval, moralizing tradition," according to the art historian Erwin Panofsky. Such images, copied by Richard Wilson (1713–1782), Welsh founder of the English school of landscape painting, in his *Ego fui in Arcadia* (1755), and by Sir Joshua Reynolds (1723–1792), president of the Royal Academy of Art, in his *Et in Arcadia Ego* (1769), recurred in verse and in actual landscapes designed to stimulate philosophy if not fantasy in the visitor's mind.[15] Poussin's more complex duet of narrative paintings, *Landscape with the Body of Phocion* and *The Ashes of Phocion Collected by His Widow* (both 1648), were important influences in the history of picturesque landscape design. In the first, a mount, a tower, and bodies of water create a complex terrain interspersed with temples, sarcophagi, and tombs to which the shrouded body of Phocion is borne while mourners linger hither and yon, grieving or meditating in a naturalistic funerary setting. A town is visible in the distance, indicating the practice of extramural burials. In the second, time has passed and the landscape has changed with the addition of structures and the growth of trees. These images revolutionized English garden aesthetics and eventually provided prototypes for new kinds of burial places.[16] (Fig. 2.1.)

With the death of Charles II in 1685, funeral elegies idealized naturalistic landscapes as conducive to the contemplation of mortality. Edmund Arwaker's ode evokes such a place:

> *Behold a* Grove, *whose* Melancholy *shade*
> *Appear'd for* Sorrow's *last retirement made,*
> *Where in confus'd disorder grew,*
> *Bidding Defiance to the Sun's bright Eye*
> *The* Mournful *Cypress and* Unlucky *Yew:*
> *So closely interwov'n they were,*
> *His Mid-day Beams were Strangers There.*

Another poet, "J.H., Esq.," described a setting where "the melancholy Muse," overcome by "the horror of the Dismal News" of the king's death, languishes "Beneath a Doting Willow's Shade," one of the first references to the willow as site and symbol of mourning, while a Cavalier ode by "Sir F.F., Knight of Bath," set grieving among "*Ruins*, that to Religions Sacred were of *yore*." These verses suggest some of the landscape elements

Fig. 2.1. Nicolas Poussin, *Landscape with the Ashes of Phocion*, also known as *The Ashes of Phocion Collected by His Widow*, 1648. © National Museums of Liverpool (Walker Art Gallery).

that would later characterize English gardens as well as the stylized imagery of mourning pictures.[17]

Philosophical as well as literary and artistic trends encouraged the development of English gardens as meditative places. Notions about individual freedom and the goodness of "natural man" fed the growing taste for Nature. The writings of the Cambridge Platonists, academics derisively labeled Unitarians by the Calvinists, emphasized a natural, rational moral sense. The rise of the landscaped garden also coincided with a period of free religious expression, the heights of Deism, from 1685 to 1742. Given the central role accorded the senses, especially the visual, in Lockean epistemology, it seems inevitable that thinkers who rejected the Church as the prime source for instilling and fostering spiritual values would urge the creation of sensually rich, naturalistic environments for the purpose of advancing moral philosophy—places that differed greatly from the formally structured, symmetrical, enclosed gardens inspired by French and Dutch tastes.

The first philosopher to do so was Anthony Ashley Cooper, third Earl of Shaftesbury (1671–1713), grandson of the founder of Whiggism. Educated by John Locke (1632–1704), he became a leading Deist and Whig politician. In his *Characteristicks of Men, Manners, Opinions, Times* (1711), he deified and personified Nature as the Genius of Place, "Wise Substitute of Providence!" Nature became "All loving and All-lovely," and "Rural Meditations" sacred. Shaftesbury's writings influenced English literati and many on the Continent who read him in Diderot's translation.[18] He considered taste a civic virtue. For him, aesthetics and ethics were closely related, indeed virtually the same. Shaftesbury thought of the "moral sense" as a "natural virtue," the ability to distinguish not just good from evil but beauty from ugliness. Equating the sense of beauty with the moral sense, he found both inherent in the mind when associated with emotions activated by the elements of a naturalistic environment, especially a funerary environment, where the solitude of graves and the sacredness of Nature appealed to the emotions as well as the intellect. For the like-minded, enamored of beauty in the "romantick way," a country seat was an asylum, a place of healing leisure from the profane sphere of commerce and politics.[19]

The essayists Joseph Addison (1672–1719) and Richard Steele (1672–1729) disseminated similar ideas internationally through articles in *The Spectator*. Reaching about 10,000 originally and more in reprints, the journal, founded in 1711, popularized the liberal philosophy of thinkers such as Newton and Voltaire, bridging the gap between theology, science, and aesthetic taste, blending Nature and Reason. Addison was the first, in 1711, to attack publicly the artificial, linear formality of garden design borrowed from the French, as he praised the new, naturalistic gardens as "Elysia."[20] Another of Shaftesbury's followers, Sir William Chambers (1723–1796), introduced readers in his *Dissertation on Oriental Gardening* (1722) to a different precedent for naturalistic landscapes: the Chinese garden "especially laid out for the purpose of evoking a mood of agreeable melancholy and the sense of the transitoriness of all natural beauty and human glory."[21] Francis Hutcheson (1694–1746), professor of moral philosophy at Glasgow, echoed Shaftesbury's ideas about the relationship of the moral sense to the external senses. His advocacy of the "natural garden" appeared in his *Inquiry into the Origins of Our Ideas of Beauty and Virtue* (1725).

Shaftesbury's impact on shaping landscape design is also reflected in the work of the poet and aesthetic theorist Alexander Pope (1688–1744). In *Moral Essays* (1731–1735) and other writings, Pope built upon Shaftesbury's notions of Nature's moral powers, asserting the capability of man to shape a naturalistic environment that would stir emotions and associations. Pope believed in the ability of Art to improve Nature. Blending classical and contemporary philosophy, literature, and art, Pope laid down rules for the rising vogue in garden design and described the functions of many recommended garden elements. In his *Essay on Man* (1734), for instance, he asserts the "moral utility" of commemorative statuary when engraved with instructive messages of the past. Like Horace, Pope considered the death of an individual, unknown and unwept, an unfortunate fate. He proposed using poetry and material commemoration in garden settings as a remedy for the failure of memory.[22]

Estate proprietors ambitious to create their own gardens eagerly followed Pope's guidelines. In a poetic epistle to Richard Boyle (1674–1753), Earl of Burlington, Pope cautions his friend not to forget the goddess Nature in laying out his suburban grounds at Chiswick, which he designed with the aid of the landscape painter William Kent (1684–1748) between 1730 and 1737. In his *Moral Essays* (1731), Pope advises Burlington and other aspiring designers:

> *To build, to plant, whatever you intend,*
> *To rear the Column, or the Arch to bend,*
> *To swell the Terras, or to sink the Grot;*
> *In all, let Nature never be forgot.*
> *Consult the Genius of Place in all:*
> *That tells the Water or to rise or fall;*
> *Or helps the ambitious hill the heav'ns to scale,*
> *Or scoops in circling theatres the Vale; . . .*
> *Joins willing woods, and varies shades from shades;*
> *Now breaks, or now directs, th' intending Lines;*
> *Paints, as you plant, and, as you work, designs.*

With "good sense," sensitivity to natural topography and indigenous plants, and a flexibility of design to take advantage of "spontaneous beauties" arising "from Chance," the estate owner could create an aesthetic utility in gardens in which "Parts answ'ring parts shall slide into a whole." Then, Pope promises, "Nature shall join you; time shall make it grow." The naturalistic gardening he recommends contrasted dramatically with the formal French style, though it was scarcely less labor-intensive in design, construction, and maintenance.[23]

Literary depictions inspiring the "amateur" who wished for his own English garden advanced the new poetics of space. Pope's was one of many poetic prescriptions for "modern" landscaped gardens that made designing a picturesque estate easier for a well-read, tasteful proprietor. Paraphrasing Pope was an anonymous letter in verse to Viscount Irwin:

> *O study Nature! and with thought profound,*
> *Previous to laying out with taste your ground;*
> *O mark her beauties as they striking rise.*
> *Bid all her adventitious charms surprise!*
> *Eye all her shining, all her shadowy grace,*
> *And to conceal them every blemish trace:*
> *Yet there's a happiness that baffles Art,*
> *In showing* Nature *great in every part,*

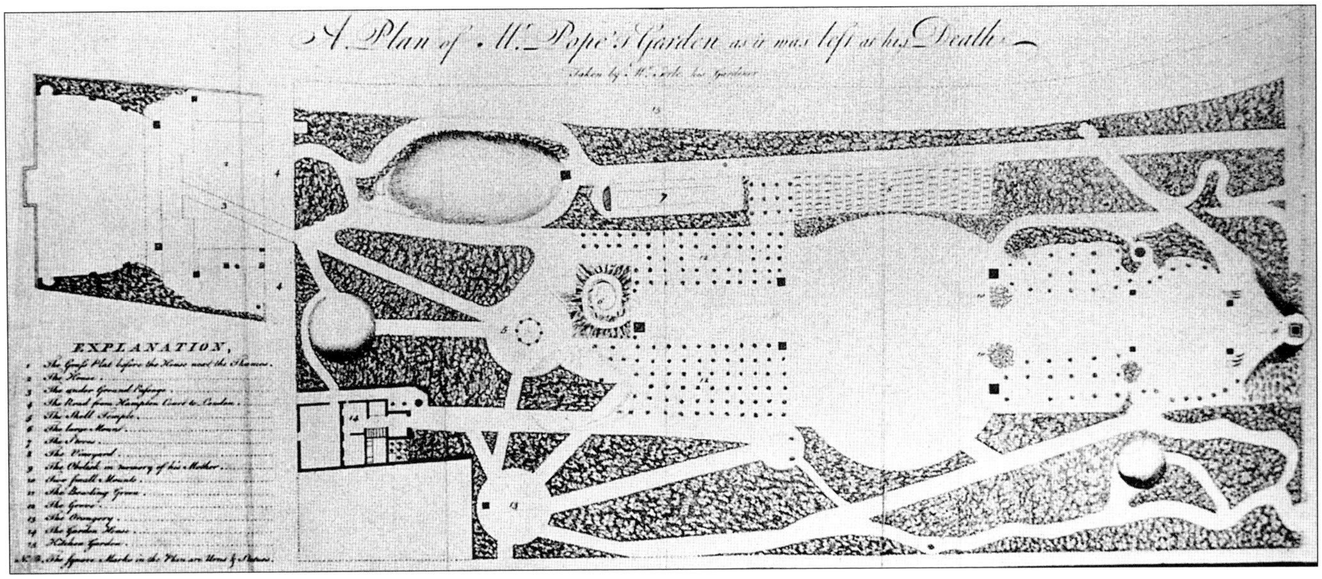

Fig. 2.2. "A Plan of Mr. Pope's Garden as it was left at His Death," Twickenham. Engraving by John Serle, his gardener, 1745. BMGL.

Which chiefly flows from mingled lights and shades,
In lawns, and woods, hills, rivers, rocks and glades;
For only happy's that assemblage made,
Where force of light contends with force of shade.[24]

Instead of the old dualism of good and evil, the contending forces in the garden would be light and shadow, voids and solids, stirring both cheerful and melancholy associations in ever-shifting dynamic relationships in three-dimensional space. Forging a compromise between Milton's *L'Allegro* and *Il Penseroso*, this vision represented an entirely new worldview.

Following Pope's lead, the anonymous poet speaks of "improving" Nature with monuments and structures to focus the reflections stimulated by the garden. He urges placing "spiry temples" on hills and "sculptur'd obelisks with statues crown'd" as focal points. Another major fixture of such gardens was the grotto, a secluded, sheltered, dark and damp private spot, made of rustic rock and located near a "weeping rill." The term "grotto" comes from the Latin *crypta*, literally a place in which to hide, but suggesting death. Since ancient Greece, grottoes were sacred places for meditation. Pope writes:

Here widow'd love, pale woe may rest their head,
Or, with the suddening Spring soft sorrows shed;
Here meditation may pursue her theme,
And of celestial joys enraptur'd dream.

This landscape where "weeping willows kiss the *watry glades*, / And rills still murmur thro' the pensive shades," where "horrid rocks," architectural ruins "moulder'd by Time," and mausoleums on "pin-crown'd hills" marked perspectives, and narrow, winding paths provided for solitary contemplation was intended to stir the spirit of melancholy.[25]

Pope practiced what he preached, making a "poetical villa" of his five-acre estate at Twickenham in Middlesex, fifteen miles west of London on the banks of the Thames near Horace Walpole's Strawberry Hill, a Gothic Revival mansion. There, between 1718 and 1743, he composed a sequence of outdoor spaces, light and shady, open and closed, including a grotto, through which the visitor passed before reaching the focal point nestled in a grove of mournful cypresses—the poet's mother's tomb, complete with an obelisk erected in 1733. Pope's friend William Kent described a picture the poet cherished of himself "in a mourning gown with a strange view of the garden to shew the obelisk as in memory of his mother's Death." Pope made his garden a "Musaeum," that is, "a place where his muses communicated with his best self." Pope's muses were melancholy ones. Albeit small in scale, Twickenham became the "Paradigm of the Picturesque Garden" with groves and "wildernesses" leading to a tower atop one of three "mounts" reached by a serpentine path.[26] (Fig. 2.2.)

Pope combined his melancholy, commemorative theme with a taste for classicism. Many urns dotted the heavily planted landscape reached by a subterranean passage, a rustic "grotto" or "cryptoporticus" leading from the Thames, its entrance inscribed with a quote in Latin from Horace, "A Hid Recess, Where Life's Revolving Day, In Sweet Delusion Gently Steals Away." Pope applied studies of Roman antiquities from the twelve-volume *Thesaurus Antiquitatum Romanarum* (1694–1699) of Johann Georg Graevius. Monuments on the river bank included busts of Virgil, Homer, Cicero, and Marcus Aurelius, plus two statues of river gods holding inscribed urns. Allusions to the Roman soothsayer Egeria were woven into his garden in the form of marble fragments imported by a friend from Egeria's grotto near the Appian Way. Pope worked closely with Kent, who had trained as a landscape painter in Rome from 1705 to 1715, and urged his transition to architect and designer of naturalistic gardens fit for philosophy and melancholy.[27]

The historic sensibility evident in English gardens was more ancient than modern in focus. Arcadian gardens were meant to be allegorical places with complex spiritual and commemorative allusions, usually classical. According to the historian Peter Gay, enlightened Englishmen sought "discovery of their true ancestors" in pagan antiquity.[28] Interest in classical literature and art revived especially because the style stirred in the mind the melancholy awareness of the inexorable passage of time. Langley and others discovered a kindred taste for classical ruins and ancient architectural styles in books and engravings by Andrea Palladio (1518–1580) and Giambattista Piranesi (1720–1778). The demand for classically influenced monuments was intense. Batty Langley placed a notice in the *Daily Advertiser* in 1731 announcing that he would provide sculptured "bustos of gentlemen and ladies, living or dead, at five guineas each," as well as vases, urns, columns, obelisks, temples, and other garden ornaments commemorative "of all the most eminent emperors, kings, generals, admirals, ministers of state, philosophers, mathematicians, architects, poets, and painters."[29]

Other writers joined Pope in shaping the new taste for landscape gardening. The poet James Thomson (1700–1748), dubbed the "English Virgil," is judged by many as having equal influence with Milton and Pope. A member of the Graveyard School of poets, he specialized in patriotic eulogies. His long poem *The Seasons*, published in four parts from 1726 to 1730, foreshadowed romanticism in celebrating Nature's melancholy potential. For the 1730 edition Kent designed plates showing neoclassical temples and monuments in picturesque landscapes. Thomson praised the "Sacred Influence" of Nature which "inflames Imagination" and "Philosophic Melancholy." He yearned to meditate in "twilight groves and visionary vales," in "weeping grottoes and prophetic glooms." Thomson echoed Shaftesbury and Pope in his belief that Nature could inspire a beneficial state of mind.[30] Other Graveyard School poets—Robert Blair, Thomas Gray, Henry Kirke White, and Edward Young—spread the taste for pastoral melancholy in the 1740s.

Stephen Switzer (1682–1745), the royal gardener, also promoted the taste for the "Rural or Forest Garden" in his three-volume *Ichnographia Rustica; or, The Noblemen, Gentleman, and Gardener's Recreation* (1718). Switzer drew from Milton a regret for Eden lost, and his garden designs aimed to temper the burdens of the Fall from God's grace. The garden visitor would imbibe lessons from Nature on solitary walks along narrow paths. Switzer admired classical gardens where "the ancient Attick and Roman Worthies erected magnificent Statues, and decreed Annual Honours to be paid to their Rural and Hortensial Deities," and he considered sculpture "one of the noblest Ornaments of our best Gardens and Plantations." Although he preached pantheism and pastoralism, his gardens remained linear, though asymmetrical and lacking the order of fashionable French gardens. Still, Switzer's "natural" garden theory drew clear equations between Whiggish notions of liberty and the new, informal style of gardening, suggesting political, philosophical, and emotional as well as aesthetic influences.[31]

Significantly, Switzer recommends landscaped gardens as appropriate for burials. He ends his *Ichnographia Rustica* with the wish to be buried in a country garden "Cover'd with flowers, free from noise and pain":

> *Let ever-greens the turfy tomb adorn,*
> *And roscid dews, the glory of the morn,*
> *My carpet deck; then let my soul possess*
> *The happier scenes of an eternal bliss.*[32]

The garden would be an Eden as before Adam's Fall where the dead could rest in paradise rather than in a place symbolic of hell. Another fashionable eighteenth-century writer who ranted against formal parterres and topiary was Batty Langley (1696–1751), whose *New Principles of Gardening* (1728) urged proprietors to make "a beautiful rural garden" of their land, precisely at a time when the ranks of estate owners were swelling with men newly wealthy from trade. Langley, like Switzer, advised them to place structures in their gardens that would stir noble emotions. He called naturalistic gardens Arcadias, versions of a primordial, idealized countryside. This was occurring just at the time when the traditional relationship of the peasantry to the land was undergoing upheaval with the Enclosure Acts. Ironically, the creation of many "natural" landscape gardens was made possible by such social disruption and hastened the displacement of agrarian communities, an upheaval lamented by Oliver Goldsmith (ca. 1728–1774) in his long poem *The Deserted Village* (1770) about a fictional town, Sweet Auburn, destroyed by estate building. The land itself came to hold nostalgic associations of families and towns that were no more.[33]

The second quarter of the eighteenth century was the heyday of English garden design. Highly literate landowners, amalgamating the era's philosophical, political, and patriotic themes, played major roles in creating gardens that objectified a poetics of place drawn from the classic tales as well as their own era's writers. Despite poetic assurances that garden-making would be simple, these landscapes in the "natural" manner were artfully contrived and arduously built. The garden-maker had to tastefully place *fabriques*—neoclassical monuments, buildings, ruins, or other architectural features, often commemorative—in spaces designed to mimic nature. (The term *fabrique*, initially referring to such structures in landscape paintings, came to signify elements meant to compose or "embellish the picturesque" in landscape gardens.) Sometimes estate owners enlisted the aid of Kent or even Pope to design didactic, evocative landscapes; but others were conceived by their proprietors alone. Aaron Hill (1685–1750), a poet, dramatist (he adapted Voltaire's *Zaïre* for the English stage), and friend of Pope's, created a small "Moral Garden" at Petty France, Westminster, in 1735, whose grottoes, cave, winding paths, and statues of virtues and vices were meant to inspire moral instruction. Eventually the picturesque garden gained international currency as *le jardin anglais* or *Englische landschaftskultur*— the English garden.[34]

The Grand Picturesque English Gardens

Sir Richard Temple (1669–1749), raised to peerage as Viscount Cobham in 1718 by King George I, took decades to develop the highly celebrated gardens at Stowe in Buckinghamshire, a property fronting on an old Roman road. Here Cobham preserved the fourteenth-century Saint Mary's parish church and churchyard of old Stowe village, ruined during the Civil War (1642–1647). He and his heirs expanded the estate to over 400 acres by 1727, to over 585 acres by 1775, and to over 1,300 acres by 1815 with lakes, rivers, and streams, woods, and peripheral "parks" for deer and livestock. The process required considerable earth-moving, even the making of "mounts" and sculpting of valleys; hydraulics to reshape water bodies and create cascades; and plantings of mature trees, some imported. (Fig. 2.3.)

Cobham hired the architect Charles Bridgeman (1680–1730) to begin the gardens in 1719. Sir John Vanbrugh (1664–1726), another leading Whig, designed the first *fabriques*: the Rotondo or Temple of Venus (1721), copied after the open, circular Hellenistic Temple of Venus at Cnidus, the Greek city in Asia Minor described by Vitruvius; the two Lake Pavilions (1723), colonnaded porticos with entablatures; and the slim, sixty-foot pyramid rebuilt in 1726 in memory of its designer. As early as 1731, in the first of many literary notices of Stowe's allegorical landscape, Cobham's friend Pope lauded Stowe's aesthetic excellence. He acclaimed it in his "Epistle to Burlington" as the epitome of gardening art.[35] (Fig. 2.4.)

Taking over the project by 1730 until his death in 1748, William Kent applied "picturesque" aesthetics to major areas in a manner reflecting the complex symbolic and antiquarian literary associations of his era and representative of Cobham's Whiggish notions. Along a meandering stream, Kent shaped a shallow valley called the "Elysian Fields" (ca. 1733), with reference to the ancient pastoral haunt of men made immortal by divine favor. Kent's semicircular Temple of British Worthies

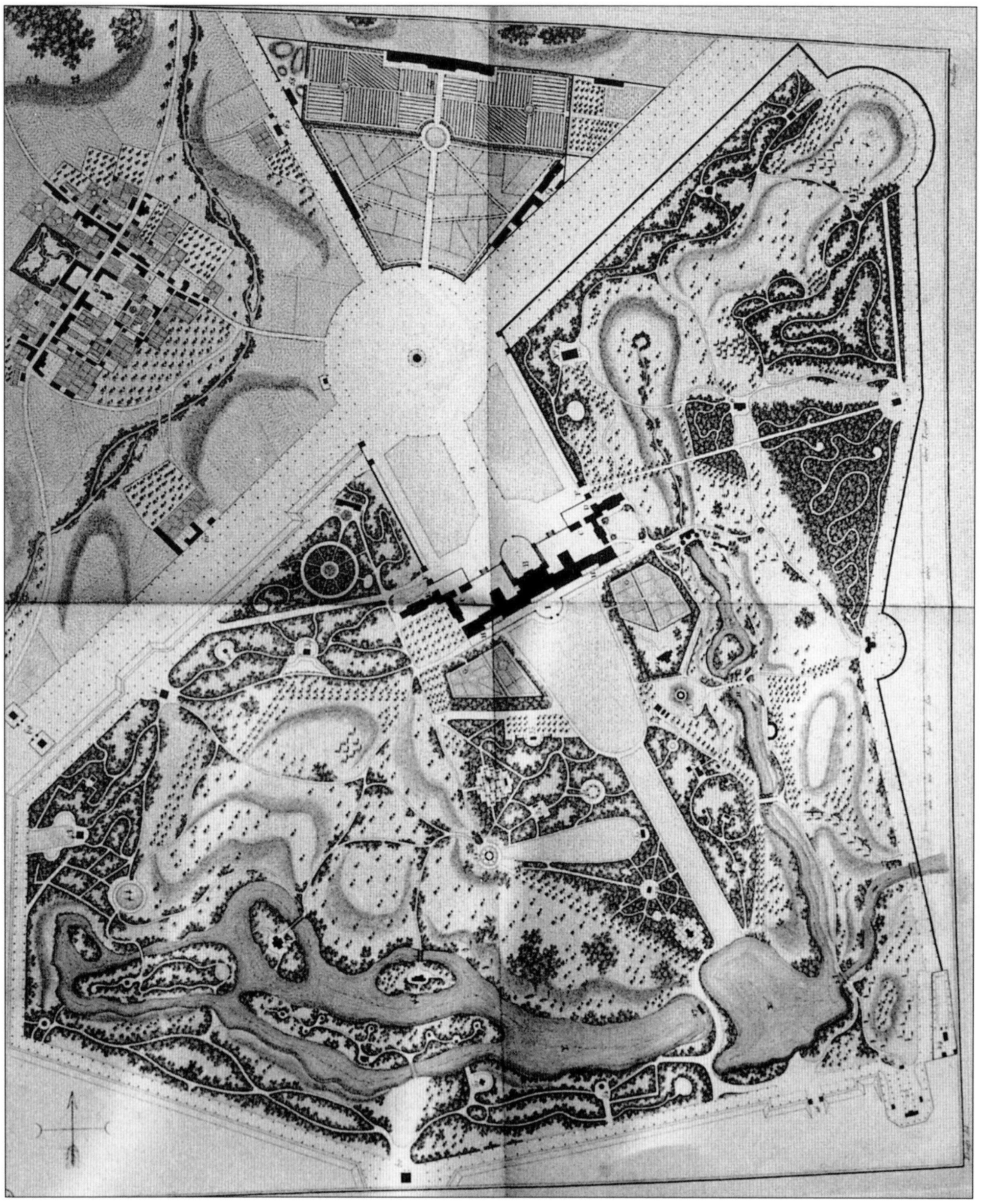

Fig. 2.4. Stowe, fabricated ruins, 1985. Photograph by BMGL.

Fig. 2.3. Stowe, engraved plan by Jean-Charles Krafft, from Krafft, 1810.

(1735), a sort of exedra topped by a small central pyramid, frames sixteen busts by John Michael Rysbrack and Peter Scheemakers of kings, queens, and writers, including Shakespeare, Milton, Bacon, Newton, Locke, Pitt, Penn, and Pope, arranged with political figures on the right and cultural figures on the left. All esteemed by Whigs, these were "Patriots and Heroes [who] founded Constitutions, stemmed the Torrent of Corruption, battled for the State, ventured their lives in the Defence of their country, and gloriously bled in the Cause of Liberty." A verse from the *Aeneid*, minus its reference to priests, proclaims the passage of the spirits of the Good across the river Styx to the "Elysian Fields."[36] (Fig. 2.5.)

On the opposite bank of the meandering stream, Kent placed his circular Temple of Ancient Virtue (1737), inspired by the Ionic Temple of Vesta at Tivoli, sheltering statues of the philosopher Socrates, the poet Homer, the lawmaker Lycurgus, and the soldier Epaminondas, all by Scheemakers. A rostral column (1747) topped by a statue of Clio, muse of history, honors Cobham's nephew Captain Thomas Grenville, who had just died in a naval battle with the French. (Fig. 2.6.) Among its lengthy Latin inscriptions are two reading, "The Muse Forbids Heroic Worth to Die" and "None But Heroic Deeds I Sing." Kent added other structures elsewhere in the grounds. His Temple of Venus (1731) features a concave Ionic colonnade inspired by ancient

Roman baths; busts of Nero, Cleopatra, Faustina, and Vespasian occupied exterior niches. His Hermitage (1731) mimics the look of rustic ruins, with its pediment and bell tower. Benches and niches line its dark interior. Kent placed triple-arched artificial ruins over a cascade at the end of the largest lake, designed the covered, colonnaded Palladian Bridge (1738) at the end of another, then built the freestanding rustic Grotto (1739) over a stream. (Fig. 2.7.) A second grotto, Dido's Cave (ca. 1727), named to recall the grief of the queen of Carthage on being deserted by her lover Aeneas, was later mounded over to appear subterranean amid masses of foliage, a "wilderness." An inscription quotes Milton's praise of the goddess's "thick embower'd cave . . . and twilight groves, and shadows brown, which Sylvan loves."[37] (Fig. 2.8.)

Fig. 2.5. Stowe, Temple of British Worthies, designed by William Kent, ca. 1735, with busts by Rysbrack and Scheemakers, across the artificial water body called the River Styx. Photograph by BMGL, 1985.

Most of Stowe's *fabriques*, added and relocated throughout the century, alluded to cultural heritage, made political statements, or commemorated individuals. In 1723, a small obelisk was erected to memorialize the Reverend Robert Coucher, chaplain to Cobham's dragoons. John van Nost the Elder produced the cast-lead equestrian statue of King George I in Roman armor, modeled after a statue of Marcus Aurelius on the Capitol in Rome. Rysbrack set statues of George II and Queen Caroline atop high columns. (Fig. 2.9.) Kent's modest pyramidal cenotaph (1736) to William Congreve (1670–1729) recognizes Cobham's friend, the master of comedic theater, who is buried in Westminster Abbey. (Fig. 2.10.) The Temple of Modern Virtue resembled a "Gothick" ruin. A small monument, another cenotaph, to Captain James Cook (1728–1779), the "Great Ocean's Greatest Explorer," includes a globe of the world, which he was the first to circumnavigate in both directions, opening the South Pacific for British colonization before he was slain by the Hawaiians. An urn on the banks of a lake honors Prime Minister William Pitt the Elder, first Earl of Chatham (1708–1778), called "the Great Commoner."

Fig. 2.6. Stowe, Temple of Ancient Virtue (Kent, ca. 1734) and Roman rostral column in memory of Captain Thomas Grenville (1747), topped by allegorical figure of Heroic Poetry pointing to a scroll with the Latin inscription, "None But Heroic Deeds I Sing," and facing the Temple of British Worthies. Photograph by BMGL, 1985.

Commemorative nationalism of this sort permeated the spirit of Stowe. The Scottish architect James Gibbs (1682–1754) designed a Tuscan Temple of Friendship (1739), sheltering busts of Cobham and nine political friends who opposed Sir Robert Walpole after the Excise Bill of 1733. In 1741, just before Walpole's fall from power, Cobham had Gibbs design the triangular, turreted "Gothick" Temple of Ancestral Liberty, made of rusty ironstone; his family's Saxon coats of arms adorn its vaulted, circular core (Fig. 2.11.) Once surrounded by cedar groves, it overlooks the Octagon Lake. The histo-

Fig. 2.7. Stowe, Grotto on the River Styx. Engraving by T. Medland from J. Seeley, 1797.

Fig. 2.8. Stowe, "The Serpentive River [Styx] and Grotto in Stow [*sic*] Gardens." Engraving, ca. 1760. BMGL.

rian John M. Robinson explains that "to the Whigs 'Saxon' and 'Gothic' were interchangeable, associated with freedom and ancient English liberties: trial by jury (erroneously thought to have been founded by King Alfred), Magna Carta, parliamentary representation, all the things which the Civil War and Glorious Revolution had protected from the wiles of Stuart would-be absolutism, and to the preservation of which Lord Cobham and his 'Patriots' were seriously devoted."[38] In 1749, in memory of her husband, who had died that year, Lady Cobham had Gibbs design a 115-foot tower, actually a column with eight enormous convex flutes topped by a portrait statue of Cobham. Visitors climbed a spiral staircase inside to reach a platform in the belvedere with distant, panoramic views of five counties. The cenotaph bears inscriptions from Cicero and Pope about gardening and the proper use of riches.

The young Lancelot "Capability" Brown (1716–1783) served as Stowe's head gardener from 1741 to 1751, when he left to begin his own practice. In 1747, by considerable earth-moving and planting of mature elms and limes, he laid out the Grecian Valley, its focal point the Greco-Roman Temple of Concord and Victory. Perhaps modeled on temples in Baalbek and Heliopolis, it was rededicated in 1764 to honor the end of the Seven Years' War. Brown erected a 117-foot obelisk to the empire, later dedicated to General James Wolfe, who died fighting the French in Quebec. Brown's work at Stowe softened Bridgeman's formalities, expanded the "naturalized" gardens into a manmade valley, and created imposing spaces and vistas on the grand scale of his later work in the peripheral deer park, well beyond the human scale of Kent's symbolic walking gardens. Richard Grenville, Earl Temple, Cobham's nephew, took over, developing Stowe from 1749 until his death in 1779. When George Grenville, first Marquess of Buckingham (1753-1813), inherited the estate, he had Kent's Queen's Temple (1742) redesigned and rededicated in 1789 in honor of Queen Charlotte, who nursed the seriously ill George III back to health, saving the government of Grenville and William Pitt the Younger. From 1809 on, the marquess pursued a massive program of plantings.

Many visitors marveled at Stowe. Poems, articles, and guidebooks invited visitors to discover and "read" its wonders, rich in both ancient and recent symbolism and highly inscribed. Sarah Bridgeman, widow of the landscape designer Charles Bridgeman, published a book on Stowe with fifteen engraved views and a plan in 1739. The publisher Benton Seeley kept revising his slim, illustrated *Description of the Gardens* annually from 1744 to 1750, then periodically until 1827. The engraver George Bickham produced *The Beauties of Stowe* (1750), "a necessary Pocket Companion for such as Visit those Gardens," with sixteen illustrations. William Gilpin urged, "I would have our Country Squires flock hither two or three times in a Year, by way of Improvement,

Fig. 2.10. Stowe, monument to William Congreve designed by William Kent, 1736. Photograph by BMGL, 1985.

Fig. 2.9. Stowe, Monument to Queen Caroline by Rysbrack, ca. 1730. Photograph by BMGL, 1985.

Fig. 2.11. Stowe, Temple of Ancestral Liberty. Photograph by BMGL, 1985.

and after they have looked about them a little, return Home with new Notions, and begin to see the Absurdity of their clipped Yews, their Box-wood Borders, their flourished Parterres, and their lofty Brick-walls."[39]

Called the "national Valhalla," Stowe evidenced the era's new commemorative consciousness. One visitor in 1744 described Stowe as featuring "buildings dedicated to . . . men of ingenuity and invention," adding that "they receive a dignity from the persons to whom they are consecrated. Others that are sacred to imaginary powers raise pleasing enthusiasms in the mind." She concluded, "At Stowe you must walk amidst Heroes and Deities, powers and persons whom we have been taught to honor, who have embellished the world with arts, or instructed it in Science, defended their country and improved it." Visiting in the 1760s, Madame du Boccage, friend of Voltaire, translator into French of Milton and Pope, and a prominent figure in French literary circles, praised the way the English "immortalize their great men: the statues erected to their honour are, like seed, capable of producing others to all eternity." Stowe celebrated an "aristocracy of merit," a concept with particular appeal to Whigs and the like-minded.[40]

Fig. 2.12. Rousham, Oxfordshire, Octagon Pond in the Vale of Venus with statue of Pan. Photograph by BMGL, 1985.

Fig. 2.13. Rousham, Octagon Pond in the Vale of Venus. Photograph by BMGL, 1985.

Colonel Robert Dormer and his brother General James Dormer, Cobham's friend, drew inspiration from Stowe's early development to begin a twenty-five-acre garden at Rousham in Oxfordshire (1720–1737) with Bridgeman's aid. When Robert died, James called in Kent, who worked from 1738 to 1741 to fashion an Elysium, a commemorative walking garden in contrast to the panoramic, bucolic Arcadia seen beyond from its "mount," punctuated by Kent's sham ruin or "eye-catcher" and a medieval-style bridge on the meandering river Cherwell. On the hill's vantage point, Kent placed an arcaded structure modeled after the ancient Temple of Fortune in Praeneste, or Palestrina. He built other neoclassical structures dispersed throughout the wooded grounds, constructed on a diminutive scale to emphasize a sense of intimacy when the visitor was close and an illusion of monumentality and exaggerated distance when seen from afar—a series of views along a sinuous path past irregular rills, cascades, and lakes. The grounds contain a Vale of Venus, a small, shaded pond with a central memorial to the owner's favorite dog. Kent provided benches to encourage visitors to sit and appreciate key picturesque views. (Figs. 2.12, 2.13.)

Rousham's classic interpretation of an Augustan garden recalling ancient Rome, termed "Kentian," offers pleasure walks through "romantic woodland arbors" underplanted with yews and flowering shrubs. Visitors enjoy views over open pastoral fields and stroll through a varied terrain, experiencing extremes of shade and sun metaphoric of life's vicissitudes. Rousham is a prime example of the walking garden amid an "artful wildness," Pope's phrase for the place he frequented, offering sequences of multisensory experience structured in an informal series of naturalistic scenes meant to stir emotions and associations with classical and contemporary literature. Pope may even have contributed to Rousham's design. Open to the public since the 1740s as a tourist attraction, with a welcoming gateway designed by Kent, Rousham survives unaltered and unmanicured, a fine example of the picturesque.

John Aislabie (1670–1742), once chancellor of the Exchequer, began laying out his estate at Studley Royal near Ripon in North Yorkshire when he went into self-imposed exile in 1721 after being expelled from Parliament for sponsoring the speculative mania that led to the South Sea Bubble, an ill-fated financial venture to pay off the national debt. In the wooded valley of the river Skell, with its ancient associations with Robin Hood, Aislabie spent two decades creating gardens that borrowed much from the topography, plantings, and architecture seen at Stowe and Rousham. His son William completed the composition by building a neoclassical Temple of Filial Piety nestled in the woods, its colonnaded façade reflected in a "moon pond" in a greensward. (Fig. 2.14.) In 1768, William purchased some adjacent land, including the monumental monastic ruins of Fountains Abbey, to complete a major vista along the river from the garden's heights. (Fig. 2.15.) Medieval ruins such as these were favored garden elements, additional reminders of the transitoriness of life, the toll taken by time, and the nation's long history; if they did not exist on site or could not be moved from elsewhere, they were fabricated.[41]

Others undertook garden-making as a ritualistic act of melancholy in response to personal tragedy. At Hagley in Worcester, George, first Baron Lyttelton (1709–1773), secretary to the Prince of Wales, Cobham's cousin, and Pope's friend, composed a garden around a ruined castle to assuage his grief after the deaths of his wife in childbirth in 1747, his friend the poet James Thomson in 1748, and his father in 1751, publication of his verses in *Dialogues of the Dead* (1760) evidently not sufficing. Lyttelton dedicated an urn to Pope and to Thomson a half-octagonal building bearing a Latin inscription, "To the Immortal Genius of James Thomson, Sublime Poet, Good Man." The Hagley gardens epitomized the ideal of Elysium as personal retreat for spiritual exercise.

Fig. 2.14. Studley Royal, Temple of Filial Piety, erected by William Aislabie in memory of his father. Photograph by BMGL, 1985.

Fig. 2.15. Studley Royal, Yorkshire, ruins of Fountains Abbey on the legendary River Skell. Photograph by BMGL, 1985.

Henry Hoare the Younger (1705–1785), a member of the financial elite, inherited the 2,650-acre Wiltshire estate of Stourhead on the death of his widowed mother in 1741. It already had melancholy associations from its inception in 1717, having been built by his father on the remains of a Catholic royalist estate sacked and seized by Cromwell's Parliamentary troops during the Civil War. For the younger Hoare, it held personal significance owing to a series of bereavements. Two of his children died in 1735 and 1740 and his wife in 1743, leaving him with three children, only one of whom survived to adulthood. He never remarried but directed his melancholy into developing his landscape garden over the next four decades.

Hoare built a landscape even more explicitly allegorical than Stowe's. With designs by the architect Henry Flitcroft (1687–1768), he created a place reminiscent of settings in Virgil's *Aeneid*, the epic of Rome's founding, but which also represented his own aim to found a family estate despite death's toll. Like Virgil's Elysium, the site had "cool meadows" watered by streams. By damming a small river, Hoare created a reflective, rambling water body he thought of as Lake Avernus, crossed by Aeneas to reach Hades. In 1748, Flitcroft built a rough-hewn rock grotto over a spot called the entrance to the netherworld, marked with the Latin motto "Easy is the descent to Avernus!" For the visitor, descending along a path into the cool, dark enclosure and then reemerging into the light, the grotto represented death and rebirth. These solitary, contemplative places became standard features in many English gardens. (Fig. 2.16.)

In 1744, Flitcroft, a protégé of Lord Burlington and close to Kent, built Stourhead's Roman Doric Temple of Flora, with an altar and marble busts of Marcus Aurelius and Alexander the Great, inscribed with the Sibyl's words before she led Aeneas through the underworld in search of his father, Anchises. In 1753, Hoare added a domed Pantheon or Temple of Hercules with a Corinthian portico to shelter other statues of classical figures, such as the moral hero Hercules by Rysbrack. Inspired by a painting by Gaspar Poussin (1613–1675) of the Roman Campagna, Hoare completed in 1762 the major picturesque scene across the lake to the Pantheon with a five-arched Palladian bridge copied after one in Vicenza. Then 1765 saw completion of Flitcroft's Temple of Apollo, modeled after a round structure excavated at Baalbek and illustrated by Robert Wood in a book Hoare purchased in 1757. The view across the water virtually replicated Lorrain's 1672 painting depicting Aeneas at the Temple of Apollo at Delos, "picturesque" indeed, and more so with the addition of the lake and bridge.

Fig. 2.16. Stourhead, Wiltshire, Pantheon or Temple of Hercules, 1753–1754, by Henry Flitcroft. "Lake Avernus" and bridge inspired by Palladio's original at Vicenza. Photograph by BMGL, 1985.

Allegorical themes also functioned to redefine the national past. Stourhead contained a collage of mnemonic forms representative of a past that was both symbolic and mythological, as well as real. Aeneas' search for his father paralleled the search for British history, which some in fact traced back to Aeneas following the oft-repeated story originating with the twelfth-century monk-chronicler Geoffrey of Monmouth's *Historia Regum Britanniae* (1138) that Brutus the Trojan, Aeneas' great-grandson, founded the British race. Other historical references appeared in 1765, when Hoare acquired the High Cross (1373), commemorating eight royal

Fig. 2.17. Stourhead, old village chapel and the High Cross, 1373, acquired from Bristol in 1765. Photograph by BMGL, 1985.

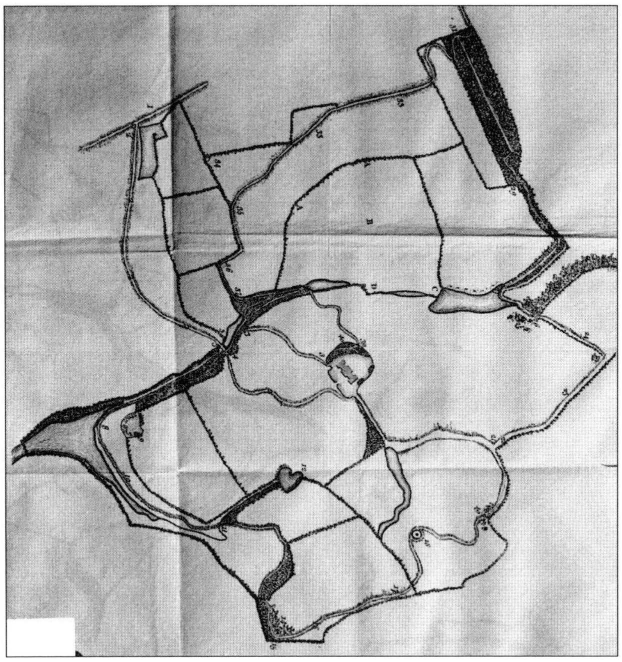

Fig. 2.18. The Leasowes, Halesowen, Worcestershire, William Shenstone's estate. Plan engraved by Shenstone, 1764. BMGL.

patrons of Bristol, which city residents inspired by Cromwell had discarded as a superstitious relic. (Fig. 2.17.) The visitor following the Circuit Walk experienced each *fabrique* up close in a ritualistic way and afar as in memory.

In 1772, Flitcroft completed an imposing triangular, crenellated brick tower 160 feet tall, dedicated to King Alfred and inscribed, "On this summit [he] erected his standard against Danish invaders. To him we owe the origin of Juries, the establishment of a Militia, the creation of a Naval Force. Alfred, the light of a benighted age, was a philosopher and a Christian, the father of his people, the founder of the English MONARCHY and LIBERTY." Visitors climbed the circular staircase inside to marvel at the panorama from the top, two miles from the house. Adding to the sense of historicism are the remains of an old village and a church and churchyard, traditional burial place of the Hoare family. Stourhead was second only to Stowe in attracting international recognition and emulation. By the 1760s, it was drawing so many visitors that an inn was built. In 1765, Horace Walpole (1717–1797) judged that "the whole composes one of the most picturesque scenes in the world."[42]

As elegiac as William Shenstone's (1714–1763) moralistic, pastoral poetry was his idyllic garden in Shropshire (1745–63), carved out of his fifty-eight-hectare farm on a hilly site in Halesowen near Dudley, with panoramic views into Worcestershire. (Fig. 2.18.) There, Shenstone promulgated his ideas of "landskip or picturesque-gardening" as in his *Unconnected Thoughts on Gardening*, a guidebook and treatise on taste published posthumously in 1764. He declared: "Water should ever appear, as an irregular lake or winding stream. Art, indeed, is often requisite to collect and epitomize the beauties of nature; but should never be suffered to set her mark upon them. . . . Objects should indeed be less calculated to strike the immediate eye than the judgment or well-informed imagination, as a painting."[43] The Leasowes, begun after the death of Shenstone's mother, was a personal garden of remembrance or "consecrated grove" with serpentine paths through dark valleys—ideal for melancholy reflection. A circuit walk took visitors past a sequence of "pictures," such as a ruined, ivy-draped Gothic priory, a Grecian temple, and assorted urns, seats, and memorials to literary friends, living and deceased, including Thomson, Lyttelton, and William Somerville. Shenstone advocated turning historical sites into gardens but realized that where historical significance did not exist, monuments could create a sense of the past. He designated one small, deep valley crossed by a mossy cascading stream and hemmed in by overgrown banks as "Virgil's Grove,"

Fig. 2.19. Engraving of funerary urn erected to the proprietor's cousin in the woods from the posthumous edition of Shenstone's "Elegy I," 1764.

erecting an obelisk, nearly hidden among ancient oaks, as a cenotaph to the ancient poet. He dedicated a funerary urn, also inscribed as a cenotaph, to his cousin Maria Dolman, who died at age twenty-two of smallpox. (Fig. 2.19.) His garden was intended to stir visitors' sentiments, to elicit nostalgia, and to refresh spirits wearied by the bustle of city life.[44]

Many visitors to The Leasowes, greeted by the poet and elegist Shenstone "in his own hair," without the formality of a wig, left with ambitions to create similar places. He granted the general public access to the grounds, noting in 1749, "It is now Sunday evening, and I have been exhibiting myself in my walks to no less than a hundred and fifty people." The thirty-five-page description of The Leasowes (1761) by his publisher, the poet Robert Dodsley, prescribed walking a circuit past the estate's major features. It was widely read and influenced the nascent romanticism of the likes of Sir Walter Scott. Samuel Johnson and James Boswell visited The Leasowes in 1774 and recommended it to friends. It became a place of pilgrimage for the Whig intelligentsia—Oliver Goldsmith, Edmund Burke, Adam Smith, and others. Parties including the Grenvilles, the Pitts, the Lytteltons, and the Reverend Richard Jago frequented the place. The greatest tribute of emulation came from the marquis de Girardin, who developed his gardens at Ermenonville in France in the 1770s and honored his friend and adviser Shenstone with a cenotaph. Shenstone also became a mentor to Joseph Spence (1699–1768), friend of Pope and Dodsley, who wrote on the *ferme ornée* style of gardening, calling The Leasowes "a Place, that is so much every Body's Favourite." Arthur Young's *Six Months' Tour through the North of England* (1771) featured stops at The Leasowes and Hagley gardens. A popular guide, *A Companion to The Leasowes, Hagley, and Enville* (1789), sold for two shillings.[45]

Melancholy, Memory, and Monuments

The popularity of naturalistic gardens among the liberal elite conditioned and reflected the fascination of English poets and essayists with such places for spiritual renewal and philosophic inspiration. Shortly before her death in 1737, the "bluestocking" poet Mrs. Elizabeth Rowe wrote of her pleasure in solitary, "mournful" meditation in such a setting:

> *While drooping winds among the branches sigh,*
> *And sluggish waters heavily roll by.*
> *Here to my fatal sorrows let me give*
> *The short remaining hours I have to live.*[46]

Similarly, Thomas Warton the Younger (1728–1790) celebrated such places in his blank verse poem "The Pleasures of Melancholy" (1747):

> *Beneath yon ruin'd abbey's moss-grown piles*
> *Oft let me sit, at twilight hour of eve. . . .*
> *Amid the mould'ring caverns dark and damp,*
> *Or the calm breeze, that rustles in the leaves*
> *Of flaunting ivy, that with mantle green*
> *Invests some wasted tow'r. Or let me tread*
> *Its neighb'ring walk of pines . . . thro' the gloomy void.*[47]

Nature tamed by human hands produced the sacred places of asylum to which one repaired, like Voltaire's Candide retreating from the world's vicissitudes to his garden for stoical meditations on life and fate. Only John Wesley (1703–1791), founder of Methodism, warned of the danger of such gardens in seducing visitors to pantheistic idolatry.

Thomas Gray (1716–1771) expressed a fashionable melancholy in his "Elegy Written in a Country Church-

Yard" (1751), but he found an edifying usefulness in frequenting the graves of humble, rural Englishman rather than those of men of "Grandeur." Shifting focus from the dead to the living, Gray praised the conduciveness of such a landscape to the contemplation of death. He favored old rural burial places where the ancient folk custom of planting trees and flowers on graves with rude markers persisted despite High Church opposition to such practices. Gray advocated cultivating a tender, sweet response to death, a soothing state of mind relieving the world-weary "far from the madding crowd's ignoble strife." His brand of melancholy suggests a return to the lost rhythms of Arcadia.[48] Many garden owners and designers had preceded the poets in creating landscapes that expressed and cultivated such sentiments. Gray advised his friends to visit landscaped gardens as well as rural churchyards to find reminders of "transience and decay." He particularly favored Charles Hamilton's Painshill in Surrey, developed from 1738 to 1773, with its "narrow gloomy path" that revealed picturesque scenes along a "broad, sinuous, island-studded river apparently without beginning or end." One area focused on a Roman mausoleum.[49]

Others with poetic sensibilities began to dream of similar resting places. Melancholy monuments, especially urns and obelisks, already used as allegorical or commemorative fixtures in landscaped gardens, increasingly took on funerary connotations. An urn erected by Copleston Warre Banpfylde in the Hestercombe gardens near Taunton honors Stourhead's Henry Hoare, depicting him as Virgil. A major feature at Hawkstone Park in Shropshire, the picturesque seat of Sir Rowland Hill, is a 112-foot Tuscan column (1795) topped by a statue of the family founder, the first Protestant Lord Mayor of London, holding a copy of Magna Carta. So great was the demand for such monuments that some proprietors fashioned them of wood painted to resemble stone, the ideal sort of cenotaphs favored by Leone Battista Alberti, whose *Ten Books on Architecture* (1450–1485), first published in English in 1726, influenced many theorists of the "modern" style of gardening.

Ambitious estate owners accumulated multiple commemorative objects, displaying a sort of ancestor worship. Castle Howard's park in Yorkshire featured an obelisk to William Lord Howard erected by his son, another dedicated in 1714 to the Duke of Marlborough, and a pyramid built in 1728 to honor a female ancestor whose marriage had united properties to create the estate. Lady Ann Irwin, daughter of Charles Howard, third Earl of Carlisle (1669–1738), proprietor of the estate, praised her family's idealized landscape, shaped by Vanbrugh:

Fig. 2.20. Castle Howard mausoleum, 1731–1742, by Nicholas Hawksmoor, in Yorkshire. Photograph by BMGL, 1985.

> *Buildings the proper points of view adorn*
> *Of Grecian, Roman and Egyptian form*
> *Interspersed with woods and verdant plains*
> *Such as possess'd of old th' Arcadian swains.*[50]

The focal point is a huge family mausoleum designed by Nicholas Hawksmoor in 1742 to replace the Howards' use of the local parish church and churchyard, destroyed by consolidation of the estate. (Fig. 2.20.) The domed classical mausoleum, rivaling the proportions of the castle's famed central dome, was the first funeral structure standing free of a church built in England since ancient times. It inspired poetic descriptions:

> *How rich the columns—and how light the dome!*
> *A Temple worthy of immortal Rome!*
> *O'er the Mosaic floor O lightly tread,*
> *Beneath's the sacred mansion of the dead;*
> *Where with his race th' illustrious founder lies.*[51]

Horace Walpole thought that it "would tempt one to be buried alive."[52]

Rejection of Anglican burial by some of the elite made the century's final decades "the great age of mausolea," according to the art historian Nicholas Penny.[53]

Literally and figuratively unconnected to the Church, dozens of mausoleums were erected on private country estates, and architects produced designs for hundreds of others never built. The mausoleum (1792) at Park Place in Remenham on the Thames in Oxfordshire, estate of General Henry Seymour Conway (1721–1795), friend of Thomas Gray and Horace Walpole, is a pyramid set atop a square base with a low relief depicting a sarcophagus; it is surrounded by some of England's first poplars. At West Wycombe Park in Buckinghamshire, Sir Francis Dashwood (1708–1781) built his family mausoleum as an eyecatcher atop an adjacent hill. The great architect Robert Adam (1728–1792) designed a Gothic mausoleum for a prominent hilltop in the Claremont Gardens in Surrey.

Commemorative cenotaphs not containing burials but intended to suggest death and the past proliferated as well. The ninety-foot-tall, colonnaded Rockingham Mausoleum (1791) in Wentworth Park in Yorkshire, by the architect John Carr (1723–1807), contains busts of eight of the Marquis of Rockingham's Whig friends on the first floor, an empty sarcophagus on the second, and a Roman cupola on the third. A long inscription by Edmund Burke states that its purpose is "to instruct the mind" and calls on the English to "Remember. Resemble. Preserve." This neoclassical structure inspired the Temple of Liberty at Woburn Park, which contains busts of another leading Whig, Charles Fox, and his allies, who supported the American cause but opposed the French Revolution.[54]

The architectural eclecticism associated with melancholy structures in English gardens in turn influenced the styles of funerary monuments in churchyards and churches. An article in a 1755 issue of *Connoisseur* criticized the neoclassical taste for having "introduced the heathen mythology in our gardens." The prescient author predicted that these pagan forms and allegorical figures pointed to trends that would introduce Egyptian hieroglyphics and even Chinese forms into the English garden.[55]

Preaching the Picturesque

Theory and literature spread the popularity of the garden form. In *A Philosophical Inquiry into the Origin of Our Ideas of the Sublime and the Beautiful* (1756), the Whig political theorist Edmund Burke (1727–1797) crystallized the ideas and design formulas of picturesque gardens, linking philosophy, politics, and poetics. His theory that all emotion is sensation expanded on Lockean epistemology. Like many of his contemporaries, Burke considered the solitary contemplation of mortality sublime and favored the creation of environments to foster it, believing that such refined taste would be socially beneficial, counteracting the baser motives of the "rabble." The sublime, he believed, arises from a pastoral landscape or classical architecture because they present no boundary to the eye and the imagination. Melancholy associations are particularly important when traced to classical precedents, said Burke. Sensations stirred by the sublime, "melancholy as they are," give pleasure. Paraphrasing Homer, he wrote:

> *Still in the short intervals of* pleasing *woe,*
> *Regardful of the friendly dues I owe,*
> *I to the glorious dead, for ever dear,*
> Indulge *the tribute of a tear.*[56]

In his "Introduction to Taste" in the *Philosophical Inquiry*, Burke argued the relationship of taste to sensations and emotions. Thoughts of pain when pain is not present produce melancholy. Burke describes the capacity of the "affecting" arts to graft "a delight on wretchedness, misery, and death itself," even onto the "dark, uncertain, confused, terrible, and sublime to the last degree."[57] Hence, for him, an ideal landscape incorporated references to death, explicit or implicit, with burial sites, mausoleums, cenotaphs, places of solitude, winding paths leading from sunny spaces through cool dark woods, damp grottoes reminiscent of the tomb, dark and reflective bodies of water, streams, material evidence of the ravages of Nature such as blasted tree trunks, deciduous plants displaying nature's inexorable cycle of seasons, and vistas of great distance, height, or depth—all elements of the sublime.

Demand for such gardens, albeit simpler, grew and for a time spurred the rise of professional landscape gardeners with a different aesthetic, of the "beautiful" rather than the "picturesque." Lancelot "Capability" Brown's "grand vision" for "beautiful" landscapes lacked many of the complex philosophical and literary underpinnings of the "picturesque." Brown's work was generally more subtractive than additive. Instead of contributing to a sense of intimate melancholy accessible to the individual on a meditative stroll, his "landscape parks" of wide, undulating greenswards framed by sinuous bands of trees were meant to be seen from a distance, panoramically, from the windows of the house, from a commanding vantage point, or from a carriage in transit, more pastoral scene than garden.[58]

Yet the taste for melancholy increased toward the century's end. Encouraged by new theorists of the "picturesque," a wilder, untamed version of nature won favor among those who rejected the vogue for Capability Brown's vast, sweeping, impersonal lawns. The Whig Parliamentarian Sir Uvedale Price (1747–1820), the poet Richard Payne Knight (1750–1824), and the architect Sir William Chambers (1723–1796) articulated an aesthetics of the "picturesque" as a better catalyst for evoking deep emotions than Brown's groomed, expansive "beautiful." (Figs. 2.21, 2.22.) Price described the picturesque as having the qualities "of roughness and sudden variation, joined to that of irregularity." Drawing on experience from his own estate at Foxley, he declared the picturesque within the practical reach of any gentleman able to undertake his own landscape "improvements." With such encouragement, some began to study horticulture.[59]

Chambers favored landscapes that would display the "vicissitudes of seasons" through varied plantings, particularly those that in autumn "afford in their decline a rich variegated colouring" representative of impending mortality. Resplendent autumn colors, like those in New England, were particularly desirable for inspiring a sense of melancholy. Appropriate garden structures, which would "indicate decay, being intended as mementos," might include "the tombs of predecessors." Others were "ruins of castles, palaces, temples . . . or half-buried triumphal arches and mausoleums, with mutilated inscriptions, that once commemorated the heroes of antient times; or . . . sepulchres of [the owners'] ancestors, catacombs and cemeteries of their favorite domestic animals; or whatever else may serve to indicate the debility, the disappointments, and the dissolution of humanity." Such structures might "fill the mind with melancholy and incline it to serious reflections." Chambers' ideal landscape, a sequence of "surprising" or "supernatural" scenes, was "calculated to excite in the mind . . . quick successions of opposite and violent sensations." The garden itself would take command of the passive visitor's thoughts and actions: "Sometimes the passenger is hurried by steep descending paths to subterraneous vaults. . . . Sometimes the traveller, after having wandered in the dusk of the forest, finds himself on the edge of precipices, in the glare of day-light . . . or at the foot of impending rocks, in gloomy valleys, overhung with woods; or on the banks

Fig. 2.21. "The Picturesque." Depiction of how Knight envisioned the landscape at Sheringham Park, Norfolk, in a more dramatic naturalistic style. Engraving by Hearne and Pouncy, from Knight, *The Landscape*, 1794.

Fig. 2.22. "The Beautiful." This shows Sir Humphrey Repton's manicured landscape at Sheringham Park, Norfolk, which Knight criticized as not evocative of sentiment. From Knight, *The Landscape*, 1794.

of dull moving rivers, whose shores are covered with sepulchral monuments, under the shade of willow, laurel, and other plants sacred to . . . the Genius of Sorrow." For Chambers, variety in terrain and artifice worked to accentuate the sense of melancholy. Although he summarizes the elements of landscape found in English gardens, his ideal would not be fully realized until the creation of America's first "rural" cemetery, Mount Auburn, in 1831.[60]

In his *Essays on the Nature and Principles of Taste* (1790), the Reverend Archibald Alison (1757–1839), a philosopher-aesthetician, formulated a theory that further rationalized the form of the English garden and influenced designers on both sides of the Atlantic. Alison drew on studies in natural history and Scottish philosophical pragmatism, such as that of Francis Hutcheson (1694–1746), a disciple of Shaftesbury, to develop his theory of "associationism," which held that beautiful things trigger a series of mental suggestions of divine power and love. Both the beautiful and the sublime, he believed, spark moral and religious sentiment perceived through the "Emotion of Taste." Alison systematically defined and praised the standard elements of the English garden as sublime, even sacred, so long as tending by the hand of man was not too evident. He noted that "in the vegetable kingdom, the form of trees are sublime. . . . Nothing is more sublime than the form of rocks, which seem to be coeval with creation, and which all the convulsions of nature have not been able to destroy. The sublimest of all the mechanical arts is architecture, principally from the durableness of its productions; and these . . . are in themselves sublime, in proportion to their antiquity . . . or . . . their duration." In addition, "the form of temples, although very different as forms, have in all ages been accounted sublime. . . . The forms of all those things . . . employed in the burial of the dead are strikingly sublime." And the sublime was the most potent aesthetic force in stirring salutary emotions and instilling lessons of moral philosophy.[61] Americans knew Alison's theories from his book, reprinted in Edinburgh in 1811 and in Boston in 1812, or in condensed form in Francis Jeffery's article on "Beauty" in the 1816 *Encyclopaedia Britannica Supplement*.

The second and third generations of romantic gardeners and proprietors did more than carry on such taste; they proselytized. Sir William Stanhope (1702–1772), who bought Pope's Twickenham estate in 1744, sent cuttings of the willow under which the poet had meditated as mementos to friends across England and abroad. (The parent tree died in 1801; the estate was again sold in 1807 and completely demolished.) Sir Walter Scott applied Price's aesthetic principles to transform an old gravel pit he acquired at Abbotsford in 1813 into a bower. He planted thousands of trees—weeping birches, poplars, firs, horse chestnuts, elms—and confessed "how deeply" he had been bitten "with the madness of the picturesque." According to the art historian A. A. Tait, "Scott shared with [Sir Humphrey] Repton an almost evangelical enthusiasm for landscape" in gardens he planned for others in the 1820s and in the crusading zeal evident in his letters.[62] How easy it was, Scott exclaimed, for a gentlemen to lay out and plant his own grounds. His enthusiasm for landscape gardening spread the taste in Scotland, on the Continent, and in America through the popular author's writings in the *Quarterly Review* (1828) and in international correspondence. A sense of the picturesque along with melancholy retrospection suffuses Scott's celebration of his Caledonian past, represented in ruins, monuments, and the persistence of wild Nature in the land. As an honorary member of the Massachusetts Horticultural Society, he undoubtedly influenced Bostonians such as Dr. Jacob Bigelow and General Henry A. S. Dearborn as they, in turn, became leading arbiters of "rural" landscape aesthetics in America in the 1830s.

William Wordsworth (1770–1850) also preached the values of "musing in solitude" in a romantic setting. In his "Essay on Epitaphs" (1810), which plays upon "rural" tastes fostered by English gardens, he proposed relegating all burials to the countryside. Updating Evelyn's criticism of urban burials, he decried "the unsightly manner in which our monuments are crowded together in the busy, noisy, unclean, and almost grassless churchyard of a large town. He argued: "We, in modern times, have lost much of the advantages [of the hortatory power of funerary monuments]." His American contemporaries agreed with him that "tombs lose their monitory virtue when obtruded upon the notice of men occupied with the cares of the world, and too often sullied and defiled by those cares" in the midst of busy city streets. Wordsworth believed that "when death is in our thoughts, nothing can make amends for the want of soothing influences of nature, and for the absence of those types of renovation and decay, which the fields and woods offer to the notice of the serious and contemplative mind." Siting gravestones with epitaphs along country roads, following the Roman pattern, would present lessons for travelers and elicit beneficial emotions. Wordsworth commended "the still seclusion of a Turkish cemetery, in some remote place; and yet further sanctified by the grove of cypress in which it is embosomed."[63] In echoing the concerns as well as commemorative trends seen throughout the eighteenth century, he articulated a desire for burial reform that was increasingly being expressed in urban areas. His objection to the old burial ways was aesthetic and spiritual, shaped by changing ideas about death and Nature. Others would raise more practical concerns for urban real estate values or public health.

Meanwhile, English gardens inspired countless copies on the Continent as visitors took home impressions of their forms and elements or ordered books and engravings with detailed descriptions and views of picturesque landscapes. (Figs. 2.23, 2.24, 2.25.) Part of a larger vogue for English culture, or *anglomanie*, literary descriptions and poetic formulas for landscape compositions helped enlightened proprietors abroad transform their own grounds into contemplative places for com-

Fig. 2.23. Engraved view of a fictional English landscaped garden with monuments and temple. From Van Laar, 1802.

Fig. 2.24. Urn and weeping tree. From Van Laar, 1802.

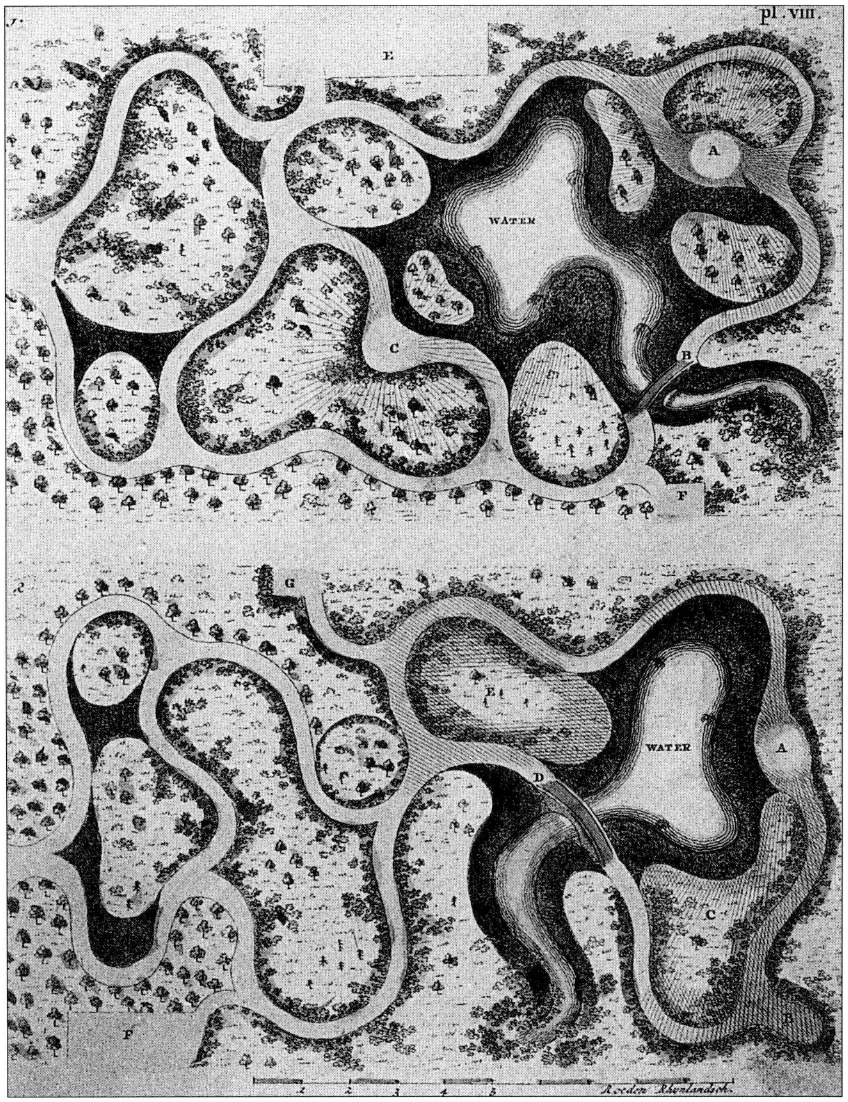

Fig. 2.25. Plan of picturesque avenues and paths. From Van Laar, 1802.

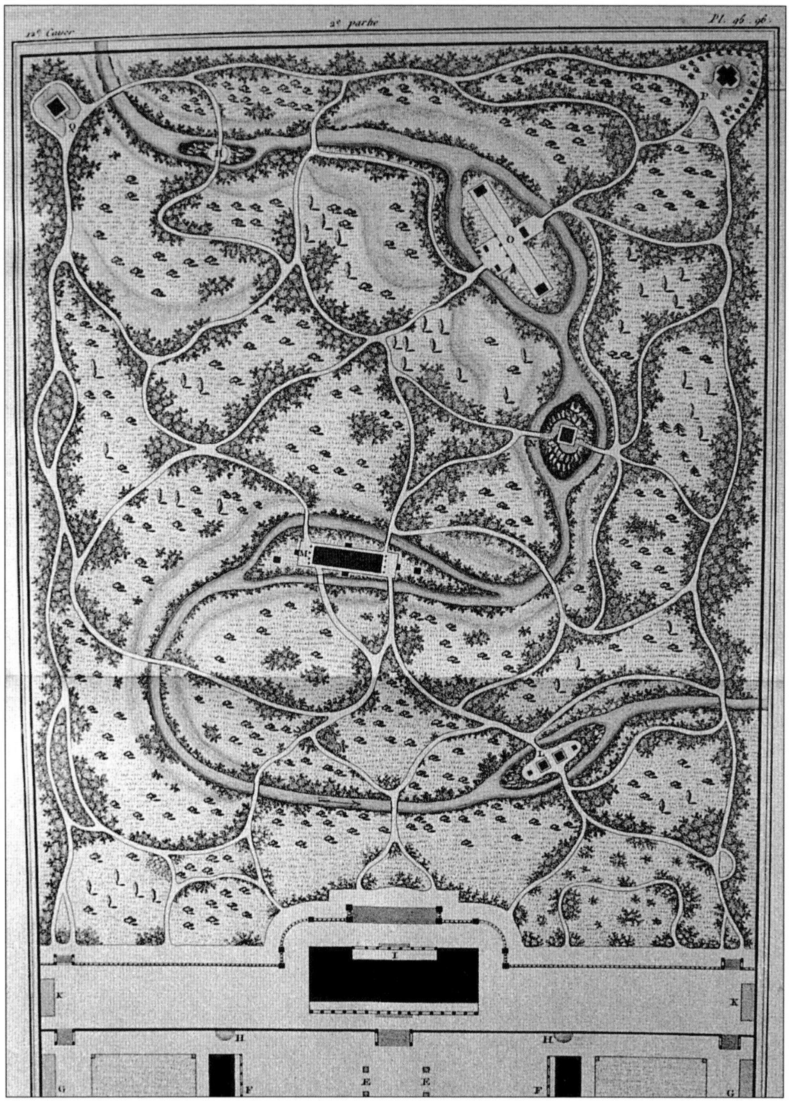

Fig. 2.26. Plan of a *jardin anglo-chinois*, based on a Mandarin estate forty-five leagues from Peking, designed by M. Stronberg, gardener. From Krafft, 1810.

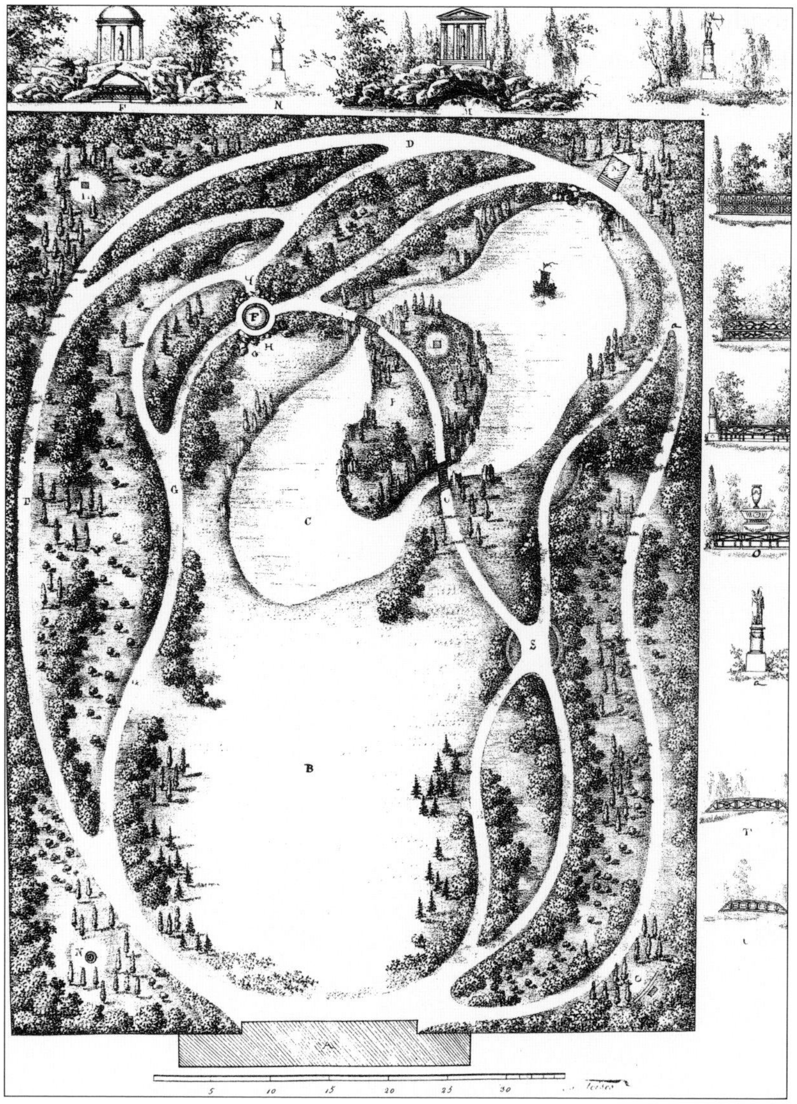

Fig. 2.27. Theoretic picturesque "pleasure" garden (*jardin champêtre*), plan number 30, drawn by Gabriel Thouin, lithograph by C. Motte. From the pattern book *Plans raisonées de toutes les espèces de jardins par Gabriel Thouin, cultivateur et architecte de jardins* (Paris: Lebégue, 1820). A third edition of this influential book was published in 1828.

memoration and objectification of the past, public and private. Whether known as *le jardin anglais*, *le jardin pittoresque et sentimental*, *le bosque melancholique*, *il giardino inglese*, or *der englische Gärten*, the English style inspired philosophical and political liberals in search of new aesthetic forms to serve as a transition from authoritarianism to rationalism and romanticism, from the old order to the new. "English" landscaped gardens with all their standard *fabriques*, follies, and eye-catchers, their monuments and other characteristic structures, now appeared in Ireland, Scotland, France, Italy, Germany, Austria, Hungary, Poland, and Russia.[64] The international influence persisted into the next century, owing to its strong literary foundation and the formation of societies in major cities following the example of the Royal Horticultural Society, established in 1804 and chartered in 1809. By 1824, it had almost 2,200 members, many outside Britain. (Figs. 2.26, 2.27.)

In 1775, Sir Horace Walpole predicted that "some American will . . . revive the true taste in gardening. . . . I love to skip into futurity and imagine what will be done on the grand scale of a new hemisphere." So numerous were the popular theorists and advocates of the taste for landscape gardens by century's end, including Walpole himself, that his prediction was bound to come true.[65] The *furor hortensis*, or pastoral gardening rage, soon extended across the Atlantic. Americans associated the English garden with ideals of Independence. The New Englander Daniel Webster declared in 1825: "A chief distinction of the present day is a community of opinions and knowledge amongst men in various nations. . . . The whole world is becoming a common field for intellect to act in. . . . A great chord of sentiment and feeling runs through two continents and vibrates over both. . . . There is a vast commerce of ideas."[66] That observation applies to the developing appreciation for Nature and the spread of English garden aesthetics. The legacy of English gardens, with their emphasis on *le genre sombre*, lay in the precedents they provided for new pastoral cemeteries, prototypes of which appeared outside Paris at Père Lachaise in 1804 and near Boston at Mount Auburn in 1831.

3

THE FRENCH CULT OF ANCESTORS AND THE BIRTH OF PÈRE LACHAISE

And finally philosophy
Teaches you to despise the horrors of the tomb
And the terrors of the afterlife.

—Voltaire, "Epître à Uranie" (1732)

Come here, all you whose meditative hearts
Love the sad joys that melancholy imparts.
Behold this tombstone where the bending birch
Like the Chinese willow, but more solemnly
With its long branches and sad falling leaves
And hanging arms weeps upon the grave . . .
In the peaceful fields, place my tomb.

—Abbé Jacques Delille, *Des Jardins* (1782)

Funerary institutions are one of the first needs of civilization.

—Nicholas-Thérèse-Bénoist Frochot, prefect of the Department of the Seine (1800)

IN THE SECOND HALF OF THE EIGHTEENTH century, the English landscape garden movement extended to the Continent along with the cult of melancholy and a revised sense of historical memory, taking with it the taste for neoclassical monuments and ruins, real or fabricated. A growing body of literature—philosophy, aesthetic theory, descriptive poetry and prose—made possible the reinterpretation of English trends in pastoral melancholy. But French writers and designers did not simply translate and adapt the naturalistic and neoclassical elements of *le jardin anglais*. They created a new institution, a "cult of ancestors," which manifested in material form a secularized historical consciousness with both public and private dimensions. The public policy aspects of this movement were formalized in the wake of the Revolution—which had overthrown not just the government but royalty and the aristocracy, Catholic worship, even the calendar—as a way to bind citizens to the radical new nation. One aspect of this policy was burial reform, resulting in the creation of the Cemetery of Père Lachaise outside Paris in 1804.

Interpreting the Picturesque

The many works of British writers recommended to French literati the creation of elegiac, pastoral landscapes in their own country. The philosopher and later famed Encyclopedist Denis Diderot translated Shaftesbury, a fellow Deist, in the 1740s. A 1785 translation of Horace Walpole's *Essay on Modern Gardening* was also influential.[1] Drawing on the *Dissertation on Oriental Gardening* (1722) by Sir William Chambers, the French began to refer to a hybrid concept, *le jardin anglo-chinois*. The Jesuit Jean-Denis Attiret, court painter to the emperor of China, wrote a report in 1743 on the famed Yuan Ming Yuan (Garden of Perfect Brightness, or Garden of Gardens), a 350-hectare park ten kilometers west of Beijing, the emperor's residence for ten months of the year, developed under the Qing dynasty from 1709 on. Attiret marveled at its man-made hills up to sixty feet high, interspersed with valleys and streams, lakes and cascades, and paths with "various Turnings and Windings, adorn'd on the Sides with little Pavillions and charming Grottos" each "diversify'd from the rest." The streams were "not faced . . . with smooth Stone and in a strait Line; but look rude and rustic, with different Pieces of Rock . . . placed with so much Art, that you would take it to be the Work of Nature. In some Parts the Water is wide, in others narrow; here it serpentizes, and there spreads away, as if it was really push'd off by the Hills and Rocks." *Fabriques* included colonnades, triumphal arches, and bridges of various kinds. In a huge central lake, "one of the most beautiful Parts in the whole Pleasure-ground," a rocky island "rais'd, in a natural and rustic Manner," commanded panoramic views of the gardens with groves of "Trees from all foreign Countries; and then, some all blooming with Flowers, and others all laden with Fruits." Flowers sprung as if randomly from hillsides and rocks, unlike in the formal parterres of Europe.[2] Another influential source, Georges-Louis LeRouge's *Cahiers des jardins anglo-chinois à la mode* (1776–1785), included drawings of Stowe and other English gardens as well as descriptions of the picturesque in Chinese gardens.[3]

Fig. 3.1. Pastoral scene with tomb, bust, temple, and tower, reminiscent of similar fictional views of the Athenian Ceramicus. From Salomon Gessner, *Oeuvres* (Paris, 1799).

The popular tales and verse of the Swiss poet and painter Salomon Gessner (1730–1788) won international acclaim with the appearance of his *Idyllen* in 1757, its translations, and a sequel. The frontispiece to the 1797 edition of Gessner's *Oeuvres* depicts a tomb in a picturesque setting. (Fig. 3.1.) Gessner was not concerned with celebrating heroes; he advocated burial customs that would perpetuate domestic sentiment and affection transcending death. His poetry reflected the increased level of sentimentality associated with the rising tide of affective individualism, and his accompanying illustrations presented rural landscapes as the proper sites for cultivation of salutary emotions, especially melancholy.[4]

Mid-century travels further whetted the French appetite for the picturesque. After studying in Italy from 1761 to 1765, Hubert Robert (1733–1808), a friend of Piranesi, dubbed "Robert of the Ruins," painted moldering classical monuments, feeding the taste for Roman antiquities overgrown by resurgent Nature that became so popular during the reign of his patron, Louis XVI. Abbé Saint-Non engraved many of Robert's paintings in *Recueil de vues dessinées d'après nature dans les villas et environs de Rome* (1765). After the 1763 Treaty of Paris reconciled France and England, the French elite again traveled to Britain, where they discovered new picturesque gardens complete with ruins and neoclassical monuments, then returned home to transform many of their own estates in that fashion.[5]

Books on the "natural" style of gardening continued to appear in France. A translation of Thompson's *Seasons* was published in 1760 and of Whately's *L'Art de faire des jardins modernes* in 1771. Whately frequented Parisian salons, preaching that "the art of gardens conceived in the elevated spirit largely places itself on the same level as landscape painting." With his *Essai sur les jardins* in 1774, Claude-Henri Watelet (1718–1786), philosopher and member of the Académie, introduced French literati to the ideas of Joseph Addison and other English garden theorists, furthering the vogue for *le paysage humanisé* (the humanized "rural" landscape) as an alternative to the linear formality of baroque French gardens. From 1779 to 1785, the five-volume *Theory of Garden Art* by the Dane Christian Cajus Lorenz Hirschfeld (1742–1792) was published in Leipzig simultaneously in both German and French, spreading the taste for the picturesque throughout Europe and linking Nature with nationalism.[6]

The poet-priest Abbé Jacques Delille (1738–1813) felt that "one must be a good heathen to relish" these pastorals. Delille, translator of Virgil and Milton, praised "the *sublime melancholy* of the English Nation" that was evident in picturesque landscape design and in Whately's ideas. In his extended poem *Les Jardins* (1782), Delille listed diverse trees, shrubs, and grasses that might be imported from around the world to create a new sort of pastoral cemetery, a horticulturist's delight. Trees would have utilitarian value, and plants of different shades and textures would form carpets of ground cover over earthen graves.[7]

Delille's friend Jean-Jacques Rousseau (1712–1778) proved a great voice of nascent romanticism. The philosopher proposed a view of death shaped by a new valuation of Nature and resigned to the belief that the natural cycle of birth, growth, degeneration, and death governs both the life of man and that of societies and polities. Calmly contemplating his impending death in *Les Rêveries du promeneur solitaire*, he found consolation in "savage solitude" during the last six weeks of his life in 1778 at Ermenonville, a landscape garden fifty kilometers northeast of Paris in the countryside of Île de France (Oise). The 2,100-acre property, dotted with lakes and traversed by picturesque rivers, reflected Rousseau's naturalistic aesthetic as if it had been created by the protagonist of his novel *Julie; ou La Nouvelle Héloïse* (1761).[8]

Ermenonville's owner and designer, René-Louis marquis de Girardin (1735–1808), was the leading authority on the English garden style in France, owing to his extensive travels before 1766 and his friendship with the proprietors of several English estates. (Fig. 3.2.) Al-

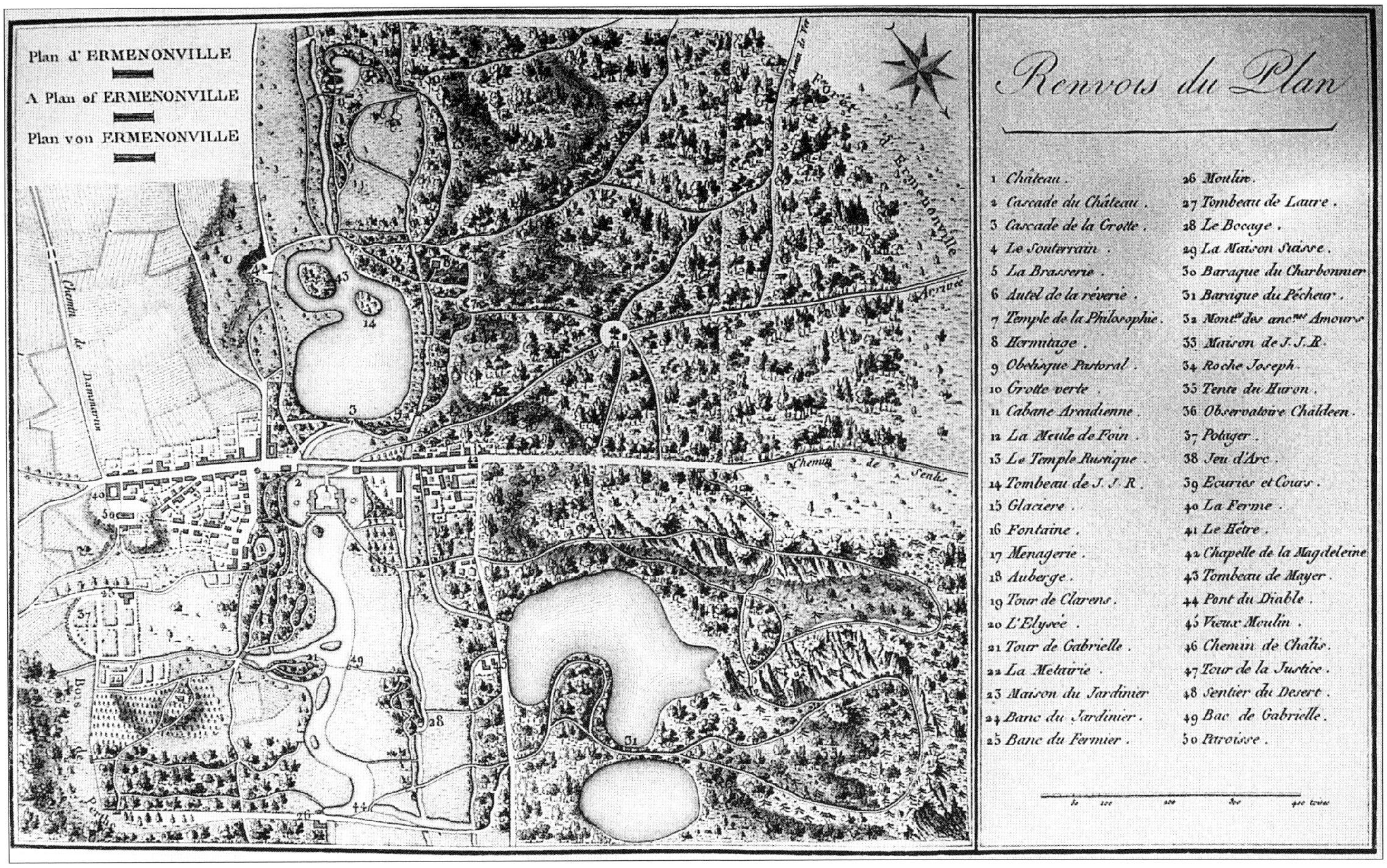

Fig. 3.2. Plan of Ermenonville gardens. From Laborde, 1808.

though Girardin boasted of his own creation of his garden, he had received advice from the poet William Shenstone, owner-designer of the famed gardens at The Leasowes; the painter, architect, and geographical engineer Jean-Marie Morel (1728–1810); and the Scottish botanist and landscape gardener Thomas Blaikie (1751–1838). Hubert Robert also counseled the marquis on the design of his *jardin paysager*, a place where visitors could meditate on antiquity, Nature, morality, and philosophy. Following the example of William Kent, Girardin even planted a few dead trees to help inspire melancholy. Girardin's *De la composition des paysages sur le terrain, ou des moyens d'embellir la nature* (On the Composition of Landscape on the Terrain, or Some Ways to Embellish Nature), published in Geneva in 1777 and translated into English by Girardin himself as *An Essay on Landscape* in 1783, adapted English garden design with the intention of promoting the secular and natural spirituality of the Age of Reason.[9]

Rousseau's death while at Ermenonville led to the decision to bury the philosopher there. Even before Girardin became aware of the use of mausoleums, graves, and cenotaphs in English gardens, he had intended to make a funerary monument a focal point at Ermenonville, initially considering an urn containing the ashes of two lovers. When Rousseau died, the marquis insisted on burying him, knowing that the Church would deny Rousseau burial. On July 4, 1778, at midnight, the time for burial of Dissenters, a small group accompanied the embalmed body by torchlight to a tomb on the Isle of Poplars, a picturesque island in a rambling lake. Rousseau's tomb was marked by a neoclassical monument topped by an urn—perhaps the one intended for the anonymous lovers. (It was replaced in 1780 by a marble sarcophagus designed by Robert, inspired by the tomb of Nero, which he and Piranesi had painted.) It is inscribed, "Here rests the man of Nature and Truth." A bas-relief by Jacques-Philippe Lesueur included allegorical figures of Maternal Virtue and a scene of natural child rearing, depicting unswaddled babies and mothers praying to the goddess Nature, inspired by Rousseau's novel *Émile*. Poplars surrounding the site suggest the columns of the Temple of Nature.[10] (Figs. 3.3, 3.4.)

Rousseau's tomb, the "Elysium," was the centerpiece among fifty ruins, broken columns, urns, cenotaphs, and other mnemonic structures scattered in the bucolic landscape, including a prehistoric tomblike dolmen that had served as a sixteenth-century ossuary. (Fig. 3.5.) The marquis also dedicated a grotto to the English poet Thomson and erected a memorial to his friend

Fig. 3.3. Ermenonville, Rousseau's first tomb on the Isle of Poplars. Engraving by J.-M. Moreau le Jeune, 1778, from Hirschfeld, 1780.

Fig. 3.4. Ermenonville, Rousseau's second tomb by Hubert Robert on the Isle of Poplars. Engraving by Alexis Donnet, 1824.

Fig. 3.5. Ermenonville, prehistoric dolmen. Photograph by BMGL, 1985.

Shenstone. There were busts of Lycurgus, Socrates, Homer, and Epaminondas. Beside a serpentine stream, Girardin placed a small red-brick pyramid honoring Theocritus, Virgil, and the contemporary poets Saint-Lambert, Thomson, and Gessner. (Fig. 3.6.) A poem about the value of thought and love by Voltaire (1694–1778), the great philosophical iconoclast of his era, inspired Girardin's Altar of Dreams. Nestled on a hill amid Scotch pines, a semicircular Temple of Philosophy, dedicated to Montaigne, bore a verse from Virgil in Latin, "Happy is he who would know the cause of things." (Fig. 3.7.) The temple was meant to appear incomplete rather than in ruins, though inspired by Robert's paintings of the Temple of the Sibyl at Tivoli in Rome. Its six Tuscan columns celebrated theories of Descartes ("Nil in rebus inane"), Newton's "enlightening" discoveries, William Penn's humanitarianism in his "Holy Experiment" in Pennsylvania, Montesquieu's defense of Justice, Voltaire's "Ridicule" of prejudice and superstition, and Rousseau's celebration of Nature. Girardin left space to honor Benjamin Franklin, Joseph Priestley, and others but went no further. The inscription from Descartes, meaning "There is no void in Nature," expressed the significance of the garden itself.

Girardin soon added other graves. In 1779, the Alsatian landscape painter Georges-Frédéric Mayer (Meier) died while at Ermenonville and was interred on another small island. When an unidentified thirty-year-old "neurasthenic" committed suicide in the park in June 1791, leaving a note signed "a victim of love," Girardin seized the romantic opportunity to bury the man, marking the grave with a stone inscribed to "an unhappy, melancholy dreamer." (Fig. 3.8.) Three years later Girardin added a cenotaph dedicated to an undistinguished painter named Gandat, who died of apoplexy at Ermenonville but was buried elsewhere. Another tombstone honored an unnamed mother and child with the grieving words, "To my son, to my wife / I lived to love them / I survive to weep them." Finally, in 1810, after Girardin's own death, admirers constructed a monument to his memory on the estate. These objects had to be sought out or found by chance during a promenade down sinuous paths through the wooded landscape.[11]

Ermenonville's didactic landscape was meant to be visited. Girardin's brother published a guidebook in 1788.[12] Benjamin Franklin, Thomas Jefferson, Sweden's

Fig. 3.6. Parc d'Ermenonville, the Philosophers' Pyramid dedicated to Theocritus, Virgil, Thomson, and Gessner. Engraving by Constantin Bourgeois, from Laborde, 1808. BMGL.

Fig. 3.7. Parc d'Ermenonville, Temple of Philosophy. Engraving by S. Gobelin, ca. 1800, after the drawing by Ballura. BMGL.

Fig. 3.8. Parc d'Ermenonville, Tomb of the Stranger, an unidentified suicide in 1791. From Laborde, 1808. BMGL.

Fig. 3.9. Désert de Retz, ruins of the church of Saint-Jacques de Roye from the deserted village. Photograph by BMGL, 1990.

Fig. 3.10. Désert de Retz, pyramidal icehouse. Photograph by BMGL, 1990.

King Gustav II, Austria's Emperor Joseph II, Louis XVI and Marie Antoinette, as well as Delille, Mirabeau, Saint-Just, Danton, Robespierre, and Napoleon all made pilgrimages there. Rousseau's tomb was considered a model of taste, a secular shrine for the old elite as well as for future revolutionaries. But revolutionary vandalism forced the closing of the gardens to the public in 1788. Six years later Rousseau's body was moved to the Panthéon in the heart of the urbanized Left Bank of Paris, an unlikely tomb for the "Apostle of Nature." Still, the site of his first tomb remains the focal point in Ermenonville's picturesque gardens.[13]

Landscapes reflecting Rousseau's romanticism spread throughout France as the pantheistic celebration of Nature replaced religious orthodoxy among some of the elite. François-Nicolas-Henri Racine de Monville (1734–1797), a multitalented horticulturist and cultural leader, then Grand Master of Waters and Forests in Normandy, developed the Désert de Retz as a *jardin pittoresque*. With his prime residence in Paris, this was his pastoral retreat and hobby. Purchased in 1774, the estate in Île-de-France abutting the Marly Forest grew to forty hectares; it included the deserted village of Saint-Jacques de Roye with its Gothic church, preserved as a ruin after removal of the vernacular structures. (Fig. 3.9.) In 1785, Racine de Monville had the architect François Barbier design a rustic pyramid that doubled as an icehouse and a gargantuan building in the shape of a destroyed column with spiral stairs leading to four stories of rooms. (Fig. 3.10.) There he stayed when in residence; guests stayed in a Chinese pavilion. Racine de Monville added a tomb, obelisk, and Temple of Pan, among seventeen *fabriques*. As work progressed, Le Désert attracted visitors including Marie Antoinette, the comtesse Du Barry, King Gustav III of Sweden, as well as Benjamin Franklin and Jefferson. Others could visit by buying a ticket.[14]

After visiting Ermenonville and the Désert de Retz, Marie Antoinette was determined to add a similar naturalistic retreat at Versailles beyond Le Nôtre's linear waters and geometrical parterres. (Figs. 3.11, 3.12.) The queen's gardens were more playfully fanciful than melancholy or philosophical, omitting ruins and commemorative monuments though including an Austrian hamlet, reflecting the queen's nostalgia for the country of her youth, and a Temple d'Amour, after a design by Hubert Robert. Louis XVI did have Robert install mock funerary monuments in the picturesque gardens of Rambouillet. His courtiers followed suit. The comte de Vaudreuil, the comte d'Albon, and even the comte d'Artois, the king's

Fig. 3.11. Versailles, Temple de l'Amour in *le jardin anglais* or *jardin champêtre*, the private domain of the Petit Trianon of Marie-Antoinette at Versailles, designed in the 1780s by the architect Richard Mique in collaboration with the painter Hubert Robert. Photograph by BMGL, 1992.

Fig. 3.13. Classical tombs by the architect Famin in the wooded Parc du Chateau de Rambouillet, in Yvelines, southeast of Paris. Engraving by Bourgeois, from Laborde, 1808.

Fig. 3.12. The rustic Grotto overlooking the little man-made lake in *le jardin anglais* of Marie-Antoinette at Versailles. Photograph by BMGL, 1985.

Fig. 3.14. Classical tombs by the architect Famin in *le jardin anglais*, an area in the wooded Parc du Chateau de Rambouillet designed from 1783 to 1793 by Charles-Claude de La Billarderie, Comte d'Angivillier (1730–1809), superintendent of the royal buildings, for King Louis XVI to please his queen, Marie-Antoinette. Engraving by Bourgeois, from Laborde, 1808.

brother, decorated their own picturesque estates with similar melancholy elements.[15] (Figs. 3.13, 3.14.)

At Maupertuis, Alexandre-Théodore Brongniart (1739–1813), architectural student of Boullée and Blondel, joined with the Scottish landscape gardener Thomas Blaikie to design an Elysium in 1780 for Anne-Pierre, marquis de Montesquiou-Fézensac, with a cenotaph to the Protestant martyr of the 1572 Saint Bartholomew's Day massacre, Admiral Gaspard de Coligny. A ruined pyramid with caryatid columns marking the entrance to an imaginary tomb was set in a dense forest amid free-standing columns with a neoclassical sarcophagus atop a high base, *fabriques* inspired by Robert's paintings of Roman ruins. (Fig. 3.15.) A huge natural rock, a principal attraction, bore an inscription from Delille about the primacy of Nature.[16]

Fig. 3.15. The "Elysium" at Maupertuis, gardens of Anne-Pierre, marquis de Montesquiou-Fézensac (1739–1798), a writer and political liberal, containing the pyramid to the memory of Huguenot martyr Admiral Gaspard de Coligny (1519–1572), one of 50,000 Protestants slain in the St. Bartholomew's Day massacre, and cenotaph to Rousseau. Engraving by Bourgeois, from Laborde, 1808.

The architect, painter, and printmaker Louis Carrogis, called Carmontelle (1717–1806), drew the picturesque plan for the forty-six-acre Parc de Monceau just northwest of Paris, built for Philippe d'Orléans, duc de Chartres, cousin of the king and Masonic Grand Master of the Grand Orient of France. Built between 1769 and 1778, the *parc à fabriques* contained a rustic pyramid, a ruined Roman temple, false Gothic ruins, and other structures inspired by Robert's drawings of Roman ruins, some designed by the architect Bernard Poyot (1742–1824). In 1783, Blaikie took over development of the irregular twenty-hectare fantasy landscape, featuring a small lake and sinuous paths among thick and varied plantings focused on a *bois des tombeaux* (woods with tombs), featuring statues, severed columns, an obelisk, and memorial stones around a huge rustic pyramid inspired by that of Caius Cestius in Rome, as well as by Masonic symbolism. Monceau soon became a favored promenade for the elite.[17] (Fig. 3.16.)

Fig. 3.16. Parc de Monceau, rustic pyramid in the Bois des Tombeaux. Photograph by BMGL, 1985.

The vogue for such scenes brought Robert many commissions for neoclassical monuments in picturesque gardens. In 1784, the deposed court banker Jean-Joseph, duc de Laborde (1724–1794), received his estate at Méréville near Étampes, seventeen leagues south of Paris on the plains of Beauce. François-Joseph Bélanger (1744–1818), architect to the comte d'Artois, Louis XVI's brother, began work on the landscape but proved to be too wedded to linearity. Robert took over, transforming the estate, with the help of hundreds of workers, into a *jardin anglais* complete with funerary structures set among some twenty *fabriques* and ruins of a medieval fortress. The diversified terrain was traversed by a sinuous river feeding ponds dotted with islands, all reshaped by a hydraulic engineer. Exotic plantings included newly acclimatized tulip trees from Virginia. Prominent amid the trees and enormous rock masses forming grottoes and secluded paths were a cenotaph to Captain James Cook, English explorer of the South Seas; a bust by the neoclassical sculptor Augustin Pajou surrounded by dark evergreens; a Trajan column, thirty-seven meters tall, built by the contractor J. André using Robert's sketches; a Temple of Filial Piety by the architect Nicolas le Camus de Mézières (1721–1789); and a simple column in memory of Laborde's two sons, shipwrecked near California in 1786. Work continued until 1794, when Laborde was arrested; he died on the guillotine.[18] (Figs. 3.17, 3.18.)

Fig. 3.17. Jardins de Méréville, sarcophagus (cenotaph) of Captain Cook designed by Hubert Robert and Augustin Pajou, white marble urn with low-relief bust surrounded by "a great number of forest trees" that "seem to reproduce the savage and remote country which contains the real tomb of that illustrious voyager." Engraving by Bourgeois, from Laborde, 1808.

Fig. 3.18. Jardins de Méréville, rostral column, "fine turkey-blue marble rostrated with bronze," in memory of the two sons of Jean-Joseph, duc de Laborde. The brothers were lost at sea in 1786 while accompanying the navigator La Pérouse to the Pacific. Engraving by Bourgeois, from Laborde, 1808.

Fig. 3.19. Parc de Betz, Temple of Friendship by Hubert Robert. Engraving by Bourgeois, from Laborde, 1808. BMGL.

Fig. 3.20. Jardins de Plessis-Chamant, tomb of the proprietor's wife, "distinguished by her goodness and virtues, mourned by daughters and husband." Engraving by Bourgeois, from Laborde, 1808.

Fig. 3.21. Parc de Morfontaine, tomb of black marble sheltered by thuyas, larch, and evergreens. Engraving by Bourgeois, from Laborde, 1808.

Robert contributed structures to the gardens of the Château de Betz in Normandy for the duc de Harcourt, focused on a "valley of tombs" approached on an avenue lined with funerary trees—cypress, sycamore, poplar, and arborvitae. Developed in the 1780s, Betz featured the central pulpit and an obelisk from the Saint-Innocents Cemetery as well as an urn-topped monument meant to encourage prayer and meditation. Mnemonic structures, eclectic in style, included gravestone steles guarded by allegorical figures of Faith, Hope, and Charity; modern tombs by Camus de Mézières for the legendary crusader Thibaut de Nanteuil, killed in 1182, and for his wife, who died of a broken heart; the ruins of a feudal castle; a Druid temple; a Pavilion of Rest; and an obelisk honoring American Independence. More than a garden, Betz was a historical museum as well as a place to enjoy the pleasures of melancholy. (Fig. 3.19.)

As in England, picturesque gardens offered models of idealistic alternatives to existing burial practices. Abbé Chaulieu, Chateaubriand, Madame Necker, and the prince de Ligne described their ideal burial places as in a grove under a majestic tree, preferably deciduous rather than evergreen. A simple tomb marked by a neoclassical monument and surrounded by an iron fence provided a focal point in the wooded garden at Le Plessis-Chamant. Le Peletier, head of the municipality of Paris, installed a black marble tomb in a picturesque setting at the center of his *jardin anglo-chinois* at Morfontaine in 1770. (Figs. 3.20, 3.21.) A cenotaph with a bust of Carolus Linnaeus was placed in 1790 in the Jardin des Plantes, the king's botanical gardens, where the grave of the naturalist Louis Daubenton became a focal point after his death in 1800.[19] (Fig. 3.22.) Michel-Barthélemy Hazon drew up detailed plans for an idyllic funerary grove on his Normandy estate, inviting friends

Fig. 3.22. Grave of the naturalist and horticulturist Louis-Jean-Marie Daubenton (1716–1800) on a rise in the picturesque half then recently added to the Jardin des Plantes, Paris. Orginally, this severed column, representative of the death of an influential man, a "pillar," was surrounded by rustic boulders and a large, circular, latticework metal fence. Photograph by BMGL, 1985.

Fig. 3.23. Parc de Cantiers, Normandie, *Bosquet religieux* ("religious bosk"), funerary site of Michel-Barthélemy Hazon and his wife, pyramid of earth and turf topped by a tree, designed by architect Alexandre-Théodore Brongniart for his own gardens. Engraving, ca. 1800. BMGL.

to choose burial places there near the central earthen pyramid under which he and his wife intended to lie. (Fig. 3.23.) So great was the vogue that the comte de Laborde, despite his taste for English gardening, lamented "those tombs of parade and fashion which some people take a pleasure in multiplying in gardens through a puerile affecting of sentiment and melancholy."[20]

Debating Funerary Reform

The French philosophes were the first to turn to English culture in search of alternatives to the forms of their old order. After returning from a three-year exile in England (1726–29), Voltaire wrote that "it is not the tombs of kings that one admires, but the monuments that the recognition of the nation has erected to the greatest men who contributed to its glory; you see their statues as in Athens one saw those of Sophocles and Plato; . . . just the sight of these glorious monuments has excited more than one soul and formed more than one great man."[21] Heeding his Whiggish friends there, Voltaire urged the social uses of honoring exemplary individuals, new heroes to replace saints, kings, and nobles. Looking to ancient models for ways to express modern ideas, neoclassicism provided him and others of like mind with a new vocabulary of commemoration, just as English gardens offered an aesthetic alternative to royalist formalism.

Voltaire aimed to dispel the image of death institutionalized by the Church. In postulating new commemorative forms, he relied heavily on classical references condemning the fear of death, particularly in *De rerum natura* (*On the Nature of the Universe*) by the Roman poet Lucretius. Voltaire saw himself, in fact, as a new Lucretius, teaching his era to "despise the horrors of the tomb and the terrors of another life." He paraphrased the Epicurean, writing: "This dread and darkness of mind, therefore, requires not the rays of the sun. . . . [O]nly knowledge of Nature's form dispels them."[22] He and other readers of Lucretius saw ancient wisdom recapitulated in the funerary elements of English gardens. In his essay "Enterrement" ("Burial"), written just before his death, Voltaire argued that the traditional canon law bans on burial within churches had been perverted over time by "some bourgeois with the vanity to change temples into charnel houses so they could rot there in a distinguished manner."[23] He preferred the example of the laws of the Twelve Tablets in ancient Rome, where few had the privilege of burial within the city. How much more rational was the Roman practice of extramural burials—burials outside the city walls, where cadavers polluted neither sacred places nor any of the secular city.

In advocating a laicized funerary cult in the name of immortality and history, the philosophes adopted a vocabulary associated with English landscape gardens and romantic poetry as much as with classical sources. In an essay in *L'Encyclopédie*, Jean Le Rond d'Alembert (1717–1783) proposed the creation of a large extramural cemetery outside Paris. Entries in that Enlightenment compendium of knowledge, published between 1751 and 1781, blamed the Church for encouraging and perpetuating the fear of death and obscuring death's natural "narcotic sweetness." D'Alembert, like Montesquieu and Voltaire, agreed with the Deist Henry St. John Bolingbroke (1678–1751) and other English philosophers that history could be reinterpreted and rehabilitated in secular and intellectual terms, and that history, framed as a compendium of good and great lives in the manner of

Plutarch, could have a socially beneficial moral and didactic function. Like Voltaire, d'Alembert reflected a trend in the consciousness of French philosophers of the time described by the historian George Armstrong Kelly as "mortal politics." This was a period when "questions of death and immortality affected historical understanding." The era was "focused more fixedly on the memory of deeds than on a metaphysics of the unchanging. Memory suggested perpetuating the human chronicle, and that chronicle is what we call history."[24]

Postéromanie, or the vogue for celebrating "virtuous fathers of families whose achievements lived on in their well-raised children, the citizens of the future," flourished among the new bourgeoisie, to the dismay of most ecclesiastics and aristocrats. Although Claude-Adrien Helvétius (1715–1771), another philosophe, preferred to celebrate the present rather than a past of royalty and nobles, other writers supported a cult of posthumous memory. Abbé Rémi, in his poem *Les Jours* (1770), a corrective to and rejection of Young's *Night*, asserted that death held no dominion over fathers who endowed their progeny with property. For in doing so, such men "journey on through the centuries under the auspices of Nature."[25]

One problem remained: creating a mechanism for transmitting memory through new landscapes, monuments, and cultural practices. The French did not consider the possibility of setting funerary landscapes in the countryside until after scientific theories had emerged to suggest that plants actually cleanse the air of pollutants by "imbibing the phlogistic matter." Joseph Priestley (1733–1804), a British Unitarian minister encouraged in scientific studies by Franklin, presented a paper in 1772 to the Royal Society in London suggesting that plants create "dephlogisticated air," a substance that the French chemist Antoine-Laurent Lavoisier later named oxygen. By 1779, Jan Ingenhousz (1730–1799), Priestley's friend and a London physician, validated this theory by his discovery of photosynthesis. Prompted by these discoveries, French cemetery reformers began to formulate ideas for burial places in "rural" (that is, suburban) or garden settings. As early as 1777, Girardin advocated that "it is without [outside] the [urban] gates that tombs and sepulchres should always be placed. It was certainly a sublime idea to deposit the ashes of great men in some picturesque situation, as was the custom of the ancients. It recalled the memory of them in a very interesting manner, instead of that repugnance which is produced by dismal burying grounds. Those masses of rottenness and corruption, placed in the midst of cities, become infectuous to the living."[26]

Theoretical plans for wooded cemeteries proliferated in France. In 1784, the famed writer and philosophe Jacques-Henri Bernardin de Saint-Pierre (1737–1814), Rousseau's friend to the end, published a detailed description of an ideal funerary garden. Based on the Lockean theory that all ideas are acquired directly from visual and other sensory experience, it would contain a variety of ideas readable in material form meant to elicit emotional and intellectual responses. Bernardin believed that rural settings inculcated republican virtues and other noble sentiments, including "gentle melancholy," which he considered "the most voluptuous of affections of the soul," gratifying man's feelings of both misery and excellence. In keeping with France's new revolutionary cults, which elevated republican virtues to the stature formerly granted saints and kings, Bernardin's cemetery would be a compendium of social and cultural history in secular terms, complete with monuments honoring those who made contributions to the nation: botanists, inventors, explorers, and dignitaries, as well as women, the keepers of family order. Merit would dictate a tomb's location, with the "most venerable"—writers, generals, and virtuous women—at the center. The monuments, in a hierarchy of shapes indicative of different degrees of merit—from obelisks, columns, and pyramids to urns, bas-reliefs, and medallions—would not be "packed together as in a store or warehouse, but distributed with taste." Sculptures would be of various materials, not all of marble from the same quarry. These objects would remind visitors of the physical appearance of the deceased during life rather than in the grave. The philosopher discouraged decorative bronzes and gilding, associated with baroque ostentation, for that would detract from the monuments' visual and psychological impact. "The more simple," he asserted, "the more energy they communicate to the sentiment of melancholy. They produce a more powerful effect when poor rather than rich, antique rather than modern, detailed with misfortunes rather than with attributes of power." Personal monuments would have as much or more importance in such a place as monuments erected to public figures.[27]

Bernardin called a tomb "a monument erected on the frontier between two worlds," the symbolic divide between the living and the dead. His cemetery, between the city and the country, would be a "middle landscape," to use the term of the historian Leo Marx. It would be a "hierophany," as much later described by the scholar of religions Mircea Eliade, an *axis mundi* or sacred spot linking the sphere of man with that of the divine. Imagined as a horticultural park with a variety of indigenous and imported trees, shrubs, and grasses, Bernardin's ideal cemetery would have none of the symmetry, the manicured lawns and topiary of Le Nôtre's formal gardens. It would contrast dramatically with existing barren burial grounds that included no signs of an Eden lost.[28]

Bernardin expanded on English garden theories in applying design principles to his "rural" cemetery. He wanted his Elysium set on an island planted with poplars in the Seine in the Paris suburbs. The river would serve to isolate burials from the city, preserving public health and eliminating the necessity for high walls, which would mar the appearance of the pastoral and block the healthful flow of air. It would also function as a route for funeral barges and for boats bearing visitors. Views of distant vistas would evoke thoughts of infinity, causing the visitor to muse on the distance between past and present, the vicissitudes of human affairs, man's fleeting existence, his smallness but yet his immortality. Bernardin's essay "On the Pleasure of Tombs" was widely read even in nineteenth-century America. Its initial influence would be felt in French burial reform, but the culmination of his vision would come with the founding of Boston's Mount Auburn in 1831.[29] Of similar influence was Hirschfeld's *Theorie der Gärtenkunst.* Hirschfeld praised the gardens at Stowe and urged the addition of real tombs and family burials to similar gardens in place of cenotaphs. His quarto volumes included engravings of monuments in picturesque settings, as well as a descriptive model for a cemetery where a variety of trees would purify the air while their varied foliage hues intensified a sense of melancholy. Many German, French, and American landscape gardeners used Hirschfeld as a text well into the next century. (Figs. 3.24, 3.25.)

Fig. 3.24. Moonlit obelisk over the tomb of Johann Georg Sulzer (1720–1779), Swiss aesthetic philosopher and naturalistic garden theorist who taught at the Berlin Academy of Sciences, "*Sentimentale Parkszene mit Sulzer-Denkmal.*" Engraving from Hirschfeld, 1780.

Fig. 3.25. Anonymous, idealized funerary urn in a forest. Engraving by Hirschfeld, 1780.

French plans for wooded cemeteries proliferated. Bélanger sketched a funerary scene reminiscent of Rousseau's tomb. Jean Lecointe proposed a cemetery with monuments, mausoleums, and a ceremonial gateway, a heavily planted landscape that would blend into the countryside and not reduce the supply of arable land near the city. As advocated by John Evelyn, fruit trees and aromatic plants, including medicinal plants, would maximize the land's usefulness. These theories developed independently of the growing criticism of conditions in Church-controlled burial sites. Many other funerary reformers simply advocated removing burials from cities but failed to present detailed proposals for alternative landscapes of death.

The iconoclasm of the French Revolution far surpassed that of the English Civil War. The Revolutionary policy of de-sacralizing or de-Christianizing all cemeteries, not just the tombs of the privileged, fueled discussion of new deathways and commemorative forms. The Revolution had created a "problem of the past," which some arbiters of culture considered solvable through monuments that would mark and define the start of a new national history, often through innovative commemorative places incorporating secularized, romantic notions of death and Nature to celebrate the lives of new kinds of heroes. Joseph Fouché (1759–1820), the virulently anticlerical Jacobin deputy to the Convention, wanted cemeteries to represent the new reign of secular Reason. He ordered a statue of Sleep to be erected to replace the central cross in the Lyons cemetery. To objectify "the sweet repose that the dead enjoy," he placed the motto "Death Is Eternal Sleep" at entrances to burial grounds throughout the Department of Nièvre. Fouché ordered the planting of shade trees, also symbolizing the sleep of death. Inspired by Ermenonville, he favored poplars, rejecting cypresses and other evergreens, funerary plantings associated with sadness. Everything in his cemetery would be calculated to inspire "sweet, agreeable, and touching ideas, like the virtue that made men respectable." Fouché's ideal funerary landscape would convey patriotic pride and even the pleasure of survivors at having had a virtuous friend or a relative "worthy of his equals and of the Republic." Nothing would remind the visitor of hell or purgatory, concepts "invented to make priests indispensable" through their efforts to "eternalize sadness" in images of bare bones, death's-heads, and other medieval iconography. In this way Fouché implemented Robespierre's declaration that death is "the beginning of immortality."[30]

On 28 Vendémiaire, Year II (19 October 1793), Pierre-Gaspard Chaumette (1763–1794), radical anti-Girondin Procureur-Syndic of the Paris Commune, ordered that funerary honors be the same for all. He wanted cemeteries to reflect the classical concept of the Elysian Fields, complete with odoriferous, deciduous trees. Planting graves with flowers would permit the citizen to "breathe the soul of his father in the rose." This secularized ideal represented an official rejection of old forms of fear and mourning and a desire to develop a commemorative consciousness, the same sentiment expressed on the banners that Jacobins bore at the head of their funerary processions: "The just man never dies; he lives in the memory of his fellow citizens." Chaumette also ordered the Commission of Public Works to remove from cemeteries all crosses and other objects that radical revolutionaries considered too somber and repellent, the old iconography of death.[31]

The next day, the Commune of Arts and Jean Baptiste Avril's Administration of Public Works petitioned the National Convention to have cities move their cemeteries "to the four corners of their circumference." Temples of Liberty and Humanity would be surrounded by "humble and respectable tombs of heroes, friends of the fatherland, on which one will read touching inscriptions" while strolling "under the lugubrious shadow" of cypresses. Avril proposed enclosing these cemeteries with low hedges and wide grass-lined ditches, a soft border or "ha-ha" characteristic of English gardens, unlike old graveyards' forbidding walls. A lawn would cover the entire site, in contrast to the arid dirt in parish churchyards. Only a few notables would merit perpetual burials, as under the old order. The egalitarian, anticlerical Chaumette opposed Avril's plan for that reason. The Convention responded by ordering the construction of four new cemeteries on "simple, rustic, isolated" sites outside Paris; but it left implementation of the decree to the local government, the Commune.[32] Before any extramural sites could be created, however, the mass executions of the Reign of Terror forced the city to open new burial grounds inside Paris. One open pit a few blocks north of the square where the guillotine sat received the headless bodies of Louis XVI and Marie Antoinette. Chaumette himself soon joined many of his fellow *sans-culottes* in a common pit. The bodies of Danton, Robespierre, and their partisans were deposited in the Parc Monceau.

The proposals for creating a "cult of ancestors" through the design of pastoral cemeteries were a response to the debate over preserving and reinterpreting a historical consciousness through artifacts of the past. Abbé Henri Grégoire (1750–1831), Constitutional Bishop of Blois and deputy to the Convention from Loire-et-Cher, issued a forceful plea in 1794 after the fall of Robespierre to undo the damage caused by the "vandalism" of antidespotic patriots during the Terror. Grégoire proposed establishing a museum where artifacts could be assembled, preserved, and displayed, as well as archival records of French history, no matter how distasteful to Revolutionaries, to foster nationalism and moral improvement of the citizenry in a didactic way.[33]

Moderate reformers also feared the destructive influence of the Terror's devaluation of life on public morale and civilized behavior. More than functional burial reform, they advocated creation of a "cult of tombs" to instruct posterity in their duties to the Supreme Being (the Revolution forbade references to God—the more radical referred to the Goddess of Reason) and to society through memory of the goals and lives of the nation's forebears. Delille stressed the necessity of the funerary dimension to any new *cultes domestiques*. In his 1794 poem "L'Imagination," he urged government support for ceremonies and places that would permit ordinary families to honor their dead. Abbé François-Valentin Mulot (1749–1804) agreed, congratulating him: "Thus a society of families, of which the large part of human society is formed, will extend the limits of life into the hereafter and will perpetuate the stay of the dead. Delicious ideas! How consoling you are!"[34]

Having descended to the brink of chaos through anarchy and demagoguery, the French now recoiled from iconoclasm and tried to reassemble pieces of a shattered culture. Revolutionaries became reformers. They realized that a change in public sensibilities and practices could not be decreed or legislated but would have to be instilled as a new vogue. Mulot observed: "No, the law cannot oblige me to employ what faculties I have to honor those who were dear to me. In the closed garden, in the open field where I will have placed my father's, wife's, or son's body, if there remains to me the means to obtain the help of an able artist, I must have constructed on their bodies a monument which retraces their virtues for me." It was time to reaffirm the rights of property, even if that meant permitting privileges of class and wealth. Theorists began to consider the institutionalization of postmortem property in the privatization of graves and agreed that "proper" burial should reflect both a citizen's spiritual and material worth.[35]

The prosecutor Nicher-Cérisy noted that ancient Egyptian legislators had found that nothing contributed more to social stability than solemn public burials. Citing Herodotus, who observed that such customs assured religious observance as well as payment of debts, Nicher-Cérisy declared that "it is among funeral monuments that man comes to study his heart and tie the knots that attach him to the fatherland and humanity . . . among tombs that he appreciates the past and foresees life to come."[36] If the graves of average citizens were to be held sacred, how much more so should be those of political and cultural leaders? In planning the creation of new rites and burial places based on the classical traditions of Greece and Rome and a heritage traced to the Gauls, the French aimed to honor new national heroes. They created a repository for notables on the Left Bank in Paris in the former neoclassical church of Sainte-Geneviève, renamed the Panthéon, and reinterred Voltaire there in 1791, Rousseau in 1794 shortly after the Jacobin radical Marat. In considering cemeteries, however, most theorists preferred naturalistic landscapes in the English fashion rather than grand architectural structures amid the urban fabric.

Scholars at the Lycée des Arts took up burial reform in 1796 following a call by the National Institute of Sciences and Arts for papers on the creation of cults. On 15 Messidor, Year IV (2 July 1796), the National Institute held a public meeting on the social uses of marking deaths. In 1798, it obliged its members to attend the funerals of their confrères. With a mandate from Minister of the Interior Pierre-Charles-Louis Baudin, who declared that "the first principles of morals, of medicine, and of social science demand prompt reform of the state of inhumations," the institute offered a prize for the best essay on new funeral ceremonies and sepulchral sites.[37] Forty essays by architects, writers, teachers, functionaries, and citizens were judged on 14 Vendémiaire, Year IX (5 October 1800). Some included detailed plans and instructions for rigid new systems; others were conceptual essays. Amaury Duval and Abbé Mulot shared the prize.

Duval, antiquarian scholar and former ambassador to Naples, thought that all cemeteries should be outside city limits, following the example of the ancients, for placing tombs near dwellings inspired public fear and disgust. Only national heroes deserved urban burials. A reading of Bernardin informed Duval's observations on Italian burial places, and especially his praise for the ancient Roman cemetery the Elysian Fields ("Champs-Elysées" in French) on the "smiling hill" overlooking the river near the old city of Messina. High poplars and ruined tombs garlanded with vines created a picturesque atmosphere, inviting melancholy meditation. Yet Duval wanted to avoid the ostentation of Roman tombs as well as the Egyptian funerary style designed for kings and aristocracy at the people's expense. He feared that "moderns will fall into the same excesses as ancients," that "the rich and distinguished will always be buried magnificently" while the bourgeois will ruin himself financially "to be interred with almost equal pomp." Without government regulations, "the poor and the proletariat will again be thrown into the gutter." To eliminate class jealousies stirred by "theatricals" in public cemeteries, Duval advocated forbidding tombs of stone, symbols of rank and "foolish ambition." Members of all religions would lie side by side in his "asylum of peace," diminishing the factionalism that was detrimental to national unity. He would permit only graves of earth and grass in small, private cemeteries on stretches of lawn where families could install plantings and erect small stones over their dead. Duval approved of epitaphs, especially those expressing domestic sentiments, though he advocated listing the faults as well as the virtues of the deceased so as to teach youth to "profit from [their] errors." He frowned on any display of titles and accomplishments.[38]

Duval wanted his grave, like Rousseau's first, to lie under poplars by a stream, an idyllic spot near his hometown, planted with lilacs and violets. "There several times each year, I will conduct my friends. . . . I will tell them, soon one of us will be cold and insensible under this earth. Since we can remain together for so little time, let's put hatred and enmity away. Only death can separate us. . . . And we will renew this vow always to remain united." Duval considered such sentiments the basis of social stability. In the republican cemetery, each body would rest in its own grave with a modest marker for a prescribed time—about three years, with quicklime added to ensure decomposition—before removal of the bones to an ossuary. Duval felt that "if the world was populated with loving and sensible souls, there would be no need to order respect for the dead."[39] Again, sensibilities had to be cultivated, not legislated. Duval recommended two sorts of burial places, preferring private property, after Roman custom, as more personal and better able to foster sentiment and strengthen individual ties to family and the state. For those without rural land, he proposed public cemeteries in infertile fields at opposite ends of the city. The poor would develop closer ties to the nation, as these cemeteries would be "almost property for those who have none." Duval countered charges that putting cemeteries near cities wasted good land: "A graveyard planted with trees and covered with grass will not be lost to the living." Useful plants would provide produce, making the space self-supporting. The social role of citizens would not end at death, since bodies buried would "fertilize the soil so that trees and vegetables to nourish their posterity will use their substance." Small size and lack of concentration of burials would keep the air pure and free of "pestilential miasmas." Following the fashion of English gardens, Duval proposed surrounding his "field of death" with "ha-has" (linear trenches) and "a hedge of sad evergreens."[40]

Abbé Mulot agreed that burials should be left to private initiative for those with land outside the city. For yeoman farmers, such sepulchers would become personal sanctuaries: "How happy is he who, in the garden he saw his father plant, can deposit the precious remains of that dear parent, who can go to the simple mound that covers him to render respectful and flattering homage of the heart that makes him live again, to recall the lessons of childhood and to receive new ones." For those without land, the government would create "places of rest" with "simple but noble" family tombs even for the laboring classes, "where all have the right to be received without distinctions." There would be no "terrible" mass graves "where a friend will seek his friend in vain! Where the thankful nation will not be able to distinguish the remains of its benefactor when the law finally permits it to render him honors and to pay him the tribute of its gratitude!" Mulot had no wish to return to the days when birth or royal benevolence allowed a few to raise themselves to superior rank with magnificent tombs, "marble imposters"; he nevertheless hoped that modest monuments would encourage art patronage.[41] Whereas Duval proposed a lawn cemetery with optional plantings, Mulot described a wooded terrain, where carpets of ferns covered graves. The picturesque landscape would elicit melancholy. Dark cypresses, lilacs, and roses would be "living emblems," making the "place of sadness" naturally consoling. The grounds would be planted with indigenous trees to thrive in the soil nourished by human remains, hastening sanitary decomposition and enhancing a melancholy mood. Although this natural environment would remain unpolluted, Mulot stipulated that it be located at least half a kilometer from the city.[42]

Other essayists presented variations on Duval's and Mulot's proposals. François-René-Jean de Pommereul, prefect of Indre-et-Loire, envisioned several "fields of rest" of two hectares each, set at least a kilometer from the city on elevated terrain to clear the air of pollutants and hasten decomposition. Those with means could purchase family burial space and construct tombs, decorating them according to their means and taste and enclosing the property with a fence or grille. There, only individuals bearing the family surname could be buried. Families would be responsible for upkeep. If no heir survived, the plot would revert to the Commune; but existing graves would remain inviolate in perpetuity. The poor would be buried at public expense, in mass graves holding at most a hundred bodies each in the "silent shade of the woods." As under the old system, burial would be for a limited time, although he set no time limit for their removal. The central square in Pommereul's plan would be a place of national apotheosis, the "field of honor," where those distinguished for virtue as designated by the state would be buried at public expense. At the center would be a marble statue of the Genius of Life extinguishing the flame of his torch. Horticulturists from the botanical gardens, the Jardin des Plantes, would maintain the plantings, mainly dwarf cypress.[43] (Figs. 3.26, 3.27.)

With one exception, all the National Institute essayists suggested garden settings. Everyone seemed to agree with Athanase-Charles Détournelle that future cemeteries should correct both the social inequalities of the ancien régime and the excesses of the Revolutionary leveling of status. Détournelle proposed siting

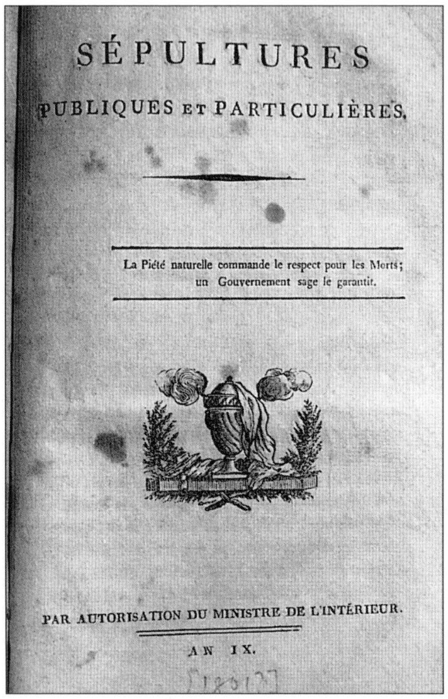

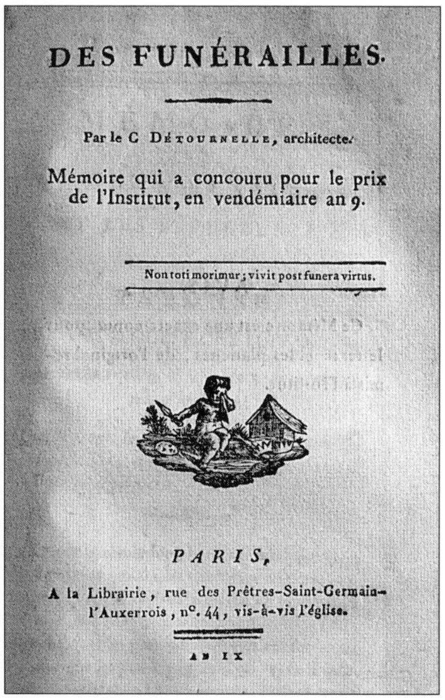

Figs. 3.26, 3.27. Covers to two published essays on funerary reform submitted to the (French) National Institute, 1801.

twelve cemeteries around the periphery of Paris. Though an architect, he frowned on mausoleums, declaring, "Only the state of nature should surround the simple, rustic places destined to become the asylum of tombs." He added, "The most solitary and most silent place charms sorrow and is most fitting for sad reflection."[44] He and Abbé Jacques-Michel Coupé both speculated that future cemeteries would become useful—socially, psychologically, and practically. In Détournelle's plan, fruit trees would assure productivity of the land. Crops of grain and hay would cover earthen pyramids over the graves. Coupé proposed six Parisian cemeteries; these would be models of decency and grandeur, as well as places to produce fruit and wine. He envisioned that other French and foreign cities would emulate the plan.[45]

Jean-Baptiste Leclerc, representative from Maine-et-Loire, presented a similar argument to the Council of Five Hundred on 9 Fructidor, Year V (25 August 1797), advocating civil institutions such as marriage, public education, national holidays, and funeral practices as means to ensure stability and social order, writing, "Respect for elders, memory of relatives and friends, veneration commended by the memory of those who were notable by actions dear to the fatherland are too useful sentiments for public morale, for religious principles, to be abandoned exclusively at random by the legislator." Through "cults" celebrating these virtues, the French could establish "a chain of sociability in which factions join in the hands of the government and keep the unity on which reposes the survival and internal peace of the State." Nevertheless, Leclerc warned, "break that unity, show the citizens that they have only transitory, earthly ties with one another, continually put before their eyes the image of eternal separation, and you considerably contribute to the natural tendency of sects to segregate themselves one from the other. . . . Instead of one big family, you will have numerous jealousies." Summarizing the essays received by the National Institute, Leclerc counseled his fellow legislators to foster new burial practices that would promote political and social stability. In his "Report on Institutions Related to the Civil State of Citizens," delivered 16 Brumaire, Year VI (7 December 1798), he proposed to the legislative body that public cemetery plots be allotted to families for that reason.[46]

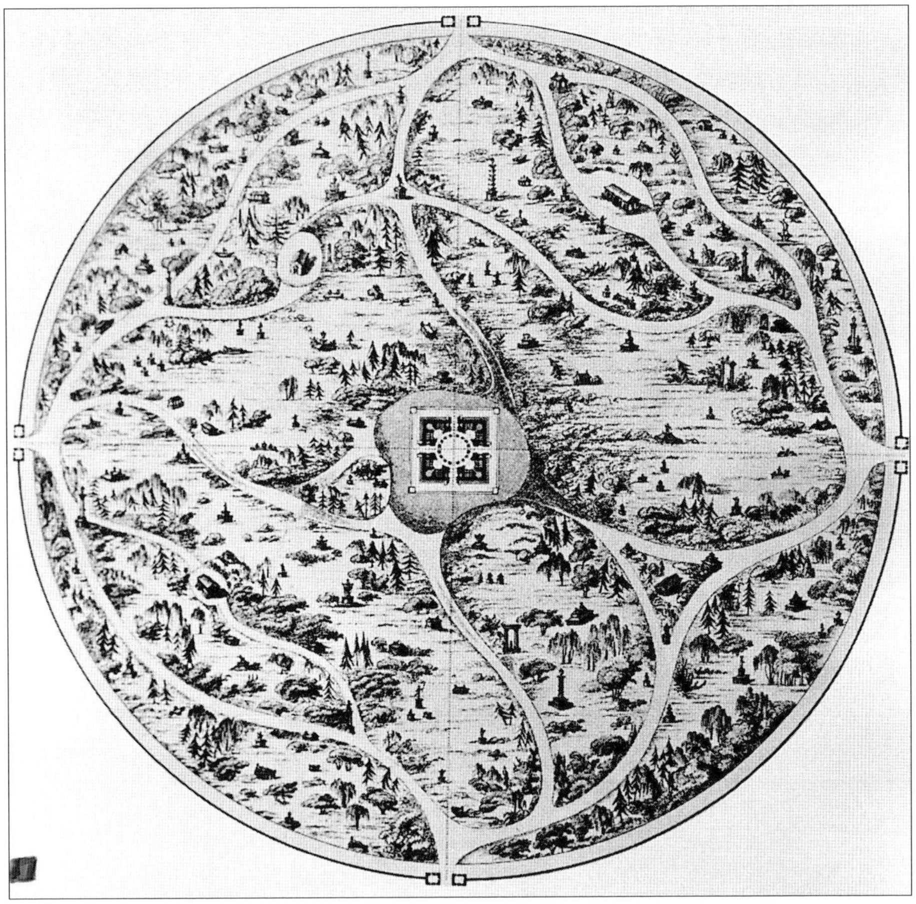

Fig. 3.28. *Champs de repos* ("Field of Rest"), design for a picturesque, circular cemetery by Jacques Molinos, 1799, a funerary-reform proposal for converting the varied topography of the Montmartre quarries in Paris. At the center would have been a monumental pyramidal chapel containing a crematorium, introducing that practice in modern Europe. BMGL.

In 1799, administrator Jacques Cambry urged the department of the Seine to build a circular, pastoral funerary landscape designed by Jacques Molinos, architect and inspector of civil buildings. Cambry proposed a site in the Montmartre quarries north of the city. (Fig. 3.28.) The Molinos design permitted sinking private crypts on the site and construction of common catacomb-like ossuaries. The cemetery would include picturesque plantings and be crisscrossed by serpentine paths. A monumental pyramidal temple at the center, symbolic of the sacred mount or tomb, would contain a crematory and columbarium, or repository for urns. Molinos hoped that the rich would employ artists for their monuments, serving an added cultural function. Cambry's long essay on funerary reform accompanying the design echoed ideas from the National Institute contest.[47] Molinos and Cambry were not just public-spirited reformers but members of a company intent on developing and managing a thirty-year monopoly on a new municipal cemetery with crematory. The French, however, unlike the English and some Americans later, would not turn funerary reform over to entrepreneurs.

In 1800, Antoine-Chrysostome Quatremère de Quincy (1755–1849), archaeologist and theoretician of art and architecture and prominent member of the Académie, delivered an impassioned plea that any cemetery project would include restoration of monuments. He criticized the perversion of aesthetics by iconoclasm: "Sophisticated ignorants, stop finding pleasure in ruins! Yes, those made by time are respectable, those of barbarism are horrors. Ruins of time, monuments to human fragility, are a lesson to man, the other a shame." He advised, "Tombs without sculpture and graves without epitaphs say nothing." Without patriotic shrines, France would "present a terrible example to Europe." Establishing grand cemeteries for the capital would be one step in the government's efforts to revive commerce and the arts, to secure the confidence of the nation's household heads, and to win the respect of the rest of the world.[48] Other calls were heard for a cult of tombs. According to a former Revolutionary, professor of history Pierre Doliver, writing in 1801, a cult of ancestors would "resurrect public morale, almost extinguished in all hearts, or rather give it a new existence, better conceived and worthy." He asked: "What is more powerful than funeral religion? The honors rendered to mortal remains are a homage addressed to the party that survives, and the cult of tombs is a tie between the living and the dead. The development of a cult of the dead would be one of the most powerful ties to attach men to the Nation, the most effective way to instill duty, to praise great virtues and talents, and the last duty of the country to its citizens."[49]

The essayist Joseph de Girard summarized the desire of many to create a "religion of memory" based more on personal ties than on the creation of national heroes. Allowing family graves on private property would bind citizens "to the soil that gave them birth." Indeed, "he who cherishes his father's land is more attached to his country by that simple bond than the proud philosopher." Property and melancholy were "the elements of which true love of country is composed." The landscape would contain the usual elements of the Elysium or *jardin anglais*: hills, streams, and paths for melancholy promenades. Burial would take place under an oak's shade in one's own field or under symbolic aspens, cypresses, or weeping willows.[50]

Fortunately for the French, a wealth of the nation's past cultural glory had escaped the campaigns of spoilation to be preserved and displayed at the new Museum of French Antiquities and Monuments, a "veritable cemetery of the arts," incorporated under the auspices of the Louvre in 1796, the creation of painter and architect Alexandre Lenoir, who had begun in 1791 by supervising a warehouse of architectural ruins placed in the Château d'Anet, formerly a Petits-Augustins convent. Lenoir saved many tombs and ecclesiastic relics from the Church of Saint-Denis, traditional burial place of royalty, and elsewhere, reassembling fragments to make monuments to Turenne, Molière, Descartes, Boileau, La Fontaine, Abélard and Héloise, and others. Lenoir displayed them as cenotaphs, like *fabriques* or ornaments, clustered in the small garden or park he laid out around the museum as an Elysium. Some praised its creation of a "cult of heroes." The historian Jules Michelet found in its chronological arrangement of historic artifacts "the true order of the ages," drawing from recollections of youthful visits there a sensibility that would inform his career. This Revolutionary interpretation of history, however, attracted powerful foes, especially Quatremère de Quincy, and led to the museum's closing in 1817. But by then a better site had been created to display such monuments.[51] (Figs. 3.29, 3.30.)

Fig. 3.29. Lenoir's Elysium Gardens at the Museum of French Monuments, Paris. Engraving by Robert, ca. 1800. BMGL.

Fig. 3.30. Tomb of Abélard and Héloise (*right*) reconstructed by Lenoir and placed amid other funerary monuments in his Elysium gardens. Engraving by Robert, ca. 1800. BMGL.

Père Lachaise

On 21 Ventôse, Year IX (12 March 1801), the Paris prefect of police ordered establishment of three cemeteries, each one mile beyond city walls. That winter the legislature allocated funds for the purpose. On 7 Germinal (27 March 1801), the legislature set up procedural mechanisms by which communes might purchase land outside their legal boundaries for public cemeteries. The department of the Seine, headed by Prefect and Minister of General Police Nicholas-Thérèse-Benoist Frochot, created the office of health commissioner (Conseil d'Hygiène) in 1802 to oversee sanitary inspection of cemeteries. On 17 Floréal, Year XI (6 May 1803), Frochot won authorization to purchase land for cemeteries for the Commune of Paris.[52]

Frochot tried but failed to acquire Parc Monceau for one cemetery. He finally succeeded in purchasing an estate east of Paris on the slopes and ridge of a hill twenty-seven meters tall, an escarpment called the Butte

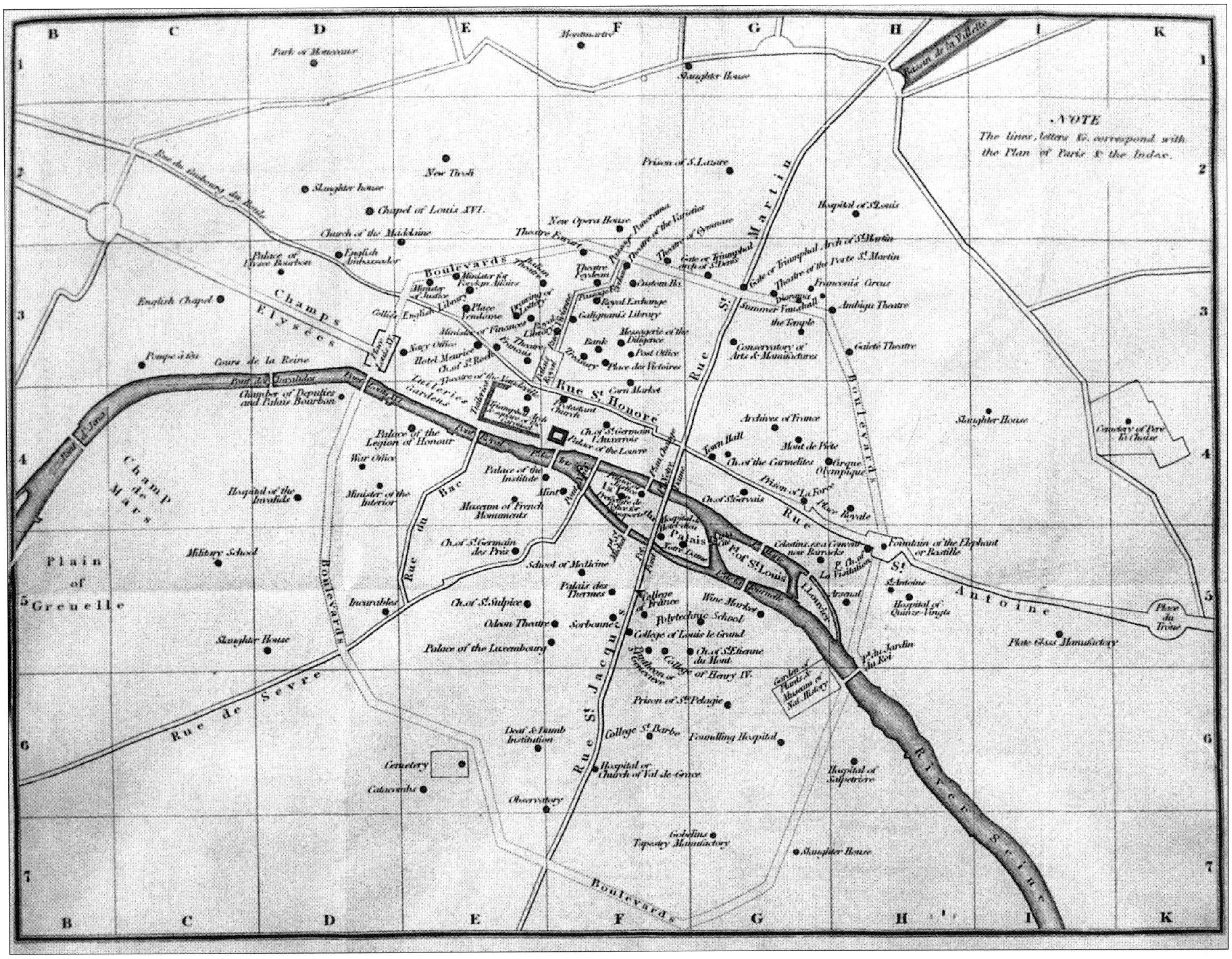

Fig. 3.31. "Guide to the Principal Objects of Curiosity in Paris," map showing the location of Père Lachaise on the periphery to the east, along with other urban institutions and asylums. From Planta, 1819.

Saint-Chaumont. (Fig. 3.31.) It had been a Jesuit country seat called La Folie-Regnault until Louis XIV let his confessor, Père François d'Aix de la Chaize, rename it Mont Louis. The property commanded views over Belleville, Montmartre, and Ménilmontant to the north, Bicêtre and Meudon on the southern horizon, and the fertile banks of the Marne in the east. Visitors admired the panorama of Paris to the southwest. No other site of such compact size presented more picturesque and varied views or had more irregular topography. Though near the burgeoning city, the site remained rural, still bordered by arable land, although its gardens had fallen into disrepair. The soil was ideal for burials, with a thick, sandy layer over a deep, chalky mass, perfectly constituted to aid decomposition of bodies without allowing escape of gaseous exhalations to pollute the city's air. Besides, the location assured that prevailing winds would carry any effluvia away from Paris. The old estate conformed to Napoleon's decree on 23 Prairial, Year XI (12 June 1803), that each municipality establish a nondenominational cemetery of at least thirty-five square meters on the most elevated site possible, preferably exposed to the north. Acquisition of the land permitted the closing of several old burial grounds, including the Clamart.[53]

Frochot appointed Brongniart, the neo-antique architect of the department of the Seine, to create the new cemetery. Brongniart had designed French estates in the

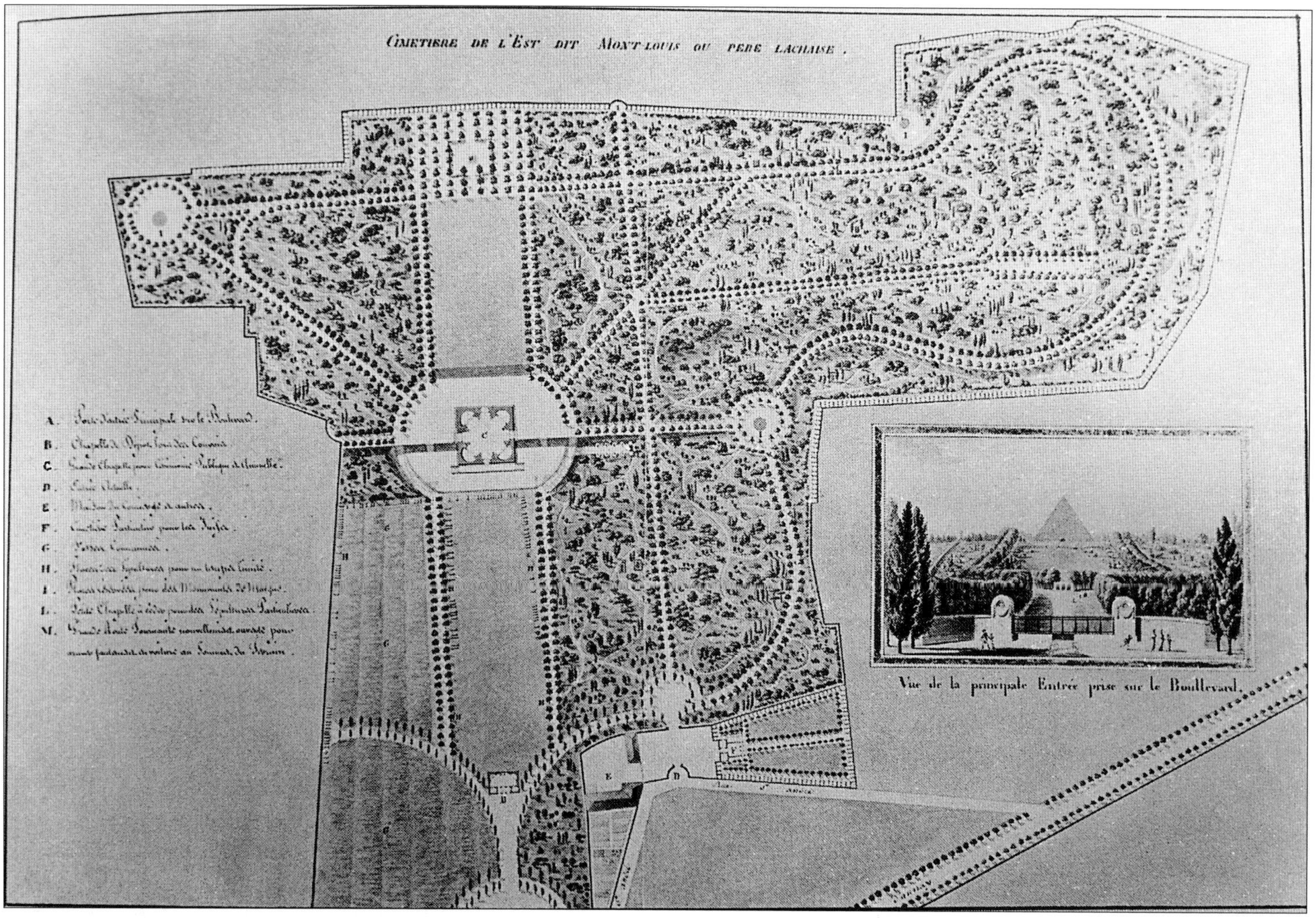

Fig. 3.32. Map of Père Lachaise with inset engraving of the design of the pyramidal chapel proposed by Brongniart, ca. 1812, but never built. BMGL.

style of *jardins anglais*; but he modeled his Cemetery of the East on the Ceramicus, just beyond the Dipylon gates at Athens, the place where the Greeks had buried their heroes. Brongniart's design emphasized landscape rather than heroic architecture. Frochot, who participated in the design, urged the architect to plan a funeral chapel as a focal point to elicit a spiritual yet secular melancholy. Literally and figuratively central was to be a pyramidal chapel two hundred feet high, to be visible from the city below. Had it been built, it would have recalled in modified scale the monumental funerary structures of Brongniart's teacher Boullée and the eye-catchers or *fabriques* of English gardens. Napoleon heartily approved of the Egyptian-style chapel, but construction had to be postponed owing to the wars that raged throughout the decade. Brongniart's plans for the cemetery entrance were modest. At first, he wanted to build a gate composed of heaps of false ruins scattered as if by chance on half-destroyed pillars, but friends criticized the idea as too poetical. Perhaps the emperor's advisers also considered it negatively prescient. So Brongniart drew a simpler, more austere plan—a grilled entry set into a high, pillared wall adorned with carved wreaths and low reliefs of flaming torches. It defined the semi-circular exterior space. The gate stood throughout the cemetery's first two decades. (Fig. 3.32.)

At Mont Louis, Brongniart laid out winding footpaths and both straight and sinuous carriage avenues leading separately through the irregular terrain. He preserved some of the old estate's gardens and the central entry axis, lined with old chestnut trees. Poplar-lined roads and acacia-shaded paths followed the curve of the hill to the summit, where another straight road defined by ancient chestnuts stretched behind the old mansion to the east. The combination of picturesque footpaths with a formal central axis and linear avenues had precedents in the English "forest" or "rural" garden as well as in the design for Paxton Manor depicted in Stephen Switzer's *Ichnographia Rustica*, an early treatise on the "modern" style in gardening. Brongniart's design for the Cemetery of the East similarly placed major monuments at nodal points between intersecting avenues. He augmented vestiges of the old garden, neglected for half a century, with fruit trees, plane trees, lindens, sycamores, cypresses, and weeping willows, although the site lacked the conventional symbolic streams or ponds of English gardens. The cemetery remained pastoral for at least a decade after it was consecrated on the first day of spring, 1 Prairial, Year XII (20 May 1804).

Most of the burial sites consisted of five- and ten-year leaseholds on flat ground to the left of the central alley. A temporary marker of wood or stone was permitted on each single burial until the disinterment. Gone were the mass graves; but this area of "public graves" lacked the scenic seclusion of lots for the elite purchased in perpetuity on higher terrain. As Brongniart's plan slowly took shape, the enthusiasm of the monied classes was not quick in coming, although until 1824 innovative perpetual freehold concessions, costing 250 francs for two meters of land, were exclusive to Père Lachaise, as the place was dubbed in reference to the former Jesuit owner. Throughout the first decade, monuments remained widely scattered. Observers speculated that the slow acceptance of Père Lachaise by the elite for perpetual burials resulted from the post-Revolutionary disruption of social values. Whatever the reason, the common people loved the cemetery as a dramatic improvement over the old system. One French engineer lauded it in 1821 as evidence of a happy new era of simple, affectionate sentiments combined with the "desire for immortality," a positive reaction against the "horror of nothingness." Still, it took time before the bourgeoisie, many of whom could bury their dead on private estates, acquired the means and the taste to make Père Lachaise the most fashionable cemetery of the capital.[54]

In 1817, officials tried to hasten the acceptance of Père Lachaise among the new bourgeoisie by moving from the Museum of French Monuments the so-called tomb of Abélard and Héloise, constructed of twelfth-century Gothic fragments by Lenoir. (Fig. 3.33.) Under other cenotaphs fashioned in ancient style, they claimed to reinter the remains of La Fontaine and Molière, although the writers' bodies had long since been lost in the common pits. Soon, new notables joined the old to increase the prestige of the place. Chopin and Géricault lay near Napoleon's heroic marshalls. The deaths of other popular figures—the poet Delille, Marshall Ney, General Foy—fostered a sense of patriotic melancholy. Their elaborate funerals set the fashion for national obsequies attended by thousands. These events served a dual purpose, helping to create a "cult of heroes" while popularizing the new cemetery.[55] (Figs. 3.34, 3.35, 3.36.)

Fig. 3.33. Monument of Abélard and Héloise moved to Père Lachaise from Alexander Lenoir's Museum of French Monuments, Paris. Engraving by Frederick Nash, 1822. BMGL.

The author of an 1820 guide to Père Lachaise, Marchant de Beaumont, felt that this sort of publicity alone would not suffice to make the new, secularized burial landscape acceptable to Catholics without a general change in sensibilities. The cemetery was slow to find favor because "public opinion, which submits everything to its laws, has not yet attributed a number of essential virtues to families: respect for the ashes and memories of their kin." The shift in mentality, he said, had responded first to the larger political and economic fortunes of the nation. During the empire's heyday, "people drunk with glory and victory-proud ignored sad subjects, anything that would remind them of the fragility of happiness." As Marchant de Beaumont remarked, "The dead are soon forgotten during days of prosperity."[56]

Only seventy-two permanent monuments were erected in the cemetery's first four years; but as the Napoleonic wars progressed and France suffered defeat, death became again a vivid reality. As an index of the shift in attitudes toward commemoration, the speed

Fig. 3.34. Tomb of the nature poet Abbé Jacques Delille (1738–1813). Engraving by Jolimont, 1821.

Fig. 3.35. Monument to Général Maximilien-Sébastien Foy, whose funeral in 1825 drew more than 100,000 people. Engraving by Augustus Pugin, 1829. BMGL.

Fig. 3.36. Grand tombs and monuments to Massena, Lefèvre, and other military heroes. Engraving by Pugin, 1828. BMGL.

with which private monuments were added escalated annually from 51 in 1808 to 113 in 1812, 242 in 1813, 509 in 1814, and 635 in 1815, the year of Waterloo. The government encouraged the installation of memorials by providing the services of a marble sculptor on the premises. The concierge sold wrought-iron fences "for the protection" of monuments and plants for private plots. By the 1820s, a funerary industry had grown up in the neighborhood with twenty marble cutters, an ironworker for decorative fences, florists, and architects, all catering to proprietors of perpetual freeholds. Drawings of grand monuments and mausoleums by Brongniart and other architects promoted building on the ambitious scale that came to characterize Père Lachaise. (Figs. 3.37, 3.38, 3.39, 3.40, 3.41.)

Fig. 3.37. Pyramidal tomb of Craufurt. Engraving by Jolimont, 1821.

Fig. 3.38. Colonnaded temple over the sarcophagus, topped by a crown of the comtesse Demidoff. Engraving by Jolimont, 1821.

For that reason, the cemetery's appearance changed dramatically, and for the worse. Delille once admitted, "We enclose where it is not necessary, we crowd our buildings upon one another, and fritter away every thing into small parts." After only fifteen years, an Englishman observed, "many of the best and costliest monuments are fallen to pieces, having like so many other things in that country been made for display and not for duration." So many vandals and thieves preyed on the stones that large guard dogs now patrolled to prevent the removal of bronze and gilt copper decoration. By 1830, with over 31,000 monuments in place, the original look of the picturesque had been obliterated. Prosperous Parisians rejected the simplicity of earthen graves for elaborate structures occupying entire family plots. The layout of lots allowed no margins to be preserved as green borders or open space. Mausoleums fronted directly on avenues and paths, nearly touching like buildings on city streets. The aesthetics of the English garden had been merely a passing fancy, superseded by the taste for grandiose funerary architecture.[57]

Other circumstances prevented the realization of several features of Brongniart's design. Both the cemetery's architect and its administrator, Brongniart and Frochot, died in 1813. Brongniart was buried in his relatively mod-

Fig. 3.39. Monument to Jean-Louis Lefèvre, 1812, showing other monuments widely scattered in the landscape. Engraving by Arnaud, 1817.

est family lot near the tomb he designed for his friend the poet Delille, the "French Virgil," who had preceded him with a grand public funeral by only a month. (Fig. 3.42.) By the end of the war, with Napoleon in exile, the plan for a central pyramid was abandoned. The old estate house was demolished in 1822, making way for a simple, classical Doric granite chapel designed by Étienne-Hippolyte Godde (1781–1869). It was completed in 1824. (Fig. 3.43.) The following year, Godde built a new cemetery gate, overturning Brongniart's plan.

By 1814, the vogue for Père Lachaise as public space had caught on as it began to function as a park. Guidebooks spread its popularity among non-Parisians, many of whom went home with the idea of creating such a

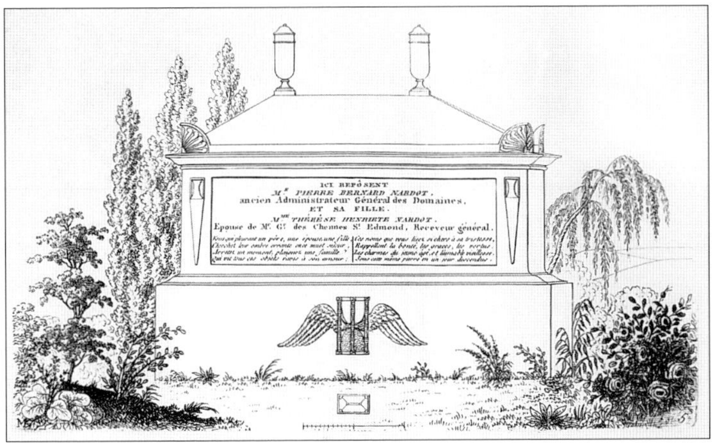

Fig. 3.40. Sarcophagus of Pierre Bernard Nardot and his daughter. Engraving by Arnaud, 1817.

Fig. 3.42. Brongniart family lot at Père Lachaise with monument to the architect (*right front*) with the low-relief of the Paris Bourse (treasury or stock exchange) he designed in 1826. Photograph by BMGL, 1990.

Fig. 3.41. Sarcophagus "to the immortal memory" of Damme Marie Anne de Cetto, topped by an urn and still surrounded by dense trees including a weeping willow, 1811. Engraving by Arnaud, 1817.

Fig. 3.43. Design for the Doric Chapel at Père Lachaise by Etienne-Hippolyte Goddé. Engraving by Jolimont, 1821.

Fig. 3.44. Panorama of Paris from the General Foy monument in Père Lachaise. Engraving, Rouargue Frères, ca. 1825. BMGL.

place for their cities. The British architect Augustus Charles Pugin (1762–1832) exclaimed in 1829: "Burial grounds *à la pittoresque*, laid out for a promenade. . . . This invention is indeed original in the people of Paris." (Fig. 3.44.) Not anticipating that similar cemeteries would be founded near the British capital in the 1830s, he declared that "it would hardly happen in London that we should have a Guide to the burying-grounds, as a fashionable promenade; that parties would be made to visit them . . . that taverns and drinking-houses should be established close beside them for the accommodation not only of these parties of pleasure but for mourners also!" Ignoring the British origins of the design, Pugin asked, "What Englishman will undertake either to condemn or entirely approve it, unless he could enter completely into the minds of the French themselves?"[58]

Indeed, no other city had managed burial reform and the spatial handling of death in such an aesthetically innovative way. Marchant de Beaumont, the most poetic of the cemetery's publicists, told visitors that they could find settings "shaded by the leaves of eternally green trees," tombs "surrounded with flowers and decorated with wreaths that seem to make reign in this abode a continual spring." There, "the charms of nature enjoy the power to banish grief, sadness, and melancholy from the soul, where one breathes pure air, where under a magnificent sky the soul soars to its most sublime thoughts, where one feels at home in an Elysium conversing freely with the new residents of the celestial regions." The novelist Honoré de Balzac, who loved to walk there, used it as the setting for a dramatic moment in *Le Père Goriot* (1835).[59]

Such a place had international appeal at a time of budding romanticism. A dozen Americans had been buried in Père Lachaise by 1830, and articles in American periodicals further spread the fame of the place. In 1826, *Atlantic Souvenir*, published in Philadelphia, lauded the French cemetery's "appearance of a wide and variegated garden . . . where trees and shrubs conceal and disclose wild romantic beauty, tombs and temples." The French had institutionalized the cult of the melancholy, and Americans admired this first attempt at creating a public place objectifying new interpretations of history as well as the sentimental pastoralism of romantic literature while solving practical urban problems.[60]

The French had made a major advance in landscape design by adapting a style formerly associated with estate gardens for use in a public funerary institution meant as a refuge for the living as much as for the dead. Marchant de Beaumont recognized the importance of the arrangement of space, which conducted the visitor through a programmed landscape intended to teach lessons of history and moral philosophy and to rouse emotions, expanding on principles proposed by English design theoreticians and aesthetic philosophers. Space became dynamic, "now rising into an amphitheater at the crest of the plateau, now hidden by the undulations of the irregular terrain." The landscape was an active agent leading the visitor on a passive promenade. Ser-

Fig. 3.45. Panorama of Paris from Père Lachaise with the dome of the Pantheon, by then made the place of honored entombment of notables like Voltaire and Rousseau. Engraving by Pugin, 1829. BMGL.

pentine walks, rocky and smooth roads and paths, the rising and falling topography directed one through the grounds as a "variety of sights and vistas incessantly struck the eye to keep the heart from saddening." New "pleasures of melancholy" supplanted the old fear of death.[61] Père Lachaise explicitly contrasted the realm of the living and the dead, the city and the "rural" cemetery, the present and the past, especially in the panoramic view over Paris from its highest central point. (Fig. 3.45.)

Just as the Gothic cathedral functioned as an encyclopedia for medieval man, preaching spiritual lessons through its visual elements, Père Lachaise offered a complex compendium of secularized messages for a new era. Like the cathedral, it invited emulation. In such a cemetery, wrote Marchant de Beaumont, "all the lessons of contemporary history are inscribed for all ages, for all classes," and "each tomb would without doubt offer some special lessons." It created a "usable" past for a republic without immediate precedent and presented new heroes to its citizens. The dead "were not all virtuous, without doubt." Yet at Père Lachaise, "all become useful," providing "great examples that did not exist in previous cemeteries nor in church crypts." Marchant de Beaumont concluded, "The reunion of the majority of memories of a vast city within the same wall is in this manner the most powerful stimulant to live well in that city."[62]

Parisians were justly proud. As Père Lachaise attracted international acclaim, it came to provide the model for multifunctional funerary landscapes in the cities of another republic also attempting to create a sense of history and social order in the wake of its own revolution. Bostonians referred to Père Lachaise as an inspiration and point of comparison for the creation of Mount Auburn Cemetery in 1831. Although, as the landscapes of Père Lachaise and Mount Auburn developed, they reflected differences between French and American material culture, they were both conceived as responses to similar problems and designed in emulation of English gardens.

4

AN AMERICAN SENSIBILITY TO MELANCHOLY

So live, that when thy summons comes to join
The innumerable caravan, which moves
To that mysterious realm, where each shall take
His chamber in the silent halls of death,
Thou go not like the quarry-slave at night,
Scourged to his dungeon, but, sustained and soothed,
By an unfaltering trust, approach thy grave,
Like one who wraps the drapery of his couch
About him, and lies down to pleasant dreams.

—William Cullen Bryant, "Thanatopsis" (1817)

As Puritanism declined in both Old and New England, melancholy gradually became perceived as the ideal emotional response to death, replacing Calvinistic fears of man's postmortem fate. Liberalizing ministers prescribed it to their congregations and readers. In 1714, the Reverend Increase Mather (1639–1723) preached that contemplating the flight of the saved soul to heaven "should make the Believer long for death." The Reverend Leonard Hoar (1629–1675) declared it "an error in the saints [i.e., the Puritans] and people of God to be so much affrighted at death and to goe so mournfully out of this world." Excessive fear might be a sign of perdition, but cessation of doubt was no longer seen as false assurance. Intense introspection on mortality served as a new sort of spiritual exercise, recommended by the poet John Milton (1608–1674), heeded on both sides of the Atlantic. According to the historian David Stannard, writing about the Puritans, "a tumultuous and exalted depression became their psychological ideal, the symbol and expression of their ultimate Salvation. This symbol suffered the fate so common to religious symbols, of being sought for and treasured as an end in itself . . . without regard for the . . . original inner meaning that it had possessed."[1]

Hence, a predisposition to melancholy was common among the descendants of the Puritans even before it emerged among other Americans of the colonial period, especially Anglicans. It served as a major theme during the flowering of New England's material and literary culture in the early nineteenth century, though, as with other imported cultural trends, not until decades after it flourished in England. As they became more fully aware of the power of a naturalistic environment to epitomize larger ideals, New Englanders began to envision landscapes to serve as catalysts for melancholy or to commemorate a common past. Early evidence of a new consciousness linking Death and Nature and emphasizing the individual contemplation of those ideas appeared during the Revolutionary era, when Americans first adopted the taste for melancholy and celebration of the simplicity of Nature from the English Graveyard poets. The rebellion against British imperialism did not impede Americans' exposure to and acceptance of new Whiggish cultural trends, which ran counter to Tory culture. Robert Blair's poem "The Grave" (1743) and Thomas Gray's "Elegy Written in a Country Churchyard" (1751) first appeared in popular editions from American publishers in the early 1770s and were reprinted repeatedly thereafter.

On both sides of the Atlantic, the English style of landscape gardening was also considered a countercultural response to Tory power. It asserted notions of individualism, natural rights, and memory of personal merit, great or humble, over elitist dictates and traditional practices. The political significance of the aesthetics of melancholy helped spread the seeds of romanticism among Americans. Early-nineteenth-century American leaders recognized the partiality of their Parliamentary allies for romantic gardens and monuments as "a sort of party issue," symbolizing new political principles and an enlightened worldview.[2]

English garden design influenced Thomas Jefferson's 1771 plans for a romantic landscape at Monticello. He wanted to organize his garden around a burial site and monuments in "some unfrequented vale in the park, where is 'no sound to break the stillness but a brook, that bubbling winds among the weeds; no mark of any human shape that had been there, unless the skeleton of some poor wretch, who sought the place out to despair and die in.'" Jefferson decided, "Let it be among the ancient and venerable oaks, intersperse some gloomy evergreens" with "a small Gothic temple of antique appearance" illuminated at night by a dim lamp, a mausoleum to contain urns and inscriptions, and a pyramid of "rough rockstone" over the grave of "a favourite and faithful servant." He wished to represent the symbolic contrasts between life and death, present and past, by contrasts between secluded lawn, sheltering woods, and open vistas and panoramas. Jefferson pondered whether "a view of the neighboring town would have a good effect." In 1773, he buried his best friend, Dabney Carr, under a large elm where they had often read together. The gravestone was inscribed with lines from the *Iliad* paraphrased by Alexander Pope:

If in the melancholy shades below,
The flames of friends and lovers cease to glow,
Yet mine shall sacred last; mine undecayed
Burn on through death and animate my shade.

In 1808, Jefferson planted a double line of weeping willows around the site of his own intended grave. Although most of Jefferson's intentions to lay out his property in the English fashion were never realized, his plans reveal the influence and resonance of British Whiggish sentimentality on post-Revolutionary America.[3] (Fig. 4.1.)

Contemporaneously, themes of melancholy appeared in the writings of Philip Freneau (1752–1832) and Charles Brockden Brown (1771–1810), writers described by the historian Henry F. May as "the leading radical intellectuals" of the Revolutionary and Federal eras.[4] Freneau introduced the new nation to the imagery of sacred groves, the possibility of reattaining Eden through Nature, and the sublime significance of ruins. Yet, as in the case of Jefferson's dreams for Monticello, the time was not entirely ripe for a wholehearted American espousal of such aesthetics. Freneau's generation nevertheless began to reject old images of death as represented in dismal traditional graveyards. In "The House of Night" (1786), Freneau recounts a deathbed scene, ending on a note of optimism with the light of dawn, a questioning of old pessimism, and a new resolve:

What is this Death, ye deep read sophists, say?—
Death is no more than one unceasing change;

Fig. 4.1. Jefferson's burial ground at Monticello. Postcard, ca. 1900. BMGL.

New forms arise, while other forms decay,
Yet all of Life through creation's range. . . .
When Nature bids thee from this world retire,
With joy thy lodging leave, a fated guest;
In Paradise, the land of thy desire,
Existing always, always to be blest.[5]

Fred Lewis Pattee calls the poem "the first distinctly romantic note heard in America." Although literary celebration of melancholy à la Freneau was rare during the Federal period, it presaged new notions about death and history that would gain currency in the next decades.[6]

Fig. 4.2. Cherubs on markers (1777, 1799) on Longfellow family graves in the Old Eastern Cemetery, Portland, Maine. Postcard, 1908. BMGL.

Popular Iconography

In the late eighteenth century, manifestations of naturalism and sentimentalism appeared in the form of the willow-tree-and-urn motif commonly used on gravestones and in mourning pictures, an iconography borrowed from the memorials in pastoral English gardens. Images of willows and urns, a combination of modern origin compatible with neoclassical taste, began to replace cherubs on gravestones, just as cherubs had replaced death's-heads. White marble markers began to win favor over the Puritans' comber gray slate, and the words "In memory of" replaced the blunt "Here lies the body" or "Memento mori." The willow-and-urn motif symbolized secular, commemorative burial in a natural setting, an ideal as rare in fact in colonial America as in England.[7] (Figs. 4.2, 4.3, 4.4, 4.5.)

The weeping willow (*Salix babylonica*) gained popularity after its introduction in the West from its native China in the 1730s. Alexander Pope planted one in his elegiac gardens at Twickenham. Masons carried willow and acacia branches at funerals. Folklore held that the willow dispelled evil, purified, and facilitated contact with the spiritual realm. Its pensive drooping branches

Fig. 4.3. Two cherub markers flank the willow-tree-and-urn motif on slate gravestones of the Stone family in the first Concord burial ground. Photograph by BMGL, 1978.

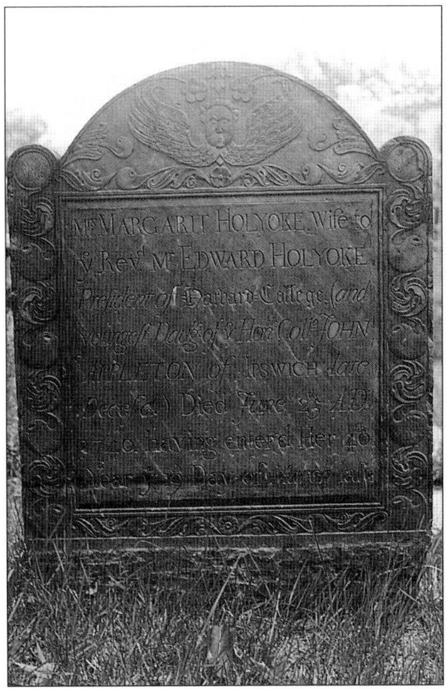

Fig. 4.4. Cherub on the slate marker of Margarit Holyoke, 1740, in the first Cambridge burial ground. Photograph by BMGL, 1978.

Fig. 4.5. Willow-tree-and-urn motif on slate marker of Captain Joseph Lindsay, 1826, Marblehead, Massachusetts, hillside burial ground. Photograph by BMGL, 1979.

predisposed it for symbolic usage. The *New England Farmer* reported in 1827 that, in addition, "it weeps little drops of water . . . like fallen tears upon the leaves."[8] As one of the first trees to turn green in spring and the last to shed its leaves even in the cold New England climate, it represented the persistence of life. Its ease of regeneration from cuttings further intimated immortality.

Although Lombardy poplars had been chosen for New Haven's New Burying Ground in 1797, that tree never gained widespread use in New England owing to its lack of longevity and its linear formality. In rare depictions in mourning pictures, poplars are seen in the distance or clustered to the side. In 1828, the *New England Farmer* reprinted a comparative assessment of the poplar and the willow: "That prim, stiff, unmeaning, shadowless, dirty, exotic, the Lombardy poplar, ranks and files of which have invaded our shores, and driven back the natives of our own woods, is now, we hope, proscribed by universal consent, and will be exterminated as soon as possible. Among the kinds in our view most worthy of propagation, as well as from ease of culture, as on account of its intrinsic beauty and density of shade, is the weeping willow."[9]

English aesthetic theorists such as the Reverend Archibald Alison popularized the weeping willow because they found its emotional associations both melancholy and conducive to the creation of a "picturesque" landscape. It made a fine contrast with the oak in garden compositions as in mourning pictures. The oak bore older funerary associations from Germanic lands, where folklore emphasized its powers of protection against evil. It represented temporal human strength and the male family head. Depicted with trunk and branches severed, as on many nineteenth-century funerary monuments, especially Germanic, it symbolized the end of a family line. Many considered both the willow and the oak suited for funerary planting for functional reasons as well. William Prince II, head of the Linnaean Botanical Gardens and Nurseries in Flushing, New York, noted in 1828 that the willow's root system served to dry the soil in graveyards and that the oak also had widely spreading roots.[10]

Through the early nineteenth century, the urn-and-willow iconography recurred in popular mourning pictures, stylized painted and embroidered compositions regularly produced by genteel schoolgirls and young ladies for display in family parlors or lithographed for those who did not have daughters with leisure time and the training or talent to make them. The best were complex crewelwork pieces copied from illustrated pattern books, exercises learned at "female academies." Sarah Pierce taught such skills in her Litchfield Female Academy (1792–1833) in Connecticut. Around 1815, mourning picture work became popular at the Moravians' Linden Hall School of Girls (1746) in Lititz, Pennsylvania. These standardized compositions commonly included a weeping willow, a "venerable" oak, an urn or obelisk atop a monument, set within a melancholy rural funerary landscape peopled by mourners or simply a lone, grieving woman in Empire dress or later in "widow's weeds." Usually there were distant views of the landscape of the living left behind, seen across symbolically reflective streams or ponds. The popularity of these images indicated a new, secularized, nondenominational spirituality conditioned by liberal religion, the rise of affective individualism, and the "domestication of death."[11] (Figs. 4.6, 4.7.)

Mourning pictures appeared again and again, handmade or mass-produced, copied and reinterpreted in different media, in all parts of the nation—in German and Dutch Protestant households in Pennsylvania and New York, among French Huguenots, in Calvinist-Reformed homes in the Carolinas, and in Congregational, Presbyterian, and Unitarian homes in New England. The willow-tree-and-urn motif was prevalent for over half a century—on decorative panels over mirrors, on furniture in silhouette or low relief, and in miniature on lockets, rings, and other jewelry. Some uses even served patriotic, public purposes. Mourning scenes on cotton or silk fabric, even on wallpaper, memorialized Washington, Franklin, Lafayette, Commodore Perry, and other national heroes. Snuffboxes, bellows, andirons, fans, and, appropriately, handkerchiefs bore the conventional design. English Staffordshire and Liverpool dishware manufacturers turned out mourning pictures commemorating the deaths of patriots for the American market. An allusion to one such scene appears in the song "Sing All a Green Willow" from *Shakespeare's Dramatic Songs to All His Dramas*, a volume of music published in London in 1815 and imported in quantities by Americans. It can be found even in Jefferson's Monticello library.[12]

The landscape of mourning pictures was imaginary, stylized, symbolic, and picturesque, with no precedent

Fig. 4.6. Mourning picture inscribed "To the Memory of Susan K. White . . . 1833," with other names added in 1843 and 1848. Engraving and watercolor. BMGL.

Fig. 4.7. Mourning pictures inscribed "Sacred to the Memory of Sarah, wife of James Merry . . . 1836." Engraving and watercolor. BMGL.

in actual American burial places. The pictures popularized the imagery of the paintings titled *Et in Arcadia Ego* by Nicholas Poussin (1630 and 1640) and Sir Joshua Reynolds (1769), but instead of shepherds pondering a sarcophagus there was a sole female or group of mourners sadly musing over a funerary urn in a romantic setting. These images introduced Americans of all classes, who were for the most part not conversant with theories of landscape design, to the melancholy and commemorative elements of the picturesque English garden.

The focal point and constant in these pictures was the neoclassical monument—whether an urn, squat obelisk, or pyramid raised on a base or sarcophagus—rather than the traditional flat colonial stele. When slab gravestones did appear in mourning pictures, they were secondary to the scene, as if relics of the past. The central monument bore the name of a dead family member or friend with dates of birth and death and often a bit of sentimental verse, further emphasizing the composition's literary roots. The urn was merely symbolic of death, without reference to a cremation, a process that would not become an issue for discussion until the 1870s. The urn had been used as a funerary vessel for centuries by European royalty and nobility to hold the heart, often in a different location from the body, such as in the place of birth, or for a second burial of bones removed from a temporary grave. In English gardens, it generally was evidence of neoclassical taste, a reference to ancient Greece and Rome. A stone, vase-like ornament on a pedestal, it was sometimes inscribed with a dedication.[13]

The mourning picture setting was usually pastoral, rolling terrain. A distant view of a town or at least of a church or country house could usually be seen off to one side. Often the burial place was also set to one side or isolated in the foreground by a body of water, establishing landscape variety or enhancing the vista as in English gardens, but also carrying the classical connotations of rivers and lakes as passages to the hereafter. Only occasionally did trees form the entire backdrop for the monument.

According to the historian Philippe Ariès, mourning pictures played the role of a portable tomb or memorial adaptable to American mobility.[14] Even though such artifacts of melancholy did not substitute for secure, permanent commemorative burial places, they certainly helped spread the demand for more attractive funerary landscapes. Although most graveyards remained settings quite unlike the romantic ideal, the desire for material commemoration was growing. The vogue for mourning pictures preceded by decades the fashion of placing elaborate family monuments in pastoral cemeteries, but it conditioned public opinion in favor of burial reforms that would eventually make the ideal real at Mount Auburn and other "rural" cemeteries.

New Haven's New Burying Ground

The desire to ensure the perpetuity of graves dates from the period immediately after the Revolution, when the impermanence of property became a concern. James Hillhouse (1754–1832), a prominent New Haven citizen and sponsor of many public improvements, cited this as his reason for creating, in 1796, the New Burying Ground just north of the town and Yale College. Yellow fever had ravaged the city in 1794 and 1795. But Hillhouse makes no reference to public health in the documents with which he launched his new institution. Although most New Englanders accepted the practice of burial in common rather than in private graveyards, Hillhouse conceived of his plan for permanent family lots after visiting a former family estate. Along with house and fields, he remarked, the family burying ground had fallen "with the rest into the hands of strangers, and the descendants had no control over the graves of their relatives and ancestors, which, though honorably protected in this instance, were liable, in other hands, to be neglected, injured, or entirely obliterated in the progress of time." In cases of graveyards on private estates like Jefferson's Monticello, legal arrangements might ensure the perpetuity of graves and the coherence of that portion of the property in which they rested, but such instances were rare. Strangely, Hillhouse did not cite the even greater impermanency of burials in New England's common graveyards and their threatened dissolution. He desired simply to create "a sacred and inviolable burial place" for his own and other New Haven families.[15]

By 1796, New Haven's old common graveyard was nearly full and would have to be either extended onto valuable land in the commercial city's center, which was already "over-built," or replaced by a new site. Hillhouse wanted to create a new burial place, "larger, better arranged for the accommodation of families, and by its retired situation, better calculated to impress the mind with a solemnity becoming the repository of the dead." The Yale divine Timothy Dwight thought that the old location, "in the current of daily intercourse," made the graveyard "too familiar to the eye to have any beneficial effect on the heart." Public visibility degraded it "into a mere common object." Even the orthodox Congregationalist Dwight wanted a new burial place to be "a solemn object to man, a source of useful instruction and desirable impressions" rather than a reminder of the grim, medieval fear of death.[16] Unlike old New England graveyards, such a site would include plantings and sufficient space for families to erect monuments.

Removal of the burial place from the city's center conformed to principles articulated by the British aesthetic theorist Archibald Alison, who wrote in 1790, "The seasons of care, of grief, or of business, have other occupations, and destroy, for the time at least, our sensibility to the beautiful or the sublime, in the same proportion that they produce a state of mind unfavorable to the indulgence of imagination."[17] Whether or not they were familiar with Alison's views, Hillhouse and Dwight sensed the incongruity of the old burial site with the escalating urban activity at the city's center. They wished to create a place conducive to melancholy, in a more natural setting, a place where their fellow citizens might plant weeping willows over neoclassical funerary monuments as in the landscapes of mourning pictures. Such a place had no precedent in America. Although the Dissenters' Bunhill Fields near London provided one modern example of an incorporated extramural burial ground with freehold family plots, even it did not reflect the combination of neoclassical and melancholy aesthetics that Hillhouse envisioned for the New Burying Ground.

Hillhouse also wanted to secularize his city's burials in the spirit of his age, which supported separation of Church and State. In contrast to those in most New England towns, New Haven's old graveyard was not a purely civic institution. The original settlers, diverging from Puritanism, and "following the custom of their native country, buried their dead in a Church-yard" directly next to the first meetinghouse on the central green or public square. Dwight later observed: "While the Romish apprehension concerning consecrated burial-places and . . . particular advantages supposed at the resurrection to attend those who are interred in them remained, this location of burial-grounds seems to have been not unnatural. But since, this apprehension has been perceived by common sense to be groundless and ridiculous, the impropriety of such a location forces itself upon the mind."[18]

Hillhouse persuaded thirty-one leading New Haven citizens to subscribe fourteen dollars each for the privilege of choosing one of the first 284 family lots, each measuring 18 by 21 feet, or 576 square feet, large enough for the burial of several generations. The Connecticut legislature granted an act of incorporation to the Proprietors of the New Burying Ground in October 1797, creating an institution independent of the city, the first corporation of its kind in the nation. The ten-acre graveyard contained private plots governed by rules and regulations written by a board elected by proprietors of the lots. It was not a municipal facility like previous burying grounds. The board possessed the power to sell plots, at cost and not for profit, unlike other corporations of the period, which were chartered as profit-making ventures even if they provided amenities such as bridges and turnpikes for public use. Proprietors of plots, with one vote each in the corporation, taxed themselves for maintenance and improvement of the entire burying ground. The corporate body as well as individual freeholds remained exempt from property taxes.

Josiah Meigs (1757–1822), professor of mathematics at Yale, surveyed and laid out the New Burying Ground. Workers rolled and leveled the already flat terrain to permit imposition of a highly rational and symmetrical geometric scheme, with roads eighteen and twenty-four feet wide forming a grid of parallelograms, each thirty-five feet by sixty-four feet. Hillhouse further rationalized the plan with a numbering system to permit keeping accurate records of burials and property holdings. Both the landscape and the institution were products of the same rational mind-set revealed in the drafting of the Constitution a decade before and in the laying out of the gridded land survey in the Northwest Territory after 1785. One visitor was struck by the orderly, segmented design of the "square plat, of large extent, divided by smooth walks into small squares . . . again divided by railings into still smaller squares, and these again into squares so minute as to be reasonably occupied by two families; for the square not being lost sight of for a moment, and the smallest square being too large for the generality of families, no choice is left but to divide this . . . into half squares."[19] (Figs. 4.8, 4.9.)

The New Burying Ground was symbolically and aesthetically urban. The plan reflected in miniature the order and regularity of New Haven itself, unusual among New England towns for its grid layout. Unlike earlier graveyards, it had a road system that permitted hearses and carriages to enter the premises to deliver coffins and bring mourners close to graves. Fences, mostly of wood, defined property lines as around house lots in towns.

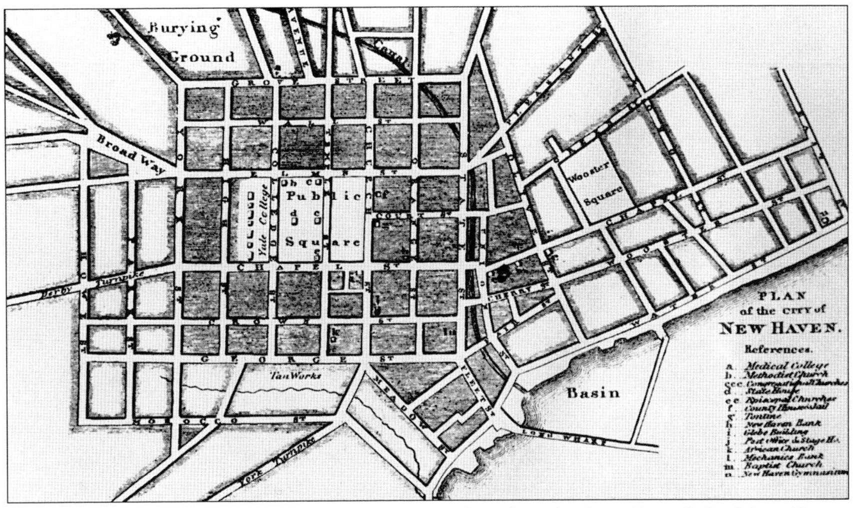

Fig. 4.8. New Haven, 1837 map of the town showing the location of the New Burying Ground. "Plan of the City of New Haven in 1838," from Edward R. Lambert, *History of the Colony of New Haven* (New Haven, 1838).

Fig. 4.9. New Haven's New Burying Ground on Grove Street, grid plan, engraving, 1839, showing sections reserved for Yale College, the Baptist and Methodist Societies, Strangers, People of Color, and the City. "Plan of the Burial Ground," from Aaron N. Skinner, *History of the City Burial Ground in New Haven* (New Haven: N. Green & J. S. Benham, 1863).

Horizontal railings painted white contrasted with black vertical posts. Hillhouse, whose street plantings had brought New Haven acclaim as the "City of Elms," planted fast-growing, columnar Lombardy poplars, expected "to grow with the least irregularity possible," in rows in the burying ground. The Lombardy poplar, which had recently been introduced to America and was much in vogue, was associated with the neoclassical and the formal, not with the naturalistic and the picturesque. These trees, as well as the regularity of tiny roads and fences, made the place quite different visually from the region's old, barren, and chaotic graveyards. Hillhouse, in the words of an observer, had undertaken "the building of a new and entire city, in the immediate rear of the old one. He builds his houses of stone, in a very solid and costly manner, and has marked out the area of a spacious square, in which are to be ornamental plantations."[20]

Dwight praised the plentiful space provided for family lots because it precluded the "use of vaults by taking away every inducement to build them." Dwight disapproved of vaults, "these melancholy and disgusting mansions [which] seem not to have been dictated by nature and certainly not approved by good sense. Their salubrity is questionable; and the impression left by them on the mind transcends the bounds of mourning and sorrow, and borders, at least, upon loathing." Following the English example, the association of earthen burial with lower-class status had made entombment in vaults popular with the American elite. Family tombs—whether subterranean chambers or shafts or aboveground rooms set in peripheral walls or mounded over with turf—proliferated in New England graveyards at the end of the eighteenth century, perhaps a sign of the desire to maintain family cohesion as communities became more complex, though more probably in response to the crowding of burials into areas not large enough to absorb the population. Or perhaps they were simply a mark of status. In any case, given the ever-diminishing space available for individual graves, if family members wanted to remain together after death, tomb building was often the only way to ensure it. (Fig. 4.10.) Dwight sanctioned the relatively new desire of families to be buried together as natural, and he approved of the way in which the New Burying Ground guaranteed it.[21]

Hillhouse considered the New Burying Ground a

Fig. 4.10. The John & James Dodd family tomb, 1821, in Boston's Copp's Hill Burying Ground. Photograph by BMGL, 1979.

semipublic institution. The trustees donated one lot to Yale College and set aside one for each of the local "Ecclesiastical Societies" (Methodist, Baptist, and others), one for burial of strangers, three for those who could not afford family lots or were not members of local congregations, and one for "people of color." In 1800, the corporation deeded a large triangle lot to the town for common use, a second for strangers, and another for blacks. A public-spiritedness thus tempered a sense of exclusivity, although a certain spatial distinction of status existed, unlike in the old graveyards.[22]

Perhaps the New Burying Ground was too innovative in concept. New Haven families, faced with the prospect of buying burial space, were slow to accept it. By 1800, fewer than half the lots had been sold, and the corporation was $16,000 in debt. Hillhouse covered expenses by purchasing 155 unsold lots. For fifteen years he personally retained control over the burying ground. Few landscape improvements were made, owing to the lack of funds. Not until 1814, when all the lots were finally sold, did the corporation add eight more acres. New Haven's citizens, meanwhile, continued to use the old graveyard on the central green. It was not officially closed until 1820, when it was finally judged to be "in a condition of total neglect and going to ruin in a manner deemed inconsistent with the religious and moral sense of this community and indicating a want of decent respect for the memory of the dead."[23]

By 1814, half of the fast-growing poplars Hillhouse planted had reached maturity and were dying and unsightly. Many were removed and not replaced. Only a few weeping willows planted by proprietors evidenced a nascent romanticism. There remained unfortunate similarities between the New Burying Ground and the region's old graveyards, especially after old markers were moved there in 1820 from the old burial place on the Common, causing crowding and increasing the number of thin, vertical head and foot stones. Many families continued to erect such markers, albeit now favoring white marble, occasionally imported from Italy. A new vogue, the simple obelisk, only punctuated the linearity and formality of the place. Monuments and markers were "universally" aligned on lots, further permitting the crowding of stones.

Although some innovations at the New Burying Ground—freehold in perpetuity of plots, a state charter for an eleemosynary corporation, and plantings in a designed landscape—offered precedents for the creating of Mount Auburn Cemetery in 1831, it was quite different aesthetically from the "rural" cemeteries of the decades to come. Still, Dwight rightly declared the New Burying Ground "altogether a singularity in the world." He took American and foreign visitors there, "not one of whom had ever seen or heard of any thing of similar nature." He was confident that the example of the place would "extensively diffuse a new sense of propriety in disposing of the remains of the deceased." The New Burying Ground, which predated the Parisian cemetery of Père Lachaise by seven years, actually created a "cult of ancestors" at a time when the French were still debating how they could do just that as a means of stabilizing society.

Founders of the New Burying Ground meant it to be a repository of history, a place for commemorating individual lives rather than a traditional reminder of the final fact of death. Dwight praised it, saying that "an exquisite taste for propriety is discovered in every thing belonging to it, exhibiting a regard for the dead, reverential but not ostentatious, and happily fitted to influence the views and feelings of succeeding generations." Hillhouse had hoped to perpetuate a sense of the past into the future, especially in terms of family. Until the 1820s, however, only a few of his fellow citizens were ready to follow his lead. Although Hillhouse's generation, that of the Founding Fathers, realized the importance of fostering a sense of their all-too-short national past as the foundation of a strong republic, they did little in material terms to achieve that goal. Only in the next generation did a taste for private as well as public commemoration really flourish. It was also in the 1820s that the debate over the poor condition of George Washington's tomb began in earnest, as a commemorative consciousness came to dominate the national culture. The deaths of the last of the Founding Fathers increased the popularity of mourning pictures and helped spread the cult of the melancholy in literature and art, as well as in monuments and landscapes. In the process, Americans domesticated the romanticism adopted from abroad and reinterpreted it to meet personal as well as national needs.

The Flowering of Melancholy Literature

One such work which cultivated an American romanticism was Washington Irving's *Sketch Book of Geoffrey Crayon, Gent.* (1819–20). Irving loved the picturesque and popularized the taste for it among Americans with accounts of his travels in the English countryside. He synthesized diverse sources of romanticism, from British aesthetic theorists and Sir Walter Scott to his friend Washington Allston, the Boston painter and poet. Irving found that "the fondness for rural life among the higher classes of the English . . . [had] a great salutary effect upon the national character." A "moral feeling" pervaded English scenery, "associated in the mind with ideas of order, of quiet, of sober, well-established principles, of hoary usage and reverend custom"—in sum, the sense of a long and stable past, which America seemed to lack. He intended to tap and reinterpret this heritage and convince his countrymen that they shared in it too.[24]

For Irving, English country churchyards, without the "haughty" memorials "which human pride has erected over its kindred dust," epitomized all that was good in English culture. There, he wrote, rural funerals still evidenced beautiful and simple ancient customs, the "remains of some of the rites of the primitive church," if not of some "still higher antiquity . . . observed among the Greeks and Romans" in "the olden time." Such folkways were like ruins, "vestiges and reminders of a former age" and a common British-American past, purer and more prototypically democratic than medieval or more recent deathways. They presented alternatives to the formalities of British High Church and aristocratic culture, rejected alike by Puritans and Revolutionaries, typified by the "mournful magnificence" of Westminster Abbey, and "teaching no moral but the futility of pride which hopes still to exact homage in its ashes and to live in an inscription." Irving declared Death the great democratizer, the ultimate revolutionary: "The equality of the grave . . . brings down the oppressor to the level of the oppressed." Westminster Abbey was a place of contradictions, "Death's great shadowy palace, where he sits in state, mocking at the relics of human glory and spreading dust and forgetfulness on the monuments of princes."[25] In contrast, Irving praised the "rich vein of melancholy" running through the English character,

Fig. 4.11. Saint Giles churchyard, Stoke Poges, inspiration for Thomas Gray's "Elegy." Postcard, ca. 1900. BMGL.

Fig. 4.12. Romantic English churchyard. Engraving from *Gleason's Pictorial Drawing-Room Companion*, ca. 1850s.

which gave it "some of its most touching and ennobling graces," traits epitomized in the simple traditions of picturesque burial grounds. (Figs. 4.11, 4.12.) A taste for nostalgia and "sweet-souled melancholy" permeates Irving's prose. Echoing John Evelyn's belief that plants, "natural hieroglyphics of our fugitive, umbratile, anxious, and transitory life," were an important presence in burial places, he urged Americans to use plantings in their burial grounds to transform them from places "of disgust and dismay" to attractive sites of "sorrow and meditation."[26] Calvinist ministers might still admonish their congregations to gaze into the grave and contemplate their fate, but Irving and his contemporaries generally recoiled from dwelling on the decay of death. Irving admitted, "There is a dismal process going on in the grave, ere dust can return to its kindred dust, which the imagination shrinks away from contemplating; and we seek still to think of the form we have loved with those refined associations which it awakened when blooming before us in youth and beauty." Irving rejected the "unlucky yew" and the "mournful cypress" along with all the old, grim iconography of death. He wondered why men sought "to cloathe death with unnecessary terrors and to spread horrors round the tomb of those we love." Agreeing with English and French romantics that "the natural effect of sorrow over the dead is to refine and elevate the mind," he counseled his readers to "go to the grave of buried love and meditate." Melancholy as a source of a purified, natural culture was to be encouraged in every way possible. The creation of naturalistic burial places would permit Americans to engage in the "pleasures of melancholy, uplifting sentiments to improve the national character." Nature would "soften the horrors of the tomb," in Irving's words, "beguile the mind from brooding over the disgraces of perishing mortality," and "associate the memory of the deceased with the most delicate and beautiful objects."[27] The desire he expressed for melancholy, "sweet-scented" burial landscapes would eventually result in the creation of Mount Auburn and other pastoral cemeteries.

Even more influential in bringing melancholy romanticism to New England was William Cullen Bryant (1794–1878), a poet whose youthful experience paralleled those of many New Englanders of his generation. The women of his family nurtured Bryant on the orthodoxy of John Calvin and the hymns of Isaac Watts, teaching him to think constantly of death. He watched his younger sister die at home, but his reaction was not that of a good Calvinist. He sought solace in the pleasant rural landscape of the Berkshire Mountains around him, indulging there in the "pleasures of melancholy" while reading poems of the English Graveyard School. Bryant's father, a religious liberal, encouraged his adolescent son's sentimentalism with poems such as Blair's "The Grave" and the works of Addison, Pope, Gray, Wordsworth, and Coleridge.[28]

The young Bryant took up the pen himself, setting the imagery of mourning pictures to verse in messages of consolation for similarly melancholy young friends. His work might have remained private had his father not sent it to Boston, where literati had just started publishing a periodical to encourage indigenous American literature and criticism. In founding the *North American Review* in 1815, William Tudor Jr. (1779–1830) hoped to disprove British criticisms that America was dangerously lacking in art and literature. Tudor and his colleagues feared the truth of British warnings that lack of a civilization, after Americans discarded much of that of the mother country, would endanger the fragile new republic. The first issue declared that the American environment provided all the stuff of culture: "These hills and forests hold romance; why may not majestic spirits have haunted them of old just as surely as they haunted the forests and mountains of Europe. Our country is alive with romantic possibilities if only one will grasp them before it is too late!"[29] Romanticism, based in the cultivation of sentiment and a sense of the local past, might stave off the deterioration of a rootless society. What Edward T. Channing, the magazine's editor, was seeking was just what the elder Bryant submitted to him in 1817.

When Channing and his cousin Richard Henry Dana, Senior, read Bryant's poem "Thanatopsis," they could hardly believe it had been composed in the small western Massachusetts town of Great Barrington. Dana exclaimed, "That was never written on this side of the water!" "Thanatopsis," meaning "meditations on death," brought to mind the Graveyard poets and Wordsworth. It treated themes of Death and Nature in a manner that appealed to Boston's Unitarian intellectuals, describing death in secular, pantheistic terms as a final reunion of the individual with the insensate earth. As in Shaftesbury's philosophy, Nature replaced God, and death became a universal force more powerful and invincible than man. Death and Nature were sublime, Man's stoic acceptance of inevitable natural processes vanquished fear, and reason tempered emotion in a modern statement quite unlike anything urged by the old Puritan preachers.[30]

Bryant brought the taste for melancholy to many Americans, not just the intellectual elite already familiar with English romantic sources and settings. In his poem "The Burial-Place," written in 1818 and published in 1821, Bryant contrasts the ideal of the English rural churchyard with the aesthetically inferior American burial grounds. Echoing Irving and the English Graveyard poets, Bryant praises the willows, woodbine, and ivy that "hide / The gleaming marble" in contrast to the "naked rows of graves" surrounded by "coarse grass, between" that "shoots up its dull green spikes, and in the wind / Hisses." Bryant delights in the power of resurgent Nature, which, "rebuking the neglect of man, / Plants often, by the ancient mossy stone, / The brier rose."[31] Pantheism dominates Bryant's melancholy; and in the same nostalgic spirit as Irving, he finds in the English country churchyard the symbol of a common past. Implicit in Bryant's celebration of England's rural burials is the encouragement of reform in America's burial grounds. Following the example of Wordsworth, Bryant urges the creation of naturalistic burial landscapes in poems such as "A Hymn to Death" (1820), "The Old Man's Funeral" (1824), and "The Two Graves" (1826).

Bryant's poetic notions about death bridged a gap between the stern Calvinist outlook on the hereafter and the liberal belief in the naturalness of death, as well as the expectation of universal salvation increasing among his generation in New England—resonant in Unitarianism and Universalism. Bryant also spoke to the sentiment of melancholy shared by many contemporaries. Dr. Jacob Bigelow, soon to become a leader of the burial reform movement and a founder of Mount Auburn, expressed his personal resignation in a letter to his sister in 1820 after the sudden death from "lung fever" of his six-month-old son and firstborn. Bigelow called it "the first domestic calamity which has befallen our house" and "our earliest discipline—how soon others are in reserve for us is only known to Providence." He concluded: "Sufferings are the lot of humanity. Few years are all that remain for any of us."[32] Bigelow, like John Quincy

Adams and their friend Judge Joseph Story, wrote sentimental verse to assuage his grief on the loss of a child even as he pursued a busy public career. Such men—proponents of a new sensibility—were not ashamed to cry in public.

Melancholy had public as well private utility. Through the works of Irving and Bryant, the Wordsworthian notion of Nature as a moral force won American proponents. Bryant and the Boston literati domesticated Wordsworth, including his advice on burial reform. After the Reverend William Ellery Channing met Wordsworth in England, the Unitarian minister returned to Boston bringing word of the naturalistic route to a new moral revival.[33]

A taste for sentimental poetry was far from limited to the readers of genteel ladies' magazines and best-selling gift books. The *North American Review* avidly defended Wordsworth against "severe and unjust criticisms" from a common foe, the *Edinburgh Review*. One review of Wordsworth's poetry in the American journal proclaimed: "Our intercourse with Nature becomes permanent; we acquire a habit of transferring human feelings to the growth of earth. . . . We are convinced that there is more mind, more soul about us, wherever we look, and wherever we move. . . . [T]here is no longer any dullness or death . . . but a sweet music . . . and the beauty of all visible things becomes their joy." By the late 1820s, themes of Death and Nature in prose and poetry were appearing in mass-circulation newspapers and magazines along with local and national news and advertisements.[34] In one typical romanticized piece, "The Grave of a Mother," in an 1823 issue of the *Boston Patriot and Daily Mercantile Advertiser*, the anonymous essayist wrote of "musing and wandering among the graves" one pleasant November evening as "the moon shone in her midnight meridian." Pausing over the grave of his mother, the son proudly notes that "no costly marble reared its head to tell that the slumberer beneath had once been great; it was marked by nought but the plain, simple stone . . . and the willow that had been planted by the hand of love." The natural setting intensifies the delight in melancholy: "Not a leaf stirred save some that were nipped by the pinching frosts of autumn from the trees, and as they slowly descended to earth, were silent monitors of the approach of winter and decay of man." The writer concludes, "There is something solemn and serious in the stillness of the graveyard; when the mind is made to feel its weakness, and to turn with reverence and admiration to that Being who governs the destinies of all."[35]

The essay described an idealized landscape of mourning, certainly not the typical New England burying ground, which offered no romantic, rural setting in which to plant the symbolic willow over the solitary grave of a loved one. Limited space would have prevented one from doing so even if the forces of religious conservatism had not protested the pagan profanation of death or had not the public sexton interfered. For liberal and romantic Bostonians in the 1820s, discrepancies between the melancholy ideal and the unpleasant reality of urban graveyards were especially dramatic. Even in rural towns, it seemed that the only consideration in graveyards was "confining the remains of the departed to the smallest portion of earth that will hide them." Graves were "indecently crowded together, and often, after a few years, disturbed."[36]

Death had yet to be returned to the Garden. Still, idealism increased every year. The old burial grounds were not exclusively an urban problem, nor were they the product of densely settled population of the living. The inherited landscapes of death reflected orthodox beliefs that did not encourage an iconography associating death with Eden, let alone heaven. The recent vogue for mourning pictures and willow-tree-and-urn motifs was the exception. But rapid urbanization and the advancing sensibility of personal affection, as well as sensitivities to unpleasant sights and smells, to say nothing of the latest trends in taste and liberal theology based on literary importation and cosmopolitanism, made the issue of burial reform more pressing in Boston than in other seaboard cities or smaller New England towns.

From Personal Melancholy to Public Memory

In 1820, William Tudor, Boston's chief cultural arbiter, attributed the new sensitivity to the remains of the dead to urbanization. During the colonial period, Tudor argues, burials were matters of community concern. There was no separation between public and private life in the small, tight-knit, traditional town. Survivors remembered where kin and neighbors lay in the common graveyard even without markers. Like oral lore, such knowledge often went unrecorded, yet it was seldom forgotten. But grave markers appeared increasingly as New England towns became more complex, commercial, and diversified in a time of community disintegration, social flux, and religious change.[37] By Tudor's era, even the few toppling gravestones would not suffice for accurate marking, let alone serving the purpose of memory. Like many of the elite, intent on creating a culture in material terms, Tudor wanted to promote public as well as private commemoration.

Even more than New Haven's James Hillhouse, leading Bostonians had "great objections to the place of sepulcher in a private field that in a few years" might pass into the hands of strangers who would "take no interest in preserving its sacred deposit from the plough." Newspaper articles bemoaned the unidentified grave of George Washington's mother in a Virginia field. Bostonians realized that the precise resting places of many of their own notables had also been forgotten, even in the city's center. For that reason, in 1827 citizens joined a subscription campaign to erect a twenty-one-foot granite obelisk or pyramid, designed by the architect Solomon Willard (1783–1862), in the Old Granary Burying Ground over the graves of Benjamin Franklin's parents, with the name Franklin inset in bronze letters and a plaque bearing their son's inscription from the original marble stone, which had deteriorated. (Fig. 4.13.) General Henry A. S. Dearborn delivered an address at a public ceremony on the laying of the cornerstone, and the governor and other state officials in attendance emphasized the importance of such a commemorative event.[38]

Fig. 4.13. Pyramid monument designed by Solomon Willard over Franklin's parents' graves in the Old Granary Burying Ground, Boston. Postcard, 1908. BMGL.

Fig. 4.14. Franklin's tombstone, Christ Church Burying Ground, a few blocks north of Independence Hall, Philadelphia. Engraving, 1873. BMGL

The elder Franklin's monument was far grander than the plain, horizontal tombstone marking the grave of their illustrious son in a crowded Philadelphia burial ground. (Fig. 4.14.) Throngs of visitors forged a path through surrounding graves to visit the Founding Father, and many of them drew negative judgments of the American character based on what they saw. One Frenchman observed, "They could have, after all, chosen for him a more honorable resting place than the obscure corner of an obscure graveyard, where his bones are thrown pele-mele with those of grossly ordinary men, under a stone that soon the weeds will hide from view." For him, the unsightly grave proved "a cruel truth: no object in America is respected for the memories it engenders. The present generation is too occupied by business to have time to venerate historic images, or ancient services rendered, or great talents that are no more; there are enough other cares. Americans pick the fruits planted by their ancestors, or rather by their immediate predecessors," without giving them their commemorative due.[39]

Boston was one of the first places in America to feel

Fig. 4.15. Dr. John Collins Warren, daguerreotype portrait with skull, ca. 1850. Courtesy Massachusetts General Hospital, Boston.

the impulse to commemorate the dead—to locate and mark the remains of the deceased in the name of history. By the 1820s, Boston's burying grounds had become places of worse chaos, disarray, and overuse than ever; but concern with marking the precise locations of graves and tombs had never been great. The remains of the hero of the Battle of Bunker Hill, General Joseph Warren, had by now been lost for a second time. In 1825, Dr. John Collins Warren (1778–1856) set himself the difficult task of finding his illustrious uncle's skeleton. (Fig. 4.15.) Its burial site in the Old Granary Burying Ground had been forgotten even within his family, despite the elaborate public obsequies accompanying the general's reinterment in 1776. After a lengthy search, Warren found the remains in the family tomb of Judge George Richards Minot, a historian, only steps from his own new Beacon Hill residence.[40] Warren identified the skull by the teeth and the fatal bullet hole behind the left ear. He moved the bones to a crypt he had recently had built in the basement of the new Saint Paul's Episcopal Church across the street. Warren considered the crypts of St. Paul's a more permanent and appropriate resting place for the relics of a hero, for his other, less distinguished family members, and for prominent Bostonians like himself—prosperous businessmen, professionals, and civil leaders who could afford such a tomb. His solution to Boston's burial problems, however, was not for everybody. The controversy that ensued revealed the complexity of conflicting interests and concerns preoccupying Bostonians as they tried to create new cultural forms expressing their changing notions of death and community, family, and postmortem fame.

5

THE NECESSITY FOR MONUMENTS

Art and Public Commemoration in the Young Republic

And you! ye bright ascended Dead,
Who scorned the bigot's yoke,
Come, round this place your influence shed;
Your spirits I invoke.

—Charles Sprague, "An Ode Pronounced before the Inhabitants of Boston . . . at the Centennial Celebration of the Settlement of the City" (1830)

As for what we generally understand as faiths, such as customs, ancient traditions, the strength of memories, up to the present I don't see a trace of them [in America].

—Alexis de Tocqueville to Louis de Kergolay [his cousin] (1831)

Although revolution did not leave social and cultural chaos in its wake in America as in France, Americans still faced the problem of creating a republican culture and finding forms with which to redefine its history. The dual impulse for public and private commemoration through the half century after independence presented a solution to the problem of defining a national past separate from that of the mother country and its colonialism. As in France, those intent on creating a culture as a unifying and stabilizing force turned to building monuments and to cultivating a taste for melancholy. By providing retrospective forms for both communities and families, they hoped to diminish the dangers of divisive factionalism—religious, political, social, and regional. Their fears for the fragility of governmental order were based on the cataclysmic view of history. The optimistic idea of progress as an operative force had yet to enter and dominate the American mind.

Monuments, it was hoped, would serve as material manifestations of and catalysts for a new civic religion: patriotism. The demand for monuments and commemorative landscapes intensified after the War of 1812, when the Treaty of Ghent (1814) assured Americans that their "experiment" in republican government could succeed if it was bolstered culturally. Eventually, the creation of public monuments and pastoral cemetery landscapes demonstrated the ingenuity of Americans in adapting borrowed aesthetic forms to create their own usable past.

New Englanders laid claim to a national history through literary as well as material forms. They drew upon a historical consciousness rooted in their Puritan past and its rejection of Anglican culture. The Puritans believed that their mission in the New World was determined by Providence, and that their founding of an exemplary Commonwealth, a "City on a Hill," was a major event in the history of mankind. Their descendants retained their forefathers' belief that their history could be a conservative social force, counteracting dispersion and dissension, a concern dating from the days of the Pilgrims, when William Bradford (1590–1657), first governor of Plimouth Plantation, wrote:

> *O New England, thou canst not boast;*
> *Thy former glory thou hast lost.*
> *When Hooker, Winthrop, Cotton died,*
> *And many precious ones beside,*
> *And still doth languish more away.*

The Reverend William Hubbard (1621–1704), first historian of the Massachusetts Bay Colony, referred in the 1650s to the founding decade as a "Golden Age," a time of God's special grace. Secretary of the Plymouth Colony Nathan Morton and Edward Johnson, a militia captain of the town of Woburn in the Massachusetts Bay Colony, also recorded the deeds of the founding generation as it was dying out. The zeal for defining and memorializing a common Puritan past increased as Calvinist orthodoxy declined in the eighteenth century.[1]

For generations, the Puritans and their heirs built no monuments as material equivalents of written histories. Iconophobia, the rejection of ostentation, and the practical needs of developing settlements provide only partial explanations. New England's gravestones were exhortations to remember death, not records of exemplary individual lives. Colonial leaders received scant commemoration in the burial place. Both the tomb of John Winthrop, first governor of Massachusetts, in Boston's first graveyard and that of the Mather dynasty of Puritan ministers on Copp's Hill were barely marked.[2] (Fig. 5.1.) A commemorative impulse nevertheless began to take root among American Puritans, as among the English, with discussion of the beneficial effects of mourning certain deaths. Architectural metaphors were common. Samuel Willard (1640–1707), later dubbed "the Last of the Puritans," pastor of Boston's South Church and president of Harvard, counseled his flock in 1683, "When a Saint *Dies* there is manifold ground of mourning: there is then a Pillar pluckt out of the Building, a Foundation Stone taken out of the Wall." Willard advised Puritans to "embalm the memory of the Saints with the sweet smelling Spices that grew in their own Graves . . . [to] remember and make mention of them with honourable thoughts and words." As the founding generation died out, ministers hoped that remembrance of the lives of the early leaders would stabilize society and perpetuate their principles. On the death of Thomas Savage (1640–1705), Willard wondered: "When the Pillars are gone, how shall the building stand? . . . When the Wall is pluckt down, and the hedge removed, who shall keep out the Bore of the Wilderness?"[3] It was hoped that memory of a past shaped by virtuous individuals and their deeds would forestall lawlessness and destruction of the social order. Such views would strike a chord with Yankees, who in the 1820s keenly felt the passing of time with the deaths of the Founding Fathers of their Republic.

Fig. 5.1. Mather family tomb, Copp's Hill Burial Ground, Boston. Engraving from King, *Hand-Book of Boston*, 1878. BMGL.

Despite his metaphors, Willard was not urging the creation of actual gardens with commemorative monuments—something the English had not yet begun to do. Rather, he echoed Milton's yearning for new material forms of remembrance to inspire retrospection and resolve. Puritans favored literary over material remembrance. "Every other monument will become old, and grow over with the Moss of time and their Titles, though cut in Brass, will be Canker-eaten and illegible," Willard wrote. Only memory of the virtuous lives of the community's "elect," those predestined to salvation, would endure "when Marble itself shall be turned into common dust."[4] Colonial New Englanders would build no monuments of marble or brass, nor had they any buildings symbolic of their Commonwealth from which to draw symbols. Yet Willard was ahead of his time in referring metaphorically to commemorative forms as a way of encouraging his community to perpetuate the examples of "Visible Saints."

The term "Saints" took on new meaning in reference to church members and individuals of civic prominence. Willard urged their commemoration through histories and biographies. Increasingly, ministers like Willard prescribed a formal, ritualized response to death that combined the growing desire for remembrance of notables with proscription of excessive grief and a moderation of emotion characteristic of Puritanism and of the Yankee culture that followed it. Memory of the exemplary individual—the "Saint" or later the secular "Great Man"—functioned in the same didactic way as Winthrop's concept of the "City on a Hill," to perpetuate notions of community ordained by Providence and based on divine law, followed strictly by his "chosen" people.

Material evidence of a historical or commemorative consciousness was also absent in colonies outside New England. Colonists in general did not develop an appreciation of monuments until they became *Americans* after their Revolution. In their rebellion, New York patriots and their slaves pulled down a statue of King George III on the Bowling Green; but the British had erected few monuments in the colonies against which patriots could vent their Revolutionary sentiments. The war did, however, produce heroes for Americans, providing names and stories ready to be invoked as independence created the need for defining a common purpose, principles, and past. Thus was born the necessity for monuments.

The brother of Major General Joseph Warren (1741–1775), the physician-patriot who fell in the Battle of Bunker Hill, Dr. John Warren (1753–1815), himself wounded there while attending the fallen, stressed the stabilizing functions of commemoration and the fragility of republican states in his 1783 Fourth of July oration in Boston, attributing the demise of the ancient republics of Athens and Rome to "a forgetfulness of *fundamental principles*." He warned, "So nearly is the most prosperous condition of a people allied to decay and ruin that even this flattering appearance conceals the seeds that finally must produce her destruction." To forestall the inevitable, Warren urged Americans to "go search the vaults, where lay enshrined the relicks of your martyred fellow citizens, and from their dust receive a lesson of the value of your freedom! . . . When virtue fails, when luxury and corruption shall undermine the pillars of the state, and threaten a total loss of liberty and patriotism, then solemnly repair to those *sacred repositories* of the dead."[5] But in the 1780s and for decades, Americans had no sacred repositories to which they could repair for philosophic or patriotic contemplation of the past personified in public or private ways.

John Warren's remarks were inspired by the discovery that the body of his heroic brother Joseph had been lost in a common grave on the battlefield "among the vulgar dead" for almost a year. When Bostonians located the hero's remains shortly after the British evacuation, they held a grand patriotic funeral at King's Chapel on April 8, 1776. The young lawyer and ardent patriot Perez Morton (1750–1837) eulogized his fellow Freemason Joseph Warren, Grand Master of the Ancient Grand Lodge of Massachusetts, promising, "Thy memory has been embalmed in the affections of thy grateful countrymen, who, in their breasts, have raised eternal monuments to thy bravery!" Bostonians reinterred Warren in the family tomb of George Minot in the Old Granary Burying Ground but showed no concern for marking the new resting place, let alone erecting a monument.[6]

Almost two decades later, the King Solomon Lodge of Free and Accepted Masons, founded in Charlestown in 1783, erected a wooden monument that combined elements of an obelisk and an urn, forms just beginning to win favor for funerary use in old graveyards. They chose a site on the battlefield, however, rather than marking the hero's place of entombment. In December of 1794 magistrates and ministers, with townspeople following, marched "with slow-step to the notes of a dirge" to the hill in still-rural Charlestown to consecrate the monument to Major General Warren and his fallen associates. Master Mason John Soley declared that his generation, not "content with having raised a monument of gratitude" in their hearts alone, now presented "one to the eye of future generations." Renaming the hill with "the graves of our departed countrymen" Mount Warren, Soley called upon the citizens to bring children there and "teach them obedience to the voice of their country; inform them that their birth-right is Freedom." The monument, he declared, would represent "the legacy left them by their country to maintain its valor."[7] The General Court passed a law making it a crime for anyone to deface or destroy the monument. (Fig. 5.2.)

In 1790, to remedy the newly perceived lack of histor-

Fig. 5.2. Masonic wooden monument to General Joseph Warren, erected in 1794 on the Bunker Hill Battle site. Engraving from G. W. Warren, 1877.

Fig. 5.3. Monument to American Independence, a wooden Doric column topped by a gilded American eagle, said to be the first public display of that patriotic icon, designed by Charles Bulfinch, erected in 1789 on Boston's Beacon Hill just before location there of the Massachusetts State House (1795–1798) he designed. Engraving, ca. 1830. BMGL.

Fig. 5.4. Revolutionary Soldiers' Monument on Lexington Common, the nation's third Revolutionary War monument, dedicated on July 4, 1799. The stocky obelisk, the first monument to fallen heroes built of stone, became overgrown with ivy clipped to reveal the inscription:

SACRED TO LIBERTY AND THE RIGHTS OF MANKIND!!! / THE FREEDOM AND INDEPENDENCE OF AMERICA, / SEALED AND DEFENDED WITH THE BLOOD OF HER SONS. / THIS MONUMENT IS ERECTED / BY THE INHABITANTS OF LEXINGTON, / UNDER THE PATRONAGE AND AT THE EXPENSE OF / THE COMMONWEALTH OF MASSACHUSETTS, / TO THE MEMORY OF THEIR FELLOW CITIZENS, / ENSIGN ROBERT MUNROE, AND MESSRS. JONAS PARKER, / SAMUEL HADLEY, JONATHAN HARRINGTON, JR., / ISAAC MUZZY, CALEB HARRINGTON AND JOHN BROWN, / OF LEXINGTON AND ASAHEL PORTER OF WOBURN, / WHO FELL ON THIS FIELD, THE FIRST VICTIMS OF THE / SWORD OF BRITISH TYRANNY AND OPRESSION / ON THE MORNING OF THE EVER MEMORABLE / NINETEENTH OF APRIL, AN. DOM. 1775. / THE DIE WAS CAST!!! / THE BLOOD OF THESE MARTYRS / IN THE CAUSE OF GOD AND THEIR COUNTRY / WAS THE CEMENT OF THE UNION OF THESE STATES, THEN / COLONIES, AND GAVE THE SPRING TO THE SPIRIT, FIRMNESS, / AND RESOLUTIONS OF THEIR FELLOW CITIZENS. / THEY ROSE AS ONE MAN TO REVENGE THEIR BRETHREN'S / BLOOD, AND AT THE POINT OF THE SWORD, TO ASSERT AND / DEFEND THEIR NATIVE RIGHTS. / THEY NOBLY DAR'D TO BE FREE!! / THE CONTEST WAS LONG, BLOODY AND AFFECTING. / RIGHTEOUS HEAVEN APPROVED THE SOLEMN APPEAL, / VICTORY CROWNED THEIR ARMS; AND / THE PEACE, LIBERTY, AND INDEPENDENCE OF THE UNITED / STATES OF AMERICA WAS THEIR GLORIOUS REWARD.

Postcard, ca. 1910. BMGL.

ical monuments in Boston, the architect Charles Bulfinch (1763–1844) designed a sixty-foot Doric column to be placed on Beacon Hill in memory of Independence. Sitting on a pedestal, and topped by a globe and an American eagle, it was made of wood and would not have lasted long, even if real estate speculators had not torn it down in 1811 so the hill could be lowered for construction of homes for the city's new elite.[8] (Figs. 5.3, 5.4.)

After the Revolution, foreign visitors began to warn Americans that their lack of a common culture and a sense of their own history could threaten the republic's longevity. Aware of their own need to create cultural alternatives to the old regime, the French, too, were particularly concerned with finding ways to bolster society through material commemorative forms. Honoré-Gabriel Riguetti (1749–1791), comte de Mirabeau, a leader in the National Assembly early in the French Revolution and a rival of Lafayette, advised Americans to "multiply your monuments, rites, and commemorative ceremonies."[9] Some Americans, fearful of French conspiracies and extremist fervor, questioned such advice; but others heeded moderate French ideas about the stabilizing utility of a "cult of heroes" or "cult of ancestors" in either material or literary form. In a 1790 oration at the University of Pennsylvania, James Wilson (1742–1798), a signer of the Declaration of Independence, proposed building a Temple of Fame in Philadelphia to honor war heroes like Warren, Montgomery, and Mercer. The Unitarian minister Jeremy Belknap (1744–1798), who moved to Boston from New Hampshire after the Revolution, aimed to become "the American Plutarch" by publishing in 1794 the first of two volumes of collected biographies of American "Adventurers, Statesmen, Philosophers, Divines, Warriors, Authors, and Other Remarkable Characters." Belknap founded the Massachusetts Historical Society (1794), the first such organization in the new nation.[10]

Washington's Tomb

No other hero had the nationally unifying potential of George Washington, who died on December 14, 1799. His death sparked a commemorative consciousness with patriotic dimensions, as the Reverend Peter Whitney (1770–1842) suggested in an 1800 funerary sermon, "Weeping and Mourning at the Death of Eminent Persons a National Duty."[11] Washington's burial site on his Mount Vernon plantation evoked the imagery of mourning pictures and funerary verse, a pastoral ideal then coming into vogue which would inspire the design of American "rural" cemetery landscapes. Washington's burial place—as it existed and as it was idealized—contrasted markedly with most burial grounds, especially in the cities. Just as French visitors made pilgrimages to Rousseau's tomb in the romantic landscape at Ermenonville as a secular shrine, Americans flocked to Washington's grave. Descriptions in newspapers and books made the setting of Washington's tomb familiar to many in the first quarter of the nineteenth century. Paintings, engravings, and mourning pictures depicted the place as romantic and picturesque, as people wished it to be rather than as it was. Nevertheless, the idealized images reflected the new "rural" or pastoral aesthetics so central to the budding cult of melancholy and provided a model for "improved" burial places. (Fig. 5.5.)

Travel narratives of Mount Vernon proved popular, preceding by decades efforts to restore and preserve the estate. In 1823, one writer in the Republican *New-England Galaxy* lauded the simplicity and nobility of the rural setting, with extensive gardens where long gravel walks and alleys wound through fruit trees and shrubbery. Citing scriptural references to the garden as a place of sepulcher, the traveler, visiting the vault "in which the dust of the hero reposes," could not imagine "a more romantic and picturesque site for a tomb." On the hill, "a curtain of forest trees" separated it from the Potomac's banks, "breaking the glare of the prospect yet affording glimpses of the river when the foliage is the thickest." Huge native oaks, symbolizing for him the virile president, "venerable by their years," surrounded the tomb, "annually strew[ing] the sepulcher with autumnal leaves, furnishing the most appropriate drapery for such a place." Contrasting in winter "to the hoary and leafless branches of the oak," a copse of red cedar formed an evergreen backdrop. Deciduous foliage symbolized the decay of the body, while the cedars' "eternal verdure" furnished "a beautiful emblem of the immortal spirit." The account embroidered on reality, drawing

Fig. 5.5. George Washington's original tomb at Mount Vernon. Engraving from Theodore Dwight, *Things as They Are; or, Notes of a Traveller through Some of the Middle and Northern States* (New York: Harper & Brothers, 1834).

more on garden aesthetics than on a true description of Mount Vernon's tattered formality after a quarter century's neglect. It offered a romanticized ideal, yet to be achieved but achievable. It also offered more rational imagery than popular depictions of the apotheosis of the first president borne from his tomb heavenward in triumph by an angel and Father Time, leaving behind mourning Columbia, an Indian, mothers and children.[12]

Despite interest in Washington's tomb, by the 1820s it had become a ruin of the sort that failed to appeal even to tastes conditioned by English garden aesthetics in which ruins signified a vanished past. Mount Vernon continued to deteriorate as Washington's heirs and their fortunes dwindled. British visitors criticized the shabbiness of the place as evidence of a weak civilization, boding ill for the republic's longevity. One traveler scorned the plain tomb, lacking an inscription, as "an insufficient memorial of the mighty dead."[13] To E. T. Coke, a British army officer, the neglect stood as an indictment of American taste: "The situation is a very pretty one, but scarcely any thing has been done by art to add to the natural beauty. The grounds are laid out in a tasteless style and kept in a slovenly manner, high coarse grass growing up to the very door. The Americans possess generally but little taste for ornamental gardening, or at least make no display of it." Coke wondered why the nation did not purchase the property. He declared that the people's failure to erect a monument to the "man who was their idol while living and whose memory is still so revered amongst them" was a "subject of surprise and reproach among foreigners."[14]

Others liked Washington's burial place, calling it characteristically American. The historian J. S. Buckingham found a pleasing "air of simplicity" there, though it would not appeal to those "accustomed to seeing the splendid mausolea erected to the memory of rulers, statesmen, and heroes in the old world."[15] Americans treated their first president's tomb no differently from those of other heroes of the Revolution, or of ordinary citizens. By the 1820s, however, as the debate over Washington's tomb demonstrates, many had grown uneasy with the lack of material forms of postmortem remembrance in general. Some tried to rationalize disregard of gravesites, saying that the names and virtues of notables were perpetuated in other places or patterns. According to Coke, Americans felt that the city of Washington and its public buildings were a sufficient memorial to the president. Others remained reluctant to copy new English and French practices of creating monuments or shrines to notables. Still, visitors expected to find monuments at the grave and in the capital city, and they urged the creation of an appropriately melancholy environment at the burial site, to be patterned after English gardens.

When the Washington family refused to exhume and reinter the president's remains in the national Capitol, legislators proposed establishing a Congressional Cemetery at Mount Vernon. Many preferred to leave things as they were. Those with "romantic sensibilities," wrote Caroline Howard Gilman, questioned whether "there is not something more touching in the lonely burial-place of our country's idol, even if its waving trees and natural flowers" did not stir "deep musings." The issue was one of aesthetics, that is, whether "improvements" on the rural plantation to create a commemorative landscape reminiscent of the English garden, complete with a funerary monument, would be preferable to leaving evidence of natural decay and ruin indicative of time's passage and Nature's resurgence. Americans had no taste for ruins, but they could not force removal of Washington's body to a more fitting site. Some asserted that Mount Vernon, even in disrepair, epitomized American values: respect for private property, celebration of virtues grounded in the land, the equation of nation with Nature, the rejection of ostentation associated with Old World aristocracy. One visitor observed: "If feeling and taste be consulted, his dust will forever rest in the shades of his favourite retirement. I would prefer for myself or for a friend, the solitude and quiet of this rural spot where 'the birds sing over the grave' to the proudest columns of marble which a grateful country could rear." Mount Vernon became "the American Mecca" associated with "the agricultural pursuits and domestic concerns of the American Cincinnatus."[16] The Reverend Hosea Ballou (1771–1852), a leading Boston Universalist, echoed patriotic moralists' advice to visit the site, observing that "the American traveler, who visits the tomb of the hero and patriot whom we call the *father* of his country can never read the inscription of the beloved name of WASHINGTON without having a crowd of recollections, embracing the events of that momentous conflict which led to the independence of our happy republic, press on his mind." A visit, he urged, would "awaken and strengthen sentiment and resolutions favorable to the defense and perpetuity of those political institutions which are the purchase of that valor which won our independence."[17]

Following such advice, parents took children there as if on pilgrimage. Bostonian James Russell Lowell (1819–1891) visited Washington's grave at age eight in 1827 with his father. Fifty-nine years later, the poet took his own grandson to the site. The Federalist writer Theodore Dwight (1764–1846) found his visit to Washington's tomb gratifying precisely because of its simplicity: "There is something much more congenial to my mind in the simple and indeed humble depository of the ashes of Washington than in the most splendid monuments of Italy or even of Egypt. Where there is no attempt made to captivate the eye, the mind is left at perfect freedom to form her own conceptions." Dwight had no objection to monuments to Washington and hoped the day would come when every city, town, and village would have one "constructed in the purest taste"; but he insisted "that any fabric of art" at Mount Vernon would only be "an impediment to the mind, which, if left to itself will create the noblest conceptions out of nothing."[18]

The landscape did not remain pristine and picturesque; it simply deteriorated. Even worse, owing to the abolition of primogeniture and the economic vicissitudes of the new republic, many private burial grounds were lost by families along with their other property within a generation. Not until 1831 did Washington's executors follow the request in the president's will for a simple brick family vault and a marble sarcophagus "of the ancient Roman shape . . . sculptured in relief, an eagle with the national escutcheon of America, the stars and stripes of her Union, and the word 'WASHINGTON,' only." John Struthers (1786–1851), an English marble mason working in Philadelphia, did the carving. It was not completed until 1837.[19] (Fig. 5.6.)

Fig. 5.6. Washington's second tomb at Mount Vernon (1835) designed by architect William Yeaton. The president's request for a vault topped by a sarcophagus of "ancient Roman shape" was followed, but the vault is sheltered in an open room behind the brick Gothic Revival façade and visible through iron bars. The burial ground, with hundreds of unmarked graves of Mount Vernon's slaves and some of the freed blacks emancipated by his last will and testament, is about fifty yards to the southwest. Engraving by W. H. Brooke, ca. 1840. BMGL.

Republican Uses of Art

The efforts of voluntary associations rather than the government made the second quarter of the nineteenth century an age of monumental building. As American leaders turned their attention to stabilizing the nation in symbolic ways alluding to patriotism and moralism, sacred yet secular and nondenominational, citizens debated the uses of art. In 1811, Benjamin Henry Latrobe (1764–1820), architect, landscape painter, new immigrant from England, and a republican, had declared that "the history of Grecian art refutes the vulgar opinion that the arts are incompatible with liberty," for "Greece was free when the arts flourished."[20] Accordingly, he designed public buildings in the national capital that would double as monuments, and he encouraged the taste for neoclassical styles to express republican ideals. Not until the 1820s, however, would the likes of Nicholas Biddle (1786–1844), a prominent Philadelphian and president of the Bank of the United States, take up the call for public works of art as proof of national and civic character. Mention of the arts in this debate referred to sculpture, architecture, and monuments and their place in the landscape, or to paintings depicting historic events and notables.[21]

John Adams (1735–1826) and Thomas Jefferson (1743–1826) debated the use of the arts in the correspondence of their declining years. Adams opposed a public policy for developing the arts, which he considered "subservient to Priests and Kings, Nobles . . . Monarchies," for "Sculpture, Painting and Poetry have conspir'd against the Rights of Mankind."[22] Adams's iconoclasm lingered from his Puritan and Revolutionary past. Art remained a symbolic enemy for those of his thinking. The historian Neil Harris notes that for those of like mind, art was a sign of "dangerous age and decay," and the emergence of artists portended "the beginnings of national declension." For many Americans, the condition of classical *objets d'art*, "the broken and mutilated torsos, suggested the shattered state of the societies which produced them."[23] Sculpture and architecture thus symbolized society in form, duration, and preservation, and the inevitable decay of monuments heralded a civilization's decline. Americans at the semicentennial of independence were loath to create material forms that might prove to be harbingers of their nation's demise. Lacking a taste for ruins, many remained wary of monuments.

Jefferson, by contrast, saw art and architecture as agents of history, a means by which his age could transmit its principles, even if durability was limited. Efficacy, however, depended on style, and for him the neoclassical represented "not what was to perish with ourselves, but would remain, be respected and preserved through other ages." It suggested a negation of luxury destructive to the republic. Its simplicity, visual purity, and restrained ornament were metaphoric of civic virtue, orderly and logical like the Constitution, an emblematic denial of the baroque tastes of monarchies and aristocracies. It strengthened the conscious association of America with the heights achieved by classical cultures and political principles derived from ancient Greece and Rome. Jefferson wanted his generation's material culture to transmit a sense of national purpose just as its federal and state documents did. He remarked to James Madison that monuments would present "to travellers a specimen of taste in our infancy, promising much for our mature age."[24] Many Americans agreed with Jefferson. Soon, neoclassical funerary monuments—urns, obelisks, steles, and sarcophagi—began to appear among the flat colonial markers in old graveyards.

Debate over the uses, values, and problems of art persisted through the first quarter of the new century. If art represented the decay of an aging civilization, as some believed, lack of art indicated to others a society that was too immature and therefore weak and tenuous. This latter view fed fears that even after surviving the War of 1812, the United States would remain merely an "experiment" resting on shallow foundations. Even John Adams wondered, "Is it possible to enlist the 'fine arts' on the side of truth, of virtue, of piety, or even of honor?"[25] News of the restoration of a monarchy in France in 1814 and then of another revolution in 1830 renewed American insecurities. Jefferson, after all, had asserted each generation's right to revolt against the last. Conservatives feared a coming democratic revolution.

A father and son who shared the name William Tudor played integral roles in their respective generations, that of the Revolution and that of the creation of a commemorative culture. William Tudor the elder (1750–1819), cousin of Abigail Adams, an attorney who had read law with John Adams, served as judge advocate general of the Continental Army. A friend of Washington, Jefferson, Adams, and other Founding Fathers, he helped form the Society of the Cincinnati, an organization of Revolutionary War officers, and in 1799 suggested that the new nation be renamed "Columbia." The younger William Tudor (1779–1830), a merchant ship owner and prolific writer, was among the first fourteen members of Boston's literary Anthology Society (1805) who united to edit the *Monthly Anthology* and the *Boston Review* and who founded the Boston Athenaeum (1807), an exemplary subscription library. He was the biographer of James Otis as well as a founder and first editor of the quarterly *North American Review* (1815), a friend of Emerson, and a Unitarian. He was the first, in 1819, to compare Boston ambitiously with Athens, giving rise to Boston's nickname "the Athens of America." He also played a leading role in the association that planned and built the Bunker Hill Monument.[26]

When the younger Tudor declared in 1810 that every city should erect a statue to Washington and hold annual ceremonies to honor him with "the delicious feelings of filial gratitude," he was personalizing his patriotic sentiments, which derived in part from his father's connections; but he sincerely hoped that perpetuating reverence for the "Father of his Country" would forestall destructive political factionalism. He became a great advocate of the role of commemorative art in creating a usable past for Boston, New England, and the nation. Yet in a more general sense, he believed that artists had a high duty to their country and "should feel something of a *missionary spirit*," their goal being "to excite the taste of the publick." He considered it his personal mission to enrich the national culture, to counteract foreign criticism like those in the *Edinburgh Review* that great art, architecture, and literature would not suffice for the creation of a culture if they were borrowed and not indigenous. Tudor called upon Boston's Whig elite to accept the challenge and prove the critics wrong. Philanthropically minded merchants and professionals created institutions to foster cultural nationalism, motivated by the belief that "correct taste" could strengthen "republican virtue" and ensure a good and stable society. In addition to his literary efforts, Tudor urged the creation of a repository for art in Boston that would enable American artists to improve their work and connoisseurs to refine their taste. Models and casts acquired from Europe would provide aesthetic inspiration and education for a time if no original art was forthcoming.[27] George Watson Brimmer (1784–1838), another merchant, assembled an art collection at Boston's Athenaeum in 1827. Tudor hoped to make it a "fashionable resort," but it remained private and inaccessible to those without proper connections.

After the War of 1812, leading Americans speculated that devising props for the Founding Fathers' principles by creating a unifying culture might convince all of the republic's validity and permanence and muster patriotic sentiment for its preservation. Summarizing that philosophy well into the monument-building era, the Reverend Hubbard Winslow (1800–1864), Boston's 1838 Fourth of July orator, predicted that art would "check the growing tendencies to insubordination and render all classes of citizens more humane, peaceful, and happy." In this, Winslow repeated the messages he and other Bostonians had been hearing from their Federalist cultural leaders. As in England and France, Americans came to feel that commemorative monuments, landscapes, and other institutions of memory would embody their political ideals and exert stabilizing powers of social control.[28]

Baltimore Takes the Lead

Baltimore, incorporated by the state of Maryland in 1796, and with a much shorter history of mercantile prosperity, acquired the name "Monument City" for its structures erected in memory of Washington and local heroes of the War of 1812. As early as 1809, the Maryland legislature granted permission to a voluntary association to raise $100,000 by lottery for a monument to the first president, the nation's first; but war postponed the effort. Finally, on July 4, 1815, Baltimoreans laid the cornerstone on a hill north of the city in a public ceremony.

Baltimore's monument building captured the interest of Boston owing to that rising port city's mercantile and religious ties. The Boston physician Jacob Bigelow received the news with envy from his brother Henry, who was in Baltimore on business. Henry, however, did not report on the controversy over the choice of a site.[29] Town house residents had rejected placement in the city's center, fearing the stability of tall structures that might attract lightning. They insisted that the column be placed at the periphery. General John Eager Howard (1792–1827), himself a hero of the Revolution, donated land on his huge Belvedere estate, known as Howard's Woods, on a hill overlooking the town from the north. Robert Mills (1781–1855), America's first native-born "professionally trained" architect and later designer of the Washington Monument in the national capital, won $500 in the design competition of March 1813. An estimated thirty thousand people assembled from miles around for the laying of the cornerstone. Although local quarries provided the marble, costs had already exceeded $200,000 by 1824 just for the Doric column and its capital, symbolic of strength for Masons, forcing Mills to omit carvings. Because of the cost, his initial proposal for a statue of Washington clad as a Roman warrior in a horse-drawn chariot gave way to a sixteen-foot statue depicting Washington resigning his commission as commander in chief of the Continental Army. The sculptor Henrico Causici of Verona, Italy, won that design competition of 1826. Causici, who had sculpted panels for the Rotunda of the U.S. Capitol, carved the statue from three seven-ton marble blocks. The monument, reaching 178 feet on the hill, was dedicated on November 25, 1829, as a crowd marveled at the placement of the statue on top. The summit, reached by 228 internal steps, offered an extensive panoramic view, considered symbolic of liberty.[30] (Fig. 5.7.)

In the summer of 1815 a subscription campaign of the Committee of Vigilance and Safety raised funds for

Fig. 5.7. Baltimore's Washington monument, designed by Robert Mills. The cornerstone was laid in 1815. It was topped by a portrait statue of Washington by Henrico Causici and dedicated in 1829. This prompted John Quincy Adams to dub Baltimore "the Monumental City." Engraving by William Henry Bartlett, ca. 1835, from Nathaniel Parker Willis, *American Scenery* (London: George Virtue, 1840).

Fig. 5.8. Baltimore's marble Battle Monument, designed by architect Maximilien Godefroy. Its cornerstone was laid in 1815 and it was dedicated in 1825. Engraving by W. H. Bartlett, ca. 1835, from N. P. Willis, 1840.

a second monument to citizens who died defending Baltimore against the British siege the previous fall in the Battle of Fort McHenry. (Fig. 5.8.) The cornerstone was laid on the newly designated Monument Square on Calvert Street in September in a ceremony reminiscent of a public funeral, with tolling bells and a processional of about twenty thousand following a hearse bearing the plan of the monument. The site, in the middle of a street surrounded by buildings, was designated Monument Square. Construction of this fifty-two-foot column designed by French émigré architect Maximilien Godefroy with sculpture by Antonio Capellano took a decade. Atop a truncated Egyptian Revival base with four eagles rises a stocky column bearing reliefs of two battles depicting the death of Major General Robert Ross and the bombardment of the British fleet. A ten-foot-tall female allegorical figure, "Fame crowning the deeds of the slain," representative of the city, holds the laurel wreath of victory and a ship's rudder symbolic of the city's thriving port or the stabilization of the "ship of state." Perhaps it seemed ironic to Bostonians that such civic spirit and a sense of history were displayed in that new commercial city before theirs. In any case, this example of monument building to the south supplied additional impetus for Bostonians to debate and plan their own commemorative structures and landscapes.[31]

The Yankee View of History

The thinking of this era revealed a latent pessimism premised in the cataclysmic view of history that permeated much of Western thought in the early nineteenth century, the notion that dramatic, violent beginnings and endings characterize the fate of cities, states, and civilizations, just as human life is defined by birth, maturation, decay, and death. This notion of history seemed correct to a generation with fresh memories of recent revolutions. Only Nature was eternal, constantly renewing itself, resurgent even after civilization's fall, overgrowing the ruins. The cataclysmic concept of history paralleled the cult of melancholy with its emphasis on individual mortality. The only difference was that one pertained to the public sphere and the other to the private; one to a city or state, the other to the individual. Some Americans, as we have seen, argued for commemorative monuments as a means to preserve memories of a past worthy of emulation and a present soon to be past; others argued that the very act of monument building could forestall the inevitable decay of civilization.

The young Dr. Jacob Bigelow (1787–1879) shared his era's cataclysmic philosophy of history, first expressing it in his 1816 address at Harvard upon being made Rumford Professor: "The power which men and nations exercise in regard to each other is temporary and transient. The greatest individuals have lived to see the decline of everything upon which their greatness reposed. Societies and political institutions, which have been distinguished in their ascent, have not been less remarkable in their fall. Those nations and governments which, in former times, have subdued their competitors and controlled, for a time, the destinies of the great portion of the world, are now erased from the list of empires, and perhaps, recognized only in name." Only knowledge was "permanent and progressive," immune to the vicissitudes and revolutions of Time. As an antidote, Bigelow urged Bostonians to expand all fields of learning and recognize the accomplishments of those who had done so.[32]

Bigelow saw the past as a source of inspiration and encouragement for those "who would despond as to our future destinies." He proclaimed the importance of recognizing and preserving the memory of great Americans. Commemoration of notables would attract "the honorable notice of foreigners" and reflect "lustre upon the country of their birth." He proposed celebrating "men unambitious of fame, whose lives have passed in obscurity" yet who contributed to the nation's development and improvement in various ways: "If gathered from the ashes of obscurity, [their names] might serve to shed a gleam upon our literary reputation." Bigelow remained confident that there had lived many men as learned as Franklin, "a native of New England," or as patriotic as any of the Founding Fathers. Only posthumous commemoration would resurrect such exemplary figures from oblivion.

Fame came naturally to those fortunate enough "to live in times of political importance" or lucky enough "to find paths untrodden by predecessors," whereas the patriots, philosophers, and scientists of his own era, said Bigelow, went unacclaimed and seemingly would have no place in history. He regretted that his generation did not have the advantages of that of the Revolution, for an era's importance intensified and immortalized men's reputations. Bigelow and his peers were eager for fame. They strove to be Renaissance men, to excel in many fields, to assert their individualism, and to establish their family names. He proposed creating a history for his generation composed of monuments, biographies, and recognition of individual merit.[33] Bigelow had articulated a new sense of mission for Bostonians to commemorate and celebrate their present as well as their past. John Adams congratulated Bigelow for refuting the criticisms in the *Edinburgh Review* predicting the decadence of American culture. Adams added, "Our honors and glories and constant good fortune may make them giddy, as well as Napoleon."[34]

The leading Unitarian divine, William Ellery Channing (1780–1842), agreed: "Let the records of past ages be explored to rescue from oblivion, not the wasteful conqueror, but the benefactors of the human-race." He protested glorifying military heroes as symbols of superiority, triumph, and power. His ideal heroes were the intellectuals and philanthropists working diligently to elevate local and national culture. Altruism and cultural responsibility were, for him, prerequisites for gentry status. Channing encouraged the elite in active stewardship of their wealth and urged on all citizens a sense of duty toward community. He believed that commemoration would instill such lessons.[35] Other Unitarian ministers encouraged Bostonians to anticipate their mortality throughout the course of their lives and not to rely on a written will for the benevolence required of all good men in recognition of the wealth that God permitted them to accumulate. The textile entrepreneur William Appleton (1786–1862) noted in his journal his sense of "duty to distribute [his] income, which is large, giving religious objects the first thought, and uniting with others in promoting the Arts and Sciences." The Unitarian industrialist Amos Lawrence (1786–1852), acting as "his own executor," decided to keep only one tenth of his income, giving away the rest, thus earning the reputation of "the greatest philanthropist of his age."[36]

In addition to shaping the mind-set of a generation of leaders, themes of cataclysm persisted in works of American literature and art such as the novel *Zenobia; or, The Fall of Palmyra* (1827) by the Unitarian minister William Ware (1797–1852), the story "The Fall of the House of Usher" (1839) by Edgar Allan Poe (1809–1849), and visionary paintings by Washington Allston (1779–1843) and Thomas Cole (1801–1848) in the 1820s and 1830s. James Fenimore Cooper (1789–1851) summarized the philosophy in his novel *The Crater* (1847): "The earth revolves, men are born, live in their time, and die; communities are formed and are dissolved; dynasties appear and disappear; good contends with evil; and evil still has its day; the whole, however, advancing slowly but unerringly towards that great consummation, which was designed from the beginning, and which is as certain to arrive in the end, as that the sun sets at night and rises in the morning."[37] Their fatalism also fed the commemorative impulse. Although the intellectual elite knew Sir Thomas Browne's warning that no one could become immortal in name alone through funerary inscriptions, leading Bostonians wished to leave to posterity material evidence of their social and cultural greatness, their republican principles, and their reputations as citizens who distinguished themselves in service to society. They took heart that their country was yet young, pristine, and bound to endure through a maturation period of indefinite length; but they believed that the United States still would go through the process depicted in Thomas Cole's five-painting series *The Course of Empire* (1833–36), graphically tracing the lifespan of a fictional classical civilization from savage and Arcadian periods to a flourishing of ostentatious high culture and its inevitable destruction. (Figs. 5.9, 5.10.)

Fig. 5.9. Thomas Cole, *Arcadian or Pastoral State*, painting from the five-part series *The Course of Empire*, 1833–1836. Courtesy New-York Historical Society.

Fig. 5.10. Thomas Cole, *Destruction*, painting from the five-part series *The Course of Empire*, 1833–1836. Courtesy New-York Historical Society.

Many Yankee leaders accepted the moral mandate to band together in voluntary associations to develop projects for the common good. On the 1820 bicentennial of the Pilgrims' landing at Plymouth, celebrated with the designation of Plymouth Rock, Daniel Webster (1782–1852), then a Boston lawyer practicing before the U.S. Supreme Court who had recently moved from Portsmouth, New Hampshire, to Boston, chose a similar message acknowledging "a sort of *genius of place*" and elevating local associations to the level of national significance. (Fig. 5.11.) Webster proclaimed that "by ascending to an association with our ancestors, by contemplating their example and studying their character, by partaking [of] their sentiments, and imbibing their spirit, and rejoicing in their successes and triumphs, we seem to belong to their age and to mingle our own existence with theirs. We become their contemporaries." Monuments perpetuated the memories of individuals who built them as well as the subject commemorated. Through monuments, the present generation could experience significant historical events, if only vicariously. Declaring that "a moral and philosophical respect for ancestors elevates the character and improves the heart," Webster urged

Fig. 5.11. Plymouth Rock, dedicated in 1820, with its first cast-iron enclosure. From a stereographic photograph by Kilburn Brothers (Benjamin and Edward, based in Littleton, N.H.), ca. 1867. BMGL.

his generation to consider themselves as "interested and connected . . . through all time, links in the great chain of being." He exhorted his contemporaries to leave "honorable memorials of themselves for the day when they would sleep with the fathers."[38]

Not only did Webster reinterpret the French debate on the "cult of ancestors" he also applied to public life the cult of melancholy which had been imported from England. These were precisely the qualities, public and private, that seemed to him lacking in Boston in 1820. The city's rapid growth and advances in technology had widened the gap between Webster's age and the past. Like many civic and cultural leaders of his era, Webster advised commemorative remedies to stabilize society for the future. As the nation celebrated its semicentennial, it simultaneously mourned the deaths of Adams and Jefferson, which fell on the fiftieth anniversary of independence in 1826. In eulogizing the two Founding Fathers, Webster asserted a bold and unprecedented confidence when he declared that America itself would be their memorial: "Marble columns may, indeed, moulder into dust, time may erase all impress from the crumbling stone, but their fame remains; for with AMERICAN LIBERTY it rose, and with AMERICAN LIBERTY ONLY can it perish."[39] In similar terms, Edward Everett (1794–1865), then a Unitarian minister teaching Greek at Harvard, presiding over belated "funeral solemnities" for Adams and Jefferson at the site of the Battle of Bunker Hill on August 1, 1826, proclaimed: "The faithful marble may preserve their image; the engraven brass may proclaim their worth; but the humblest sod of Independent America, with nothing but the dew drops of the morning to gild it, is a prouder mausoleum than kings and conquerors can boast. The country is their monument. Its independence is their epitaph." He struck a fatalistic note, however, acknowledging that "the contemporary and successive generations of men will disappear. In the long lapse of ages, the Tribes of America, like those of Greece and Rome, may pass away. The fabric of American Freedom, like all things human, however firm and fair, may crumble into dust." But, he concluded, "the cause in which these our Fathers shone is immortal. . . . Their eulogy will be uttered in other languages, when those we speak, like us who speak them, shall be forgotten."[40]

The natural rights of man might be immutable and the righteousness of the American republic confirmed by Providence. Even so, as the nation celebrated having endured half a century, a pressing need was felt for some tangible commemoration of heroes and key events. An awareness of the uses of history was in the air, especially as a counterbalance to escalating and unsettling social changes that worried many. Ralph Waldo Emerson (1803–1882) observed that with industrialization, "a cleavage is occurring in the hitherto firm granite of the past and a new era is nearly arrived."[41] Rapid, perceptible change fed a spirit of restrospection. In Boston, despite recent successes in industrializing the hinterland, uncertainties arose about the city's future as New York, Philadelphia, and Baltimore eclipsed it in prosperity. Some wondered whether their city had not already, according to the anticipated pattern, had its heyday and entered a period of irreversible declension. According to William Tudor Jr., it appeared that "Boston does and must decline," and that other cities would inevitably run away with the "population and capital" of the "Metropolis of New England."[42]

Tudor and his circle of friends were sensitive to criticisms from abroad, such as that of the British essayist Sidney Smith, writing in the *Edinburgh Review*, who urged the commemorative impulse as a way to preserve the republic, for "great men hallow a whole people and lift up all who live in their time."[43] But Tudor wished to redefine greatness in a particularly American way. Holding to the doctrine of original equality that there is no natural ascendancy or subordination, he insisted that the criteria for recognition be based on talent, intellect, achievement, and service rather than on lineage. His personal sense of mission to improve local and national culture, character, and intellect led Tudor to define gentry status in terms of voluntary acceptance of the stewardship of wealth and civic responsibility, traits that became criteria for elite status in Boston. Indeed, his generation worked assiduously to create a sense of history that would serve their purposes, and Whiggish Bostonians led the crusade. Cultivation of the arts and material commemoration were thus justified. In 1813, Josiah Quincy had described the first attachment of the citizen to the nation as a filial affection that transcends death. "There is my fireside; there are the tombs of my ancestors," Quincy declared as proof of his attachment to his hometown. Time and time again, in the 1820s and subsequently, leading Bostonians called upon their fellow citizens to turn funerary commemoration to patriotic purposes.[44]

These were, of course, national questions, but they seemed particularly acute in Boston. It was incorporated as a city in 1822, leaving behind the traditional town form of government, the last vestiges, it seemed, of traditions dating back almost two hundred years, a past longer than that of any other major American urban area. Nathan Hale composed a long meditation on the state of community life in his *Chronicle of Boston and the Book of Retrospections and Anticipations*, bemoaning the lack of material evidence of the past:

> I looked for the monuments [the rich] had erected, either to adorn the age in which they lived, or to humanize the age that was to come.
>
> For . . . "Without memorials of the past men would conceive that their own age was the original and father of all excellence, and thence would be vain and conceited."
>
> In contemplating antiquity . . . the mind itself becomes antique; it contracts from such objects a venerable rust, far preferable to the point and polish of those wits who profane the memorials of former days with ridicule. . . .
>
> Yet how few among the great men of the world have founded their own monuments? Romulus, Alexander, Constantine, Peter, Washington, founded cities, those eternal monuments, which conquest cannot annihilate, nor time impair, but which all generations strengthen, extend, polish, and admire.
>
> But the monuments of the rich men of the city, where are they?[45]

Boston and America might be stronger for the absence of aristocracy; cities might be monuments to their developers; but Hale and others worried that city and the nation would suffer from the lack of monuments traditionally erected by the rich in classical times and more recently in English gardens. In fact, leading colonial families such as the Bowdoins, the Jays, and the Boudinots had been eclipsed economically, culturally, and politically by a new elite on whom fell the new duty of redefining the past through monuments.

The 1830 celebration of the bicentennial of the planting of the Massachusetts Bay Colony added another regional focus to this retrospection. Yankees sought their own historians' perspectives on the sense of mission of the past, intending to adapt it for their own era's needs. Tudor, ever the avid urban booster, insisted that the example of Boston proved the value of a legacy of a principled past and provided ample evidence of its citizens' continuing worth. He concurred with William Ellery Channing's exclamation, "What a monument is a city to the immortal energies of the human mind; and what a witness to man's spiritual destiny." Such men were confident that through voluntary associations meant to create an indigenous high culture, they could truly turn Boston into the "Athens of America," a latter-day "City on a Hill."[46]

The Bunker Hill Monument

The call for private and public monuments arose at a time when the few that already existed seemed destined to fall into decay or oblivion. Old burial grounds were crowded, chaotic, and threatened by legislated displacement and urban development. Only temporary memorials to the Revolution had been erected in Boston. There were no permanent or durable commemorative structures or civil statuary in public places; and open space that might be appropriate for them was rapidly disappearing, owing to congestion and rising land values. Although many lauded the New England tradition and mind, leading Bostonians felt increasingly discontented with the intangibility of their history, especially at a time when their spirit of urban competition was piqued by Baltimore's monuments. This provided the impetus Bostonians needed to plan their own commemorative structures and landscapes. William Tudor Jr. unsuccessfully urged erection of an equestrian statue to Washington in 1816, though he knew that the city had no fitting place then. Although Massachusetts was full of major Revolutionary sites, ideal locations for monuments to commemorate the sacrifices of local heroes and to emphasize the importance of the region in Revolutionary events seemed scarce. Tudor favored hilltop locations that would be visible from a distance, especially from the city. He considered a variety of non-sculptural monuments—pyramids, obelisks, triumphal arches, and columns—finally concluding that "the most ancient, the most durable monument of human labor on the surface of the globe is a tomb!" But burial grounds in the city were completely unsuitable even for accurately marking the graves of notables, let alone for commemorating them with great monuments or mausoleums. Americans also lacked the technological capabilities to quarry the enormous blocks of granite needed for building obelisks or pyramids. Indeed, Tudor acknowledged, "no nation in modern times could have prepared the endless blocks of granite with the nice exactness of their fitting." He still urged construction of a suitable Revolutionary War monument on "an advantageous situation . . . insulated as much as possible from others and not difficult of access." Despite daunting difficulties, Boston's leaders became determined to build just such a major monument.[47]

Another obstacle was the historical controversy that was raging in 1818, pitting a Federalist faction, which credited General Israel Putnam (1718–1790) of Connecticut with leading the Patriots at Bunker Hill, against Republicans, who backed the leadership claims for Colonial William Prescott (1726–1795). Major General Henry Dearborn (1751–1829), who had been a young captain in the battle, led the charge against Putnam, drawing verbal volleys from Colonel Daniel Putnam (1759–1831), the patriot's son. General Henry Alexander Scammell Dearborn (1783–1851) then weighed in on the side of his father and the Republicans, while Daniel Webster, son of a patriot veteran from New Hampshire, joined the memory battle on the side of Putnam and the Federalists, fearing the destabilizing consequences of revisionism as the power of that party was on the wane. Partisans jousted in the *Port-Folio*, the Federalist *Columbian Centinel*, and the Republican *New-England Galaxy* and *Boston Patriot*, as well as the literary *North American Review*. For a time, with the fiftieth anniversary of the battle fast approaching in 1825, it seemed that history was more divisive than unifying.[48]

For these reasons, Tudor's call for a patriotic monument in Boston to rival Baltimore's was not answered for seven years. Finally an appropriate site presented itself. In the spring of 1823, a notice appeared in the *Boston Patriot* newspaper that three acres of land on Breed's Hill in Charlestown would go up for auction. The site, across the mouth of the Charles River from Boston, contained the remains of the patriots' earthen redoubt and breastwork as well as mass graves of about five hundred soldiers from Massachusetts and Connecticut who fell in the Battle of Bunker Hill. Henry A. S. Dearborn protested to the newspaper: "Here repose the ashes of the brave. Let not the glorious sepulchre of our Revolutionary warriors be profaned." He proposed "that some patriotic gentleman of wealth" purchase the site and "have it enclosed with a stone or iron fence, to be held sacred." Dr. John Collins Warren, nephew of Dr. Joseph Warren, who had fallen heroically on the site, purchased the central parcel of land in November 1822.[49] (Fig. 5.12.)

Tudor recognized the need to preserve the entire site of the "American battle of Marathon." Its summit, he thought, was the ideal location for a monument, atop heights commanding a view of the city, the harbor, and the countryside for miles around.[50] Though connected to Boston by a bridge, it remained rural. Tudor and Henry A. S. Dearborn easily mustered support from many of the city's intellectual and financial elite—Edward Everett and George Ticknor of Harvard, Dr. John Collins Warren, Daniel Webster, Judge Joseph Story, and Dr. Bigelow—a coalition of Republicans and Federalists ready to put their squabbles aside to focus simply on commemorating that pivotal event. Colonel Thomas

Fig. 5.12. Portrait of General Henry A. S. Dearborn, a painting, copied by Jane Stuart in the 1850s from the original by her father, Gilbert Stuart, ca. 1827. Courtesy Massachusetts Horticultural Society (hereafter MHORT).

Handasyd Perkins, Boston's "merchant prince," hosted an organizational meeting at his house in May 1823, a few days before taking the issue to the public at the Merchants Exchange.[51]

Dearborn played a central role in the planning. Born in 1783 in Essex, New Hampshire, he was far from provincial. While his father served as Jefferson's secretary of war, young Henry attended William and Mary College. On graduation, he asked the president for a diplomatic post abroad, but Jefferson genially refused, explaining that "no man ought to go to reside for any time abroad under the age of forty, for he would lose his American tastes and ideas . . . and grow incapable of becoming a loyal, useful, and contented citizen at home." The young Henry, determined to become the sort of citizen Jefferson described, took his advice and returned to New England to read law in Salem under Judge Joseph Story, then a Jeffersonian and a friend of John Marshall. During the War of 1812, young Dearborn commanded the defense of Boston's harbor as brigadier general of the militia. He superintended construction of harbor fortifications in Portsmouth, New Hampshire, and was elected commander of the Ancient and Honorable Artillery Company in 1816. After the war, tired of the law, Dearborn developed wide-ranging expertise in civil engineering, architecture, politics, and horticulture. He became a leading member of Boston's new elite and participated in various voluntary associations to bolster local and national culture, especially as vice president of the New England Society for Promotion of Manufactures and Mechanical Arts and as first president of the Massachusetts Horticultural Society. Dearborn was a force to be reckoned with, not only in terms of institutional influence but also for his high style. He was a recognizable figure, driving through the city streets in his stately carriage drawn by a double span of horses with postilion.[52]

In 1823, a group of twenty-six prominent Bostonians, including Dearborn, petitioned the legislature, stating: "As 'the first impulse to the ball of the Revolution' was given in the North; and the plains of Massachusetts were first stained with the blood of patriots,—THERE should be reared the FIRST PILLAR of the Republic." The declaration noted that there were no monuments at Charlestown, Saratoga, Trenton, Monmouth, or Yorktown. "No statue, not even of Washington, adorns the Capital, nor do his ashes reposed under a national tomb." The petition concluded with a nationalistic argument: "If great actions, having for their object the public good; if individuals, renowned for their civil and military virtues, have in all ages, illumined the history and claimed the admiration of nation;—if they have been decreed worthy of the triumphal arch, the column, the temple, or the mausoleum,—what people have had more cause thus to cherish the memory of their statesmen and heroes than those of the United States?[53]

Granting the petition, the General Court chartered the Bunker Hill Monument Association as an eleemosynary corporation to purchase the land and build a monument. At its first meeting, on June 17, 1823, the association elected twenty-five directors. Dearborn solicited members for five dollars each to buy twelve additional acres of the battlefield and to reimburse Dr. Warren for the three he had bought. New Englanders were determined not to let southerners usurp all of the credit for the foundation and preservation of the nation. A circular letter issued in the fall of 1824 soliciting donations argued, "Our fellow-citizens of Baltimore have set a noble example of redeeming the arts to the cause of free institutions in the imposing monuments they have erected. . . . If we cannot be the first to set up a structure of this character, let us not be other than the first to improve upon the example. The group issued a circular letter in July announcing its intention to erect "a simple, majestic lofty and permanent monument, which shall carry down to remote ages a testimony . . . to the heroic virtue and courage of those men who began and achieved the independence of their country." It would display "the names and dates of all the distinguished characters and events which originated in New England." It would be of national importance but also "dedicated to the Revolutionary glory which belongs to this portion of the Union." Edward Everett tried to raise funds nationally, focusing his efforts on obtaining small donations from all classes in neighboring states. By 1825, the association had bought the entire battlefield.[54]

Through 1824, directors of the association and others debated the merits of various monumental forms. Dearborn preferred a large but simple Ionic column as more economical and quicker to build, for he wanted to see it completed in his lifetime. He opposed topping the column with a portrait statue, asserting that the monument "should be purely national" rather than commemorative of any individuals, which would have been controversial. (Although Washington had later assumed command of the Continental Army on Cambridge Common, his name was not mentioned because he was not present at the Battle of Bunker Hill.) Only William Ladd, president of the American Peace Society, proposed a mausoleum, so as not to produce "mortified pride" and increase "hatred and revenge" in the British that might lead to renewed hostilities. A mausoleum could serve as Boston's Westminster Abbey, a place of burial and commemoration for patriots and notables. There, promised Ladd, "an American might meet with an Englishman as a reconciled brother, who might join him in admiration of English principles carried to perfection by descendants of Englishmen." Although the notion of creating a funerary depository for notables did not appeal to the rest of the Bunker Hill Monument Association, it lingered in their minds, eventually giving Dearborn and Bigelow another inspiration for the creation of Mount Auburn Cemetery.[55]

The design competition, announced on January 22, 1825, solicited plans for a granite column about 220 feet tall but promised to remain open to any suggestions. The design committee was composed of Loammi Baldwin, George Ticknor, Samuel Swett, Dr. Bigelow, and the painters Washington Allston and Gilbert Stuart. Allston dissented, remarking that a giant column "would remind him of a peripatetic candlestick. A man's leg . . . though a very handsome support for his body, when cut off, becomes abhorrent."[56] Judge Joseph Story, vice president of the association, as well as Webster and others, preferred the idea of an obelisk. Their taste prevailed.

The design committee awarded a $100 "premium" to sculptor Horatio Greenough (1805–1852) for his wooden model of large-scale obelisk based on the proportions of one at Thebes but larger. Greenough called the obelisk "the most purely *monumental* form of structure," preferable to the column, which rightly stands as part of a building. Many contemporaries agreed, to judge from the number of obelisks used in lieu of slab gravestones in burying grounds. Baldwin had placed a small one atop his family tomb. Immediately after submitting his design with an explanatory essay, Greenough sailed for Europe to study sculpture in Rome. Baldwin (1780–1838), now acclaimed as "the father of civil engineering in America," altered Greenough's design by eliminating the stone platform or plinth intended as a base, surrounded by ranges of twenty steps on all sides, and by enlarging the dimensions of the obelisk's base. (Fig. 5.13.) Greenough, who had proposed the platform

Fig. 5.13. Engraving from the membership certificate of the Bunker Hill Monument Association, ca. 1833, envisioning the structure complete with the entire battlefield preserved. BMGL.

for display of sculpture and related artifacts, complained long-distance that omission of the platform left the monument looking like "a great spire of asparagus springing out of the ground." He never collected his award and did no further work. In the end, the association designated Solomon Willard "Architect and Superintendent," charging him to oversee construction, thus precipitating a controversy over authorship of the design, which, after all, was simple and derivative except in its immense size and provision of an internal circular stairway leading to a viewing platform inside the pyramidal top, which commanded a "glorious and boundless prospect" for 360 degrees around the metropolitan region and out to sea. The monument's simplicity of design was far overshadowed by its scale, so ambitious as to be beyond belief given the lack of materials and technology appropriate for its building.[57]

The cornerstone of the Bunker Hill Monument was laid atop the foundations of the old earthen fort on June 17, 1825, the fiftieth anniversary of the battle, in what George Ticknor (1791–1871), the German-educated Harvard professor of languages and humanities and curriculum reformer, described as "the most solemn ceremonies that have happened since Pericles made his funeral oration in the Ceramicus," referring to the cemetery outside the gates of Athens. A procession from Boston was led by 190 veterans of the battle, followed by dignitaries and tens of thousands of citizens who came from miles around. Alexander Parris (1780–1852) served as "official architect," the title of the presiding officer in the Masonic ceremony. The visiting marquis de Lafayette, French hero of the American Revolution, gave a brief speech. Then, John Pierpont (1785–1866), a popular Unitarian minister with a growing national reputation, read an ode he composed for the occasion emphasizing the funerary significance of the monument:

Here sleeps their dust; 't is holy ground;
And we, the children of the brave,
From the four winds are gathered round,
To lay our offering on their grave.

Bunker Hill Monument would endure for millennia, testifying to the distant future and distant nations about the republican principles on which the United States had been founded and of the prominent role that the city had played in the Revolution. Daniel Webster, by now a congressman on his way to a political career of great national importance, gave the chief oration, urging Bostonians to "cherish every memorial of these worthy ancestors" so as to teach future generations "to venerate their piety." He proclaimed, "Our object is, by this edifice to show our own deep sense of the value and importance of the achievements of our ancestors . . . to keep alive similar sentiments, and to foster a constant regard for the principles of the Revolution." Webster revealed his belief in the familiar cataclysmic model of history. "We wish," he said, "that in those days of disaster which as they come on all nations must be expected to come on us also, desponding patriotism may turn its eyes hitherward and be assured that the foundations of our national power still stand strong."[58]

Such fatalistic yet lofty ideals had impelled the ambitious undertaking of a construction project of a scale and difficulty unprecedented in America to that time. Designated the architect by the association, Solomon Willard (1783–1861) presented the final plan for a 221-foot structure based on the cost estimates of engineer Gridley Bryant (1789–1867), who in 1825 purchased the Quincy quarries twelve miles south of Bunker Hill which would provide the granite for the monument. Bryant paid $250, then sold the quarries to the association for $350. Although Willard offered to donate his services, the association insisted on paying his expenses, at least. Essentially a contractor, Willard, later dubbed "Father of the Granite Industry," and Bryant had to develop new technologies for quarrying and transporting the heavy stone before work could begin in 1827. In the process, Bryant invented what would be known as the Granite Railway, the first railroad in America, pulled by horses, which transported cut stone from the quarries four miles to the shore, where it was loaded on sloops and schooners for the short trip north along the coast to Charlestown. Deliveries averaged six tons each. Colonel Thomas Handasyd Perkins bankrolled the innovative operations.[59]

Construction proceeded at a ploddingly slow pace. Some viewed the incomplete structure as a negative sign, a message of foreboding for the future of the republic. In 1830, when the obelisk still rose only forty feet, "surrounded by the massive stones prepared for the rest lying promiscuously at its base, like a sublime ruin," one pessimistic observer predicted that it would remain "like a broken column, emblematic of a Republic of magnificent promise in its rise, but prematurely dismembered and inglorious in its fall."[60] (Fig. 5.14.) Not all observers were skeptical. In 1836, the diplomat Alexander Hill Everett (1790–1847) envisioned that the monument would stand as evidence of a Golden Age even "when our . . . metropolis and her sister cities shall have had their day of power, prosperity and glory, and passed away; when Boston, New York, and Philadelphia shall have been what Rome, Athens, Memphis, and Babylon at their proudest period never were, and shall have sunk again, in conformity with the immutable law that regulates all human things, into the state of ruin in which those celebrated seats of empire are now; when . . . the hand of Time shall have swept away everything except that simple granite obelisk, which will probably outlast all the structures it is destined to overlook." In that remote future, he predicted, "the friends of liberty and virtue will come up from distant lands," perhaps from "Australasia," in pilgrimage to that monument to the once-great American republic.[61] (Fig. 5.15.)

Lack of funds further slowed the work. The corporation, virtually penniless by 1830, received only meager contributions, a situation complicated by the nation's plunge into hard economic times caused by the Panic of 1837. Finally, a national fund-raising campaign, initiated by Sarah Josepha Hale (1788–1879), editor of the popular magazine *Godey's Lady's Book*, permitted completion of the monument. By 1838, however, it was evident that the association's goal of preserving the entire battlefield as a national historic site would be impossible. The association reluctantly sold ten acres, all except the square block of land immediately around the monument, to developers of domestic real estate. (Fig. 5.16.) The capstone was not put in place until 1843. The cost and difficulties of the project discouraged Bostonians from planning similarly ambitious public monuments for years to come.[62]

Fig. 5.14. Bunker Hill Monument with construction just begun and stalled. Engraving from Caleb H. Snow, *A Geography of Boston* (Boston: Carter & Hendee, 1830).

Fig. 5.15. Bunker Hill Monument with portrait of General Joseph Warren. Engraving from Nathaniel Dearborn, *Boston Notions: Being an Authentic and Concise Account of "That Village," from 1630 to 1847* (Boston: N. Dearborn, sold by W. D. Ticknor & Co., 1848). Nathaniel Dearborn (1786–1852) was one of Boston's major engravers, his publications often reissued in subsequent editions after his death. BMGL.

Fig. 5.16. Bunker Hill Monument completed, with a small plot of property remaining as residential development begins to surround the square, ca. 1845. BMGL.

cial stability by strengthening family cohesion, like the French "cult of ancestors."

Thaddeus William Harris (1795–1856), a gentleman horticulturist and Harvard Librarian, described a historic and commemorative rationale for creating a new kind of funerary landscape, a "rural" cemetery: "Had such a cemetery with prophetic forethought of posterity, been laid out in the settlement of the country, and all our venerated dead—the eminent in church and state—been deposited side by side, with plain but enduring monuments, it would possess already an interest of the most elevated and affecting character." Harris anticipated that "in a Rural Cemetery the names and virtues of the departed would live in perpetual freshness and their souls seem to commune with those who come to do honor to their names." It would become more than a simple, functional burial place. It would attract local and foreign visitors alike, who would come to view monuments honoring "the names and memory of great and good men, whenever or wherever they have died." Harris suggested that his cemetery's summit be "consecrated" to George Washington "by a cenotaph inscribed with his name."[64] In that way, Boston, like Baltimore, would have two patriotic monuments, one commemorating local participation in a war founding the nation and the other honoring the Father of the Country along with other notables. Once a dramatic, hilly site was chosen, General Dearborn, by now Massachusetts Historical Society president, judged its summit "an admirable place for a monument intended to be seen at a distance," the best in the vicinity of the city. The cemetery's founders predicted that "public sentiment will often delight in these tributes of respect, and the place may gradually become the honorary mausoleum for the distinguished sons of Massachusetts."[65]

Dearborn believed that a cemetery, even more than patriotic monuments in public places, should be representative of the highest culture of the city and the nation. All agreed that the abysmal condition of Boston's grave-

Commemoration Turns to the Cemetery Idea

Bostonians' thoughts on memorializing the past turned toward a less ambitious, more personal sort of commemoration, toward projects that might be accomplished more quickly, on a less grandiose scale, and bit by bit as a series of smaller voluntary efforts to celebrate individual merit and inspire historical consciousness. They remained avidly retrospective. As Josiah Quincy, no longer mayor of Boston but now president of Harvard College, observed on the 1830 bicentennial of Boston, the "natural and generous affections of man . . . connect him with ancestry . . . enlarge the sphere of his interests; multiply his motives to virtue; and give intensity to his sense of duty to generations to come, by the perception of obligations to those which are past."[63] Many members of the Bunker Hill Monument Association readily responded to Jacob Bigelow's 1825 appeal to found a cemetery. Henry A. S. Dearborn took a lead in that project through the new Massachusetts Horticultural Society. Appropriately, the topic of the 1832 Harvard commencement address by the graduating student Joseph Stevens Buckminster Thacher was "Respect for Public Monuments, whether Triumphal or for the Dead." Thacher advocated a sort of commemoration that would serve so-

yards indicated only disregard for the past, and that the pressures of urbanization on the limited space of the Shawmut Peninsula made postmortem commemoration impossible in Boston, necessitating an extramural setting, a site outside city limits. Land close to the city, like that in Charlestown, was too valuable to reserve in large parcels for commemorative purposes. In founding Mount Auburn Cemetery on land four miles west of Boston on the Cambridge–Watertown line, Dearborn and his associates chose a site that would not be threatened by rising land values or urbanization for decades. In doing so, they made possible the creation of a vast "commemorative landscape" even larger than that initially proposed for the expanded setting of the Bunker Hill Monument. The new cemetery would be full of complex commemorative structures—public and private—based on precedents from Egyptian and classical times as well as recent experiments in the picturesque, the melancholy interpretive landscapes of England and France. Dearborn made specific reference to "the great Egyptian Cemetery . . . on the farther shore of the Lake Acherusia, near Memphis, ornamented with trees and water-courses, and answering to the Elysian fields of later times," a place produced by the Golden Age of Egypt before the wealthy "sacrificed their true taste for nature to their ambition of splendor."[66] The allusion had a particular local appeal certainly not lost on the Boston elite. Dearborn, the idealist, hoped to make his own era a new Golden Age.

Dearborn and his friends looked to the best of ancient civilizations for models to emulate or recycle in their new Arcadian age. They sought inspiration from the Elysian Fields, where the Greeks "supposed the souls of the virtuous and illustrious retired after death and roamed through bowers, forever green, and over meadows spangled with flowers and refreshed by perennial streams," and from the "rural" Athenian Ceramicus outside the Dipylon Gate. Dearborn suggested that in planning Mount Auburn, Bostonians were compensating for the loss of the entire Bunker Hill battlefield, itself often equated with the Ceramicus, which he described as "a pleasant resort for all who wished to borrow inspiration to noble deeds," a commemorative place where "the illustrious men, who had either died in the service of their country or were thought deserving of the most distinguished honors" were buried. The Ceramicus had been a pastoral "public promenade" for Athenians. There, Plato and his Academy conducted their philosophical discussions. To Bostonians, who named their private library the Athenaeum and dubbed their city "the Athens of America," the analogy bore particular significance.[67] Alexander Everett also cited classical public gardens as models for Bostonians in their quest to fashion a pastoral landscape for burial and commemoration. He referred to the Ceramicus as an exemplary "public garden" and "near the spot appropriated to the sepulchers of distinguished men." (Fig. 5.17.) Aristotle's Lyceum was "another Athenian garden of the same description."[68] This analogy too struck a chord with his fellow Harvard men, who for decades had used "Sweet Auburn," the estate destined to become the new "rural" cemetery, as a retreat in student days. Intent on modeling the new nation and its institutions on such classical examples, the founders chose to preserve, refine, and extend the analogy of place at Sweet Auburn.

As the French visitor Gustave de Beaumont observed after he and Alexis de Tocqueville dined with Alexander Everett and his friends on September 16, 1831, two days after consecration of the new cemetery, Boston's elite were preoccupied with shaping urban aesthetics. As heirs of the Puritans, they wanted their art and architecture to be useful and morally meaningful.[69] Everett hoped that the funeral ground of Mount Auburn, "consecrated to the memory of the patriots and heroes of the Revolution," would be the first of many such institutions and

Fig. 5.17. Imaginary view of the "Academic Grove" or Ceramicus, a place of philosophic study amid funerary monuments in a naturalistic setting, with Athens seen in the distance. Engraving drawn by H. W. Williams, 1839. BMGL.

would inspire the reform of Mount Vernon, with its "central situation in the Union, natural picturesque beauties, and noble position upon the banks of one of the finest rivers in the world." He proposed an imposing monument to George Washington at Mount Vernon similar to the one suggested for Mount Auburn. "Towering majestically above the clumps of trees that adorn the grounds," it would be visible from afar to "citizens as they ascended the river to visit the place." With memorials to other Founding Fathers, Mount Vernon would become "a sort of sacred ground, like the plains of Elis in ancient Greece, where the Olympic games were celebrated.[70] Ralph Waldo Emerson correctly observed in 1836, "Our age is retrospective. It builds the sepulchers of the fathers. It writes biographies, history, criticism."[71]

Planned from the start as a prototype for other commemorative landscapes, Mount Auburn was to be exemplary. Like Boston itself when it was first founded by Puritans, Mount Auburn would be "a City on a Hill" and "one of the chief ornaments of the neighborhood . . . superior in its natural advantages of position to the famous sepulchral grounds of the ancient world," declared Everett. It would "record examples . . . of public and private virtue" that would teach the entire nation. It would become a catalyst for developing "high national spirit," "public virtue," and fine arts worthy of a durable republic.[72] But at the same time, and in the short term, Mount Auburn would help to solve more practical problems of public health, urban land use, cultural differences, and social factionalism evident in the burial controversy of 1823.

6

GRAVE PROBLEMS

Urban Burial Controversies

The burying-place continues to be the most neglected spot in all the region, distinguished from other fields only by its leaning stones and the meanness of its enclosure, without a tree or shrub to take from it the air of utter desolation.

—William B. O. Peabody, "Mount Auburn Cemetery" (1831)

The citizens of this metropolis buried their deceased friends in frequented parts of the city, crowding to the utmost capacity the spaces provided for them, and filling with sepulchres the cellars of their most central churches.

—Dr. Jacob Bigelow, *A History of the Cemetery of Mount Auburn* (1860)

Public health concerns provided one motivation for the creation of Mount Auburn and other "rural" cemeteries but not, as some historians have suggested, the primary one. To be sure, the question of burial reform preoccupied Bostonians and other urbanites in the 1820s and 1830s; but the impulse to improve burial practices and places stemmed as much from changing sensibilities as from fears that burying the dead in the midst of busy cities endangered public health and precipitated epidemics. Throughout the Western world at the time, the spread of genteel tastes and behaviors to ever-larger segments of the population gave rise to new criteria for urban cleanliness and sightliness as well as new definitions of proper ways to treat the dead. Many urbanites became sensitive to an unprecedented degree to the foul smells pervading their environment and began to consider repulsive the garbage and dirt collecting in their streets. Burial reform was only one of many steps taken to improve their cities.

The growing impulse to reform burial practices also reflected new attempts by municipalities to extend their powers over other corporate entities within their geographic limits. Attempts to regulate corporate practices as well as public services supplied by the municipality came about of necessity at a time of crowding within urban boundaries. Cities lacked adequate resources to solve the problems of too rapid growth and the strain it placed on traditional ways of providing services. Voluntary associations often filled the void. The burial controversy that broke out in Boston in 1823 reveals the complexities underlying the reform impulse and illuminates many of the reasons behind the founding in 1831 of Mount Auburn, the nation's first "rural" cemetery.

The tripling of Boston's population in the half century following independence created a number of environmental problems that confronted the first city government, installed in 1822. Little vacant land remained on the Shawmut Peninsula, portions of which were intensively overused. Sanitation and health were matters of growing concern, as were real estate values and the question of the city's appearance. Reform-minded civic leaders disapproved of the narrow, treeless, dirty streets, so unlike the winding rural roads near the country towns from which many of them had only recently moved. They especially focused their attention on the old, chaotic burial grounds, barren pockets of disorder in the bustling city. (Fig. 6.1.)

Filth and pollution of all sorts made cities in that era unpleasant if not downright unhealthy. The Boston Board of Health, created in 1799, had been slowly "correcting the atmosphere" for two decades, with vague authority to regulate the handling of fish and untanned hides, sewers for refuse, privies, harbor dumping, and the depth of graves, in addition to quarantining ships suspected of carrying disease. The board had power "to establish the police of burying grounds, appoint and locate the places where the dead may be buried, and cause the places for the deposit of the dead to be repaired and properly enclosed."[1] Yet the board was subject to political pressures, and, characteristic of most municipal authorities at the time, it took little regulatory action, especially with respect to quarantines, which slowed commerce and interfered with the city's mercantile economy and the prosperity of its new elite. Regulating burials, unlike quarantines, did not conflict with any powerful interest group, however. As a result, the subject received public support, provided that no drastic changes in existing graveyards were proposed.

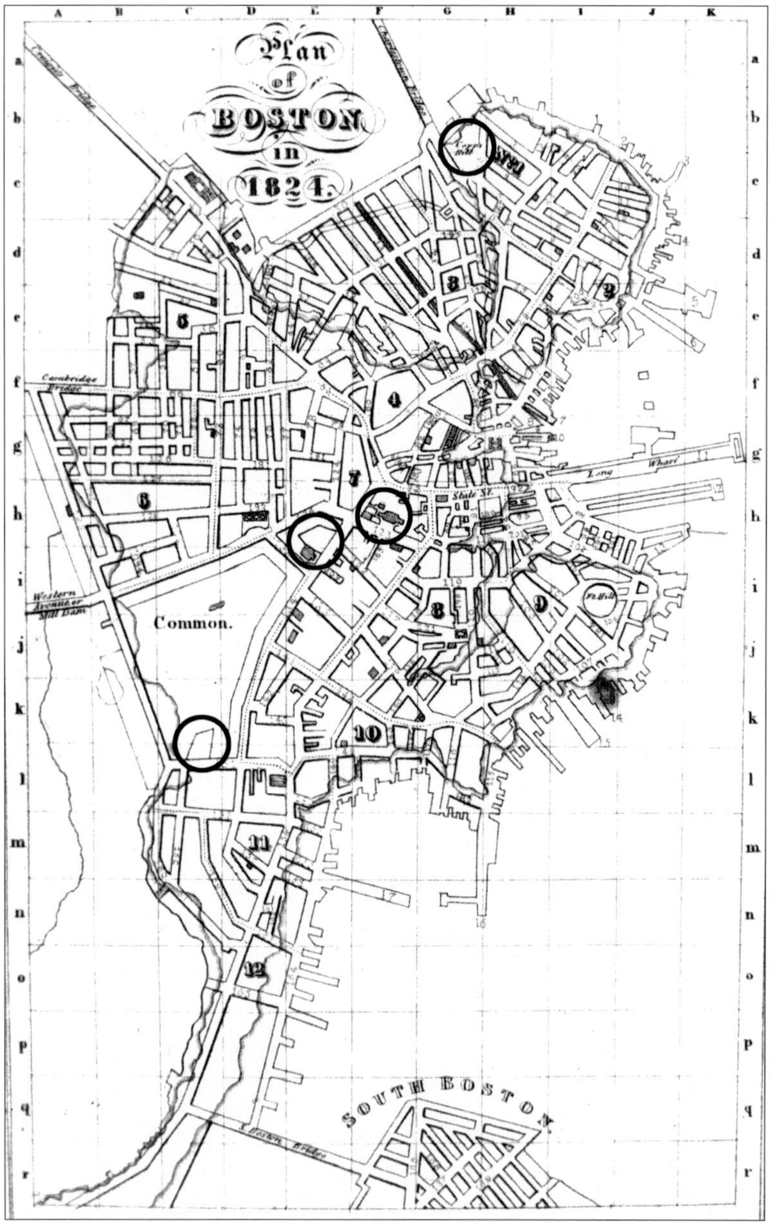

Fig. 6.1. Map of Boston on the Shawmut Peninsula. The locations of the four original burial grounds (circled by the author) are, from top to bottom: Copp's Hill (1660), King's Chapel (1630), the Old Granary (1660), and the Common (1756). Engraving by Abel Bowen, 1824. BMGL.

Bostonians had long been aware that their graveyards posed chronic problems. As early as the 1730s, Boston's first three burial grounds—now King's Chapel, Copp's Hill, and the Old Granary—became so crowded that burials often had to be made four deep or in small, common trenches. (Figs. 6.2, 6.3.) A fourth graveyard was opened on the south end of Boston Common in 1756. Tradition holds that it was the first one used by blacks. There, during the Revolution, the British buried their common soldiers who died in Boston in combat or of disease. By the 1790s, physicians fearful of disease causation advised the town to ban the grazing of cattle in the burial grounds, as was the traditional practice. Water from the Granary Burying Ground flowed onto the Common and thence into the Back Bay and Boston Harbor. Poor drainage increased foul odors and led to further complaints, although Bostonians depended on individual wells for their water supply, and few expressed worries that burials would pollute them. Creation of a fifth graveyard in 1810, South Burying Ground on the Shawmut Peninsula Neck, failed to alleviate the problems. Even with this additional space, Boston's total available land for burials remained under five acres, much of it filled to capacity.

A flurry of public complaints about unsightly, overused burial grounds prompted the Massachusetts General Court in 1810 to honor Boston's request for powers to regulate burials more closely. With new authority, in

Fig. 6.2. King's Chapel Burying Ground, Boston. Engraving from F. W. P. Greenwood, 1833.

Fig. 6.3. Copp's Hill Burying Ground, Boston. Engraving from Bridgman, 1851.

Fig. 6.4. Old family tombs in Old Granary Burying Ground, Boston. Photograph by BMGL, 2006.

1811 the town ordered disinterment of many old burials to gain space for new ones. The action was not unprecedented in light of the regular dissolution of graveyards in other cities whenever centrally located land was needed for construction. Yet the idea of desecrating the graves of their forebears greatly offended some Bostonians and was not easily forgotten. Ironically, Bostonians, who showed little concern about identifying the precise resting places of many heroes of the Revolution, nevertheless reacted with strong emotions to the threat of displacing the community of the dead. A decade later, a disgruntled citizen wrote to the *Boston Patriot and Mercantile Adviser* of his lingering animosity over the plan to move the "mouldering bones of our ancestry respected by all nations, civilized and savage, from the long silence of the tomb for some pitiful object of economy."[2] Some Bostonians even cited this issue as justification for their opposition in 1822 to abandoning town government for a city charter, feeling that they could not trust elected officials.

Overcrowding had forced the town to ban burials in individual graves in 1816. Within two years, unmarked graves, four deep, had taken up the remaining space in the Granary Burying Ground, with not all burials related. Bits of old coffins and bones regularly turned up when new burials were made in common or family tombs, many of them vertical brick-lined shafts. (Fig. 6.4.) The Board of Health permitted construction of a few more tombs as late as 1823. An inventory a decade later found that the King's Chapel yard had about 80 of these narrow, subterranean structures; Copp's Hill had 226, with one for infants erected by the town; and the new Neck Burying Ground had 172. By 1823, alderman Stephen Hooper found that even these were nearly filled, despite the compacting of remains. As he told Dr. John Collins Warren, "the question must soon by met by us or some other counsel which will not shrink from its responsibility, whether new and extensive places of deposit shall be opened within or without the city."[3]

Many Bostonians remained reluctant to bury their dead far from their homes and the center of town. They did not support the creation of new burial places distant from around-the-clock public scrutiny. The new South Burying Ground, set on damp, marshy land of the "Neck" leading off the Shawmut Peninsula, contained primarily the graves of the poorer classes, including paupers from the Alms House and the House of Industry. It was further considered undesirable because the public gallows were located there, and it was surrounded by dirty industries—candle manufacturers, slaughterhouses, and rope makers. Furthermore, its peripheral location made it subject to periodic violations by grave robbers who removed individual bodies or vandals who ransacked the graves. Outbreaks of such incidents in 1822 and 1829 shocked the public. The regularity of body snatching led health commissioners in 1823 to offer a $500 reward for information concerning the "resurrection men" who provided physicians with a constant supply of cadavers for their anatomical research and teaching.[4]

This concern for the security and permanency of burials was new. Bostonians had tacitly accepted the fact that when a family died out, its tomb would probably be given or sold to another family. They regularly heard of unscrupulous gravediggers who "speculated in tombs," erasing family names on markers, emptying vaults of their contents at night, or compacting remains in order to resell the entire space to a new family or to bury dead strangers, charging from eight to twelve dollars for each.[5] Such corruption added to the chaos that resulted from the lack of general maintenance and persistent depredations. Until the 1820s, most Bostonians took for granted that their burial grounds would be places of horror—horrors created by the living. For instance, urban lore held that despite elaborate obsequies for Governor John Hancock (1737–1793), following his lying in state for eight days, vandals severed the Founding Father's arm the night of his interment in the Old Granary. Vagrants occasionally took shelter in tombs and harassed passersby. Such remained the status quo until changing sensibilities led to unprecedented demands for assurances of permanency of burials and for more pleasant burial places conducive to commemoration and even to ornamentation of the city center.

Crisis in New York

From periodic reports in their newspapers, Bostonians knew that other cities faced even greater problems. Boston escaped many of the epidemic diseases that sporadically ravaged major mercantile cities along the Atlantic coast and were often attributed to "miasmas" or foul air near burial grounds. New Yorkers traced their recurrent epidemics to the area near the overcrowded Trinity Churchyard. (Fig. 6.5.) A New York Board of Health study in 1806 determined the "malignant epidemic fever" to be greatest in that neighborhood, where "a vast mass of decaying animal matter produced by the superstition of interring dead bodies near the churches, and which has been accumulating for a long lapse of time, is now deposited in many of the most populous parts of the city." The board, concluding that it was "impossible that such a quantity of these animal remains should continue to be inoffensive and safe," recommended prohibition of future burials in the city. Rather than proposing dissolution of existing churchyards, however, board members suggested that old burial places "might serve extremely well for plantations of grove and forest trees, useful and ornamental to the city." Plantings would cleanse the soil, hasten natural decomposition of corpses, and purify the air.[6] With the exception of New Haven's New Burying Ground (1796), however, there were few precedents for plantings in urban graveyards, and New York failed to implement these recommendations. City authorities ignored the report and continued to permit churches to extend crypts and tombs, even under streets.

Late in the summer of 1822, Bostonians read that yet another epidemic had rendered New York a "desolate city," resembling "a place afflicted with the panic, confusions and disorder of a siege." New York's "magnificent edifices" looked "like painted sepulchres; the spirit of life and gaiety had departed." While the rich fled

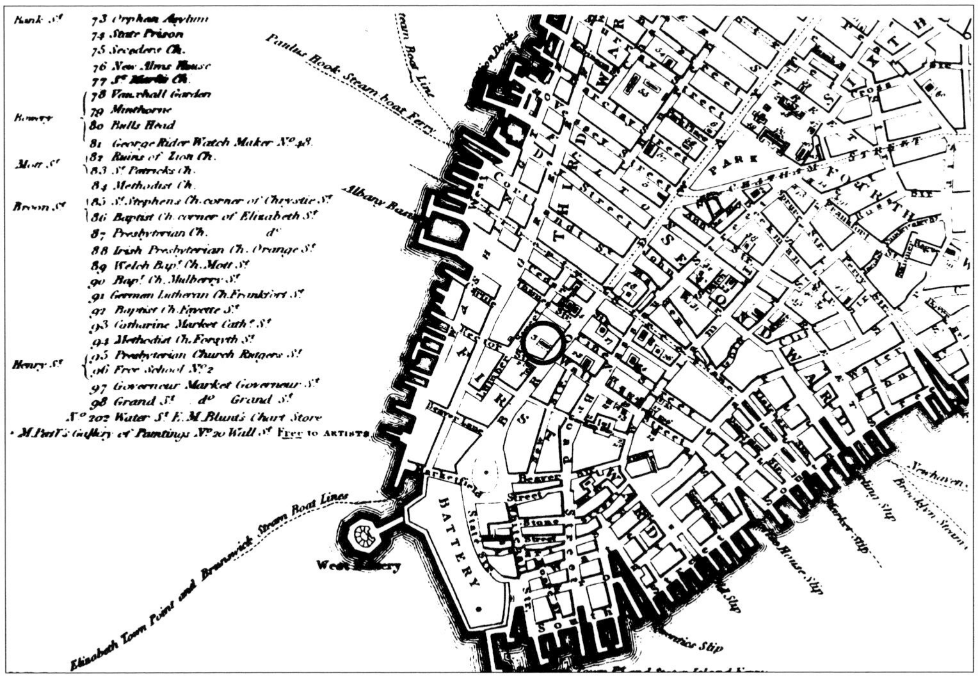

Fig. 6.5. New York City map, ca. 1820, showing the location of Trinity Churchyard on Broadway at the head of Wall Street (circle added by the author). BMGL.

north from the city center near Manhattan's southern tip to the "little village of Greenwich" to breathe fresh, rural air, the poor had no choice but to stay and take their chances with the fever in the polluted atmosphere.[7]

The New York publisher Francis D. Allen wrote a pamphlet, *Documents and Facts, Showing the Fatal Effects of Interment in Populous Cities*, blaming the epidemic on the graveyards. He cited European examples to prove the deleterious effects of burying the dead in the midst of cities and urged removal of all burials to extramural sites, citing French burial reform. Allen knew that the American urban public would be slow to accept the idea of suburban graveyards, despite growing fears and frequent outbreaks of epidemic disease. "There are many whose feelings would revolt at the idea of taking their kindred and friends to a general cemetery three or four miles from the city," he wrote. That was the fate of the poor consigned to a potter's field. Proximity to the deceased's family community had taken on a similar, if secularized, importance in the American mind to burial near the church altar in High Church cultures.[8] Such old patterns and preferences, however, were becoming anachronistic in rapidly growing cities like New York and Boston in the 1820s, as people began to separate home from the place of work and to draw greater distinctions between the public and private spheres of life. No longer did tolling bells summon the entire community to accompany bereaved family members on foot from their home to bury their dead in the graveyard. Bells might still be tolled at the expense of the state; but unless the deceased was notable, funerals were no longer public events. Such a tradition conflicted with the new pace of urban life. Urbanites were no longer expected to draw valuable lessons of moral philosophy as they heedlessly hurried past burial grounds. Hence, Allen discounted the notion "that grave-yards within the city are absolutely necessary as mementos to the living."[9]

Allen published Dr. Samuel Akerly's opinion that Trinity Churchyard was "a great cause" of the yellow fever ravaging the city in 1822. Akerly (1785–1845), one of the city's most eminent physicians, advised the New York Board of Health that "an impure state of the atmosphere, caused by these and other masses of putrid matter greatly aggravates the malignity of the disease where it exists." In use since 1698, Trinity contained almost 120,000 bodies, some in graves less than two feet deep. The stench of decay was obvious for blocks around. Many New Yorkers, if not all medical professionals, agreed with Akerly that there were real dangers associated with such "noxious effluvia."[10]

Uncertainty about disease causation complicated the response of physicians and the public to problems of urban sanitation and burial reform. Most physicians were aware at the time that smallpox, measles, and other diseases causing skin eruptions were contagious. Yet anticontagionist theories maintained that those diseases were exceptions to the rule. The belief was that miasma or foul air engendered diseases, especially those involving fevers. Dr. Benjamin Rush (1746–1813) of Philadelphia had been a vocal miasmatist, and his influence on American medical opinion was great. Boston physicians attributed the "bilious remittent fever" that ravaged the southern portion of their city in 1796 to miasmas. Self-interest impelled business leaders in mercantile cities to favor such anticontagionist theories. Quarantines, the contagionist device for stemming the spread of disease, interfered with the free flow of trade. Cleaning up the urban environment, as advocated by the anticontagionists, was less costly and at the same time increased real estate values and appealed to new sensibilities offended by foul smells and visible filth. The medical historian Erwin Ackerknecht rightly observes that "powerful social and political factors" colored the scientific discussion of disease causation. The public debate over the sources of effluvia and the sorts of ills engendered by miasma reflected religious, intellectual, and economic concerns as well.[11]

When Akerly urged burial reform in New York, therefore, his arguments were more economic than medical. He warned New Yorkers that property around churchyards would be "greatly injured and depreciated unless something effectual" was done to correct the overcrowding. The shift of opinion in the medical community was again evident after the City Council passed a law in March 1823 banning burials south of Canal Street under penalty of a $250 fine. Dr. David Hosack (1769–1835), professor of materia medica at Columbia College of Physicians and Surgeons and head of the medical faculty of Rutgers College, collected signatures from 130 local physicians petitioning that the law be rescinded in the name of property rights. Churches took the city to court in 1825 for infringing on their corporate property, but the New York State Supreme Court upheld the legality of the ordinance in 1827. Some New Yorkers boasted that their city was in the vanguard of a burial reform movement soon to be followed in other major cities. Bostonians, however, handled the matter of reform quite differently.[12]

Boston's Burial Controversy

Since no major epidemics had recently struck Boston to raise questions of the association of disease, miasmas, and burials, Bostonians' interest in burial reform centered instead on issues of space and aesthetics. The Boston burial controversy began in December 1822, when directors of the new Saint Paul's Episcopal Church (1818) petitioned Boston's first City Council for "leave to erect tombs"—that is, crypts in the church basement—and for that cellar to be "recognized as a public cemetery." A committee appointed by councilmen to study the matter readily approved the proposal, provided that the City Council direct construction and retain perpetual control over the condition of the crypts. Alderman Ephraim Eliot, a druggist soon to become first president of the Massachusetts College of Pharmacy (1823), declared that such burials could cause "no possible injury to the public health," that "no other mode, in common use, is more secure and less objectionable." Eliot quoted the authority of eight prominent local physicians that "decomposition of animal substances neither generates infection nor produces diseases." Furthermore, he noted that tomb burial had long been practiced in King's Chapel and at the Episcopalian Trinity and Christ churches with "no evil results." The Board of Health and its president, Benjamin Whitman, remained silent on the issue, thus lending tacit support to approving the crypts.[13]

It was religious factionalism rather than public health that emerged as the main issue of public concern in the controversy following Saint Paul's receipt of approval for crypts. Denominationalism had been increasing in Boston for several decades, inserting a new element of discord into many civic discussions. Until the 1820s, most Bostonians harbored an antipathy toward the Church of England which they had inherited from the Puritans, heightened by the attempted late-seventeenth-century imposition of Anglicanism on them along with revocation of the Puritans' charter for the Commonwealth of Massachusetts. Since the days of Sir Edmund Andros's tyrannical governance over the Dominion of New England from 1686 to 1689 and, more recently, the Revolutionary-era debates over the appointment of American bishops in the episcopacy, many Bostonians despised that denomination as aristocratic, papist, corrupt, and, worse yet, an agency for exerting control over them and their affairs. Many, especially Unitarians, who rejected dogma and sectarianism, feared that the establishment of Saint Paul's in 1819 signaled the beginning of a new British attempt to impose Toryism and High Church practices. The noted journalist and publisher Joseph T. Buckingham (1779–1860), a Freemason and Unitarian, outspoken editor of the *New-England Galaxy*, one of the nation's earliest weekly newspapers, articulated the region's traditional antipathy to Episcopalianism, writing, "We have long looked upon the English form of worship as at variance with our republican institutions and repugnant to the views and feelings of our forefathers."[14]

Members of the new congregation of Saint Paul's came almost exclusively from the town's new social, economic, professional, political, and cultural elite, including Daniel Webster, George Sullivan, David Sears, and William Shimmin. Some local critics accused Saint Paul's of being a "movement on the part of men of wealth and prominence in the community to build a costly and impressive church building." Major subscribers for the building fund included Dr. John Collins Warren, Harrison Gray Otis, William Tudor, Stephen and Henry Codman, William and Samuel Appleton, and Lucius M. Sargent. Parishioners, however, proclaimed it the beginning of a new era, as "men from the Orthodox, Unitarian, and Episcopal churches banded together to build a Church that would be of historic order but modern in spirit; of English inheritance, but American in character."[15]

The cornerstone of Saint Paul's was laid in September 1819, and the completed edifice was consecrated the following June. Its architect, Alexander Parris (1780–1852), assisted by Solomon Willard (1783–1861), designed the church in the form of an Ionic Greek temple. It occupied a prime site, which alone cost $18,000, on Tremont Street near the corner of Boston Common, less than a block from the Granary Burying Ground, and close to the new homes of many of its members on Beacon Hill. The *Boston Intelligencer and Evening Gazette* declared that "the whole design indicates the origin of a new taste among us by which high and uncouth steeples erected upon low buildings in bad proportions, will be abandoned,—and a purer ideal of architectural beauty will be introduced." The local historian Caleb H. Snow praised the project in 1825 as "the commencement of an era of art in Boston" and predicted that the new church would have "a sensible influence on taste in architecture."[16]

The builders of Saint Paul's spared no expense. (Fig. 6.6.) The congregation budgeted a generous $50,000; but when the structure alone cost $83,000 and total expenditures reached over $100,000, the congregation

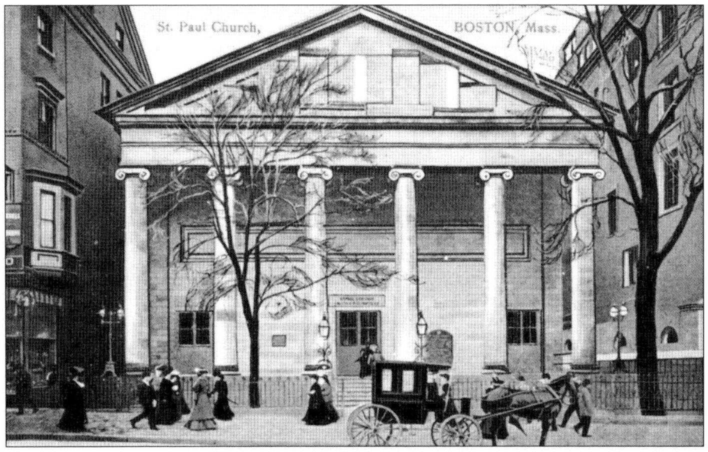

Fig. 6.6. Saint Paul's Church, Boston. Postcard, ca. 1900. BMGL.

found itself in debt for over half that amount, an astronomical figure, considering that the entire town budget in 1820 was only $150,000.[17] Dr. John Collins Warren (1778–1856), a surgeon, anatomical specialist, and Harvard professor (in 1811 he founded the Massachusetts General Hospital with Dr. James Jackson) who was approaching the zenith of his medical career and social leadership, joined Saint Paul's in 1820. Serving as both vestryman and senior warden for the new congregation, he tackled its high initial debt. It was Warren who decided to alleviate the congregation's financial difficulties by building and selling forty-seven family tombs in the church's cellar. At the same time, sales would help defray building costs and the crypts would also provide a secure and dignified place of burial for Boston's elite, who might not own family tombs in the burying grounds. Warren favored church burials, traditional in Anglicanism for the elite, although the form was one against which the founders of Massachusetts had deliberately reacted in creating common, secular graveyards situated away from meetinghouses. Although some previous examples of crypt burials existed, they certainly were not central to the Boston tradition.[18]

Even before the City Council voted to approve Saint Paul's crypts, the Federalist *Columbian Centinel* observed that the issue had "excited some interest."[19] A number of Boston newspapers covered the controversy as a question of public health. The Republican *Boston Patriot and Daily Mercantile Advertiser* explicitly condemned church "cemeteries," meaning crypts, and churchyard burials in general, as conducive to disease: "A very fertile and reprehensible source of poisonous vapours contaminating the air is that of Church-yards in the middle of populous towns. The practice of depositing dead bodies in Churches is still more liable to censure, as this forms a constant source of putrid vapours, however imperceptible, which cannot fail to prove greatly destructive to health." Journalists sought to convince Bostonians that all urban burials posed health problems, yet no one seemed ready to ban them entirely. Indeed, the burial controversy became mainly an exercise in rhetoric, with issues defined primarily in religious and political rather than medical terms. Medical opinions were invoked only to strengthen other arguments about crypts.[20]

The fear that miasmas from burials might cause epidemic disease was only one of many powerful arguments mustered against Saint Paul's crypts. Joseph T. Buckingham, who oriented his Republican *New-England Galaxy* toward laborers and the "middling sort," launched a vehement journalistic crusade against the City Council's support of Saint Paul's petition. Emphasizing the traditional Yankee condemnation of the "ignorance and bigotry" underlying belief in the sacredness of church burials, he challenged proponents to show where the Bible stated "that there is anything sacred in stones and mortar, or that one piece of ground is more holy than another." He warned that they would ultimately find the cellars of their churches to be, on the contrary, "the most dreadful of temporal curses." Buckingham called on "the common sense of the community" to reject church burials, adding, "We have long looked upon the English form of worship as at varians with our republican institutions and repugnant to the views and feelings of our forefathers." For him, Episcopalianism in general and the crypts in particular represented "undue attachment to a foreign nation and a haughty and aristocratic spirit"; he concluded that "the quicker we get rid of them the better." Buckingham pitted his era's nascent egalitarianism against the creation of new marks of privilege, charging that "a more impudent and high-handed attempt to affect the selfish purposes of a purse-proud and obstinate aristocracy at the expense of the comfort, convenience, health, and even lives, of the whole city, is not on record."[21] His sensationalistic effort to stir public opinion against church crypts relied heavily on anti-elitist humor. Buckingham printed one long piece of doggerel lampooning the wealthy churches. In part, it read:

Not many years ago, (as it is well known,)
Some "meek and lowly" men wishing to hear
The gospel *preached unto themselves, alone,*
From the vulgar, (so it would appear,)
Did build a costly *house to make each pew*
Come high as possible—for seats so dear
Could not be purchased by the poor, they knew—
Beside, they had no gallery, *for fear*
That low and vulgar herd should creep in there.

And when the HOUSE *was* dedicated, *they*
Would let none in without a ticket*; well,*
Not satisfied with having their own way
In worshipping alone, in their stone shell,
They now *do "want the liberty," they say,*
"Of building TOMBS *in it!—No—not to* sell,
They wish to SLEEP *alone, as well as pray:*
Perhaps it yet *may be our lot to tell*
They have engaged a private *room in* ———

Their petition might be granted, (as
'Twas doubtful) they did get eight learned men
To say, "that every catching *fever" had*
Been caused by "putrid vegetables*!" Then*
The common-council did decide it best
To grant them their request, "for," say they "when
They rot their smell *no* FEVER *can molest;*
For butchers, too have ever *been*
Snuffing such scents, *and they are* healthy *men!*

. . . .

But sure, in mercy, we've already got
Enough of burying grounds *beside the* MALL*;*
There's not a mortal walks there now, but what
He grasps his nose with all his might; nor shall
The greatest snuff-taker *that ever had*
A stuffed-up snout step on the common, and
Not grow quite sick—the stench is now *so bad*
None but a Council-man unmoved *can stand*
Upon that PUBLICK WALK—THE CITY'S LAND*!*

Therefore, I hope ST. PAUL'S *will not be made*
A Tomb, *though, I must say, I always thought*
It looked like one—but then I was afraid
To go and see if 'twas,*—besides I sought*
Not to creep in a place I should not go,
(Having no ticket, *for none could be bought).*

Apropos*: when the* tombs *are built d'ye know*
If TICKETS *will admit the* dead*? They ought—*
For then each DEAD intruder *will be caught.*[22]

Democratic leanings played a stronger role in Buckingham's opposition to the crypts than did any other concern, and he repeatedly stressed that issue in his own editorials as well as in poems and articles he reprinted from other periodicals. He selected one item for a March 1823 issue of the *New-England Galaxy* addressing the question "What is death?":

'Tis to be free! . . .
To join the great equality;
All alike are humbled there!
The mighty grave
Wraps Lord and slave;
Nor pride nor poverty dare come
Within that refuge-house, the tomb![23]

Buckingham even suggested that bribes had bought the favorable vote of the aldermen authorizing "the location of charnel-houses and reservoirs of filth, corruption, rotten carcasses, plague and yellow fever, in the neighborhood of that spot consecrated to the goodness of health [the fifty-acre Common and the tree-lined promenade of its Great Mall],—the only spot in the city where all classes may meet on terms of equality."[24] (Fig. 6.7.) He credited "the industry, prudence and firmness" of the old town's Board of Health with keeping Boston free for over twenty years from the epidemics that devastated other American cities, making Boston an asylum with "pure and healthful atmosphere." Buckingham was exaggerating. Boston literally lay under tons of filth that had to be removed by the wagonload from the streets during Mayor Quincy's administration. It was true, however, that yellow fever and cholera had not been the scourge in Boston that they were in New York and Philadelphia. Yet Buckingham generally favored traditional ways of doing things and opposed what he saw as rampant changes under the new city government.[25] He predicted that permitting Saint Paul's to build tombs would precipitate other requests for church burials, leaving Bostonians "fugitives compelled to desert their homes and fly from a pestilence of their own creation" or forcing them "to snuff up the effluvia of rotting carcasses when they take their morning promenades and inhale the pestiferous odour of animal putrefaction with every breeze," turning the city into a "congregation of tombs and charnel-houses."[26] He appealed to growing urban pride to oppose such crypts.

Buckingham was right that Saint Paul's petition would not be the last. Leaders of other churches quickly realized the economic benefits of crypt burials. The Prudential Committee of the Park Street Church proposed selling crypts to reduce its debt in 1822. Congregational-

Fig. 6.7. Boston Common Mall or shaded "publick walk." From a stereograph by American Views, ca. 1860. BMGL.

Fig. 6.8. Park Street Church, adjacent to the Old Granary Burying Ground on Tremont Street. Postcard, ca. 1900. The Egyptian gateway to the graveyard was added in 1840 by the architect Isaiah Rogers. BMGL.

ists had built the Georgian church in 1809. (Fig. 6.8.) As early as 1816, fund-raisers considered erecting tombs beneath it to produce revenue. Although many of the vaults in the Old Granary Burial Ground were virtually in the basement of the church, which was built over part of the old graveyard, the congregation did not petition to build their own crypts inside until Saint Paul's set the precedent. Leaders of the Park Street Church then argued that crypt burial was "not an uncommon practice by religious societies of the day." Furthermore, since their cellar was "large and deep," crypt burials would not differ greatly from burials in family tombs in the adjacent burial ground. Church spokesmen denied any potential danger to public health and insisted that church cellars were standard repositories for the dead in all Christian nations.[27] The City Council permitted the Park Street Church to erect a range of tombs on each side of its cellar, provided that the foundation not be injured; but the Board of Aldermen rejected a proposed "strangers' tomb" there for travelers who died while in Boston. This second issue intensified public controversy over Boston's burials. The Unitarian Buckingham's dislike for the orthodox Congregationalists, as much as his antipathy toward Episcopalians, tinged his rhetoric against the place already dubbed "Brimstone Corner." He even suggested that some civic-spirited Bostonian might resort to arson: "Fire, mingled with a suitable portion of refined flour of sulphur," he wrote, would be capable of settling the matter by disposing once and for all the bodies of the dead in that church cellar.[28]

To keep the debate alive in order to sell newspapers, Buckingham reprinted articles from the British press critical of church crypt burials. One traveler's account of a Dublin church condemned curiosity seekers who invaded the privacy of the dead on tours guided by a disrespectful sexton. "It is a poor privilege," the visitor concluded, "to hold together for a century or so until your coffin tumbles in about your ears, and then to reappear, half skeleton, half mummy, exposed to the gazes of a generation that can know nothing of your name and character." Such "indignities" he found scarcely less "humiliating" than being "hung up in dissecting rooms," an argument with particular meaning for those concerned about the theft of bodies snatched from graves for anatomical study. Buckingham also published articles with an edge of religious criticism appealing to heirs of Puritans who remained contemptuous of Catholic display and veneration of saints' relics. Others appealed to newer sensibilities that recoiled from the medieval depiction of death and the display of cadavers, mummies, skeletons, and skulls.[29]

Buckingham mustered some opposition to crypt burials. But Bostonians were becoming increasingly tolerant of religious diversity, exemplified by the proliferation of ecclesiastical structures built by various denominations. Boston's first mayor, John Philips, as well as the aldermen and the City Council, were not prepared to rescind their permission for the Episcopalians or Congregationalists to build church crypts. When Josiah Quincy (1772–1864) became mayor in May 1823, however, Buckingham found a new champion for opposition to crypt burials. Mayor Quincy asserted his intention to improve the "health, security, and cleanliness" of Boston and to run an active administration that would define and extend municipal powers. In his inaugural address he proclaimed, especially to those with "restricted fortunes," that he would use his executive authority to improve public health: "The rich can fly from the generated pestilence. The sons of fortune can seek refuge in purer atmosphere. But necessity condemns the poor to remain and inhale the noxious effluvia." The problem of urban burials was one of many issues Quincy tackled. He urged preventive measures, declaring it "not sufficient that the law, in its due process, will ultimately remedy every injury and remove every nuisance." For Quincy, "the criterion of an efficient government is that [nuisances] should be removed before complaint and without complaint." His motto was "Prevention should be the object of solicitude, not remedy."[30]

Throughout his mayoral tenure, Quincy stood on the side of Boston's mercantile interests. He became known as the "Great Mayor" owing to his innovative program of city planning and municipal management. His concern with burial reform was part of a larger program that included cleaning the streets, improving the antiquated sewerage system, initiating a city water supply, and creating new market facilities. A consummate politician, he enjoyed the wholehearted support of leading Bostonians of various classes, including Buckingham, advocate of the "middling sort," as well as William Tudor, spokesman for the cultural elite. To all of them the mayor represented the forces of modernization in the new city government. He emphasized "efficiency" and was instrumental in rationalizing the procedures and authority of the municipal corporation and in imposing its authority over other corporations—schools, churches, and businesses. Those that would not conform to new regulations were asked to relocate beyond Boston's corporate boundaries. Because of his own extensive speculation in Boston real estate, Quincy had a vested interest in improving the environment. He made sure that porches of churches did not infringe on new public sidewalks, that privies did not drain into the streets, and that crypt burials did not emit foul smells that would be noticeable on the Common.

Quincy was familiar with New York's burial controversy, for his wife, Eliza Susan Morton, came from a mercantile family there. He concurred with Tudor's opinion that "it is solemn to place the remains of our friends within that sacred temple dedicated to God; it is affecting to offer our devotions, surrounded by the graves of those we have loved; but in great cities, it becomes as noxious to the living as it is useless to the dead." Urban cemeteries "must in time become so heaped up with the spoils of mortality as to require removal to prevent pestilence." Ultimately, a clean city and issues of public health mattered more than the rights of religious institutions to determine their own individual burial places and practices.[31] In Tudor and others of similar mind, he had the support of a major faction of Boston's elite in his crusade to reform the burial system.

For Quincy, the first order of business was to try to undo the "dangerous precedent" set by the first city administration in permitting crypts, given that more churches would try to take advantage of the precedent, "considering the pecuniary advantage." Indeed, on June 4, 1823, the mayor received a third petition for a crypt permit from proprietors of the Bromfield Street Methodist Episcopal Church. Quincy knew that to reverse permissions already granted would be difficult if not legally impossible. Prominent members of Saint Paul's and the Park Street Church still held influential positions in city government and could argue that their crypts were already in use. Nonetheless, on June 25, Quincy ordered a complete investigation of all urban burials and charged the City Council to present a report "on the expediency of prohibiting or limiting the erection of any New Cemeteries or tombs within the precincts of the city." To ensure that it would not bow to special interests, Quincy chaired the committee.[32]

Boston Debates Burial Reform

One physician supported Quincy's decision to scrutinize all urban burials. On July 4, 1823, Buckingham enthusiastically reported publication of a pamphlet dedicated to the mayor that would surely "have a tendency to counteract the pernicious effects of our late city council." In his *Remarks on the Dangers and Duties of Sepulture*, the fortuitously named Dr. John Gorham Coffin (1769–1829) argued against urban interments in a moderate, rational tone. He signed the pamphlet simply "A Fellow of the Massachusetts Medical Society," attesting to his character, reputation, and knowledgeable authority, which he pitted against those of the eight Boston physicians who supported crypt burials, discounting the dangers of miasma. Coffin distinguished himself from the other local physicians by his long crusade on behalf of preventive medicine of all sorts. Like so many members of the city's new elite, he was a relative newcomer from Essex County, north of Boston. He shared Quincy's interest in the welfare of the underprivileged and made recommendations for constructive action to create an urban environment conducive to public health. Both Coffin and Quincy, along with the young Dr. Jacob Bigelow (1787–1879), preferred the preventive approach over dramatic actions and "heroic" cures at the point of medical crisis—the standard bleedings, purgings, and quarantines of the day.[33]

By synthesizing various arguments against urban burials, Coffin's pamphlet emphasized anti-contagionist and miasmatist views, drawing heavily on the experience of France to condemn the role of animal putrefaction in fostering disease. Coffin reprinted portions of Francis D. Allen's pamphlet suggesting that "morbific exhalations" from New York's Trinity Churchyard created conditions in which fevers repeatedly ravaged the city. Addressing burial crypts under Boston churches, Coffin cautioned that although they might be "harmless while they remained without being moved," there was no telling what would happen if a churchyard located "amidst the revolutions of a busy population" were disturbed by increasing urban activity or natural disaster. Like Buckingham, Coffin played on new sensibilities as well as old hostilities to the idea of moving existing graves. "It is not long indeed," he remarked, "since we have seen in this populous city, the mangled remains of the dead transported from one burying-ground into the other. We have also seen two church-yards opened, and deeply broken on extensive spaces, leaving exposed to our reluctant and pensive curiosity, shattered limbs of corpses and their decayed coffins, till they were closed again by a range of brick vaults."[34] Americans began to reject for themselves such sights, which were commonplace in London and Paris.

As an alternative to urban burials, Coffin advocated creating a "rural" burial place. Following New Haven's example, Bostonians might transfer remains and gravestones from the city's center to a suburban location, whose grounds would be extensive enough to permit only single burials in harmony with the natural process of decay. Using shrouds that readily decomposed would hasten the process. As in Europe, after a fixed interval of time bones could then be disinterred and the grave reused. Coffin proposed a ban on all burials in family tombs, vaults, and even coffins—anything that separated the body from the surrounding earth and unnaturally inhibited decay. He considered multiple burials a "pernicious custom" since vaults had to be reopened for additions before "the time prescribed" for decomposition of previous burials. Coffin anticipated opposition from those whose religious views held that the dead would rise intact on Judgment Day and thus wished to preserve the corpse in the tomb or grave. "If the perished body is to be restored, it must be done by an act of creative power," he argued. "To believe that human intervention is to have any influence in the case, is to suppose that human agency can interfere with the purposes of the Almighty."[35]

The physician advocated naturalism and simplicity as essentially American, democratic, and anti-aristocratic, and his ideal burial landscape reflected these principles. The graves, set amid "the simplicity of nature," would be "eloquent" in teaching lessons to the living. Death was the great equalizer, the ultimate democrat, more evident in the common grave than in the "haughty" tomb, symbol of artificial status. Coffin closely followed the work of French theorists on burial reform, for whom pollution was figurative as well as real. Putrefaction from urban burials symbolized social and cultural corruption. Set apart, it became natural and harmless. As if echoing Buckingham, Dr. Coffin suggested that, in choosing between the tomb and the grave, Bostonians were choosing between aristocracy and democracy, superstition and natural law, human pretensions and the inexorable will of God.[36]

His ideal burial site also reflected the era's nascent romanticism. He envisioned a mourner's repulsion and hasty retreat from the grotesque sight of a parent's tomb in a crowded urban graveyard, where no lingering affection or quiet, commemorative melancholy would be possible. In contrast, he observed, "I am differently affected when with the rising sun, or by the light of the melancholy moon, I go alone to my mother's grave. There I love to linger; and while there I hear the wind over one that sighed over me. I breathe an air refreshed by herbage, which draws its strength from the source whence I drew mine: and in the drops of dew that tremble on its leaves, I see the tears which so often bedewed her eyes as she breathed forth a prayer that her children might cherish her memory and escape from the pollutions of the world."[37] The funerary landscape Coffin described was that of the English Graveyard School of poets, Wordsworth, and William Cullen Bryant, or imagery familiar from mourning pictures and the iconography of the willow tree and urn. In America, few such landscapes existed. Coffin's naturalistic burial site would epitomize these changing notions about death and Nature, harmonizing them with the taste for antiquity of Boston's elite. It would embody the liberal religious vision of the hereafter as Eden, a garden, rather than the fearsome place handed down from the medieval era and the Puritan past.[38]

Coffin's suggestions were not new. Such calls for a "rural" burial space, sanctified by Nature, had been heard frequently in Boston in the years before the burial controversy. Just months before Coffin's pamphlet appeared, the *Boston Patriot and Daily Mercantile Advertiser* reprinted a piece from a Charleston, South Carolina, newspaper praising the moral influence and simplicity of rural burial grounds, for "what individual gazes upon the most obscure cemetery, without feeling the uncertain tenure of human existence?" It would be a "melancholy pleasure" to visit such "habitation of the dead and meditate on the 'hoary text' that 'teaches the rustic moralist.'"[39] Such emotions were lost in graveyards crushed by urbanization or left behind in hometowns by rural New Englanders moving to Boston to establish careers and make their fortunes.

Even before the controversy over crypts arose, the idea of creating a cemetery in a suburban location had occurred to Bostonians interested in founding new urban institutions. As an alternative to crowded graveyards, with their "desolate look of abandonment," William Tudor had proposed in 1820 that "an ample piece of ground . . . in the vicinity of large towns" be selected for all urban burials in Boston, New York, and other cities. "It would be easy, without great expense," he wrote in some detail, "to give the walls and entrance an appropriate appearance. The cypress, the willow, and other funeral trees, would form suitable ornaments within. A sufficient space might be allowed to different families to decorate as they choose, and where their remains would repose for ages untouched." Tudor suggested that "such a cemetery would be an interesting spot to visit," a morally uplifting place representing both the refinement of the city and its respect for the past.[40]

Not surprisingly, when Mayor Quincy reported on behalf of his Joint Committee on Urban Interments, he recommended banning additional crypt burials—an issue tabled with no alternative available.[41] He managed to win denial of the request by the Methodist Episcopal Church on Bromfield Lane to build crypts; a third formal municipal permit would definitely set a precedent. In his report he questioned the medical opinion of the physicians who had deemed such burials of no danger to public health, speculating that "it would not be surprising, if within the compass of the present generation, an entire revolution of opinions should take place and that of effluvia arising from the decomposition of animal matter *again* be held to be injurious to, or even destructive to health." Ultimately he deemed the medical debate irrelevant, only one manifestation of the "very great and honest diversity of opinions" of Bostonians concerned with issues of commonality versus privilege, the authority of the municipality versus interests of private property. Quincy concluded, "Grant that burying that dead within the city may be possibly innocent;—burying the dead out of it is certainly so." He could only keep his concerns alive by declaring it "the duty of this and every other city council to limit as much as possible, consistent with existing property rights, all future burial within the precincts of this ancient peninsula; and also to adopt a prospective system, which shall terminate, ultimately, in some distant years the burying within it altogether."[42]

Ideally, Quincy wanted to open a common municipal burial place with "wall and watch" and to "maintain the sanctity of the sepulchres," a place "where will finally repose all the inhabitants of the city," where "all classes [would] meet together." Not only would such a place solve the problem of crowding in Boston's old graveyards, but also it would "unite the interests and the natural prejudices and affections of the whole community," creating civic spirit. The elite, with their kin buried there, would not tolerate the lapses of security that permitted grave robbing in the undesirable Neck or South Burying Ground, the basis of the "powerful repugnance at present existing to being buried without the limits of the peninsula." Existing family tombs in the old graveyards and churches would remain in place out of respect for property rights, but additional burials would cease as soon as these became full.[43] After filing their forty-page report, Quincy and the aldermen formed a second committee to select a site for creation of this new cemetery. The City Council authorized the commission to erect tombs that the city might sell. (Unlike Dr. Coffin, they had no general opposition to the idea of entombment.) Yet this second commission accomplished little.

In July, the mayor wrote to Dr. John Collins Warren to elicit suggestions on how to end urban interments, but Warren replied that he would only favor finding additional land within the city "such as can conveniently be devoted to the purpose without injury to more important interests." Careful not to endanger the interest of Saint Paul's, Warren noted that "it would be advantageous to the health and beauty of the city to open new cemeteries in different parts and especially in the vicinities of churches, in order to obtain the ventilation and comfort of such open spaces." Increased density of building along Boston's narrow streets impeded the circulation of fresh air, Warren argued. Trained in medicine in Paris, he was probably familiar with French urban planning theories that open spaces and city squares might function to circulate fresh air. The idea that burial grounds could provide open space beneficial to air quality was new and ran counter to miasmatists' arguments that all "domestic" interments fouled the urban atmosphere; but then, Warren's suggestion was compatible with his antimiasmatic beliefs.[44] The proposal was, however, unrealistic, considering the paucity of space left on the Shawmut Peninsula. Already some dared suggest that parts of the Common be developed for residences and businesses. Mayor Quincy reappropriated a strip of property south of the Common in 1824 and held a referendum on its use, offering citizens five choices, including creation of a new burial ground. But since additional land would have to be made by filling in the salt marsh or flats acquired by the city in 1824 from ropemaker proprietors to preserve views over the Charles River, and since the resolution that the site be "kept open . . . for the use of the citizens" precluded its development as a cemetery, nothing was done for over a decade, at which point the site became the Public Garden in 1837.[45]

Only as an afterthought at the end of his letter did Warren note that interments might not be restricted to the bounds of the peninsula. The physician speculated that a country site might be preferable to one in Boston "if a sufficient number of persons would be ready to defray the expense." He did not suggest that the municipality purchase land beyond its limits. Rather, the elite could continue to buy tombs in the city, associated with their churches, while everyone else would have to bury their dead outside the urban bounds.[46] Quincy did not take up this proposal, for he wanted to reestablish a common burial place for all Bostonians while at the same time riding the city of interments.

Although Quincy's second committee never produced a report establishing a site for burials beyond the municipal limits, the Ordinance on the Burial of the Dead, passed in 1826, closed the Central (Common), King's Chapel, and Old Granary burying grounds, banning the opening or digging of new graves and the building of additional tombs there. Under Quincy, the city also ended the use of the old section of the North or Copp's Hill Burying Ground, while permitting additional tomb construction in the new sections there as well as in the South Burying Ground on the Neck. The North and South graveyards alone retained sufficient room for continued use for a short time under increasingly careful regulation by a new "Superintendent of Burying Grounds." From then on, Bostonians regulated interments more closely by municipal codes. New restrictions permitted a family to reserve a spot for twenty years after a first burial if it placed a small stone engraved with the name, age, and lot number there. Burials would not be in perpetuity, though the ordinance made no mention of how the remains would be disposed of and the space recycled after the allotted time. Burial grounds would henceforth be "sufficiently secured by locks and bolts."[47]

Quincy had done all he could for burial reform under his administration until 1828, which, after all, produced unprecedented municipal action and beautification. Quincy, who had extended the tree-lined Great Mall up the new Park Street to the State House in 1826, was never able to close the Middle Burial Ground on the Common and extend the "The Mall" because a few families rejected the destruction of their tombs. He lamented that "one law we lack yet, not only for the promotion of health, but for other cogent reasons," was that "no dead body in the future shall be buried or otherwise deposited with the city, or nearer than half a mile from its limits." At the start of his sixth term, Quincy noted that Bostonians remained "disgusted and sickened by the foulness which infects and contaminates the noble city of New York" and wanted to prevent such conditions in his city. But Bostonians were not all sickened by the idea of burials in their midst. Quincy's crusades for public health and cleanliness eventually gave way to more materially successful projects: building Quincy Market, widening streets, improving public schools, and creating a new workhouse or House of Industry.[48] He cannot be faulted for diverting his attention from burial reform. He did succeed in curtailing the use of crypts by additional churches, cleaning up the city, and creating an atmosphere of reform conducive to the founding of alternative institutions and landscapes through voluntary associations rather than under municipal auspices. Bostonians knew that under Quincy the urban death rate had fallen significantly, to a point "less than in any other city of equal population of record."[49] Given that accomplishment, burial reform in the name of public health was not a pressing matter. Interments under churches persisted until 1862. Saint Paul's crypts remained in use until 1878. Even the founders of Boston's "rural" cemetery, Mount

Auburn, decided to acquire a crypt under the Park Street Church for use as a receiving tomb for those who could not be buried immediately.

The spirit of urban improvement fostered by Josiah Quincy depended on voluntary action by citizens. The new municipal corporation could more easily act negatively by banning, regulating, or removing environmental abuses than positively by innovating with creative alternatives. The mayor once remarked that "a city would be noble if man would do but half as much for himself as nature as done for him." In his *Municipal History of Boston* (1852), Quincy wistfully noted that while the City Council had failed to act on his proposal for founding an extramural burial ground, he was proud that his policy had finally "been sanctioned by the establishment of the cemetery at Mount Auburn by an effective organization of private citizens."[50] In the end, Quincy was buried there atop a hill facing east over Boston. Buckingham, too, purchased an oversized family lot in a wooded area in the heart of the grounds.[51]

7

THE CEMETERY IDEA AND THE FOUNDING OF MOUNT AUBURN

The holiness of nature is ever a lofty contemplation; and it is well amidst the quiet wildwood and beneath the forest shades, to be reminded sometimes of death.

—Cornelia Walter, *Mount Auburn Illustrated* (1847)

When Mayor Josiah Quincy proved unable to create an extramural cemetery under municipal auspices, Joseph Buckingham advised Bostonians to take matters into their own hands. Addressing a growing spirit of reform and philanthropy, the journalist asked, "If we in life make sacrifices for the public good, shall we be selfish in death?" New Haven had already laid out its new and improved burial ground apart from the civic center; Bostonians might do likewise. As Buckingham wondered in the pages of his *New-England Galaxy*: "Who would wish to be buried in a close city and a crowded graveyard, to be deranged and knocked about, separated and disjointed, long before the last trumpet sounds? Would we not rather lie serenely where the pure breeze rustles the honeysuckles, and the field flowers, the long grass and the drooping willow, which cover and hang over our graves? Where, secure from unhallowed footsteps and boisterous mirth, the reeling tread of the drunkard, or the daily vapid gaze of the thoughtless, we lie quiet, undisturbed and happy?" He popularized the ideal of rural burials among Bostonians not familiar with the literary exhortations of William Cullen Bryant, Washington Irving, and William Wordsworth, let alone the ideals of creating a "cult of ancestors" which informed French funerary reform or the Enlightenment moral philosophy, and which in turn provided an underpinning for the eighteenth-century English landscape gardens that enshrined Nature through picturesque design.[1]

Support for a pastoral cemetery appeared in other newspapers as well. "A Traveller" suggested to the Federalist *Columbian Centinel* that an ideal site for a cemetery would be on two lofty hills for sale in South Boston, "superior to any thing in the vicinity" and "susceptible of great elegance at a trifling expense." Said to have natural beauty, it would be far better than "a noisome appalling enclosure" in the city "from which we turn with disgust and dread." He urged the city to buy, enclose, and convert the property "into a delightful burying ground, which might be called the *Field of Repose*, as that of Père Lachaise of Paris," or like New Haven's New Burying Ground. In this way, "many objections to shutting up the old yards would be removed at once." The writer waxed poetic: "When we should behold from afar, a lofty column, or the more humble testimony of affectionate remembrance, a *white* stone, reared amidst waving willows, often would our feet thither turn, with mournful satisfaction." There, Bostonians might pass "most pleasant and improving hours in 'converse with the departed'" and learn "the lessons of our own mortality," believing that in such a setting "from those we love, even death itself cannot separate us." Visible from the city, "the summits of these beautiful hills" illuminated by the "last rays of the setting sun," an emblem of death, the place would stir "the recollection that *there* was laid in peace the remains of a dear husband or wife or child" and "would assuage our grief and chasten our sorrow; and many of those gloomy thoughts which come over the mind in the hours of sadness would thereby be dispelled."[2] The prescribed symbolism was already familiar from the era's conventional mourning pictures, with their neoclassical monuments beneath weeping willows and venerable oaks, framed in greenery in the light of the setting sun—a romantic landscape of death set apart from the city glimpsed in the distance.

Some merchants with rural estates around the urban periphery had begun to install tombs and burial grounds on their own properties. Thomas Green Fessenden, editor of the *New England Farmer* and author of *The American Gardener* (1828), decried the practice as "gloomy." He urged banishing "tombs and cemeteries" from private gardens, as "they always awaken melancholy reflections in old people for they remind them of their approaching end." Tombs in estate gardens might have been a solution to the ban on new church crypts. But, sharing a propensity toward collective action as well as fears of the chronic impermanence of property, most New Englanders rejected private burial places.[3]

Proposals for alternatives to Boston's graveyards after the 1823 burial controversy focused nascent cultural trends: a budding historical consciousness, the desire to create exemplary institutions through voluntary associations, the wish to ameliorate urban life, a sentimentalism shaped by affective individualism, and new notions of death conditioned by liberalized religion. As several cemetery proposals appeared in the wake of the controversy, one person took action. Following the public and private discussion of reform, Dr. Jacob Bigelow (1787–1879) later recalled that in about 1825 he became aware of "certain gross abuses in the practice of Sepulture as it existed under churches and in other receptacles of the dead" in the city.[4] (Fig. 7.1.) But Bigelow was not content to complain or debate. He launched the project to create America's first "rural" cemetery.

Fig. 7.1. Dr. Jacob Bigelow, portrait photograph, ca. 1855. Photographer unknown. BMGL.

Bigelow was like others in Boston's new elite, sons of ministers, craftsmen, or farmers who moved to the city from the hinterland after the Revolution to establish careers. They would become the class that Oliver Wendell Holmes later labeled "Brahmins." Ambitious for a prosperous professional future that could only be had in the region's "metropolis," Bigelow uprooted himself from his hometown, just to the west, leaving his rights to burial there. Like other newcomers to the city—Daniel Webster, Joseph Story, General Henry A. S. Dearborn—he had no family tomb in a Boston graveyard; and Mayor Quincy's regulations made certain that no new ones could be built.[5]

By 1825 Bigelow was an ambitious thirty-eight-year-old physician. He had settled in Boston in 1811 after earning a degree from Harvard in 1806 and an M.D. in 1810 from the University of Pennsylvania, the nation's first medical school, founded in 1765. His elder brother Henry, a merchant whose life was cut short in 1815 by an accident in Baltimore, had helped him weather initial financial difficulties.[6] Alexander H. Everett, Bigelow's Harvard classmate, who had read law in the office of John Quincy Adams, introduced him to a social circle with scholarly interests, including Nathan Hale and Edward

Channing. Everett was the brother of Edward Everett, a Harvard professor of the classics who had been the teacher of Ralph Waldo Emerson. They would meet on Saturday nights in George Ticknor's study for literary discussions of classical and English romantic works. Bigelow won election to the Anthology Club, the Athenaeum, the Massachusetts Historical Society, the American Association of Arts and Sciences, the American Philosophical Society, and a number of international medical and scientific societies.[7]

At Harvard College and its new medical school, Bigelow taught botany and materia medica (medicinal plant use, not yet termed "pharmacology") from 1815 to 1855 and a course on the "application of the sciences to the useful arts" from 1816 to 1827, a field he termed "technology," introducing the word into American usage. He published *Florula Bostoniensis* (1814, 1822, and 1848) and the three-volume *American Medical Botany* (1817), illustrated in color with sixty copper-plate engravings produced by an aquatint process he adapted to produce the first American book containing color prints. He expanded the latter work in 1820 as *The Pharmacopeia of the United States of America*, the first ever, and in 1822 published *A Treatise on the Materia Medica Intended as a Sequel to the Pharmacopeia of the United States* with practical advice for clinical use. These landmark books won him international acclaim, marked by a certificate of "hommage" from the Société Linnéenne de Paris and commendation by the Royal Horticultural Society of London.[8]

Dr. James Jackson (1777–1867), professor of theory and practice of medicine at Harvard from 1812 and 1836 and a founder of the Massachusetts General Hospital with Dr. John Collins Warren, took the young Bigelow into his prosperous medical practice. Jackson was one of the physicians who testified to the City Council that the crypts at St. Paul's would not endanger public health. No records remain of Bigelow's position on the controversy, but his medical philosophy was opposed to the traditional, "heroic" bleedings and purgings of his era as interference in natural processes. Later termed "therapeutic nihilism," his theories reflected his belief in the natural, "self-limiting" nature of many diseases. While Bigelow seemingly shared the anti-miasmatist view of Boston's medical leaders, the young physician's sympathies lay with the more naturalistic solutions to the problem of burying of the city's dead than with Dr. Warren's promotion of church crypts for the wealthy. Bigelow favored both the tone and substance of Mayor Quincy's report on urban burials.

In November 1825 Bigelow invited to his Summer Street home several influential friends—John Lowell, William Sturgis, George Bond, Thomas W. Ward, John Tappan, Samuel P. Gardiner, and Nathan Hale—members of the Bunker Hill Monument Association and other new cultural institutions. Hale, son of a Yale classmate of James Hillhouse, knew about New Haven's New Burying Ground. Bigelow proposed that they form a voluntary association to create a similar extramural place composed of family burial lots, separated and interspersed with trees, shrubs, and flowers, in a wood or a landscape garden.[9] The idea appealed to those who were familiar with the arguments for such a place posed by advocates from Wordsworth, Scott, Pope, and Addison to the Scottish rationalists, French reformers, and the American Washington Irving. Their tastes were informed by the literature of pastoralism and melancholy familiar from Anthology Club readings and from the Athenaeum's shelves. Several prominent citizens not at the meeting also promised their support. The proposed "rural" cemetery would put into practice their historical philosophy, summarized by Bigelow in his 1816 address on his installation as Harvard's first Rumford Professor. It would provide space to preserve the memories of notables, to the credit of the region and the nation, and to perpetuate bonds of familial affection.[10]

Bond and Tappan began the search for a fitting site. They tried to acquire Augustus Aspinwall's Brookline estate, just west of Boston, but he refused to sell. They then considered land near the "Punch Bowl" on either side of Western Avenue, the road leading west from the Shawmut Peninsula; but so close to the city, it proved too expensive at a time of soaring real estate values. Some landowners refused to sell property to create a burial ground or to have one nearby. Since none of those sites would in any event have lent itself to creation of a pastoral landscape, it is fortunate that those efforts did not succeed. Otherwise Boston might simply have gained an extramural burial ground like that of New Haven, not a site imbued with the Genius of Place, the topographical features conducive to design of a picturesque landscape.[11]

Bigelow's proposal languished for several years, and

his group put no more work into the project. He had more pressing priorities, including publication in 1829 of *Elements of Technology*, his Harvard lectures "on the application of science to the useful arts," with his own mechanical and architectural illustrations. The national depression, which curtailed many projects requiring substantial expenditures, also delayed the cemetery's founding, as it did construction of the Bunker Hill Monument. Bigelow nevertheless continued to win support for his broader agenda of making Boston the "Athens of America."

Pantheism and the Unitarian Factor

Although Bigelow favored preserving the memories of dead loved ones and notables, he considered attempts to preserve the corpse unnatural. In a lecture in 1831 he assured Bostonians that decayed physical matter did not become "extinct and useless" but served as the substance "from which other living frames are to be constructed." The dead body "contributes its remains to the nourishment of plants around it." Without "this law of nature, the soil would soon be exhausted, the earth's surface would become a barren waste, and the whole race of organized beings, for want of sustenance, would become extinct." Existing burial places were unnatural, he said, because they upset the equilibrium of nature's system.[12] Bigelow condemned the use of "preservative agents" to interrupt the process of decay, although embalming was as yet rare and cremation nonexistent in Western culture. He likewise condemned "subterranean vaults and walls of brick" in graveyards as evidence of the pretension "to divide the clay of humanity from that of the rest of creation, and to preserve it separate for a time, as if it were for future inspection," as was the case in church crypts. Such "resistance to the laws of nature" could "at best only preserve a defaced and degraded image of what was once perfect and beautiful." He preferred a system in which "nature is permitted to take its course, when the dead are committed to the earth under the open sky, to become early and peacefully blended with its original dust." Writing in the *North American Review* in 1834, he remarked, "Convenience, health, and decency require that the dead should be removed from our sight. The law of nature requires that they should moulder into dust, and the sooner . . . the better." This should occur "not in the immediate contiguity of survivors" but "in the retired valley of the sequestered wood, where the soil continues its primitive exuberance."[13]

The question for Bigelow was one of sensibility, not public health. Similarly, General Dearborn observed, "We cannot speak confidently with respect to the danger of health which arises" from entombing the dead in churches. Indeed, he believed that the threat to health from urban burials had "probably been overrated, if, indeed, it exists at all."[14] Like Bigelow, Dearborn was drawn to notions of the naturalness of death such as those expressed in William Cullen Bryant's "Thanatopsis" (1817), in which thoughts of Nature assuage the fear of death by inspiring acceptance of the inevitable surrender of individual existence: "To mix forever with the elements, / To be a brother to the insensible rock / And to the sluggish clod." Nature was the great democratizer, "the great tomb of man." In proposing a pastoral cemetery, Bigelow might have been quoting Bryant:

The groves were God's first temple . . .
Ah, why
Should we in the world's riper years, neglect
God's ancient sanctuaries, and adore
Only among the crowd, and under roofs
That our frail hands have raised?[15]

Bigelow believed that the natural processes of decay as well as worship of the divine belonged "in the retired valley or the sequestered wood, where the soil continues its primitive exuberance, and where the earth has not become too costly to afford to each occupant at least his length and breadth." There, decay would "take place peacefully, silently, separately," the body "merged and lost in the surrounding harmonies of the creation." Each burial would have its own earthen grave, untouched in perpetuity.[16]

In his essay "On Burials," Bigelow declared natural decay "in the embrace of nature" beautiful. He cited the discovery of the remains of Major John André, a British officer executed for spying with Benedict Arnold. Workers disinterring the body from a grave overlooking the Hudson River found the roots of a massive tree wound through the Englishman's skull. It was, remarked Bigelow, "a natural and most beautiful coincidence" that "a faithful sentinel" had been posted "to watch till the obliterated ashes should not longer need a friend."[17] Such sights even on Boston streets inspired wonder rather than horror. Colonel Joseph May, a Unitarian merchant, recounted such a discovery on his morning walk along Tremont Street past the Old Granary Burying Ground, when he gazed into the gaping Cunningham family tomb where the Revolutionary leader James Otis lay: "Behold! the coffin was full of the fibrous roots of the elm, especially thick and matted about the skull." The sight reinforced May's thoughts on Death and Nature in proto-Transcendental terms. In that "noble elm," May saw "in transfigured glory . . . all that was material of James Otis."[18]

Fig. 7.2. Portrait of the Reverend William Ellery Channing in his prime, ca. 1840. Unidentified lithograph. From George Cary Eggleston, *The American Immortals*, 1901. Courtesy Mount Auburn Cemetery (hereafter MAC).

Bigelow and friends wished to create a secluded site where such processes could take place in peace and privacy, not incongruously in the bustling city's center. In a wooded cemetery, trees would hasten decomposition and stand as monuments to the deceased whose substance they consumed in the divinely ordained system of Nature. To permit and encourage decay "in the embrace of Nature" spoke to a pantheistic belief that was shared by Unitarians. The Reverend Joseph Stevens Buckminster (1784–1812) thought that God could be seen in Nature's design. The Reverend William Ellery Channing (1780–1842) proclaimed, "God is in Nature, God is in History." (Fig. 7.2.) He considered Nature a source of civilization. "If we . . . are destitute of the antiquity of human institutions," he wrote, "we should never forget that we possess the antiquity of Nature." Such thinking suffused Unitarian thought and premised Bigelow's proposal for a "rural" cemetery where "the forbidding and repulsive conditions which attend on decay" would be "merged and lost in the surrounding harmonies of creation."[19]

These pantheistic sentiments attest to a deep-seated and widening rift between the old orthodox Calvinists and the increasing numbers of Unitarians, a rift that predated the anti-Anglican sentiments that tinged Boston's 1823 burial controversy. In the escalating evolution of Protestantism, Unitarians took individualistic belief to a level previously espoused only by the Society of Friends—the Quakers. Although Unitarianism had its roots in eighteenth-century England, the American version arose in reaction to the resurgence in Calvinism resulting from the evangelical revivals of the Great Awakening beginning in the 1740s. About the only point of consensus between Calvinists and Unitarians was their distrust of "papism" and similar forms in Anglicanism or Episcopalianism. Like the Calvinists, Unitarians eschewed High Church symbols such as the cross.[20]

Unitarianism had been flourishing since that liberal Christian faction won the appointment of Henry Ware (1764–1845) as Hollis Professor of Divinity at Harvard in the Unitarian Controversy of 1805. That aroused the animosity of orthodox Calvinists and precipitated theological debate and finally schisms in Congregational churches. The faction intent on preserving Calvinist theology founded the Andover Theological Seminary in 1808, although Yale remained a stronghold of orthodoxy. The old establishment decried Unitarians as Arminians (deniers of predestination) concerned only with secular "moral philosophy." Henry Ware Jr. (1794–1843) followed in his father's footsteps as pastor of Boston's Second Unitarian Church from 1817 to 1830 and then as a professor in Harvard's nonsectarian Divinity School, founded by William Ellery Channing and others in 1816, then a Unitarian stronghold.

Unitarians proposed a "natural religion" based on

reason, considering it the ideological basis for the new republic. Channing set forth Unitarianism's basic tenets in a sermon, "Unitarian Christianity," delivered in 1819 on the ordination of the Reverend Jared Sparks (1789–1866) at Baltimore's First Independent Church. The American Unitarian Association, an alliance of 125 churches founded in 1825 and based in Boston, aimed to proselytize, as did its publication *The Christian Examiner*, launched in 1829. Rejecting the notion of original sin, Unitarians espoused "salvation by character," defending reason and the "moral nature of man" in "self-culture" as a striving for a "likeness to God," ideas expanded upon by Ralph Waldo Emerson and the Transcendental Club, founded at Channing's suggestion.[21]

Universalists, at that time a separate sect, shared similar liberal beliefs. Declaring themselves Independent Christian Universalists in 1785, they believed in ultimate universal salvation, or "salvation irrespective of character." The Universalist Church of America, founded in 1793, issued a statement of faith, the Winchester Profession, in 1803 and began publishing the weekly *Universalist Magazine* in 1819. The English-born Reverend John Murray (1741–1815), called the "father or Universalism in America," and the Reverend Hosea Ballou (1771–1852) contributed to the proliferation of new Universalist "societies" in New England towns, with Boston as the center, but members of the sect tended to be less urbane and prosperous than Unitarians. Universalists claimed to have taken the lead in avowing Unitarianism.

Although Unitarians decried the Deists as "heretics" and "infidels," Alexis de Tocqueville (1805–1859) saw more similarities than differences, writing in 1831, "It's evident that the Protestants whose minds are . . . logical, the *argumentative* classes, the men whose habits are intellectual and scientific, are grasping the occasion to embrace an entirely philosophic faith which allows them to make almost public profession of pure Deism" without shocking "public opinion." That October the French observer of American mores heard Channing charge that Calvinism was anachronistic: "We claim to go ahead; we maintain that if human reason is steadily perfecting itself, what it believed in a century still gross and corrupted cannot altogether suit the enlightened [one] in which we live. . . . The human spirit has need of a positive religion." Channing in his landmark 1819 sermon had insisted on "the duty of . . . charitable judgment, especially toward those who differ in religious opinion," a mandate for interdenominational tolerance that Mount Auburn's founders carried out in declaring the cemetery nondenominational with absolutely no discrimination based on creed, knowing how they themselves had been discriminated against.[22]

The Unitarians opposed the conservative Trinitarians' fight to hold on to power through tax-supported churches and colleges. When, in 1819, Channing decried "the impure union . . . between church and state," he expressed the frustrations of Unitarian, Universalist, Quaker, and Baptist societies, which stood outside the established church in his state and others. In 1811 Republicans passed the Massachusetts Religious Freedom Act, asserting the constitutional right of all citizens to specify which churches or religious societies, even if not incorporated, should receive their tax monies. Republicans at the Commonwealth's 1820 constitutional convention favored voluntarism rather than state support of churches; although they did not succeed in disestablishment, they did manage to expand corporate rights to churches and other voluntary associations. The Religious Freedom Act strengthened many churches outside the Congregational establishment when it was extended to all denominations in 1824. As the Unitarians won control of churches in town after town in eastern Massachusetts, the legislature finally voted for disestablishment in 1831, removing public financial support from Congregational churches. An 1833 amendment to the Massachusetts constitution confirmed religious freedom and prohibited any form of "established," state-sponsored religion.[23]

Bigelow and fellow Unitarians as well as Universalists rejected the old Calvinist fears of death along with the belief in predestination and human depravity traced to Adam's Fall. As the Reverend William Ware (1797–1852) declared in 1827, "Death, we regard not so much as even a temporary, momentary extinction of being, but simply as the appointed manner in which we shall pass from one stage of existence to another—from earth to heaven." Reverend Ballou concurred: "Our fleshly bodies, like the grass of the earth, are composed of the elements of nature; these elements support both the grass and our fleshly bodies; and as the grass finally withers and returns back from whence it came, is decomposed and joined with the elements of which it was composed, so do our bodies return to the earth from whence they came." To the virtuous, "death has no terror, it is the gate of life." The religious liberals rationally accepted the old message of death's inevitability, but without its Calvinistic suggestion of imminent damnation. Although they saw no horror in the old iconography of skull and bones, they used more naturalistic and optimistic symbols of death. Those of like mind found only sublime beauty and even intimations of immortality in the work of Nature on the human body in life and after death.[24]

Until the flowering of liberal Christianity, nascent romanticism, and a new elite taste for horticulture and picturesque landscapes in the 1820s, most New Englanders did not care about cleaning up graveyards, let alone making a burial place beautiful by placing plantings there. Bigelow was one of the first to suggest such a thing. Edward Everett made the argument: "Trees, whose inexpressible beauty has been provided by the hand of the Creator as a great ornament of earth, have rarely been planted about our graveyards; the enclosures are generally inadequate and neglected, the graves indecently crowded together and often, after a few years, disturbed; and the whole appearance as little calculated as possible to invite the visits of the seriously disposed, to tranquilize the feelings of surviving friends, and to gratify that disposition which would lead us to pay respect" to the dead.[25]

Bigelow's proposed cemetery would not just dispose of the city's burial problem. It would fill many cultural needs as well: honoring the deceased, cultivating the civilizing emotion of melancholy, teaching moral lessons, fostering a sense of the past as pertinent to the present and future, and celebrating Nature. It would permit a sort of commemoration impossible in graveyards. An early supporter, Thaddeus William Harris (1795–1856), the Harvard librarian and a lecturer on natural history, remarked, "In the public graveyard it is not always in the power of an individual to appropriate . . . space enough for the purposes of decent and respectful ornament." At the new cemetery, however, it would be "in the power of every one . . . to provide a place of burial for himself, which, while living, he may contemplate without dread or disgust; one which is secure from the danger of being encroached upon, as in the graveyards of the city; secluded from every species of uncongenial intrusion; surrounded with every thing that can fill the heart with tender and respectful emotions; beneath the shade of a venerable tree, on the slope of a verdant lawn, and with the seclusion of the forest, removed from all the discordant scenes of life."[26]

The emergence of a pattern in Boston of creation of culture, similar to that of post-Revolutionary France but through voluntary associations rather than government action, is not surprising. Boston's cultural leaders shared Jean-Jacques Rousseau's belief in the excellence of human nature and the perfectibility of man. As the literary historian Vernon Louis Parrington observes, "Changing its name and arraying itself in garments cut after the best Yankee fashion, the gospel of Jean Jacques presently walked the streets of Boston and spoke from its most respectable pulpits, under the guise of Unitarianism." Mount Auburn's founders, while abandoning their Calvinism, retained a sense of didactic mission from their Puritan ancestors. Their cemetery would be a silent "city on a hill," an institution representing communitarian ideals. For those who still insisted on the useful and the moral but remained skeptical of empty, meaningless leisure, it would also be a place of constructive spiritual and physical recreation.[27] Bigelow and his colleagues echoed Wordsworth in urging that burials be removed from "the tumultuous and harassing din of cities" and placed "amid the quiet verdure of the field," where "the harmonious and ever-changing face of nature reminds us, by its resuscitating influences, that to die is but to live again."[28] They had distinct ideas about the qualities such a site should possess: soil fit for burials, without heavy boulders to impede gravedigging but loose and sandy to hasten decomposition. It would also have to be far enough from the city to be isolated from urbanization yet close enough to permit easy access, given the limitations of transportation at the time.

The Massachusetts Horticultural Society

While their cemetery proposal languished, Bigelow and his friends founded the Massachusetts Horticultural Society, chartered by the state legislature in 1829 to develop the quality and diversity of plants grown in New England. (Fig. 7.3.) Like various other societies for the promotion of agriculture or useful manufactures that sprang up after the Revolution, it aimed to further regional prosperity and to strengthen American civilization through economic independence. Founders Henry A. S. Dearborn (1783–1851) and John Lowell (1768–1840) considered horticulture "the most distinguished of the fine arts." They perceived an intricate relationship between the "culture" of plants and the "culture" of the nation, playing on the ambiguity of the term.[29]

Dearborn, the society's first president, traced the history of horticulture to ancient Egypt, where "stupendous temples, pyramids and obelisks" became wonders of the world along the Nile's fertile banks, "adorned by a succession of luxuriant plantations." Dearborn saw the foundations of the arts and sciences in the horticultural achievements of ancient civilizations. Despite advances in ancient Greece and Rome, he believed that the greatest developments came only with the "improved style of gardening" of eighteenth-century England described by Milton, Addison, Pope, and Kent. If these precedents could be followed, and if Americans would seriously develop their stock of plants and their skill in arranging gardens, history pointed to America as the next great civilization. Dearborn proposed transforming the Charles River into an artery of prosperity and culture similar to the ancient Nile. Such a call to action appealed to Bostonians engaged in ransacking historical precedents for forms with which to fashion their own culture.[30]

Fig. 7.3. Membership certificate of the Massachusetts Horticultural Society, 1829. The iconography, including horn-of-plenty agricultural produce in a picturesque setting, epitomized the founders' ideals of productive pastoralism. MHORT.

Scientific naturalism spread internationally, conditioning the taste for pastoral landscapes as well as aiding practical attempts to diversify plants for both crops and ornamentation. The Massachusetts Horticultural Society was not America's first such organization but followed the New York Society (1822) and the Pennsylvania Society (1827) in Philadelphia. As with monument building, Bostonians were determined to keep pace. As the society's first corresponding secretary, Bigelow expanded his extensive international contacts to include the likes of Sir Walter Scott, an honorary member of the society from its inception. Zebedee Cook Jr. (1786–1858), the society's vice president, stressed the importance of a "reciprocal interchange of opinions and sentiments" between Boston and Paris, where a similar organization had been formed in 1826, following the model of the London Horticultural Society (1805).[31] Boston, however, did not have the resources of other urban areas to furnish ornamental plantings. Complaints arose that those in the Boston area had no cultivators on whom to call for a supply of the most common plants, no nurseries to supply plants to ornament grounds. The Massachusetts Horticultural Society offered one way to remedy the deficiency as Bostonians tried to compete with the amenities of "Sister Cities." Dearborn expressed his hope that the society, an "association of men of taste, of influence, and industry," would serve as a "branch of our domestic industry" by "generously and patriotically" developing fruits, vegetables, and ornamentals.[32]

The society's gentleman horticulturists aimed to spread "rural" taste so Americans could draw upon indigenous sources in creating a new culture. The term "rural" implied more than tilled fields. It reflected the perception that the green, tree-covered countryside was rapidly disappearing along the Atlantic seaboard, recalling the deforestation that had preceded the rise in taste for the picturesque in England a century before. "Rural" taste involved a nostalgia for America's original semi-forested landscape and a desire for a way of life in harmony with Nature associated with the vanishing or vanished primeval past. Gustave de Beaumont, traveling with Tocqueville in 1831, observed that in Massachusetts, "the virgin forest disappeared long ago and no trace of it is now found."[33]

Even ancient and "venerable" trees, considered sublime, seemed threatened. Some old and notable trees served as landmarks or historical sites: oaks used by Indians as council sites or Liberty Trees with Revolutionary associations. Cambridge had the Whitefield Tree on the Common, where the Wesleyan evangelist George Whitefield had preached in 1740 when denied a Puritan pulpit. The Rebellion Tree in Harvard Yard was the place where students traditionally gathered to protest against the faculty. Even more revered was the elm on Cambridge Common under which Washington was said to have assumed command of the Continental Army on July 3, 1775. (Fig 7.4.) The Massachusetts Historical Society, founded in 1791, solicited specimens representing New England's natural history as well as documents and historical artifacts for its collection. Horticulturists, however, wished to preserve ancient trees individually, or entire pastoral properties. Judges Samuel Fay and Joseph Story led a crusade in Cambridge in 1830 to plant trees on the Common, which had been largely denuded to fuel Patriot campfires during the Revolution.[34]

By the 1820s, a few old farms and estates ringing Boston were the sole preserves of woodland and orchards—enclaves of the picturesque—from the hills of Milton and Roxbury to the south, to Cambridge and Watertown in the west, to Salem and Essex County to the north. In this belt of rural culture, New England's first small nurseries sprang up. As urbanization spread, real estate values around the periphery of cities soared. Horticulturists feared that because of America's lack of primogeniture, such estates would be sold and subdivided to meet the increasing demand for truck farmers, and that owners would hesitate to plant trees that would not mature in their lifetime. Soon, mills would line the region's once bucolic rivers and streams.[35]

Stone Farm or "Sweet Auburn"

George Watson Brimmer (1784–1838), a merchant and member of the same social circles as Bigelow, shared these concerns. In 1825 he purchased seventy-two acres of rolling wooded land four miles west of Boston on the border between Cambridge and Watertown, quiet towns undergoing rapid transition. (Fig. 7.5.) Cambridge had a population of only 6,072 in 1830, yet rural land on its western border seemed destined for inevitable dissolu-

Fig. 7.4. Elm tree next to Cambridge Common under which Washington assumed command of the Continental Army. Engraving from *Gleason's Pictorial Drawing-Room Companion*, ca. 1845. BMGL.

Fig. 7.5. Deacon Simon Stone farmhouse on the Charles River, before the founding of Mount Auburn. Painting by Josephine M. Stone, ca. 1830. Courtesy Watertown (Massachusetts) Free Public Library.

tion. Charles Francis Adams, Ralph Waldo Emerson, Bigelow, and Brimmer all had fond memories of time spent in the overgrown remnants of the high ground of Simon Stone's farm, dating from the early colonial period. Harvard students had frequented the place, once called Stone's Woods, dubbing it "Sweet Auburn" in 1801 after Oliver Goldsmith's nostalgic poem "The Deserted Village" (1770), lamenting the erstwhile "loveliest village of the plain," one of many small English and Irish towns destroyed during the eighteenth-century consolidation of estates, many ironically to make way for the creation of picturesque gardens.[36]

The poet Caroline Frances Orne (1818–1905), who grew up in nearby Cambridgeport, described the farm, one of the most naturally picturesque places in the Boston area, as a spot where "willow, bending downward, kissed the stream" of the Charles River, which made "a graceful sweep" on its southern boundary. "Beneath the shade of its trees, generation after generation of my ancestors have played as children," she recalled. Orne considered it a "fairy place," magical because "the first dwelling, falling to decay, was left deserted, mouldering away," a ruin that touched a chord of nostalgia in those with a romantic turn of mind. The place evoked for them New England's colonial past, now undergoing obliteration just as surely as the culture of the Indians who had used the site for war councils before selling the land to Stone. Orne had spent her youth in Sweet Auburn's grounds, its "cool retreats, the favorite walks, the hills covered with the fragrant wild strawberry or the various and beautiful tribes of mosses," which she described as scenes of "pristine beauty." (Fig. 7.6.) The poet James Russell Lowell (1819–1891), who recalled his childhood experience of picking hazelnuts and watching chipmunks skirting the bogs there, exclaimed in 1837, "Show me a place so sweet as that most delightful of spots, Sweet Auburn!"[37]

Brimmer desired to preserve the trees, some over sixty years old—oak, beech, cedar, and pine. There was a walnut grove as well, and an ancient pear orchard. Had he not been determined to retain the natural parklike landscape "for some public or appropriate use," it might have been a prime site for development on a major public way, the River Road, which connected to the Boston Post Road, the overland route to New York.[38] (Fig. 7.7.) The navigable tidal Charles, its banks lined with salt

Fig. 7.6. Wooded view of Fresh Pond looking north from the summit of Sweet Auburn. Engraving by [William S.] and [John B.] Pendleton, Boston, ca. 1833. Courtesy American Antiquarian Society (hereafter AAS).

marshes, stretched along the south of the property. Mills, factories, warehouses, and wharves were being built upstream at Waltham, where the Boston Manufacturing Company opened its first textile mill in 1813. In Watertown there were new soap and candle factories, a paper mill, and a dye-house. In 1816 the federal government built the core of what would become a massive arsenal, a complex of storehouses, barracks, workshops, and wharves, on forty acres half a mile from Sweet Auburn and across the river from the New England Lace Factory.

Brimmer made a wise choice in buying Sweet Auburn. Initially he intended to create his own residence there, just west of Cambridge's prestigious old Tory Row, renamed Brattle Street, and near new rural estates. Lowell's country seat, "Elmwood," later home of Harvard's presidents, was just to the east. To the west and north lay Charles Davenport's "Fountain Hill" and Harrison Gray Otis's "Oakley." John P. Cushing settled on his property, named "Bellmont," in 1831. Sweet Auburn's natural qualities resembled the landscape achieved through artifice in English landscape gardens. Several acres of "wildwood" were separated by natural lawns, grassy knolls, rambling ponds, wetlands, rugged slopes, and valleys. (Figs. 7.8, 7.9.) A glacial ridge or esker crossed the property amid a varied terrain of seven hills, dells, and bogs, a landform created over four successive Ice Age periods, part of the Boston basin which stretched up the Charles into Watertown. Unlike elsewhere in the metropolitan region, there were few rock outcroppings. The soil consisted of sand plains and clay

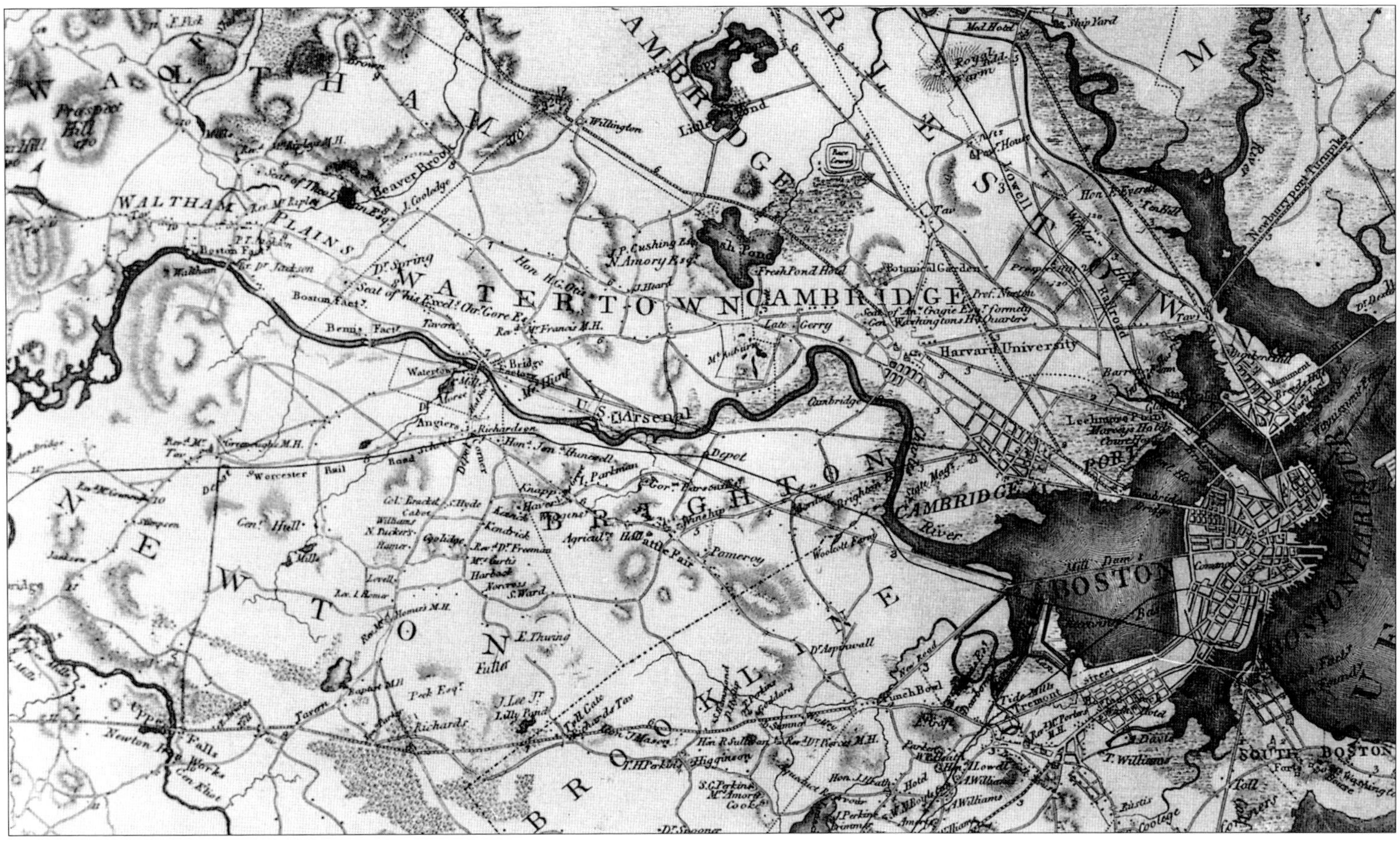

Fig. 7.7. "Map of Boston and Its Vicinity from Actual Survey with Corrections in 1833," by John G. Hales. The hills of Sweet Auburn lie four miles northwest of Boston and a mile from Harvard College, on the Cambridge–Watertown line. BMGL.

Fig. 7.8. Forested hills around the dell. Photograph by BMGL, 1986.

Fig. 7.9. Forested hills above the dell. Photograph by Carol Betsch, 2005.

beds over an underlying ledge of slate fifteen to two hundred feet below the surface.

Brimmer planted some ornamental trees amid the volunteer forest growth and laid out a few winding roads through the hills. Although he had staked out sites for a new house and stables, construction was impeded by the depression and by 1830 had not yet begun. Increasing ill health altered Brimmer's plans, but he remained motivated to preserve the pastoral site rather than to develop it as a country seat. Brimmer may have visited Père Lachaise in Paris. In any event, he felt that Sweet Auburn would be the perfect place for a similar burial landscape, though it is unclear whether Brimmer first approached Bigelow with the proposal that his property be considered as a cemetery site or whether Bigelow suggested it to his college friend.[39]

Many other characteristics recommended Sweet Auburn for the purpose. Peripheral to the expanding city, the site was typical of those chosen for the "undesirable" institutions then being removed from urban centers—insane asylums, hospitals, and orphanages. The historian David Rothman characterizes such "asylum" sites as having "tranquil, natural, and rural" grounds of ample proportions centered on "a low hillside with an unobstructed view of the surrounded landscape." Nathan Hale, Bigelow's publisher friend, wrote that Sweet Auburn was as near the city "as is consistent with perfect security from the approach of . . . [industries], usually found in the neighborhood of a large town, but not in harmony with the character of a place of burial." It was extensive enough to provide ample high ground for burials, with the lower periphery reserved as a buffer zone.[40]

Sweet Auburn was also newly accessible to Bostonians. Through the eighteenth century the Charles River remained a barrier to easy travel from Boston to Cambridge and areas to the north and west. Except for ferries downstream, the sole crossing had been just below the falls along the Post Road Bridge a couple of miles upstream from Sweet Auburn and the original Watertown center nearby; but in 1794, when the West Boston Bridge (later rebuilt as the Longfellow Bridge) was constructed, the eight-mile trip by land from Boston to Harvard College was shortened to two and a half miles. In 1795 daily stage runs began along this route, becoming hourly in 1826, the first high-frequency route in America, preceding similar service in the vicinities of Paris and London by two or three years. Thus Bostonians, who had previously considered only hilltops south of the city as locations for a "rural" cemetery, began to look to the north and west. Hearses had been introduced in 1796 in Boston for bearing coffins beyond the immediate vicinity of the deceased's house; now carriages, newly available for hire, could be used to carry mourners to burial places farther from home than had been possible in the old days when funeral processions proceeded on foot, following the coffin borne by pallbearers to a nearby graveyard.

Sweet Auburn's outstanding feature was its central mount rising 125 feet above the river, commanding what Bigelow called "one of the finest prospects which can be obtained in the environs of Boston." Dearborn reported to fellow horticulturists that the summit could be "reached by a gentle ascent, which winds like a road around the hill, with valleys on each side, and is so exact in its bearing that it is difficult to persuade one's self that man had no agency in forming it." From the top one saw the serpentine Charles leading to the sea, its course lined with tidal salt marshes, a broad swath of open space between the city and the proposed cemetery. All around stretched dramatic panoramas. On a clear day, one could see as far as the Blue Hills of Milton to the south, Mount Monadnock in New Hampshire to the north, and the ocean to the east.[41]

In short, the topography was ideal for creating a landscape in the English fashion, a standard feature of which was a "mount" or high point, reached by a sinuous path, from which to survey the surrounding territory. Often a temple, pavilion, or tower was built atop it, providing a place for contemplation of the sublime, deemed inherent in distant horizons. The first-century Greek philosopher Longinus, recently translated and popular among eighteenth- and early-nineteenth-century literati, considered wide horizons, panoramic vistas, and broad rivers sublime, emblematic of infinity and the divine, capable of casting the imagination into "a pleasing astonishment." Similarly, in the "General Scholium" to his *Mathematical Principles of Natural Philosophy* (1687), Sir Isaac Newton (1643–1727) described God's literal presence in space. Distant vistas and panoramas suggestive of infinity were not just representative of the divine but actual attributes of it. Adding a political perspective to the theological, the British essayist Joseph Addison had written that "a spacious horizon is an image of liberty." Such theories of landscape aesthetics were known to Boston literati and appealed to their liberal religious sensibilities.[42]

The enthusiasm for sweeping views was explained by the belief that dramatic perspectives and panoramas triggered powerful emotional associations like those elicited by vistas in "picturesque" gardens, where English landscape gardeners arranged plants and distant architectural elements called "eye-catchers" so as to maximize such prospects from appropriately chosen hilly terrain. Artists tried to capture their sublime qualities in popular painted dioramas exhibited in major cities. Painted landscape dioramas were often fashioned in a complete circle, with dimensional effects created by lighting and multiple transparencies. One British writer described the surprising sensations he experienced on viewing a diorama in London in 1823: "The decided effect of the thing is that you look over an area of twenty miles. . . . You have, as far as the senses can be acted upon, all these things [realities] before you; and yet in the midst of all this crowd of animations; there is stillness, which is the stillness of the grave. The idea produced is that of a region—of a world—desolated; of living nature at an end; of the last day past and over." The panorama of Paris seen from Père Lachaise contributed to the renown of the Parisian cemetery. Even Edgar Allen Poe described the sublime emotions elicited by distant, panoramic views as catalysts for melancholy and moral meditations. It is important to remember how rarely people of the era actually got to experience such a vantage point, accustomed as they were to crowded city streets and low buildings that offered no distant views from their rooftops. Only the new State House dome (1797), designed by Charles Bulfinch, provided Bostonians with such a vantage point.[43]

For all these reasons, a site similar to that of Père Lachaise seemed appropriate for an innovative American cemetery inspired by English landscapes. The example of the French cemetery, as well as the desire to preserve the highest point at Sweet Auburn for its unsurpassed views, suggested to Brimmer and Bigelow the ideal use for the property. In addition to accommodating burials, the hilltop might also, they speculated, provide a fine site for a monument to George Washington to complement the still incomplete Bunker Hill Monument atop Breeds Hill, with a view of Boston just to the west across the Charles River. Sweet Auburn provided a location visible for miles around for a second monument, as advocated by William Tudor.

Sweet Auburn's other topographical features were also perfect for a romantic cemetery. Its bodies of water and wetlands lent themselves to the design of a picturesque landscape replete with allegorical meaning. Folklore held that lakes and ponds as well as trees had the power to contain spirits. One dark pond amid a deep, naturally circular dell could function even better than Thoreau's expansive Walden Pond as a "mystic center" or *axis mundi*, or, as the historian Leo Marx explains, like the "naval of the earth" in the archaic myths studied by Mircea Eliade. It had the secluded feel of the grotto, the womblike or tomblike enclosure of earth or rock sheltering dark pools, brooks, or cascades—a common fixture of English gardens. Père Lachaise had no symbolic bodies of water and therefore offered no opportunities to fashion such a contemplative place.[44]

The Making of the "Rural" Cemetery

Brimmer's willingness to part with Sweet Auburn gave new life to the proposal for an extramural cemetery. At the September 1830 festival of the Boston Horticulturists, Zebedee Cook Jr., an insurance executive, lauded the idea of a multifunctional place "devoted to public uses," including "a public cemetery similar in its design to that of Père Lachaise in the environs of Paris, to be located in the suburbs of this metropolis." It would advance both horticultural and historical consciousness. Made "more alluring, more familiar, and imposing, by the aid of the rural embellishments," the place would connect "the present with the past" in a manner "peaceful and salutary to the physical and moral nature of man." Cook believed that "every generation of man is a link in the great chain that has been forming from the creation of the world, connecting the present with the past, and to be lengthened out through succeeding ages." That connection would be strengthened by the proposed cemetery. He advocated a landscape drawing on the English style of gardening: "The skill and taste of the architect should be executed in the construction of the requisite departments and avenues; and appropriate trees and plants would decorate its borders, the weeping-willow, waving its graceful drapery over the monumental marble and the somber foliage of the cypress should shade it, and the undying daisy should mingle its bright and glowing tints with the native laurel of our forests." Flowers "in their budding and bloom and decay" would be "silent and expressive teachers of morality," reminders of the fate of men and nations.[45]

Cook declared that the same salutary influences of the "American System" backed by John Quincy Adams and Henry Clay, a program that was charging "the energies and hopes of our yeomanry," could be carried out locally by voluntary associations undertaking projects like the cemetery and garden to acculturate, educate, and produce better citizens by instilling "a spirit of emulation." Through institutional and material means, the elite would foster respect for authority and the work ethic as they elevated the taste of the "middling sort," thus stabilizing and improving the republic. The cemetery, said Cook, would be a new kind of educational institution, affording "instruction and admonition" to all who visited it. The "rural" cemetery would "teach those who have wealth and leisure, how they may make themselves happy not only without injuring others but with direct benefit to their fellow-men, to show them that in order to secure enjoyment for themselves, there is no need of inventing new pleasures . . . that Nature opens a never-failing paradise to those who are content to be innocent and well employed." There, "the heart [would be] chastened and the soul . . . subdued, and the affections purified and exalted." There, "ambition [would survey] the boundaries of its powers, of its hopes, and its aspirations." These notions echo those of the French philosophes who advocated the "cult of ancestors" prior to the establishment of Père Lachaise.[46]

On November 23, 1830, Henry A. S. Dearborn and John C. Gray joined Bigelow in calling a meeting at the Exchange Coffee House to consider developing the cemetery under Massachusetts Horticultural Society auspices. Brimmer offered to sell his land for $6,000, taking a loss; and Horticulturists voted to purchase it, contingent on selling enough family burial lots to cover the cost.[47] About forty acres were initially reserved for burials. As president of the society, Dearborn enthusiastically agreed with Bigelow and Brimmer that Sweet Auburn was ideal, "consistent with perfect security" of burials, yet sufficiently distant from the urban growth that threatened existing Boston burial grounds. Dearborn assembled a committee of Bigelow, Brimmer, George Bond, Edward Everett, Abbot Lawrence, and John C. Gray to work out details. A week later, Dearborn announced a plan for both a cemetery and an experimental horticultural garden to be created separately on the grounds. Bigelow felt that the "young, active, and popular" Horticultural Society would ensure public acceptance of the innovative cemetery. The venture would enable the Horticulturists to fulfill their aspirations to establish an experimental garden.[48]

Seconding Cook's moralistic ambitions, Dearborn asserted that the cemetery would "teach the community to pay more respect to the dead," an activity in which he judged that Americans lagged "behind other countries." Visitors would engage in secular meditation, an equivalent of religious activity in the sacred context of Nature, an idea that appealed to Unitarians. The cemetery would teach nondenominational lessons of moral philosophy and renew ambitions of self-improvement through work and self-denial.[49] It would teach historical lessons as well: "There can be formed a public place of sepulture, where monuments can be erected to our illustrious men, whose remains, thus far, have unfortunately been consigned to obscure and isolated tombs instead of being collected within one common depository, where their great deeds might be perpetuated and their memories cherished by succeeding generations. Though dead they would be eternal admonitors to the living—teaching them the way, which leads to national glory and individual renown." The historical mandate Dearborn articulated would be, for many, the most compelling reason for creating such an innovative funerary institution.[50] He predicted that within three years it would "rival the most celebrated rural burial grounds in Europe and present a garden in such a state of forwardness" as to be a credit to its sponsoring institution and to the city as well.[51] The argument for the need to compete with European cities in urban amenities so as to display their own history and high cultural achievement convinced the Boston elite that the cemetery was necessary and justified, not an idiosyncratic luxury.

As soon as the Massachusetts Horticultural Society agreed to sponsor the cemetery, Dearborn sent to Paris and London for books and maps of funerary landscapes and monument designs, including over two hundred engravings of art, architecture, and landscape from Père Lachaise. He translated French accounts of "that celebrated burial place, from a belief that it would be interesting to members of the Society," knowing that "establishment of rural cemeteries similar to Père Lachaise, has often been the subject of conversation in this country, and frequently adverted to by the writers in our scientific and literary publications." Before the creation of Père Lachaise, "all was confusion, disorder, and irreverence towards the ashes of the dead in Paris. Causes, adverse to the indulgence of a recollection of our predecessors, seemed to have combined in the accumulation of everything which was capable of exciting terror and disgust." The model of the French cemetery offered many advantages. Père Lachaise was "the place of rendezvous for all the great and the opulent" of that city—in life and after death—"for the illustrious in letters, the sciences and the arts; for those who were successful in commerce, and the numerous branches of national industry, for persons eminent for their public stations, and for men distinguished in political events." There, said Dearborn, "families are reunited, all opinions are confounded." The cemetery unified society, both on a private and public, a personal and national level. Bostonians, and indeed America, needed such an institution.[52]

Dearborn admired Père Lachaise for reflecting English landscape design and was determined to incorporate the best aspects of it in his new cemetery. He lauded Bacon, Milton, Addison, Pope, Kent, Bridgeman, and famous English gardeners as "the champions of true taste." He quoted John Evelyn's condemnation of "the custom of burying in churches, and near about them, and especially in great cities," aware that his opinion would have resonance in Boston. He ordered all three of Sir Humphrey Repton's works on landscape gardening and consulted them in designing the new cemetery's landscape. Like the best English landscape gardeners, Dearborn permitted Sweet Auburn's terrain to dictate a design that accorded with Sir Uvedale Price's conception of the "picturesque" rather than displaying the broad lawns, trimmed vistas, and specimen trees associated with Capability Brown's aesthetics of the "beautiful."[53]

Dearborn stressed the compatibility of a cemetery with an experimental garden. Invoking the sacredness of gardens in all cultures while advocating practical development of plants to bolster the American agricultural economy, he mustered support from Bostonians more interested in horticulture than in burial reform. On June 8, 1831, the Massachusetts Historical Society assembled potential subscribers to hear about Mount Auburn's plans, purposes, and functions. Purchase of the property would be complete as soon as one hundred subscribers were found, paying sixty dollars each. Subscriptions would then be final, obligatory, and collectible in one lump sum. Each subscriber would get a family burial lot measuring fifteen by twenty feet, a total of three hundred square feet. Lots were offered on egalitarian terms, ability to pay being the sole criterion for becoming a proprietor. The elite were accustomed to buying burial space for tombs in common graveyards, though not in perpetuity or in fee simple (that is, without restrictions on inheritance by heirs). Many may have considered an investment in a burial lot equivalent to buying a church pew. Yet the only precedents for private burial plots other than on family estates were New Haven's New Burying Ground and Père Lachaise.[54]

On June 23, 1831, the state legislature amended the Massachusetts Horticultural Society charter, permitting it to acquire real estate valued up to $10,000 for a "rural cemetery or burial ground" and "to plant and embellish the same with shrubbery, flowers, trees, walks, and other rural ornaments, and to enclose and divide the same with proper walls and enclosures" as a "perpetual dedication." Dearborn enlarged his committee, chaired by Judge Joseph Story, by assembling twenty Bostonians, including the Whig senator Daniel Webster and professor Edward Everett, as well as ministers, merchants, lawyers, scholars, businessmen, and of course Bigelow and Brimmer. The select committee met repeatedly throughout the summer of 1831 and publicized the cemetery among their friends.[55]

Bigelow consulted many about what to name the cemetery, for this was the first time an American burial ground was to be given a proper name. Some suggested the classical but generic "Necropolis" (City of the Dead), but others countered that the name suggested an urban place rather than a "rural" landscape. Edward Everett, then *North American Review* editor, favored Bigelow's choice of "Mount Auburn," a simple change in the property's popular name but also symbolically descriptive. "Auburn" reminded classical scholars of the mythical Lake Avernus, a circular crater nestled into a hilly landscape in Campania near Naples. It was the reputed entrance to Hades sought by Virgil's Aeneas in search of his deceased father, and an allegory built into the landscape of the famed English gardens of Stourhead in the 1740s. Everett also though that "Elysian Fields" would be a "pretty" name, though as objectionable to the religious as "Sweet Auburn" because of its classical literary reference; yet he rationalized that "use diminishes surprisingly all such associations, as is seen in the case of the new towns in New York [State]—Troy, Utica."[56] The name "Mount Auburn" was of good Anglo-Saxon origin. It was also suggestive of allegorical sites visited in the Reverend John Bunyan's *Pilgrim's Progress* (1678) by Christian, an Everyman en route to the Celestial City, such as Mount Marvel, Mount Innocent, and Mount Charity. The name, like those of subsequent "rural" cemeteries, resembled names given to the era's new "rural" (suburban) estates. By midsummer 1831, Bigelow and the Horticulturists were calling their proposed cemetery "Mount Auburn."[57]

Dearborn, Bigelow, and the others promoted their cemetery in circulated subscription papers and placed many articles and progress reports in local periodicals. They encouraged visits by their friends to appreciate "the scenery and natural advantages of the spot," emphasizing the importance of preserving its endangered pastoral qualities. Dearborn continued to stress the potential historical and commemorative functions of the cemetery, and suggested that it might contribute to solving one of Boston's urban problems. In addition, an experimental garden would "develop the vast vegetable resources of the Union, give activity to enterprise, increase the enjoyment of all classes of citizens, advance the prosperity, and improve the general aspect of the whole country." Dearborn urged Bostonians to support the venture as a matter of civic duty, looking both to their past and to their future.[58]

Although the Horticulturists declared their proposed cemetery nondenominational, it was the product of liberal religion. Toasts at the 1831 festival of the Horticultural Society revealed the new cosmology while indulging in mockery of the old. Malthus A. Ward drank to "*Eden*—the first abode of the living—Mount Auburn, the last resting place of the dead. If the Tree of Life sprung from the soil of the one, Immortality shall rise from the dust of the other." The Reverend John Pierpont's toast displayed the levity with which the founders treated the old orthodoxy: "The tables turned since man first attended to Horticulture—then he had his worst *fall* in the Garden—now he has his best Garden in the *Fall*." In 1829 Dearborn had spoken of the inherent sanctity of any garden, citing the Almighty's sanctioning of its "peerless beauties and refined pleasures," epitomized by his "planting that of Eden, and consecrating it as a terrestrial paradise." Three years later he described Mount Auburn as a new Eden, reflecting "the beneficent precepts of our religion, the dictates of an exalted morality, a holy respect for the ashes of the dead, the kindest sympathies of the heart, and that active spirit of improvement which pervades every section of our country."[59]

Speaking in support of the cemetery, Dearborn acknowledged that "there is something unpleasant to many in the idea of cultivating the place of death. This may be owing to the old prejudice, which regards nature and art as opposed to each other." He praised the concept of creating a natural setting for burials as compatible with a new respect for the dead that "does not seem to partake of superstition." This new sensibility with regard to death was based on "enlightened, just, and manly sentiment, influencing not only the intelligent" but also common Americans, "who in general seem to be strangers to strong and delicate feeling." Dearborn urged the cultivation of sentiment as "giving a direction to public taste," a way to strengthen the republic by creating moral citizens. He equated the "rural" cemetery with the "grandeur" of Niagara Falls. Both were places where the inexorable forces of Nature instilled a sense of the sublime, where "the mind loses itself in earnest conjecture respecting destiny." Although Mount Auburn would be an educational institution, its lessons would be spiritual, conveying a realization of morality in aesthetic as well as intellectual terms.[60]

Such arguments, along with articles on international burial reform, appeared in many Boston periodicals almost as if they were advertisements. By the first of August, 1831, ninety-one families had purchased Mount

Auburn's first hundred lots. Brimmer claimed ten himself in various locations. Owing to that favorable response and the need to raise more funds to provide for embellishments and security, the subscription roll was enlarged to two hundred and then four hundred.

The Consecration Ceremonies and Joseph Story, Mount Auburn's First President

Fig. 7.10. Joseph Story, portrait from the crayon drawing by William Wetmore Story, engraved by J. Chaney. From W. W. Story, ed., *Life and Letters of Joseph Story*, 1851.

The Society prepared consecration ceremonies for September 24, 1831. Brimmer headed a committee that selected U.S. Supreme Court Associate Justice Joseph Story (1779–1845), one of its members, to serve as chief orator. (Fig. 7.10.) Story, a Unitarian, had been active in the Horticultural Society and in cemetery planning for two years. A national figure with regional roots, he was representative of the sort of notable individual Bigelow wanted the cemetery to recognize for the historical record. Though a newcomer to the Boston–Cambridge area, Story was so eminent that he was generally deemed the best choice to deliver the address.[61]

Born in Marblehead, son of Dr. Elisha Story, a surgeon who had participated in the Boston Tea Party before joining the Continental Army to care for the wounded, Joseph Story graduated from Harvard in 1798, then read law with Samuel Sewell and Samuel Putnam before setting up practice in Salem in 1801. Initially a Jeffersonian Republican, Story served in the Massachusetts House of Representatives from 1805 to 1811 with a hiatus while entering the Tenth Congress with Josiah Quincy in 1808–9. When President James Madison appointed him to the Supreme Court in 1811 under Chief Justice John Marshall, Jefferson opposed the appointment, knowing that Story would favor nationalization of the law over the rights of the various states to retain discrepancies. Simultaneously, for a time, the indefatigable Story rode the New England circuit, traveling over two thousand miles annually to preside over court in Massachusetts, Rhode Island, New Hampshire, and Maine when not serving three months a year on the Supreme Court.

As an overseer of Harvard, Story was instrumental in getting Josiah Quincy, former Boston mayor, appointed president of the college in 1829. That same year the noted attorney Nathan Dane (1752–1835) and Quincy persuaded Story to move from Salem to become Harvard's first Dane Professor of Law and create a model legal curriculum. Together, they shifted control of the college from Calvinist clergymen to secular attorneys and businessmen, mainly Unitarians and Whigs.[62] Old friends called Story simply "the poet of Marblehead," but his national reputation grew immensely during his thirty-four-year tenure of the nation's highest court and with his three-volume *Commentaries on the Constitution of the United States* (1833). Story eventually expanded his legal commentaries to twelve volumes that went through multiple editions, earning him the reputation of "the American Blackstone" and a "Father of American Jurisprudence."[63] The historian Arthur M. Schlesinger Jr. ranks Story second only to John Marshall as the "main pillar" in the "fortress of conservatism" built in that era. Story became a legal advocate of "the sacred rights of property" and corporations, private and eleemosynary. He allied himself nationally with Henry Clay, Nicholas Biddle, and other Whigs against the Jacksonian Democrats and sided with Danial Webster in the Charles River Bridge case in 1831, insisting that the common law protected the sanctity of private property. Along with John Quincy Adams, Massachusetts governor Levi Lincoln, and Alexander Everett, writes Schlesinger, Story's ideas assisted in the eventual rise of the national Republican Party out of the Whig Party in defense of the "American

System." Like his Whig colleagues industrialists Nathan Appleton and Abbot Lawrence, Story wished to create an American culture for political purposes.[64]

Mount Auburn was an appropriate cause for him. It achieved the goal his ally Quincy had promoted as mayor of establishing an extramural cemetery for Boston. Its design borrowed from the ideologically loaded landscape aesthetics of the English garden, with its Whiggish associations, and from the aim of French cemetery reform to restore social order through a "cult of ancestors." Furthermore, the rights of property were ensured and enshrined at Mount Auburn as nowhere else in America through legal assurances from the state that family burial lots could be held in perpetuity and could not be lost because of debt. Most important, Mount Auburn, a nondenominational yet spiritual institution, appealed to Story, a Unitarian and close friend of his Harvard roommates, the noted Unitarian ministers William Ellery Channing and Joseph Tuckerman. In his Supreme Court decisions, Story insisted on "private rights of conscience and the freedom of religious worship" while declaring that the nation's essential Christianity "ought to receive encouragement from the State," though he meant this "encouragement" to come through reformed corporate law and tax exemptions rather than outright state support. In his 1829 inaugural address at Harvard, Story declared that "Christianity becomes not merely an auxiliary, but a guide, to the law of nature."[65]

Story played a leading role in developing Mount Auburn despite his numerous academic and national commitments. Indeed, the cemetery was one of many local improvement causes he championed. Mount Auburn also seemed an appropriate project for Story because of his well-known penchant for melancholy, influenced by the deaths of several of his children, his first wife, his father, and others close to him. His son William Wetmore Story realized this after receiving a long autobiographical letter from his father, aged fifty-two, in 1831, prefaced by the observation, "Perhaps, when I am in my grave you will take comfort in these little details." Story's elegiac outlook was evident in his emphasis on the mystical significance of the simultaneous deaths of Jefferson and Adams on the fiftieth anniversary of Independence in his 1826 Harvard Phi Beta Kappa lecture, "Characteristics of the Age."[66]

William Wetmore Story, who left the law to become a sculptor, recalled that his father wrote Mount Auburn's consecration oration "to solace his wounded heart" following the death of his daughter, the fifth child lost in fifteen years: "In writing his address, he found a refuge from busy cares, and an outlet for crowding recollections, which found in utterance their best relief."[67] This illustrates still another reason why so many Bostonians in the professions, business, politics, and intellectual pursuits chose to found Mount Auburn. The cemetery provided a ritualized mechanism by which men, unlike women in their private sphere, might manage their grief—so frequent in an age of high infant and maternal mortality—through a controlled expression of mourning, permitting them to get on with their life and work. They would master their sorrow by putting it aside, away from daily view, while going about their business in public. Women had the newly prescribed etiquette and garb of the stages of mourning, but men could not retreat into seclusion. Removing the visible reminders of the deaths of loved ones from urban graveyards would help enable them to carry on as usual in their official capacity.[68] Story, Dearborn, Bigelow, and many of their friends were unabashed sentimentalists, a quality that only later would acquire negative connotations in male culture. They mourned publicly, and they wrote as much melancholy verse—and just as devoid of literary merit—as the published "scribbling women" of their day. Yet they began to try to be stoic in public, consigning their emotions to their leisure time and to places beyond the hustle of urbanization. They created Mount Auburn for those reason among so many others.[69]

The revamping and ritualization of deathways represented by the "rural" cemetery did not simply represent a "beautification of death," historian Philippe Ariès's assessment, or a "denial of death," which belongs to twentieth-century American culture. Rather, it reflected that era's new sensibilities shaped by the exigencies of a modernizing way of life: the rise of affective individualism, intensified cohesion of the nuclear family, a growing cult of efficiency in business and industry, and separation of the public sphere of men from the private one of women. Changing tastes were also crucial: a revulsion toward foul odors, whether of refuse or of bodies decomposing in burial; a new appreciation for the salutary influence of Nature on the emotions through cultivation of reason and sentiments; and a growing insistence on the canons of taste and gentility.

The contrast between the newly perceived inappropriateness of the city as a place of burial and Mount Auburn's fitting naturalism proved a major theme in descriptions of the consecration and in Judge Story's address on that occasion. (Fig. 7.11.) Story's son described the afternoon as ideal, "one of the serenest of those melancholy days which mark the early New England autumn." As Dearborn put it, "the deep blue vault of heaven canopied the immense area with a dome of more resplendent grandeur than all that genius can conceive or art accomplish; whispering zephyrs rustled the many twinkling leaves . . . the glorious sun gilded, with his cheerful beams, the smiling landscape." One broad, shady avenue had been cleared into the grounds from the entrance, marked only by bars to be opened or closed. Boston's elite drove their carriages into the site, leaving them in a grove of walnut trees, and walked into a deep dell near the center of the property, a natural amphitheater that easily accommodated an estimated two to three thousand on "rude benches." One newspaper likened the crowd to "the assembled Athenians in the venerable groves of Ceramicus," the cemetery and place of intellectual rendezvous of the ancient Greeks. Sixteen members of the Boston Band were paid three dollars each to lead the procession of speakers, ministers, and dignitaries to a stage "fashioned of unshorn pine boughs and young trees, and decorated with festoons of flowers interwoven with the variegated leaves of the forest." To the right of the platform an orchestra and choir performed in a hillside grove, overlooking the pond like angels singing from on high. According to the younger Story, the scene was "novel and impressive beyond description, and the whole assembly seemed subdued to reverential feeling by this simple service in the great church of nature."[70]

Henry Ware, Harvard's Hollis Professor of Divinity and a leading Unitarian, intoned the first prayer. Then the band played the music of the "reverend psalm of 'Old Hundred,'" a hymn composed by the Reverend John Pierpont, sung by the crowd "in one vast choral, that swelled into the sky and sounded down the aisles of the wood with a grandeur of effect beyond that of dome or cathedral."[71] Pierpont, nationally known for his popular, sentimental poetry, reinterpreted the message of

Fig. 7.11. Wooded hills above Consecration Dell. Photograph by BMGL, 1986.

Bryant's "Thanatopsis," emphasizing the universality and naturalness of mortality:

Decay! decay! 'tis stamped on all!
All bloom in flower and flesh shall fade,
Ye whispering trees, when we shall fall
Be our long sleep beneath your shade.

Here to thy bosom, Mother Earth,
Take back, in peace, what thou hast given;
And all that is of heavenly birth,
O God, in peace, recall to heaven.

The judge's son observed that "an electric thrill seemed to pervade the air when the last sound of voices died away."[72]

Judge Story then rose to speak; but "so overpowered was he by emotion that he could not begin," his son recalled. Regaining his composure, Story "faltered out" his first words; "several times, during the delivery of his discourse, he was so much overcome as to be obliged to pause, and his own emotion communicated itself to the audience, who listened in reverential silence and with glistening eyes." The man, still mourning the death by scarlet fever that spring of his ten-year-old daughter, had written his oration "in his heart's blood," and it "could not fail to reach the hearts of all who had suffered like himself." That was the same Joseph Story whom Andrew Jackson called "the most dangerous man in America." Some historians have described Unitarianism as a cold and rational religion devoid of emotion; but the sentimentalism in Story's address, the emotional response of his audience, and Unitarians' writings about Mount Auburn contradict that assessment.[73]

Judge Story's address summarized the intention that the cemetery solace survivors by providing a place for personalized commemoration. He declared: "It is to the living mourner—to the parent, weeping over his dear dead child—to the husband, dwelling in his own solitary desolation—to the widow, whose heart is broken by untimely sorrow . . . that the repositories of the dead bring home thoughts full of admonition, of instruction, and slowly, but surely, of consolation also." Old graveyards, he said, with their "sad spectacle of promiscuous ruins and intermingled graves," offered little comfort to the grieving and only intensified the bitterness of their loss. Even in rural towns, burial grounds were "left in a sad, neglected state, exposed to every sort of intrusion with scarcely a tree to shelter their barrenness or a shrub to spread a grateful shade over the new-made hillock." Familiar with the literary celebration of melancholy, Story praised the influence of contemplative visits to graves in a pastoral setting. Such a place admonishes, instructs, and instills "reminiscences of the past, sources of pleasing melancholy reflection." He explained:

> As time interposes its growing distances between us and [the dead], we gather up, with more solicitude, the broken fragments of memory, and weave . . . into our very hearts, the threads of their history. As we sit down by their graves, we seem to hear the tones of their affection whispering in our ears. We listen to the voice of their wisdom, speaking in the depths of our souls. We shed our tears; but they are no longer the burning tears of agony. They relieve our drooping spirits, and come no longer over us with a deathly faintness. We return to the world, and we feel ourselves purer, and better, and wiser, for this communion with the dead.

Story appreciated the "pleasures of melancholy" to be cultivated in the "Garden of Graves." Mount Auburn would be a place "to gratify human feelings, or tranquilize human fears; to secure the best religious influences, and to cherish all those associations which cast a cheerful light over the darkness of the grave." It objectified the new way of thinking about death. He viewed Mount Auburn "rather as means than as ends, rather as influences to govern human conduct, and to moderate human suffering." He observed: "Our cemeteries, rightly selected and properly arranged, may be made subservient to some of the highest purposes of religion and human duty. They may preach lessons, to which none may refuse to listen, and which all that live must hear. Truths may be there felt and taught in the silence of our own meditation, more persuasive, and more enduring than ever flowed from human lips." The "rural" cemetery would teach moral philosophy as well as history. It would serve along with the church as a source of spiritual activity.[74]

Story predicted that Mount Auburn would become an asylum for the world-weary, especially those overwhelmed by the new pace and demands of urban life, a place where visitors might "indulge in the dreams of hope and ambition, or solace their hearts by melancholy meditation." Its site objectified the contrast between urban and rural, creating a place of compromise and conciliation with its "variety of natural and artificial scenery." Story presented the symbolic juxtaposition:

> All around us there breathes a solemn calm, as if we were in the bosom of a wilderness, broken only by the breeze as it murmurs through the tops of the the forest. . . . Ascend but a few steps, and what a change of scenery to surprise and delight us. We seem, as it were, in an instant, to pass from the confines of death to the bright and balmy regions of life. Below us flows the winding Charles, with its rippling current, like the stream of time hastening to the ocean of eternity. In the distance, the city—at once the object of our admiration and our love—rears its proud eminences, its glittering spires, its lofty towers, its graceful mansions, its curling smoke, its crowded haunts of business and pleasure, which speak to the eye, and yet leave a noiseless loneliness on the ear.

In the cemetery, "we stand, as it were, upon the borders of two worlds," between the living and the dead as

ial or worship and passageways to the afterlife were consciously revived and reinterpreted at Mount Auburn.[75]

Fig. 7.12. "View from Consecration Dell." Lithograph by [Louis] Prang and [Julius] Mayer, Boston. From Flagg, 1861.

One English visitor observed that the ceremony "seemed to touch the hearts of all who witnessed this impressive scene, with the spirit of humility, devotion, reverence, and awe." The Boston press referred to the spirit of urban pride that resounded after the consecration. Joseph T. Buckingham effused that "there is not in all the untrodden valleys of the West, a more secluded, more natural or more appropriate spot for the religious exercises of the living." He predicted that in a few years, "when the hand of taste shall have passed over the luxuriance of nature, we may challenge the rivalry of the world to produce another such residence for the spirit of beauty." He was confident that Mount Auburn would "soon be a place of more general resort, both for [Bostonians] and for strangers, than any other spot in the vicinity." Indeed, there was "no better spot for the rambles of curiosity, health or pleasure; none sweeter for the whispers of affection among the living; none lovelier for the rest of our kindred." (Fig. 7.12.) Buckingham, who had so vehemently and publicly opposed the construction of crypts under Boston's churches during the 1823 burial controversy, became equally active in promoting and publicizing the new cemetery and was one of the first hundred subscribers.[76]

Despite the naturally picturesque advantages of the site, Mount Auburn still required landscape design, sculpting, and planting. Dearborn's plan, inspired by the contemplative, commemorative elements of English gardens and Père Lachaise, was only the first step toward realizing Mount Auburn's great potential.

well as between the city and country. The place was a hierophany, a link between earth and heaven, a sacred space. Its topography further symbolized this role. Mount Auburn lay west of Boston, where the setting sun daily emphasized that it was a place of death. Ancient associations attached to the garden, the mount, the valley, the pond, and the river as sacred and symbolic places of bur-

8

CEMETERY OR GARDEN?

Landscape Design and Conflicting Institutional Purposes

First follow Nature, and your judgment frame
By her just standard, which is still the same:
Unerring Nature, still divinely bright,
One clear, unchanged, and universal light.

—Alexander Pope, *Essay on Criticism* (1746)

Nature is a setting that fits equally well a comic or a mourning piece. . . . Within these plantations of God, a decorum and sanctity reigns. . . . In the woods, we return to reason and faith. There I feel that nothing can befall me in life,—no disgrace, no calamity, (leaving me my eyes,) which nature cannot repair. . . . I become a transparent eye-ball; I am nothing; I see all; the currents of the Universal Being circulate through me; I am part or particle of God. . . . In the tranquil landscape, and especially in the distant line of the horizon, man beholds somewhat as beautiful as his own nature.

—Ralph Waldo Emerson, "Nature" (1836)

The leaders of the Massachusetts Horticultural Society naïvely anticipated that creating a picturesque cemetery would require little work and very little expense for "the hand of art to fit it" for its purposes. As Edward Everett put it, "Nature has already done almost all that is required. Scarcely any thing is needed but a suitable enclosure, and such walks as will give access to the different parts of the enclosed space, and exhibit its features to the greatest advantage."[1] The land on which the cemetery was to be situated was "so abundantly covered with forest trees," many over sixty years old, that nothing was required but the laying out of earthen avenues, planting of borders, clearing of underbrush, and erection of fences, gateways, and a few appropriate edifices "to put the grounds in a sufficiently complete state for the uses designated to render them at once beautiful and interesting." Here, "among the hills, glades, and dales . . . may be selected sites for isolated graves and tombs." These would serve as focal points seen from sinuous avenues laid out "to approximate the landscape of the most admired English gardens." The process was not that simple.[2]

Dearborn's Initial Design

It was General Henry A. S. Dearborn, president of the Massachusetts Horticultural Society, who led the planning of the landscape. On the front periphery, in the flat land northeast of the glacial esker called Indian Ridge, he proposed conversion of "small ponds and morasses into picturesque sheets of water, their margins diversified by clumps and belts of our most splendid native flowering trees and shrubs." The garden would be a buffer zone, screening burials from the Cambridge–Watertown road. Cleaning and deepening the ponds would produce sludge, invaluable for fertilizer for the "successful cultivation" of this experimental garden. Dearborn doubted that the area designated for burials would require much "improvement." He predicted that the cemetery could be completed in two years. The task would have taken forty years, he said, had not large forest trees, "the venerable monarchs of the grove," and their "luxuriant progeny, which, in umbrageous contiguity, cover each hill and plain and sloping vale," already cloaked most of the grounds.[3]

Fig. 8.1. First receiving tomb, Green Briar Path. Engraving from *Picturesque Pocket Companion*, 1839.

The Horticultural Society appointed a nine-member Garden and Cemetery Committee, five of them burial lot owners. Most of the work of designing and laying out Mount Auburn's landscape, however, was done by a subcommittee consisting of Brimmer, Bigelow, and Dearborn.[4] Dearborn was away for months at a time, serving in the United States Congress from 1831 to 1833, but he attended half of all meetings from 1831 through 1834. Joseph Story, albeit an associate justice on the U.S. Supreme Court, took over in his absence, though by this time plans for the system of avenues and paths and other landscape features were well on the way to completion.

George Brimmer's task was to procure a "receiving tomb" in the city for winter use when digging graves with the tools available at the time was difficult, or for temporary storage of bodies to be interred later at Mount Auburn in tombs or graves that were not yet ready, or to be shipped elsewhere. Use of a receiving tomb may also have been elected by some to ensure against "suspended animation," or burial of the living (perhaps in a coma), a common fear in that era. He paid $300 for a crypt under the Park Street Church, belying the argument that a prime motivation behind advocacy of an extramural cemetery was the belief that burials under urban churches endangered public health. The cost of placing a body in the tomb was $1.50, paid to the sexton.[5] John C. Gray and Benjamin A. Gould oversaw construction of an additional receiving tomb at the cemetery, a simple quadrangular tumulus of granite blocks covered with sod, functional rather than ornamental. (Fig. 8.1.) Bodies deposited from April through September could remain there for up to two months; four during the rest of the year. Analysis of deposits from the 1830s reveals that only a third were recent deaths (within one month). Another third had died within the past year. The rest were prior deaths retrieved from old graves or tombs, perhaps the equivalent of the second burial common in many cultures. Despite the required posting of a bond, bodies often lay unclaimed for longer periods or were simply abandoned, to be buried anonymously at the cemetery.

Mount Auburn's leader and landscape designer for the first three formative years, Dearborn was self-taught in the principles of classical design. He wrote and illustrated by hand a two-volume "Treatise on Grecian Architecture" (1828), dedicated to his children and urging their self-improvement through the study of historic design. He looked to ancient Greece as an ideal place where "ev'ry mechanic who excelled in his vocation was enabled to eternize his name, which was considered the greatest possible blessing, as the most important prayer which the Greeks address to their Gods was for the conservation of their memory." He anticipated that the new cemetery would offer such opportunities to enterprising Bostonians.[6]

Even before Mount Auburn's consecration, Dearborn was at work on the grounds, chalking and staking out a few eighteen- to twenty-foot-wide avenues to provide access to all parts of the property for horse-drawn hearses and carriages and five- to six-foot-wide paths for pedestrians. Creating a picturesque landscape "in conformity to the modern style" required laying out avenues that curved to fit the site's remarkably varied terrain. Dearborn followed the land's natural features in positioning avenues and paths and tried "to run them as nearly level as possible by winding gradually and gracefully through the valleys and obliquely over hills, without any unnecessary or unavoidable bend." He used elliptical or parabolical curves to replace "stiff circular lines," which he found "incompatible with elegance of form and a pleasing effect." This graceful shape was, he claimed, "a discovery of the Greeks, for all the mouldings in their architecture and the beautiful forms of their vases are profiles of the sections of a cone, and are either parabolical, elliptical, or hyperbolical."[7] The cemetery was to be a walking garden with paths separated from carriageways, following the example of Père Lachaise. This permitted pedestrians to stroll through much of the grounds without distraction by carriage traffic, except at intersections. At both cemeteries, the carriage avenues made all of the grounds accessible even to the aged and others not able to walk the hilly terrain, minimizing the distance pallbearers had to carry the coffin from a hearse. (Fig. 8.2.) Those interested only in the experimental garden could visit without venturing into the area reserved for burials. Dearborn drew further inspiration from English landscape gardens in his design of a sinuous path system. Perhaps he knew the poem by William Mason (1724–1797), "The English Garden" (1771), which lauded the "smooth, simple path" with "undulating line" as "emblem pure of legal liberty."[8]

Through the autumn of 1831, Dearborn labored "with hands as well as mind, without money and without price." As soon as he returned from Congress in the spring of 1832 he was there, "hoe in hand, day after day, at the head of his laborers, levelling and grading the walks, taking his dinner with him. . . . He would step into the Wyeth House [an inn] across the road to eat." Using oxen to help with the heavy earth-moving, Dearborn and his workers plowed, leveled, and rolled the ground to retain the character of the original terrain while refining it.[9] After the April rains, the more arduous work began of laying roadbeds of fine gravel and smoothing the earthen paths. Dearborn's journal detailed his activity. In 1832 alone he completed nearly six miles of avenues and paths, providing carriage access to the summit. He even laid a road outside the grounds around the eastern periphery (now Coolidge Avenue) to the Charles River and to existing highways on the south and northeast, "thus furnishing a new and most interesting approach" from Brighton, Brookline, Roxbury, and other towns to the south, as well as from the city. Laying out avenues and paths cost $3,000, one third of the initial income from the lot sales. Before long, Mount Auburn was acclaimed "the pleasantest place of resort" in the area as visitors, "numerous beyond all expectations," thronged to the grounds throughout the fall.[10]

After leveling the ground along the Watertown road for a fence, Dearborn set aside his tools for several months to attend the House of Representatives' winter session. A resident manager had yet to be hired. Charging Brimmer to oversee whatever landscape work remained, Dearborn sent detailed instructions, stipulating how thick to lay surfaces for avenues and paths, how to sod gutters, and where to get good gravel. Should Brimmer have to go south, Dearborn suggested that Bigelow take over. Brimmer oversaw the building of a rustic gardener's cottage following Dearborn's designs. Unfinished tree trunks served as columns along the porch.[11]

Determined that "the general appearance of the whole grounds should be that of a well-managed park" in the English fashion, Dearborn sketched planting plans showing shrubs and flowers in generous ten-foot-wide borders along major avenues but not otherwise deliberately clustered to frame vistas. The flowers would include new bulbous varieties and perennials as well as the native "wild" sort. Ideally, ornamental plantings would appear naturalistic rather than as a "dense and wild coppice or a neglected garden whose trees and plants have so multiplied and interlaced . . . as to completely destroy all the airiness, grace, and luxuriance of growth which good taste demands," even where proprietors "improved" lots with their own plants. Dearborn, by his own account, "established as a principle the method pursued in England in laying out extensive ornamental plantations of forest trees, shrubs, and flowers," transplanting elms and other forest trees from his estate nurseries at Brinley Place in Roxbury into open areas near the front. He recommended moving and rearranging trees later to "render their plantations a picture, varying and contrasting the masses by different tints," as an artist creates "factitious scenes," each "connected with the whole design." He thinned the woods in places to admit sunshine in "lawns" (then meaning clearings), especially along Central Avenue, which was "more open to the sun" than the rest of the cemetery.[12]

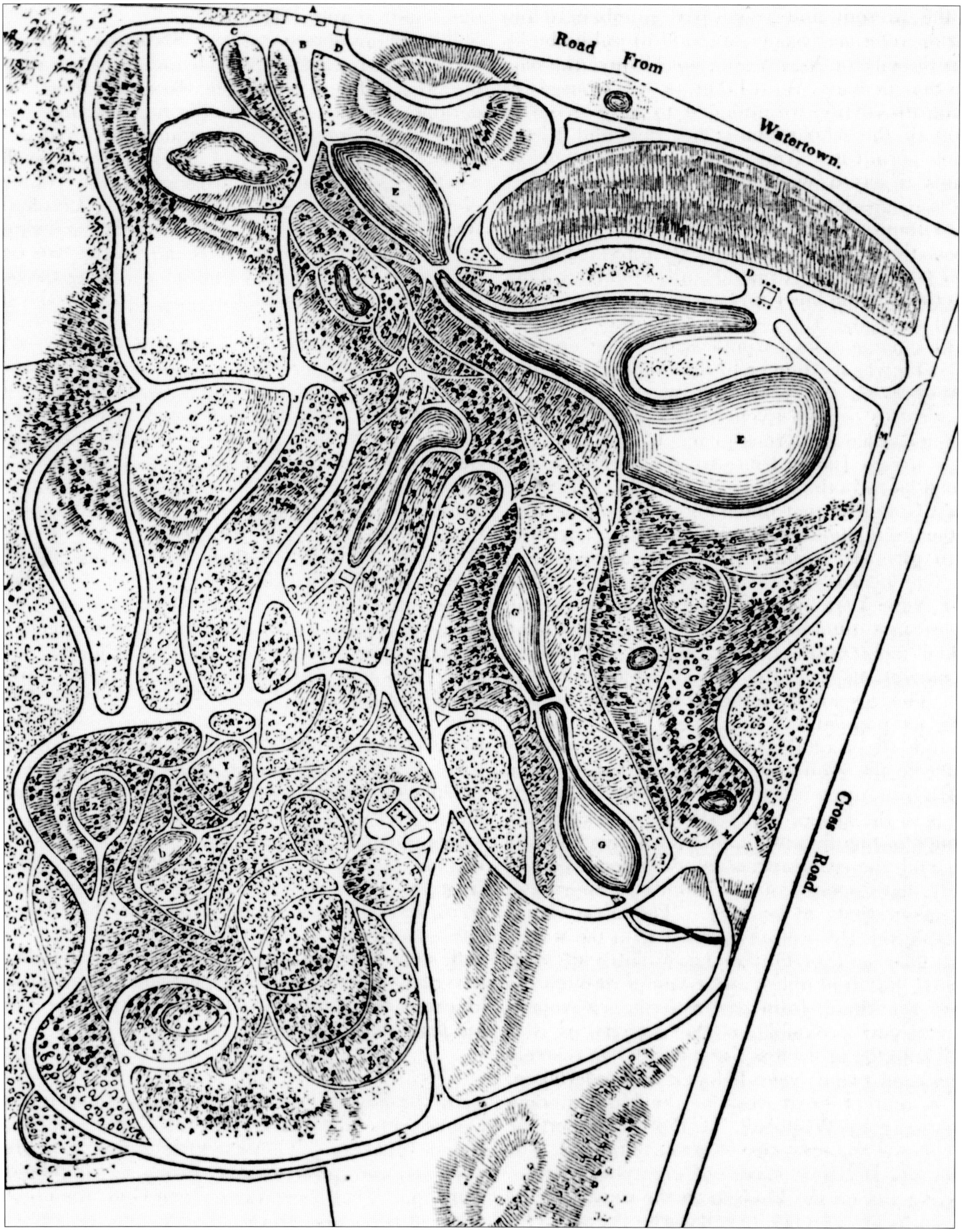
Road From Watertown.
Cross Road.

By 1833, Dearborn had carved "sheets of water" from bogs and shallow ponds to provide settings for aquatic plants as well as rhododendrons, azaleas, magnolias, and other species requiring damp, rich soil. In order to preserve Mount Auburn's "rural" nature and ensure that it would not become built up in a congested fashion as was already the case at Père Lachaise, he created six-foot margins or setbacks between lots and each avenue or path and reserved at least three feet between lots. The standard 300-square-foot lot therefore required at least 550 square feet. But Mount Auburn's 72 acres (increased to 110 by 1833) seemed so large in contrast to old graveyards that the Garden and Cemetery Committee agreed to be generous with space, preserving margins to ensure the naturalistic aesthetics into the future. No lots would be set in designated focal point areas such as Central Square near the core of the grounds, where the main avenue branches out near Consecration Dell. The committee also preserved wooded areas on hillsides unless there were special orders for building tombs there.

Through that formative period Bigelow was subordinate to Dearborn in the design process. The doctor's professional and academic careers and his activities in local literary societies kept him busy. Bigelow spent the summer of 1832 in New York City, investigating an Asiatic cholera epidemic, returning to Boston surreptitiously to evade quarantine. In 1833 he traveled to Europe for five months with the Whitwells, the Kembles, Dr. Oliver Wendell Holmes, Thomas Appleton, Mrs. Kirk Boott, and their families. One of the first things he and his friends did when they reached Paris in May was to visit Père Lachaise. The doctor wrote to his children, "It truly equals our expectations, especially in its superb view of the city." Although it was more crowded than he had anticipated, Bigelow deemed some of its monuments "magnificent." Sentimental inscriptions of familial affection touched him "most deeply."[13]

Although Bigelow had called for creation of a "rural" cemetery in 1825, he never specified what the landscape design should be like. It was Dearborn who made most of the initial decisions about trees and landscape. Bigelow carried them out, buying $100 worth of shrubs, directing their placement by workmen, and giving plant names to avenues and paths identified by signs painted on small, white "guideboards" made of red cedar cleared from the property. He had them raised seven feet high on posts and painted white. Naming, rather than landscape design, is what Bigelow's biographer referred to in crediting the doctor with "designating" the cemetery's ways. While Dearborn was busy laying out Mount Auburn, Bigelow was often absent, though he attended all but four Garden and Cemetery Committee meetings in the first four years, a record surpassed only by treasurer George Bond. Then, when Dearborn returned to Boston in the summers of 1832 and 1833, Bigelow happened to be away. Dearborn missed most of the committee meetings Bigelow attended. In the spring of 1833, Dearborn was supervising setting hitching posts outside the gate, finishing paths in the experimental garden, grading the public lot, laying a path around Forest Pond, and staking out fifty more lots with the assistance of surveyor Alexander Wadsworth (1806–1898). The need for someone to oversee construction, lay out lots, direct Wadsworth's topographical survey, and take on the increasing demands for burials, record keeping, and overseeing individual monument building forced the Garden and Cemetery Committee to hire a full-time superintendent, David Haggerston, in March 1833. By 1834, Dearborn was conspicuously absent.[14]

Fig. 8.2. The first map of Mount Auburn, 1831. Engraving after the landscape design of General Henry A. S. Dearborn, transcribed by Alexander Wadsworth. Reprinted in *The American Magazine*, 1846. MAC.

The Fate of the Experimental Garden

The controversy that would arise later over whether Dearborn or Bigelow deserves credit for Mount Auburn's founding and design was a distant echo of a more substantial controversy that plagued its first years. Bigelow and other cemetery proponents resented that permanent structures could not be built right away. Horticulturists, by contrast, begrudged development of the cemetery at a time of limited funds and at the expense of the experimental garden. Ambitious plans to make Mount Auburn an "Institution for the Education of Scientific and Practical Gardeners" were thwarted, though Dearborn urged them on: "In this age of general improvement, when institutions and associations have been formed for inculcating intelligence in every branch of knowledge and among all walks of society . . . it is not only desirable, but highly important, that measures should be taken for extending similar advantages [as in instruction in the mechanical arts] to those persons who may wish to become accomplished Gardeners." He proposed a practical school of horticulture with instructors in "a science and an art . . . requiring an extensive acquaintance with Natural History and Physics, Botany, Mineralogy, Hydraulics, Mechanics, Architecture, Chemistry, and Entomology." There would be lessons in topographical analysis, drawing, projection of maps, laying out of grounds, and design of "rural" buildings to "embellish" the "modern" or English style of landscape gardening. Here gardeners would teach both theory and practice so "that science and skill may be contemporaneously acquired . . . in a well-managed establishment," as was only possible then in England and in parts of Europe. Indeed, he wished Mount Auburn to become a school of design, complete with library, models, maps, and plans and elevations of buildings. There would be studio space where students would learn to create "rural architecture" as well as gravel walks, artificial caverns, fish ponds, and observatories extending over at least half the grounds.[15]

Dearborn's plan was not unprecedented. London's Royal Horticultural Society (1804) leased Chiswick Gardens, which proved an important training ground from 1823 on for Joseph Paxton (1803–1865), who achieved fame second only to John Claudius Loudon (1783–1843) as one of a new generation of English landscape gardeners. The Royal Botanic Society Gardens in London's Regent's Park, developed between 1811 and 1818, attracted aspiring professionals such as Adolph Strauch (1822–1883) from Prussia, who later became a major American cemetery and park designer based in Cincinnati. Dearborn hoped that his experimental garden and school combining design and horticultural curricula would become another such center for professional training. Its interdisciplinary focus would resemble that of Bigelow's pioneering Harvard course on technology. Ultimately, no ambitious, formalized program of landscape study would be available in America until seventy years later, with the development of the first such curriculum at Harvard.[16]

The need for an experimental garden to develop better and more diversified plants preoccupied other founders. As Zebedee Cook Jr., the society's vice president, reminded his colleagues: "We have been too long accustomed to rely upon foreign nurseries for fruit trees and other plants. . . . We should depend more upon our own resources." Cook recalled a time when "everything that bore the impress of a foreign original was sought after, admired and eulogized without much regard to its intrinsic merits." Now, he observed, "these antinational prejudices and predilections are fast receding before the beaming and unquenchable light of intellect and patriotism." Cook aimed to domesticate foreign plants at Mount Auburn and develop new hybrids, with parts of the garden devoted to fruit trees, timber trees, ornamentals and shrubs, flowers, orangeries, hotbeds, vineries, and greenhouses. Nurseries, melon grounds, strawberry fields, and a "culinarium" for vegetables would fill the northeastern section of the grounds and a bit to the southeast—tiny parcels for such ambitious uses. Dearborn agreed about the need for an experimental garden to "develop the vast vegetable resources of the Union, to give activity to enterprise, increase the enjoyment of all classes of citizens, advance the prosperity of all classes of citizens, and improve the general aspect of the whole country." In this way, Mount Auburn would become an institution of the "American System."[17]

Horticulturists wanted to discover which seeds from various parts of the country and other nations could be naturalized. In the spring of 1832, anxious over delays in planting new varieties of potatoes, corn, peas, and carrots, Dearborn charged Brimmer to hire a gardener to prepare the soil in the flat area north of the Indian Ridge glacial esker. Although it was to remain separate from the burial area, Dearborn staked out walks and chose locations for bridges connecting the two areas at several points over extensive wetlands named Garden Pond, "a line of demarcation rather than of disconnection," with the garden shielding the cemetery from the public road. As in English gardens, borders and barriers were to be inconspicuous.[18]

News of the joint garden and cemetery venture spread internationally through a network of horticulturists who sent contributions. The *New England Farmer* regularly listed plants received: *Magnolia acuminata* seeds from Ohio forests, trees from an upstate New York nursery, scions of plums and apples from Montreal, vegetable seeds from the London Horticultural Society, and a hundred seed varieties from the Calcutta Botanical Gardens. The Naples Botanic Gardens sent a large box of mixed seeds. By the end of 1833, Dearborn had inventoried over 1,300 forest, ornamental, and fruit trees, a wide array of vegetables, and 450 seed varieties—strawberries, wild rice, skinless oats, Normandy garden cress, tree of heaven, and a newly discovered vegetable from Chile, the *Oxalis crenata*, which some hoped would rival the potato as a staple crop. Since Mount Auburn had yet to install greenhouses, he cultivated many in his own Brinley Place estate nurseries in Roxbury.[19]

When David Porter, American chargé d'affaires to the Ottoman Empire, read discussions in American newspapers of trees "most proper to decorate or to conceal the gloomy aspect of our neglected Grave Yards," he sent seeds of the oriental cypress, the beauty of Turkish cemeteries, earmarking his gift specifically for the cemetery. In Turkey, he wrote, "death is divested of half his terrors, by the cheerful aspect which [the] cemeteries present. They are places of resort during festivals and are visited by Christians as the most pleasant place for recreation." Porter predicted that when the cypress "decorates" American graveyards, "death will be deprived of his sting, the grave of its victory."[20]

Dearborn welcomed gifts for the cemetery and the garden, and he tried to develop both sections simultaneously. In 1833 he persuaded the Horticultural Society to go $5,000 into debt and got thirty-five Bostonians to loan $100 apiece to buy twenty-five acres of hilly, wooded land just to the west of Mount Auburn, arguing that the terrain would permit better development of the picturesque landscape and provide "beautiful sites for monuments." The land was quickly surveyed and sold for burial lots, which proved so desirable that many exchanged their lots for new ones there. Mount Auburn now encompassed 110 acres, in comparison to Père Lachaise, which began with only 55 acres, expanding to 72 by the 1830s.[21]

Despite enlarging the cemetery, Dearborn never did accomplish his goal of dividing the garden into "compartments" or "departments" to conduct the "comparative experiments on the modes of culture . . . to attain a knowledge of the most useful, rare, and beautiful species, the best processes of rearing and propagating them, [and] the most successful methods of insuring perfect and abundant crops, as well as useful and ornamental planting."[22] Joseph Bradlee, George Pratt, and Elijah Vose unsuccessfully tried to raise funds specifically earmarked for the experimental garden, since proceeds from lot sales were absorbed by improving the burial area. Nevertheless, Dearborn hired David Haggerston, a commercial gardener from Charlestown and a Horticultural Society member, as superintendent in the spring of 1833. With two laborers and the porter at the gate, the "practical gardener" Haggerston planted hotbeds for vegetables and decorative plants. They set out three hundred forest, ornamental, and fruit trees. Dearborn still hoped to develop a mutually beneficial, symbiotic relationship between the garden and the cemetery, but he was growing pessimistic. Tensions escalated between horticulturists and lot owners over public access to the grounds. Brimmer noted indifference if not outright opposition to an experimental garden among cemetery proprietors. By that summer a disheartened Dearborn realized that he would have to abandon his hope of creating a landscape gardening school. Behind the scenes Bigelow may well have been one of these opponents, despite his knowledge of plants and his Horticultural Society leadership. He later suggested that the garden plan had just been a matter of expediency to secure institutional auspices under which to begin developing the cemetery.[23]

Early Public Acceptance and Uses

An auction was held in November 1831 for subscribers who paid a premium to select lot locations. The merchant-philanthropist Samuel Appleton paid the most, $100, to get first choice; Bigelow and Dearborn each paid $72.50 and Brimmer between $60 and $71 for each of his ten lots. Other premiums ranged from $15 to $65. The lots chosen were dispersed throughout the grounds, some on flat land near Central Avenue, others on hills and in valleys. No section seemed more desirable than another. The first four hundred lots were in the areas surveyed first. Appleton, a major benefactor of Harvard, claimed the top of Cedar Hill on a path leading to the cemetery's highest point. Josiah Quincy, former Boston mayor and now Harvard's president, picked a lot nearby with a commanding view of the city and the college to the east. (Fig. 8.3.) Bigelow chose two contiguous lots on Beech Avenue near Central Avenue. Story preferred a secluded spot in the tiny valley of Forest Pond reached only by an earthen path. Dearborn and the journalist Buckingham chose lots overlooking the other end of that pond. The heirs of industrialist Francis Cabot Lowell selected a location for a chamber tomb on a steep hillside reached by a path extending into the central dell with its dark, natural, circular pool. Most preferred more visible lots on sinuous avenues accessible to carriages.

In the spring of 1832 the society designated Bigelow and Charles Curtis as agents "to go round" and solicit lot sales. Treasurer George Bond placed advertisements in newspapers. Subscribers received assurances that they would not be subject to any charges beyond those for the burial lot. Location was to be determined by a chance drawing similar to the land distribution lottery used by the Puritans in forming towns. Just having a plot was supposed to be prestigious. A pamphlet in the fall of 1832 listed existing proprietors in order to encourage sales to Bostonians aspiring to associate themselves with members of the elite who had already accepted the new cemetery.[24]

According to Dearborn, Mount Auburn immediately won favor among "the affluent, the enlightened, the virtuous, the patriotic, the industrious and enterprising among all classes," an optimistic assessment of lot sales tinged by promotionalism in his public statements. He believed that this ready acceptance evidenced a strength of local and national character, a moral and patriotic sensibility in Boston beyond "that active spirit of improvement which pervades every section of our country." He urged that spirit on, hoping to increase lot sales. In that first year, lot purchases and premiums brought in $10,488.50. Of the first 250 proprietors, some 122 were merchants, gentlemen, or physicians; 41 were mechanics or skilled workers; 3 were widows; and the rest were unclassified. Mount Auburn appealed particularly to those with Harvard ties and fond memories of having lingered there as students. Henry Blake McLellan wrote to his mother in 1833, shortly before his death at age twenty-two, that he wanted to be buried there because "with those pleasant places my college days are tenderly connected, *and I would love there to sleep my long, cold sleep.*" Despite the newness of the cemetery, McLellan believed that "to such a place there is a permanence which is wanting to the common churchyard; the bodies there deposited rest quietly forever." His family promptly bought a lot. The college received a donation from Dr. George Shattuck's family of a large 5,226-square-foot lot for burial of students and professors who did not have burial rights in family lots of their own or who could not be shipped back to distant homes for burial. Decades before the regular use of embalming, rarely would a body be shipped to a distant home. Supplementing the Harvard corner in the crowded old Cambridge graveyard, the wooded site near the cemetery's highest eminence was named Harvard Hill.[25]

Fig. 8.3. Josiah Quincy lot on the corner of Rose and Sweet Briar Paths. Photograph by BMGL, 1983.

In contrast to Dearborn's assessment, Bigelow found the public slow to accept Mount Auburn as a burial site. He later recalled that the "change of place from the city to the country was not effected without difficulty." The idea of graves in "a distant wood" initially "met with lukewarmness, prejudice, and direct opposition." After all, burial outside the town center had been the fate of social pariahs or the poorer sort, their graves often ravaged by "resurrection men" who supplied corpses to physicians for anatomical study. Some even questioned the motivations of a doctor recommending a rural cemetery; but fears for the vulnerability of graves were calmed by passage in 1831 of a Massachusetts law making human dissection legal, hence eliminating much of the illicit traffic in cadavers supplied by grave robbers. Bigelow countered people's reluctance to bury their dead far from their homes by arguing that the city's crowded burial grounds might soon have to be abandoned and "the original tenants'" bones "ejected" and removed to parts unknown. Other burial places "must be formed in the country—the primitive and only proper location" for interment. Bigelow overcame some hesitancy by "quiet interviews with selected friends of good judgment, of public spirit, and of high social influence," many of whom helped advance lot sales.[26]

Nevertheless, as Bigelow's biographer, the Reverend George E. Ellis, wrote, many Bostonians "were grieved and shocked at the proposal of carrying [their dead] far away across the river and burying them in wild, desolate woods, their graves exposed to violation." The location required negation of superstitions, especially the old taboo against transporting the dead across water. Random lot placement at Mount Auburn was not an issue. The need to fit burials into crowded graveyards had already ended the traditional alignment of graves on an east-west axis, based on the belief that bodies had to be positioned so the "elect" could sit up in their graves on Judgment Day to face the Second Coming with the rising sun.[27]

Most people had yet to adopt the practice of visiting graves, just becoming accepted in Paris after burial reform, and could not understand the desirability of creating a pleasant, pastoral setting for interments. Even those who envisioned such an ideal setting through the era's mourning pictures and sentimental poetry balked at the associated costs. Public hacks were scarce and expensive. Despite the regular stage and new bridges, there was little transportation for those not rich enough to own carriages, a luxury. With good Yankee frugality, many potential proprietors might have considered it an excessive expense to rent a hearse for funeral transportation and carriages for those who would follow it to a place four miles from the city.

Yet publicity in various Boston newspapers was aimed at persuading "mechanics" or skilled craftsmen, members of the growing middle class, to join the elite in buying lots. Still, many could not consider Mount Auburn because of the initial cost of $60 for a family lot, an expenditure not always necessary in the old graveyards, though crypts under city churches sold for about $300. Women working in the Lowell mills of the Merrimack Manufacturing Company earned about $98.80 a year after paying for board, and this was more than schoolteachers received. Male operatives in the Lowell and Waltham mills took home about $292 annually before rent. Common laborers in Boston grossed about $230 a year, a master mason $500. Estimated annual expenses for a family of four living frugally were $450. Purchase of a family lot at $60 would have been difficult to afford with no provisions for paying over time. Even a minister and academic of the caliber of Henry Ware, Hollis Professor of Divinity at Harvard, who officiated at Mount Auburn's consecration, declared himself "ill able to spare the sum of money"; yet he did.[28]

Dearborn proposed scattering less expensive single graves throughout the grounds among the family lots, but other founders vetoed that idea. Mount Auburn did provide a "public" lot, sixty by ninety feet in size, divided into four sections for 160 permanent single graves at $10 each for those who would not or could not buy a family lot. (Fig. 8.4.) Surrounded by a simple iron fence, it was deemed adequate for widows, orphans, travelers, and those of the "middling sort." Mount Auburn had no provisions for the working class or poor, who were still consigned to anonymous graves in municipal burying grounds. Landlessness was only a recent and limited, urban and industrial phenomenon in 1830. Great tides of

Fig. 8.4. Saint John's Public Lot on Fir Avenue, Mount Auburn's second public lot. Photograph by Carol Betsch, 2005.

poor immigrants had yet to arrive; and when they did in the 1840s, the Catholic Church made other provisions in small consecrated grounds.[29]

The Tremont House, Boston's new "modern" hotel (the first of its kind in the nation, opened in 1829), applied for a land grant to erect a tomb for out-of-town guests who died while staying there. The request was denied; the trustees deemed the "public" lot adequate. Maintaining its reputation for innovation with the best new amenities, in 1833 the hotel purchased its own lot on Hawthorne Path and erected a pentagonal tomb of Quincy granite for guests who became permanent. The six-foot-tall structure with sunken chamber contained three rows of horizontal cells of mica slate, aligned three across, along all four sides, a total of thirty-six spaces, each to be sacrosanct and sealed with a marble tablet bearing the name and dates of the deceased. (Fig. 8.5.) By 1839 it held two interments, one a visitor from New York and one from Smyrna, the Ottoman port, which actively traded with Boston.

The Horticultural Society deemed Mount Auburn egalitarian, declaring, "Every citizen should have an opportunity of participating in the advantages of the establishment." Although granting that there were few provisions for the "humblest citizens" of the "Metropolis of New England," Dearborn spoke of lots "which every man in the community might acquire upon the same terms," and "at an expense considerably less than that of a common tomb [in a Boston graveyard] or a vault beneath a church, to deposit the mortal remains of his friends or to provide a place of burial for himself, which, while living, he may contemplate without dread or disgust . . . removed from the discordant scenes of life." Farmers, mechanics, and dealers in building materials might pay for lots in labor or goods. The neighboring farmer, Leonard Stone, built a two-story clapboard superintendent's cottage with shingled roof, following Dearborn's specifications, in exchange for a plot. Indeed, Dearborn noted that a large part of the cost of "constructing roads, fences, gate-ways and other edifices may be defrayed by compensation in cemetery lots." Bartering lots for services and goods continued on a limited basis for decades.[30]

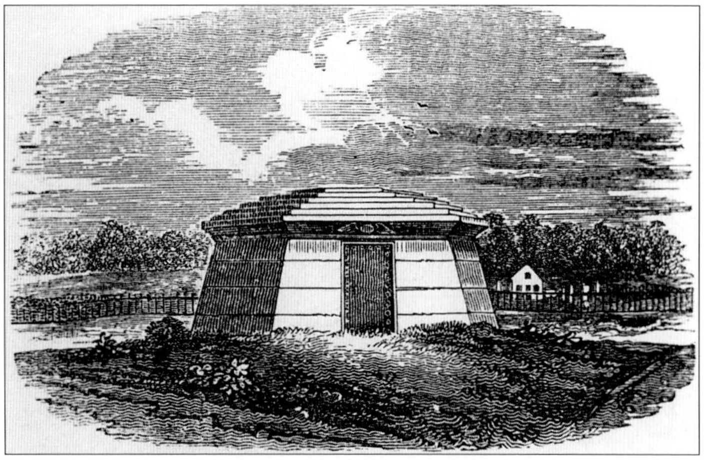

Fig. 8.5. Tremont House, or "Strangers'" Tomb, Mount Auburn. Engraving from *Picturesque Pocket Companion*,1839.

In its first year Mount Auburn proved more popular than Père Lachaise (1804) had been in its first two decades. Père Lachaise won acceptance slowly and only after a "revolution in customs and manners" brought about by the "universal gloom" following Napoleon's Waterloo defeat, as Dearborn explained in 1832. It had taken a full decade for the Parisian cemetery to become "a resort of the admirers of the arts, the opulent and enlightened, as well as the common place of sepulcher for the most illustrious in letters, science, and arts, and of the humblest citizen in Paris." By contrast, prosperous Bostonians lost no time in buying space at Mount Auburn. More lots were sold in its first four years than in the Parisian cemetery's first ten, and monument and tomb construction also exceeded that at Père Lachaise for the first years of both.[31]

Among the first proprietors, John Pierpont (1785–1866), ordained the Unitarian pastor of the Hollis Street Church in 1819, whose hymn was sung at Mount Auburn's consecration, lauded "The Garden of Graves" in *The Token*, a sentimental gift book, in 1832: "At last, we are to have a place in which, with our friends, we may be laid when we are dead, and upon which we can look with pleasure while we live. Sweet Auburn, a spot consecrated already in the hearts of many, by the associations and remembrance of early friendship, by the recollections of many a solitary walk, and many a day dream of revery, is to become a garden, sacred to sepulture and to botanical science." Pierpont anticipated being "beautifully mingled" there, "life and death." He predicted:

> Vegetable beauty and frailty and strength and grace shall there be peculiarly emblematical and instructive. The rose shall hang its head and blush

over the resting-place of modesty; the lily shall tell of the innocence that is buried beneath its stem; the oak shall shade the inflexible patriot's grave; and the laurel shall dress the poet's bed. . . . The young widow will, with her own hands, plant a weeping willow where she has herself bent in sorrow; the mother will scatter snowdrops upon the earth that covers her child, that was cut off in the first days of its opening spring; the lover, carry the graceful myrtle that his mistress nursed while she lived and bid it take root and watch her in his stead where now she sleeps alone; the husband, lead the grapevine around and over the arbor that hides the mother of his children; while all the trees of the garden, that fade at the touch of the frost, shall remind the laborer and the mourner, alike, that all must die; and the cedars that even now, in dead winter, look green upon the sides of Sweet Auburn, shall stand up over the remains of the Christian preacher, and intimate eternity to man.[32]

Pierpont bought a lot on Magnolia Avenue, which curved around the mount. He visited it often to savor the "pleasures of melancholy" and meditated on his inevitable fate. He described the site in the verse "To My Grave":

My grave! I've marked thee on this sunny slope,
The warm, dry slope of Auburn's wood-crowned hill
That overlooks the Charles, and Roxbury's fields,
That lies beyond it, as lay Canaan's green
And smiling landscape beyond Jordan's flood,
As seen by Moses.

The spot had an intensely personal significance for the minister, who gazed back across metropolitan panoramas while recollecting his career:

There stands the church, within whose lofty walls
My voice for truth, and righteousness, and God . . . .
. . . . I chose this spot,
And marked it for my grave, that, when my dust
Shall be united to its kindred dust,
They who have loved me—should there be any such
E'er stand beside it and let fall a tear.

There Pierpont contemplated the "Kingdom" of God, where "Life, death, earth, heaven, eternity, and time / Lie all within it." Such were the lessons of pantheistic moral philosophy that visitors were supposed to read in the picturesque wooded landscape.[33] (See Fig. 10.27.)

Many locals still frequented the old "Sweet Auburn." Two visitors, Mary Tyler Peabody (1806–1894) and Sophia Dana Ripley (1803–1861), went home after a three-hour stay in 1833 "loaded with wild flowers." Mary Peabody gloried in Mount Auburn's romantic melancholy in a letter to Miss Rawlins Pickman of Salem in the fall of 1835, praising the wonderful emotions stirred by a visit one evening: "How can I describe the feeling with which I looked again upon our gorgeous woods and heard the song of the wind in the pine groves. I should like to sleep there, with that beautiful soul sighing my requiem. Nothing that the hand of man has done was so interesting to me as the grave of a young wife, whose simple monument is surrounded by a railing and decked with beautiful flowers." The young teacher concluded, "I always feel as if I want to stay when I get there."[34] For those inspired by Enlightenment literature and romanticism, by the "picturesque" appeal of English gardens, and by new liberal religious notions about Death, Nature, the individual soul, and the divine, Mount Auburn served as a catalyst for an efflorescence of prose and poetry, and even for the development of Transcendentalism out of Unitarianism. George Ticknor Curtis (1812–1894), Story's son-in-law, observed in 1834 that the cemetery permitted people "to rid themselves of Time among the final homes of those who have exchanged it for eternity."[35]

Ralph Waldo Emerson continued to visit as during his college days. His journal tells of a visit in the spring of 1834, a whole day spent in the woods except for a brief lunch at the Fresh Pond Hotel, a "pleasure ground" nearby. Emerson "forsook the tombs and found a sunny hollow where the east wind would not blow." There he sat against a tree all day, communing with Nature, "and let what would pass through [his eyes] into the soul." He delighted in the sight of various plants, four gliding snakes, a "chick-a-dee," and a "black-capped" titmouse: "I saw no more my relation, how near and petty, to Cambridge or Boston; I heeded no more what minute or hour our Massachusetts clocks might indicate—I saw only the noble earth on which I was born, with the great Star which warms and enlightens it. . . . It was Day—that was all Heaven said. The pines glittered . . . and seemed to challenge me to read their riddle. . . . This gay and grand architecture, from the vault to the moss and lichen on which I lay,—who shall explain to me the laws of its proportions and adornments?" Scholars now see that as Emerson's epiphany, "his extraordinary vision" that led him from Unitarianism to Transcendentalism, a religious philosophy he articulated in "Nature" in 1836 and other essays.[36]

Jones Very (1813–1880), a tutor of Greek at Harvard from 1836 to 1838, took his students for discussions to Mount Auburn as if it were the Athenian Ceramicus. More important, there he also meditated to imbibe the mysticism that led him from Unitarianism to Transcendentalism and informed his sonnets "Nature," "The Garden," "The Dead," and others, which Emerson edited, arranged for publication in 1839, and reviewed (calling them "almost as pure as the sound of Surrounding Nature") in the Transcendentalist journal *The Dial*, then edited by Margaret Fuller (1810–1850). Fuller also sought out such enclaves of unsullied Nature for reading and contemplation, often frequenting the wooded terrain dubbed Sleepy Hollow in Concord in the company of Nathaniel Hawthorne and others of the Transcendentalist Club. Personally troubled and made melancholy by her decision to leave New England to write for Horace Greeley's *New York Tribune*, she spent one last afternoon amid the "heavenly beauty" of Mount Auburn in May 1844, musing deeply on her past and future. Such were the intended spiritual uses of the cemetery.[37]

Others found Mount Auburn a recreational amenity, constantly improved with access for all by foot, horseback, or carriage. They sought only leisure, not the "pleasures of melancholy." Extensive publicity in regional and national newspapers, guidebooks, and travel narratives attracted more visitors than proprietors. Immediately, Mount Auburn earned an international reputation. In April 1833 the famed British actress Fanny Kemble (1809–1893) judged Mount Auburn "a pleasure garden instead of a place of graves."[38] Many used the cemetery "in a manner very different than expected, destroying the solemnity and quiet." Proprietors complained that conditions were becoming worse than those in the city's old graveyards. Some mutilated trees, broke fences, and trampled lots. Dearborn's hand-lettered signs were not effective:

VISITORS ARE DESIRED TO CONFINE THEIR WALKS
TO THE AVENUES AND PATHS
AND TO AVOID TREADING ON THE BORDERS.
PAUSE—THIS IS HALLOWED GROUND, SACRED TO
THE DEAD AND THE LIVING.
PLUCK NOT A SHRUB—TOUCH NOT A FLOWER.
LEAVE EVERY THING IN ITS BEAUTY.
WALK YOUR HORSE.

Visitors on horseback proved both disruptive and destructive, riding on narrow paths intended for contemplative strollers and tethering their mounts to trees and shrubs. Joseph T. Buckingham complained about the prevalent "vice" of graffiti: "Even Mount Auburn,—where, one would think, was assembled all that could touch, subdue, and elevate . . . has not been spared. The marble monuments have been scribbled upon, the chains . . . broken, and the grounds and shrubbery injured." The society employed officers to police the grounds on holidays such as the Fourth of July; but behavioral problems were chronic and intolerable for those interested in peaceful burials.[39]

Trouble in the Garden and Institutional Schism

Some lot owners may have feared for the security of graves because of the free public access to the grounds or the offensive behavior of visitors. In any event, the first proprietors insisted on making Mount Auburn a congregation of private family burial grounds in a single landscape. After all, among the objections to the old urban graveyards was that they were so very public, exposed to the view of, if not physically accessible to, passersby. To provide security if not privacy, Zebedee Cook and George Bond oversaw enclosure of the grounds in the spring of 1833. Dearborn ordered seven-foot cedar and spruce fenceposts from Maine, to be connected by iron rails and painted a dark color. Some observers described "neat and substantial" pickets, others "rough sawed pales." An open fence was chosen because it was "not so liable to be shaken and injured by the wind" and would remain "secure against cattle" until the society could afford to build a "stone or brick wall all round." Above all, a sturdy fence was crucial in winning public confidence that the dead would remain safe from grave robbers. One Newton resident queried Dearborn in 1833: "How will the bodies be protected at Mount Auburn? by some ponderous concave rock placed over the grave for a time and lifted and moved from place to place by powerful machinery?" In lieu of a system to protect against grave robbing, that letter suggested the use of mortsafes, temporary iron grilles rooted in the ground over graves.[40]

Horticulturists still charged that cemetery proprietors had no interest in their activities, although the lot owners made up an increasing proportion of the Society's membership and automatically received life tenure with purchase of a burial lot. Through 1833, society meetings became increasingly stormy. By 1834, many lot holders professed "a positive aversion" to the idea of an experimental garden. Dearborn sided with the Horticulturists, Bigelow with cemetery advocates. Others also took sides. According to Zebedee Cook, Dearborn always felt that Mount Auburn "was purchased with the intention of establishing a Garden of Experimentation, that the *cemetery* was secondary, the proceeds thereof to be devoted to the *garden and* the cemetery." Despite Cook's urging, Dearborn hesitated to state that in writing. He remained on friendly terms with Bigelow, but his increasing commitments in Congress and elsewhere eased him away from the growing unpleasantness. By 1834, Dearborn, the sole conciliator between the two factions, was seldom seen. Brimmer resigned in 1832 owing to ill health, to travel abroad. He died in Florence in 1838, and though it was rare in that era, his body was shipped back to the cemetery he had been so instrumental in creating.[41]

Dearborn resigned as president of the Society on September 10, 1834, citing his intention to move west, although he never did do so beyond traveling through upstate New York to Buffalo. He attended his last Garden and Cemetery Committee meeting in July. Cook, who briefly succeeded him as president, left a month later to head a major insurance company in New York City. Perhaps Dearborn or Cook eventually could have reconciled the two factions had they stayed on. It was Judge Story, rather than Bigelow, who took over from Dearborn and Cook despite intensely pressing professional concerns. He had only a passing interest in horticulture and lent a sympathetic ear to proprietors' complaints that visitors with free access "destroyed the solemnity and quiet" of the place and even perpetrated real damage. The great judicial defender of property rights supported their claims that the cemetery should be a collection of private holdings ensured in perpetuity under institutional auspices rather than a public place open and accessible to all. He heeded fears that "indiscriminate admissions" impeded the cemetery's growth after some potential proprietors told him they would not purchase lots while Mount Auburn remained so open.[42]

After eighteen months of diminishing lot sales and proprietors' complaints that the grounds were being "used in a manner very different from what they had expected," Story persuaded the Garden and Cemetery Committee to deny entrance to all persons on horseback or in carriages, with the exception of those attending funerals. Proprietors protested. Story modified the regulation to admit lot owners, family members, and guests in carriages if they presented to the gatekeeper a nontransferable ticket, to be issued annually. No provision was made for society members without lots. The public could still enter freely on foot from sunrise to sunset, but lack of public transportation to the site, four miles from Boston and a mile from Cambridge, limited access to the grounds for a time. Only proprietors could enter on Sundays, the one day of rest for the working classes and a day that had brought "unusual concourses of people." Story noted "that the injuries done to the grounds and shrubbery were far greater on that day than on any other." Only committee members could make exceptions to restrictions by issuing tickets to out-of-town visitors. Sabbath meditations in the sacred groves would no longer be interrupted by pleasure seekers who lacked a proprietary stake in the place, possession of which was like purchasing a pew in one of Boston's fine churches.[43]

Six days a week, nonproprietors who came by horse or carriage without tickets could secure their animals at hitching posts outside the gate and proceed on foot. Story ordered the south gate locked so the porter at the main north gate could scrutinize everyone entering or leaving. Many bought lots just to have the privilege of entering in carriages, and those who already owned lots liked the exclusivity. Still, the committee insisted on supplementary legislation, passed March 21, 1834, making it a misdemeanor to "destroy, mutilate, deface, or remove any tomb, monument, gravestone or other structure . . . tree, shrub, or plant" or to discharge firearms in the cemetery, under penalty of a fine of $5 to $50 and prosecution for trespass. Story deemed such regulations "indispensable to the quiet and good order of the grounds." New signs detailed them and warned proprietors in carriages to go no faster than a walk.[44]

Despite new rules and restricted admissions, Mount Auburn's popularity grew, justifying Dearborn's 1831 prediction that it would be "a holy and pleasant resort for the living . . . one of the most instructive, magnificent and pleasant promenades in our country. From its immediate proximity to the Capitol of the State, it will attract universal interest and become a place of healthful, refreshing and agreeable resort." Story's Garden and Cemetery Committee did not ban visitors altogether. Its members merely wanted them to be fewer in number and better behaved. Indeed, the committee placed benches at various spots for those walking miles through the grounds. Mount Auburn, in fact, was envisioned as a walking garden precisely at a time when Boston, rapidly expanding, was ceasing to be a compact walking city.[45]

Story was gratified in the fall of 1834 to report that Mount Auburn remained "a place of general resort and interest, as well to strangers as to citizens; and its shades and paths, ornamented with monumental structures, of various beauty and elegance, have already given solace and tranquilizing reflections to many an afflicted heart, and awakened a deep moral sensibility in many a pious bosom." Once rowdy visitors were excluded, Alexander Everett could muse: "How salutary the effect which a visit to its calm and sacred shades will produce on souls too much agitated by the storms of the world! It was surely fitting that Art and Nature should combine their beauties to grace a scene devoted to purposes so high and holy." Ironically, visiting Mount Auburn had not calmed the souls of those whose behavior brought the "storms of the world" into it. The place was for those whose gentility was already confirmed.[46]

The regulations prompted public criticism reminiscent of the charges of elitism leveled against the St. Paul's and Park Street churches in the 1823 burial controversy. Only this time Joseph Buckingham's Republican *New-England Galaxy* was not leading the crusade against "privilege." He was a cemetery proprietor and an ardent advocate. Story tried to dispel the "erroneous" public opinion that Mount Auburn was a "private speculation for the private benefit of members of the [Massachusetts Horticultural] Society, or of the individuals, who originally advanced the money to purchase the grounds . . . and that considerable profits [had] been already realized from it." The cemetery was instead "in the truest and noblest sense a public institution . . . of which the whole community [might] obtain the benefit upon easy and equal terms . . . the usual sum fixed for the purchase of a lot." Story denied that anyone had "any private interest" in the venture. In fact, by the end of 1834 cemetery development had produced a $2,000 deficit.[47]

By then, differences between Horticulturists and proprietors proved irreconcilable. A major cause of friction, leading to official separation into two separate institutions, was the failure of lot sales to produce enough revenue for development of the experimental garden. Limited admissions and strict regulations increased the contention. For their part, few of those with burial lots had any interest in the activities and aspirations of the Horticulturists and demanded that land for the garden be given over to burials, although there was no pressing need for space. Nevertheless, development of the cemetery as a pleasant, picturesque place was more important to them than experimental gardening and was a personal priority for Bigelow, Story, and others who, unlike Dearborn, Cook, and the avid Horticulturists, owned no country estates on which to create family burial grounds in the fashion of English gardens. Dearborn and Cook, however, sympathized with proponents of the cemetery because they supported providing for interments outside of the old graveyards and because such an institution would have other functions as well. Indeed, both men later helped found other "rural" cemeteries—Forest Hills in Roxbury south of Boston and Green-Wood across the East River from Manhattan in Brooklyn, respectively.

Horticultural Society officers Marshall Pinckney Wilder and Elijah Vose did not own burial space at Mount Auburn. They lacked Dearborn's enthusiasm for the cemetery venture and realized that an experimental garden would not be forthcoming for years, if ever. The Garden and Cemetery Committee belatedly and half-heartedly ordered some improvements to make the garden "productive and profitable" late in 1834. By then, cemetery proponents Bigelow and Story insisted that major structures mentioned in the original plan—a granite gateway, a permanent enclosure, a chapel, and an observatory tower—be built before further energy and funds were allotted to the intricacies of cultivating better cabbages and cauliflowers. Neither Horticulturists nor cemetery proprietors remained satisfied with Mount Auburn's development under society auspices. Dearborn distanced himself, literally and figuratively, from the fray.[48]

The New Corporation

During the nation's first five decades, New Englanders pioneered in creating autonomous nonprofit corporations for multiple civic uses, unknown under English common law, for the "public good" but not necessarily for all of the public. Initially, certain churches and colleges receiving state tax support were considered public institutions and their trustees de facto public officers. With the shift of political power from the Federalists to the Republicans after 1810, matters changed as court cases affirmed that charters granted corporate control and property rights to trustees of "charitable" institutions, some deemed perpetual, no longer public nor receiving public monies yet exempt from taxes and from state interference. Daniel Webster successfully argued before the New Hampshire Supreme Court the definitive case of *Trustees of Dartmouth College v. Woodward* in 1817. When the case was appealed to the U.S. Supreme Court in 1819, Justice Joseph Story joined Chief Justice John Marshall in declaring that a charter vested property rights in trustees, who could perpetuate themselves as a board without outside interference. Trustees might ask the legislature to amend or expand a charter, but the legislature could not interfere as long as the trustees followed stipulations of corporate powers within the law. By 1820, Massachusetts had readily granted more nonprofit charters than existed in all of Europe, many to institutions assuming functions formerly provided by the state, the town, or the family, if at all, thus privatizing and systematizing those services.[49]

As an expert in redefining the law, Story headed a committee to negotiate an institutional separation from the Horticultural Society by acquiring a charter for Mount Auburn as an eleemosynary corporation. On March 31, 1835, the Massachusetts General Court issued a new charter in the name of the Proprietors of the Cemetery as a nonprofit corporation in perpetuity, an inviolable contract. That was the first time the term "cemetery" was officially used in American English for a burial landscape and only the second time that a burial place had been incorporated as separate from another institution. The Horticultural Society relinquished ownership of the land designated for the experimental garden. By signing the charter on April 21, 1835, proprietors ceased to be members of the Horticultural Society, unless they joined individually, and they in turn elected a president and trustees. On June 19, the Horticultural Society deeded all land to the new corporation. The state exempted the cemetery from taxes. The new charter empowered the trustees to add fifty more acres of land and to receive money to maintain buildings, tombs, monuments, and grounds yet to be developed. Most established rules, regulations, and procedures remained in effect, although the new charter formalized bans on shooting firearms, playing music, or harming monuments, structures, and plants, which became misdemeanors. Bigelow and Story devised a new seal for Mount Auburn bearing the Latin motto *Sic panditur via immortalitatis*, "Thus extends the path of immortality."[50] (Figs. 8.6, 8.7.)

The agreement separating the two institutions stipulated that the cemetery pay the Horticultural Society a retroactive and henceforth annual sum of one-fourth of the proceeds from lot sales after deducting $1,400 per year for operating expenses, provided that the society apply that money only to an experimental garden or "promotion of the Art and Science of Horticulture." The society failed in an attempt to claim a quarter of burial fees in addition in 1845. With minor modifications in 1858 and 1910, which excluded applicability to new purchases of cemetery land, this arrangement remained in effect until 1975. For over a century, officers of the Horticultural Society reserved the right to inspect Cemetery

Fig. 8.6. Corporate seal of the Massachusetts Horticultural Society, 1829. MHORT.

Fig. 8.7. Corporate seal of the Proprietors and Trustees of Mount Auburn Cemetery, devised by Jacob Bigelow and Joseph Story, 1835. MAC.

financial records. Although the society never tried to establish another experimental garden, Mount Auburn funds made possible the building of three Horticultural Halls—the first designed by Richard Bond on School Street in 1845, the second by Gridley J. Fox Bryant and Arthur Gilman at a central Tremont Street location in 1865, the third a large three-story English baroque structure across Massachusetts Avenue from Symphony Hall in 1901, designed by Edmund March Wheelwright, the city architect. Horticultural Society president Leverett Saltonstall deemed the establishment of Mount Auburn "one of the most fortunate events" in the financial history of his organization because of, not despite, the institutional schism.[51]

Mount Auburn's charter vested ownership of the entire cemetery in "proprietors," owners of family lots of at least three hundred feet square, and provided for preservation of perpetual control of each lot within the family that purchased it in fee simple. Proprietors could not use lots for speculation by selling burial rights or subdividing. The new corporation kept meticulous records of proprietors and burials, facilitated from the start by an innovative system of numbering lots consecutively as surveyed, not in sequence along avenues and paths in the manner of street addresses. Books were kept registering names and dates of interments and other vital information—city of residence, dates of birth and death, original place of interment in cases of bodies moved from previous graves and receiving tombs. A lot remained indivisible once occupied by burials and passed intact to heirs of the original proprietor unless part of it was reconveyed to the corporation. In naming a lot representative after the death of an original proprietor, trustees gave preference to male over female heirs, with "proximity of blood and priority of age having due regard" in addition to "proximity of residence" to the cemetery, for it would not have been wise policy to vest responsibility in a son who had moved far away unless there was no alternative. Trustees acted as a jury, selecting a new lot representative to assume the sole vote in the corporation after the original owner's death, thus providing for continuous family control over each lot through a sort of primogeniture. The rules also meant that there were few women with voting rights in the corporation unless they were proprietors in their own right or sole surviving widows or descendants, a reflection of the Victorian social order.[52]

The notion of perpetuity of burial as guaranteed at Mount Auburn was unprecedented. Although the cemetery provided a place for individualized, permanent burials, not all of the original proprietors took advantage of that privilege. Fewer than half of the first four hundred lots sold were actually used for burials. Many owners arranged with the corporation to exchange their lot for another site they later found preferable as new roads and paths were graded. Sometimes they exchanged lots to be nearer those of friends or relatives elsewhere in the grounds. Others sold their lots back to the corporation when they moved away. Often when that happened, it meant moving burials also. Family members continued to move their relatives' bodies from one burial place to another, often several times, from Mount Auburn as from other burial places in that era.[53]

Proprietors met annually at a time and place in Boston advertised in newspapers. Usually they simply cast votes or proxies to elect anywhere from seven to twelve trustees. The occasion resembled the old New England town meeting in procedure and function. Trustees were like selectmen. Many of the first nine trustees elected had been active on the Garden and Cemetery Committee. They met monthly, first at treasurer George Bond's Boston home, then at Charles Curtis's office, and by 1844 at Bigelow's Summer Street house—though rarely at the cemetery. Through the 1830s, attendance was so erratic that trustees often lacked a quorum for months, delaying the few decisions to be made. Responsibility for cemetery development and maintenance was shared by four committees: Grounds, Lots, Finance, and Regulations and Interment Records. Prime responsibility usually rested with Bigelow.

The officers were distinguished men who could devote only limited time to the cemetery. The first president, Joseph Story, was busy serving as a justice of the U.S. Supreme Court when not teaching law at Harvard. Benjamin R. Curtis (1809–1874), the secretary, was paid $100 a year for his services. He was a young lawyer who would follow in Story's footsteps, gaining a U.S. Supreme Court seat in 1850 but resigning seven years later (after writing the minority opinion in the Dred Scott case) to serve as chief defense counsel in President Andrew Johnson's impeachment trial. Although Bigelow held no cemetery office other than trustee until 1845 and continued his Harvard teaching and medical practice, he played a new leading role in directing day-to-day decisions. The newness of the eleemosynary corporation and the distinguished status of its officers and trustees created public skepticism toward the cemetery as elitist and antidemocratic. Despite the relatively high prices of the lots, the trustees disclaimed any "design to confine the sale of lots to any class of citizens." Burial space, they declared, was "advertised for sale without discrimination." And indeed many of Boston's "middling sort" accumulated enough money to purchase lots as the cemetery made efforts to draw proprietors from the ranks of prosperous mechanics and farmers in the metropolitan area.[54]

Mount Auburn marked its first interment in July 1832, a stillborn infant. Of seventeen burials that year, only two were recent deaths. Others had been dead anywhere from four months to twenty-one years before being reinterred from older graves or tombs. Dearborn moved his recently deceased parents to his new lot; Joseph Story moved the remains of five of his children, four from Salem and one from the Cambridge burial ground. When Mary Hastings died at age twenty-six, her father reburied with her the bodies of two infants, perhaps her sisters, who had died in 1815 and 1819. Sometimes graves in lots without family tombs were used for multiple burials. Reinterments made up the majority of burials through Mount Auburn's first decade, most from Boston, and most performed during the cool spring months of April and May. Many proprietors were anxious to move bodies of loved ones from old urban graveyards, fearing that those grounds would be forcibly discontinued and the bones carted away to unknown sites. But there were few attempts to move the remains of colonial ancestors. Precise locations of many burials, even of grandparents, had been forgotten. Mount Auburn's records reveal that the earliest death dates of reinterments were 1792 for Mary Sargent, 1796 for Simon Elliot and Captain John Stanton, 1797 for a Mrs. Green and John S. Ellery, and 1798 for Jeremy Belknap. Many other family members reinterred at Mount Auburn had died in the 1820s. Bostonians took renewed consolation, as Bigelow observed, in the pleasant, pastoral place for postmortem reconstitution of immediate families.[55]

Though an urban institution, Mount Auburn was called "rural" because of its "picturesque" landscape laid out on a wooded suburban site over irregular terrain, sculpted with earthen avenues and paths. Trees, native and planted, formed a major element of the landscape structure, as in the forest gardens advocated by English designers such as William Kent, Uvedale Price, and William Chambers. Trustees ordered in 1838 that no burials or tombs should "be injurious to any valuable tree," charged the superintendent in 1841 with being "personally responsible for the preservation of the trees," and in 1842 expended $200 for a variety of forest trees, many imported from abroad.[56]

The next year, the trustees contemplated ways to improve the wetlands and ponds that were small, scattered, and stagnant. Their subterranean water source entered from the north in the vicinity of Fresh Pond, and they "communicated with each other by filtration through the sand or gravel" as water percolated under Indian Ridge and into Meadow Pond, originally a "bog meadow covered with grass and bushes," before draining into the Charles River. The trustees hoped to excavate them and to improve the flow of water to create picturesque lakes and streams, as had been done in English gardens; but fearing that this would need the approval of the legislature and proprietors, requiring expansion of corporate powers, they tabled the massive engineering project in favor of first expending surplus funds from lot sales on structures to "embellish the picturesque."[57]

By 1835, Mount Auburn's basic corporate and landscape structure was in place in forms that would endure relatively unchanged, providing precedents to be emulated in the founding of many other "rural" cemeteries. Into the 1860s, the landscape reflected its founders' application of a formula derived from eighteenth-century English theorists, from the literary proponents of romanticism, and from French cemetery reformers. In this way, Mount Auburn took shape as a fitting site for development of an American cult of commemoration and melancholy.

Crediting the Initial Landscape Design

Cornelia Wells Walter, *Boston Transcript* editor and Bigelow's friend, gave prime credit for creating the cemetery to Bigelow in her book *Mount Auburn Illustrated*, published in 1847, a year before Dearborn founded and designed Forest Hills, the second "rural" cemetery in metropolitan Boston. Echoing Bigelow's claims, Walter wrote, "By him the plan for the rural cemetery was first conceived." Here again, the ambiguities of the term "plan" become complex, referring in this case to a concept rather than to a map, and certainly not to a landscape design. Walter did note that General H. A. S. Dearborn initially "gave his aid in a disinterested and indefatigable manner" in studying the "capabilities of the ground" and laying out avenues and paths and planting the belt of trees along the cemetery's front at his own expense. She was correct only in writing that since Mount Auburn's founding, "much of its care has, by the Trustees, been vested in the direction of Dr. Bigelow," but that was after the separation from the Horticultural Society.[58]

Others credited Dearborn with Mount Auburn's design. Five months after the general's death in 1851, Samuel Walker, then Massachusetts Horticultural Society president, asserted in a national publication that "the history of Mount Auburn will be a record, in all coming time, that the members of this Society . . . were founders of that 'Garden of Graves,' . . . and that to its first President, General Henry A. S. Dearborn, are the public indebted for the beautiful and chaste arrangement." No mention was made of Bigelow, an officer of the society at the time and, of course, Dearborn's colleague.[59]

The controversy heated up after Dearborn died. The Reverend George Putnam eulogized the general as "the head and the working member" of the subcommittee that laid out Mount Auburn. "With an eye so keen to detect the beautiful and a heart so warmly loving it, he knew how to make the most of every nook and dell, the tangled bog, the sandy level, the abrupt declivity, every tree and shrub and rock. In a word, he, after God, created Mount Auburn." Putnam conceded that "the first *conception* of a Forest Cemetery in America is not claimed for" Dearborn; but he minimized the originality of Bigelow's 1825 proposal for an extramural cemetery: "Scores of men through scores of years had doubtless thought and talked of the subject; but it was when [Dearborn] as president of the horticultural society took up the project, and not before, that any thing was *done*." Dearborn was not "the man to take a secondary and subordinate part in a matter in which official right and duty gave him a leading one . . . in which he felt perfectly at home, which was congenial to his life-long tastes and pursuits, and for which he had at the time entire leisure." Putnam insisted that "the *inception* and accomplishment of the *work*" were Dearborn's. Mount Auburn was "empathetically his creation," if "not his alone."

Dearborn played "a leading and efficient part in changing a people's whole system of burial, in redeeming the waste places of death, in surrounding the very grave with nature's choicest adornments, and investing the dreary sepulchre with the scenes and objects that are fraught with the most soothing and elevating associations." He "directed the steps of the living multitudes of cities and villages to the abodes of the dead, as the quietest shades and the loveliest resorts." When the eulogy appeared in newspapers, Bigelow found himself simply listed among others "associated with [Dearborn] in maturing and executing the plan." Despite their essential truth, these were harsh words for Bigelow, then the cemetery's president, to read.[60]

Bigelow tried to disprove contentions of Dearborn's prime instrumentality in the cemetery's founding. In 1860, at age seventy-three, he published his *History of the Cemetery*, characterizing himself as "a witness and an agent in most of the movements" that produced Mount Auburn. He insisted that the avenues and paths were laid out by a committee including himself, Dearborn, and Brimmer.[61] Although in his account of early landscape development Bigelow skillfully used the passive voice to avoid the question of agency, he made a persuasive claim for himself as prime mover and decision maker. He concluded, undoubtedly with Dearborn's Forest Hills in mind, "Mount Auburn, in most respects, takes precedence over other cemeteries which have been founded in imitation of it." Bigelow thus continued to wage a war of words even after Dearborn could no longer retort in the competition to claim principal credit for the founding of what had become America's prototypical burial institution and picturesque landscape.[62]

Soon after publication of Bigelow's history, the *Mount Auburn Memorial*, a small weekly paper produced by the cemetery gatekeeper and his son, featured a biographical sketch of Dearborn in 1860, asserting that "it was he who performed the chief part of the work of laying out the grounds. . . . The skill and taste with which he performed his task is fully acknowledged in the admiration of those who have seen the beauties of that sacred ground . . . a magnificent and beautiful monument to him—to his industry and taste."[63] Again in 1866, Bigelow complained to the Horticultural Society that "in all the late publications, discourses, and records of the Society, all notice of my name has been avoided, and the credit given to other parties, whom I now gratefully recall as friendly, and efficient collaborators." He protested, "For 36 years, I have officially devoted to the care and improvement of Mount Auburn most of the leisure time which I had to spare . . . and have gratuitously watched its interests as of those of my own child." He correctly claimed responsibility for the design of major structures; but although he brought the rural cemetery idea to Bostonians' attention, it certainly was not "his" innovation. William Tudor, Josiah Quincy, and even Joseph T. Buckingham offered earlier proposals for such a place. Nevertheless, on December 29, 1866, the society tried to lay the controversy to rest by issuing a resolution acknowledging Bigelow's "aid and counsel."[64]

Two decades later, Bigelow's eulogist, the Reverend George E. Ellis, took up the cudgels, claiming that the doctor "was called upon to lay out and adorn Mount Auburn, to designate its avenues and paths, to draft its lodges, gateway, and fences, and to plan its tower and chapel" with the aid of his "taste and skill, and knowledge of materials, and eye for proportions, and judgment of construction." After attributing the design of the cemetery and its structures to Bigelow, Ellis boldly declared that Bigelow deserved the greatest praise as "the first—we may say, in Christendom—to conceive, propose, and earnestly and patiently to guide on to a most complete triumph, the plan of an extensive forest-garden cemetery, combining the wildness of nature with the finish of culture, with all appropriate arrangements and adornments." Ellis thus claimed originality for Bigelow's idea, conceived "without aid or guidance from any similar device in this country, nor on the scale which it was organized and carried out, had he any previous example in Europe to follow." His choice of the seldom-used term "forest-garden" indicates an attempt to discredit Putnam's eulogy of Dearborn and undermine praise of Forest Hills Cemetery in Roxbury, which Dearborn founded and laid out under town auspices. Ellis's assertion that Bigelow did not look to European precedents contradicted Dearborn's early published accounts of the use of printed materials from France and England and his repeated references to the example of Père Lachaise. It also ignores what Bigelow as president did by eliminating half of Mount Auburn's forest growth in the 1860s.[65]

To complicate matters, two local historians stated in

1973 that "[Alexander] Wadsworth's imaginative solution—no doubt supervised by Bigelow who is traditionally credited with the design—was to wind the roadways around the hills and ponds, their routes dictated by terrain in order to achieve picturesque vistas and make efficient use of the ground." Wadsworth, a civil engineer, surveyor, and mapmaker, worked for Dearborn to produce "an accurate topographical survey and to locate the numerous avenues," simply drawing a detailed map or "plan," in the parlance of the day, in 1831 to show "general outlines of the projected improvements" as Dearborn staked them out. (Fig. 8.8.) That did not mean that he designed the landscape (just as his 1833 "Plan of the Village of Old Cambridge," a map, certainly does not imply that he provided the urban design in 1630). Mount Auburn's trustees voted him "Surveyor of the Corporation" in 1848, charged with creating detailed lot "plans" showing the locations of monuments, tombs, and burials. Wadsworth revised maps into the 1860s as Bigelow and the Committee on Grounds laid out additions to the avenue and path system. After the trustees altered the terrain through grading and infill and extended a new hydrology system in the 1860s, they agreed "to contract with a competent surveyor for a topographical survey," indicating that Wadsworth's expertise was limited.[66]

Fig. 8.8. Alexander Wadsworth (1805–1898) portrait, 1889. Oil on canvas board by Frank Duveneck (1848–1919). Gift of Eliot Wadsworth. MAC.

The debate over assigning credit for founding Mount Auburn obscures the fact that it remains an important and influential *designed* landscape. Although trends in professionalization proceeded at an irregular place in the flux of nineteenth-century society, it is wrong to call the likes of Bigelow and Dearborn "amateurs" in landscape design and architecture. They excelled in many fields, though not on the full-time, income-earning basis later defined as "professional." As in England historically, members of the well-read gentry became physicians, clergymen, barristers, politicians, architects, landscape gardeners, and more, often combining fields of expertise. In Boston in the 1830s, members of the new elite—Bigelow, the physician, horticulturist, professor, writer, and architect, and Dearborn, the nonpracticing attorney, politician, engineer, architect, horticulturist, and landscape gardener—easily became Renaissance men. Working together in the Massachusetts Horticultural Society and similar new institutions, they fostered and applied their eclectic expertise and developed many projects to improve their society and culture.[67]

9

ART AND NATURE BALANCED

Creating a Marble History in the Forest Cemetery

Nature and Art here harmonize with each other, and mingle their powers "to lend enchantment to the scene."

—Enoch Cobb Wines, *A Trip to Boston* (1838)

The care with which the rural aspect of the enclosure is preserved affords the best illustration of the harmony which exists between Nature and Man, even in his decay.

—"Burial," *North American Review* (July 1861)

Visiting from Philadelphia in 1838, the Reverend Enoch Cobb Wines, a noted penology reformer, found "an accumulation and variety of classical beauties" and "scenes of Arcadian loveliness" at "the most romantic of burial-places," Mount Auburn, "which certainly no spot in America can match and which probably few places can equal in any part of the world." Wines concluded that "though corruption is not less foul here than elsewhere . . . yet death would seem disrobed of half its terrors, if one could be assured of a final resting place beneath the deep shadows of its trees and amid its profusion of flowers." Similarly, the journalist John Ross Dix was delighted by Nature's presence at Mount Auburn: "There is a life, joyous life beneath, around, and above us—insects chirp in the grass—bright-eyed, variegated squirrels run gracefully up the boles of trees, or peer curiously out from amongst turfed grass—bright-winged birds glance athwart the leafy gloom . . . yea, every thing tells of life." Wines and Dix echoed Keats in noting that it "would almost make one in love with death to be buried in so sweet a place." The same sentiments were repeated by many others, including Thoreau, who wrote in *Walden* (1845), "There can be no very black melancholy to him who lives in the midst of Nature."[1]

The "picturesque" spirit of place reigned throughout the cemetery's first decades. Mount Auburn's founders valued Nature's power to soothe grief and to serve as balm for the world-weary. One writer observed in 1835, "A wise man, indeed, would not complain if his child were buried in the bed of the ocean or entombed in a far distant region; but it would be his choice that some neighboring grove or valley afford it a grave, which he may visit and there dwell upon the virtues of the beloved one," a place that mourners "could visit without publicity and without interruption." Mount Auburn's creation came at a time marked by the formalization of mourning customs privatizing grief, especially for women. The relocation of burials from the city's streets to a secluded domain permitted discreet mourning, even making possible the attendance of women at funerals, a practice eschewed in town burial grounds.[2]

Once the landscape had been laid out and the corporate institution established, until the mid-1840s most of

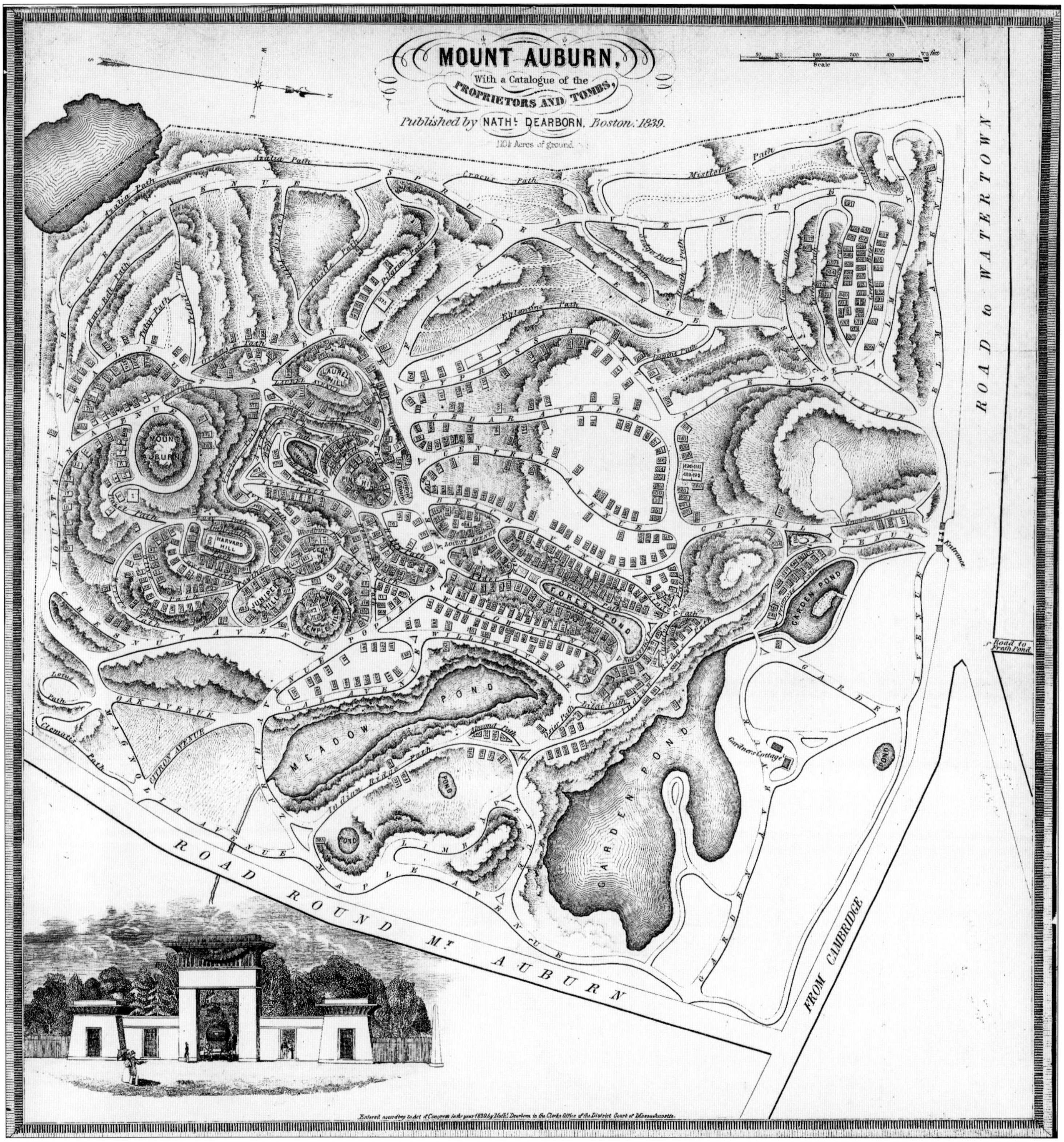

Fig. 9.1. "Plan of the Cemetery of Mount Auburn" by surveyor Alexander Wadsworth, showing the landscape design of General Henry A. S. Dearborn. From N. Dearborn, *Catalogue*, 1839. MAC.

the trustees showed little concern for development and maintenance, delegating authority to Bigelow and a few others who, as the committees on lots and grounds, visited the cemetery and made minor decisions. By and large, they assumed that the naturalistic landscape required little work. Development proceeded slowly, impeded by the conflicts that ended in the separation of the cemetery from the Massachusetts Horticultural Society and hard times following the Panic of 1837. For a while, proprietors' "improvements" did not mar the woodsy rusticity of the site as Dearborn had left it. Mount Auburn remained the same size until land purchases in 1842 and 1844 expanded it to 116 acres. Art and Nature remained in balance until the late 1850s. (Fig. 9.1.)

In 1834 John W. Russell became the second superintendent, primarily serving as a caretaker in exchange for the handsome annual salary of $600 plus a house owned by the corporation, where a few laborers boarded with his family for $2.50 a week. He had the use of some land for a vegetable garden to satisfy the needs of his household. He also functioned as sexton, employing gravediggers, supervising funerals, and enforcing bans on music and the firing of guns.[3] He directed surveyor Alexander Wadsworth's laying out of lots so as to permit the digging of graves without damaging trees. Preservation of forest trees remained a priority; the layout of the grounds was determined by their location. Trustees dictated the placement of new avenues and paths. Many lots were distinguished from the surrounding landscape by stepped or terraced grading commissioned by proprietors. As superintendent, Russell maintained records listing numbered lots, sales and improvements, burials and vital statistics, and structures erected. He was left unsupervised until 1838, when the trustees began to suspect that he was "permitt[ing] many trees to be removed improperly," probably to facilitate surveying and gravedigging. They dismissed him in 1841, charging that he had been selling firewood. In those hard economic times, the cemetery needed the revenue as much as the superintendent did.

Russell was replaced by Rufus Howe, the first and last superintendent elected by the proprietors rather than hired. The trustees held him "personally responsible for the preservation of trees," allowing none to be removed without the approval of the Committee on Lots. Howe had to account to the treasurer for all brush or wood produced by tree trimming. Bigelow insisted on controlling each tree planted or removed. Grass was allowed to reach meadow length before the scythes went through about twice a season. Sale of hay from grass-cutting produced more income for the cemetery. Howe served for fourteen years, until 1855.[4]

Through Mount Auburn's first decade it remained "almost a wilderness." Graveled avenues and paths, barely staked out, created a labyrinth through the wooded grounds "perplexing to the stranger." Descending from the mount with its panoramic view, visitors found themselves "within the shadows of the deep forest and secluded glade . . . shut off from the visible world, as if . . . a thousand miles from any habitation." Yet, as journalist Joseph T. Buckingham observed, "what a change has a period of seven years produced! The native wildness of the place is softened and subdued, but not destroyed, by the hand of labor and art," a place where "the visitor now sees in all directions the marble urn, the sarcophagus, and the granite obelisk. . . . Seven years ago, Mount Auburn was the habitation only of the field-mouse and the squirrel, or of wild animals and reptiles more unfit for the companionship of man; it is now a City of the Dead, populous with all degrees and qualities of our race, rich with the treasures of memory, of love, or friendship, and affection."[5] (Figs. 9.2, 9.3.)

Bigelow took personal pride in the cemetery, to which he devoted increasing amounts of time and effort after its split from the Horticultural Society. Through the 1840s he retained his taste for the "picturesque," enjoying Mount Auburn's rough, naturalistic landscape, sanctified by the pantheistic sentiments of Wordsworth, Delille, and Bryant, as well as Boston's Unitarians and Transcendentalists. The physician even tried to capture the poetics of place, privately penning his thoughts before burying his poem amid the correspondence of his wife and children:

> *Mount Auburn! thou divine enchanting spot*
> *Whom Nature has embellished and adorned*
> *With all the pride of her luxuriance,*
> *Thee I salute: and Muses invoke thine aid*
>   *To guide me through the maze of poesy*
>   *Which I have entered heedless and alone. . . .*
> *Auburn! it is not language can express*
> *The majesty and beauty of thy groves;*
> *Description's efforts are inadequate*
> *To paint the charms of the thrice favoured spot*
> *Whose gifted soil supports thy forests wide.*
> *Let him who wills to know thy beauties fair*
> *Come to thy depths and pay his homage there.*

As the man who took credit for proposing creation of the "forest cemetery" and as a founding trustee conscien-

Fig. 9.2. Contemplative visitors in the "forest" cemetery at the lot of the merchant Elijah Loring, Esq., on Oxalis Path. Engraving by R. Hinshelwood, 1847, from a drawing by James H. Smillie (1807–1885).

Fig. 9.3. The "picturesque" cemetery landscape with Henry Oxnard's Gothic Revival monument on Narcissus Path. Such grading, berming, elevating, and terracing of individual lots was done by proprietors rather than the cemetery. Engraving by Rice and Buttre, 1847, from a drawing by Smillie. MAC.

tious about stewardship, Bigelow uttered invocation and invitation. At Mount Auburn, he wrote, the businessman could find moral recreation and self-renewal:

Let him forget,
Reposing on thy soil, the toilsome cares,
Vicissitudes, and labours of the little world
Which he inhabits. Let his weary soul
Find rest amid the silence of thy groves
And let the waving of thy foliage breathe
A pleasing calm throughout his harassed soul
And lull him into visions of repose.

Nature would also soothe the mourner seeking privacy for solace:

Let him come sit amid thy solitudes,
And meditate on his departed friends:
Let him recline upon the turf, and list
To the sweet song of heav'n inspired birds,
Till all his faculties are deep absorbed
In Nature's charms. Then let his stricken soul
Spurn the stern shackles of despondency,
Shake off the cares that clung around his soul
And turn towards home, a new created man.[6]

Bostonians and visitors from beyond increasingly heeded Bigelow's advice.

Cornelia Walter, Bigelow's friend, celebrated the "forest umbrageousness" in verse in 1847, lauding the lakes "so cleansed, deepened, and banked as to present a pleasant feature in this widespread extent of forest loveliness." Mount Auburn sheltered "thickly wooded vales, yet fresh with the growth of centuries." (Fig. 9.4.) New plantings of acacias and willows, chosen for their symbolic significance, added a note of cultivated melancholy: "The sombre shade of its groves, the solemn calm of all things around, appeal to the religious sense." Unlike her Puritan ancestors, Walter found this "deep, dark wood . . . holy."[7]

Despite the separation of Mount Auburn from the Horticultural Society, a taste for ornamental plantings developed among the cemetery's proprietors and trustees such as Bigelow, who made many of the aesthetic decisions. Buckingham praised the blend of cultivated plants with the indigenous: "The native oak now waves its foliage over an exotic shrubbery; the anemone, the vi-

Fig. 9.4. Forested area on Vine and Aster paths winding up toward the cemetery's summit and overlooking Consecration Dell. This portion of the cemetery is the only area retaining the original display of the "picturesque." Photograph by Carol Betsch, 2005.

Fig. 9.5. Monuments from the 1830s on Ivy Path overlooking Consecration Dell. Photograph by Carol Betsch, 2005.

olet, and the aster, long the lonely and the unobtrusive spontaneous product of the soil, now gracefully mingle with the daisy, the narcissus, and the lily; the wild rose and sweetbriar unveil their blushing beauties and exhale their incomparable fragrance in the presence of more gaudy varieties of foreign origin. Most of the trees and shrubs that are indigenous to our New England forests are to be found within the limits of Mount Auburn, and the nurseries of exotic plants have made bountiful contribution to add to the native establishment." Greater transformations were soon to follow.[8] (Fig. 9.5.)

In the words of one visitor in 1849, Mount Auburn was "a large extent of wild, unreclaimed, hilly ground, covered with oak and pine . . . enclosed for a public burial place."[9] To augment the "picturesque," the Grounds Committee planted more forest trees in close proximity to one another in areas where they did not already exist. In 1841 the trustees approved a more efficient plan by Waldo Higginson, which called for laying out lots in the southeast section prior to planting. By its second decade Mount Auburn was a forested, truly "rural" cemetery, with secluded "lawns" or open areas "thickly overshadowed" by a canopy, as captured by the drawings of James Smillie in the mid-1840s. Although Art and Nature remained balanced, with each passing year and the accumulation of more and more artifacts, the landscape's "rural" character gradually faded.[10]

Early Monuments

For many, however, the consoling, emotionally salutary influence of Nature was not enough. Proprietors and voluntary associations intent on commemorating notables at Mount Auburn strove to create a "marble history" of "the good and great." They believed that mnemonic monuments could "improve" on Nature by ornamenting the grounds in the style of English gardens. Most such additions to the landscape in its first decade were the products of private initiative, such as the monument to Hannah Adams, which erroneously proclaims the deceased writer the cemetery's "First Tenant." She was actually the ninth, moved there in November 1832, a year after her death. Hers was nevertheless the first monument, erected by a voluntary subscription of her female friends to recognize the "Historian of the Jews and Reviewer of Christian Sects." As the only woman yet granted access to the Athenaeum library and a member of one of Massachusetts's most distinguished families, she was deemed worthy of public commemoration. The Horticultural Society donated a lot on Central Square and even appropriated $35 for an iron fence to protect her neoclassical marble stone. (Figs. 9.6, 9.7.)

New Englanders began to take an unprecedented interest in erecting marble monuments and protecting them with iron fences, a marked change from the stark slate markers and crude wooden enclosures of the old town graveyards. Many were copied from the designs of early monuments Dearborn had imported from examples at Père Lachaise, easily copied locally by new monument dealers. During Mount Auburn's first decade, proprietors built 190 tombs and 164 monuments. Through the 1840s, most proprietors chose simple neoclassical monuments, which stood out to good advantage in the wooded landscape, appearing as if placed in niches to form a series of tableaux where trees had been cleared away. Occasionally the material chosen was Connecticut freestone or brownstone, whose reddish hue harmonized with the surrounding earth that constituted the surface of most family lots, paths, and avenues before grass groundcover became popular at mid-century. Inscriptions on the freestone were usually gilded to make the engraved writing clearer. Those carved on marble monuments were often accentuated with black paint or gilded. A few of the early monuments were made of bluestone.

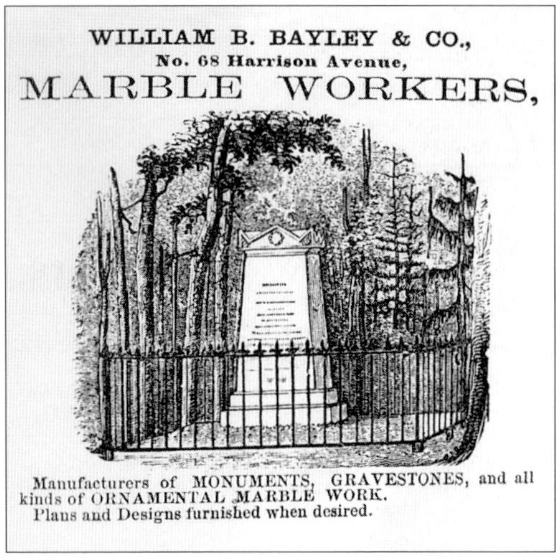

Fig. 9.6. Hannah Adams monument. Advertisement by William B. Bayley & Co., Marble Workers. From Stevens, 1860.

Fig. 9.7. Hannah Adams monument on Walnut Avenue, near Central Square. Engraving by Smillie, from Walter, 1847. MAC.

Despite the increasing availability of granite, marble remained the stone of choice until after the Civil War, when new technology made the harder stone cheaper and easier to carve. Marble gained popularity after it was first quarried in Vermont in the 1780s and began to replace slate as the preferred stuff of gravestones in New England's burial grounds. The material proliferated elsewhere for funerary use. In New Orleans it was imported beginning in the 1820s for that city's highly architectural cemeteries, since it was better for aboveground tombs than the traditional stuccoed brick. Marble could be easily and ornately sculpted, an important consideration in that era of diversifying iconographic taste. Although it was known not to be very durable outdoors, the whiteness of the stone provided a newly desirable, optimistic symbolism consonant with new attitudes toward death and the hereafter, more appropriate in the mind of the times than the grim gray slate of old. The mass of marble stood out in the landscape, glowing against the greenery or the gray granite walls of mausoleums. It also suggested the purity of heaven-bound souls and the assurance of salvation provided by liberal religion, serving visually as an affirmative spiritual statement in contrast to the flat, austere slate incised with death's-heads, linked with the old Puritan view of death and predestination.

New Englanders also associated marble with

Fig. 9.8. Joseph Story monument in its original wooded setting. Lithograph by Pendleton, 1834, from a drawing by William Hunt. AAS.

Fig. 9.9. Joseph Story monument on Narcissus Path with iron fence added. Engraving from *Picturesque Pocket Companion*, 1839. MAC.

classical art, another reason for its being chosen increasingly over materials and forms from the immediate past. Insistent that their new cemetery not resemble old graveyards, Mount Auburn's founders issued a circular letter in 1833 prohibiting thin, perpendicular slab markers, and slate in particular. Dearborn and his associates felt that the "stiff and ungainly" slate would "give a gloomy aspect to the scenery" and "would not harmonize with the natural and artificial beauties of a rural cemetery . . . intended to banish the cheerless associations connected with the burial-places in our cities and country towns." The few old gravestones that were moved to Mount Auburn in the course of reinterments had to be set horizontally in the earth so as to be eventually consumed by it. Only monuments "of a form approved by the committee" of trustees, such as marble steles, were permitted.[11]

Both Story and Bigelow chose for their own lots simple, neoclassical monuments, two of the first nine scattered in the wooded landscape by the spring of 1833. Story's, erected when he reinterred his five deceased children, is a marble obelisk atop a pedestal. (Figs. 9.8, 9.9.) Its simple Egyptian iconography is similar to that Bigelow used on the cemetery's gateway. The obelisk form was already a favored style for funerary monuments, especially for heroes, in the late eighteenth century. (Fig. 9.10.) English landscape gardeners had borrowed it from Italian villa gardens; hence it was considered more Roman than Egyptian. Bigelow placed a monument on his lot before the 1834 reinterment of his six-month-old son William, who had died in 1820. (Fig. 9.11.) Like others who erected monuments in the first years of Mount Auburn, he contracted for it himself, in 1832, possibly based on his own design, using precut marble from the Massachusetts State Prison. He hired the architect Solomon Willard to carve a low-relief festoon of olive leaves around the severed column (now lost), symbolic of life cut short, set atop a neoclassical plinth and pediment. It cost $168.13, plus $22.63 for three men and a derrick to set the stones. A simple iron fence by Safford

Fig. 9.10. George Bond monument with its iron fence in a wooded setting on Indian Ridge Path. Lithograph by Pendleton, 1834, from a drawing by Hunt. AAS.

Fig. 9.11. Jacob Bigelow monument on Beech Avenue (the original column and iron fence with torchières are now missing). Engraving from *Picturesque Pocket Companion*, 1839. MAC.

& Low cost $13.70; sodding added $10. By 1834 the cost of the lot, with a premium paid for site choice, and improvements, none of them ostentatious, came to over $300, more than the annual income of a common laborer, an index of expenditures by the "average" proprietor in the 1830s.[12]

In his writing and by personal example, Bigelow urged building monuments before a death in the family. Erecting one was a way to learn the lessons of moral philosophy, to come to terms with mortality, and to ensure commemoration of one's self and one's family. Mount Auburn's founders urged each family head "to provide a place of burial for himself, which while living he may contemplate without dread or disgust . . . surrounded with every thing that can fill the heart with tender and respectful emotions . . . removed from all the discordant scenes of life." Publicists stressed the civic function of "improving" the landscape with tasteful structures like the cenotaphs and other architectural features that decorated English gardens.[13] Mount Auburn provided a place where one might create and personalize the sort of "rural" burial place celebrated in the melancholy, nostalgic verse of England's Graveyard poets, of Wordsworth, and of Bryant, but rarely found in reality. There, patriarchs could fulfill their responsibility as teachers of spiritual values, a role long proclaimed by ministers but increasingly relegated to matriarchs. There, too, they could give material expression to the value of family at a time when that institution was being weakened by geographic mobility. Through self-commemoration, they could ensure longevity of the family name. Bigelow urged his peers to be conscious of creating a personal reputation and establishing a lineage, of contemporary if not historical origin, as in America "prescriptive and hereditary positions [were] declining in social influence." In his essay "On the Limits of Education" he declared it "better to be the founder of a great name than its disreputable survivor." Rephrasing the French aphorism "I am my own ancestor," referring to a new individualism, he observed, "In this great and original country, which is now treading in the vanguard of a new reformation, we have thousands yet untaught who are to become ancestors in fame, ancestors in fortune, ancestors in science, ancestors in virtue. May their descendants be worthy of them."[14]

Regulations concerning the erection of monuments conformed to tastes espoused by the likes of the critic Henry Russell Cleveland, who as early as 1836 cited Mount Auburn as the first place in the nation to display fine "sepulchral architecture," discounting consideration of "the rude gravestones of our burying-grounds" as art. He cautioned proprietors to keep the new cemetery "in good taste," in contrast to the excessive "display of magnificence" at Père Lachaise in Paris. Noting that "the few models for monuments . . . have been eagerly copied, and with no great variety," he wrote: "It is of great importance that the public taste . . . should be well directed, before the cemetery becomes filled up with uncouth structures," by which he meant Egyptian styles "with no connexion with our religion." Cleveland urged instead what he considered "the architecture of Christianity, the sublime, the glorious Gothic." Many of Mount Auburn's founders, while rejecting New England's old material culture of death, retained the characteristic Yankee aversion to ostentation and shunned baroque ornamental tastes. Joseph Story preached that monuments should not be "for the poor purpose of gratifying our vanity or pride" but should serve as texts from which man might "read" his "destiny and duty."[15] (See Fig. 9.3.)

Manifestations of a new symbolic consciousness were apparent throughout Mount Auburn's landscape in its first decades. As we have seen, there would be none of the grim, medieval symbolism of death's-heads and skeletons. Declared nondenominational, Mount Auburn attracted many Unitarians and Universalists, who eschewed traditional Christian symbolism, even the simple cross, sharing their Puritan ancestors' antipathy to displaying as "an object of veneration" the "ignominious engine used for the destruction" of Christ. Instead, many of their first monuments often bore the carved symbol of a lit oil lamp or flame, an ancient image representing enlightened reason, truth, wisdom, and life.[16]

To expand the range of expressive iconography, proprietors turned to examples set by political and philosophical liberals in Britain and France, a diversity of symbols and architectural styles derived from Egypt, Greece, Rome, and other pagan precedents, including images of plants. Dearborn had ordered books illustrating such patterns from France, depositing them in the Massachusetts Horticultural Society to inspire the purchasers and makers of monuments. (Figs. 9.12–9.15.) Such symbolism gained currency through literary and mass-circulation newspapers and journals, sentimental poetry, pattern books, and guidebooks. Masons also drew from an extensive vocabulary of formal symbols used in commemorative sites such as Mount Auburn and other cemeteries modeled after it. Antebellum American taste was consciously molded into an "aesthetic ideology" representing current notions about life, death, nature, and the sacred.[17]

Fig. 9.12. Monument of Q. M. Q. Verhuell at Père Lachaise, engraving from Arnaud, 1817. Dearborn ordered such books from France as a source of monument patterns that proprietors of Mount Auburn burial lots might consult. MHORT.

Fig. 9.13. Monument of Nansouti at Père Lachaise, engraving from Jolimont's *Les Mausolées français*, 1821, another book obtained by Mount Auburn founders and made available at the Massachusetts Historical Society. MHORT.

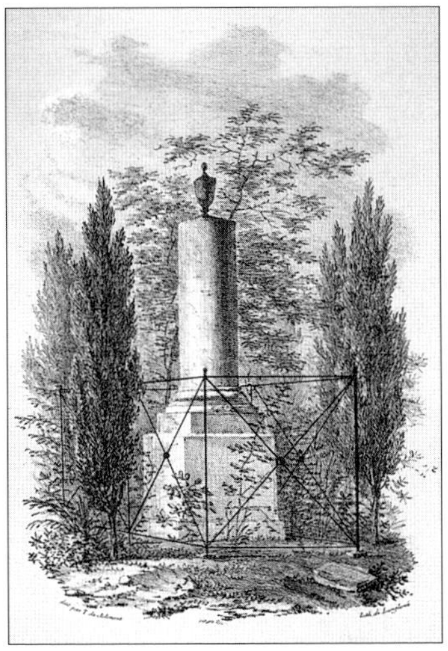

Fig. 9.14. Monument of Méhul, Père Lachaise. Engraving from Jolimont, 1821. MHORT.

Fig. 9.15. Monument of Dugazon, Père Lachaise. Engraving from Jolimont, 1821. MHORT.

Even before the founding of Mount Auburn, many who could afford to do so had begun to choose simple neoclassical marble structures in lieu of traditional gravestones, even though they were set amid the slabs and rude tombs of old burial grounds. The shift from flat, thin stones to more sculptural monuments indicates an intellectual transition from the dualism of orthodoxy to a more modern view of history, a move away from the influence of a fixed and formal community culture to a multidimensional individualism. Yet in the case of monuments of notables, most of the new ones commemorated not just a single individual but several members of a family, broadly defined, and frequently acknowledged friends who had contributed to erect them. Often built over chamber tombs, such monuments evidence anticipation of mortality and an assertion of family cohesion in the face of the disruptive forces of mobility and modernity as well as death.

By providing a more advantageous setting for the new structures, Mount Auburn increased the desire for them, although initially there were few local craftsmen or architects to meet the demand. But designs were available in books on Père Lachaise by C.-P. Arnaud and François Jolimont. Bigelow himself ordered sketches for two standard neoclassical monuments from Solomon Willard in 1832 and recommended the architect's services to others. William Kenrick of nearby Newton expressed the hope that "indigenous artists" might produce such monuments for sale once the railroads made available large blocks of marble. The merchant Robert Gould Shaw anticipated the growing demand for marble monuments, sending to Italy in 1833 for an assortment of neoclassical structures "as an adventure, thinking they would be wanted."[18] (Fig. 9.16.) In 1837 the trustees allocated $100

Fig. 9.16. Robert Gould Shaw monument, Pine Avenue, ca. 1832, one of the monuments he imported from Italy for use at the new Mount Auburn. A bronze plaque was later added to honor his grandson, Colonel Robert Gould Shaw, the Civil War hero, buried in a common grave with his troops where they fell in South Carolina. Engraving from N. Dearborn, *Guide*, 1852. MAC.

to commission various designs to be made available to proprietors wishing to order custom-made monuments from local quarries. In 1838 Bigelow offered a prize of $50 for the best monument design, but no record remains of submissions. Many early monuments were designed or produced to order by Alpheus Cary, a local stonecutter and engraver. Dearborn had raised a lone voice in favor of eliminating stone monuments altogether: "Let the monuments be found in the noble forests of our land, let them not be such as the elements waste, but such as time only strengthens and repairs."[19] His advice went unheeded. While Bostonians rapidly acquired the taste for plantings on their graves, they were also determined to set memories of their dead in marble, and they demanded new and varied monument designs.

When James Silk Buckingham visited Mount Auburn in 1838, he praised the "beautiful design" of many monuments, "executed from the finest Italian marble, having indeed been made in Italy." Others had been made in Boston "with great taste and skill; though this is a branch of art but recently cultivated in the city." The *American Magazine* saw such monuments as evidence of "a pure and classical taste"; some were "elaborate and highly ornamented," but the majority were "elegant but plain."[20] The neoclassical style harmonized with the valuation of Nature as the ancient, sacred source of law and culture. Bostonians particularly looked to ancient civilizations for purer political forms representative of an Arcadian era when man was closer to Nature and natural law. Classical columns were inspired by the tree trunks of the forest, while the burial mound or mount suggested pyramids. Obelisks were hierophanies, symbolic and ceremonial points of linkage between the sacred and the profane, heaven and earth.[21] Athenian grave markers of the ninth and eighth centuries BC, an era the art historian Vincent Scully describes as having tried to reconcile perceived oppositions between Man and Nature, inspired many early monuments. The funerary stones and urns of the ancient Greeks, like their latter-day equivalents at Mount Auburn, "celebrated the family cult and contrasted in all major ways with nature's forms around them."[22] Elite Bostonians, who considered themselves citizens of the "Athens of America," commissioned sculpted busts of their notables depicted in classical togas in the Greek style for display at their own Athenaeum. (Figs. 9.17–9.20.)

In the popular press and periodicals, writers reiterated the desire of Mount Auburn's founders to create a place that was "beautiful, attractive, consoling—not gloomy and repulsive." One correspondent believed that Americans had formerly neglected their dead because "we are inclined, *generally*, I know, to disparage external appearance. We have a contempt for ceremonies. We are a hard, practical people, intensely absorbed in business, surrounded by circumstances which accustom us to the livelier kinds of excitement, educated and impelled in every way to undervalue and lose sight of what may be called the graces of civilization." That became less true in Boston in the 1830s, especially among those who were successful in international commerce and industrial capitalism. Charges of a "want of feeling" toward the dead as a national "fault" were rapidly being disproved at Mount Auburn and the many cemeteries subsequently fashioned after its example. Indeed, one writer noted in 1839, "We are not, in our mortuary observances, quite so heathenish as we have been."[23]

Mount Auburn supported a cult of ancestors enshrined in family burial lots even more than a cult of heroes meriting public commemoration. Some used the cemetery to honor family founders for genealogical purposes even though their bones lay elsewhere. Dr. George Shattuck's father had in 1833 disposed of one lot on flat ground near Central Square and donated another of 5,226 square feet on a prime hilltop to Harvard College. Shattuck bought a large 1,600-square-foot lot on an as yet unsurveyed elevation covered with oak, cedar, and walnut trees in the western portion of the grounds in 1836 and persuaded Bigelow to name the walkway to his

Fig. 9.17. Stone and Stevens family obelisks on Beech Avenue. Engraving from N. Dearborn, 1852. MAC.

Fig. 9.18. John W. Webster family monument, Narcissus Path. Engraving from N. Dearborn, 1852. MAC.

Fig. 9.20. Martha Coffin Derby sarcophagus on Iris Path overlooking Consecration Dell. Drawn and engraved by Smillie, from Walter, 1847. MAC.

Fig. 9.19. Alexander Wadsworth monument, originally on Indian Ridge Path before being moved to a more conspicuous location on Spruce Avenue in the 1860s. Engraving from *Picturesque Pocket Companion*, 1839. MAC.

Fig. 9.21. Dr. George Shattuck Jr., family lot on Pilgrim Path. Engraving by Smillie, 1847. MAC.

Fig. 9.22. Shattuck family monument with detailed genealogical inscriptions. Photograph by BMGL, 1988.

lot Pilgrim Path in lieu of a plant name.[24] (Figs. 9.21, 9.22.) His intention, he wrote cemetery treasurer George Bond, was to commemorate a forefather who had come to Massachusetts in 1638. He constructed an underground tomb ample enough to hold several generations; and he commissioned a simple rectangular sarcophagus designed by the painter Washington Allston, built by Alpheus Cary, and inscribed with a genealogy including the name of another ancestor who had left no male descendants to carry on his name. Each side of the simple sarcophagus lists members of maternal as well as paternal branches of the family tree, including ancestors buried elsewhere, particularly one "Pilgrim Father, One of a Handful God Hath Multiplied into a Nation," though he did not try to retrieve and reinter their remains. "I wish to associate in the minds of my children the names of their maternal ancestors at the family burial place," he said. A simple iron fence topped by symbolic acorn finials surrounded his lot.[25]

The other side of the monument traces the family lineage to Bartholomew Cheever, born "in Canterbury,

Kent, in 1607." The patriarch "came to America in 1637 and died in 1693, aged 86." It also recognizes Caleb Davis, "Born in Woodstock, Connecticut in 1739 . . . Educated a Merchant, Resided in Boston; Died July 6, 1797, Aged 58. Caleb was Speaker to the First House of Representatives under the Commonwealth's New Constitution, Distinguished alike for Piety and Patriotism" and "Eleanor Cheever, Daughter of William Downs Cheever, was Born February 1, 1749/50—Married to Caleb Davis, September 9, 1787—Died January 2, 1825, Aged 75 Years." The inscription notes, "The Records of the Boston Female Orphan Asylum Tell of Her Associated Labors in the Cause of Suffering Humanity" and proclaims to God that Richard, Bartholomew, Daniel, William Downs, Eleanor, and Elizabeth, "Who Now Likewise Rest from Their Labors, Were of the Generations Who Have Risen Up to Bless Thy Name." Such was the testimony and gratitude of that generation for predecessors' accomplishments, the sort of detail once recorded only in family Bibles but now chiseled in stone.

Fig. 9.23. Samuel Appleton family lot between Woodbine and Hawthorn Paths leading to the cemetery's summit. The marble temple was made in Italy ca. 1838. An Egyptian Revival façade of a chamber tomb nestles into the hillside in the right rear. Engraving by Smillie, from Walter, 1847. MAC.

Mount Auburn's first guidebook urged contemporaries in 1839, "Let us employ some of the superfluous wealth now often expended in luxury worse than useless in rendering the place where our beloved friends repose decent, attractive and grateful at once to the eye and the heart."[26] The monuments and tombs were a sign of the new expendable wealth in the region arising from industrialization and international commerce; but Mount Auburn's moral mission resisted displays of conspicuous consumption. Story advised proprietors to maintain a balance in using the monuments to represent virtues and family prosperity, the fruit of the work ethic and evidence of righteousness—old lessons taught in a new style. Trustees reserved the right to ban any monuments or inscriptions they considered offensive or in poor taste.[27]

When a curmudgeonly visitor from Pennsylvania complained to the *Boston Evening Transcript* in 1839 about the "ostentatious display of tombery" and "pomp and aristocracy of the city in these precincts of mortality," arguing, "The towering homes and pride-swollen fronts do not frown from the heights of Beacon Street up on the Boston Common . . . with a colder superciliousness, than the $10,000 obelisks from out their cast-iron exclusions," the editor retorted, "We Bostonians pride ourselves upon two things . . . the Common and Mount Auburn." He protested that not one obelisk "cost a tenth" of the alleged sum, the "vast majority" being "distinguished in their plainness and modesty." Their simplicity had "attracted the attention or admiration of visitors" who favorably "compar[ed] our establishment with the most distinguished and beautiful foreign ones," finding it "a decent monument to the dearly cherished and sometimes illustrious dead, such as may gratify the heart's best nature in the survivors, or kindle a glow of noble emulation in the breast of all who survey it." He exclaimed facetiously, "This, forsooth, is aristocracy!"[28]

The visitor, however, was not entirely off the mark. The merchant, textile industrialist, financier, and philanthropist Samuel Appleton (1766–1853) had erected a miniature Grecian temple, fashioned of marble in Italy. Measuring twelve by six feet, it is set on a tiered base and topped by carved sepulchral lamps. Low-relief Corinthian columns appear to support the entablature.

Fig. 9.24. Appleton monument detail. Photograph by BMGL, 1983

Its sides bear symbolic elements—a snake or serpent eating its own tail, with spread wings over it representing eternity and evergreen wreaths for perpetual remembrance. (Figs. 9.23, 9.24.) A grove of evergreens originally framed the marble's whiteness, creating a theatrical composition on a dramatic site near the cemetery's summit. From a distance it seems to take on far grander proportions that its diminutive size might suggest. Costing $10,000, it was the most costly private monument at Mount Auburn, and perhaps in the nation, in the 1830s.

Monuments to Notables

The distinction between civic and private funerary monuments soon became blurred. Story wanted Mount Auburn's monuments to teach "our destiny and duty," to elucidate exemplary and notable lives in the same manner as Jared Sparks's collected biographies. Bigelow encouraged developing a cult of ancestors within each family as well as a celebration of heroes for the community, region, and nation. Mount Auburn's purpose, he insisted, was to "afford the means of paying tribute of respect by monumental erections to the name and memory of great and good men, whenever or wherever they have died." Through the first decades, many cenotaphs, monuments unrelated to actual burials but honoring those buried elsewhere, were erected.[29] For instance, Thomas Dowse (1772–1856) of Cambridge, a philanthropist and self-made man, erected a large obelisk to Benjamin Franklin, his master during his printing apprenticeship, next to a smaller one for himself. (Fig. 9.25.) It commends the "Illustrious Example" of Franklin's "Industy, Integrity, and Self-Culture." A bachelor, Dowse made a fortune as a leather dresser, providing fine sheepskins for bindings to publishers such as Little & Brown. He opened his fine house and gardens to the public, and willed his huge library to the Massachusetts Historical Society.[30]

Mount Auburn provided a place for teaching future generations about that era's accomplishments in shaping a new American civilization. Bigelow was intensely conscious of his contemporaries' advances in developing the thriving republic's industries, institutions, art, and literature, and he wished to contribute to that progress. He intended that his era's monuments and epitaphs would challenge posterity to strive to surpass his generation's accomplishments, thus meriting a status in turn as distinguished ancestors. Monuments, it was believed, could instill ambition by perpetuating the fame of a new breed of American hero as role models. The first guidebook to Mount Auburn expressed the hope that one day the cemetery might display as many great names as its Parisian archetype: "See how the dust of Père Lachaise teems with them! What monuments—what historical and classical accumulations—what scholars, conquerors, and bards—what hints and helps to patriotism and perseverance and high ambition!" At Mount Auburn, "even the pilgrim who comes from other climes to visit . . . may

Fig. 9.25. Obelisks erected on Gentian Path by Thomas Dowse to himself and Benjamin Franklin. Lithograph by Louis Prang, in Flagg, 1861. MAC.

read wherever he wanders on the face of the soil, the character and praise of the living generation in the works which shall indicate their remembrance of those that have passed away."[31]

When the famed Prussian phrenologist Dr. Johann Gaspar Spurzheim (1776–1832) died while lecturing in Boston, local leaders decided to honor him at the new cemetery. His theories had so captured the imagination of the scientifically minded that Mayor Quincy, Boston's aldermen, Harvard faculty, and the city's entire medical profession marched en masse through the streets to his funeral, which featured an ode composed for the occasion by the Reverend John Pierpont. After the *Edinburgh Review* charged in 1815 that he was a charlatan preaching "trash," Bostonians responded with fervent espousal of his theories and a determination to commemorate his life. Literary Bostonians were steadfast champions of anyone criticized by that British journal. They also knew that in 1828 the British Phrenological Society had erected a monument with portrait bust over the tomb in Père Lachaise of Franz Joseph Gall, another noted phrenologist, acclaimed for locating the "hump of crime" on the skull. Spurzheim epitomized the sort of scholar that elite Bostonians wished to honor at Mount Auburn.[32] William Sturgis (1782–1863), a China trade merchant, contributed the largest sum to a subscription campaign to buy a burial lot for Spurzheim and a polished Italian marble sarcophagus in imitation of the Roman tomb of Scipio Barbatus. (Fig. 9.26, 9.27.) A simple iron fence surrounded the monument in a prominent spot atop the first hillock on the left of Central Avenue just inside the cemetery entrance, a site "to excite in the minds of some a classical recollection" as it corresponded to a description of a place of sepulcher in Virgil's ninth eclogue. The English visitor Harriet Martineau nevertheless complained that she and others did not understand how a sarcophagus was appropriate for Spurzheim. Perhaps it was a matter of expediency, she thought, saving the committee the trouble of commissioning a custom-made monument. In fact, the sarcophagus had fortuitously arrived in Boston just before the phrenologist's sudden death, one of the first monuments imported on speculation by Robert Gould Shaw.[33]

Fig. 9.26. The cenotaph of the famed phrenologist Gaspar Spurzheim, a marble sarcophagus imported from Italy. Engraving from *Cyclopedia of Useful Knowledge*, 1836.

Fig. 9.27. "Tomb of Spurzheim" on the Indian Hill rise above Central Avenue. Engraving by Smillie, from Walter, 1847. MAC.

Many voluntary associations adopted the monument-building cause. In 1834 the Garden and Cemetery Committee granted a lot to the "Committee of the Young Men of Boston," headed by Charles Francis Adams, H. F. Baker, and L. M. Walter, for construction of a cenotaph in memory of the marquis de Lafayette. The association must have failed to raise sufficient funds, because no monument was ever erected, and the lot was forfeited without record.[34] The purpose of commemoration was twofold in that it proclaimed the values of the present as well as the virtues of the deceased. A subscription campaign by "friends" funded a monument to Clement Durgin (1802–1833), associate princi-

Fig. 9.28. Clement Durgin monument on Narcissus Path. Engraving from *Picturesque Pocket Companion*, 1839. MAC.

Fig. 9.29. Monument "In Memory of our Teacher, Martha Whiting . . . Erected by the Pupils of Charlestown Female Seminary" on Poplar Avenue. Engraving from N. Dearborn, 1857. MAC.

Fig. 9.30. Edwin Buckingham monument on Willow Avenue. Engraving from *Picturesque Pocket Companion*, 1839. MAC.

Fig. 9.31. Buckingham family lot, including monument erected by a subscription campaign to son Edwin, who died at sea, and the more simple slab markers of the publisher-journalist Joseph T. Buckingham, his wife, Melinda, and her sister Lucinda. Photograph by Carol Betsch, 2005.

pal of the Chauncey Hall School. The inscription reads: "A Student and Lover of Nature, In Her Wonders He Saw and Acknowledged and Through Them Adored Her Beneficent Author. His Life Was a Beautiful Illustration of His Philosophy; His Death of the Triumph of Faith. His Pupils Have Reared This Monument as an Imperfect Memorial of Their Grateful Affections and Respect." Students at the Charlestown Female Seminary erected a monument to their teacher Martha Whiting, who died in 1850. Other subscription campaigns honored the deceased as well as their relatives. Boston mechanics funded a cenotaph to Edwin Buckingham, who died at sea in 1833 at age twenty-three, son of the newspaper editor who championed the mechanic class. (Figs. 9.28–9.31.) It bears the inscription "The Sea His Body, Heaven His Spirit Holds."

Story instigated a campaign among classmates to build an Egyptian sarcophagus on the Harvard Hill grave of his colleague John Hooker Ashmun

(1800–1833), Royal Professor of Law, after eulogizing him at the "funeral obsequies" in the university's chapel. Charles Chauncey Emerson, his student, composed the epitaph: "He Went Behind Precedents to Principles; And Books Were His Helpers, Never His Masters. There Was the Beauty of Accuracy in His Understanding, and the Beauty of Uprightness in His Character. Throught the Slow Progress of the Disease which Consumed His Life, He Kept Unimpaired His Kindness of Temper and Superiority of Intellect. He Did More Sick Than Others in Health. He Was Fit to Teach at an Age When Common Men Are Beginning to Learn, And His Few Years Bore the Fruit of Long Life. A Lover of Truth, An Obeyer of Duty, A Sincere Friend, And a Wise Instructor. His Pupils Raise This Stone to His Memory." Ashmun's monument was a spiritual tract, a sermon preached so visitors might resolve to live similarly in hopes of being equally righteous, accomplished, and remembered.[35]

Attempting to assemble Harvard's late notables on Harvard Hill, Bigelow and Story joined an appeal to the widow of John Thornton Kirkland (1770–1840), Harvard president at the height of the Unitarian controversy, to permit reinterment of her husband; but she refused "to disturb the repose of his present resting place" in the Cambridge burying ground across the street from Harvard Yard. Mrs. Kirkland replied to a committee of alumni that despite "the peculiar beauties of Mount Auburn," she had "no pleasing associations with the new and great city of the dead." She suggested that perpetuating her husband's memory could be accomplished "without the removal of what at best must soon be dust." Undeterred, a committee consisting of Bigelow, Charles P. Curtis, F. W. P. Greenwood, Charles Francis Adams, and Jared Sparks raised funds for a cenotaph at Mount Auburn. As Mrs. Kirkland predicted, few visitors "pause to think if he sleep beneath the marble."[36] Rather than marking mortal remains, the monument imparts the lesson of a life. (Fig. 9.32.)

Fig. 9.32. Harvard Hill, with monuments to President John Hooker Ashmun (foreground) and John Kirkland (left). Photograph by Carol Betsch, 2005.

Following William Ellery Channing's advice, many rejected the notion that military bravery and dramatic deeds alone constituted heroism. They wanted to celebrate exemplary lives reflecting personal virtue in the service of the community. Channing preached self-culture and self-improvement to workingmen, the lesson that character and learning mattered more than power and prestige. The melancholy tale of a promising life cut short appealed more to proponents of "conspicuous commemoration" than bold deeds or accumulated wealth.[37] Such was the case with the Reverend Samuel H. Stearns, born in 1802, graduated from Harvard in 1832, and ordained at the Old South Church in 1834. He resigned his ministry in 1836 owing to illness and, like other invalids of means, went traveling through Europe in the hope of regaining his health. He died in Paris and was buried at Père Lachaise. In 1839 his family, friends, and former congregation arranged for his body's reinterment at Mount Auburn, erecting an obelisk proclaiming him "Discriminating, Tasteful, Magnanimous, Devoted, Uniting Uncommon Eloquence with Fervent and Confiding Piety . . . A Full Believer in the Doctrines of Grace." (Fig. 9.33.)

Even if it required the ritual of reburial at the risk of reviving the veneration of relics, Bostonians were particularly eager to commemorate their liberal ministers. In 1837 the Reverend John Murray, who died in 1815, was reentombed at Mount Auburn under a marble monu-

Fig. 9.33. Rev. Samuel Stearns monument on Moss Path. Engraving from from *Picturesque Pocket Companion*, 1839. MAC.

Fig. 9.34. Rev. John Murray's monument on Vine Path at the entrance to Consecration Dell. Photograph by BMGL, 1986.

ment, a severed fluted column topped by an urn. (Fig. 9.34.) "Erected at the Recommendation of the United States General Convention of Universalists," the monument was intended, wrote the Reverend Hosea Ballou, "to accommodate future generations with a knowledge of the spot" so they might learn "to cherish and preserve the memory of those whom the wisdom of God has distinguished as benefactors of mankind." Since his death Murray "had mouldered in the Sargent [family] tomb in the Granary Burying-Ground, without a stone or inscription of any kind to denote the ashes of the man who had stirred the country with the tidings of universal love." Ballou urged commemoration while warning "against the pageantry of pride, displayed in costly garnishings, and also against monkish superstition, which attributes efficacy and merit to that which is but dust." A visit to Murray's new burial place, in its natural setting, might supplement the reading of the great man's biography but would not lead visitors astray in the superstitious way associated with High Church forms.[38] Similarly, in 1839 George Bond and George W. Coffin, on behalf of others, petitioned Theodore Lyman of the Brattle Street Church "Society" to have the remains of the Unitarian minister Joseph Stevens Buckminster (1784–1812) moved from a common graveyard to a Mount Auburn lot donated by Amos Lawrence, where a proper monument could be erected.[39]

Most monuments in Mount Auburn's first decades celebrated the importance of ministers, mothers, merchants, and mechanics—considered the bedrock of the new republic. The cemetery attracted self-commemoration of businessmen and industrialists active in New England's economic development. Still, many of their monuments are quite unpretentious, reflecting the frugality and restrained taste of even the most prosperous New Englanders. The business associates of Francis Stanton financed a simple one to "An Upright Merchant, A Useful Citizen, A Valued Friend." The family of Jesse Putnam, who died in 1837 at age eighty-three, erected a discreet monument of Italian marble with simple emblems under a "noble" oak on Beech Avenue to mark the grave of the "Father of Merchants of Boston, A Distinction Not Claimed by Himself, But Accorded by Others in Consideration of the Intelligence, Energy, and Integrity with Which for More Than Half a Century at Home and Abroad, He Followed and Adorned His Profession." Putnam's wife, Susannah, is also remembered: "Having Discharged with Unwearied Fidelity and Devotion the Duties of this Relation as well as Those of a Daughter and Mother, She Sank into the Sleep of Death with Hope Full of Immortality." Such epitaphs reflected the notion that exemplary women had important social functions, albeit in a sphere separate from the business world of their husbands.

Fig. 9.35. Family lot of Thomas Handasyd Perkins, Boston's "Merchant Prince," over a subterranean chamber tomb on Central Avenue and with the marble Newfoundland watchdog sculpted by Horatio Greenough, ca. 1840s. Photograph by BMGL, 1979.

Thomas Handasyd Perkins Jr., son of the "Merchant Prince," eschewed proclamation of his family's central position in the city's economic life, commissioning a single monument for his lot on Central Avenue over a full-chamber masonry tomb hidden beneath ground. No epitaphs adorn the marble monument, which stands less than two feet high. There is simply a reclining watchdog, a faithful Newfoundland sculpted by Horatio Greenough. The family surrounded the lot with a fine iron fence. (Fig. 9.35.)

Bostonians also commemorated those whose teaching or scholarship furthered their city's cultural and commercial success. One early monument was to Frederic P. Leverett, superintending teacher of the Boston Latin School and author of the nationally known *Latin Lexicon* which went to press the day he died. It celebrates his work, which "Reflects Honor Not Only on the Person Engaged in its Preparation, But on Our Country . . . the Result of American Ability and Industry and American Enterprise." Another honors the example, "Cherished for Imitation," of Warren Colburn, a mathematician who died at age forty in 1833. As an educational reformer introducing the Pestalozzian system of education, asserting that belief in the self is the only guide to knowledge, Colburn authored texts on arithmetic and algebra used in New England schools, providing a practical education for a new generation of industrialists and engineers who might later take Bigelow's course on technology at Harvard. Colburn also served as a superintendent in developing the Waltham and Lowell manufactories in 1814 and 1822. (Figs. 9.36, 9.37.)

Requests from commemorative committees for land became so numerous that in 1838 the trustees declared it henceforth "inexpedient to make gratuitous appropriations for erection of monuments to distinguished individuals."[40] Perhaps they feared that those already honored were not as inherently "distinguished" as they had hoped, or they may simply have realized that granting honors at a time of industrialization, technological innovation, and cultural renaissance would soon lead to a landslide of requests for free space. The Massachusetts Horticultural Society had to buy a lot on Yarrow Path in 1838 for Thomas Green Fessenden (1771–1837) as the Massachusetts Society for Promoting Agriculture joined them in financing the monument to the editor of the *New England Farmer*, a neoclassical marble structure set in place in 1839. Trustees permitted the "gratuitous ap-

Fig. 9.36. Frederick P. Leverett marble monument topped by the flame of life on Vine Path overlooking Consecration Dell, erected ca. 1833. Photograph by Carol Betsch, 2005.

propriation"—their final one—of a small, irregular lot in 1839 for the Reverend Noah Worcester (1758–1837), an abolitionist dubbed the "Friend of Peace." His friends moved his remains, first entombed near his Brighton home, to Mount Auburn and erected a handsome monument over them.

The trustees deviated from their new rule against granting whole lots for commemoration in donating a lot on Central Avenue for a stocky twenty-foot marble obelisk decorated with low-relief swags of roses in memory of members of the U.S. Exploring Expedition—Lieutenant Joseph A. Underwood and Midshipmen Wilkes Henry (nephew of Captain Charles Wilkes), James W. E. Reid, and Frederick A. Bacon—"Pioneers in Civilization," who died in the "Feejee" Islands in 1839–40, their graves "unknown, for every vestige of the interment was carefully effaced, in order that the cannibals might not disinter the remains." The expedition, Thoreau complained, had been the object of much "parade and expense." Associate officers and the scientific corps funded the cenotaph at a cost of $200. It was designed by Joseph Drayton (1795–1856) and erected by John Struthers and Son of Philadelphia. It proclaimed the men heroes of a venture of international import. Since cenotaphs had been dedicated to "the Great Ocean's Greatest Explorer," Captain James Cook, in the famed English garden of Stowe and in the picturesque landscape garden of Méréville in France, Mount Auburn was thought to provide a fitting site for a monument honoring the heroes of an American venture of such prominence.[41] (Figs. 9.38, 9.39.)

Fig. 9.37. Warren Colburn monument on Locust Avenue. Engraving from N. Dearborn, 1852. MAC.

Fig. 9.38. Nathaniel Bowditch monument at the junction of Central and Cypress Avenues, prominently sited along the processional leading into the cemetery, a bronze portrait statue by Robert Ball Hughes, 1847, with the stocky obelisk to members of the U.S. Exploring Expedition behind it. Drawn and engraved by Smillie, from Walter, 1847. MAC.

Fig. 9.39. U.S. Exploring Expedition monument, detail. Photograph by Arthur C. Haskell, 1937. MAC.

Fig. 9.40. Nathaniel Bowditch monument at the junction of Central and Cypress Avenues, prominently sited along the processional leading into the cemetery, a bronze portrait statue by Robert Ball Hughes, 1847, with the stocky obelisk to members of the U.S. Exploring Expedition behind it. Drawn and engraved by Smillie, from Walter, 1847. MAC.

The death of the astronomer and mathematician Nathaniel Bowditch (1773–1838) inspired commemoration by mercantile leaders who owed their prosperity in international trade to his refinement of navigation techniques and instruments. Although Bowditch was initially laid in a tomb in Boston's Trinity Church, an association of urban leaders formed in 1843 to build a cenotaph as a focal point at Mount Auburn, despite the fact that when Harmony Grove Cemetery was founded in his hometown of Salem in 1840, a central lot had been dedicated for a funerary tribute to him so that "generation after generation shall thus be permitted to see an enduring memorial of what unaided self-training, united with high moral worth, can accomplish." His minister, the Reverend Alexander Young, felt that Bowditch had "built his own monument, more enduring than marble," but he nevertheless supported erection of "material and visible" commemoration: "Let the shipmasters and mates throughout the United States and all seamen who have actually used the *Practical Navigator* give one dollar each (those who please may give more) towards the erection of a monument of white marble in a style of severe and simple grandeur, befitting his character; and let the amount be collected in every seaport by the Chamber of Commerce, the Marine Society, and if neither of these exist, by some Insurance Company, or by the Collector of the port."[42] (Fig. 9.40.)

The committee contemplated an obelisk but agreed on a life-sized seated portrait statue of the scientist with globe, navigational quadrant, and book—the most elaborate form attempted to that time for an individual in any American funerary setting. The work by Robert Ball Hughes (1806–1868), an Englishman recently settled in Boston, was the first large bronze cast in the United States. In 1847 Hughes exhibited a plaster copy in the vestibule of the Athenaeum, where it remains. Since the Mount Auburn trustees believed that Bowditch and his statue represented the latest advances in American industry and art, the corporation reserved a prime piece of land across Central Avenue from Spurzheim's sarcophagus on the rising ground, a focal point, allotting funds to protect the monument with an iron fence while reserving a band of space around it in perpetuity for ornamental purposes. The Bowditch statue sits on this elevated site as if gazing northward towards the cemetery entrance to welcome visitors. (Fig. 9.41.) One observer wondered, "Who shall estimate its propitious influence upon the minds of those ingenuous youth, who, generation after generation, shall thus be permitted to see an enduring

Fig. 9.41. Bowditch statue, detail. From a stereograph, ca. 1870. MAC, BMGL.

memorial to what unaided self-training, united with high moral worth, can accomplish?" Placement of the Bowditch statue just in front of the cenotaph to the American explorers of the South Seas was also a proud nationalistic assertion of seafaring competence, linking the accomplishments of both. In this respect Mount Auburn's trustees shared the same agenda as the management of Père Lachaise in its first years, who realized that collecting notables, or at least their cenotaphs, would not only help enshrine a new version of national history but also confer prestige on an innovative new cemetery, thus attracting patronage and visitors.[43]

The trustees, however, did not want to act as a jury, deciding who merited commemoration, nor did they want to give away land only to have to raise lot prices inordinately or else sacrifice income needed for cemetery improvements. Already, owing to the Panic of 1837, they had found that they could not afford to build the structures planned to embellish the grounds. The decision to stop granting land did not impede the commemorative impulse of groups intent on putting up cenotaphs and funerary monuments. It simply meant that subscription campaigns had to be organized to raise the money to purchase lots if the individuals in question did not already have the right of burial there. Because of irregularities in the rolling terrain and the winding system of avenues and paths, there were odd patches of ground that could not be sectioned into regular lots. In 1840 the Committee on Lots reserved these for "public monuments," to be sold for 26⅔ cents per square foot plus a premium of $20 for site choice, provided that perpetual care be paid for.

The trustees stuck to this new policy and did not make special provisions when William Ellery Channing, the "Apostle of Unitarianism," died in 1842. (Fig. 9.42.) Channing's family exchanged their lots on Chestnut Avenue, which had become a busy road winding up to the cemetery's summit, for two secluded plots along the newly surveyed Greenbriar Path on a low rise southwest of the entrance. Then 112 members of the Federal Street Church congregation contributed $1,780 for a monument to a subscription campaign run by Thomas Handasyd Perkins, the "merchant prince." The landscape painter and poet Washington Allston (1779–1843), Channing's classmate and brother-in-law, designed the sarcophagus-like monument, which defies precise description as neoclassical. Alpheus Cary, the new local

Fig. 9.42. Rev. William Ellery Channing monument on Greenbriar Path. Engraving by N. Dearborn, 1852. MAC.

monument dealer, constructed it of Italian marble. The inscription on the front reads: "In Memory of William Ellery Channing Honored Throughout Christendom for His Eloquence and Courage in Maintaining and Advocating the Great Cause of Truth, Religion, and Freedom This Monument is Gratefully and Reverently Erected by the Christian Society of Which During Nearly Forty Years He Was Pastor." The rear notes that the "Minister of Jesus Christ to the Society Worshipping God in Federal Street Boston [died] October 2 1842 While on a Journey to Bennington, Vermont."[44]

Upon the death from tuberculosis of the Congregationalist minister Charles Turner Torrey (1813–1846) after two years in a Baltimore prison for antislavery activism, an association called the Friends of the American Slave brought his body back to Boston for a grand public funeral at the Tremont Temple and a public meeting at Faneuil Hall after the burial at Mount Auburn. They took advantage the new policy of selling irregular parcels of land for "public monuments," acquiring a small triangular parcel at the intersections of Spruce and Fir Avenues. A native of Scituate, Massachusetts, and graduate of Yale, Torrey became known as the "Martyr for Liberty." His monument, a short, capped obelisk designed by the Carew firm, bears Torrey's words taken from one of his last letters: "It Is Better to Die in Prison with the Peace of God in Our Breast Than to Live in Freedom with a Polluted Conscience." Affixed are bronze reliefs of a weeping black woman in chains, a medallion or tondo relief portrait of Torrey, and

Fig. 9.43. Charles T. Torrey monument at the junction of Spruce and Fir Avenues, erected ca. 1846 to the abolitionist who died in a Baltimore jail. Daguerreotype by Albert Sands Southworth and Josiah Johnson Hawes, ca. 1850. Courtesy George Eastman House.

a crown of thorns, all exhibited at the Boston Athenaeum in 1859. (Fig. 9.43.)

The noted sculptor Thomas Crawford (1814–1857) produced the marble monument of Dr. Amos Binney (1803–1847), a merchant, co-founder in 1830 of the Boston Society of Natural History, and noted expert on American mollusks. Crawford, who moved his studio to Rome in 1835, met Binney before he died there while traveling to regain his health. Binney's widow, Mary Ann, commissioned the monument and had her husband's remains shipped to a newly purchased lot near Fir Avenue, where she also reinterred his parents. The neo-Roman composition, nine feet tall and over seven feet wide, draped with a shroud and adorned by inverted torches and a laurel wreath, features high-relief sculptures set in niches on two sides—Binney rising to heaven, a soul effigy cloaked in a toga, and a mourning woman bearing an urn, representing the widow who brought the remains home. Installed in 1850 within an ornate cast-iron fence, it became a major attraction.[45] (Fig. 9.44, 9.45.)

The cenotaph of Margaret Fuller Ossoli (1810–1850) was installed on her family's lot between Pyrola and Belwort paths. Her father, Timothy, who died in 1838, was a U.S. congressman, but his stone did not draw the visitors who beat a path to the stone in memory of Margaret, feminist, Transcendentalist, and the first woman admitted into Harvard's library. She had edited the *Dial*, written for Horace Greeley's *New York Tribune*, and established an international reputation before, on a visit to Italy, she met and married Giovanni Angelo, Marquis Ossoli, a captain in the Italian Civic Guard and ten years

Fig. 9.44. Dr. Amos Binney monument on Heath Path by the sculptor Thomas Crawford, with soul effigy ascending to heaven. Photograph by Harvard Film Service, ca. 1930. MAC.

Fig. 9.45. Mourning woman on opposite side of the Dr. Amos Binney monument. Photograph by BMGL, 1986.

her junior. After working on behalf of the ill-fated Roman Revolution of 1848, Margaret and Giovanni sailed for New York, only to meet with a tragic death by shipwreck off Long Island's Fire Island on July 19, 1850. The bodies of wife and husband were never found, despite Thoreau's exhaustive search of miles of beaches. Sailors retrieved the body of their son Angelino "Nino" Ossoli and temporarily buried his small body in a sea chest in the sand until the family could remove it to Mount Auburn in 1854. (Figs. 9.46, 9.47.)

Thomas Carew (1819–1894), Cary's competitor in the local funerary monument business, custom-made Fuller's arched marble stone inset with a bronze plaque reading: "By Birth a Child of New England / By Adoption a Citizen of Rome / By Genius Belonging in the World / In Youth an Insatiate Student Seeking the Highest Culture / In Riper Years Teacher, Writer, Critic of Literature and Art / In Mature Age Companion and Helper of Many Earnest Reformers in America and Europe and of Her Husband Giovanni Angelo, Marquis Ossoli. / He Gave Up Rank, Station and Home for the Roman Republic and For His Wife and Child / And That Child, Angelo Eugene Philip Ossoli / Born in Rieti, Italy, Sept 5, 1848, Whose Dust / Reposes at the Foot of this Stone. / They Passed from This Life Together / By Shipwreck JULY 19, 1850. / United in Life by Mutual Love, Labors, and Trials, The Merciful Father Took Them Together, and in Death They Are Not Divided." The star above Fuller's low-relief portrait medallion was the signature she used on her writings. A book represents her literary career; a sword the Italian struggle she and her husband shared. The oak and laurel suggest strength and accomplishment.

Fig. 9.46. Cenotaph of the famed Transcendentalist writer Margaret Fuller Ossoli, with low-relief profile portrait, on her father's family lot between Pyrola and Bellwort paths. The memorial is called a cenotaph because her body was lost at sea and is not buried here. Engraving from N. Dearborn, *Guide*, 1875. MAC.

Fig. 9.47. Cenotaph of Margaret Fuller Ossoli. Photograph by BMGL, 1994.

When Boston native Frances Sargent Locke Osgood (1811–1850), prominent in literary circles in England as well as America owing to her prolific contributions of prose and verse to leading periodicals and her own anthologies, died of tuberculosis at home in New York, she was buried at Mount Auburn on Orange Path in her parents' lot. Her colleagues, "most of the celebrities of the time," contributed pieces to a "gift book" or "souvenir" titled *The Memorial* (1851), whose proceeds were to be devoted to building her monument. Finding the grave unmarked on a visit in 1854, Fanny Fern was impelled to lambast her friends and the widower in *Fern Leaves from Fanny's Port-Folio*. Samuel Osgood (1808–1885), a renowned painter, protested to the *New York Evening Post* that before Fern's book went to press, he had designed a marble monument at his own expense and placed it on a prominent lot visible from Walnut Avenue as it winds uphill to the mount. A bronze lyre crowned by a laurel wreath, inspired by her poem "The Hand That Swept the Sounding Lyre," stands fifteen feet high atop a rectangular white marble base. The Greek lyre, like the Saxon or Old English *hearpa*, was strummed during the reading of poems and tales. Initially, four of the five strings of the lyre were cut to symbolize the silenced voice of the poet and her three children. Samuel later requested that his second wife sever the fifth string when he died.[46] (Fig. 9.48.)

The monument of the famed neoclassical architect Charles Bulfinch (1763–1844) on Bellwort Path is

Fig. 9.48. Frances Sargeant Osgood monument on Walnut Avenue, topped by the bronze lyre with broken strings, symbolic of the poet's voice silenced. Photograph by Carol Betsch, 2005.

Fig. 9.49. Charles Bulfinch monument on Bellwort Path, with urn from the Tontine Crescent. Photograph by Haskell, 1945. MAC.

Fig. 9.50. Rev. Daniel Sharp Gothic Revival monument on Chapel Avenue, designed by architect George Snell, 1856. Engraving by N. Dearborn, 1857. MAC.

crowned by the "great urn," modeled after a design by Robert Adam which he had bought in England to use as a focal point in Franklin Place, a small elliptical park in the Tontine Cresent, an elegant residential block in Boston that Bulfinch designed and developed, named in memory of the Founding Father born nearby. (Fig. 9.49.) The urbanist Bulfinch had improved Boston's plumbing infrastructure and street lighting. Best known for designing the domed Massachusetts State House (1798), he completed Benjamin Henry Latrobe's work as official architect of the U.S. Capitol in the 1830s, both major monuments to his expertise. Bulfinch was initially placed in his family crypt in King's Chapel until his son Thomas moved all the remains to Mount Auburn in 1854. The urn meant to commemorate Benjamin Franklin was moved from Boston to do the same for Bulfinch.

Religious societies also solicited contributions to buy lots and erect monuments. Baptists raised funds for a monument to the Reverend Daniel Sharp (1783–1853), who died at age seventy near Baltimore. Designed by the architect George Snell and erected in 1856, it was, as described by one guidebook, "in the early English style of pointed architecture," and displayed "refined taste which distinguishes this monument from most of the miscalled Gothic structures in the grounds." Although many Yankees shared a taste for the Gothic Revival, which had begun to replace the neoclassical in favor, others reflected their Puritan forebears' rejection of things considered "papist" in their descriptions of the style.[47] (Fig. 9.50.)

In 1859 Charles Tufts, Silvanus Packard, and Maturin M. Ballou petitioned for permission to unite contiguous lots on Central Avenue, eliminating the intervening spaces, to create a site for a life-sized marble statue of the Reverend Hosea Ballou (1771–1852), the famed Universalist. To extend the privilege of contributing to Universalists nationally, the Boston Society ruled that no subscription should exceed one dollar. Ballou died at age eighty-one after a long career in which he "assaulted the

Calvinism of his day" and denied the inevitability of postmortem punishment. In the thirty-four years Ballou served as pastor of Boston's Second Universalist Society, he contributed to the religious liberalism that presaged the founding of Mount Auburn as a new Eden innocent of Adam's Fall. In 1859 the sculptor Edward Augustus Brackett (1818–1908) completed the statue of Ballou "in full vigor of adulthood" and looking sterner than his liberal theology would have suggested.[48] (Fig. 9.51.)

Professional colleagues of inventors and innovators also contributed to build monuments. A simple obelisk memorializes Barnabas Bates (1785–1853), founder in 1825 of New York's weekly Unitarian *Christian Inquirer* and acclaimed the "Father of Cheap Postage," an attempt by Whigs to claim credit for the postal reform attributed to Jacksonian Democrats. The remains of what was once a more elaborate monument on Spruce Avenue proclaim Thomas Blanchard (1788–1864), "An Eminent American Inventor, Whose Great Mind Conceived the Ideas and Brought into Operation Works of Art That Will Live for Ages." Two sides bear a low relief of the lathe he created to manufacture gunstocks, axe handles, shoe lasts, and wheel-spokes, the other a printing press, two of the twenty-five inventions he patented. The back takes note of other family members. (Fig. 9.52.)

In 1866 the "express companies of the United States" contributed to have Thomas A. Carew design an elaborate monument to William Frederick Harnden (1813–1845). It replaced a modest marble stone depicting a dove clasping a broken flower in its beak. Harnden, the quintessential self-made man, began the most innovative private postal company in Boston in 1839, with door-to-door pickup and delivery between Boston and New York, the first to use the word "express." He expanded links to Philadelphia, Albany, Liverpool, London, Paris, Scotland, Germany, and Ireland, in the process securing cheap passage for about 100,000 immigrant couriers. By 1844 over forty such firms existed in Boston alone. Inscribed "Founder of the Express Business in America" and "Because the King's Business Required Haste" (1 Samuel 21), the monument with canopy supported by Corinthian columns shelters a draped marble urn guarded by a faithful dog. Two low-relief sculptural panels on the sides of the interior lion-clawed base depict scenes of mail being sent and received from a home and railroad station. The grand

Fig. 9.51. Rev. Hosea Ballou portrait statue by Edward Augustus Brackett. Photograph by BMGL, 1979.

Fig. 9.52. Monument of Thomas Blanchard, ca. 1865, with low reliefs of machines he invented. Photograph by BMGL, 1988.

monument is not unlike an advertisement for the new and growing industry, although the trustees assiduously rejected other proposals for images considered promotional.[49] (Figs. 9.53, 9.54.)

Successful abolitionists erected a sculpted stone on the grave of the former fugitive slave Peter Byus (ca. 1807–1867) on Citron Path at Magnolia Avenue near the cemetery's periphery. It bears a low relief of a slave breaking his chains, copied from Josiah Wedgwood's famous black and white jasper cameo *Am I Not a Man and a Brother?* (1787), made for the Society for the Abolition of the Slave Trade and widely circulated via Franklin among American antislavery advocates. Byus's stone celebrates the life of a man "Born in Hampshire County, Virginia, A Slave. At the Age of About Thirty-Six He

Fig. 9.53. William Frederick Harnden monument on Central Avenue, 1866. Photograph by Carol Betsch, 2005.

Fig. 9.54. Harnden monument, detail of low relief (woman passing package to courier), "The Express Business." Photograph by BMGL, 1979.

Fig. 9.55. Peter Byus monument, 1867, with low relief of freed slave adapted from the cameo by Josiah Wedgwood. Photograph by Jennifer Johnston, 2006. MAC.

Fled for Freedom to Boston, Where He Resided for the Last Thirty Years of His Life." It proclaims him to be "A Sincere Christian, A True Friend, And An Honest Man." (Fig. 9.55.)

In the wake of the Civil War came a shift in ideas about a usable American past comprised of notables to be commemorated as exemplary in a funerary setting. The original goal at Mount Auburn had been to create for Boston, New England, and the nation a new Ceramicus, Valhalla, or Westminster Abbey. The new trustees either would not or could not promote the place as the nation's chief historical, let alone funerary, repository. Other "rural" cemeteries had arisen in major cities to challenge that claim, even across town at Forest Hills in Roxbury and in other towns within a carriage ride of Boston. But even more important was the failure of Bostonians to reach consensus about their own public heroes and where they should be commemorated—in cemeteries, parks, or squares and commons.

The story of competing claims on behalf of the "discoverer" of anesthesia illustrates the point. When William Thomas Green Morton (1819–1868), a dentist, died at age forty-nine, an ongoing dispute raged over whether he should receive credit for the discovery. Morton's friends decided to erect a grand monument over his grave on Spruce Avenue since he had died without funds, having expended much of his estate and vitality over two decades in an attempt to claim credit for discovery of sulfuric ether, use of which he first demonstrated at the Massachusetts General Hospital in 1846 during an operation by Dr. John Collins Warren. The fluted column topped by a draped urn acclaims, on behalf of "Citizens of Boston," the "Inventor and Revealor of Anaesthic Inhalation / Before Whom in All Time Surgery Was Agony / By Whom Pain in Surgery Was Averted and Annulled / Since Whom Science Has Control of Pain." (Fig. 9.56.) A Boston "chemist" (pharmacist), Dr. Charles T. Jackson (1805–1880), Emerson's brother-in-law, who initially had recommended that the dentist try sulfuric ether, despite being skeptical of Morton's experiment, belatedly tried to claim the credit. When Jackson died, he was buried atop the mount in his family lot across from the tower. His modest stone proclaims him the discoverer of anesthesia: "Eminent as a Chemist, Mineralogist, Geologist and Investigator in All Departments of Natural Science. Through His Observations of the Peculiar Effects of Sulphuric Ether on the Nerves of Sensation, And His Bold Deduction Therefrom, The Benign Discovery of Painless Surgery Was Made." Jackson's family added: "Thy Godlike Crime Was to Be Kind / To Render with Thy Precepts Less / The Sum of Human Wretchedness / And Strengthen Man with His Own Mind." (Fig. 9.57.)

The controversy became more regional after the Civil War. Morton received increased acclaim with international acceptance of the use of ether in surgery, but some in the medical profession credited Crawford Williamson Long of Georgia with its first use in 1842 for removal of a neck tumor, although that was not publicized until 1849. Thomas Lee, "a citizen of Boston" and philanthropist of the Public Garden, tried to solve the dilemma after receiving ether during an operation by donating in 1867 a grand monument "In Gratitude for the Relief of Human Suffering by the Inhaling of Ether." He skirted the controversy by simply proclaiming the discovery of anesthesia with local pride. Placed in the new Public Garden, the elaborate Victorian monument by sculptor John Quincy Adams Ward (1830–1910) is topped by a figure of the Good Samaritan kneeling over a wounded man and includes low-relief scenes of anesthesia use during the Civil War and in an operating room. The inscription reads: "To Commend the Discovery That the Inhaling of Ether Causes Insensibilty to PAIN—First Proved in the World at the Massachusetts General Hospital, Boston, October, A.D. MDCCCXLVI." It

Fig. 9.56. William Thomas Green Morton monument, 1868, on Spruce Avenue. Photograph by Jennifer Johnston, 2006. MAC.

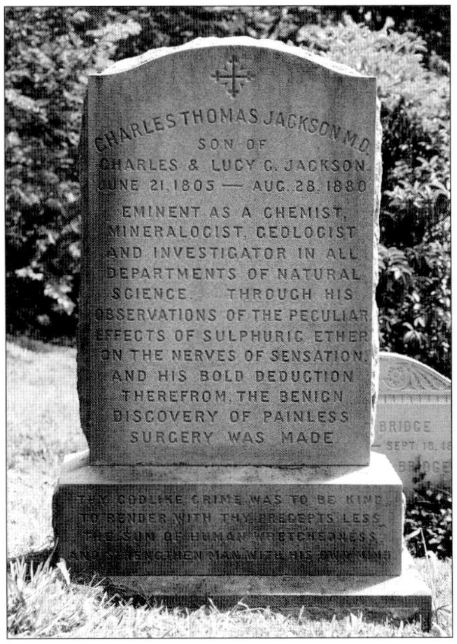

Fig. 9.57. Charles T. Jackson memorial marker, ca. 1880, on Mountain Avenue. Photograph by Jennifer Johnston, 2006. MAC.

Fig. 9.58. Ether monument, topped by a statue of the Good Samaritan with four low-relief plaques under the Gothic arches by sculptor John Quincy Adams Ward (1830–1910). The architects William Robert Ware (1832–1915) and Henry Van Brunt (1832–1903) designed the forty-foot-tall structure of marble and granite donated by Thomas Lee, Esq., and dedicated in 1868 in the twenty-four-acre Boston Public Garden (1859). Postcard, ca. 1908. BMGL.

simply quotes from Isaiah, "This Also Cometh Forth from the Lord of Hosts Which is Wonderful in Counsel and Excellent in Working." (Fig. 9.58.)

Space for Tombs

Bigelow encouraged the enclosure of lots and monuments with fences but tried to discourage the construction of crypts and tombs so "that the resources of art shall not be wasted in vain efforts to delay or modify the inevitable course of nature," that is, decay of the corpse, which could be hastened by earthen burial. He perceived natural decomposition in a proper place apart from the living and amid Nature as something good and beautiful, citing the Bible: "Then shall the dust return to earth as it was, and the spirit shall return to God who gave it." He reasoned that "the common grave affords the most simple, natural, and secure method by which the body may return to the bosom of the earth, to be peacefully blended with its original dust." He thus urged improvements "above the surface of the earth—not under it," for "a beautiful monument is interesting to every one . . . a far more soothing object than the most costly charnel house." Besides, the cemetery provided abundant space for individual graves guaranteed in perpetuity by the charter. There was no longer any need to cram the remains of one's family members into a crypt to provide postmortem proximity or even identifiable burial space. Mount Auburn could accommodate tombs large enough for several generations.[50]

Unlike Bigelow, Dearborn did not discourage attempts to isolate the dead from contact with the soil. He only cautioned that entrances to hillside tombs could easily seem "offensive to good taste," preferring chamber tombs built inconspicuously underground. Indeed, he suggested that those who could afford to do so might consider combining a tomb and monument in a single large structure, though none was built at Mount Auburn until the 1870s. In offering this advice, Dearborn might have had in mind the grandiose freestanding mausoleums that came to characterize Père Lachaise, after which he had modeled Mount Auburn; but he hardly could have wished the "rural" cemetery to become as built up with structures as had quickly become the case in Paris, giving new cemeteries there a distinctly urban feel.[51] (Fig. 9.59.)

Dearborn simply counseled that graves could be "so constructed as to possess most of the advantages of tombs." On request, the cemetery's gravedigger could build a brick platform to hold the coffin a foot above the bottom of the grave and construct brick arches over the coffin before filling it all with dirt. The grave thus would be "more secure" and remain undisturbed when other adjacent graves were dug. The preference for a tomb over earthen burial, however, stemmed more from the fear of grave robbers and the wish to keep the remains away from the ground than from the desire to preserve the corpse. There were no attempts through the 1840s to seal tombs hermetically to prevent decay. Embalming was rare. Accounts of visits to tombs included graphic descriptions of decomposition. Opponents of tomb burial described in grisly detail the sight of bodies in tombs periodically reopened to accept the new dead. Some complained of this as an invasion of the privacy of the dead; others seized the opportunity to look into the face of death of their loved ones as a "determination to pro-

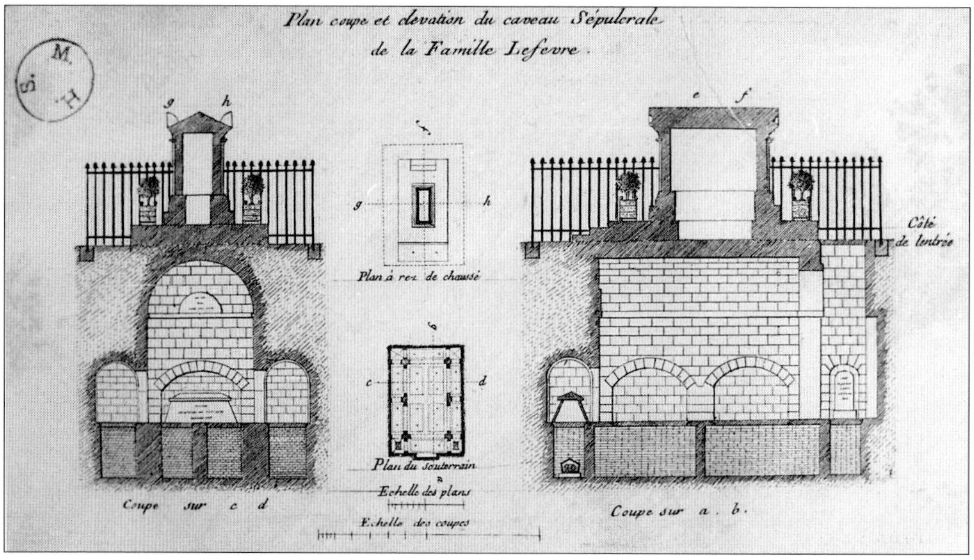

Fig. 9.59. Structure of a typical subterranean chamber tomb at Père Lachaise, Paris. Engraving from the book by Arnaud, 1817, used as reference for building the same at Mount Auburn. Henry A. S. Dearborn purchased the book for cemetery proprietors' reference and deposited it at the Massachusetts Horticultural Society. MHORT.

Fig. 9.60. Monument with Masonic symbolism, 1841, of Jacob Foss of Charlestown, on Snowdrop Path. Note the door set flush with the ground, allowing access to the subterranean chamber tomb, one of the only remaining examples of what was common on such lots in the cemetery's first decades. Photograph by BMGL, 1978.

long and caress" their "intensity of grief" and mourning, considered salutary.[52]

Despite Bigelow's advocacy of earthen burials, the trustees did not ban them as they had slate gravestones. Many proprietors built single-chamber tombs—in the first year alone eighteen subterranean tombs but only sixteen monuments, many on the same lots. Through the 1830s, about twenty tombs were built annually. By 1841, 190 lots, almost half of all sold, were used for tombs, most invisible underground, punctuated by 164 monuments. Some proprietors, including merchant Thomas Handasyd Perkins, built subterranean rooms with eight-foot-high ceilings under two feet of earth, following the designs of Père Lachaise tombs illustrated by Arnaud, larger than the shaft or chamber tombs in New England's old burial grounds. Such a tomb cost about $190 if made of brick or cement block, $270 if built of stone covered with mica slate and flat granite. Entrance was by a locked iron door at the top of a flight of steps covered by a removable stone that could be turfed over so that no evidence was visible to the casual visitor. Usually a single monument on such a lot recorded the names and vital dates of some of those lying below, though such a monument is not automatic indication of a subterranean tomb. (Fig. 9.60.)

Similar tombs were nestled into hillsides or mounded with dirt to conceal masonry, revealing only stone façades with locked doors. These cost from $300 to $1,500. The first extensive use of granite appeared on the façades, simple slabs forming a front wall and protective wings or crafted in the Egyptian style. Many had iron doors or marble inserts with inscriptions. The twin neoclassical tombs of W. Read and S. O. Mead on Ailanthus Path off Central Avenue were settled within a hillock and surrounded on all sides by an ornate cast-iron fence. An exception is William P. Winchester's Gothic Revival brownstone mausoleum, almost freestanding, designed by architect Arthur Gilman (1821–1882), erected on Narcissus Path by Forest Pond before 1848.[53] (Figs. 9.61–9.65.)

Fig. 9.61. Dual family chamber tombs on Central Avenue. Photograph by BMGL, 1979.

Fig. 9.62. Family chamber tomb between Deutzia and Lily paths, with original wrought-iron enclosure. Photograph by BMGL, 1984.

Fig. 9.64. George W. Coffin chamber tomb, topped by an obelisk, on Chestnut Avenue. From *Picturesque Pocket Companion*, 1839. MAC.

Fig. 9.63. Neoclassical façades on the William Read and Samuel O. Mead tombs on two 481-square-foot lots on Ailanthus Path off Central Avenue. Daguerreotype by Southworth and Hawes, ca. 1850. Courtesy George Eastman House.

Fig. 9.65. William P. Winchester mausoleum, ca. 1844, by architect Arthur Gilman in the "Pointed" style, nestled into the hillside on Narcissus Path, then overlooking Forest Pond. Daguerreotype by Southworth and Hawes, ca. 1850. Courtesy George Eastman House.

By the 1850s, Bigelow realized that antipathy to earthen burials had grown. Indeed, many who might have rejected crypt burials in the city's center chose Mount Auburn for chamber tombs since they thought that no nuisance or danger to public health would result in such a place. Site choice and the design of many tombs seem to have corresponded to "geomancy," the topographical siting of domestic and burial structures developed by the Chinese, whose descriptions of proper tomb burials emphasize the acceptance of death as "an inherent aspect of the cosmos," a natural process in terms close to those used by Bigelow and the Unitarians. *The Burial Book* (*Tsang Shu*), written by Kuo P'u in the fourth century BC, and subsequent *feng shui* literature by siting theorists explain how proper burial extends the fortunes of the dead to the living. The ideal burial site has a view of water, symbolizing, among other things, money. The Chinese located their tombs in parabolic land formations where sheltering hills afforded protection from the elements. Hills and ridges were places of vital *ch'i*, the force thought to circulate between heaven and earth and along such land formations. Topography influences the flow of *ch'i* to "energize" the dead, preserving links with living and future progeny and ensuring their prosperity. The Chinese also favored white stone as lucky. Even more than the post-Revolutionary French, the Chinese cultivated a cult of ancestors in their burial landscapes. Some Bostonians knew about geomancy through contacts from the China trade, and they may have borrowed from it in siting their own tombs in Mount Auburn's terrain, rich in geological formations such as Indian Ridge.[54]

The prevalence of chamber tombs indicates that there was little concern with theories that miasmas from decaying bodies endangered health in the cemetery's first decades. Indeed, the family of Dr. John Gorham Coffin, outspoken crusader against the dangers of urban crypt burials, built one of Mount Auburn's first tombs. The Committee on Lots deemed it the trustees' duty to prevent construction of "any tomb without its being so secured as to prevent the escape of effluvia from within," but little was done to follow through. Just as they had banned selling graves in family lots, the trustees ruled in 1841 that no proprietor could rent or sell tomb space, a departure from the common practice in old graveyards resulting from the chronic need for temporary deposit of bodies, especially in winter. Lucius M. Sargent (1786–1867) complained in the *Boston Evening Transcript* about the "highly offensive" practice of tombs being opened often "for the admission of the dead, at all times; and, of course, when the worms are riotous, and the corruption is rankest, and the pungent gases are eminently dangerous, and disgusting." Even when closed, an "intelligible odor" surrounded them. "Again and again," he declared, "visitors at Mount Auburn have been annoyed by this effluvium."[55]

Concerned with the detrimental effects of burials on public health decades before the germ theory of disease causation gained currency, Bigelow failed to persuade the trustees that the form, number, and location of tombs had to be regulated. Tombs would have to be constructed "in imitation of the ancient columbaria, in which a subterranean apartment is provided on one or both sides, with cavities like pigeon holes, 'catacomb' slots, the mouths of which are to be tightly closed with bricks and cement, or with a flat stone." New bylaws in 1854 stipulated that tombs had to be "strong, tight, and durable" with "every part including the door at least two feet under ground." Tombs must be covered with earth and the door "properly secured against nuisances." From 1851 to 1915 superintendents gradually persuaded lot representatives to allow the final sealing of single-chamber tombs.[56]

With monuments accumulating, ornamental plants set amidst the indigenous, and iron fences surrounding lots in the forested landscape, Mount Auburn's initial, Arcadian phase was passing. Buckingham complained in 1848 that in areas near Central Square, "the monuments thicken upon the view." Tombs, "embosomed in the deep shade of a grove of pines," ranged to the south.[57] Another observer in 1853 saw the woods "hewn away in various spots for the purpose of sepulture and to open the many avenues . . . and afford to those who love such a holy and secluded plot, the most interesting retreats and delightful walks."[58] This proliferation of structures was the wave of the future, altering the "rural" or "forest" cemetery even before Bigelow and the trustees hastened the transformation.

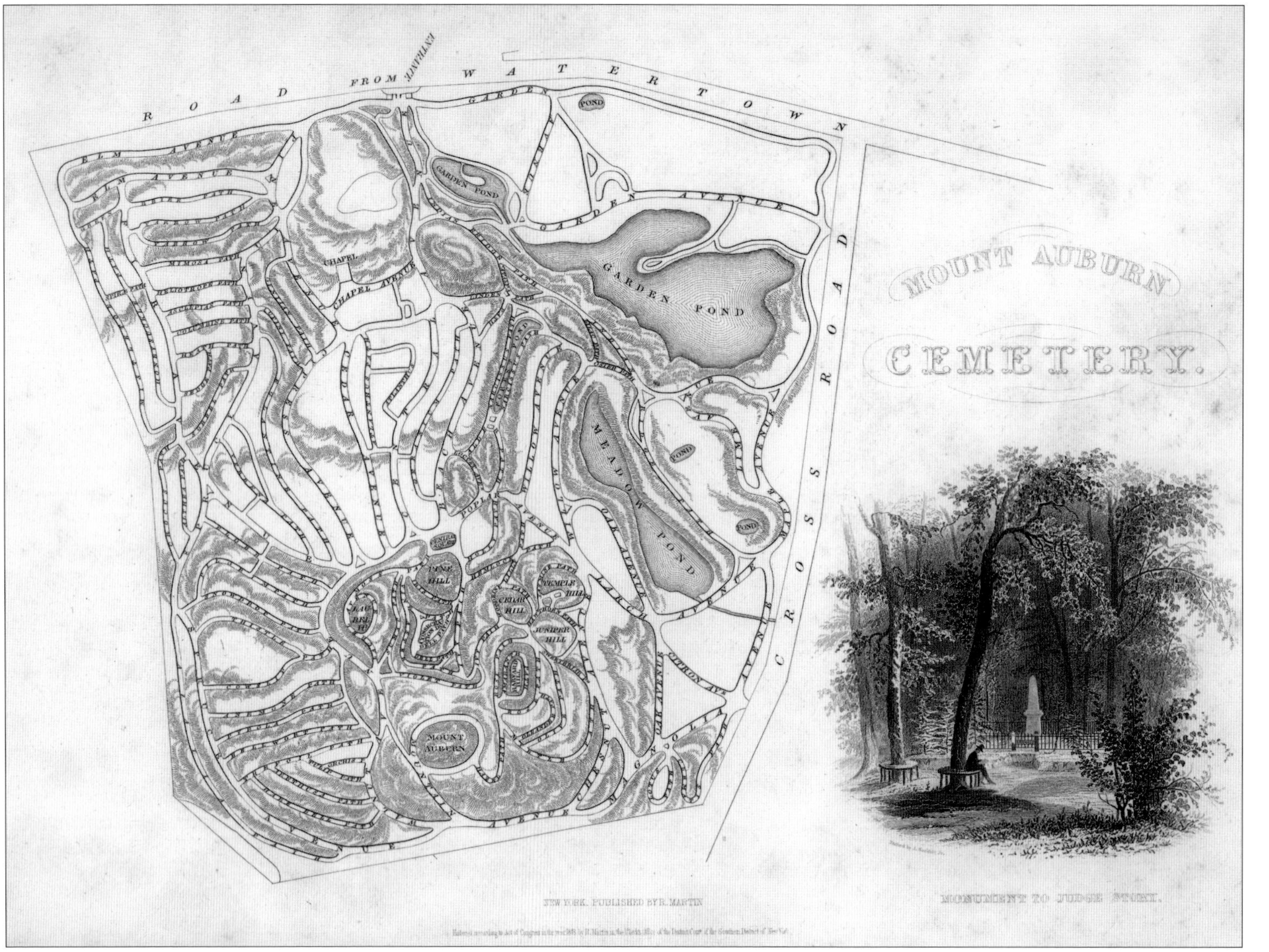

Fig. 10.1. Map of Mount Auburn. Engraving by Smillie, from Walter, 1847.

10

EMBELLISHING THE PICTURESQUE

Structures in the Landscape

> The Rhine has its castled crags, its vine-clad hills, and ancient villages; the Hudson has its wooded mountains, its rugged precipices, its green undulating shores—a natural majesty, and an unbounded capacity for improvement by art. . . . Without any stretch of the imagination we may anticipate the time when the ample waters shall reflect temple, and tower, and dome in every variety of picturesqueness and magnificence.
>
> —Thomas Cole, "Essay on American Scenery" (1835)

> *There sits the Sphinx at the road-side, and from age to age, as each prophet comes by, he tries his fortune at reading her riddle. There seems to be a necessity in spirit to manifest itself in material forms.*
>
> —Ralph Waldo Emerson, "Nature" (1836)

Mount Auburn's founders realized that creating a picturesque funerary landscape would entail more than simply choosing an appropriately varied terrain with scattered reflective ponds, laying out sinuous drives and paths, and planting ornamental trees and shrubs amid the natural forest growth. (Fig. 10.1.) As we have seen, they planned from the start to "embellish" the grounds with "public" structures meant to be mnemonic, ornamental, and functional. Art would "improve" upon Nature. After all, English gardens featured the grottoes, temples, towers, chapels, monuments, and gateways that served as eye-catchers as well as reminders of a real or mythical past. The Scottish aesthetic theorist Archibald Alison described such assembled structures in English landscaped gardens as intensely sublime, amplifying upon the picturesque.[1]

The French architect Brongniart had such intentions for Père Lachaise in Paris in 1804, for which he designed a central pyramidal chapel (never built) and other funerary structures of diverse revivalistic styles. Henry A. S. Dearborn was well aware from his reading of the importance of architectural elements in planning the French cemetery, although he did not concern himself with how the rage for architecture had completely changed its landscape aesthetics after only three decades. He also knew that Londoners, formulating plans for an extramural cemetery, intended to display "exact models of the superb temples, triumphal arches, columns and public monuments of Greece and Rome, as receptacles or memorials of departed worthies of the empire."[2] In aspiring to create such a landscape blending the pastoral with structures bearing associations to a long and venerable past, Mount Auburn's founders applied the recent taste for English landscape gardens, the historicism of their age, and the newly felt necessity to fabricate monuments. Such ideas were in the air.

They agreed with the English-born landscape

painter Thomas Cole (1801–1848), who emigrated to America in 1818 and epitomized the rise of American art, helping found the National Academy of Design in 1826 and becoming the de facto founder of the Hudson River School of painters, although he focused as much on New England's natural landscape and romantic allegories in settings of the fancied picturesque and the sublime. Cole's "Essay on American Scenery" (1835) proclaimed that "Poetry and Painting . . . purify thought by grasping the past, the present and the future—they give the mind a foretaste of its immortality." Cole complained that American scenes had few historical and legendary associations; but the lack of monuments and structures was a problem "not so much of the past as of the present and the future." Cole explained: "You see no ruined tower to tell of outrage—no gorgeous temple to speak of ostentation. . . . We are still in Eden; the wall that shuts us out of the garden is our own ignorance and folly." How could being "in Eden" shut Americans "out of the garden" through "ignorance and folly"? Lack of towers and other ancient structures might mean that Americans had nothing to represent old "outrage" or "ostentation," certainly not from their primitive colonial past; but it also signified lack of material reminders for principles of "the present and the future," even reinterpreted with derivative styles from the ancients.[3]

Like Boston's Unitarians, Cole considered Eden achievable or recreatable through Art. He applied Burkean theories of sensory creation of emotion to his paintings, knowing that Burke himself had referred to landscape gardening. Many scenes Cole depicted contain the same mnemonic, picturesque elements common to both English landscaped gardens and Mount Auburn—aerial perspectives heightening a sense of distance and stirring thoughts of the past, the future, or the infinite. Mirror lakes and dark pools encouraged melancholy introspection. A varied terrain of hills and valleys framed perspectives. Luxurious and "venerable" trees testified to the inexorable processes of Nature and Time. Most important, neoclassical and medieval structures or their ruins covered by clinging ivy represented a long and distant past. Cole's paintings *The Departure* and *The Return* (1837), as well as *Thanatopsis* (1850) by Cole's friend Asher B. Durand (1796–1886), bear exaggerated resemblance to Mount Auburn's landscape as it was being developed with seemingly ancient structures and tombs added to embellish the picturesque. (Figs. 10.2, 10.3.)

The cemetery's founders were eager to erect ornamental structures as soon as lot sales produced a sufficient surplus or a subscription campaign had been mounted by philanthropists desirous of improving native cultural institutions. Although design competitions were to be held for the structures, Bigelow submitted models and drawings of a Gothic tower, a Grecian tower, and a Doric temple even before consecration of the cemetery. He also urged that at a later date a "stupendous monument" to George Washington might be erected at Mount Auburn.[4]

In that preprofessional era, both Dearborn and Bigelow were well qualified to design Mount Auburn's landscape and buildings. Historian Walter Muir Whitehill observed that "at the beginning of the nineteenth century the practice of architecture was considered to be within the grasp of any literate gentleman who had a mind to try his hand at it."[5] Neither Dearborn nor Bigelow can be considered a dilettante, dabbler, or amateur at design. Both were multitalented Renaissance men and shared a sense of mission to create a usable past in material terms for their nation, region, and city. Their ideologies and taste for the revival and reapplication of ancient architectural styles, as well as for Nature, were alike. Both deserve credit as founders and designers of America's first "rural" cemetery because of various tasks and responsibilities each assumed in its first four years.

Whereas Dearborn provided the initial landscape design, Bigelow's major contribution, beyond first proposing the cemetery, was architectural. Bigelow was as qualified as any American architect of his generation to prepare a design. At Harvard, as first Rumford Professor of the Application of Science to the Useful Arts, he lectured on architecture and building technology using a set of models and drawings he made himself. The budding architect Alexander Jackson Davis (1803–1892) honed

Fig. 10.2. Thomas Cole, *The Departure*, 1837. This first painting in a pair of Gothic fantasies shows an urn-topped monument (left) in a picturesque landscape with river and distant Norman castle. Courtesy Corcoran Gallery of Art.

Fig. 10.3. Cole, *The Return*, 1837. The second painting in the pair shows the same monument that appears in *The Departure*, with the addition of a Gothic chapel similar to that later designed by Bigelow for Mount Auburn, but with steeples. Courtesy Corcoran Gallery of Art.

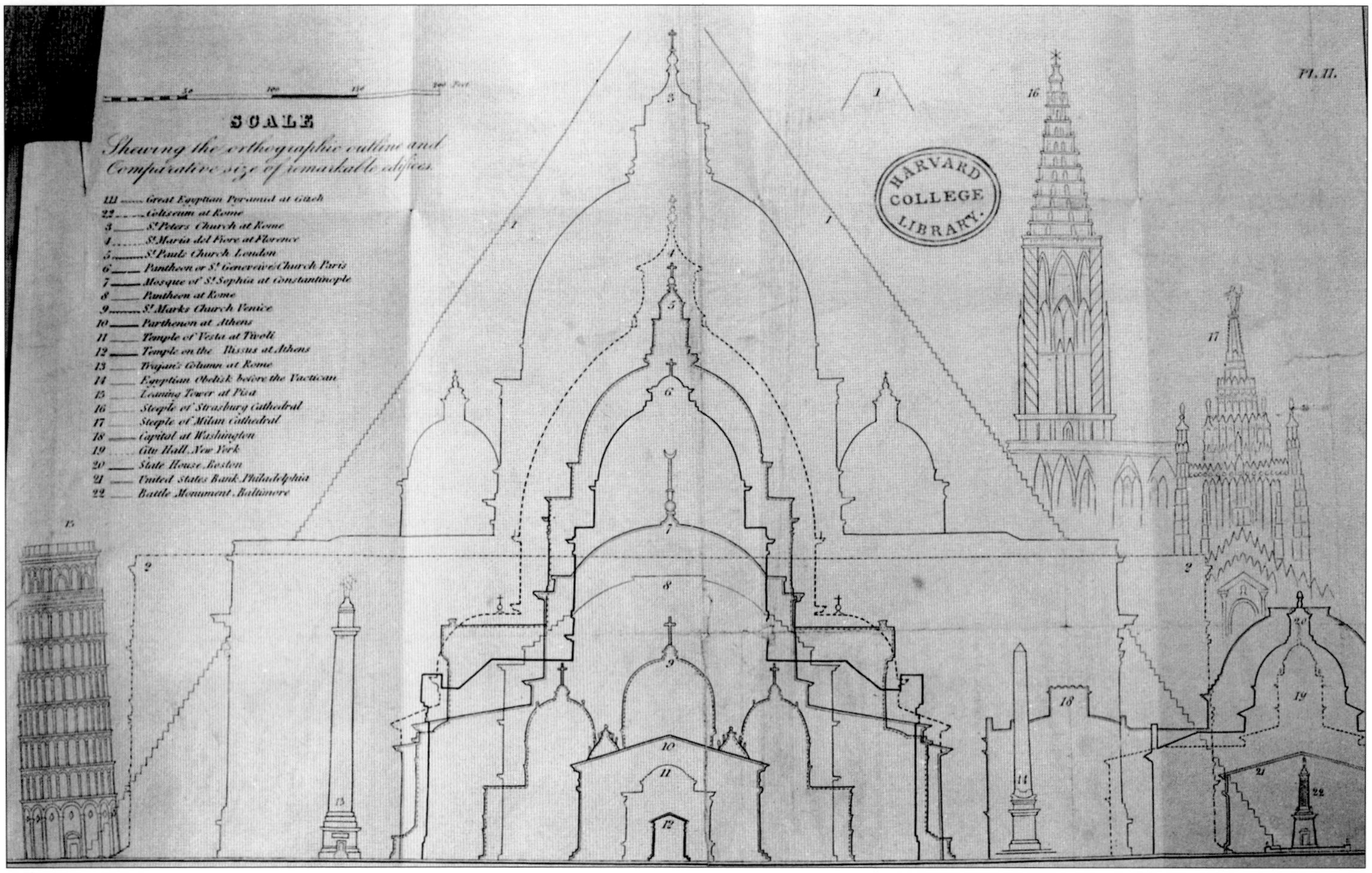

Fig. 10.4. Jacob Bigelow, "orthographic outline and comparative sizes of remarkable edifices." Frontispiece in his *Elements of Technology*, 1829.

his drafting skills in 1827 and 1828 in Bigelow's extensive architectural library under the doctor's tutelage, "reading" design as aspiring attorneys "read the law" in the offices of established professionals. Bigelow drew his own comparative scale illustration of major classical and modern buildings for his 1829 book *Elements of Technology*, declared accurate by the famed architect Charles Bulfinch. Bigelow's architectural expertise reflected itself in his ambitions for Mount Auburn.[6] (Fig.10.4.)

The Egyptian Gateway

Bigelow provided designs for the gate, claimed to be his own. He also closely supervised its construction by local farmers and mechanics who traded their labor for burial plots. Work began in 1832 on the twenty-five-foot structure of wood, painted gray and dusted with sand while wet to simulate stone. (Fig. 10.5.) The gate was to be a temporary full-scale facsimile until sufficient funds from lot sales permitted its reconstruction in stone. Bigelow gave attention to iconographic detail. He wrote Dearborn in Washington in January 1833 that "the winged globe is a splendid ornament, worthy of being oftener copied in modern times. . . . In most of the Egyptian cornices there is on each side of the globe, a fabulous sort of animal with an inflated body and a head like a serpent or crocodile." (Fig. 10.6.) Nevertheless, some friends suggested "that an uncouth Egyptian Idol might give offense of some persons." Bigelow directed carving of the decorative detail, modifying it by positioning a drooping Egyptian lotus, symbolic of eternal life, "so as to conceal the head of the monster, leaving the spectator to imagine what he pleases behind it."[7] Perhaps Bigelow, intent on recreating Eden at Mount Auburn, was loath to place a snake at the entrance.

Because of economic restraints during the cemetery's founding and hard times after the Panic of 1837, the first

Fig. 10.5. Mount Auburn's twenty-five-foot Egyptian gate, designed by Bigelow, originally built of wood painted and sanded to resemble stone in 1832. It was reconstructed in Quincy (Massachusetts) granite in 1843. Engraving by Smillie, from Walter, 1847.

Fig. 10.6. Detail of Egyptian iconography modified by Bigelow on Mount Auburn's gate. Photograph by Harvard Film Service, ca. 1930. MAC.

corporate structure, and the one major addition during the first decade, was the Egyptian Revival gateway. It came to be representative of Mount Auburn. Symbolic in many ways, it was more often used and recognized as a logo for the cemetery than the seal that Bigelow and Story devised. It appeared on engraved views in guidebooks, on stationery, and even on memorabilia such as teacups as an unprecedented architectural element for an American burial landscape. (Fig. 10.7.) Most graveyards had only simple openings in enclosing walls or pale fences with a simple gate. The architect Goddé's 1835 design for the Père Lachaise gateway in Paris was not as grandiose as Bigelow's. The unprecedented addition of such a ceremonious entrance, more elaborate than those of Boston's new churches, indicates the complexity of new notions about the cemetery and expectations that it would be a place of great civic and cultural importance.

Bigelow's choice of the Egyptian style responded to intellectual and cultural trends. From the Renaissance on, a few elite western Europeans had used obelisks and pyramids in funerary monuments, but more elaborate and explicit use of Egyptian architecture and symbols was radically new. Interest grew through the first decades of the century with publication of the archaeological findings of Napoleon's Near Eastern campaigns. A major catalyst came in 1822 with a discovery that challenged the basis of Western thought. News of Jean-François Cham-

Fig. 10.7. China teacup decorated with the Mount Auburn gate, ca. 1850. MAC.

pollion's deciphering of Egyptian hieroglyphics precipitated an international debate on the origins of knowledge, perfectly coinciding, in the spirit of the time, with the quest for taxonomies of reality in varied forms—linguistics, mastery of modern languages, codification of the law, and the increasing use of numbers in all aspects of everyday life, technology, and history.

In 1833 Edward Everett wrote two articles in the *North American Review* on the importance of Champollion's work in the intellectual history of the era. In 1831 he ranked the discovery with those of Leibniz and Newton, "destined to throw a flood light on a chapter of the history of mankind." Indeed, as John T. Irwin observes, "the decipherment of the hieroglyphics and Darwin's theory of evolution were probably the two severest blows delivered by nineteenth-century science to the credibility of Genesis and accepted Biblical chronology." In England, wrote Everett, it excited "violent party spirit." Such a discovery appealed to religious liberals who challenged old orthodoxies, rejected traditional superstitions, and refused to believe in the universal wages of sin resulting from Adam's Fall.[8] The Fall was reinterpreted as symbolizing man's discontinuity with the natural world rather than referring to the literal expulsion from Eden. The Egyptian style, therefore, represented the restoration of naturalism, perfectly appropriate for the entrance of a gardenlike cemetery established by liberal Protestants.

Champollion's discovery struck a chord in scientific minds intent on developing hieroglyphical methods of interpreting physical shapes through signature analysis, physiognomy, and phrenology. Bigelow, who attempted to found a Linnaean Society in Boston in order to catalogue New England plant materials and who taught the principles of technology at Harvard, was an enthusiast of things Egyptian because of the implications of Champollion's work. His taste for the Egyptian was further whetted by arrival of the first Near Eastern artifacts in Boston in 1823—a Theban mummy of Padihershef, a stonecutter in his sarcophagus, donated by a Dutch merchant to the Massachusetts General Hospital—strengthening associations of the Egyptian style with death.

The Egyptian style also captured the imagination of arbiters of culture seeking to find new symbols representative of their nation. Many Americans in the 1830s equated their country with Egypt, another "first civilization" capable of providing an alternative cultural idiom to that inherited from England. They nicknamed the Mississippi the "American Nile" and named new towns along its banks Memphis, Cairo, Karnac, and Thebes. One amateur archaeologist even theorized in 1839 that Egyptians had migrated to America via Asia; and Joseph Smith claimed to have translated his *Book of Mormon* (1830) from hieroglyphics he personally deciphered. Furthermore, Freemasonry fostered the taste with its exotic symbolism and publications such as Jeremy Cross's *True Masonic Chart; or, Hieroglyphic Monitor* (1819).

Egyptian elements had appeared in English landscaped gardens by the 1830s. Now the Egyptian style interested American architects searching new archaeological texts for designs to meet the growing demand for public buildings on a grand scale. The aspiring young architect Alexander Jackson Davis spent his two years with Bigelow in Boston copying illustrations from the doctor's architectural library as well as from that of Dr. George Parkman and from works in the Athenaeum.[9] Davis and Bigelow pored over French reports from Napoleon's 1798–99 expedition and avidly read Dominique Vivant Denon's three-volume *Voyage dans la Basse et la Haute Egypte pendant les campagnes du général Bonaparte*, first published in New York in 1803. They used its illustrations as models for their own fanciful drawings of Egyptian cemetery gates and buildings, predating Mount Auburn's founding by three years. Bigelow's design of the cemetery gateway closely resembles those Davis drew: vertical structures with flaring cavetto cornices and flanking pylons inspired by gates of Thebes, Karnac, and Denderah, entrances to burial grounds along the Nile. It is also strikingly like the tomb of the scientist Gaspard Monge in Père Lachaise, a design Bigelow knew from the Jolimont book Dearborn had ordered.[10] (Figs. 10.8, 10.9.)

Davis favored cemetery gates "constructed so that even in ruins" eventually they would "testify to posterity the sense which the age had of the event commemorated." Mount Auburn's gateway did not commemorate an event as did the Bunker Hill Monument; but Bigelow created a design to be as durable, anticipating that once rebuilt in granite, it would stand even after the parent civilization lay in ruins. His was a fatalistic, cataclysmic view of history shared with many of his era. Yet at the

Fig. 10.8. Archaeological view of the gate at Thebes from the books of Denon, 1802–1823.

Fig. 10.9. Egyptian Revival tomb of the scientist Gaspard Monge (1746–1818), Père Lachaise, Paris. Engraving from Jolimont, 1821, the book Henry A. S. Dearborn ordered as an aid for design in Mount Auburn.

same time, Bigelow and others interpreted the Egyptian style as promise and symbol of permanency, an architecture that had endured longer than other ancient monuments—even the famed wonders of the world. It was intrinsically historic as well as sublime, stirring awe by reminding viewers of a nonrecurring past. Bigelow noted, "No man can look upon the splendid ruins of Karnac without feeling humbled by the greatness of a people who have passed away."[11] It indicated the pastness of the past and the mortality of all. It bore subtle hortatory messages updating and reinterpreting the medieval *memento mori*. For that reason, association with ancient funerary structures aside, it seemed particularly appropriate for a cemetery.

A British visitor agreed, praising the gateway "which looms up in all its gloomy grandeur and exhibits on its front the awful emblems of Time and Eternity! It stands like a solemn milestone on life's broad highway, intimating to every traveller that he is another stage nearer the end of his journey, and that when the weary race shall terminate, 'THEN SHALL THE DUST RETURN TO THE EARTH AS IT WAS, AND THE SPIRIT SHALL RETURN TO GOD WHO GAVE IT.'" The quotation was from Ecclesiastes 12:7, added by Bigelow to the face of the plinth to be read by all entering the grounds.[12]

Yet Egyptian style and symbols baffled some critics, who considered them reminiscent of tyrant kings and heathenism. John Frazee of New Jersey, founder of the National Academy and a specialist on funerary sculpture, wrote in 1835 that the Egyptian would "never harmonize with the glorious principles of republican achievement nor with Christianity." Henry Russell Cleveland presented a similar opinion on "American architecture" in 1836, calling the Egyptian style "anterior to civilization," reminiscent of the "most degraded and revolting paganism which ever existed" and "the architecture of embalmed cats and deified crocodiles." Although he praised Mount Auburn's potential as a model for sepulchral architecture, he doubted whether the Egyptian design so prevalent in "uncouth structures" there was "appropriate to a Christian burial place." Although it was "solid, stupendous, and time-defying," the critic thought it out of place where "religion should be present to the mind."[13]

Cleveland acknowledged that few Bostonians had the same disagreeable associations with the Egyptian that he did. The style had the "great merit of combining cheapness and durability," considered preferable by many to the more expensive and fussy Gothic, which was furthermore associated with papism. Many of the first proprietors followed the lead of Joseph Story and chose the Egyptian style for their monuments. Sometimes, as on Samuel Appleton's, only a symbol or two appeared eclectically on a neoclassical structure. Others, like Kirk Boott, superintendent of the first textile mills in Lowell, or the descendants of Francis Cabot Lowell, the mills' chief entrepreneur, favored it for their hillside chamber tombs with full façades aboveground. (Figs. 10.10–10.12.)

Dearborn defended the Egyptian as "the architecture of the grave, particularly adapted to the abode of the dead" with an "enduring character" emblematic of immortality.[14] He interpreted the Egyptian, like Mount

Fig. 10.10. Egyptian façade of the family tomb, built into the hillside, of Kirk Boott, superintendent of the Lowell, Massachusetts, textile mills, ca. 1840. The tomb sits on a 453-square-foot lot on Amaranth and Rose Paths as they ascend to the cemetery's summit. Photograph by Carol Betsch, 2005.

Fig. 10.11. Egyptian façade of the Francis Cabot Lowell II family tomb on a 1,620-square-foot lot on Ivy Path near Consecration Dell and under Harvard Hill. Photograph by BMGL, 1980.

Fig. 10.12. Hicks–Endicott Egyptian tomb façade, Violet Path. Photograph by BMGL, 1988.

Auburn's entire landscape, as symbolic of death. Addressing members of the Massachusetts Horticultural Society, he traced to Egypt the practice of "placing the tomb in the midst of the beauty and luxuriance of nature." He equated Mount Auburn with "the great Egyptian cemetery . . . on the farther shore of the Lake Acherusia, near Memphis, ornamented with trees and water-courses."[15]

Bigelow's friend the writer Cornelia Walter presented one of the best explanations for the extensive use of the Egyptian at Mount Auburn, arguing that "the now mythologized doctrines of Egypt seem to have been the original source of others more ennobling; and hieroglyphical discoveries have traced and are tracing them far beyond the era of the pyramids to an unknown limit, but to a pure, sacred, and divine source. When the art of writing was unknown, the primeval Egyptians resorted to symbols and emblems to express their faith; and these, as correctly interpreted, certainly present many sublime ideas in connection with those great truths which in an after age constituted the doctrines of *Christianity*." Walter noted that some Egyptian sculptures and paintings were "undoubtedly symbolical of the resurrection of the soul, a dread of the final judgment, and a belief in Omnipotent Justice."[16]

Walter expanded on Bigelow's reasoning, suggesting that the symbolism of Mount Auburn's landscape itself had Egyptian origins. The pyramid was representative of "*the mountain*, the holy hill, the divine sanctuary cut in the mountain, i.e., *the tomb*," she wrote. "The *mountain* was sacred among the Egyptians as the abode of the dead, and was identical with the sepulcher . . . the future state." Walter observed that for Mount Auburn's founders, as for the ancient Egyptians, "the image or figure of a hill became an emblem of *death*, and the pyramidal form, which imitated it, was a funereal symbol—an object consecrated to the abode of the departed." She omitted consideration of more recent precedents in English gardens or at Père Lachaise.[17]

Walter specifically defended the symbol of the winged globe that appeared so frequently at Mount Auburn in its early years as "a most beautiful emblem of benign protection." The image of the sun with outstretched wings was "the primitive type of the divine wisdom—the universal Protector." There could be no "more fitting emblem than this for the abode of the dead," for the symbol represented "the protecting wings of Him who is the great author of our being—the 'giver of life and death.'"[18] Mount Auburn's founders considered the Egyptian sacred and sublime. Equally, it appealed to cosmopolitan and nondenominational tastes.

Some critics of Mount Auburn's gate objected to the replication of the style in wood. One visitor from Philadelphia in 1838 called it a "paltry deception" and belittled "the taste that could paint wood in imitation of granite at the entrance of a City of the Dead." He tried to shame his hosts: "In a city like Boston, rich beyond most others and proverbial for its liberality," cost "never ought to be an obstacle; it *cannot* be now, when vast sums must have been realized from the sale of lots."[19] He ignored the frequency with which ornamental structures in English gardens were fashioned of wood and then painted to resemble stone, with the full intention of permanency without replacement. Sir William Chambers, for instance, placed a number of ornamental buildings of wood at the Kew gardens outside London; and they were strong enough to withstand the nearby blast of German bombs in World War II.

Inspired by Mount Auburn, the Boston architect Isaiah Rogers designed a small Egyptian gate, constructed of Quincy granite in 1840, for the Old Granary Burying Ground. Three years later he used an almost identical granite structure for the old Touro Jewish Cemetery in Newport, Rhode Island. The technology of cutting and carving that hard stone had newly been perfected. Until the 1840s, use of granite remained expensive and difficult, slowing completion of even the Bunker Hill Monument, a simple but immense structure in the form of an obelisk, until 1843.[20] (Fig. 10.13.)

Fig. 10.13. Egyptian gate by architect Isaiah Rogers, 1840, at Boston's Old Granary Burying Ground. Engraving by Moses King, from *King's Hand-Book of Boston*, 1878.

Return of financial prosperity by the spring of 1841, investment of proceeds from lot sales in different securities—primarily federal bonds, banks, and textile mill or railroad stock—and accumulation of savings of over $26,000 by 1843 and $82,000 in 1844 permitted the trustees to undertake major construction projects intended to embellish the picturesque landscape as originally intended. They also planned on obtaining subscriptions "from munificent individuals in aid of such funds," since they were reluctant to sell stock to finance projects. They chose Octavius T. Rogers of Quincy as contractor for the $9,535 project of reconstructing Bigelow's wooden gate in fine hammered granite "of substantially the same form, mode, and dimension." Rogers was the only one capable of making and raising the twenty-two-foot-long monolithic cap or cornice stone in a single piece, the largest piece of sculpted granite placed in an American structure to that date. Rogers shipped the stone by barge from Quincy, south of Boston, and up the Charles River. Teams of oxen dragged the stone from the nearby riverbank to Mount Auburn, where it was raised into place by means of screws on a wooden frame. Yet despite his expertise, Rogers left an "unseemly" joint, and the monolith had to be reset. Work was complete in October 1843.[21]

The new gate could be locked at night, and it had a signal bell for summoning the gatekeeper after hours. In 1852 a larger bell was installed, "which could be heard throughout the grounds for giving concerted signals to workmen, ringing out visitors at sundown and the like."

The central carriage entry was flanked symmetrically by two pedestrian doors and two rooms used as porter's and superintendent's offices. Obelisks, separated by short expanses of cast-iron fence, punctuated the entrance on either side.[22]

Next, the trustees determined to complete the front and the eastern side of the grounds by removing the fence of wooden pales and replacing it with a permanent one. They abandoned the original idea of erecting "a wall of stone of a substantial and elegant design." By the 1840s, the taste for ornate cast-iron fences reigned supreme. In England, for example, John Claudius Loudon advocated use of iron railings rather than high walls around public gardens as more secure than the "ha-ha's" or inconspicuous trenches used to keep cattle out of English landscaped gardens while preserving distant vistas of the countryside. Mount Auburn's trustees were confident that metal could provide "due protection and security" for their grounds. In the spring of 1844, Bigelow submitted a design for a ten-foot-high fence with the Egyptian motif carried out with lotus flower finials. Octavius Rogers laid a firm foundation, granite posts set four feet deep to prevent dislocation by frost heaves. The firm of Adams, Whitredge and Cummings of Boston prepared and assembled the cast iron. The corporation expended $15,000 for the granite base alone, three times more than the trustees committed to the initial construction of the chapel. Although the trustees allocated only $15,000 to $17,000, expenses soared because of the need to regrade the Old Cambridge Road along the entire front of the cemetery. Eventually, the trustees sold $10,000 in stock to complete the work—the portion along the front by 1848 and the Coolidge Avenue side in 1851, a total length of 4,364 feet, costing $26,958.[23]

The new iron fence made the interior of the cemetery visible from exterior streets. Approaching visitors glimpsed monuments west of the gate in "the surrounding verdure, like bright remembrances from the heart of the earth."[24] Some still found fault. James Silk Buckingham, an Englishman otherwise praiseful of the landscape, found "one defect," the combination of cast iron with the Egyptian style. He criticized the fence's "diminutive" scale compared to the "colossal size . . . and durability of material" of authentic Egyptian structures. He concluded that "the effect of the whole is to produce a strange combination of heaviness and littleness, quite unworthy of the place, and leave a most unfavourable impression on the visitors." Buckingham especially opposed "the cumbrous and inappropriate gates and railings along the entrance." He hoped that the Egyptian entrance might eventually be replaced by a Greek or Roman one, a truly "triumphal gateway," perhaps "with a fine open colonnade of the Ionic order."[25]

The cemetery's south and west borders were enclosed in 1851 by a "substantial timber fence," replacing the original flimsy palisade. To increase protection, the trustees voted to plant a live hedge of buckthorn or a similar protective, thorny shrub, "believing that in a few years in this way a very handsome and permanent hedge may be obtained at a comparatively trifling expense," under $1,000. There was no need to provide an ornamental enclosure for the rear periphery, which would not be seen by large numbers of passersby from outside and which might be screened by plantings from within.[26]

The Chapel

Although Mount Auburn was nondenominational, the founders planned from the start to construct a chapel for funeral services. Original plans called for a Doric temple on one of the minor hills in the eastern portion of the grounds near Consecration Dell. The site was even labeled "Temple Hill" on the 1831 map in anticipation. Bigelow prepared a design "of simple and classical character" and obtained an estimate for its construction in the fall of 1834; but the legal separation of the cemetery from the Horticultural Society followed by the Panic of 1837 delayed construction until the mid-1840s. By then, tastes had changed.

Whereas Mount Auburn's proprietors favored Egyptian or neoclassical styles for monuments in the 1830s, by the 1840s many had turned to the Gothic, perhaps heeding the advice of Henry Russell Cleveland, brother of the later famed landscape architect, that that style should be "chosen for the prevailing architecture" of the cemetery. American interest in the Gothic was fueled by discussion of the writings of British architectural theorist Augustus Welby Pugin (1812–1852). The Winchester family commissioned architect Arthur Gilman to design a brownstone Gothic Revival tomb overlooking Forest Pond, a very picturesque setting. (See Fig. 9.6.) Criticism of the Egyptian and the Greek as pagan lessened the vogue of those styles. By 1845, Andrew Jackson Downing could happily proclaim that "the Greek temple disease has passed its crisis. The people have survived it." The elite New Yorker George Templeton Strong (1820–1874), who had something to say about just about everything, decried both the Egyptian and the Greek as the "revived Pagan style." He felt that "this recurrence of heathen taste and anti-Christian usage in architecture or art of any sort is, or should be, unreal and unnatural everywhere." The Boston architect and sculptor Hammatt Billings (1816–1874) remained skeptical in 1857 that "the symbols, utterly unmeaning to our unsymbolical minds are supposed to convey some suggestion of immortality." "Utterly . . . unsymbolical minds"? Billings had no idea what would result a half century later with the demise of cultural Victorianism and the rise of modernism, erasing the complex symbolism in his era's popular culture. Yet he represented the next generation of architects, who favored the Gothic. Many theories and rationalizations were mustered to justify the new Gothic vogue.[27]

The Gothic weathered controversy through the eighteenth century when it was revived in English gardens and elsewhere. Bigelow told his students that "Gothic" was a derisive term traced to Sir Christopher Wren. Many English and American Whigs associated the style with Tory politics and High Church ideology. Some Whiggish English garden proprietors contemptuously rejected the "Gothick" as "barbarous and tasteless," while others enshrined actual ruins or built revivalistic "Saxon" replicas as "eye-catchers." The French critic Quatremère de Quincy wrote that the style was "born not in the infancy but in the decrepitude of the social state," thus signaling impending ruin; but that was in the context of his nation's revolution against the old order. Addison considered it symptomatic of a "meanness of manner" of an outmoded, decaying order rather than of a youthful, simple civilization.[28]

Yet the English aesthetician and landscape gardener Batty Langley (1696–1751), an early and influential advocate of rehabilitating the style, preferred to call it "Saxon" and to associate it with an era of simple Christianity and an English tradition of freedom. Other advocates, following the German critics August Wilhelm Schlegel (1767–1845) and Friedrich Schlegel (1772–1829), wrote that the Gothic represented "a spiritual striving for the infinite" as well as for a mythical past. Influenced by the Schlegels, Coleridge wrote, "Grecian architecture is a thing, but the Gothic is an idea" or "symbolical expression of the infinite." From the 1770s, romantics on both sides of the Atlantic favored reinterpretations of the Gothic for that reason.[29]

Proponents of the revival associated the Gothic with Nature, referring to the arboreal theory of the style's origin made current in England in Bishop William Warburton's 1751 edition of Alexander Pope. In his *Elements of Technology* (1829), Bigelow provided one of the first American descriptions of the Gothic, also tracing the style to "the imitation of groves and bowers under which the Druids performed their sacred rites." John Henry Hopkins (1792–1868), Episcopal bishop of Vermont, repeated this theory in 1836 in the first American book on Gothic architecture, researched at the Boston Athenaeum (where his path must have crossed Bigelow's). Even Emerson echoed such notions of the origins of the style in the *Dial* in 1841. Bigelow, Hopkins, Emerson, and others therefore associated the Gothic with pantheism rather than Christianity, with Nature rather than the Roman Church, thus finding it acceptable for modern applications. A renewed taste for the Gothic had common origins and proponents with the taste for romantic landscape gardening. Bigelow and other proponents preferred to use the simply descriptive terms "pointed" or "perpendicular" and to trace the style to an arcadian past more distant than the Dark Ages.[30]

A firm believer in derivative culture, Bigelow identified the "Greco-Gothic" or "Romanesque" as early manifestations of the style. A similar account appeared in an anonymous essay in the *American Journal of Sciences and Arts* that drew comparisons between the Gothic and older Greek forms while speculating that the style originated in Rome. These arguments dissociated the Gothic from the popish, making it suitable for use by Low Church Protestants. Although Bigelow got most of his information from the archaeological writings of Pugin, he favored the Gothic for the same symbolic reasons as did his friend the architect Alexander Jackson Davis. Neither Bigelow nor Davis used the Gothic in an archaeological spirit but rather as a symbolic and poetic form suggesting the passing of time. That, after all, was a major function of the picturesque landscape of the cemetery itself and English gardens before it. That was also the aspect of the Gothic captured by Thomas Cole in his 1837 paintings *The Departure* and *The Return*, so suggestive of sections of Mount Auburn's landscape yet to be built. (See Figs. 10.2, 10.3.) Like other revival styles, the Gothic reminded Americans of a past much longer than what they had as a nation but which they could still make their own.[31]

Certainly the role of Sir Walter Scott (1771–1832) as a corresponding member of the Massachusetts Horticultural Society, and the popularity of his historical novels, whetted the interests of Bigelow and his friends further. Even Nathaniel Hawthorne exclaimed in his *English Note-Books*, "Oh, that we had cathedrals in America were it only for the sensuous luxury." Intellectual Bostonians realized Art's power to revive faith through the senses amid Nature.[32] Such were the powers attributed to picturesque English garden landscapes. Bigelow knew, too, that the Gothic as well as structures of other diverse ancient styles were favored by Richard Payne Knight and Sir Uvedale Price as architectural ornamentation for such gardens because their of rich romantic associations.

The style's growing popularity bolstered Bigelow's decision to adapt the Gothic for the cemetery's chapel. Once dissociated from papism, it appealed even to Unitarians. In 1809 William Ellery Channing had requested that his friend the architect Charles Bulfinch design the new Federal Street Church in the Gothic style. The architectural firm of Town and Davis began using the Gothic in 1832. The detailing of the estate house at Lyndhurst in Tarrytown, New York, designed in 1838 by Alexander Jackson Davis, a decade after he and Bigelow read architecture together, is similar to that of Bigelow's chapel. George Washington's second tomb (1835), by William Yeaton of Alexandria, Virginia, took the form of a plain brick façade with Gothic entry, reflective of literary and artistic depictions of the first president's grave in a romantic setting. The architect Solomon Willard, Bigelow's friend, who provided some working drawings for Mount Auburn, had used the Gothic for granite structures, including the Bowdoin Street Church (1830), Temple Street First Methodist Church (1833), and Saint Peter's (1833) in Boston and

Fig. 10.14. Harvard's Gore Hall, (now destroyed), designed in the "Pointed" style by Richard Bond, 1838. Postcard, 1903. BMGL.

the First Unitarian Church of Salem (1836). Another local Gothic structure, Gore Hall, Harvard's library, designed of Quincy granite by Richard Bond in 1838, was a Latin cross 104 by 81 feet, vaguely reminiscent of King's College Chapel in Cambridge, England. Boston proved a fertile field for the growing American taste for the Gothic.[33] (Fig. 10.14.)

Development of mortuary chapels in cemeteries produced a new building type akin to architectural follies in English gardens and provided opportunities to use the Gothic. Henry Edward Kendall won the competition over forty-five other entries with his Gothic design for a chapel for London's new Kensal Green Cemetery in 1832. John Notman, a Scotsman settled in Philadelphia, designed a Gothic chapel in miniature (50' by 24½') in 1837 for Laurel Hill, the joint stock cemetery founded in partial emulation of Mount Auburn in 1836. Henry Russell Cleveland praised the Gothic in an 1836 article in the *North American Review*, finding its Christian ornamentation reminiscent "of the joys of life beyond the grave." Cleveland's only reservation was that the style would prove too expensive for American projects, a point Bigelow had made in 1829.[34] Trends in taste and rising prosperity made it virtually inevitable that a number of Gothic monuments and structures would become part of Mount Auburn's eclectic landscape. (Fig. 10.15.)

By the 1840s, the style reached its heyday, urged on by the aesthetic preaching of Ecclesiologism, an Anglican-Episcopalian movement devoted to propagation of Gothic taste with renewed religious associations. The Cambridge Camden Society, organized in England, began publishing the *Ecclesiologist* in 1841 to counteract the

Fig. 10.15. Gothic chapel designed by architect John Notman in 1837 for Philadelphia's Laurel Hill Cemetery (1836), which he had laid out. Mount Auburn did not add its chapel designed by Bigelow in a similar style until 1846.

iconoclastic effects of Puritanism on church architecture. Americans were already familiar with the simple or Norman architecture of the rural English parish church through illustrations in the *Gentleman's Magazine and Historical Chronicle*, imported regularly from England from the 1780s on. Missionary work of Ecclesiologists along with the simultaneous rise of Episcopalianism, especially new and noteworthy in New England, hastened acceptance of the "Christian" style.[35] (See Fig. 1.1.)

Bigelow cited such examples to the trustees. The spirit of cultural competition as well as the availability of surplus funds by 1843 encouraged them to allocate $5,000 for a chapel, provided a like sum could be raised by subscription within one year. The trustees did not sell stock, as they had done to pay for the granite gateway and fence. Philanthropic Bostonians contributed to the project; Dr. George Parkman, despite a reputation for miserliness, donated $100, Samuel Appleton and Dr. George C. Shattuck $1,000 each. Although $7,000 in contributions was raised, the board learned that the chapel would cost at least $25,000.

Some proprietors, however, saw no need for a chapel. To heirs of Puritans, it amounted to making Mount Auburn into a churchyard. Most held funeral services in their own homes, an old custom from the days when Puritans treated burials as a civil rather than a religious matter. Only in the late eighteenth century did a few of Boston's new religious liberals began to conduct obsequies in churches, services more often held for prominent citizens rather than for other members of the congregation. Given the pleasant landscape of the new cemetery in season, many proprietors held services in the open at the grave or tomb rather than in their homes. Bigelow urged construction of a chapel before any other "public" structures to provide shelter for services in inclement weather. Still, Cornelia Walter speculated that the chapel would probably serve Episcopalians primarily for a more formal burial service than other, more liberal Protestants.[36]

In the spring of 1844 the trustees invited half a dozen prominent local architects, including Richard Bond, Gridley J. Fox Bryant, and Ammi B. Young, to submit designs for a chapel "in a chaste style and taste and of the most durable materials, and upon a plan which will admit of great additions and enlargments at a future period without injury to the symmetry and proportions" of the original building "when the religious services and erection of monuments" inside would necessitate expansion. It would "constitute the Nave or part of the Nave of a future Church which shall become with its future transept a Latin or Greek cross." The lack of built-in pews or pulpit would permit varying uses. Movable furnishings would be of iron or wood. Although the concept of movable seating differed greatly from that of New England meetinghouses and churches with pews as permanent structural interior divisions sold to congregation members, it was the pattern in most European churches.

The trustees intended that the chapel, like English churches, "become the repository of Marble Busts and Statues and other sepulchral monuments which may from time to time be placed there by liberal Benefactors and Friends in memory of the Dead, and which would not bear the exposure of the open air" in the harsh New England climate. They also suggested that the chapel be lit by a dome, lanterns, or skylight to leave the walls free for display of commemorative monuments and plaques. Such lighting would have a dim quality appropriate to the funereal nature of the place. Coming from above, it would symbolize the light of heaven and life after death.[37]

Bigelow "anonymously" placed his own entry in the competition. When the trustees met at Bigelow's house to select a design, they unanimously chose his. Bigelow proposed a structure of the style he termed "Protestant Gothic," although his plan called for simple motifs sug-

Fig. 10.16. Façade of Mount Auburn's first chapel viewed from the south. Lithograph by John Henry Bufford (1810–1870) of Boston, *Catalogue of Proprietors*, 1846. MAC.

Fig. 10.17. Façade of Mount Auburn's first chapel viewed from the south. From a stereographic photograph by D. Appleton, ca. 1870, before the addition of the Sphinx and removal of curbing in the foreground. BMGL.

Gothic from being sublime, but he also knew that a structure built in granite could not include elaborate detail. His design resembled Harvard's Gore Hall library in its simplicity. As architectural historian Douglass Shand-Tucci observes, this chapel, like so many other Boston buildings of its era, possesses "fundamental characteristics that proceed, if not from the Greek Revival, not from the Gothic either. Rather, . . . from one thing all these buildings . . . have in common: granite." He labels this and other such structures from the 1840s examples of the "Boston Granite Style."[38] (Figs. 10.16, 10.17.)

Bigelow's claim to complete authorship of the chapel, however, is open to question. In November of 1845, trustees accepted a letter from Ammi B. Young "in relation to a design and plans furnished by him for a Chapel" and voted to respond with thanks for "donation of his bill for a valuable design." Yet Young, known for his Boston Custom House (1837), excelled in the use of granite for a neoclassical rather than a Gothic idiom.[39]

When Bigelow persuaded the trustees to choose his design for the chapel, he also won acceptance of a new location. The low Temple Hill on the carriage drive winding to the summit of the cemetery already had several family lots and a receiving tomb. Moreover, it did not have the appropriate flat topography or central location for proper siting of a Gothic structure. Bigelow favored use of the plateau just west of Central Avenue nearer the cemetery's front. (Fig. 10.18.) The corporation had to repurchase four lots to lay out a new avenue, providing access to the chapel and making it one of several major focal points in the landscape. They expanded the road in front of the chapel to seventy feet wide, creating plentiful space for the parking of horse-drawn hearses and carriages from funeral corteges. The double doors were on the groundplane so caskets would not have to be carried up steps.[40]

Bigelow served as contractor for the chapel's construction. On the recommendation of D. R. Hay of Edinburgh, author of a philosophic treastise on harmony of

gestive of the Egyptian, including exterior octagonal columns rather than buttresses. Its simple nave, sixty by forty feet and eighty feet high, is lit only by small, circular clerestory windows, a high rose window over the entrance, and a tall "painted glass" window at the end of the nave, leaving plentiful wall space. Bigelow undoubtedly knew that aestheticians like Archibald Alison and Pugin thought that detailed ornamentation kept the

Fig. 10.18. Mount Auburn's chapel viewed from the north from Lawn Avenue near the cemetery entrance. Carte de visite photograph by G. K. or W. S. Warren, Cambridgeport, Massachusetts, ca. 1865. MAC.

Fig. 10.19. Bertel Thorwaldsen's often-copied, low-relief medallion sculpture, *Night*. From a stereographic photograph, ca. 1860. BMGL.

colors, Bigelow hired the firm of Ballantine & Allan of Edinburgh, noted for its "glass painting" and appointment by the Royal Commission in the Fine Arts to execute the painted windows for the House of Lords, rebuilt in 1836. He rejected their suggestion for distinctly biblical scenes, with major windows depicting the Resurrection and the Ascension and smaller semicircular panes picturing the twelve Apostles in the style of the thirteenth century.[41] Rather, Bigelow sent them templates for the north rose window inspired by the famous low-relief carving *Night*, by the internationally acclaimed sculptor Bertel Thorwaldsen, with a winged female figure alight, cradling two sleeping infants and accompanied by a dove. (Fig. 10.19.) Wilson Flagg said it was meant "to symbolize the tranquility of death." Cornelia Walter remarked that it reminded her of Mrs. Hemans's sentimental verse:

> *Free, free from earth-born fear,*
> *I would range the blessed skies*
> *Through the blue divinely clear,*
> *Where the low mists cannot rise.*

Bigelow requested that the rose window on the front or south of the chapel depict two cherubs from Raphael's painting of the Madonna di San Sisto gazing upward to a source of heavenly light, representing belief in immortality. He suggested that the representation of Death in the north window be in cold or somber tints, while that of Immortality facing the sun be in bright and dazzling colors.[42] (Figs. 10.20, 10.21.)

Bigelow commissioned Gridley J. F. Bryant, architect of Boston City Hall, to draw up working plans for the chapel. Octavius T. Rogers constructed the building quickly, completing work in 1846. The effects of the haste became evident, however, in less than a year. The granite pieces were flawed by veins of iron which discolored the entire structure. In the spring of 1848 Superintendent Rufus Howe spent $100 on experiments to remove exterior stains, but the defective stone had already begun to disintegrate, creating chronic leaks in the roof that grew worse each year. Inspectors from the firm of Washburn, Treadwell & Standish complained that in addition, "the walls of the clerestory cracked as if shaken by the wind," making a very disquieting noise. Engineers convinced the board in 1851 that the defects were great enough to raise doubts about the safety of the entire chapel. The pinnacles were particularly unstable, and walls admitted wind and rain. No restitution could be obtained from Rogers, despite conclusive evidence of "gross violation of the building contract," a result of subcontracting.[43]

Piecemeal reconstruction was impossible. In February 1852, when a storm damaged the precariously mounted north rose window, the trustees concluded that there was no alternative to razing and rebuilding the en-

Fig. 10.20. Great Nave Window on the north end of the chapel, stained glass by Ballantine & Allan, Edinburgh, Scotland, 1845. The firm pioneered the rediscovery of medieval techniques for making stained-glass leaded windows. The cemetery restored the window in 2006. Photograph by Harvard Film Service, ca. 1935. MAC.

Fig. 10.21. Great Rose Window on the chapel's south end, stained glass by Ballantine & Allan, Edinburgh, Scotland, 1845. Bigelow commissioned the stained glass and designed the chapel, which was erected in 1846. The cemetery restored the window in 2006. Photograph by Harvard Film Service, ca. 1935. MAC.

tire chapel if it was to be functional rather than rapidly going to ruin. Work began late in 1853 and proceeded slowly and cautiously, completed in 1858 at a total expense of $34,023. Reconstructed it was essentially the same as the first one but six feet longer and with only minor ornamental differences. Interior paving with multicolored English burnt tiles was installed in 1861. The building needed only one minor cleaning of lime marks and proved entirely strong and satisfactory except for an unsettling flaw. An echo, annoying if not eerie, made proprietors reluctant to schedule funeral services there. They also complained that the structure still seemed damp and cold. Although the trustees provided suitable books and a reading desk, hoping that it would serve as a place for quiet, melancholy contemplation like the hermitages in English gardens, the chapel never received much use.[44]

In her 1847 book on Mount Auburn, Cornelia Walter had repeated Bigelow's hope that the chapel would become a museum. The English visitor Sir Charles Lyell wrote in 1849 that the building was "to serve as a Westminster Abbey, Pantheon, or Valhalla," commemorating "distinguished men." Some proposed to trustees that the cemetery charter might even be interpreted to allow heirs of notables to contribute artifacts and "relics" for a permanent, museum-like collection to be displayed in the chapel and entrusted to corporate care. No one discussed on record who would evaluate credentials of historical note or share curatorship, but newer trustees were vehemently unwilling to assume that task. They wanted Mount Auburn to be simply for burials and opposed attempts to make something more of the cemetery, especially if it involved the creation of "high culture."[45] Yet many proprietors continued to complain that the trustees should not have expended proceeds from lot sales on such a building in the first place. They opposed plans to make the chapel a historical museum housing "a collection of mere curiosities or relics of ancient times," no more appropriate to the general purposes of the cemetery than "establishment of an historical library, though that [would be] in some sense the best monument to the worthy dead." Others countered that it was entirely fitting to make the chapel, and indeed the entire cemetery, a historical repository.[46]

Historical Statues

Advocates of commemoration seized upon the opportunity presented by the death of Joseph Story in September 1845. Bigelow mounted a subscription campaign to fund a statue of the Supreme Court justice and Mount Auburn's first president for placement in the chapel. Bigelow, Charles Curtis, and Martin Brimmer formed a Statuary Committee to find an artist. In January 1845 they reported that the son of the deceased, the young lawyer William Wetmore Story (1819–1895), despite a lack of formal art training, had designed a bust of his father and a small model for a life-sized statue, "both of which bid fair to convey a more just impression of the character, expression, and likeness of the deceased." They made a contract with the twenty-nine-year-old Story, who promptly left his Boston law practice for Rome to set up a studio.[47]

By 1847 the trustees had collected $2,630, more than enough to complete the commission. They invested the surplus in a special account eventually used for further embellishment of the cemetery. Work on the statue took longer than anticipated. In 1851 the sculptor asked for an extension of the contract, which some newer trustees wanted to cancel. Bigelow urged Story to return to Boston to complete the work, believing that American marble would produce a satisfactory statue and that work would progress quicker under the trustees' watchful eyes; but Story refused, resigning his commission. The trustees reconsidered, persuaded Story to continue work in Rome, and negotiated a new contract.[48] Story promised delivery in October of 1854, three years after first contracted, but the statue did not arrive in Boston until the following spring. Edward H. Eldredge exhibited it in the Athenaeum vestibule and kept it insured until cemetery trustees procured a suitable pedestal, designed by Richard Saltonstall Greenough. In ceremonies at the Athenaeum, Mount Auburn's trustees accepted the statue, deeming it "an exact and living likeness of its distinguished original, a just conception and appropriate expression of character," and "a truthful and life-like embodiment of what marble can give successfully to commemorate the dead."[49] (Fig. 10.22.)

William Wetmore Story returned briefly for the ceremonies and halfheartedly resumed his law practice, but in 1856 he went back to Italy to devote his life to sculpture. Hawthorne visited Story's studio and modeled the romance *The Marble Faun* (1860) on the life of the expatriate. Mount Auburn's commission launched the career of a major American sculptor; and his two sons, Julian Russell and Thomas Waldo, also found careers in art, while his daughter married a Medici. It was relatively easy for cultured young American men or women to take up sculpture in Italy from the 1820s through the 1850s without worrying about lack of craftsmanship. They routinely hired teams of skilled stonecutters, some specializing in the intricate carving of drapery or skin and hair texture, to execute their designs in marble. Story and the others produced sculpture for American patrons, who, inspired by neoclassical taste and the desire to commemorate notable individuals, provided a stream of commissions, many for cemeteries.[50]

Bigelow proposed other historic statues for the chapel in his 1853 annual report, quoting Joseph Story's report a decade earlier on possible uses of the chapel and his expectation that "marble busts and statues and other sepulchral monuments . . . *may from time to time be placed there by liberal benefactors and presented in memory of the dead.*" For a year Bigelow argued with trustees that Mount Auburn's original plan included addition of statuary at corporate expense to the buildings and grounds, a provision in the charter. He quoted from the *Dictionary of the English Language* (1755) of Samuel Johnson (1709–1784) the definition of "embellishment" as "adventitious beauty" and "adscititious grace," or "that which is taken in to complete something else, though originally extrinsick." Noah Webster's 1828 dictionary described "embellishment" as "any thing that adds beauty or elegance, that which renders anything pleasing to the eye, or agreeable to the taste, in . . . the fine arts." A majority of the trustees voted to allocate $15,000 for three "commemorative" marble statues of "persons distinguished in American History"; but those dissenting demanded proof of legal authority to undertake the project under the charter.[51] (Figs. 10.23–10.25.)

Fig. 10.22. Joseph Story portrait statue by William Wetmore Story, 1854. At the time, the statue, one of four later donated to Harvard University, stood in the first chapel. Note the ornate cast-iron fence meant to keep visitors at a distance. From a stereograph, ca. 1865.

Fig. 10.23. John Winthrop portrait statue by Richard Saltonstall Greenough, 1857. The statue originally stood in the first chapel. From a stereograph, ca. 1865. MAC.

Fig. 10.24. James Otis portrait statue begun by Thomas Crawford and completed by Randolph Rogers, 1857–58. The statue stood in the first chapel. From a stereograph, ca. 1865. MAC.

Fig. 10.25. John Adams portrait statue by Randolph Rogers, 1857. From a stereograph, ca. 1865. MAC.

Trustee Charles Curtis and Secretary Henry M. Parker rendered their legal opinion that "*commemorative statues* are an embellishment of a Cemetery," making it "a more attractive resort," and therefore within the lawful power of the board to commission. They added that the articles of incorporation could also be construed "properly [to] allow the heir of any of our military heroes to hang the trophies of his father's victories above a mural tablet in the chapel," entrusting the artifacts to corporate care. Since a "good estate" usually reserved about $360 for funeral expenses if a burial lot or tomb had already been purchased, the bulk paid for a gravestone, some trustees speculated that a similar sum might be expended on a portrait of the deceased—a painting or low relief—for display in the chapel rather than as a monument on a lot. Curtis and Parker joined with Bigelow in hoping that "memorials of the worthy dead might thus gradually accumulate under [trustees'] care and eventually the number of these relics of various kinds may make up such a collection that [the corporation] would not be authorized, in the first instance, to establish as an independent thing, as an embellishment of the Cemetery . . . appropriate to and in harmony with the place." Mount Auburn might have a collection of historical artifacts and art, not unlike the Parisian Museum of the Invalides attached to the funerary chapel housing Napoleon's tomb, or it might amass "a historical library . . . in some sense the best monument to the worthy dead." Curtis and Parker agreed with Bigelow that the cemetery was empowered to fund the statues but not to instigate a museum collection or library "as an independent thing" using corporate funds.[52]

In a split decision, the trustees allocated $15,000 to be divided for three full-length statues "to be prepared under contracts to be made with proper artists, the said statues to be those of persons distinguished in American History." Bigelow's Statuary Committee encountered "great difficulty" in choosing subjects because of "the equality of conflicting claims, especially of those which crowd about the revolution." Bigelow felt that the "difficulty would be somewhat diminished by selecting a representative man," using Emerson's term, "for each of four distinct epochs or periods in our history"—the colonial settlement of America and foundation of Boston, the first resistance to "aggression of British power," Independence and establishment of republican government, and the triumph of constitutional law or "realization growing out of the others of the period of supremacy of law and of intellectual, moral, and social progress." Story's statue already epitomized the last stage, said Bigelow.[53]

Extensive discussion focused on the choice of notables to symbolize the other three periods. Bigelow solicited advice from the likes of John Gorham Palfrey, then writing a history of Massachusetts. Former mayor and Harvard president John Quincy suggested John Jay, John Marshall, and John Pickering as representative Americans on criteria of "morals, motives, and intellect." Others proposed John Cotton and John Eliot. The decision finally rested on sons of Massachusetts—John Winthrop, James Otis, and John Adams—to reflect a characteristically regional interpretation of national history.[54] Still, opposition to the statuary remained, generally among new proprietors and trustees who argued that the cemetery was founded for functional reasons, to remove burials from the city, and not to become a museum. They encouraged a public debate that filled local newspapers and carried over to the 1856 annual proprietors' meeting.[55]

The *Boston Advertiser* supported the statues. W. F. Brown of the *Boston Daily Courier* praised the ability of sculptors to show "a just appreciation of the historic enterprise to which they have given their talents," believing that "the appropriate ornaments of cemeteries are memorials of the dead, and of these memorials, works of statuary are, by common consent in the enlightened world, the most beautiful, expressive, and desirable. Their historic truth enhances their value, and their costliness restricts their multiplication." Brown defended the rights of trustees to embellish the cemetery and expressed confidence that the effort would be respected by "a cultivated and discerning community."[56]

J. M. Wightman countered in *The Atlas* that defenders of statues were not acquainted with the opinions of the majority of proprietors. He complained that the $15,000 allocated for the statues was especially objectionable after the $50,000 spent on the chapel, "for which there has not been and probably will not be any use." Wightman did not categorically oppose commemorative statues. He merely thought that it would be better if they were financed by voluntary subscription and placed in Faneuil Hall, the State House, or the Athenaeum, public sites in the city where a larger portion of the population would see them: "The statues of Winthrop, of Otis, and Adams ought not to be immured within this monument [Mount Auburn's chapel]; their dust rests in other places; they have no connection with this cemetery. . . . [T]heir statues should stand out boldly in the light of day—in places which when living, they had graced and honored by their presence, their virtues and their patriotism, and where they may be often present to the eye, as bright exemplars for the present and future generations."[57]

A writer to *The Christian Examiner* favored the statues: "How rich we shall be in works of art when these have arrived to reconsecrate, by their almost speaking presence, the hallowed regions of our unforgotten dead!" The writer cautioned proprietors, however, not to be swept along by materialism, for they were capable of evil as well as good in attempts to commemorate the great and the ordinary: "The chief charm of Mount Auburn is the peaceful shade which its deep groves fold around the sorrowing heart—and marble shafts are no compensation for destroyed trees—least of all, is one of these gloomy tombs a grateful substitute for the blended beauty and fragrance of pine and elm."[58]

Debate continued. A letter to the *Daily Courier* alleged that the cemetery corporation had diverted money "from its legitimate purposes without even consulting proprietors." The writer, identified only as a lot owner, judged it a "decided impropietory [*sic*] to place statues of statesmen in such a place," questioning trustees' authority to do so based on his "experience in corporations." Corporations were so new and so rapidly growing, multiplying in scale, that few could differentiate between the status of Mount Auburn and the region's burgeoning mill systems, so it is not to be wondered why Bostonians, some of them Mount Auburn proprietors, might have doubts about the authority of the trustees. The writer favored the idea of producing historic statues but proposed that they be put in "suitable public places or buildings."[59] Two days later, another letter to the

Courier from one of Mount Auburn's first proprietors defended the decision to commission statues and complained that the controversy served only "to keep off persons who are disposed to purchase lots," warning that "agitation and party excitement" would doom Mount Auburn "to the fate of too many modern corporations"—dissolution and bankruptcy. The controversy, in other words, created bad public relations.[60]

Wightman stepped up his criticism of the financial impropriety of corporate commissioning of statues a week later in the *Atlas*. He would not object to display of costly works of art, he argued, if proprietors were "not taxed for them without their consent." He mustered a summary of Mount Auburn's budget to prove his point. In 1855, corporate expenditures were $37,342, but receipts totaled only $26,439, depleting investments by $10,650, while there was no permanent fund to ensure future maintenance and preservation of the grounds. Even worse, limited corporate investments of $30,000 had only a $25,000 market value. Wightman reminded Bostonians that Bigelow had announced at the 1856 annual meeting that, "if, for the next thirty years, the trustees should sell all the available lots, and spend as they have been doing since the first establishment of the cemetery, at the end of that time the Corporation would be without any income with which to keep the grounds in order." Furthermore, the annual interest on each statue would pay for one grounds worker for a year. By mid-1856, alterations and additions under way on the gate and superintendent's house had to be stopped because of the statuary expenses.[61]

Wightman echoed the views of insurgent trustees who had proposed six weeks before that the contracts for the statues be canceled, that monies saved be placed in a permanent fund, "and the income derived from it be spent upon the grounds,—in keeping them in more perfect order than has hitherto been the case, that it would be far more for the reputation of the place and the pleasure and comfort of the visitors and proprietors than would be the exhibition of the statuary, however beautiful." To curb future spending, this minority faction amended Article 25 of the bylaws to stipulate that no new expenditure over $1,000 could be made unless voted on by the trustees at a meeting held at least seven days after the proposal had been presented. This measure would prevent a few influential trustees, like Bigelow, from rushing through projects that the other trustees might oppose if given time for deliberation.[62]

The insurgent trustees were not averse to spending money for amenities to the grounds if the additions provided new facilities or conveniences for proprietors and visitors. In 1855, new trustees Mace Tisdale and Isaiah Bangs joined Bigelow on the Committee on Grounds. They urged installation of benches, improvement of lighting in the lodge, and placement of privies in the grounds, the last item strongly opposed by Bigelow. Tisdale, who had narrowly won reelection in 1855, threatened in turn to resign over the statuary controversy, following the example of George W. Crockett, a trustee for twelve years. Isaac Parker dissented so vocally that he lost his sixteen-year seat, and like-minded proprietors elected three new trustees who joined Tisdale in opposition to the statues, forcing the trustees to issue majority and minority reports for and against rescinding the contracts, although there were already two empty pedestals and one statue of Story framed by a cast-iron fence already in the chapel.[63]

Bigelow pointed out that the corporation had entered into binding contracts with three sculptors and had given a $1,000 down payment to two of them after approving four daguerreotype views of maquettes. Richard Saltonstall Greenough (1819–1904), designer of the Story statue pedestal, was chosen to make the statue of Winthrop, and Thomas Crawford (1814–1857) won the commission for the Otis portrait. He was one of the first American sculptors to settle in Rome to study with the famed Danish neoclassicist Bertel Thorwaldsen (1770–1844) after working with John Frazee and Robert Launitz in New Jersey carving funerary monuments. Randolph Rogers (1825–1892), who had settled in Rome in 1855 to become the center of the American colony of sculptors, was to do the portrait of John Adams. Work, however, did not progress smoothly.[64]

Crawford began working on his Otis portrait by completing a seven-foot-tall plaster model, but he died suddenly in 1857 before it could be executed in marble. Crawford's widow, the sister of Julia Ward Howe, arranged for Rogers to complete the work. Rogers had just finished his Adams "of the heroic size, in the costume of the period when he lived and all in admirable taste," and shipped it off to Boston; but it was lost at sea, and Rogers had to make a duplicate. In 1859 the ship bearing the second Adams statue put in to Savannah harbor in distress, and the statue was not forwarded to Boston until the following year. John Adams, who had always been skeptical about art, even when used in the name of history, would have found the difficulties ironic. Throughout the delays, however, Bigelow remained confident that the wait for such "a valuable and most appropriate embellishment" was well worthwhile and would ultimately give Mount Auburn "precedence over all other cemeteries in this country" at a relatively minor expense. Bigelow had higher ambitions for Mount Auburn, not content with relying on its landscape alone to make it famous.[65]

The editor of the short-lived *Mount Auburn Memorial* echoed Bigelow's confidence in the commemorative value of statues, wondering, "What parent as he conducts his son to Mount Auburn will not, as he pauses before their monumental statues, seek to heighten his reverence for virtue, for patriotism, for science, for learning, for devotion to the public good?" Luxuriating in the twilight of a Whiggish historicism, he exclaimed, "Winthrop, Otis, Adams, Bowditch, Story—these are our jewels, these our abiding treasures." He only bemoaned the lack of a memorial to John Hancock, either in Boston or at the cemetery, and proposed that the trustees select a prime site for the Founding Father's reinterment from Boston's Old Granary Burying Ground and suitable honors: "Let there be placed upon his mausoleum a colossal figure of the Genius of America, supporting upon her left arm an emblematic shield of the American Union, and in her right hand grasping the staff surmounted by the 'Cap of Liberty.'"[66]

A poem by "Justitia" published the next week in the *Memorial* reissued the call for commemoration of Hancock, his tomb then as mundane as all the others in the Old Granary without appropriate monumentation:

> *First of the band who rent Britannia's chain,*
> *And her proud mandate sent back o'er the main,*
> *Is there no shrine or urn to speak thy fame?*
> *No spot where youth may learn thy deeds to name?*
>
> *Shame to thy natal place, shame to the land,*
> *Neglecting thee to grace, itself doth brand,*
> *And to the stranger's eye seemeth imbrued*
> *With crime of deepest dye—Ingratitude.*
>
> *"Give honor," saith our God, "Where honor's due."*
> *Who broke the tyrant's rod, claims it of you.*
> *Raise where his ashes sleep, a marble bust;*
> *Place it where willows weep o'er his dust.*
>
> *But write no eulogy upon the stone;*
> *Under his bust let be his name alone.*
> *No epitaph or song his fame shall swell;*
> *For in proud history his deeds shall dwell.*[67]

The same honors would be due Sam Adams, the editor suggested; but "no one present could say positively" where his bones "reposed" in the Old Granary.[68]

The 1856 controversy over historical statues signaled a nascent unwillingness of some to use Mount Auburn as a place of public commemoration. Indeed, with the exception of Bigelow, most trustees discouraged it. In 1858 they defined "public monuments" paid for by subscription campaigns as "memorials" and stipulated that endowment of a perpetual care fund be mandatory before their erection. Since the corporation stopped granting land for such memorials of historic significance, subscription campaigns would have to raise funds to buy lots and to assure their care as well as for the monuments. Bigelow knew from experience the necessity of such a regulation to ensure repair as well as routine maintenance. Since 1845 the corporation had held a $72 endowment fund for the memorial to Dr. Kirkland, Harvard president; after less than a decade, it was needed for repairs.

The cemetery did not hold such funds for the statue of Nathaniel Bowditch. Since 1853 Bigelow had been trying unsuccessfully to repair damage done to the cast bronze by New England weather. Piecemeal efforts to stop the many holes that developed and to cover the patching with bronze paint proved insufficient and unsightly. In 1886 the statue of the mathematician and astronomer had to be taken down and shipped to Paris for recasting at Gruet, one of Europe's best foundries.[69]

Bostonians willing to contribute to commemorative monuments began to look to public sites rather than Mount Auburn. In 1867, when a subscription campaign raised funds for William Wetmore Story to sculpt a life-sized portrait statue of Edward Everett (1794–1865) in a dramatic histrionic pose, cast in Munich, they chose a site in the Public Garden. There, passersby could easily

Fig. 10.26. Edward Everett portrait statue by William Wetmore Story, cast in bronze in Munich, 1867. The monument then stood in the Boston Public Garden. From a stereograph, ca. 1870. BMGL.

Fig. 10.27. Edward Everett neoclassical funerary monument on Magnolia Avenue (lower left) with Rev. John Pierpont's rose granite sarcophagus designed by architect George Keller (upper right) on Lavender Path, the hillside beneath the summit. The latter is said to represent the Ark of the Covenant. Photograph by Carol Betsch, 2005.

read that Everett had been an "Orator, Minister, Classics Professor, Magazine Editor, Statesman, Congressman, Governor, Ambassador, President of Harvard, Secretary of State, Senator." Everett has a fine neoclassical monument of red and white granite proclaiming his *curriculum vitae* even more extensively on his burial lot on the steep hillside near Mount Auburn's summit, where it simply blends in with the stones of other proprietors. (Figs. 10.26, 10.27.)

Washington Tower

Well before Mount Auburn's founding, in 1811, Josiah Quincy and Joseph Story had suggested organizing to erect a monument to the nation's first president in the "Capital of New England." William Tudor encouraged the venture to "do honour to the good taste and judgment of those who erect it . . . to the state and town" as well as to Washington; but he worried about the lack of appropriate sites at that time in the city for even a small statue. Tudor had favored an architectural rather than a sculptural monument, considering as sites steep hills that were "not difficult of access" and near Boston. Although the Massachusetts legislature appointed commissioners and allocated some funds in 1816, nothing came of the project.[70]

In Mount Auburn's first years, Dearborn had speculated that "a stupendous monument to the most illustrious benefactor of his country" might be built at the cemetery "when the munificence of the citizens shall be commensurate with their debt of patriotic gratitude"; but at the time, the Bunker Hill Monument was still in the shambles of early construction. Bigelow provided Greek and Gothic designs for a tower, arguing that when the hill rising 125 feet above the Charles River was so "crowned," it would become "a most interesting place of resort, as commanding an extensive panoramic view of that richly variegated region of magnificent scenery, embraced within the far distant heights which encircle the metropolis." Dearborn rightly predicted that a tower would "present a prominent and imposing feature in the landscape, of which it becomes the center," serving for commemoration and giving the city historical monuments atop a prominent hill to the west as well as on Bunker Hill to the east.[71]

After the death of cemetery president Joseph Story in 1845, differences emerged among the trustees over what other amenities the corporation should fund; yet they unanimously agreed to begin the observatory or tower as soon as the chapel was built, as anticipated by cemetery founders. Bigelow as new president declared that the tower would "serve the double purpose of a landmark to identify the spot from a distance and of an observatory commanding an uninterrupted view of the country around it."[72] It would also "embellish the picturesque" in a way characteristic of many English gardens. Mount Auburn's founders knew that towers imbued with mythical or historical associations were common elements in such landscapes.[73] There seems to be an ancient funerary analogy between the tower and the tree. Lore holds that King Alfred was buried in a hollow oak trunk. Dedication of many towers to Alfred, making them cenotaphs, may have drawn inspiration from that story. Claremont in Surrey had a Belvedere Tower designed in 1715 by Sir John Vanbrugh for the summit of the principal knoll, called the Mount. Studley Royal in North Yorkshire contained a short, octagonal tower atop the estate's highest hill. Henry Hoare, proprietor of Stourhead in Wiltshire, commissioned architect Henry Flitcroft to erect an imposing 160-foot "Gothick" tower in 1762 on Kingsettle Hill, where King Alfred reputedly planted his flag against Danish invaders in 879. Voltaire in his *Histoire Générale* venerated Alfred, "The Father of His People" and "Founder of the English Monarchy and Liberty," as quintessential guardian and founder of trial by jury, a militia, and a naval force, the king who confirmed the old Saxon institution of Parliament, an image that reflected British Whigs' ideals. Many revered Washington as the American Alfred. (Figs. 10.28, 10.29.)

Fig. 10.28. Octagon Tower on Constitution Hill added in 1738 to the landscape garden at Studley Royal, Yorkshire, by its proprietor, William Aislabie, to replace a classical pavilion. Photograph by BMGL, 1985.

Fig. 10.29. Norman tower, 160 feet high, commemorating King Alfred's victory over the Danes in 879 AD, on Kingsettle Hill in the gardens at Stourhead, Wiltshire, designed by Henry Flitcroft, 1762. Photograph by BMGL, 1985.

Frequent placement of "Gothick" towers in English gardens was also a matter of taste. Sanderson Miller, an English "gentleman architect," played a seminal role in England's Gothic revival in the 1750s and 1760s as linked to the picturesque. The octagonal battlemented tower he built at his estate at Radway Grange in Warwickshire was on the spot where legend held that King Charles I raised his standard in the 1642 Battle of Edgehill. Many of Miller's other towers were follies or garden ornaments without specific historical significance, simply embellishing the naturalistic landscape, suggesting more. Miller specialized in sham castellated ruins, especially round towers providing panoramic views suggestive of infinity. Sir Horace Walpole and Richard Payne Knight, apostles of the picturesque, favored the castellated "Gothic" over the Greek or Roman. Archibald Alison, the Scottish aesthetic philosopher read by many of Mount Auburn's founders, remarked that "an old tower in the middle of a deep wood," like ruins, stirs emotional responses similar to the sublime, triggering a realization of the passage of time and the pastness of the past. Towers continued to be favored for British commemoration into the nineteenth century. In 1811 the banker Sir William Paxton built a castellated tower at Dyfed in Wales in memory of Lord Nelson.[74]

Not until the summer of 1852 did work on Mount Auburn's tower begin. No architectural design competition was held. Bigelow took credit for the concept of the circular, castellated Norman-Gothic structure, although a carpenter, M. S. Dodd, produced a wooden model and architect Gridley J. Fox Bryant provided working drawings. Indeed, one newspaper reported that it was "designed by the indefatigable G. J. F. Bryant under direction of Bigelow, President of the Corporation."[75] Bryant was Boston's leading commercial architect, specializing in granite construction, including the Mercantile Wharf Building, the State Street block, City Hospital, City Hall, and the second Horticultural Hall. The contracting firm of Whitcher & Sheldon of Quincy, which rebuilt the chapel, used granite to build the sixty-two-foot-tall round tower. Each massive stone was smooth hammered to form both exterior and interior surfaces. A spiral stone staircase ascended inside to two levels of open platforms on top. Whereas some referred to it, like the chapel, as being of "Dissenters' or Perpendicular" Gothic style, Bigelow called it Norman. Perhaps he, like the writer Henry Adams a generation later, thought of the Norman as a source of the Yankee heritage.[76] (Fig. 10.30.)

Although it was called Washington Tower, no dedicatory ceremonies were held. Its meaning was overshadowed by its immediate popularity as a tourist attraction. Guidebooks had long boasted of the spectacular panoramic view from the cemetery's summit. The tower only dramatized and maximized the view further for those willing to climb the dark, circular staircase to the platformed deck and the top. One visitor judged the view "equal perhaps to what is obtained from the monument of Bunker Hill or the cupola of the Capitol" atop Beacon Hill. No other such manmade vantage points existed. The "observatory" was acclaimed "a work of art and public enterprise." On a clear day one could survey the entire metropolitan region as far as the ocean, the Blue Hills of Milton, and the mountains of New Hampshire.[77]

With construction of the tower, the trustees completed all the major projects initially intended to "embellish" their picturesque landscape. Further "improvements" for the rest of the century would be left to proprietors. Bigelow increasingly turned his attention to diversifying ornamental plantings, especially as American landscape tastes shifted from the "picturesque" to the "gardenesque" and the "beautiful." Although the cemetery's landscape would go through successive chapters of change, losing much of its original woodsy charm, the eclectic "public" structures remain as durable and timeless as the granite from which they are made.

Fig. 10.30. Mount Auburn's 62-foot-high Norman tower, designed by Bigelow to be dedicated to George Washington and erected by Gridley J. Fox Bryant in 1853 on the cemetery's summit. Engraving from William Cullen Bryant, ed., *Picturesque America; or, The Land We Live In*, (New York: D. Appleton & Co., 1872). BMGL.

Receiving Tomb

Bigelow's increasing concern about Mount Auburn's salubrity led to his interest in constructing catacomb tombs. In 1856, inspired by Superintendent Mann's findings on a surveying tour of Green-Wood, Laurel Hill, and Green Mount Cemeteries in New York, Philadelphia, and Baltimore, Bigelow ordered alterations in the cemetery's original Receiving Tomb by constructing single compartments to prevent escape of effluvia; but he did not consider abandoning Mount Auburn's receiving vault under Boston's Park Street Church until several proprietors of other tombs in that Congregational church petitioned the cemetery in 1861 to say that they had voluntarily agreed to give up their own crypts "on the ground that such tombs are a nuisance." That was under increasing pressure from the Boston municipality given increasing public health concerns bolstered by new medical opinions. The church purchased a lot at the

Fig. 10.31. Victorian receiving tomb designed by Gridley J. F. Bryant in 1859 and constructed in Indian Ridge on Rosebay Avenue from 1862 to 1876. Anonymous photograph, ca. 1890.

Company began construction in 1862; but, as happened with the chapel, bad stains appeared on the façade. It had to be taken down, re-hammered, and replaced. Two years later the stains proved ineradicable and the face was again removed. The new building remained under construction until 1876. (Fig. 10.31.) Heavy, ornate wrought-iron gates set into the arched façade led into a central hall (45' by 10') lined with 120 columbaria and lit by a circular stained glass window at the end, with ventilation and more light from above. Iron sheeting was added to the entrance in the winter to keep out the elements.

cemetery and moved the remains in 1862, marking it by one central monument without individual names. Following this petition, Mount Auburn surrendered its vault there that year, moving abandoned bodies to a cemetery lot.[78]

A receiving tomb was still necessary for temporary deposit of bodies that could not be buried during the cold winter when graves could not be dug or while awaiting shipment elsewhere. Fearing burial alive, some people also favored delaying interment to be sure that death was real and not merely "suspended animation." Through the 1850s, the number of bodies in Mount Auburn's two receiving tombs averaged twenty-five per year; some were never reclaimed. To prevent such abandonment, the corporation required the posting of a $20 bond for each and set limits to the duration of deposit—two months from April through September and four months in the winter. Bodies unclaimed thereafter would be buried by the cemetery after fifty days.[79]

To compensate for the loss of the Park Street Church tomb, trustees commissioned architect Gridley J. F. Bryant in 1859 to design a new and larger receiving tomb to be nestled into the glacial moraine called Indian Ridge on Rosebay Avenue facing the bridge over Auburn Lake. Bryant, who had built the chapel and the tower, received $250 for the plans. The Granite Railway

The Sphinx

Bigelow's last major contribution to Mount Auburn was his personal donation "to the proprietors" in 1870 of "a monumental statue imitated from the Sphinx of antiquity and designed to commemorate the Great War of American Conservation." He initially proposed use of surplus corporate funds to augment a subscription campaign for erection of a "public monument" to the Union dead as early as 1865, although there was no single lot reserved for the war dead at Mount Auburn as at other "rural" cemeteries like Cincinnati's Spring Grove and Louisville's Cave Hill. In 1864 a campaign in Cincinnati raised $25,000 to finance a statue of a Union "Soldier of the Line" by Randolph Rogers, cast in bronze in Munich, for placement near a large soldiers' burial section funded by the state at Spring Grove.[80]

Despite the controversy over corporate funding of historical statuary a decade before, patriotism in the wake of the Civil War led Mount Auburn's trustees to agree tentatively to allocate part of its funds, not exceeding $15,000; but the subscription campaign to raise an equal sum failed. Major regional campaigns to erect Civil War monuments focused on urban spaces, especially commons as public spaces. The trustees could not agree on an artist or a design in their informal discussions. Perhaps some considered sufficient the monument erected by the Company of Independent Cadets in 1867 in memory of eight members who died "in Defense of the Union during the Rebellion" in the South, though it also mentioned previous wars fought by members. Many proprietors erected monuments on their lots to their own war dead, some richly carved with military paraphernalia. Other efforts were underway throughout the Boston metropolitan area to erect truly monumental tributes to the dead as well as the living who had contributed to the effort.[81] (Figs. 10.32, 10.33.)

Nevertheless, Bigelow determined to proceed at his own expense and with his personal sense of mission to embellish Mount Auburn with commemorative structures compatible with the goals that inspired the cemetery's founding. He insisted on "a general and comprehensive" structure at Mount Auburn "to apply either to the magnitude of these events or to the greatness of their consequences." He felt that "the wide range of architectural ideas and combinations exhibited in pillars, pyramids, obelisks, altars, sarcophagi, and mausoleums, have been produced and reproduced in inexhaustible variety," while "the more signification creations of expressive sculpture have hitherto been less frequently attempted" in America "because they are more difficult of satisfactory execution," especially for placement outdoors.[82] He resolved to give his cemetery a monument of heroic size and form, like the lion erected by Belgians on the Waterloo battlefield or the dying lion carved in a natural sandstone cliff at Lucerne in memory of Swiss Guards massacred by the mob at the Tuileries Palace in Paris in 1792 in defense of the family of Louis XVI, considered the first monument erected in modern times to dead soldiers.[83]

Bigelow personally commissioned Martin Milmore (1844–1883) to sculpt a monumental sphinx out of a single block of Hallowell (Maine) granite, fifteen feet long and eight feet high with a face three feet long. Bigelow undoubtedly drew inspiration from the painting *The Questioner of the Sphinx* (1863) by Elihu Vedder in the collection of Mrs. Martin Brimmer; but he explained that he chose the mythical figure with obtuse, inscrutable symbolism "to restore for modern application the an-

Fig. 10.32. Soldiers' and Sailors' (Civil War) monument, a Roman-Doric granite column on Boston Common sculpted by Martin Milmore and dedicated in 1877. Topped by the eleven-foot-tall "Genius of America" bearing a flag, laurel wreaths, and a sword, the monument was inscribed:

TO THE MEN OF BOSTON / WHO DIED FOR THEIR COUNTRY / ON LAND AND SEA IN THE WAR / WHICH KEPT THE UNION WHOLE / DESTROYED SLAVERY / AND MAINTAINED THE CONSTITUTION / THE GRATEFUL CITY / HAS BUILT THIS MONUMENT / THAT THEIR EXAMPLE MAY SPEAK / TO COMING GENERATIONS

From a stereograph, ca. 1877. BMGL.

Fig. 10.33. Monument of the Company of Independent Cadets, Mount Auburn, 1867. Photograph by Harvard Film Service, ca. 1940. MAC.

cient form" with its "associations of repose, strength, beauty, and duration," considering it "an ideal personification of intellect and physical force"—an embodiment of the Yankee culture that emerged triumphant from the Civil War.[84] (Fig. 10.34.)

Use of the form of the sphinx at Mount Auburn made sense to Bigelow, who knew of its recent international use as a garden ornament and as a ceremonial device on important public buildings. A female sphinx, intended to evoke a spirit of melancholy musing on the past, occupies a central position in the garden grotto on Goethe's summer estate on the banks of the Ilum in Weimar. Edmund Burke praised the tendency of that landscape "to fill the mind with that sort of delightful horror, which is the most genuine effect and truest test of the sublime." Whether meant to be sublime or merely decorative, the form of the sphinx recurred in the gardens of Chenonceau and Versailles in France, at Blenheim in England, and in Edinburgh, only a few examples of revivalistic uses of the form in modern Europe.[85]

The female sphinx was the sort described by Greek poets rather than the male sphinx symbolic of monarchy and Egyptian in origin. Indeed, the word *sphinx* is Greek. This suggests additional symbolic meaning that Bigelow had in mind for a monument to the Union dead. The Greek sphinx was a ghostlike monster with a female head and the body of a lion, believed to carry off youths arbitarily and to be present at fatal battles. Oedipus encounters the most famous Greek sphinx on the road from Corinth to Thebes, unknowingly to fulfill his destiny. He overcomes the ordeal, answers the riddle of the omniscient questioner, and proceeds of his way to the predetermined future. Likewise, Americans emerging from the Civil War with the Union intact could turn away from the divisive past and a pessimistic view of a cyclical history ending in disaster toward a new belief in future progress.

Bigelow chose the sphinx "to typify in the present age of social transition a result of greater magnitude in the history of the world than were all the revolutions and conquests of the primeval East" and "to express the present attitude and character of a nation perhaps as far remote in time from the building of the pyramids as was that event from the earliest constructions attempted by man. The same ideal from which . . . on the dividing ridge of time has looked backward on unmeasured antiquity, now looks forward to illuminate progress. It stands as a landmark of a state of things which the world has not before seen—a great, warlike and successful nation, in the plentitude and full consciousness of its power, suddenly reversing its energies . . . to resume the still familiar arts of peace and good will." He wondered, "What symbol can better express the attributes of a just, calm, and dignified self-reliance than one which combines power with attractiveness, strength of the lion with the beauty and benignity of woman?"[86]

Fig. 10.34. Sphinx to the Union Dead, sculpted in 1871 to the specifications of Jacob Bigelow, who donated it to the cemetery. Photograph by Harvard Film Service, ca. 1940. MAC.

Bigelow referred Milmore to views of restored sphinxes in Casas's *Voyage pittoresque en Egypte et Syrie*. There was, Bigelow wrote, great historical variety in the appearance of the sphinx, "from the almost Nubian and sometimes brute profile to the most perfect Caucasian face." Most Egyptian sphinxes, he judged, "though African . . . exhibit many examples of the most perfect intellectual human head" and even "some of the finest examples of the Indo-European face." Ironically, although Bigelow's notions of style betray a latent racism that even the most enlightened Yankee seldom escaped, his monument proclaims in Latin and English: "American Union Preserved, African Slavery Destroyed. By the Uprising of a Great People, By the Blood of Fallen Heroes."[87]

Bigelow instructed Milmore to carve the head of an American eagle rather than that of an Egyptian asp on the headdress. He included an Egyptian lotus, symbolic of human life, on the south side of the pedestal and an American water lily on the north. Some trustees wanted to place Bigelow's name on the front of the pedestal to turn the sphinx into a monument to the man who had originally proposed creation of the "rural" cemetery in 1825, who had served as a trustee for forty-eight years and as president for twenty-six, but Bigelow protested to John T. Bradlee, his successor as cemetery president, that his name should be displayed not as "ostentation rather than the gratitude to the donor" and threatened not to transfer ownership to the corporation unless such personal recognition was relegated to a less conspicuous place on the south side: "Jacob Bigelow Statuit et Dedicavit"—"he made it and dedicated it."[88]

In accepting the sphinx set facing the chapel in August 1872, the trustees described it as "illustrated and inscribed" by Bigelow's own "classic pen." It was "an evidence alike of his private virtues and of his patriotism . . . a most fitting crown to all the valuables services rendered to the cemetery, as chief among those who originated and planned it." The trustees funded installation in that central location, symbolically facing north, a space declared as "ornamental" to remain free from burials. It engendered only minor controversy when one proprietor cautioned that, encircled by a carriageway, it might "occasion fright to horses."[89]

Jacob Bigelow never *saw* the sphinx in place. Cataracts deprived him of sight. By early 1871 he complained that he could no longer read or write. The architectural historian Wayne Andrews exaggerates the story, claiming that the doctor "lost his mind—though only after translating *Mother Goose* into Latin." Bigelow did do the translation, finding intellectual recreation as he undoubtedly rationalized that it would introduce young Americans to classical studies. That does not indicate dementia, however, but demonstrates continuing intellectual acuity and the didactic intentions underlying most of Bigelow's work over his long, productive life. Andrews colors his description of Bigelow's inspection of the sphinx unsympathetically: "The day was to come when he would totter through the gates of Mount Auburn on the arms of his friends; reaching the Strange Sphinx Monument he set up in memory of the Civil War dead, he would finger it fondly." Indeed, friends led Bigelow to the statue after parking their carriage, not trekking on foot through the gate, and watched sympathetically as the blind physician feebly and fondly fingered its contours. Over the next six years Bigelow succumbed to deafness and paralysis as well, spending his last years bedridden but rationally complaining of his diminishing physical capabilities.[90]

On Bigelow's resignation as president and trustee in 1871, the eleven-member board sent "the originator and founder of Mount Auburn" a "unanimous and urgent solicitation" that he delay retirement. Bigelow complied, attending his last board meeting on September 25, 1872, forty-one years and a day after the cemetery's consecration. The trustees issued the resolution that "every object [at Mount Auburn], its entrance gateway, its chapel, its beautiful avenues, paths, and fountains, all bear witness to his science, skill, and taste, and signally identify him with Mount Auburn." Bigelow was not, as we have seen, solely responsible for creation of the landscape, its initial design having been produced by Henry A. S. Dearborn and others including Bigelow, trustees, workers, and superintendents. But Bigelow must be credited with major contributions in its subsequent development. The trustees commissioned a marble bust of Bigelow from the sculptor Henry Dexter (1806–1876). This "suitable testimonial and token of appreciation of the long and continued and faithful services" of the physician was placed in the chapel in November 1872.[91] (Fig. 10.35.)

Fig. 10.35. Portrait bust of Dr. Jacob Bigelow by Henry Dexter, 1872, placed in Mount Auburn's first chapel. MAC.

Bigelow drew consolation in his last days from letters of thanks from the likes of a Brookline, Massachusetts, mother who wrote that his gift of the sphinx assured her "that the blood of her sons had not been shed in vain." With his wife, Mary, who hosted meetings of the Widows' Society in their home, he spent even more time than most in mourning Civil War losses. Bigelow's eulogist, the Unitarian minister George E. Ellis, portrayed him in his final hours as "placid and tranquil, occasionally speculating as to what he was or what he was waiting for." In the end, Bigelow even rationalized his blindness, reminding a friend "that it was our human wont, as we lay down at night, to close our eyes before we actually fell asleep." Bigelow died on January 10, 1879. After services at the now Unitarian King's Chapel in Boston, he was buried under the modest neoclassical marble sarcophagus on Beech Avenue which he had erected more than four decades before.[92]

Dr. Jacob Bigelow's death marked the passing of Mount Auburn's formative era, characterized by development of a picturesque landscape and a Whiggish historical sensibility. A younger generation, which began to assume control of the corporation in the 1850s, had less complex ambitions for the institution as an agency of culture than did its founders. They did realize, however, that Mount Auburn was an important place to preserve, given legal requirements, although not in static form, given changing tastes and the need to develop more burial space. Even after the cemetery had ceased to attract throngs of visitors and to be emulated for its landscape design, it would remain through the next century very usable for burials, personal commemoration, and display of horticultural taste—if not for creation of a usable past for future eras' public commemoration. Indeed, it was not until after 1988 that Mount Auburn as an institution took on a reinterpretation and revival of all that.

11

THE RAGE FOR MOUNT AUBURN

Sacred Site or Pleasure Ground?

Where else shall we go with the musings of Sadness, or for the indulgence of Grief; where to cool the burning brow of Ambition, or relieve the swelling heart of Disappointment? We can find no better spot for the rambles of curiosity, health, or pleasure; none sweeter for the whispers of affection among the living.

—Joseph T. Buckingham, "Cemetery of Mount Auburn," *Boston Courier* (September 28, 1831)

Then let this haunt be sacred. For the feet
Of strangers, here in future days shall turn,
As to some Mecca of philosophy;
And here the admiring youth shall come to seek
Some relic of the great and good—whose fame
Shall gather greenness from the hand of Time.

—Mrs. Lydia Huntley Sigourney, quoted in Cornelia Walter, *Mount Auburn Illustrated* (1847)

Mount Auburn immediately captured the public imagination, its popularity extending far beyond the local gentry. It became a favorite "resort" for visitors, who came to read the inscriptions on the monuments or simply commune with Nature. (Fig. 11.1.) Couples frequented Mount Auburn for courtship walks, cultivating sensations of melancholy by reading the sentimental verses engraved on the stones of those who died young. Teachers urged their students to visit and learn from the exemplary lives of notables interred there so that they might acquire the appropriate ambitions and aspirations. Liberal ministers and moralists preached that the place served as a catalyst for spiritual enlightenment and virtue, and that it embodied family values and cohesion in the face of the ultimate disruptive force—death, particularly of mothers and children.

Mount Auburn's popularity then can be understood only in the context of the period's sentimentalized romanticism and secularization of devotional values. The rise of neoclassicism also fostered an appreciation of its pastoral landscape as a new Arcadia or Eden, an optimistic symbol of the young nation. The spread of Whiggish aesthetics and historicism further encouraged the taste for picturesque landscapes that multiplied across the nation in the following decades, drawing inspiration from Boston's new cemetery as a prototype. Many found in Mount Auburn simply an "asylum" from the hectic life of the burgeoning city, a place for pleasant pastoral promenades, one of the few parklike settings in the metropolitan area at a time when the Mall on the Common, shaded by a "triple colonnade of weeping elms," was Boston's only green, open space.[1] (See Fig. 6.7.) The vicinity of Mount Auburn gained favor as a place for leisure even before the making of the cemetery. In 1792

Fig. 11.1. "View from Mount Auburn," panorama looking north from the Mount toward the chapel and Fresh Pond. Engraving by Smillie, from Walter, 1847. MAC.

Fig. 11.2. Solitary contemplation by the Judge Story monument on Narcissus Path, etching by Smillie, from Walter, 1847. MAC.

Jacob Wyeth began to develop an eight-acre "rural resort" on his father's farmland on Fresh Pond, just to the north. He built a tavern or "hotel" there in the 1830s. Until the Civil War, it enjoyed a thriving business, offering diversions such as lawn bowling and boating; but the genteel sort frowned on such amusements, preferring contemplative strolls through Sweet Auburn or the rural countryside, which still lay close to the city.

Mount Auburn's founders intended to create a place appropriate to the Yankee concept of leisure. Just as their Puritan forefathers had rejected merrymaking and frivolity at the Maypole festivities at Merrymount, Yankees disapproved of new forms of recreation they considered idle and unproductive. The editor Thomas Wentworth Higginson (1823–1911) remembered the "Cheerful Yesterdays" of his childhood: "We had Mayday parties, usually at Mount Auburn, and showed in the chilly May mornings that heroic courage which [James Russell] Lowell plainly attributes to children on these occasions." Higginson, Lowell, and their childhood friends, with their parents' approval, frequented the place "to sort out butterflies in summer or divide our walnuts in autumn." The reformer Julia Ward Howe recalled that Senator Charles Sumner (1811–1874), "on a certain Fourth of July . . . had given his office boy, Ben, a small gratuity, and had advised him to pass the day at Mount Auburn, where he would be able to enjoy quiet and profitable meditation" rather than the festivities on the Common, however patriotic.[2] (Fig. 11.2.)

Mount Auburn provided edifying recreation for the humble and the great, young and old, but especially for those whose family owned a burial lot, ensuring free access to the grounds—by carriage for the elite, if they could afford one. The diary of textile industrialist Amos Lawrence (1786–1852), who had renounced drink, tobacco, and theater in his youth, tells of many days spent at Mount Auburn, where he and his three brothers had enclosed their large family lot. (Fig. 11.3.) Lawrence mused, "A better taste is grow-

Fig. 11.3. Family lot, 1,300 square feet, of the four Lawrence brothers, textile mill entrepreneurs, between Cypress and Chapel Avenues. Photograph by Carol Betsch, 2005.

ing. . . . decidedly better than the old fashion of making these tenements look as dreary as anything in the world can look." He hoped that simpler tastes would encourage proprietors to avoid ostentatious monuments and "induce them to labor to merit . . . a good word from the future lookers on." Lore holds that when a messenger came to notify Franklin Pierce that the 1852 Democratic convention in Baltimore had nominated him its compromise candidate, he found the future president sitting under a tree at Mount Auburn. The Free-Soiler and Republican Charles Sumner used the cemetery as a retreat in the years from 1856 to 1859, while recovering from injuries inflicted when a pro-slavery congressman from South Carolina attacked him on the Senate floor.[3]

Such was the use the founders intended. In consecrating Mount Auburn in 1831, Judge Story promised that it would "preach lessons to which none may refuse to listen, and which all that live must hear." Three decades later, the poet and naturalist Wilson Flagg (1805–1884) called the place "a school of both religion and philosophy," adding, "To these consecrated grounds we would resort as we attend service in the house of God, to indulge in serious meditation and to ponder on those themes which are neglected by the multitude during the hurry of business or in the idle whirl of pleasure." In the interim, many followed the advice they received from clergymen, Transcendentalists, and sentimental writers alike promoting Mount Auburn as a new kind of sacred place, an Eden minus Adam's Fall, where Nature was resanctified and each visitor that much more likely to be saved for communing there.[4]

Mount Auburn in Literature

The historian Ann Douglas, though mistaken in many judgments about Mount Auburn, rightly observes that "the cemetery functioned not like experience but like literature." Literary descriptions of melancholy landscapes inspired its design, and it was intended that the landscape function like literature in instilling particular sentiments in visitors. Mount Auburn inspired numerous poems, religious tracts, short stories, moralistic essays, and travel narratives, which augmented its fame nationally and internationally, in turn inspiring the creation of similar "rural" cemeteries modeled after it.[5]

The cemetery's naturalism harmonized with the spirit of liberal Christian optimism, such as that expressed by the Reverend John Greenleaf Adams (1810–1887), a Universalist, who wrote: "Old and crude notions of the ghastly and the awful should be exchanged for sentiments more befitting believers in Him who is the Resurrection and the Life. . . . If earth must be a sepulchre, let it also be a garden." Other Unitarian ministers such as William Ellery Channing, Henry Ware, George Putnam, and John Pierpont proved instrumental in promoting Mount Auburn in print and from pulpits as an educational institution imparting moral lessons in a nondenominational way. Wilson Flagg observed, "We need not be the disciples of a theological faith to feel the truth," to hear "a new gospel of consolation," albeit secularized, and to learn lessons of "moral philosophy."[6]

Many secular writers also stressed Mount Auburn's moral influence, urging visits there to rouse "religious sentiments" even in unbelievers caught up in "uncertainty of religious truths." (Fig. 11.4.) The journalist Joseph T. Buckingham prescribed the cemetery as spiritual medicine in 1838: "Reader! if you would have the sympathies of your nature awakened, your earthly affections purified, your anxieties chastened and subdued, go to Mount Auburn. Go not for the gratification of idle curiosity, to comment with the eye of a critic upon the forms

Fig. 11.4. Mount Auburn's chapel. Engraving by Smillie, from Walter, 1847. MAC.

Fig. 11.5. Monument and fence, both of brownstone, of John H. Gossler of Hamburg on Yarrow Path. Engraving by Smillie, from Walter, 1847. MAC.

of monuments or the taste of those who placed them there. . . . Go not there with cold indifference to shock the sensibility of the bereaved with your antic and unseemly behavior. . . . But go to read and to learn the lesson which you must transmit to those who come after you." He believed that "it is wise and beneficial for men to familiarize themselves . . . with the certainty of that death from which none can hope to be exempt, to contemplate more frequently the tomb to which they must all descend." What better place to do so than in a natural setting, where the seasonal processes of birth, maturation, decline, and renewal reminded one that death was part of an inexorable system. "There can be no good reason," wrote Buckingham, "why death should be associated with sorrow and gloom," as in the Puritan past. Mount Auburn represented a more optimistic approach to death, "the still higher and more ennobling light of a passage from mortality to immortality—from the darkness, doubt, and ignorance of mere humanity, to the light, the confidence, and the full meridian of intelligence and happiness to which this immortality will lead the spirit." It promised to teach the visitor to accept death "with resignation and joy."[7] (Fig. 11.5.)

Cornelia Wells Walter (1813–1898), editor of the *Boston Daily Evening Transcript*, advocated in her book *Mount Auburn Illustrated* (1847) "meditative wanderings" through which we might "gain a lesson from nature" and "learn to conform our lives to the order of her works in view of both the present and the future." She praised the cemetery, with its lessons of moral philosophy built into its landscape. "Those periods of meditation," she promised, "derived from the enticements of Mount Auburn will remain constantly fixed in the recollection as bright oases in the pilgrimage of life." It was a place of "intellectual indulgence" for those preferring the "pleasures of melancholy" to more frivolous leisure.[8] Walter's philosophy was familiar to literary Bostonians who read Shaftesbury, Pope, Burke, and other British advocates of the philosophic virtues of landscaped gardens: "Thus it is seen that *taste*, whether exhibited in flower-crowned mounds, or in the chaste and classic monument, may exist in a rural cemetery in close connections with *morals*; and it is no less true that every pure ideal of religion and virtue grows in beauty by the food upon which it feeds."[9] Bostonians hoped that their cemetery would not only provide spiritual nourishment but also serve as an agent of cultural as well as moral excellence, exerting social control through acculturation, the means to a great and ambitious end. (Fig. 11.6.)

In *The Mother's Book* (1831), a prolific writer then prominent in Boston literary circles, Lydia Maria Francis Child (1802–1880), had urged women to take their children on Sunday walks to visit graves. (Fig. 11.7.) "So important do I consider cheerful associations with death, that I wish to see our graveyards laid out with paths and trees and beautiful shrubs as places of promenade," the Unitarian author wrote. Mount Auburn fulfilled her desires. Indeed, illustrations by James Smillie (1807–1885) of Mount Auburn in the 1840s show parents introducing toddlers and children to the cemetery.[10]

Fig. 11.6. Father and son contemplating the John Lowell monument on Willow Avenue. Engraving by Smillie, from Walter, 1847. MAC.

Fig. 11.7. Mother bringing children to the Rev. William Ellery Channing monument. Engraving by Smillie, from Walter, 1847. MAC.

Yet some sentimental writers displayed a mournfulness too dark for the cemetery's Unitarian proponents who wished to assert a positive view about death. The Reverend William Ellery Channing found the verse of Mrs. Felicia Dorothea Hemans (1794–1835) too gloomy, "her sense of the evils of life . . . too keen." Mount Auburn's purpose was to cultivate proper Chrisitan optimism. Channing loved "to be touched, moved, but not depressed" in such a way. He resented the exploitation of melancholy in a negative way. Still, tragic personal loss, nostalgia, and durable family cohesion despite death were formulaic themes in the era's popular culture, purveyed by the likes of Mrs. Hemans, Mrs. Lydia Huntley Sigourney, and especially Mrs. Sara Payson Willis (1812–1872), who, known as Fanny Fern, sold almost a hundred thousand copies of *Fern Leaves from Fanny's Port-Folio* in 1853, the first year of its publication.[11]

Social critics also saw the virtues of Mount Auburn. The essayist and poet Henry Tuckerman (1813–1871) opined in 1836 that the cemetery fostered "that association with the past essential to intellectual dignity," a quality that he feared was fast disappearing. Lessons learned there would counteract the growing materialism that was leading Americans to live only in the present, forgetting their personal and collective past. According to Tuckerman, "sentiment is the great conservative principle of society; those instincts of patriotism, local attachment, family affection, human sympathy, reverence for truth, age, valor, and wisdom . . . constitute the latent force of civil society." In 1838 another writer in the *Christian Examiner*, a Unitarian periodical, suggested that the cemetery would stir "the sentiment of retrospection and reverence" for a common American past and also provide antidotes for the disagreeable effects of "the busy competition . . . the hurried, ambitious spirit" that was rampant in American cities. Mount Auburn objectified these positive qualities. Emotional and moral "primal instincts" rediscovered there would bolster and renew the people's republican virtue.[12]

Nostalgia for a romantically imagined personal past also colored the opinions of many authors who considered Mount Auburn moralistically didactic. One Lowell "mill girl" wrote in 1840: "Mount Auburn! how soothing and tranquilizing is the remembrance of thy deep and quiet beauty! . . . As we stray through thy pleasant woods . . . we go back in imagination to our own homes and stand by the graves of our loved ones; and we remember the crushing weight of utter loneliness which pressed upon us as the green turf hid them from our view." This young woman found Mount Auburn an asylum from the industrial workplace into which she had been thrust, a severe contrast to life in rural New England hometowns she and her co-workers remembered so fondly. Those yearning for a sense of community lost or for the timeless rhythms of preindustrial life found gratification at Mount Auburn, which, after all, drew its name from Oliver Goldsmith's "Sweet Auburn," a deserted village.[13]

Moralistic sentimentalism focused on Mount Auburn recurred in newspapers, ladies' magazines, and gift books through the 1850s. One writer in the *Ladies' Repository* observed that "a poet looking for a time" upon Consecration Dell "will have his heart stirred and may indite words of holy import or be reminded of the soul-language of a brother bard, 'Thou, God, art here; thou fill'st the solitude. Thou art in the soft winds that run along the summit of those trees.'" The visitor, so moved, should "kneel down and consecrate his soul to God." The essay urged the visitor to select his own burial spot, to be "occasionally visited and cultivated" as a reminder of mortality and "of the great work we have to do prior to our departure to the other world, and of the value of that faith which makes it safe to die."[14]

Mrs. Sarah Josepha Hale (1788–1879), a prolific sentimental writer, expressed in verse Bigelow's promotion of earthen burial: "Away with human pageantries, the Temple's solemn gloom! / No need for Mausoleum, if ye give the Death but room."[15] The theme of a cemetery hallowed by Nature rather than by the Church appealed to another Cambridge poet, Caroline Frances Orne (1818–1905). Her long poem "Sweet Auburn and Mount Auburn" (1844) nostalgically describes how the Arcadia of her childhood had been transformed into a "City of the Silent . . . sacred to the deepest affections":

> *Two hundred years! and, lo! the forest deep*
> *Becomes the silent land of dreamless sleep.*
> *Ye spirits of my sires! while earth shall stand,*
> *Be guardian genii of this hallowed land.*
> *Methinks your spirit voices oft I hear.*

Orne sensed her relationship to the past as a physical presence during her visits to Mount Auburn and recognized the spiritual functions of the place for others, inviting her readers, "Unto their Cities of the Silent come, / And look with faith's clear eye beyond the tomb." Orne reminded visitors to be on their best behavior: "'Tis holy ground—this City of the Dead / Let no rude accents of untimely mirth / Break the calm stillness of this sacred earth."[16]

Nathaniel Hawthorne (1804–1864) found the stuff of "romance" in Mount Auburn's allegorical landscape. His tale "The Lily's Quest," published in 1839 in the first guidebook to the cemetery, described lovers' futile search for a place on which to build a Temple of Love. Adam Forrester and Lilias Fay are followed through various, seemingly ideal picturesque landscapes by a melancholy black-caped old man who repeatedly quashes their plans with tales of tragedies associated with each site. In the end, after they have selected a spot on an old rural estate, they begin to construct their temple with white marble columns and dome "planned after an ancient mausoleum." When it is nearly complete, Lilias dies. Hawthorne concludes, "The pilgrim lovers were seeking not a temple of earthly joy but a tomb for themselves and their posterity." Each place to which they are attracted is reminiscent of some aspect of Mount Auburn. The story reads almost like a promotional brochure offering desirable romantic plots where real-life couples might erect their own elegaic structures.[17]

So does "The New Adam and Eve" (1843), which appeared in Hawthorne's *Mosses from an Old Manse* (1846). It depicts a day of wonderment for a young couple, newly created as cognizant adults, wandering through a Boston and Cambridge depopulated by the "Day of Doom," which left everything else in place. Setting forth on "a ramble through the city" and "commissioned" by their Creator "to pass subconscious judgment upon the works and ways of the vanished race," they are befuddled by what they see: the dry-goods store, a church, the court of justice, the hall of the legislature, a prison, a Beacon Street mansion, a bank, the Bunker Hill monument, and the Harvard library. At the end of their day of discovery, "these pilgrims, who derive their being from no dead progenitors," finally stumble into Mount Auburn "with light hearts—for earth and sky now gladden each other with beauty." There, "they tread along the winding paths" amid the diverse monuments, "sometimes pausing to contemplate these fantasies of human growth, and sometimes to admire the flowers wherewith Nature converts decay to loveliness." Hawthorne wonders: "Can Death, in the midst of his old triumphs, make them sensible that they have taken up the heavy burthen of mortality, which a whole species had thrown down? Dust kindred to their own has never lain in the grave. Will they then recognize, and so soon, that Time and the elements have an indefeasible claim upon their bodies?" To symbolize their "idea of Death," they are drawn to monuments adorned with "the Butterfly soaring upward, or the bright Angel beckoning them aloft, or the Child asleep, with soft dreams visible through her transparent purity." At last, they choose to sleep next to the marble effigy of such a child, assured that they will "always be together."[18]

Margaret: A Tale of the Real and the Ideal, Blight and Bloom (1845) by Sylvester Judd (1813–1853), a Unitarian minister and the only Transcendental novelist, tells a similar story. Judd described this romance as "a New England book . . . designed to embody the features and improve the character of our own favored region" by promoting "liberal" or "pure" Christianity while preserving "some reminiscences of the age of our immediate fathers . . . a period of which we have no enduring monuments, and one the traces of which are fast evanescing." Believing that "Calvinism has [run] its 'Course of Time,'" he intended his book as a substitute for the "orthodoxy" of Bunyan's *Pilgrim's Progress*. Its protagonists, a young man and woman, Evelyn and Margaret, establish a utopian community called Mons Christi, an earthly paradise where men of all nations meet. Mons Christi is meant to embody liberal religious principles, despite its landmark, a huge, centrally located cross. Like the cemetery, it fosters culture in many ways, with a tasteful display of marble statuary and sites named after plants. There are fountains and gardens, music rooms, observatories, halls of art, crops of rye and corn planted on adjacent land, statues of Peace and Truth, and marble muses, many of the amenities Dearborn had proposed for Mount Auburn—except the cross. Undoubtedly Judd drew inspiration from Mount Auburn, which he frequented while a Harvard divinity student from 1837 to 1840.[19]

Edgar Allen Poe (1809–1849) offers a more critical description in his tale "The Landscape Garden" or "The Domain of Arnheim" (1846). Ellison, Poe's fictional landscape gardener, chooses "a spot not far from a populous city" for his estate on "land of wonderful fertility and beauty, affording a panoramic prospect very little less in extent than that of Aetna, . . . surpassing the far-famed view from that mountain in all true elements of the picturesque." There, "the thought of nature still remained, but her character seemed to have undergone modification. . . . Not a dead branch—not a withered leaf—not a stray pebble—not a patch of brown earth was anywhere visible. . . . [I]t bewildered the eye." When Poe revisited Boston, the city of his birth, Mount Auburn's maintenance had yet to reach that level of perfection, although as the decades progressed, professionalizing superintendents aspired to that ideal. Describing Arnheim as an unnatural attempt to re-create a "Paradise" or Eden on a foundation of inheritance, Poe warns that "in the most enchanting of natural landscapes, there will always be found a defect or an excess—many excesses and defects. While the component parts may defy, individually, the highest skill of the artist, the arrangement of these parts will always be susceptible of improvement." Poe sees "geological disturbances . . . of form and color grouping" in the terrain "prognostic of *death*," as Arnheim's landscape matures and changes over time. Such messages had currency throughout the romantic era, but they struck a particular chord of recognition with those familiar with Mount Auburn. The highly controlled garden at Arnheim signifies an effort to transcend natural change and death, but continual attempts at "improvement" contain the seeds of destruction of "pure" Nature in Poe's fictional world, as indeed they did eventually in transformations of Mount Auburn's "rural" landscape.[20]

Only a few accounts contain truly negative opinions. The orthodox Congregational minister Nehemiah Adams (1806–1878) of Boston's Essex Street Church, later author of the sentimental "Agnes and the Key of Her Little Coffin," worried in 1834 that public enjoyment of Mount Auburn would encourage pantheism and obliterate the fear of death that theological conservatives were still trying to foster. The Reverend Adams wrote: "If it is possible by natural means to lose the dreadful associations of dissolution in the grave, a burial in some of the lovely places of Mount Auburn seems sure to assist it. All that meets the eye there above and around the grave is pure and beautiful." He decried the serene submission to death which the cemetery suggested, preferring the sterner Calvinistic conception of postmortem fate. He exhorted the orthodox to picture instead the moment when the graves give up their dead on Judgment Day. Adams did not foresee the purely recreational enjoyment that many would find at Mount Auburn, independent of spiritual meaning. The love of nature expressed itself in a secular way, despite the best efforts of ministers and cemetery guidebook writers.[21]

Indeed, guidebooks and pamphlets functioned as spiritual guides in addition to pointing out sites of interest and often contained more romantic prose and poetry than descriptions of the landscape. *The Picturesque Pocket Companion and Visitor's Guide through Mount Auburn* (1839), the first one intended for the public, included an essay by the Reverend John Pierpont, "The Grave and the Tomb," advocating earthen burial, as well as Hawthorne's "Lily's Quest" and sentimental poems by William Cullen Bryant, Mrs. Felicia Dorothea Hemans, Charles Sprague, and others. The editor interspersed additional verse with engravings of over fifty monuments and tombs, asking: "Will [the musing moralists of future generations] not think how once, with the first flush of spring's verdure, and how again in the summer's sultry hours, the denizens of the city's populous streets *here* at least could wrap themselves so in solitude and gloom? How *here*, even those to whom trial and toil had made the world a weariness for the time, might learn from the depths of nature in intervals of solemn but refreshing meditation to look forth with complacency and renew themselves as they looked through the tree-tops of the mountain-summit on many a glorious vision."[22]

If the guidebook aided use of the cemetery for spiritual retreat and philosophical recreation, Nathaniel Dearborn (1786–1852), a woodcut engraver and publisher, had the same intent in issuing *Dearborn's Guide through Mount Auburn . . . for the Benefit of Strangers*, a compact fifty-page booklet published annually through the 1850s and 1860s and sold for twenty cents. It contained a map, over sixty engravings, and a good deal of moral philosophy and verse. *Dearborn's Guide* urged wisdom, diligence, work, moderation, humility, stewardship of wealth, and other civic virtues while expressing melancholy personal sentiments transcribed from some of the monuments, many of them with practical, hortatory messages reminiscent of *Poor Richard's* aphorisms. (Figs. 11.8, 11.9.) For instance, when the visitor reached the monument to Robert Gould Shaw Sr., he read:

Be wise to-day, 'tis madness to defer:
Next day the fatal precedent will plead;
Thus on, till wisdom is push'd out of life
Procrastination is the thief of time;
Year after year it steals, till all are fled,
And to the mercies of a moment leaves
The vast concerns of an eternal scene.

A verse next to the view of Richard Haughton's monument offered advice for the visitor harried by the pace of urban life:

We censure Nature for a span too short;
That span too short, we tax as tedious too;
Torture invention, all expedients tire,
To lash the lingering moments into speed,
And whirl us (happy riddance) from ourself.

A similar truism accompanied the illustration of S. P. Allen's lot:

At thirty, man suspects himself a fool;
Knows it at forty, and reforms his plan;
At fifty, chides his infamous delay,
Pushes his prudent purpose to resolve;
In all the magnanimity of thought
Resolves and re-solves; then dies the same.

Although Nathaniel Dearborn published independently of the corporation, the trustees made sure that the gate-

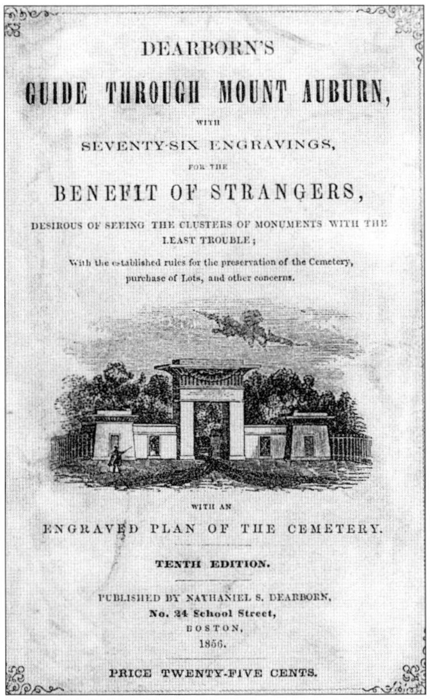

Fig. 11.8. Cover of (Nathaniel) *Dearborn's Guide*, 1856. MAC.

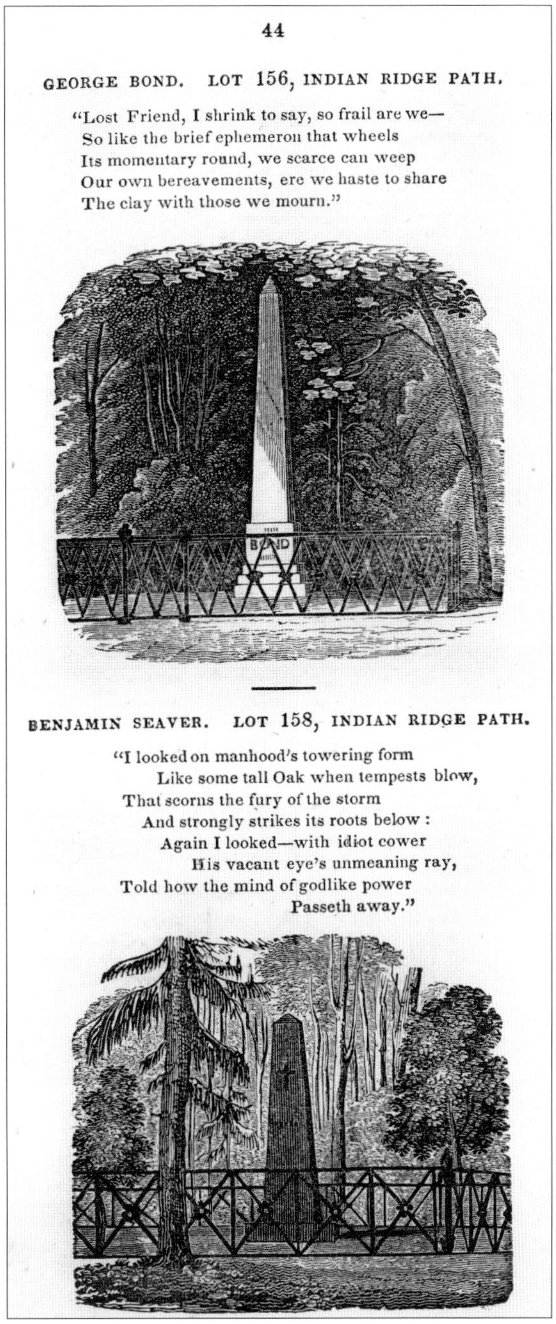

44

GEORGE BOND. LOT 156, INDIAN RIDGE PATH.

"Lost Friend, I shrink to say, so frail are we—
So like the brief ephemeron that wheels
Its momentary round, we scarce can weep
Our own bereavements, ere we haste to share
The clay with those we mourn."

BENJAMIN SEAVER. LOT 158, INDIAN RIDGE PATH.

"I looked on manhood's towering form
Like some tall Oak when tempests blow,
That scorns the fury of the storm
And strongly strikes its roots below:
Again I looked—with idiot cower
His vacant eye's unmeaning ray,
Told how the mind of godlike power
Passeth away."

Fig. 11.9. Illustrations and verse in *Dearborn's Guide*, 1856. MAC.

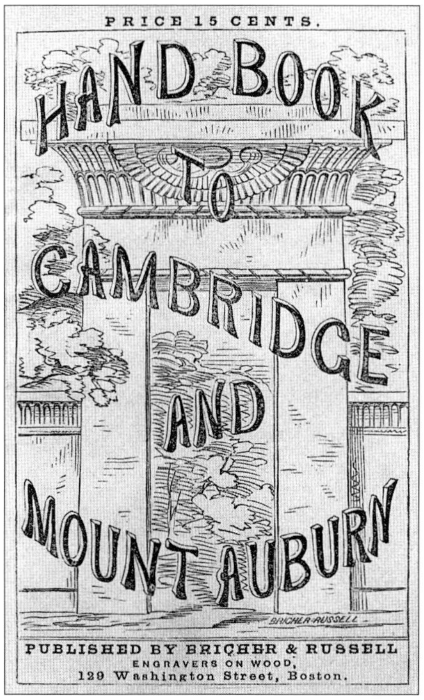

Fig. 11.10. Cover of the fourth edition of Levi Merriam Stevens's *Handbook for Passengers over the Cambridge Railroad* (1860).

keeper kept on hand a supply of these guides with their maps and their catalogues of proprietors.[23]

Levi Merriam Stevens claimed that his competing *Guide through Mount Auburn: A Handbook for Passengers over the Cambridge Railroad* aimed "not to describe Mount Auburn as any one thinks it should be, but to lead the visitor through the most interesting portions of the Cemetery, to call attention to everything on the route worthy of observation, and thus enable him to view Mount Auburn as it is—as Nature, Art and Affection have made it." His seventy-five-page guide, first published in 1856 and updated into the 1880s, contained engraved illustrations and detailed descriptions of major monuments, as well as selected epitaphs and funerary verse that emphasized Mount Auburn's moralistic functions. (Fig. 11.10.)

Echoing Buckingham, Stevens asked, "To what better place can we go to cool the burning brow of ambition, or to relieve the swelling heart of disappointment? We can find no better spot for the rambles of curiosity, health, or pleasure; none sweeter for the whispers of affection among the living." He urged his contemporaries to visit the cemetery to "renew our failing resolutions for the dark and boundless future."[24]

The era's popular new illustrated weekly newspapers, which enjoyed a wide national circulation, promoted Mount Auburn as a major attraction to be visited and touted its influence in inspiring the founding of similar cemeteries in other large cities. *Gleason's Pictorial Drawing-Room Companion*, published in Boston in large format and circulated nationally, also offered in decorative semiannual bound volumes for parlor display, devoted two large pages to Mount Auburn in 1853 with a woodcut engraving.[25] (Fig. 11.11.) Views of Mount Auburn appeared in various European pictorial compendia of the sights of America and Europe, attracting more visitors from abroad. One German illustrator, Verlager, even composed a fanciful view of the landscape, a pastiche of real and nonexistent monuments as imagined along the banks of Forest Pond, just as fictional as any Hawthorne romance yet equally capturing the intended spirit of place. Through multiple editions from the 1830s into the 1860s, that book sparked the imaginations of far more armchair travelers than any of the locally circulated guidebooks. It also places Mount Auburn among "the most noteworthy in Nature and Art in the Whole World."[26]

Wilson Flagg's *Mount Auburn: Its Scenes, Its Beauties, and Its Lessons* (1861) praised "the moral influence of graves" in a picturesque setting. Flagg believed that visitors benefited "from scenes that tend to conquer an excess of frivolity, or to moderate that entire devotion to mammon which, like intemperance and vice, has ruined many a noble heart." The visitor was "not to be saddened, but to be sobered, to think more earnestly of the higher purposes of life, of its transient duration, and of the importance of neglecting no duty of religion, charity, or benevolence." At Mount Auburn, one would

104 GLEASON'S PICTORIAL DRAWING-ROOM COMPANION.

MOUNT AUBURN.

Herewith we present an accurate view of the entrance of this "city of silence." The style of architecture is Egyptian, and is very beautiful in effect. It is constructed of granite, and most substantially built, to defy the ravages of time, and bears this inscription:—"*Then shall the dust return to the earth as it was, and the spirit shall return unto God who gave it.*" The porter's lodge and the office of the superintendent flank the lofty portal on either side, as seen in the picture. Ever since the completion of Mount Auburn, it has been a favorite resort of the thoughtful, and as a place where to lay the mortal remains of dear and loved ones. It was consecrated as a place of burial September 24th, 1831, since which it has been vastly beautified and improved for its legitimate purpose. It possesses peculiar advantages for a cemetery, and is diversified in its surface and beautified by a most extraordinary variety of foliage, wild flowers, and rare exotics. It has been the pattern followed by nearly every city in the United States, and has the honor of being the first of the character ever completed in the country. We give likewise in the present series a view of the Gothic Chapel, erected within the grounds, on Central Avenue. It is a very picturesque building, composed of granite, 66 feet by 40 in dimensions, being surrounded by octagonal buttresses and pinnacles. Here those persons who so desire it may perform the last religious services over the dead, and the chapel also forms an appropriate place for the reception of such statues, busts, and the like, as would be soiled by exposure to the weather. In this series is also exhibited a view of Forest Pond, and the tombs and monuments on its banks. It is on the shore of this simple little lake that the last resting-place of Joseph Story (Judge) rises its simple pyramidal form. Probably this is one of the most beautiful localities in the entire grounds. On the opposite page may also be found the well-known Bowditch Statue, of

ENTRANCE TO THE CEMETERY AT MOUNT AUBURN.

some years since by Dr. Bigelow of this city: "The manner in which we dispose of the remains of our deceased friends, is a subject which has begun, of late, to occupy a large share of the public attention. It involves, not only considerations which belong to the public convenience, but includes also the gratification of individual taste and the consolation of private sorrow. Although, in a strictly philosophical view, this subject possesses but little importance, except in relation to the convenience of survivors, yet so closely are our sympathies enlisted with it, and so inseparably do we connect the feelings of the living with the condition of the dead, that it is in vain that we attempt to divest ourselves of its influence. It is incumbent upon us, therefore, to analyze, as far

fall asunder almost as soon as life has ceased. The materials of which animals and vegetables are composed, have natural laws and irresistible affinities, which are suspended during the period of life, but which must be obeyed the moment that life is extinct. These continue to operate until the fabric is reduced to a condition in nowise different from that of the soil on which it has once trodden. In certain cases art may modify, and accident may retard the approaches of disorganization, but the exceptions thus produced are too few and imperfect to invalidate the certainty of the general law. If we take a comprehensive survey of the progress and mutations of animal and vegetable life, we shall perceive that this necessity of individual destruction is the basis of general safety. The elements which have once moved and circulated in living frames, do not become extinct nor useless after death;—they offer themselves as the materials from which other living frames are to be constructed. What has once possessed life is most assimilated to the living character, and most ready to partake of life again. The plant which springs from the earth, after attaining its growth and perpetuating its species, falls to the ground, undergoes decomposition, and contributes its remains to the nourishment of plants around it. The myriads of animals which range the woods or inhabit the air, at length die upon the surface of the earth, and if not devoured by other animals, prepare for vegetation the place which receives their remains. Were it not for this law of nature, the soil would be soon exhausted, the earth's surface would become a barren waste, and the whole race of organized beings, for want of sustenance, would become extinct. Man alone, the master of the creation, does not willingly stoop to become a participator in the routine of nature. In every age he has manifested a disposition to exempt himself, and to rescue his fellow, from the common fate of living beings. Although he is

Fig. 11.11. "Mount Auburn," *Gleason's Pictorial Drawing-Room Companion* 5 (Aug. 13, 1853). BMGL and MAC.

"read lessons which heaven, through nature, conveys to us in many a pleasing emblem of light and beauty. The winds represent the vicissitudes of life; but they inculcate the lesson that there is no adversity that is not followed by the tranquility of a better day. The flowers bud and bloom, and, in their vernal loveliness, represent the morning of our days and the spring-time of our life; but they perish like our own corporeal frames, to indicate by their revival that new life, of which death is but the celestial dawning. The trees that spread their branches and extend their benevolent shade over the graves . . . are a manifestation of that unseen power that has assembled the departed spirits under his providential care."[27]

Flagg, like Mount Auburn's founders, knew that sensitivity to the spiritual messages of the cemetery did not permeate all levels of society. He judged, however, that "those who possess an ordinary amount of cultivation" would benefit from the "melancholy pleasure" of meditating among the tombs. Restating the views of eighteenth-century romantics from England and the Continent, Flagg deemed "agreeable" the emotion of melancholy "when gently excited" by an elegaic landscape. For him and the like-minded, "contemplation of graves of our fellow beings produces a pensive state of mind that overcomes our natural horror of death, especially when associated with certain fanciful images emblematical of peace and immortality." At Mount Auburn, "the mind is enabled to expand its thoughts further into infinity." By implication, it would not stir such intellectualized emotions in the common man. Flagg lauded Mount Auburn's appeal to a genteel elite interested in literature and philosophy and in seeking spiritual exercise. The selected readings presented along with his own essays reveal his opinions on subjects such as the moral influence of cemeteries, epitaphs, and symbols; humility in architecture; appropriate funerary sculpture; and the use of varied plants in the landscape. He included accounts of ancient funerary practices and descriptions of Old World burial places. He reprinted Bernardin de Saint-Pierre's essay "The Pleasure of Tombs," inspired by Rousseau's burial in the picturesque gardens at Ermenonville, which in turn inspired Père Lachaise and, eventually, Mount Auburn. He excerpted passages from *Solitude Considered* by Johann Georg von Zimmerman, an eighteenth-century Swiss physician who praised the pleasures of mourning in "the salutary shades of the country." Flagg seasoned the ensemble with plenty of sentimental verse, leaving Nathaniel Dearborn's guidebooks and Truman H. Safford's weekly *Mount Auburn Memorial* to give the details.[28]

Safford, the gatekeeper, and his son DeForest enjoyed corporate support from Mount Auburn for their eight-page newspaper, edited and published weekly in Cambridgeport. In the first issue, in June 1859, the editors stated their purpose, "to open a medium of communication for [elegiac] subjects and embody the history of the place" and to present "matters of historical interest capable of awakening all the finer sensibilities of our nature and of quickening the ties of love and affection"—lofty ambitions. One letter to the editors opined, "There is more literary ability among the proprietors of Mount Auburn than was ever engaged in any literary enterprise in the world." If only they would submit prose and poetry, the new journal would prosper. Another predicted that the paper would "call attention to the condition of old neglected places of interment and aid in the good work Mount Auburn had already done . . . of renovating the burying-places of the whole country."[29]

The Saffords sold the paper at the cemetery, the Bowdoin Square railway station in Boston, the Cambridge Post Office, and the publisher's office; but it appealed primarily to cemetery proprietors. They quoted "a gentleman of taste and culture" who called the paper "*unique*, the only one in the world so far as we know, which is devoted to these chronicles of the departed, in the spirit which Scott's 'Old Mortality' would have deemed congenial in its reverent carefulness." The public was less receptive. The Saffords acknowledged skepticism overheard on the streetcar: "Isn't it rather a gloomy sort of sheet?" The editors feared that "many are at first disinclined to the reading of our paper; they say it treads mostly upon a subject the most gloomy . . . Death." But they countered, "surely no person can complain . . . if his mind is rightly directed to those things which improve and elevate."[30] Although melancholy subjects were enjoying their heyday in the 1850s, the Saffords complained, "In this jostling, whirling age of change and novelty, the greatest favor is bestowed upon any thing which presents a garish, over-showy exterior." Their paper lasted nearly two years, until the elder Safford's death. His son wished to carry on but could not.[31]

Visitors' Accounts

From the start, tourists' access to Mount Auburn and their behavior there became major bones of contention leading to the split between proprietors and Horticulturists. Caroline Howard Gilman (1794–1888), one of the popular women writers of the 1830s, a native New Englander visiting from Charleston with her Unitarian minister husband, noted in 1838, "The city does indeed throng to the spot so sacred . . . leaving the dusty world behind. Daily, hourly, a line of carriages stands at its lofty gate, and countless guests pause at the solemn inscription . . . and then enter to meditate among the unrivalled varieties of Mount Auburn."[32] Gilman neglected to note that not all visitors appreciated its genteel purposes; they came with less than pious intentions, seeking recreation rather than reverence. The young heard of the "magic wilderness" and "its beautiful and almost endless variety." As one writer described it, "You are not only lost in astonishment at what you see, but are in danger of losing yourself among its mazes, through which you might wander for hours without finding escape." As America's first designed fantasy landscape, Mount Auburn appealed to a sense of mystical excitement and even adventure, so much a part of the imagery of romanticism.[33]

Tourists flocked there, having heard that a walk or drive through the cemetery was "one of the indispensables to a stranger sojourning in or near Boston, and few places present, within an equal space, either to citizens or strangers, a more varied combination of elements to attract attention and awaken thought." They heard that "neither care nor expense has been spared in the efforts to enhance its great natural advantages." The *American Cyclopaedia of Useful Knowledge* (1835) called it "justly celebrated as the most interesting object of the kind in our country"—not unlike later museums or parks in its appeal—and noted that those Bostonians with the spirit of urban boosterism were proud that the cemetery was "a becoming appendage, and interesting ornament of the town."[34] Three years after Mount Auburn's founding, the English visitor Edward S. Abdy observed that "parties of pleasure come hither from the city in great numbers every day. No less than six hundred visitors had been there on one day the preceding week." Calling it the "daughter" of Père Lachaise, Abdy predicted that when "the novelty . . . is worn off" and it accumulated more monuments, "a visit to this hallowed spot will call up reflections and associations more impressive and permanent."[35]

Bostonians were eager to present Mount Auburn as their major showplace, designed to display regional accomplishments and taste. The author of Mount Auburn's first guidebook wondered in 1839, "What object in or near Boston will be equally attractive?" As early as the summer of 1833, a national conference of physicians meeting in Boston visited en masse. Samuel Swett took the Cuban horticulturist Ramon de la Sagra there, pointing with pride to his family monument "as if he were showing off a vacation house."[36] Visitors who made certain to see the place about which they had read so much proved the best publicists for America's first "rural" cemetery, offering accolades in numerous travel accounts, a major literary genre at the time. The Swedish naturalist Carl David Arfwedson (1806–1881), like so many others, paraphrased Keats in writing that "a glance at this beautiful cemetery almost excites a wish to die."[37] The Reverend Enoch Cobb Wines (1806–1879), noted New York prison reformer, commended the scenic drive past "the country seats of opulent citizens" as well as into the cemetery itself, "which certainly no spot in America can match, and which probably few places can equal in any part of the world." Wines concluded after inspecting the first monuments, "Nowhere else can the evidence be met with of such invariably pure taste in so large a number of persons." Having toured the "primeval forests" and ascended the "quite lofty mountain," he came away with the impression "that it was expressly designed by the Creator for its present use."[38] One Boston newspaper crowed, "Every visitor goes to Mount Auburn as a matter of course."[39]

Laudatory accounts poured in. The British phrenologist George Combe (1788–1858), a close friend of Boston's educational reformer Horace Mann, found edification at the tombs of notables, where "lessons of wisdom and benevolence may for ages be learned." He appreciated the central location of the sarcophagus of the phrenologist Spurzheim and predicted that "many a pilgrim from distant lands will preserve as a precious memorial, a flower from the sod which covers what was mortal of these saints in the calendar of a coming age," clearly not realizing that picking flowers as souvenirs was subject to a fine.[40] The journalist-poet John Ross Dix exclaimed after a visit in 1845, "There is life, joyous life beneath, around, and above us . . . every thing tells of life."[41] Sir Charles Lyell (1797–1875), Joseph Story's friend and a noted British geologist, visited in 1842 and again in 1849, praising it highly in his travel account.[42] The sixteen-year-old Emily Dickinson (1830–1886) made sure to see Mount Auburn as well as the Bunker Hill Monument, the Chinese Museum, two concerts, and a horticultural exhibition when she came to Boston in 1846, one of the few times in her life that she ventured from her home in Amherst. Of Mount Auburn, the young poet wrote that it seemed "as if Nature had formed the spot with a distinct idea in view of its being a resting place for her children, where wearied & disappointed they might stretch themselves beneath the spreading cypress & close their eyes calmly as to a nights repose or flowers at set of sun." She judged that literary descriptions of it did not do it justice.[43] Harvard president Edward Everett personally escourted Lady Emmeline Wortley, Queen Victoria's maid of honor, on a ride through Mount Auburn when she visited in 1849, and she described it favorably in her travel narrative.[44]

Arozina Perkins, a twenty-two-year-old New Haven teacher, toured Mount Auburn in 1849 for a day en route from visiting her widowed mother in Marshfield, south of the city. After a morning's stroll on the Boston Common, a climb to the State House dome (then the sole panoramic viewpoint other than Mount Auburn's highest hill), and stops at Faneuil Hall and the "Museum," she and her brothers drove to Mount Auburn "and rambled about." She declared, "I could have spent days there, and still have found something new . . . to admire." The cemetery appealed to her melancholy temperament, shaped by her father's death, the scattering of eleven siblings across the country, never to be seen again, and her separation from her childhood home in Johnson, Vermont. To the young woman suffering the personal upheavals of mobility, Mount Auburn promised the reunion of loved ones in the hereafter, even if not in a family plot there.[45]

The young English merchant Henry Arthur Bright (1830–1884), a friend of Hawthorne's, visited Mount Auburn with Longfellow in 1852 and observed, "Cemeteries here are all the 'rage'; people lounge in them, and use them (as their tastes are inclined) for walking, making love, weeping, sentimentalizing, and every thing in short." An English clergyman agreed, "It may be said that the pleasure of the people of Boston consists of going to the grave." He praised Mount Auburn: "There cannot be better scope for English landscape-gardening than it supplies." One local writer admitted that "quiet, home-keeping citizens, even in Cambridge, may not be aware of the great number of persons who daily visit Mount Auburn."[46]

Andrew Jackson Downing (1815–1852), the noted commentator on picturesque landscape design who often visited Mount Auburn and other cemeteries copied after its example, wrote in *The Horticulturist* in 1849 that the cemetery "idea took the public mind by storm. Travelers made pilgrimages to the Athens of New England solely to see the realization of their long cherished dream of a resting place for the dead."[47] It was precisely the resonance of design elements drawn from eighteenth-century English gardens reinterpreted for American culture and made manifest at Mount Auburn that led to the cemetery's great popularity and its seminal place in inspiring a legacy of landscape design at similar cemeteries in other cities and towns over the next decades. (See Appendix II for other "rural" or "garden" cemeteries fashioned after Mount Auburn's example.)

Mount Auburn's international recognition continued to grow. Notables made Mount Auburn as essential a stop as the Erie Canal or Niagara Falls on their grand tours of the United States. Isabella Lucy Bird (1831–1904), the inveterate British traveler and first woman in the Royal Geographic Society, delighted in the picturesque cemetery "far removed from the din of cities," where "the neglectfulness and dreariness of the outer aspect of the graves are completely done away with and the dead lie peacefully under ground carpeted with flowers and shaded by trees."[48] Worthies from Charles Dickens to Emperor Dom Pedro of Brazil praised the cemetery. In October 1860, trustees Uriel Crocker and Charles Nazro escorted the eldest son of Queen Victoria, the nineteen-year-old Prince of Wales, calling himself simply Lord Renfrew in deference to his

American hosts, followed by a throng who watched him plant in front of the chapel a purple Eureopean beech and a *Virgilia lutea*, a pyramidal tree drooping like the laburnum or golden chain tree. National newspapers reported that Napoleon III "gave the palm [his official award] to Mount Auburn for its natural beauty of position" and design.[49]

Bostonians savored such publicity especially because visitors' opinions echoed the rationales and ideas expressed by the cemetery's founders. Praise came from the English writer Harriet Martineau (1802–1876), a British Unitarian who received a personal tour from Joseph Story in August 1837. He had made her promise that she would not visit Mount Auburn before he could take her there. She judged it distinctly American, indicative of New England's dominance in the national culture. "As might have been predicted," wrote Martineau, "one of the first directions in which the Americans have indulged their taste and indicated their refinement is in the preparation and care of their burial places." She attributed this tendency to "the pilgrim origin of the New-England population, whose fathers seemed to think that they lived only in order to die." Thoughts of death filled "a large space in the people's mind," she explained. Despite the centrality of death in antebellum culture, Martineau saw evidence of a nascent trend in the national mentality, later labeled the "denial of death." She wrote: "A visitor from a strange planet, ignorant of mortality, would take this place to be the sanctum of creation. Every step teems with the promise of life. Beauty is about to spring out of the ashes, and life out of dust; Humanity seems to be waiting, with acclamations ready on its lips, for the new birth. That there has been any past is little more than a matter of inference." The cemetery founders seemed to have denied the past, she thought, through their emphasis on perseverance and Nature's renewal.[50]

Martineau nevertheless moderated her criticisms of American culture because she considered Mount Auburn "the most beautiful cemetery in the world," with an "air of finish and taste, especially in contrast to Père Lachaise." It epitomized hope and a softened melancholy in contrast to the French cemetery, where she perceived "no light from the future shining over the place. In Mount Auburn, on the contrary, there is nothing else." Boston's cemetery appealed "to us, in whom education, reason, the prophecies of natural religion, and the promises of the gospel united their influence to generate a perfect belief in a life beyond the grave," although she knew that the place must appear differently to the doubtful, "a mazy paradise, where every forest tree of the western continent grows and every bird to which the climate is congenial builds its nest." At Mount Auburn, in short, she found metaphors for travel and for life, lessons of transience with which she, appropriately, ended her two-volume narrative.[51]

The Question of Admissions

The question of who could come indiscriminately into Mount Auburn became "a delicate one." The trustees concluded that Mount Auburn, though "strictly a private institution," might "in some senses be considered a public one." Since it was "the pioneer of ornamental cemeteries—the delight and pride of our citizens and the admiration of strangers," they felt a responsibility to make the place more accessible, for "its fame extends wherever Boston is known," and it was repeatedly being copied in other cities. They deemed it only "natural that all strangers visiting this part of the country should be desirous of seeing it" and were determined "to grant every facility for the gratification of this desire and also for the accommodation of resident non-proprietors."[52]

Mount Auburn's popularity among many of those non-proprietors who arrived in carriages seeking admission led to the breakdown of the ticket system Joseph Story had established under pressure from lot holders to limit access to the grounds. (Fig. 11.12.) Before 1853, the secretary and nine trustees were more willing to issue tickets to "strangers" than to local residents who did not own lots. Since a fringe benefit of buying a lot was receipt of an unrestricted ticket for a carriage-load of family and guests, restricting admissions for non-proprietors encouraged lot sales, at least initially. Mount Auburn's lot prices had greatly increased, however, and it faced competition from other new "rural" cemeteries in the area. Indeed, some proprietors sold their Mount Auburn lots and purchased others that were less expensive and closer to home at Salem's Harmony Grove (1840), Roxbury's Forest Hills (1848), Concord's Sleepy Hollow (1855), and many other rural cemeteries proliferating in the metropolitan region. This competition helped to liberalize Mount Auburn's admission policy as the trustees tried to keep the place the focus of public attention.

The younger trustees relaxed restrictions to admit any visitor who appeared respectable. In 1853, secretary Henry M. Parker began issuing more than one ticket per lot, reissuing "lost" tickets, giving tickets to holders of small lots with no vote as proprietors, and even granting tickets to local non-proprietors. The trustees granted Sunday tickets to those with relatives buried in public lots and gave three to the Scots Charitable Society, owner of a large burial plot for members. They let the gatekeeper admit anyone claiming to be a proprietor or family member even without a ticket, although he and the superintendent could ask for identification and exercised the power to exclude anyone who gave a false name. The Englishwoman Isabella Lucy Bird was impressed on her 1854 visit that being an obvious stranger "produced a magic effect." The gatekeeper readily admitted her carriage and "refused a gratuity." Others criticized his authoritarian attitude; one visitor complained that he slammed the gate with "offensive alacrity." The trustees admitted that he was "an excitable person and too apt perhaps to take offense unnecessarily." Eventually, they dismissed him for taking money thrown by some leaving the grounds to supplement his $450 annual income and demanded return of the estimated $10 in tips he had surreptitiously collected annually.[53]

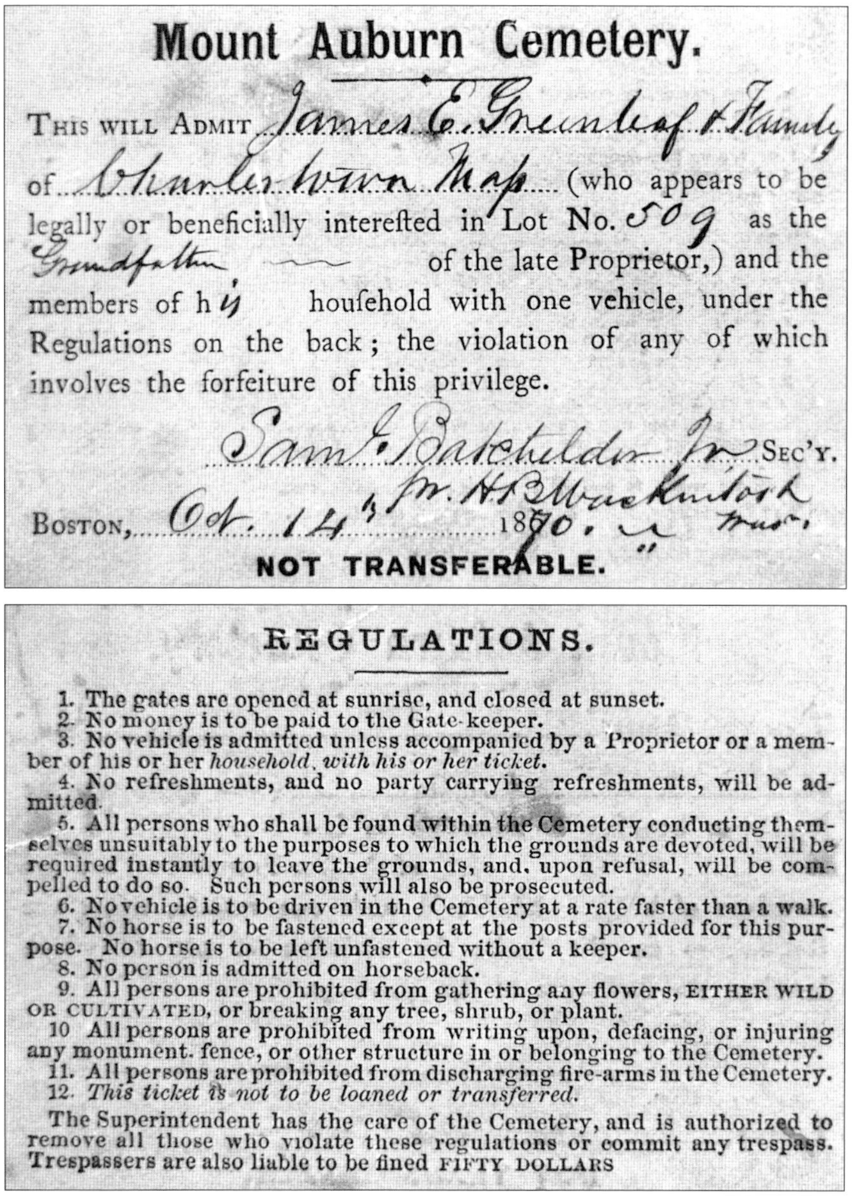
Mount Auburn Cemetery.

THIS WILL ADMIT James E. Greenleaf & Family of Charlestown Mass (who appears to be legally or beneficially interefted in Lot No. 509 as the Grandfather of the late Proprietor,) and the members of his houfehold with one vehicle, under the Regulations on the back; the violation of any of which involves the forfeiture of this privilege.

Sam'l Batchelder Jr SEC'Y.

BOSTON, Oct. 14 1870.

NOT TRANSFERABLE.

REGULATIONS.

1. The gates are opened at sunrise, and closed at sunset.
2. No money is to be paid to the Gate-keeper.
3. No vehicle is admitted unless accompanied by a Proprietor or a member of his or her *household, with his or her ticket.*
4. No refreshments, and no party carrying refreshments, will be admitted.
5. All persons who shall be found within the Cemetery conducting themselves unsuitably to the purposes to which the grounds are devoted, will be required instantly to leave the grounds, and, upon refusal, will be compelled to do so. Such persons will also be prosecuted.
6. No vehicle is to be driven in the Cemetery at a rate faster than a walk.
7. No horse is to be fastened except at the posts provided for this purpose. No horse is to be left unfastened without a keeper.
8. No person is admitted on horseback.
9. All persons are prohibited from gathering any flowers, EITHER WILD OR CULTIVATED, or breaking any tree, shrub, or plant.
10. All persons are prohibited from writing upon, defacing, or injuring any monument, fence, or other structure in or belonging to the Cemetery.
11. All persons are prohibited from discharging fire-arms in the Cemetery.
12. *This ticket is not to be loaned or transferred.*

The Superintendent has the care of the Cemetery, and is authorized to remove all those who violate these regulations or commit any trespass. Trespassers are also liable to be fined FIFTY DOLLARS

Fig. 11.12. Proprietor's ticket, with regulations printed on the back, for entrance by carriage to Mount Auburn, ca. 1860–1870. MAC

What the trustees sought was only "a mild and reasonable enforcement of the rules," not to turn Mount Auburn into "a pleasure drive for all pleasure seekers who may chance to pass that way," perhaps en route to the Fresh Pond tavern. They gave the new gatekeeper discretion to "prevent abuses which might otherwise necessarily creep in." But when he reported "surreptitious use of tickets by many residents of the area who were not proprietors," they issued a new ticket in limited numbers, including entrance by carriage to anyone requesting it, which was deemed "quite sufficient to make the grounds as public as can reasonably be required." Still, as visitors' complaints continued in 1859, the trustees again instructed the gatekeeper "to admit persons of respectable appearance and demeanor to ride into the Cemetery without tickets or permits until further orders." With over three thousand proprietors holding tickets and a constant stream of visitors, weekend traffic was heavy. Complaints arose of fast driving and damage to the grounds, especially by carriages leaving funerals. Public hackney coaches, bringing guests from hotels, were the greatest offenders. Trustees tried to ban hired hacks, but that limited access for out-of-towners. Speeders were barred from future entry, and hotels giving tickets to banned drivers lost ticket privileges for their guests.[54]

The trustees countered criticisms of exclusivity that drove the democratically minded away, changing the term "tickets" to "cards of admission" in 1861.[55] They issued these to major hotels bearing the name of the party to be admitted for one-time use and to be surrendered at the gate. Although the trustees welcomed out-of-town visitors, they were not ready for mass tourism, chara-bancs, omnibuses, and excursion wagons, and rejected trustee James Cheever's suggestion that carriages be provided for "strangers" who needed them to see the grounds along with requests from enterprising individu-als to operate carriages for hire.[56]

Improvements in public transit brought visitors in greater numbers. Initially, hourly runs by the Cambridge Stage Company from Boston to Harvard made Mount Auburn, a mile and a half to the west, accessible to any who would walk the short distance, accounting for the throngs that so annoyed proprietors. In 1834 the first large-capacity horse-drawn omnibuses went into service in Cambridge. By 1838 several regular lines offered hourly runs between Harvard and the cemetery gate. The route ending at the cemetery was so popular that in 1838 the town of Cambridge renamed the old road Mount Auburn Street, and Watertown followed suit.[57]

The station built in 1847 at Mount Auburn's north-west corner provided service by the Fitchburg Railroad and the Cambridge Branch Railroad to and from points west. The Cambridge Horse Railroad, the first in New England, extended its service in 1856 from Boston's Bowdoin Square through Cambridge to Mount Auburn's gate, making it the first central

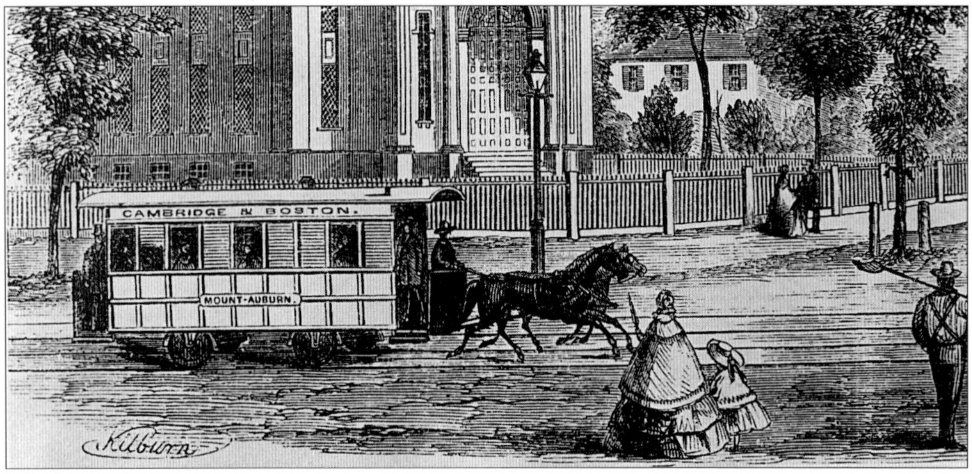

Fig. 11.13. Cambridge & Boston horse-drawn railway car headed from downtown Boston to the Mount Auburn terminus. Engraving by Kilburn, ca. 1860. BMGL.

Fig. 11.14. Cambridge & Boston horse-drawn railway car headed from downtown Boston to the Mount Auburn terminus. Engraving by John Andrew for *Ballou's Pictorial*, 1856. BMGL.

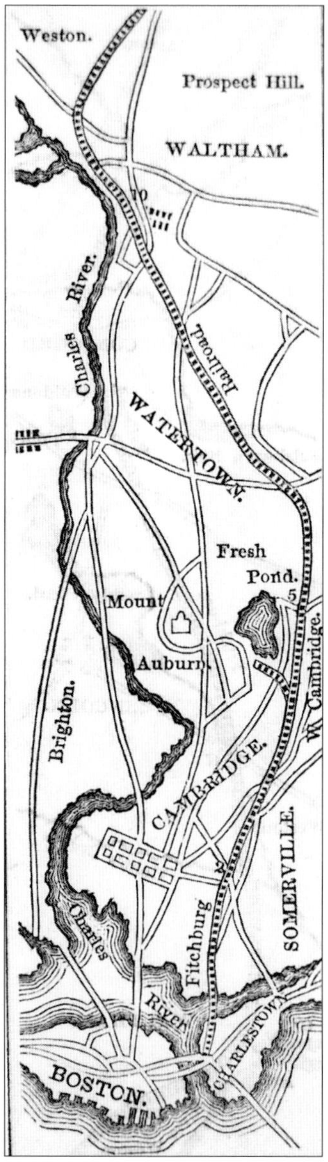

Fig. 11.15. Map of the Fitchburg railway line with a sidetrack to Mount Auburn. From the *Boston Almanac*, 1847. BMGL.

line in the metropolitan network and further increasing public access. (Figs. 11.13, 11.14.) Its cars made 175 trips each way every day at fifteen-minute intervals until 11:30 PM. Wrought-iron rails assured a smooth ride along tree-lined Brattle Street past the Longfellow House. In 1863 another line brought visitors past Fresh Pond to Mount Auburn via Garden and Craigie streets. Jacob Bigelow, like many proprietors who did not own carriages, used the horse railroad. The low fare made frequent visits possible, unlike the cost of hiring a hack. The corporation supplied trustees with tickets for the new mass transit. Although trustee Martin Brimmer wanted to limit admittance to exclude the public who arrived on the horse railway, cooperation existed between the transit company and the cemetery. The company's three founders owned burial lots, and two became trustees. Perhaps that accounted for the higher fare to Mount Auburn than to other stops, about which proprietors complained. The company kept its stables near the cemetery, with room for thirty-five cars and 220 horses.[58]

With the increased availability of public transportation, trustees feared that "the grounds [would] be overrun by crowds of persons who [would] make [Mount Auburn] a resort for pleasure and amusement and thus disturb the sacred quiet of the place"; but they remained powerless to stop trains from making the cemetery a major stop, attracting as many passengers as the Fresh Pond Hotel, a popular day resort a few blocks to the north. (Fig. 11.15.) The trustees rejected the railroad's 1853 request that they open a gate at the station for "accommodation of the great concourse of visitors which it is anticipated will thus be brought to Mount Auburn." In 1856 Philip Hickborn and twenty-five proprietors delivered a petition arguing that the station agent could be entrusted with a key to ensure that only lot owners would use such a gate. The trustees persistently rejected the idea, which was raised every few years until the century's end.[59]

Policing and Amenities

Mount Auburn's trustees confronted another chronic problem as well: that of policing. After 1841 they assigned superintendent Rufus Howe record-keeping responsibilities and hired a watchman and a gatekeeper to oversee visitors' conduct and suppress nuisances and "improper practices," needing more help. The watchman was to prevent "various depredations of late committed upon the flowers and shrubs" and to regulate behavior of "large parties assembled within the grounds with refreshments and for purposes utterly incompatible with those to which the grounds are devoted."[60] Picnicking would not be tolerated. Rules banned gathering flowers; anyone possessing them would be deemed to have picked them and would be prosecuted accordingly. Flowers brought into the cemetery had to be registered with the gatekeeper. Other forms of damage were more serious. In 1846 one proprietor complained of injury to "furniture" on his lot. The trustees offered a $100 reward for capture of the offender, who was never apprehended. As soon as the tower was built, they had to repair injury to its woodwork from cutting and defacing—in other words, graffiti. The superintendent put a fence around the large oak in front of the chapel to deter whittling and carving, a predilection that habitually damaged trees on the city streets as well. The trustees offered a $20 reward for information that would convict anyone damaging plants or monuments or committing any other acts of "trespass" and had authority from the state to deem damage to plants or structures and firing of guns a misdemeanor subject to a fine ranging from $5 to $50.

Many complained of "unseemly noises" made by those "conducting themselves unsuitably to the purposes to which the grounds are devoted." Rowdiness outside proved just as bothersome; but gatekeeper Wyeth could not control it. The publication and posting of rules and regulations proved ineffective in curtailing "obnoxious and damaging" behavior. The watchman hired in 1841 to suppress nuisances was powerless. The gatekeeper and watchmen were to be the judges of behavior, authorized to throw offenders out; but they could not enforce that authority. Superintendent Daniel Winsor posted notices warning against walking across lots, hoping to "remedy the evil," but proprietors criticized the signs as "not suitable to the character of the place." Trustees Benjamin Gould and Charles P. Curtis finally looked into deputizing a cemetery police officer.[61] When Truman H. Safford of Watertown became gatekeeper, he was given increased authority to preserve the peace in the vicinity of the gate. Isaiah Bangs persuaded the city of Cambridge to make Safford a "special policemen" on cemetery payroll. In 1857 Cambridge and Watertown deputized superintendent Jonathan Mann and two of his workers. By 1861, deputized employees wore badges on "suitable occasions" such as the Fourth of July. Until official establishment of Decoration Day in 1868 by General John Logan, national commander of the Grand Army of the Republic, the largest crowds flocked to Mount Auburn on Independence Day, necessitating extra "officers or servants." Conventions also periodically visited en masse; in 1864 a hundred members from the Grand Lodge of Odd Fellows received permission to come in a group. By 1866 the corporation was employing a "police force" during the summer months to control the throngs of visitors.[62]

Although the cemetery was open to carriages from sunrise to sunset, many accounts reveal that some roamed about after hours. After all, the Cambridge Horse Railroad scheduled runs until 11:30 PM, and many others lived nearby. Even the *Mount Auburn Memorial*, edited by gatekeeper Safford with trustees' approval, lauded the glories of the cemetery in full moonlight in 1859: "The white gleam of the monuments contrasts vividly with the sombre shadows cast by the numerous trees" and "beams from the Queen of Night shimmered down upon the beauties of Consecration Dell, the forest trees in one spot twinkling through, and flecking with fairy light some old tree-trunk, and in another, streaming down to the very bottom in long lines of brightness." Another short story by Caroline F. Orne in the *Memorial* in 1860 told of a friend traversing the cemetery as a short-cut on the way home as "A Midnight Adventure"; but in that case, the protagonist had to climb the fence after the stroke of midnight.[63]

The question of providing amenities for those who came to the cemetery preoccupied the trustees, engendering debate. Newcomers drew help in finding their way from new cast-iron signs at the corners of all avenues and paths. Iron settees were placed in the grounds. Proprietors appreciated a well with pump on Spruce Avenue near Yarrow Path, installed so many could water their plants with buckets filled inside the grounds to keep their flower beds flourishing in summer months. Trustee Mace Tisdale, new in 1850, urged the building of a well or pump house inside the gate to provide pure, fresh drinking water and shaded seats for visitors. Although some older trustees opposed such an amenity "for the benefit of outsiders," they were outvoted, and the cemetery hired architect Theodore Voelckers to design an elaborate, octagonal wooden pavilion or gazebo. (Fig. 11.16.) It was constructed just to the left of Central Avenue inside the cemetery entrance in 1853 and was soon "embowered amidst a mass of green foliage." But some disliked the structure of carved gingerbread woodwork as "so gross a violation of good taste," especially so near the Egyptian gate and incongruent in style. The artist-architect Hammatt Billings (1818–1874) criticized it too as having "rather too much of the appearance of a garden summer house to be strictly in keeping with its position in the cemetery." Complaining that "the quiet of Mount Auburn is already too much disturbed by the avalanche of foot and railroad passengers which is daily discharged upon it," the *Evening Transcript* objected that the pump house would become a "lounging place and a nuisance." It remained until 1896, when it was moved to the southern gate at the rear of the grounds.[64]

In 1860 the trustees ordered a change in the interior of the Egyptian gateway to shelter visitors from sun and rain after a temporary awning over recesses inside proved unsightly as well as providing insufficient protection from the elements. (Fig. 11.17.) They paid $1,600 to J. B. Whitcher to enclose two recesses next to the lodges with

Fig. 11.16. Victorian pump house just inside the cemetery's front gate, designed in 1853 by architect Theodore Voelckers, designer of the "picturesque" public hall for the "new town" of Winchester, Massachusetts. Carte de visite photograph by G. K. or W. S. Warren, ca. 1865. MAC.

granite walls, roofs, and Egyptian columns facing into the cemetery, following Bigelow's design modifications. Despite Bigelow's opposition in 1861, privies or water closets were built near the gate for ladies and children. Superintendent Jonathan Mann urged the trustees to lease land across the road from the entrance for a "reception house" to provide "respectable quarters" for ladies waiting for escorts or trolleys. (Fig. 11.18.) In 1869 the architect Nathaniel J. Bradlee designed the building completed in 1871 on Wyeth estate land across Mount Auburn Street with space for the superintendent's office and for Charles F. Belcher to sell refreshments. The city of Cambridge then paved the street for fifty feet on either side of the gate with granite blocks, with the cemetery and the Cambridge Horse Railroad paying half the cost.[65]

Fig. 11.17. Sheltered recesses added to the south side of the Egyptian gate in 1861, built by J. B. Whitcher for the convenience of visitors. Photograph by Haskell, 1937. MAC.

One new sort of active but genteel recreation was allowed. As winter approached in 1859, the *Memorial* observed: "If the coming season is as favorable to the lovers of skating as past years have been, soon the quiet little lake will be covered with a graceful, gliding multitude of merry ladies and gentlemen. . . . It is a fortunate circumstance that Fashion has lately countenanced this amusement as one in which the feminine part of the community can take part." Use of ponds for the new sport apparently did not seem inharmonious with Mount Auburn's dignity or its funereal purposes, and the trustees felt no need to regulate it.[66] (Fig. 11.19.)

In 1861 they considered admitting individuals on horseback but realized that "a person riding in the saddle can very easily cross through the narrow paths or

Fig. 11.18. Reception house across Mount Auburn Street from the cemetery gate, built in 1871 by William Washburn and Son, designed by the firm of engineer and architect Nathaniel J. Bradlee (1829–1888). Courtesy Historic New England (formerly Society for the Preservation of New England Antiquities).

Fig. 11.19. The skating "rage," genteel recreation in Regent's Park, London, from a stereographic photograph, ca. 1860. American engravers delighted in depicting such crowded winter scenes on Jamaica Pond, across town from Mount Auburn in Brookline, and on other frozen water bodies around Boston. BMGL.

even over the lots," injuring monuments and plants. They noted, "There is a class of persons . . . by no means a small one, who can be made to respect the rights of their fellow citizens only by the enactment of a strict code of laws and the rigid enforcement." Recognizing that they could not grant "the privilege to one without to all," they followed their proven precedent—monetary controls. They already curtailed "indiscriminate" tomb building by charging a fee for the right. They applied the same principle by charging a "bonus" of $10 for a ticket to enter Mount Auburn on horseback, provided that the rider remain on avenues and proceed no faster than a walk.[67]

The Fervor Wanes

Edward Waldo Emerson (1844–1930), the youngest child of his famed author father, observed that for the generation of Yankees born at the turn of the nineteenth century, "life was still serious, amusement occasional and secondary; they still lived in the preserve of the unseen; they worshipped and went apart for solitary thoughts."[68] The purpose of Mount Auburn was compatible with that mentality, and the founders resented its frivolous use as a "pleasure ground" by those who did not share their aversion to misspent leisure. The next generation set aside these old values and adopted new concepts of culture and leisure that diminished the cemetery's importance as an agent for transmitting moral philosophy and a consensus view of history.

Andrew Jackson Downing (1815–1852) had cited "the rise and progress" of "rural" cemeteries" as "one of the most remarkable illustrations of the popular taste" in his era. Mount Auburn's founders, he believed, had chosen "a charming natural site, finely varied in surface . . . and admirably clothed by groups and masses of native forest trees" before "tastefully" laying out grounds to be "highly embellished." He noted that "no sooner was attention . . . roused to the charms of this place than the idea of rural cemeteries took the public mind by storm." By the 1840s there was "scarcely a city of note" that did not have its cemetery. Therefore, Downing asked, "if the road to Mount Auburn is now lined with coaches, continually carrying the inhabitants of Boston by the thousands and tens of thousands, is it not likely that such a garden, full of the most varied instruction, amusement, and recreation, would be ten times more visited?"[69] According to Downing, cemetery gatekeepers estimated that over 100,000 visitors came annually. "Judging from the crowds of people in carriages, and on foot," he remarked, "I think it is plain enough how much our citizens, of all classes, would enjoy public parks on a similar scale." Through the early 1850s, William Cullen Bryant, no longer the young poet from the Berkshires who had written "Thanatopsis" but a mature, urbane journalist, lent his support in editorials in the *New York Evening Post* to the idea that achieved approval from the state for the creation of Central Park.[70]

The art critic Clarence Cook, son of Zebedee Cook, who had been involved in the founding of both Mount Auburn and Green-Wood in Brooklyn, recognized the influence of "rural" cemeteries on creation of naturalistic public parks. He wrote in 1869: "These cemeteries . . . became famous over the whole country and thousands of people visited them annually. . . . [They were] among the chief attractions of the cities to which they belonged. No stranger visited . . . these cities for pleasure or observation who was not taken to the cemeteries, nor was it long before the smaller cities, and even towns and villages began to set aside land and to lay it out for pleasure-grounds," few of which existed before in urban areas, and none of them public or of great acreage. Cook recognized that people simply "were glad to get fresh air, and a sight of grass and trees and flowers with, now and then, a pretty piece of sculpture, to say nothing of the drive to all this beauty, and back again, without considering too deeply whether it might not be better to have it all without the graves and funeral processions." Because "these cemeteries were all the rage, and so deeply was the want felt which they supplied, and so truly beautiful were they in themselves, that it was not to be wondered at if people were slow to perceive that there was a certain incongruity between a graveyard and a place of recreation."[71]

Although the first monuments to the Civil War dead, like Mount Auburn's sphinx, the generic Union soldier in Cincinnati's Spring Grove, and the massive pyramid in Richmond's Holly-Wood, appeared in "rural" or "garden" cemeteries, public places became favored from the late 1870s on, sprouting monuments honoring all those who served, even on the homefront. But even after the completion of Martin Milmore's massive Soldiers' and Sailors' Monument on Boston Common in 1877 provided a venue for public patriotic celebrations, Mount Auburn attracted throngs on Decoration Day on May 30 with a temporary platform erected in front of the chapel for major speakers such as the Reverend Phillips Brooks of Trinity Church in 1879 and Edward Everett Hale in 1880. Throughout the North, as on similar Memorial Days in the former Confederacy, this was the occasion for strewing flowers on the graves of those who had fallen in the Civil War rather than for remembering the dead in general. (Fig. 11.20)

Fig. 11.20. Crowds of visitors' carriages at Mount Auburn on Decoration Day, ca. 1875. From a stereograph. BMGL.

After the war, the cultural climate nationally became much different from that which had inspired Mount Auburn's creation and development. Gone were the genteel tastes, romantic idealism, and Whiggish intent to fashion a usable republican past and ensure national stability through funerary forms borrowed from the heights of ancient civilizations. As the cultural historian Van Wyck Brooks remarked of the new era: "Other ways were coming; and other seasons . . . ; but the spring days of the young republic, with all their aspirations and resolves, the Virgilian days, the Homeric days, were passing with the poets who pressed them. . . . Last things were in order . . . . and all the Boston men could do,—or all they thought they could do,—was to bury the dead. Mount Auburn was becoming over-crowded."[72]

The popularity of garden cemeteries waned for visitors as the public parks movement spread from the 1860s on and cities created landscapes similar to Mount Auburn's but "without the graves"—truly public places in which to picnic and ride horses, open to anyone with a carriage, welcoming all for active recreation, within the bounds of proper behavior similarly posted, and offering sites deeemed more appropriate for voluntary associations to erect monuments to notable individuals and important events. The professionalizing management of Mount Auburn and similar cemeteries at the century's end must have breathed a collective sign of relief that the "rage" for their landscapes as prime "pleasure-grounds" had run its course. Now, they could get down to the basic business of running "modern" and "efficient" funerary institutions.

12

TRANSFORMATION TO THE "GARDEN" OR "SCULPTURED" CEMETERY

In Mount Auburn, intended as the repository of the dead of successive generations, we should expect to find, as we really do, tombs, monuments, and graves embodying the changing feelings and tastes of different periods.

—Israel Spelman, Mount Auburn President, *Annual Report* (1875)

THE WIDENING GAPS BETWEEN CLASSES AND tastes which emerged in the mid-nineteenth century fragmented cultural cohesion. There were ramifications for Mount Auburn affecting its functions, its commemorative purposes, and its local prominence. The historian Ronald Story describes these as the "crisis years" in Boston, "when the entire hard-wrought infrastructure of the elite seemed in danger of dilution, seizure, and collapse," paralleling the political fragmentation, social pluralism, and escalating egalitarian demands throughout the country.[1] Boston's Brahmins felt under siege from newcomers' challenges to their institutions, including the Athenaeum in 1853, Harvard from 1850 to 1865, and the Lowell Institute through the 1850s. Insurgents solved the problem of exclusivity by founding alternative institutions—a public library granting access to all, new colleges to challenge Harvard's hegemony, and new "garden" cemeteries and a public parks system that weakened Mount Auburn's primacy as a major historical and cultural institution. In 1856 Jacob Bigelow tried to stave off attempts by insurgent proprietors and trustees to democratize cemetery administration, to lower prohibitively high lot prices, and to demand proprietary rights as corporate members over the landscape and its embellishments. After 1857 the number of trustees, elected by the proprietors, became fixed at ten to forestall expansion of the insurgency. Controversy over corporate funding of statuary, demands for investing corporate monies from new lot sales in a permanent maintenance fund, and the provision of public amenities evidenced that trend as well, as did their negation of the founders' plan to make Mount Auburn an agent of history. The impact of such sociocultural changes only escalated in the century's later decades.

In his declining years, Bigelow worried that new trustees would change Mount Auburn entirely, reshaping in radical ways the forms and policies he had developed over four decades. In 1869 he persuaded them to petition the state legislature to amend the cemetery's charter so as to provide rotating terms. This, he hoped, would lessen the threat. He noted proprietors' unsuccessful attempts to supplant the existing roster of trustees with "a new and less experienced body," worrying that "funds designed for the preservation and improvement of the cemetery [had] become so large as to tempt the cupidity of improper and irresponsible persons." Indeed, he charged, "the increased number of proprietors affords a greater opportunity . . . for clandestine and revolutionary movements." Bigelow could not account for new proprietors' tastes or anticipate what their influence might be as they became increasingly vocal about landscape care and access. With the charter successfully amended to stave off insurgency, Bigelow stepped down from the presidency in 1872, after twenty-six years, ailing but assured that his legacy would endure. Escalating change was under way, much of it his own doing, but the rest beyond his control.[2]

The "Fencing Mania"

Despite the initial intent of its idealistic founders to replicate the picturesque commemorative landscapes of English gardens, Mount Auburn was not, like a British estate, the work of one wealthy proprietor making decisions for the totality but was rather the reflection of the decisions made by many trustees and lot owners. More than the multiplication of monuments and markers, the assertions of individual rights and priorities, it was the "fencing mania" that eroded the picturesque at Mount Auburn. Proprietors increasingly enclosed their lots with cast-iron fences, creating spaces that objectified the new "domestication of death," on family property insured in perpetuity. Cemetery founders had encouraged the practice of fencing, familiar from older graveyards, but without the old need to keep cattle off graves. They banned the use of wood in favor of inconspicuous wrought-iron railings and "slight" fences or stone posts with chains, which, according to Dearborn, produced to produce "a most pleasing effect on the eye." That opinion of a "pleasing effect" pertained only to Mount Auburn's first decade, when lots remained scattered amid and framed by the woods.[3]

About forty new fences per year appeared at Mount Auburn in the 1830s. Then, from 1842 to 1857, according to the superintendents' statistics, an average of seventy-one were erected annually, ranging from simple "wire-work" or plain chains and bars with granite posts

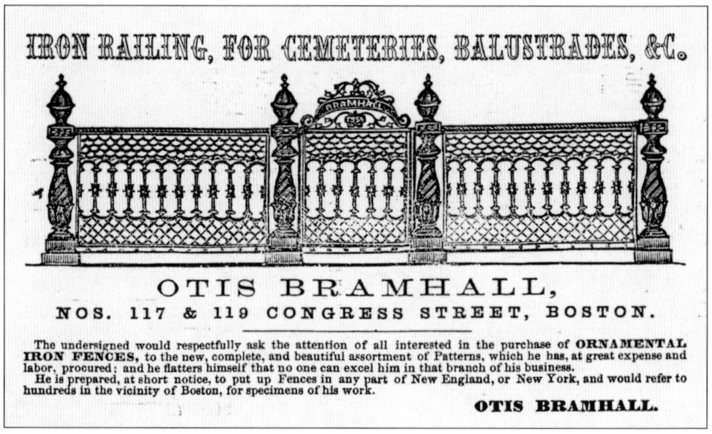

Fig. 12.2. Otis Bramhall iron railings advertisement. From Stevens, 1860.

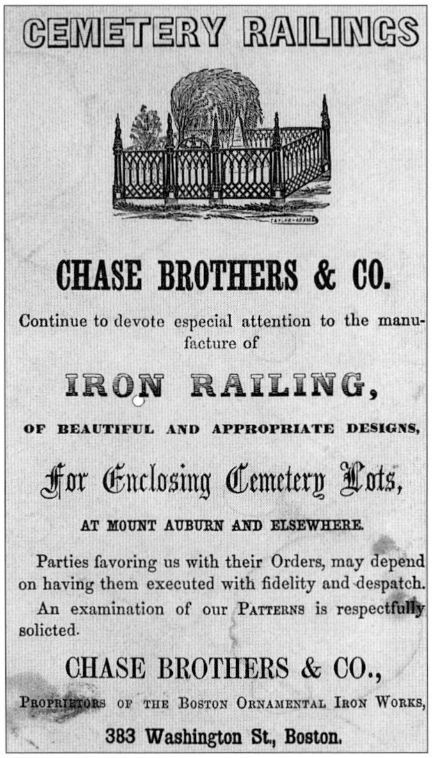

Fig. 12.1. Advertisement, Chase Brothers, "Cemetery Railings." From *Dearborn's Guide*, 1857. BMGL.

Fig. 12.3. A family lot on a wooded path at Mount Auburn, no longer identifiable because of subsequent landscape changes. The iron planter urns and cast-iron fence (no longer extant) exemplify the proliferating fences in that early era that were painted white rather than black. Unlabeled stereograph, ca. 1860. BMGL.

to elaborate structures rich in funerary iconography—willow trees, urns, inverted torches, lambs, doves, grapes, ivy vines, severed buds, roses, oak leaves, acorns, anchors of hope, wreaths. Usually the fence was set on stone blocks, although these were susceptible to displacement by frost heaves or vandalism. Some had firm foundations of foot-high granite curbing, raising the lot above the ground plane; some were even placed around, atop, or in front of chamber tombs. Many of them were manufactured in Boston by the Chase Brothers, J. L. & J. H. Roberts, or Sydney Patch. The last surrounded his own lot on cedar Avenue with "handsome palisading."[4] (Figs. 12.1–12.3.)

Fig. 12.4. Engraving of the gate and fence of the Scots Charitable Society lot, designed and drawn by the architect Voelckers. A few years later Voelckers designed the cemetery's Victorian pump house. From Walter, 1847. MAC.

The trustees encouraged the trend toward elaborate enclosures after 1856 by selling margins one to ten feet wide around lots at one third the ordinary rate per square foot, stipulating only that no interments be made in such "ornamental" space. Advertisements by new ironwork dealers fed the demand for elaborate fences as well as matching cast-iron benches, trellises, and planter urns or baskets. Some urns of terra cotta, marble, or rustic "twig-work" replicated those used in domestic gardens. The wealthy paid $2 to $5 per linear foot or $140 to $350 per lot to erect fences, some of the them more costly than the monument or accumulated markers.[5] Architects designed elaborate custom-made fences. The Scots Charitable Society in 1847 paid $1,644 for one of the finest, by Boston architect Theodore Voelckers, with figures of Saint Andrew and decorative elements of Scottish thistle and battle axes—their monument to members buried without markers in the lot under a fine turf. (Figs. 12.4, 12.5.) Voelckers also designed the fences around the large lot of the four Lawrence brothers, industrialists, as well as Samuel A. Dorr's lot and the double lot of Mace Tisdale and S. K. Hewins.[6]

Fig. 12.5. Scots Charitable Society lot fence. Photograph by Carol Betsch, 2005.

The installation of ornate cast-iron fences increased through the 1840s, given advances in both metallurgy and marketing, reaching a peak in 1853. These fences provided a solution for others who could not immediately afford a major monument. Eighteen-year-old Kate Field (1838–1896), later a journalist, wrote in her diary in 1856 that after her father died, she and her mother were consoled that at least there was the fence: "Dear Father, if there is no monument to mark the spot where lies all that remains of so glorious a nature, at least his grave is protected from all harm."[7] *The Mount Auburn Memorial*

Fig. 12.6. Cast-iron fence on Cogswell lot at corner of Central and Cypress Avenues. Photograph by BMGL, 1988.

Fig. 12.7. Samuel Turrell Armstrong (1784–1850) cast-iron fence on Sedge Path with view of tower in rear. The central monument was designed by the German architect Paul Schulze and made by Alpheus Cary. Photograph by BMGL, 1984.

praised elaborate fences. Calvin Morse's lot, the journal noted, had "a very heavy mourning fence . . . surmounted by draped incense urns. Between the posts are parallel bars. . . . [T]he upper one is ornamented, draped, and tasselled." The fence on Francis Crowninshield's lot had heavy posts and bars painted to match his tall, spire-shaped freestone monument. Alexander Wadsworth's fence was of "a very peculiar pattern; around every other bar twines a thistle shrub, with blossoms alternating," while Samuel P. Oliver's gate exhibited "the fanciful design of a rustic arch of roses, beneath which droops a weeping willow" with wreathed roses along the fence top.[8] (Figs. 12.6–12.8.)

By 1843 one visitor described Mount Auburn as a "patchwork of squares, the lots differently ornamented." The "fencing mania" had gotten out of hand, producing a clutter of cage-like enclosures, a collage of squares that marred the curvilinear, naturalistic landscape, segmenting the once "rural" into an urban-like grid. In 1853 visitors Francis and Theresa Pulszky judged that "elegant iron rails, which divide the different small lots, are neither ornamental nor . . . reverential." Fence lovers ignored all criticism.[9] The squares around lots were also defined by arborvitae hedges delineating many lots of those who would not erect fences. Delineation had become an imperative for proprietors. It cut up the continuity of the landscape, but proprietors had the right to do so. (Fig. 12.9.)

Such fencing occurred at many other "rural" cemeteries, to the dismay of the noted landscape gardener Andrew Jackson Downing. In his 1846 review of a book on New York's Green-Wood Cemetery (1838), he only criticized "the exhibitions of *ironmongery*, . . . vulgar iron railings, posts and chains, balustrades, etc., belonging properly to front-door steps . . . barbarous and cockneyish in their forms," which he found "totally out of keeping with the aspect of nature, the repose, and seclusion of a rural cemetery. A collection of such barriers . . . goes far to destroy all the harmony and rural beauty of the scene." They were "an open violation of the spirit of nature that breathes around." Lot owners, however, associated funerary property precisely with domestic space, to be personalized and defined as private, albeit in a quasi-public landscape. If proprietors insisted on them, Downing recommended "wreathing them about with some hardy and beautiful vines or twining shrubs."[10] His voice had little effect, for three years later he was still castigating "the most violent bad taste" and "hideous ironmongery" of fences, which he found "so ugly as to be positive blots on the beauty of the scene. Fantastic conceits and gimcracks in iron might be pardonable as adornments of the balustrade of a circus or a temple of Comus . . . . how reasonable beings can tolerate them as enclosures to the quiet grave of a family and in such scenes of sylvan beauty is . . . above our comprehension."[11] After Downing's death, others took over his crusade in his influential *The Horticulturist and Journal of Rural Art and Rural Taste.* William H. Scott questioned the "hideous" black iron fences in cemeteries "where *all* is *carefully* guarded" and where "cheerfulness and warmth should be constantly in view." The fact that some were painted white made them even more visually intrusive.[12]

Fig. 12.8. Cast-iron fence and gate with inverted torches at S. Dow lot. Photograph by BMGL, 1984.

At Cincinnati's Spring Grove Cemetery, founded in 1845 in emulation of Mount Auburn, the new superintendent and landscape gardener Adolph Strauch demanded reform when he took control in 1855. Trained at major landscape gardens in Europe and England, the Prussian Strauch minimized the clutter of not only new small stones, curbing, and garden furniture but fences as well, persuading trustees that "enclosures around burial lots in a well-governed cemetery detract from the sacredness of the scene by supposing it possible that such a place would be visited by persons incapable of conducting themselves properly or that the grounds were pastured by cattle." He reasoned that fences "also cause considerable inconvenience when interments are made, as well as in the erection of monuments, and cost the corporation more labor than most persons are aware of." In short, he considered them "a blemish to the whole" that "should not be suffered to destroy the effect" of the landscape. His "landscape lawn plan" set up regulations akin to later zoning codes, specifying the number and size of monuments permitted on lots, and prohibited fences and other enclosures.[13]

Fig. 12.9. Fences segmenting landscape, looking northeast from Chapel Avenue to Central Avenue. From a stereographic photograph by R. A. Miller, 1869.

John Jay Smith, a noted horticulturist and first president of Philadelphia's Laurel Hill Cemetery (1836), also frowned on the fencing craze, considering it "folly . . . to inclose a lot with a poor iron railing, that we know, beforehand, will rust and decay in a very few years, and even sooner if it is not regularly painted; indeed, iron may be said to *rot*, when exposed to all atmospheric influences, just as paper decays; the process is only less rapid."[14] Since Mount Auburn trustees refused to prohibit iron fences, many on their own lots, by the 1860s over 1,700 were in place, with almost half of all lots so enclosed. The trustees avoided infringing upon proprietors' contractual rights unless structures were "offensive" or "dilapidated." Maintenence of fences was costly, however. The high sulfur content added to make the metal fluid enough for sand or clay casting of ornate patterns made the finished product soft, requiring painting every few years to ward off rust and decay. Realization by proprietors of the expense of maintenance slowed the "fencing mania" and, from 1858 on, impelled many to begin removing the fences voluntarily, urged on by Colonel Charles W. Folsom, a Civil War veteran, who became superintendent that year.[15]

Tinkering with the Picturesque

The superintendent reported annually on lots "improved" by grading or turfing, work done by outside contractors with little effort to harmonize with the surrounding ground plane. Many lots were bermed or terraced to rise above the level of adjacent earthen avenues or paths. (See Figs. 9.2–3.) Sodding, instigated by proprietors, though haphazard, increased through the 1840s from about fifty to over a hundred lots annually; but maintaining a trimmed turf was up to the lot owner—perhaps done once or twice a season if at all. Lacking a grounds crew, the superintendent Rufus Howe hired outside "hands" in August of 1852 when trustees ordered him "to mow all brush and weeds" throughout, their first mention of such care. There was no provision for annual, systematic removal of leaves that fell in the "forest cemetery." Annually they left a thick carpet to biodegrade gradually as in the woods unless proprietors hired workers to remove them from individual lots. Bigelow himself supervised the first "draining and cleansing" of Forest and Meadow Ponds, removing much mud and muck to make them less stagnant. The desire for increased landscape maintenance was something new. It was perhaps owing to the expansion of his duties that Howe resigned in 1855 after thirteen years.[16]

The same Bostonians who created new land by filling in the Back Bay and wetlands around the Shawmut Peninsula, greatly expanding the space available for urban development, similarly tinkered with Mount Auburn's topography. The trustees approved the radical reform of reclamation by regrading to create more usable space for burials from wet or steep places and eliminating "superfluous ponds and hollows" to "improve" the appearance of the grounds with ornamental spaces. The first project called for raising dry ground around the seasonally wet area near the cemetery's gate, sculpting it into an ornamental garden, called "the Lawn" (later named Asa Gray Garden), laid out in 1854 by cemetery surveyor Alexander Wadsworth. After rejecting a "picturesque" design, the trustees settled on a circular pool curbed in stone to create an open space offering "a prospect of the Chapel from the road." A paved path reached by six radiating walkways through rough, open turf provided a view of the rear of the chapel atop the unencumbered hillside.[17] (Fig. 12.10.)

In 1856 workers began to take gravel from hills to begin filling in much of the wild, meandering, shallow, and often stagnant Garden Pond, the area in the front of the cemetery initially earmarked for the experimental garden. They began the long process on the side near the gate, then removed the old superintendent's house and associated maintenance facilities. The cemetery invited neighbors to cart away the peat and the "decayed leaves and other decomposed vegetable substances" that were excavated, whatever surplus mulch they did not reserve to enrich the soil elsewhere in the grounds for the introduction of ornamental plantings. Draining and raising dry land six feet above the surface created new burial space as Culvert Avenue (renamed Fountain in 1863) became the first part of the system of avenues and paths extended into and around the northeast portion of the grounds. In 1860, however, the pond remained a "quagmire," awaiting the carving out of a small oval "lake." In the process of sculpting this picturesque feature, the Committee on Grounds rejected the proposal of leaving a "charming little island upon which is a beautiful group of forest trees." That would have created a scene reminiscent of the Isle of Poplars, site of Rousseau's tomb, in the gardens of Ermenonville. With the stoning of the banks from 1862 to 1872, Halcyon Lake was complete.[18]

Simultaneously, they tackled the deepening of Meadow Pond, then a "bog meadow covered with grass and bushes," on the other side of Indian Ridge. After raising and stabilizing its banks with sod and stone borders, they renamed it Auburn Lake. In 1857 Abby M.

Fig. 12.10. The Lawn. From a stereograph, ca. 1870. BMGL.

Loring purchased two thousand feet at its head "to be forever kept open for ornamental purposes" and surrounded by Oxalis Path. The trustees expended corporate funds to surround the lower half with a carriage road named Rosebay Avenue; and superintendent Jonathan Mann designed a cast-iron bridge crossing the lake at the constricted center of the water body, six hundred feet long by one hundred feet at its widest. After completion of the project in 1859, one writer called it "an elegant natural mirror to reflect the beauties of earth and sky" and remarked that "Mount Auburn, until recently, has been destitute of the fine imagery and poetic pictures which a large body of water produces," ignoring how picturesque the smaller Consecration Dell and Forest Pond had always been.[19]

The trustees sent Mann on a fact-finding trip to noted cemeteries in New York, Philadelphia, and Baltimore in 1857 to gather advice on the process and to learn how to construct catacomb tombs and lay out a hydraulic system.[20] By 1859 a new drainage system running from Halcyon Lake, under Indian Ridge, and then through Auburn Lake carried seasonal excesses of water out of the cemetery to the river by percolation and underground flow. Dreaming of further embellishing the landscape with cascades as in English gardens, the trustees had wished "that the stranger in the grounds could meet unexpectedly at some point a brook winding naturally and prettily down the slope, and joining its music to that of the feathered songsters." Its bank could "be fringed with willows," providing "a place of delightful repose to the wearied tourist." Since that proved too ambitious, a system of lead pipes with a reservoir and a brick pump on the eastern periphery made it possible to raise up to four hundred gallons of water per minute. This permitted the addition of ornamental steam-powered fountain jets in the Lawn, Hazel Dell, and Auburn Lake by 1861, the last able to throw water up to sixty feet high when the reservoir was full, "an artificial grace of no mean description." In boasting comparisons, the trustees cited several new fountains installed in New York City.[21] Captain Daniel L. Winsor replaced Mann in 1861 as superintendent to carry on the engineering. In 1869, the Cemetery paid for the Cambridge Water Works main pipe to be extended into the grounds, supplementing the wells on the site.[22] (Figs. 12.11, 12.12.)

In 1863, needing more gravel for all their "improvements," such as stabilizing the bottoms of the newly carved lakes and building new carriageways and paths, the trustees ordered the shortening of Cedar and Laurel hills by up to fifteen feet, grading steep acclivities. (Fig. 12.14.) Cedar Hill was "converted into a symmetrical mound of oval shape, uniformly turfed, and made accessible to carriages by a new avenue" which circled the top around a newly curbed burial area. Even Harvard Hill's banks were regraded in 1865, followed by a portion of Indian Ridge. All the regrading eliminated much of the irregular natural terrain, which had been an element of the "picturesque," along with many trees on the steep slopes. It also necessitated laying out new paths and avenues, a project largely overseen by Bigelow.[23] The infill generated by the regrading was used to eliminate bogs as in Hazel Dell and to trim ponds to symmetrical shapes. The remaining ponds were deepened by dredginh and graveling their bottoms. Bigelow later recalled

Fig. 12.11. Meadow Lake with cast-iron bridge painted white. From a stereograph, ca. 1870. BMGL.

Fig. 12.12. Auburn Lake with fountain jet. From a stereographic photograph by O. R. Wilkinson, ca. 1869. BMGL.

Fig. 12.13. Laurel Hill, lowered and curbed. From a stereograph, ca. 1870. BMGL.

that the trustees and the proprietors had wanted a "more finished and ornamental appearance" throughout the landscape.[24]

The Demise of the "Forest" Cemetery

The preference for a woodsy, "picturesque" landscape symbolizing Nature's dominance waned in response to proprietors' demands, transforming Mount Auburn from a "rural" to a "garden" cemetery. Bigelow began the process after a fact-finding trip in May and June 1854 to "most of the celebrated cemeteries in the country," many of which he found "far superior to Mount Auburn" because "the original forest" since Mount Auburn's founding had "become so dense as to prevent or impede vegetation, injure monuments, prevent many of them from being seen to advantage." By contrast, "in other cemeteries, trees are kept trimmed high, and not allowed to grow so near to each other and proper vistas are opened." The landscape precedent of the picturesque garden had become overwhelmed at Mount Auburn by forest growth, much of it second-generation volunteers.[25]

Five years later Bigelow reported that "the ground as seen from the top of the Tower, now looks like a dense, impenetrable forest, in which most of the monuments are concealed from view by the contiguous branches." The gradual process of "thinning out the wood, pruning branches, and cutting away useless trees" would take a decade. The trustees appointed Bigelow, Benjamin A.

Gould, a founding trustee, and Isaiah Bangs, a newcomer, as a committee with power to trim or even remove trees. Selective removal of forest trees could have made the landscape look more like the English gardens that had inspired it by opening views of the chapel, tower, and major monuments from multiple perspectives, but there was no such attention to detailing the landscape with an aesthetic design in mind.[26]

Wilson Flagg commented in *Mount Auburn: Its Scenes, Its Beauties, and Its Lessons* in 1861 that the cemetery "would be at present a more beautiful place, and more convenient for the purposes to which it is dedicated, if, at the time of its consecration . . . , it had been entirely free from wood, and afterwards had been judiciously planted with young trees of the prevailing species. Very few well formed trees are to be seen in these grounds, because they are mostly the elongated trees of the forest, which occupy a great deal of space in proportion to the amount of shade afforded by them, and greatly encumber the burial lots." Yet Flagg praised the use of indigenous trees and shrubs in cemeteries, especially those with emblematic significance due to form and foliage. The Reverend A. D. Gridley opined that since "very few large trees are wanted in a cemetery . . . the frequent practice of choosing a wooded spot for the site, is found by experience to be very unwise." The roots of great trees broke through the surfaces of avenues and paths, and the trees themselves came "crashing down" in gales, "demolishing costly monuments and tearing up the very graves," so that "sooner or later, a large proportion of the trees have to be cut down, and those preserved are seldom worth preserving."[27]

To replace "the primitive forest growth," Flagg urged selection of trees with a "funereal character" that would be given space for "majestic" growth. He counseled mainly deciduous trees, with "an occasional admixture of evergreens" whose "sombre appearance" might be "too gloomy" if planted in groves. Too many proprietors had already planted weeping willows to frame their monuments, creating individual tableaux reminiscent of mourning pictures on their lots.[28] Bigelow dealt the coup de grace to the "rural" in 1864, deeming that the "growth and gradual encroachment of forest trees during the last thirty years has been, by excluding the sunlight from the ground, a great and increasing evil." He believed that "the perfection of Mount Auburn, as far as its natural features are concerned, would be attained by diminishing the trees to less than one half of their present number, leaving broad vistas and open spaces, through which the works of art could be seen; and the light of the sun might be admitted to the grass and cultivated flowers, to the health of which it is indispensable. Rows of trees are wanted only on the principal avenues . . . with a few trees only in unobjectionable places." Such alterations, he felt, "would greatly improve the picturesque effect of the Cemetery." Through that winter, a dozen workers removed "superfluous trees."[29]

That was not enough. In 1868 Bigelow persuaded the trustees to allow removal of up to *half* of the forest trees, largely second growth, which he deemed "detrimental and inconvenient," as they created "a dense shade, obstructing the views, excluding the sun in many places, and thereby killing the grass and preventing cultivation of flowers." The cemetery had no workforce to remove the immense amount of leaves and debris that fell and accumulated. By making "lawns," then defined as clearings rather than "greenswards" with trimmed turf, he could introduce ornamentals and also open up more burial space. Cultivated grasses became a new option. Bigelow recommended that proprietors plant "only low shrubs and herbaceous plants, and even these with judicious frugality," especially roses, laurels, and rhodendrons. He opined that "one elm tree is often sufficient for an acre." A "gale" in 1869 hastened the process of clearing. Bigelow thus reformed the cemetery, rejecting the "picturesque" in favor of the "beautiful," as in Capability Brown's English gardens, more open than the secluded "walking gardens" of Pope and Kent that had been the initial inspiration; but it was too late for that, given the clutter of lot enclosures and stones, about to increase even more.[30]

From 1854 to 1871, while Bigelow was president, lot sales increased from 2,425 to 4,075 with the new land available for burials, largely because of the filling and clearing campaigns. The trustees agreed in 1855 to meet the growing demand for "quarter" lots of 75 square feet each, rather than the original lots of 300 square feet—clearly no longer for an extended family of multiple generations. These smaller lots were laid out along the western side of the cemetery by 1860, then in other newly created areas such as the linear paths north of Halcyon Lake. Recognizing the growing demand for single burials, the cemetery dedicated St. Matthew's and St. Paul's "public" lots in 1863 and 1868, the latter of 28,000 square feet overlooking the naturalistic Willow Pond, yet to be purchased. Anticipating potential burials in the spaces between many lots, the trustees offered proprietors the opportunity to purchase that land to prevent insertion of smaller lots, thus reserving it as ornamental space, a recognition that Dearborn's founding intention of keeping such margins open could no longer be sustained.[31]

The Curbing Era

The aesthetics of the "picturesque" were reinterpreted and reshaped in the landscape by new trustees and proprietors, if they had ever shared the initial, idealistic vision of the founders for a truly naturalistic landscape. When some proprietors began to remove their iron fences, they replaced them with heavy granite or freestone curbing or copings, massive blocks rising twelve to sixteen inches above the ground plane, which further segmented the cemetery's naturalistic appearance, visually intruding in a very urban way, even more than the fences. The lot, trustees oberved, would be "filled up inside with good earth like a flower pot and grassed over." The first lot curb was installed in 1858; there were thirty-five added in 1859; and thirty-seven in 1860. An average of sixty-five stone enclosures were erected annually from 1861 to 1872, more than the number of fences built annually into the 1850s. Some had elaborate ornamentation and steps. Even the cemetery built stone steps on several paths in 1866 and 1867.[32] (Figs. 12.14–12.16.)

Mary Porter Tileston Hemenway (1820–1894), a Unitarian philanthropist, contributed $6,000 in 1863 for an "improvement" called Alice Fountain in memory of her daughter, who died at age two, providing for 21,000 square feet of turfed "ornamental grounds" with a fountain covenanted "to be forever kept open and in good condition"—a low jet in a large circular basin ringed in granite in an area being developed near Thistle Path by the engineering firm of Shedd & Edson. It added "to the desireableness" of the new burial lots created by filling in a bog with gravel from the lowering of Laurel Hill and defined in a basin surrounded by a semicircle of steep banks. On thirty-five of these new lots the proprietors installed curbing. The Alice Fountain "ornamental" area, distinctly different from the original landscape, was deemed to "increase the beauty of Mount Auburn," given the new tastes of the times.[33] (Fig. 12.17.)

The trustees fortuitously preserved the naturalism of Consecration Dell's rugged southern and western slopes in 1858 by withholding them from sale as proprietors were building heavy curbings on the northern side. Graveling the dell's bottom and edges four years before, emphasized by a high stone wall on an adjacent hill and curbing of nearby lots, erased much of the pantheistic symbolism originally inherent there, the "Genius of Place" embodied by a dark natural pond shrouded by high forested banks leading up to the mount. In 1862 the Committee on Grounds considered "constructing a flight of stone steps" from near the tower down the steep slope to the Dell. Fortunately, that proved too expensive and difficult from an engineering perspective, and only one short flight segment was completed under the summit. It would have transformed what remained of one of the cemetery's most picturesque sites and probably would not have stood up to the test of time.[34] (Fig. 12.18.)

The taste for curbings coincided with the trustees' decision to begin paving avenues and paths with macadamized stone. The first to be paved was the steep Mountain Avenue, in 1855, to prevent erosion. By 1865, the installation of three thousand feet of cobble-paved gutters along avenues and down other steep hillsides had eliminated flooding by freshets but intruded visually in the once "rural" landscape. Proprietors in sections newly laid out, as around Alice Fountain or between Halcyon Lake and the gateway, chose curbings so their lots would match those of neighbors. Indeed, the trustees ruled that unsold lots on the "Hemenway improvement" would be *required* to have "stone curbs substantially in accordance with the surroundings." New sections, in the height of fashion, looked entirely different from the old—"gardenesque" rather than "picturesque."[35]

The *Mount Auburn Memorial* lauded the ornateness and durability of "improvements." The imposing circular lot of hotel tycoon Paran Stevens (1802–1872), two

Fig. 12.14. Curbs segmenting the landscape on Walnut Avenue, with Osgood monument on left. From a stereograph, ca. 1870. BMGL.

Fig. 12.15. Stairs and curbing on hillside lots on Walnut Avenue. Photograph by Carol Betsch, 2005.

Fig. 12.16. Monuments and curbing along Thistle. Photograph by Carol Betsch, 2005.

Fig. 12.17. The curbed Alice Fountain with jet spray near the intersection of Spruce and Mound Avenues. From a stereographic photograph taken from Anemone Path, ca. 1870. BMGL.

Fig. 12.18. Curbing and wall on northern side of Consecration Dell. Anonymous photographer, ca. 1900. BMGL.

thousand square feet just inside the gateway, had "a very heavy granite edging . . . of fifteen curved pieces, handsomely capped," its entrance flanked by two urns matching the massiveness of the huge central sarcophagus, as prominent as if Stevens were still welcoming guests to his fashionable hotels. (Fig. 12.19.) Although the cost of even modest curbing was about double that of an iron fence, $600 to $700 per average lot for a simple enclosure, stone proved cheaper in the long run since it involved few maintenance costs.[36]

Corporation secretary Austin J. Coolidge promoted curbing in correspondence with lot owners. In 1862 he advised the Harvard College treasurer that "a neat granite edge stone" around Harvard Hill would "add greatly to its beauty and permanency." He wrote to superintendent Daniel Winsor that on Rufus Wyman's lot "the monument is so large and bold . . . that no enclosure other than a curb will answer the purpose." Wyman paid two dollars per foot for a curb one foot deep, "heavy enough for so large

Fig. 12.19. Heavy curbing on the 2,000-square-foot lot inside the gateway on Elm Avenue, owned by hotel tycoon Paran Stevens. The curbing no longer exists. "Photo-view" (photolithograph) by Louis Glaser in the small, accordion-folded *Souvenir View Book* he printed in Leipzig, Germany, 1883, distributed by Wittemann Brothers, New York. MAC.

Fig. 12.20. Ornate Victorian monument and heavy granite curbing on the Wade family lot. From a stereograph by E. C. Swain, Malden, Mass., ca. 1870. BMGL.

an area" and adequate "to protect the lot from parties crossing to and from Indian Ridge." By 1865 Coolidge considered iron fences "rather out of date," since the cemetery was "well-protected with a high iron enclosure." By this time Quincy granite enclosures had become "the almost universal fashion."[37] (Fig. 12.20.)

The Gardenesque Cemetery

As the new taste for the "gardenesque" grew, interest in exotic plants imported by expeditions to Asia and the tropics also grew along with experiments in their cultivation. Proprietors petitioned the trustees in 1856 to create a "conservatory" for "the preservation of plants during the cold season," especially the "half-hardy" or even tropical varieties that appealed to Victorian tastes but could not survive New England winters, such as palms and ferns (*Nephrolepis bostoniensis*). The trustees authorized Bigelow in 1854 to spend $300 to introduce ornamental shrubs. The doctor made an expedition with "an experienced gardener" into the White Mountains, where he located about a hundred mountain laurel shrubs (*Kalmia latifolia*), which were planted along the front of the cemetery from the gateway towards the east and around Meadow Pond. These evergreens, native to woodlands and swamps, flower in pink or white in the spring. Bigelow ordered additional ornamental shrubs from New York. An allocation of $300 the next spring permitted transplanting of trees along avenues as suggested by Alexander Wadsworth's plan, made according to Bigelow's specifications. In 1859 the trustees allotted another $500 for trees and shrubs, and Bigelow ordered rhododendrons from Liverpool for $100. The design of the Boston Public Garden by George F. Meacham that year further encouraged the taste for Victorian bedded flowering plants.[38]

In 1860 Wilson Flagg criticized proprietors' increasing planting of "exotic" shrubs to the exclusion of varieties native to New England as he described how dwarf kalmia and diverse cornels and viburnums, which gave "native harborage" to songbirds, had to "resign their places" at Mount Auburn to exotics such as costly altheas, smoke plants, and Judas trees, requiring "expensive labor or careful cultivation" by proprietors. Before the taste for ornamentals caught on in the 1850s, many lots had been in disorder with minimal plantings, while others had simple borders of cultivated perennials, replacing the wildflowers—wood sorrel, wild tulips, lilies of the valley, violets, snowdrops. A few old-timers still waxed poetic with nostalgia about the "honest dandelion," the "annual carnival of our yellow-jacketed friend" bringing out children to weave chains of them; but others now disdained the indigenous as "weeds." Realizing this growing demand for the ornamental, the trustees hired a gardener, Antone Apple, in 1857, leasing to him land next to the superintendent's new house across from the cemetery between Mount Auburn and Brattle streets. There he built a greenhouse and maintained a nursery. Proprietors could now pay him an annual fee for plants and services rather than relying on outside gardeners, who came in on a haphazard basis for lot plantings or maintenance. The gardener had no monopoly, however, and contractors still came. The trustees also permitted Apple to rent space to Alexander McDonald to "exhibit monumental specimens" for sale to proprietors; he purchased that land for his "marble shop" in 1862. The gardener and monument dealer functioned as free agents; the charter did not let the corporation sell anything other than lots.[39]

Apple went into debt and resigned in 1861. His replacement, William H. Spooner Jr., quit after five months, complaining of competition from outsiders, loss of plants from his stock, and proprietors' unpaid bills. Bigelow found that outside contractors' rude "abuses," "imposing upon proprietors" in soliciting work were bad enough. Some of them hid tools in hedges. Reluctant to ban contractors altogether, the trustees gave the superintendent control over granting permits. To retain Spooner, they decreed "stringent measures for the regulation of outside workmen" and their "untidiness." While granting him a line of credit and standardizing charges, they purchased the greenhouse he had built, sold him the stock of plants, leased him the concession for $125 per year, and had Cambridge appoint him a policeman; but that did not suffice. Neither the superintendent nor the gardener could stop outside workers from pruning or cutting down trees "in a manner prejudicial" and without approval of the Committee on Grounds. When McDonald bought Spooner's stock and greenhouse lease in 1862, the trustees abolished the office of gardener, preferring not to encourage proprietors' tastes in plantings but to take control of the ornamentals themselves.[40]

With the landscape's transition from the forested "picturesque," gradual engineering of the "beautiful," the sculpting of the land, and introduction of a new planting program far more labor-intensive in development and maintenance, the trustees realized the need to provide more management control. In 1857 they created a "permanent fund for repair and preservation of the grounds" with at least a fifth of gross proceeds from new lot sales, with the promise of that "safety fund . . . inserted as a covenant" in new deeds to accumulate as a "sacred deposit" for perpetual care of the entire cemetery and "its appurtenances," including workers' salaries; but this applied only to care of the new covenanted lots. The trustees doubted that cemetery workers "would have any right to enter and repair or otherwise alter the lots of proprietors [who had previously purchased them] without [their] consent and specific instructions"; but proprietors complained "of exorbitant charges by the Superintendent for services rendered" and asked that the new fund "apply to care of lots as well as the grounds."[41]

Fig. 12.21. Miriam lot with Victorian monument and adjacent floral parterre on Fountain Avenue. The sign in the right foreground reads "Keep Off Grass." From a stereograph by E. C. Swain, Malden, Mass., ca. 1870. BMGL.

Fig. 12.22. Historic photograph of ivy-covered Bigelow Chapel façade with topiary, ca. 1900.

Skeptical about future trustees who might succumb to growing demands for burial space, allowing new lots to impinge on focal areas, Bigelow persuaded the trustees in 1861 to set aside land as "public grounds" inside the gateway, the circular space inside the new Lawn Avenue, the lawn in front of the chapel as well as the margins around its periphery, the banks around Auburn Lake, and hillsides around the tower, "to be forever kept open for ornamental purposes." These were ideal sites for parterres edged in granite and planted by the cemetery. (Fig. 12.21.) The trustees also spent $750 to surround the lawn south of the chapel with "an edge-stone of hammered granite." (See Fig. 10. 17.) They ruled that new deeds of the lots around Lawn Avenue should restrict shrubs to under five feet "so as not to obstruct the view of the central fountain and the Chapel." Formal floral parterres filled this sunny, circular focal point in the early 1870s. "Improvements" included widening Central Avenue to twenty-nine feet, planting an allée of elms, and adding more iron hitching posts for carriage parking. In 1872 the trustees first considered paving some paths with "asphaltum" instead of macadamized gravel. The balance between Nature and Art had definitively tipped in favor of the latter by the 1870s. Mount Auburn was no longer called a "rural" or "forest" cemetery, as the terms "ornamental," "sculptured," and "garden" were increasingly used. The Victorian "gardenesque" reigned at Mount Auburn even before Bigelow's death in 1879 brought an end to the formative era.[42] (Fig. 12.22.)

From Tombs to Mausoleums

To maximize the use of all parts of the grounds and to accommodate the taste for entombment, the trustees voted in 1856 to permit tombs in hillsides, provided all but the door and granite façade were underground. On a fact-finding trip to major eastern "rural" cemeteries in 1857, superintendent Jonathan Mann inspected the structures of tombs and freestanding mausoleums, many more expensive and ornamental than those at Mount Auburn. Mann found that Brooklyn's Green-Wood, Philadelphia's Laurel Hill, and Baltimore's Green Mount permitted aboveground stone structures as long as bodies were placed in pigeonholes sealed with brick, stone, or cement. The trustees resolved to grant permits for such "catacombs," provided they be airtight and passed inspection, after the proprietor paid a $50 premium for the privilege.[43]

The architect Hammatt Billings (1816–1874) designed the neo-Gothic tomb of Jersey stone for Joseph Whall in 1858. (Fig. 12.23.) The nearly freestanding structure with a barreled-vaulted roof backed into the hillside on Lawn Avenue behind the chapel contained eighteen niches into which caskets could be hermetically sealed, preventing the release of "noxious gases." That year the trustees seized the opportunity to sell lots on "incorrectably" steep hillsides at fifty cents per square foot for catacomb tombs and developed some rougher terrain themselves. They charged Mann to contract in 1859 for the building of two granite-fronted catacomb tombs as models in the Indian Ridge hillside in Hazel Dell, the deep hollow just east of Central Avenue, no longer with wetlands in the middle. When they sold immediately, the trustees lined the dell with a semicircle of them, twelve over the decade, though construction was slowed by the Civil War, and built others to sell on Palm Avenue in 1872.[44] (Fig. 12.24.)

A few proprietors hired architects to design such catacomb tombs. Shephard S. Woodcock may have designed the simple neo-Gothic brownstone tomb for the Lodge family overlooking Auburn Lake in 1866, similar to but less complex than the Whall tomb. (Fig. 12.25.) John Lowell Gardner II, father-in-law of the famed doyenne of Boston art, Isabella Stewart Gardner, commissioned a tomb next to the Lodge structure. (Fig. 12.26.) Completed in 1868, it received three of the family who had

Fig. 12.23. Whall Tomb, 1858, overlooking the Lawn. From a stereograph, ca. 1890. MAC.

Fig. 12.24. Hazel Dell tombs. From a stereograph, ca. 1870. BMGL.

Fig. 12.25. Henry Cabot Lodge tomb. Photograph by BMGL, 1979.

Fig. 12.26. Gardner tomb on Rosebay Avenue overlooking Auburn Lake. Photograph by Carol Betsch, 2005.

Fig. 12.27. Charles W. Freeland mausoleum, designed by architect Henry Van Brunt, ca. 1870. At about the same time, Van Brunt and his partner William Robert Ware began the High Victorian Gothic design of Harvard's Memorial Hall and several Boston-area churches, with Van Brunt largely in charge of design. From a stereograph. MAC.

died earlier, including Isabella's beloved son Jackie, whose body had lain in New York's Green-Wood Cemetery since his death in 1865. The architect Henry Van Brunt (1832–1903) designed Mount Auburn's first freestanding mausoleum in the 1870s for the Charles W. Freeland family.[45] (Fig. 12.27.)

Sentimentality and the "Sculptured" Cemetery

Meanwhile, after the return of economic prosperity in the mid-1840s, Buckingham was pleased to observe the growing number of monuments that were "erected to preserve the decaying memory of one whom the world never missed when he passed away" but also "valuable as specimens of the sculptor's skill or as artistic embodiments of beauty."[46] Indeed, an unprecedented tide of affective individualism had been transforming relationships between husbands and wives, parents and children, extended family and friends, a trend that only accelerated with the spread of Enlightenment values, transformed into romanticism and sentimentalism, expressed through the "cult of the melancholy." (Figs. 12.28, 12.29.) Many families were not content with one central monument listing all burials under the patriarchal name, as on Joseph Story's monument, but insisted on a more democratic approach, erecting an additional gravestone with each new burial, with smaller ones for children. (Fig. 12.30.) By 1851 the cemetery contained 480 monuments, with an average of 30 new ones added annually, not including the smaller markers.

Although cemetery founders cited a historic sensibility of recognizing notables, the liberal spirituality it epitomized also provided for material remembrance of those who died young, rare in colonial burial grounds. Most striking are the many markers and even monuments for infants and children, an index of their high mortality but also of the era's blooming sentimentalism focused on the very young.[47] The first was the sleeping effigy of four-year-old Emily Binney sculpted by Henry Dexter (1806–1876) in 1842, Mount Auburn's first figural monument, said to be the first marble statue carved in New England. Alpheus Cary designed the open, temple-like structure supported by columns to shelter the fragile sculpture, inscribed: "Shed

Fig. 12.28. Oliver Carter family monument, Roman Revival style with a low relief of a deathbed scene. Photograph by Jennifer Johnston, 2006. MAC.

Fig. 12.29. Mrs. Henry Veazie Ward monument, ca. 1857, on Greenbriar Path. Photograph by Jennifer Johnston, 2006. MAC.

Not for Her the Bitter Tear, / Nor Give the Heart to Vain Regret, / 'Tis but the Casket That Lies Here—/ The Gem That Filled It Sparkles Yet."[48] (Fig. 12.31.)

On Fir Avenue, a marble canopy shelters the effigy of the sleeping child Susan Ella Richardson, who died in 1851. Small stones abound depicting sleeping babies and lambs or low reliefs of severed flower buds representing the early death of an innocent. (Fig. 12.32.) The sculptor Peter Stephenson (1823–1861), trained in Rome, made the marble portrait on Lime Avenue of the three Atkins children, two of whom died in 1849 aged two and nine, the other at age two in 1856. (Fig. 12.33.) The empty wicker cradle replicated in marble over the grave of Mary Wigglesworth, who died of diphtheria in 1884 before her second birthday, is unique, a design by the artist William Lyndon placed on the grave in 1888. The last two remain in relatively good condition because they were sheltered during the winter by custom-made wooden boxes.

Fig. 12.30. Curbed lot of John P. Thorndike on Rose Path, with egalitarian markers for each family burial. Photograph by Carol Betsch, 2005.

The elegant monument of Medford clipper ship building magnate Thatcher Magoun (1775–1856) has not fared as well because it was unprotected from the toll of acid rain. (Fig. 12.34.) It proclaims family sentimentality with a fine sculpture of a mourning mother and young daughter, inscribed: "Household's Tomb to Faith So Dear. / Part Have Gone, Part Linger Here / United All in Love and Hope, / One Household Still!" It exemplifies the elaborate sculpture that entered from the 1860s through the 1890s: allegorical figures of Faith, Hope, and Charity, some produced at new monument manufactories by anonymous carvers drawing from pattern books, others by major artists.

Fig. 12.31. Henry Dexter's sculpture of "Little Emily" on the family lot of C. J. F. Binney on Yarrow Path. Engraving by Smillie, from Walter, 1847. This monument virtually became a place of pilgrimage for sentimentalists. MAC.

Thomas Ball (1819–1911), a Bostonian based in Florence, made "Faith and the Angel of Death" or "The Realization of Faith" for the family of Jonas Chickering (1797–1853), the piano manufacturer whose Boston factory was said to be the nation's second-largest building after the U.S. Capitol. A marble angel holds an inverted torch while lifting a shroud from a kneel-

Fig. 12.32. Babies' markers on the Jones lot, Central Avenue. From an undated stereograph. MAC.

Fig. 12.33. Atkins children, Willie, Charlie, and Mary. Photograph by BMGL, 1980.

Fig. 12.34. Monument of Medford, Mass., shipbuilder Thatcher Magoun on Fir Avenue. The statue, "Grief," ca. 1858, depicts a mourning mother and child and is inscribed with two quatrains of the verse "One Family Still." From a stereograph. MAC.

Fig. 12.35. Chickering monument by Thomas Ball on Magnolia Avenue. Stereographic photograph, ca. 1870. MAC.

ing female clasping a cross to her breast. (Fig. 12.35.) The pedestal bears a tondo bas-relief of the grieving Muse of music holding a laurel wreath and the lyre of Apollo, inscribed "Now Faith is the Substance of Things Hoped For / The Evidence of Things Not Seen." In 1874 Martin Milmore (1844–1883) produced the marble Angel of the Resurrection with a bronze trumpet over the grave of Maria Frances Coppenhagen, who died a young woman to the grief of her mother, who made the commission. (Fig. 12.36.) In 1874 Dr. Harriot Kezia Hunt (1805–1875), for forty years one of the nation's first female physicians and an ardent reformer, had Edmonia Lewis (1845–ca. 1909), a mixed-race artist active among the American enclave in Rome, sculpt the marble figure of Hygeia, Greek goddess of health, for her family's monument. Her own small marker on the lot is inscribed "She Hath Done What She Could."[49]

Ornateness grew with the efflorescence of Victorian taste, particularly drawing on the "Language of Flowers," with international currency ascribing emblematic meaning to plants from folklore, religious traditions, and literature, loved by sentimentalists and spread through popular gift books. Alexander McDonald, Mount Auburn's resident monument dealer, provided a unique marble composition (ca. 1881) for James Garfield Sum-

Fig. 12.36. Coppenhagen monument on Yew Avenue with Angel of the Resurrection by Martin Milmore, 1872. Inscribed "My Beloved Daughter Maria" and commissioned by her mother. Photograph by BMGL, 1980.

Fig. 12.37. James Garfield Sumner monument (d. 1861), a ruined column with ferns, by Alexander McDonald, inscribed "My Husband." Photograph by BMGL, 1980.

Fig. 12.38. Williams monument (d. 1866), a rustic cross inscribed "My Husband." Photograph by BMGL, 1980.

Fig. 12.39. Sheaves of wheat symbolizing death at a ripe age on the Raymond family Victorian monument, ca. 1874 by R. Barry, on Halcyon Avenue. Photograph by BMGL, 1980.

ner on the corner of Trefoil and Arethusa paths on a hill overlooking Willow Pond. (Fig. 12.37.) Featured in engravings of the latest trend in monuments in guidebooks, it is a ruined, toppled column on a carved rocky base that seems to be overgrown with ferns and garlands of flowers. The rustic cross on the Williams family lot reflects the same imagery of ruin overcome by resurgent Nature. (Fig. 12.38.) It is reminiscent of the severed tree trunks carved in stone with similarly elaborate iconography, more popular in that era in other cemeteries and particularly among those of German extraction. Sculpted sheaves of wheat "symbolic of mature age," lives "fully ripened" for the harvest of death, adorned many monuments. A floral lexicon persisted even on simpler stones into the new century.[50] (Fig. 12.39.)

Garden furniture—arbors, urns, and settees—compounded the clutter of stones decorated with scrolls and carved flowers in a landscape segmented by ornate fences and curbs. (Fig. 12.40.) Many publications and advertisements urged proprietors to "improve" their lots with elaborate flower beds, spreading vines, and other ornamental plantings. The budding vogue reached full flower by the century's end as even the cemetery planted figurative floral parterres as focal points.[51] In

1876 the novelist Henry James (1843–1916) wistfully recalled Mount Auburn "in its infancy, and full of a sylvan charm which it has now completely forfeited." Instead, parts of it had become as cluttered with memorabilia as a Victorian parlor.[52]

Fig. 12.40. Cast iron Victorian garden furniture on the family lot of Jacob Foss on Snowdrop Path. The parlor-like arrangement epitomized the era's "domestication of death," in the words of scholar Ann Douglas (Knopf, 1977). From a stereograph by Barnum, ca. 1860. Courtesy Historic New England.

EPILOGUE

More Chapters of Change

Any landscape, designed or natural, is a living, breathing entity that changes, ages, and renews itself. It can be dramatically altered or obliterated by man or nature, or preserved, restored, and reinterpreted despite those forces. Unless wise stewardship and preservation forestall dramatic change and decay, all or part can be ruined or lost. Mount Auburn, as an institution with complex ongoing functions constantly reshaped by proprietors, trustees, and administrators, has passed through numerous chapters of change while maintaining a landscape unequaled except at the other grand "garden" cemeteries it inspired.

Changing tastes and professionalization transformed Mount Auburn's landscape as the civil engineer and railroad executive Israel Munson Spelman (1816–1907) followed Bigelow as president in 1874. (Fig. E.2.) His tenure saw the development of new areas south of the historic core according to the new aesthetics of the "landscape lawn plan" as developed by Adolph Strauch (1822–1883) at Cincinnati's Spring Grove and applied to the design and reform of many other garden cemeteries in the last four decades of the century. The idea was to simplify the landscape by banning the proliferation of small stones and lot enclosures to create "greenswards." The preference for "a smooth, closely shaven surface of grass," newly defined as a "lawn," was popularized by the emergence of public parks in major cities and by landscape architect Frank Jessup Scott (1828–1919), a student of Downing's, in his 1870 book *The Art of Beautifying Suburban Home Grounds*, lauded as a "Great Green Manifesto." These parks represented the aesthetics of the "beautiful," inspired by the eighteenth-century English gardens of Lancelot "Capability" Brown, which supplanted the "picturesque" walking gardens of his contemporaries.[1]

Application of ever-improving technologies permitted the engineering of the "beautiful," which became the wave of the future at Mount Auburn. Another engineer, James W. Lovering, Mount Auburn's superintendent from 1873 to 1895, followed the newly professionalized methods being spread nationally among "cemeterians" who followed the principles set by Strauch in hopes that modernizing the "scientific management" of burial landscapes would keep them up to par with the new urban parks they had inspired. Using "gradual and continuous efforts," Spelman's administration removed much of the clutter in older areas of the grounds to permit regrading of "unsymmetrical banks, such as Nature never makes and which she is constantly trying to get rid of." This work, of course, required proprietors' consent to eliminate some older structures—tomb façades, fences, curbings, even some deteriorating stones.[2]

The surfacing of avenues and paths, laying of turf, and introduction of additional ornamental plantings

Fig. E.1. Map of 1890 showing Halcyon Lake newly created out of Garden Pond and new sections developed according to the "landscape lawn plan." MAC.

slowly transformed the look of the landscape in the new century. (Fig. E.1.) The trustees ordered installation of a hydraulic system to carry stagnant water out of the cemetery and to bring in the fresh for irrigation and fountains. Lovering's successor, the Scottish landscape gardener James C. Scorgie, carried on his predecessor's work until 1920 to create "The Cemetery Beautiful." New regulations determining the size, number, and styles of monuments and mausoleums contributed to the simplification and standardization of design. Turn-of-the-century New England tastes favored more modest "memorials," a new term used rather than "gravestones" for smaller "markers," while "monuments" referred to larger, unique structures. New styles became fashionable and approved by the cemetery—the Celtic Revival, the Arts and Crafts, and the neocolonial styles, as well as the "flat ledger" or horizontal tombstone from English tradition and simple, rustic boulders.

Fig. E.2. Portrait of Israel Munson Spelman (1816–1907), Mount Auburn president from 1874 to 1905, oil on canvas by John White Alexander (1856–1907), commissioned by the cemetery in 1904. MAC.

Fig. E.3. One of the best examples of the revival of the Celtic cross, on the lot of the famed symphony conductor Theodore Thomas (1835–1905). The Celtic Revival at the turn of the century, like the neocolonial style in that era and other revival styles before, did not strive for archaeological or architectural accuracy, but rather underwent innovative iconographic adaptation. Photograph by Haskell, 1937. MAC.

Fig. E.4. Neocolonial markers on the lot of the Shurcliffs. The father, Arthur, and son, Sidney, were noted landscape architects who advised Mount Auburn on the design of new burial areas. The use of contemporary floral iconography replaced the old, stern Puritan symbolism as the cemetery permitted the use of slate in the traditional form, formerly banned. Photograph by BMGL, 1984.

Fig. E.5. The neocolonial marker shared by the poet James Russell Lowell and his two wives, the only death's-head symbol at Mount Auburn. Photograph by Haskell, 1937. MAC.

Fig. E.6. Rustic boulder on the Swift family lot, inset with a bronze plaque listing all burials to replace deteriorating marble markers. Photograph by BMGL, 1986.

(Figs. E.3–E.6.) All indicated a rejection of High Victorian ostentation seen in far greater profusion at other garden cemeteries.[3]

Eventually Mount Auburn added new structures or altered older ones to embellish the grounds and modernize functions. Willard T. Sears (1837–1820) designed a new chapel and administration complex (named for Justice Story in 1936) just inside the entrance in what was called the Boston Gothic or English Perpendicular style, built of red sandstone and completed in 1898. (Figs. E.7–8.) The interior of the old chapel (named for Dr. Bigelow in 1936) was refurbished with crematory retorts (furnaces) and a "columbarium" with small niches for the storage of cremated remains, as Mount Auburn entered the vanguard of the cremation movement nationally. The admission of automobiles in 1911 required the addition of two iron gates with cast-iron finials compatible with and flanking the Egyptian gateway, since its central entrance was too narrow for the new traffic. (Fig. E.9.) Completion in 1917 of the grand twenty-six-foot-tall colonnaded memorial to Mary Baker Eddy (1821–1910), founder of the First Church of Christ, Scientist, by the architect Egerton Swartwout (1870–1943), provided a focal point on Halcyon Lake reminiscent of the siting of neoclassical temples in English gardens such as Stowe and Stourhead. (Fig. E.10.) A Tudor Revival Rest House designed by architectect Ralph Hamilton Doane in 1921 provided unprecedented amenities for visitors on the cemetery's southern periphery.

Fig. E.7. The new chapel and administration building complex, 1898, designed by architect Willard T. Sears and built of red sandstone from Potsdam, New York. In the Mount Auburn *Annual Report* of 1896 Sears described it as the "English perpendicular style as exemplified in . . . English parish churches from the early fifteenth century." It was named Story Chapel in 1936. The porte cochere and steeple shown here have since been demolished. Photograph by the Heliotype Printing Co., *American Architect and Building News* 1187 (Sept. 24, 1898). MAC.

Fig. E.8. Story Chapel interior, with a nave 116 feet long by 54 feet wide, adorned with carved woodwork of Florida gulf cypress and stained glass windows by the Boston-area studios of Earl E. Sanborn and Wilbur H. Burnham. Photograph by Harvard Film Service, ca. 1935.

When Oakes Ingalls Ames (1893–1970) became Mount Auburn's eighth president in 1934, a role in which he would serve for over thirty years, Mount Auburn entered another major phase in its landscape development. Ames was the first truly full-time, hands-on president. He kept an office at the cemetery where he constantly supervised the planting of thousands of diverse ornamentals with help from his head gardener Emil Kant, especially after the devastation wrought by the hurricane of 1938. (Fig. E.12.) Speaking the following year, Ames declared his mission: "It is hoped that

Fig. E.9. Cast-iron automobile gates with Egyptian motifs added in 1913. The Trustees opined that "the architectural effect of the entrance has been enhanced rather than diminished." MAC.

Fig. E.10. Mary Baker Eddy monument, 1917, by the architect Egerton Swartwout, on Halcyon Lake. Photograph by Harvard Film Service, ca. 1930. MAC.

Fig. E.11. Rustic brick, half-timbered, slate-roofed Tudor Revival Rest House, by Ralph Huntington Doane, 1921, built with toilets and a ladies' waiting room. It was demolished in 1982. Photograph by Haskell, 1937. MAC.

Fig. E.12. Mount Auburn as arboretum. Willow Pond as newly designed during the administration of President Oakes Ames. Photograph by Haskell, 1937. MAC.

eventually all of the more desirable species of trees that thrive in this climate will be represented in Mount Auburn, thereby carrying out the original plans of the founders for a botanical collection of real interest." A survey of the inventory of new plantings reveals that "the choices of species and cultivar types show a deliberate attempt to try plants that were new or rare at the time," many of them still "unique species growing in the Boston area." Ames planted more flowering varieties and evergreens to assure seasonal interest. The trustees hired a landscape architect, Laurence S. Caldwell, to offer design advice for peripheral areas under development. They were intent on creating "cheerful landscapes, a place that will not be forbidding but will attract those who wish an opportunity to appreciate nature in its beauty and tranquility." Caldwell also redesigned the Lawn in 1937, creating a terraced, circular focal point near the entrance, renamed Asa Gray Garden after the famed naturalist buried at Mount Auburn. (Fig. E.13.) With the cultivation of diverse plantings, Mount Auburn was acclaimed in that era by the Massachusetts Audubon Society as a paradise for ornithologists as well as growing numbers of amateur birders.[4]

Fig. E.13. Asa Gray Garden as redesigned by landscape architect Laurence Caldwell in 1937. Photograph by Haskell, 1937. MAC.

While Ames cultivated his plans to make Mount Auburn one of the nation's most exemplary arboreta, civil engineer Herbert C. Philpott, who took over as superintendent in 1938, modernized maintenance as new equipment was invented. He improved road stabilization with tarvialithic, though this made the avenues more visually intrusive. Under Philpott, who served until 1966, the cemetery weathered an era plagued by storms, the Great Depression, wars, and labor problems. He met these challenges with increased efficiencies and a sense of mission to improve the status quo, even if it meant sacrificing some older structures that had been allowed by the heirs of original proprietors to sink into decay or did not appeal to contemporary taste.[5] (Fig. E.14.)

Fig. E.14. Alice Fountain on Spruce Avenue, redesigned by (Sidney) Shurcliff and (Vincent) Merrill in 1959 to convert the original, formally curbed and tiled basin with a fountain jet into a naturalistic pool with a drip fountain. (Compare the drastic change to the original in Fig. 12.17.) Photograph by BMGL, 1991.

More advice on the plan for peripheral areas under development came from the noted landscape architects Arthur Asahel Shurcliff and his son Sidney, who used their era's Colonial Revival taste. The small areas they laid out for single and double graves are characterized by standardized memorials set upright in a linear fashion, a dramatic contrast with the older sections of the cemetery except for the public lots. (See Fig. E.4.) After World War II, burials at Mount Auburn began to represent the diverse ethnicities that had come to characterize the greater Boston area—most of them going into new sections being developed on the southwestern periphery. While the cemetery had always been nondenominational, the local archdiocese finally permitted Catholics to be buried at Mount Auburn. In the 1960s the landscape architecture firm of Innocenti & Webel redesigned the circular Asa Gray Garden yet again and advised on plantings in other small areas.[6]

By this time scarcity of land for burials had become a problem, as had an aging infrastructure. A new administration met the challenges as Duncan Munro, a civil engineering graduate of the Worcester Polytechnic Institute, was promoted to superintendent in 1967 and Alan D. Chesney, a geology graduate from Johns Hopkins, became president in 1968. Philpott and Ames advised their successors, who continued to simplify landscape maintenance through mechanization. The newly developed burial areas in the back of Mount Auburn were completely different aesthetically from the historic core, following the trend set in other cemeteries toward standardized memorials for individual and "companionate" graves. Family lots were no longer in great demand. On Willow Knoll in 1981 a huge upright abstract steel sculpture by Richard Duca was dedicated. (Fig. E.15.) The surrounding area was reserved for unobtrusive "lawn markers" set horizontally in the turf, a landscape treatment inspired by "lawn plan" cemeteries following the example of the pioneering Forest Lawn (1913) in Glendale, California, and all its "memorial park" imitators.

By 1970, feeling that there was no more contiguous land to buy and projecting that burial space might last only thirty years, the trustees sent some of their members to visit "community mausoleums" in Cincinnati's Spring Grove and elsewhere in the belief "that the European practice of above-ground burial was likely to spread." In 1973 they ordered the demolition of the obsolete Victorian receiving tomb in Indian Ridge and hired the James C. Milne Company, nationally known for such buildings, to construct the modernistic Auburn Court Crypts of pink granite with a footbridge continuing the Indian Ridge Path over the flat roof. (Fig. E.16.) A "crypt" was defined as a "discrete chamber designed, constructed, and intended for use as a permanent repository for entombment of human remains encased in a casket or other suitable container." The "garden" structure was "weatherproof, outdoors, . . . as opposed to a conventionally enclosed public mausoleum," and bore inscriptions of names and dates only in a standard font with no individualized ornamentation. Another series of such structures, Willow Garden Crypts, of simplified, temple-like design by Sasaki Associates, was dedicated in 1985 on the southern periphery.[7] (Fig. E.17.)

Fig. E.15. Richard Duca's untitled abstract sculpture of cast steel was installed in 1981 on Willow Pond Knoll between Bigelow Avenue and Bradlee Road The low spiraling walls with plantings by garden designer Julie Moir Messervy and landscape architect Thomas Paine provide space for cremated remains and seating. Photograph by Richard Cheek, 2006.

Fig. E.16. Auburn Court Crypts, faced in rose granite, designed by the Canadian firm J. C. Milne Company in 1973, nestled into Indian Ridge with a continuous walkway above. The crypts provide a courtyard passage and contemplative space between Fountain and Rosebay Avenues, but there is no interior space. MAC.

The natural destruction by pests and severe weather constantly demands new solutions to problems of landscape maintenance and restoration. Cessation of DDT spraying in the 1960s required a new approach—creative, sparing use of biological pesticides. A major outbreak of the Dutch elm disease, a threat since early in the century, obliterated the prominent "canopy" which had formed a cathedral-like nave of arching branches along Central Avenue, as it did along so many Main Streets in New England towns. This loss necessitated the planting of hardier varieties of trees scattered throughout the grounds to replace the venerable old trees. Despite such periodic devastation, a replanting

Fig. E.17. Willow Garden Crypts, several postmodern but neoclassically inspired community crypt structures with exterior access only for entombment. Designed by Sasaki Associates and built by J. C. Milne Company in 1984 on the cemetery's southern periphery. MAC.

program made Mount Auburn's tree canopy more dense, with 3,635 trees inventoried in 1989 and 5,290 in 2000. Cemetery arborist Philip H. Sands and assistant superintendent Roger S. Kindred carved out small vistas in the early 1980s by selective pruning without destroying the trees and shrubbery that formed a "green wall" around every avenue and path. In doing so they nearly restored the landscape to that of the original "forest" cemetery, albeit with the diversity of species of an arboretum.[8]

The deterioration of historic structures posed chronic problems. Removal of Story Chapel's porte cochere, which was too small for modern hearses and blocked traffic inside the entrance, opened up the original vista from the gateway into the landscape. The steeple had been taken down of necessity years before. In 1980 the trustees made the controversial but necessary decision to remove most of the crumbling cast-iron fence along Mount Auburn Street, choosing to renovate only two sixty-five-foot portions on either side of the gateway by using salvageable pieces. The Society for the Preservation of New England Antiquities and the Cambridge Historical Commission vehemently protested the loss of the artifact. Yet the integrity of the landscape and its maintenance would have been compromised if a fortune had been spent on reconstructing the fence or if it had been left in disrepair to admit vandals who were plaguing the grounds at that time. Bigelow and Story chapels, Washington tower, and architecturally significant tombs and monuments have continued to require considerable restoration.[9]

A public historical consciousness stirred by the fence controversy prompted the trustees to form the Friends of Mount Auburn Cemetery in 1985 to educate the public about notable burials, monument design, genealogical resources, horticulture, geology, and ornithology. Program director Jean L. Rosenberg declared a mission in 1987 "to present the Cemetery as an historical and natural history resource; to encourage its use and enjoyment as an outdoor museum and classroom for both study and personal reflection; and to increase public awareness . . . and thus promote the use of its diverse assets for the benefit of the surrounding community."[10]

As Alan Chesney neared retirement in 1988, the trustees sought a new president with different skills to develop Mount Auburn as a historical and cultural institution, preserving a significant landscape, believing that the cemetery was nearing the end of its active life as a burial place. The mission, as they restated it for the future, was "to commemorate the dead in surroundings of exceptional beauty and tranquility that provide comfort and inspiration to the bereaved and the public as a whole, and to offer comprehensive . . . services to all faiths at a reasonable charge." Trustee Gordon Abbott Jr. recruited William Clendaniel, his deputy director at The Trustees of Reservations, a private Massachusetts land trust that became a model for the land trust movement internationally. With a history degree from Williams College, a law degree from Harvard, and experience in state government, Clendaniel had a wide-ranging background for moving Mount Auburn into a future more focused on preservation and more conscious of its role as a community resource.[11]

Becoming president in 1988, Clendaniel declared that "Mount Auburn will increasingly become a destination of those interested in horticulture, birds, sculpture, and the history represented by those buried there." It was his intention "to respond to this interest with improved interpretive materials, programs, and physical improvements without sacrificing the tranquility appropriate to . . . the essential character" of the cemetery. More than any predecessor, he saw Mount Auburn as a "museum without walls" and championed historic preservation, restoration, interpretation, and creative use of diminishing space.[12]

The trustees' Long-Range Planning Committee had already begun to consider in 1986 how to maintain the historic landscape "to preserve its uniqueness as it inevitably continues to mature and change" and to "deal with the progressive deterioration of many of our finest sculptures." Historic landscape preservation was then in its infancy, just beginning to create methodologies through the National Association for Olmsted Parks (NAOP, founded in 1980), the interdisciplinary Alliance for Historic Landscape Preservation (1978), and the National Park Service. Having been involved with NAOP during his time at The Trustees of Reservations, Clendaniel fostered programs at Mount Auburn that focused on both rejuvenation of the historic plantings and preservation of its historic structures and monuments.

He reorganized the Friends under Janet Heywood as a charitable trust in 1990, obtaining Section 501(c)3 status that expanded its fund-raising capability. Restoring the Bulfinch urn was the first of many significant projects that followed with funds raised by the Friends. (See Fig. 9.49.) New trustees, including the first women, brought expertise in environmental issues and nonprofit law. As Heywood became vice president of interpretive programs, the activities of the Friends multiplied, continuing to bring in a wide range of interest groups for special tours and programs beyond those offered the general public. The public response since then has surpassed the "rage" for Mount Auburn in the mid-nineteenth century.[13]

The idea of creating master plans for parks and arboreta was a new one. And those naturalistic landscapes were far less complex in their structures and monuments, their forms and functions, than the aging garden cemeteries that had inspired the urban parks movement over a century before. Previously, cemetery maintenance had been relatively routine, focused on the neatness of the entire picture rather than on the details. Clendaniel remarked that "the preservation of historic landscapes is a new field in which the Cemetery [should be] in the first rank." To create Mount Auburn's own master plan following a nationwide search, he hired a team from the Halvorson Company, a Boston firm of landscape architects and planners led by Craig C. Halvorson, with Elizabeth Vizza as project manager, all with experience from similar work on Boston's Franklin Park.[14]

Completed in 1993, Mount Auburn's *Master Plan* won an American Society of Landscape Architects (ASLA) award. It was the product of intensive work by teams of trustees, staff, and an extensive array of consultants. It included a visitors' survey and historical, topographical, structural, and horticultural studies. It offered recommendations for guiding "the Cemetery's future with respect for its past and awareness of the circumstances of the present" to "safeguard those aesthetic, functional, and philosophical elements . . . fundamental to the unique character and central purposes of Mount Auburn." It spoke of respecting the collection of "landscapes of varying character" dating from different eras, which represent "the historical evolution of cemetery design including monument design; changing popular tastes; and the different natural attributes of various sites within." It pledged to preserve those of "highest visual quality" while improving those deemed "less appealing." It acknowledged that "today the landscape is a complex tapestry of natural and built elements that reflect periods of taste," and that various "responses to changing tastes and needs, and thus the layering of history, have also enriched the landscape and are stories to be celebrated and not destroyed."[15]

Clendaniel declared 1993 "a watershed year" as the cemetery charted "new directions" to "sustain its financial health while making it an even more exciting horticultural landscape and increasing the public's understanding and appreciation of its historic character." Twenty years earlier, management had been "trying to make everything look the same," Clendaniel remarked. "Now we are slowly trying to accentuate stylistic differences. Mount Auburn's value to the nation is not as any particular landscape at any particular moment." The master plan aimed to make the most of limited burial space and provide additional contemplative places while preventing overdevelopment and visual clutter and preserving existing monuments as integral components. Since 1993 the cemetery has hired various landscape architects, architects, conservators, and monument designers as consultants to achieve that mission, as it has rejuvenated the historic plantings, developed new interment space with new gardens, refurbished old buildings, and built new ones.[16]

By expanding the professional expertise of the cemetery's staff and increasing collaboration with organizations such as the American Public Garden Association (formerly the American Association of Botanical Gardens and Arboreta, 1940, renamed in 2006), the Alliance for Historic Landscape Preservation (on whose board he served for a number of years), the National Trust for Historic Preservation, and many university programs, Clendaniel has again drawn international attention back to Mount Auburn. As in the nineteenth century, trustees from many other historic cemeteries from around the country came to Mount Auburn to see its innovations in preservation, landscape rejuvenation, interpretation, and fund-raising. Founder Henry A. S. Dearborn would be gratified to see how Mount Auburn now fulfilled his initial desire to make it a laboratory for the study of landscape architecture, architecture, monument design, and horticulture, with the cemetery's historic archives catalogued and preserved under first Kathleen Leslie and then Historical Collections Curator Margaret L. "Meg" Winslow.

Fig. E.18. Spurzheim with chapel in the background, the resurgent picturesque. Photograph by BMGL, 1986.

Today, remnants of various periods of changing tastes in landscape and artifacts can be found, just as Mount Auburn's president Israel Spelman predicted over a century ago, while new attitudes toward death and commemoration, as well as the region's changing demographics and an ever-altering variety of tastes, are all in evidence in the material forms of the landscape and its structures, monuments, and plants. Mount Auburn was listed on the National Register of Historic Places in 1975 and named a National Historic Landmark by the secretary of the interior in 2003, owing to "exceptional value or quality in illustrating and interpreting the heritage of the United States," one of fewer than 2,500 sites, very few of them designed landscapes and only two others historic cemeteries.[17]

A prime factor that led to Mount Auburn's creation in 1831 was the dawning of a regional and national historical consciousness. New Englanders proved to be more concerned with the "problem of the past" and contemporaneous uses of history and commemoration than most other antebellum Americans, especially when it came to creating new funerary landscapes. As Ralph Waldo Emerson wrote in his 1836 essay "Nature": "Our age is retrospective. It builds the sepulchres of the fathers." Mount Auburn in its formative years was a prototype for many other attempts to record and remember history throughout the nation, and so it is again in a new era of historic preservation. But ours is an era that offers alternative solutions for contemporaries with different expectations, given new notions about commemoration and quite different deathways, including growing acceptance of cremation.[18]

After 175 years, Mount Auburn's private, sentimental significance remains. Its designed landscape is at the height of its beauty. It has been rediscovered as a repository of history, more complex even than its founders envisioned. The author of the cemetery's first guidebook in 1839 asked: "Future generations may be prouder of it than we are, but can they be as fond? Will not the musing moralist of those days, sometimes weary of sensations and splendor, turn or seek to turn back in imagination to this uncrowded quietude and primitive simplicity—this glistening turf—these cool, sweet-winding avenues and paths—this green, fresh beauty of the woods?" Today's generation is indeed more proud, protective, and fond of Mount Auburn in an era of "sensations and splendor" beyond the comprehension of its founders. Today, it is an even more beautiful place enshrining "Nature" shaped by "Art" than it was in its founding decades.[19]

Mount Auburn still puts the past in place in a world-renowned landscape, still makes history useful for its metropolis, its region, and its nation, as well as for those with family members buried there and for countless visitors. Despite nearly two centuries of the accretion of artifacts from many distinct eras of aesthetics and the application of new technologies to meet maintenance demands, it remains vital as an "asylum," in the original sense of the term as a retreat, to refresh the spirits of those overwhelmed by the stresses of modern life. Above all, it remains the cultural institution intended by its founders in 1831. Here, one can retreat back in time and into the timeless cycles of ever-repeating seasons, ever-renewing Nature. (Figs. E.18, E.19.) As the 1993 master plan puts it, "The best memorial to the deceased is the landscape itself."[20]

Fig. E.19. Visitors' map distributed gratis to the public by the Friends of Mount Auburn Cemetery, updated in 2006. MAC.

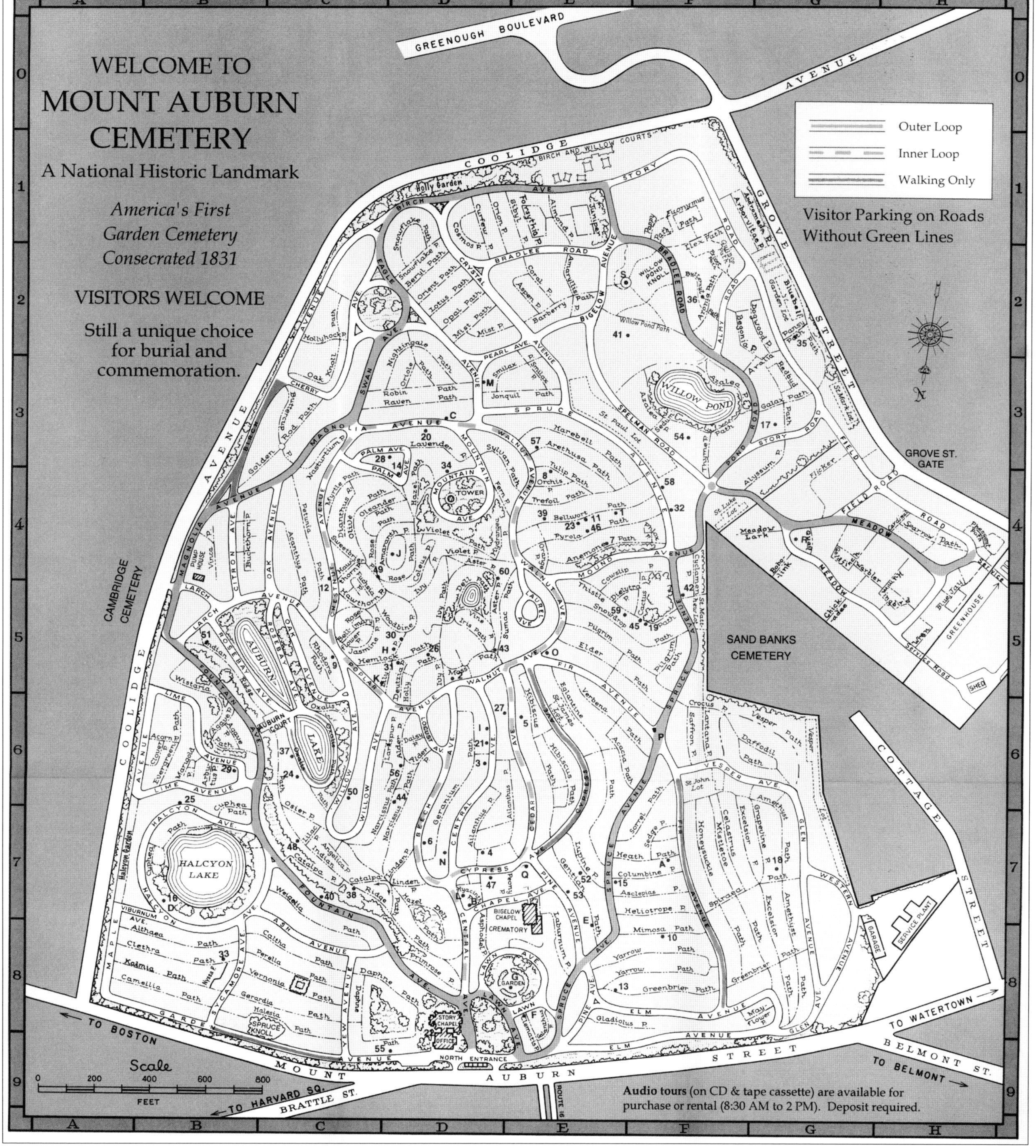
WELCOME TO
MOUNT AUBURN
CEMETERY
A National Historic Landmark
America's First
Garden Cemetery
Consecrated 1831
VISITORS WELCOME
Still a unique choice
for burial and
commemoration.
Outer Loop
Inner Loop
Walking Only
Visitor Parking on Roads
Without Green Lines
GREENOUGH BOULEVARD
COOLIDGE AVENUE
GROVE STREET
GROVE ST. GATE
SAND BANKS CEMETERY
CAMBRIDGE CEMETERY
COTTAGE STREET
MOUNT AUBURN STREET
TO BOSTON
TO HARVARD SQ.
BRATTLE ST.
TO WATERTOWN
BELMONT ST.
TO BELMONT
ROUTE 16
NORTH ENTRANCE
STORY CHAPEL
OFFICE
BIGELOW CHAPEL
CREMATORY
WILLOW POND
AUBURN LAKE
HALCYON LAKE
WASHINGTON TOWER
GREENHOUSE
SERVICE PLANT
GARAGE
Scale
0 200 400 600 800
FEET
Audio tours (on CD & tape cassette) are available for
purchase or rental (8:30 AM to 2 PM). Deposit required.

View southwest of Washington Tower toward Sylvan Path, morning, June 2005. Photograph by Carol Betsch.

View northwest from Willow Avenue, late afternoon, October 2005. Photograph by Carol Betsch.

View northwest from Mountain Avenue, below Washington Tower, late morning, June 2005. Photograph by Carol Betsch.

View southwest from Cedar Avenue, morning. October 2005. Photograph by Carol Betsch.

View west above Anemone Path, late afternoon, October 2005. Photograph by Carol Betsch.

Consecration Dell, view east along Violet Path, afternoon, June 2005. Photograph by Carol Betsch.

View south from Walnut Avenue, near Consecration Dell, early afternoon, June 2005. Photograph by Carol Betsch.

View of Gardner Mausoleum across Auburn Lake, late afternoon, October 2005. Photograph by Carol Betsch.

Auburn Lake, looking north from Larch Avenue, afternoon, October 2005. Photograph by Carol Betsch.

Spruce Knoll, morning, June 2005. Photograph by Carol Betsch.

APPENDIX I

Trustees and Officers of Mount Auburn with Terms of Service

Presidents
Joseph Story (1835–1845)
Jacob Bigelow (1845–1871)
John T. Bradlee (1871–1874)
Israel M. Spelman (1874–1905)
Prentiss Cummings (1905–1917)
William T. Richardson (1917–1918)
Charles Almy (1918–1934)
Oakes I. Ames (1934–1963)
Francis B. Richardson (1963–1967)
Oakes I. Ames (1967–1968)
Alan D. Chesney (1968–1988)
William Clendaniel (1988–)

Secretaries
George W. Pratt (1831–1832)
Charles P. Curtis (1832–1835)
Benjamin R. Curtis (1835–1844)
Henry M. Parker (1844–1855)
Austin J. Coolidge (1855–1870)
Samuel Batchelder Jr. (1870–1876)
J. Harris Reed (1876–1882)
Lewis G. Farmer (1883–1907)
John L. Dill (1907–1912)
Prentice W. Abbott (1912–1935)
Florence M. Beam (1935–1943)
T. Gordon Smith (1943–1959)
Evelyn H. Bradbury (1960–1963)
Marjorie J. Elmes (1963–1967)
J. Gardner Coolidge (1967–1984)
James M. Story (1984–2006)
Clemmie L. Cash (2006–)

Treasurers
George Bond (1831–1842)
George William Bond (1842–1867)
Austin J. Coolidge (1868–1870)
Henry B. Mackintosh (1870–1900)
John L. Dill (1900–1912)
Prentice W. Abbott (1912–1935)
John P. Knoblock (1935–1954)
Harold F. Harriman (1955–1965)
Newell W. Penniman Jr. (1966–1988)
William C. Clendaniel (1988–1989, 1991–2003)
Virginia Merler (1989–1991)
Oliver C. Scholle Jr. (2003–)

Superintendents
David Haggerston (1833–1834)
John W. Russell (1834–1840)
Rufus Howe (1841–1855)
Jonathan Mann (1855–1861)
Daniel L. Winsor (1861–1870)
Charles W. Folsom (1870–1873)
James W. Lovering (1873–1896)
James C. Scorgie (1896–1920)
John F. Peterson (1920–1939)
Herbert C. Philpott (1939–1966)
Stanley E. Robbins (1966–1967)
Duncan W. Munro (1967–1989)
Roger Kindred (Director of Cemetery Operations, 1989–1999)
David P. Barnett (Director of Operations & Horticulture, 1999–2001; Vice President of Operations & Horticulture, 2001–)

Founders and Trustees (*including dates served in other offices*)
Jacob Bigelow (1831–1879)
George Bond (1832–1842)
George W. Brimmer (1831–1832)
Henry A. S. Dearborn (1831–1833)
Edward Everett (1831–1832)
Benjamin A. Gould (1831–1859)
George W. Pratt (1831–1845)
Joseph Story (1831–1845)
Charles Wells (1831–1832)
Zebedee Cook Jr. (1832–1833)
Joseph T. Bradlee (1833–1837)
Charles Brown (1833–1837)
Charles P. Curtis (1833–1864)
Samuel Appleton (1834–1837)
Elijah Vose (1834–1837)
James Read (1835–1870)
Benjamin R. Curtis (1837–1851)
Martin Brimmer (1838–1847)
Isaac Parker (1838–1854)
Samuel T. Armstrong (1839–1840)
George W. Crockett (1843–1855)
John C. Gray (1847–1849)
John J. Dixwell (1847–1851)
Mace Tisdale (1850–1853; 1855–1858)
George H. Kuhn (1852–1855)
Charles C. Little (1852–1869)
Isaiah Bangs (1854–1859)
James Cheever (1856–1870)
Uriel Crocker (1856–1865)
William R. Lawrence (1856–1860)
Henry S. Mckean (1856–1857)
Charles C. Nazro (1856–1865)

William T. Andrew (1859–1863)
Jacob Sleeper (1859–1870)
Edward S. Tobey (1859–1863)
Edward Austin (1860–1870)
Edward S. Rand (1860–1871)
George Livermore (1864–1865)
Otis Norcross (1864–1870)
J. Ingersoll Bowditch (1865–1870)
Paul Adams (1865–1870)
Loyal Lovejoy (1865–1870)
Isaac Livermore (1866–1874)
John T. Bradlee (1870–1877)
Nathaniel J. Bradlee (1870–1880)
Alfred T. Turner (1870–1874)
Thomas M. Brewer (1870–1880)
Edward Lawrence (1871–1881)
Charles F. Choate (1871–1911)
William Perkins (1871–1880)
Samuel T. Snow (1871–1880)
James L. Little (1871–1877)
Henry W. Pickering (1872–1877)
T. Quincy Browne (1874–1899)
Israel Spelmen (1874–1905)
Charles U. Cotting (1877–1885)
Alanson Bigelow (1877–1884)
Henry A. Rice (1877–1895)
David B. Whitney (1879–1911)
William S. Eaton (1880–1899)
Roger Wolcott (1880–1893)
Jerome Jones (1880–1901; 1906–1916)
Samuel R. Payson (1880–1894)
J. Montgomery Sears (1881–1905)
Channing Clapp (1885–1892)
Richard M. Hodges (1885–1897)
Samuel Johnson (1893–1899)
Joseph Sawyer (1894–1901)
Henry S. Shaw (1894–1899)
David W. Cheever (1896–1907)
Francis C. Foster (1896–1915)
Frank W. Reynolds (1899–1905)
Joseph B. Russell (1899–1929)
Charles W. Watson (1900–1910)
Prentiss Cummings (1900–1917)
Edward W. Hutchins (1901–1929)
Thomas P. Beal (1902–1923)
Franklin W. Hobbs (1906–1952)
Alfred Hemenway (1906–1927)
William L. Richardson (1907–1932)
John G. Wright (1911–1912)
Edwin H. Abbott (1911–1927)
Charles F. Choate Jr. (1911–1927)
Wallace L. Pierce (1912–1920)
John Noble (1917–1943)
Charles E. Cotting (1917–1970)
Charles Almy (1917–1934)
Charles Walcott (1920–1935)
Thomas P. Beal Jr. (1923–1977)
Charles F. Choate III (1927–1930)
W. Rodman Peabody (1927–1940)
William H. Claflin (1928–1971)
Edward Hutchins (1929–1937)
Charles A. Coolidge Jr. (1929–1935)
Theodore L. Storer (1930–1974)
Charles M. Storey (1932–1979)
Oakes I. Ames (1934–1963; 1967–1968)
Arthur H. Morse (1935–1946)
Samuel L. Batchelder (1936–1987)
E. Francis Bowditch (1937–1939)
Charles F. Wolcott (1939–1942)
Lucius T. Hill (1941–1972)
Francis W. Hatch (1942–1969)
J. Gardener Coolidge (1944–1984)
John Noble Jr. (1946–1949)
Malcolm D. Perkins (1949–1989)
Samuel H. Wolcott Jr. (1953–1986)
Francis B. Richardson (1963–1967)
Alan D. Chesney (1968–1988; honorary trustee until his death in 1997)
Francis W. Hatch Jr. (1969–1989; honorary to 1997)
Herbert W. Pratt (1970–1997)
William H. Claflin III (1971–1980)
Robert A. Lawrence (1972–2002)
Gordon Abbott Jr. (1974–2004)
James M. Storey (1979–)
John K. Spring (1980–1995)
Hamilton Coolidge (1984–2003)
Peter S. Ashton (1985–2001)
William C. Clendaniel (1988–)
Ann M. Roosevelt (1989–)
Marion Fremont-Smith (1989–2001)
Thomas C. Cooper (1994–)
Charles T. Haydock (1994–2003)
Laura A. Johnson (1995–2002)
Oliver C. Scholle Jr. (2000–)
Clemmie L. Cash (2001–)
Louise E. Weed (2001–)
Samuel B. Carr Jr. (2003–)
Peter Shaffer (2003–)
William A. Truslow (2003–)
Mary Lee "Widgie" Aldrich (2004–)
Kim Gluck (2004–)
David Straus (2004–)
Karen Weltchek (2004–)

APPENDIX II

A Selected Chronology of Notable American "Rural" or "Garden" Cemeteries and Major Designers

Date of founding reflects incorporation or dedication rather than first use for burials, as a few of the sites had previous burials. Many are listed on the National Register of Historic Places.

1831
Mount Auburn. Boston (Cambridge/Watertown), Massachusetts; 72 acres (now 175). Gen. Henry A. S. Dearborn; Dr. Jacob Bigelow.

1836
Mount Hope. Bangor, Maine; 100 acres (now 264). Charles G. Bryant.
Laurel Hill. Philadelphia, Pennsylvania; 20 acres (now 200). John Notman; John Jay Smith; James C. Sidney.

1837
Green Mount. Baltimore, Maryland; 60 acres (now 68). Benjamin Henry Latrobe Jr.; Robert Carey Long.

1838
Green-Wood. Brooklyn, New York; 178 acres (now 478). Major David Bates Douglass; Henry Evelyn Pierrepont; Almerin Hotchkiss.
Mount Hope. Rochester, New York; 54 acres (now 196). Designer unknown.
Rural Cemetery. Worcester, Massachusetts; 24 acres (now 40). James Barnes; Timothy Paine.

1839
Harmony Grove. Salem, Massachusetts; 35 acres. Francis Peabody; Alexander Wadsworth.

1841
Rural Cemetery. Springfield, Massachusetts; 20 acres (now 26). George Eaton with Rev. William B. O. Peabody; Apollos March.
Rural Cemetery. Albany, New York; 120 acres (now 467). Consecrated 1844. Major David B. Douglass.

1842
Woodland. Dayton, Ohio; 40 acres (now 200). John Van Cleve; Adolph Strauch; Samuel Forrer.

1844
Allegheny. Pittsburgh (Lawrenceville), Pennsylvania; 100 acres (now 360). John Chislett; William Falconer.
Mount Pleasant. Newark, New Jersey; now 40 acres. Horace Baldwin.

1845
Spring Grove. Cincinnati, Ohio; 166 acres (now 733). Howard Daniels with Joseph Earnshaw; Adolph Strauch; William Salway.

1847
Cypress Hills. Kings and Queens Counties, Long Island, New York; 25 acres (now 400). Enlarged in 1873 with a national cemetery section. Designer unknown.
Swan Point, Providence, Rhode Island; 60 acres (now 200). Dr. Thomas C. Hartshorn; Niles Bierragaard Schubarth; H. W. S. Cleveland.

1848
Cave Hill. Louisville, Kentucky; 47 acres (now 300). Edmund Francis Lee; David Ross; Robert Ross; Robert Campbell; Benjamin Grove.
Woodland. Xenia, Ohio. Howard Daniels.

Oakwood. Troy, New York; 150 acres (now 625). John Clarke Sidney; Major David Bates Douglass; John Boetcher.
Forest Hills. Boston (Roxbury), Massachusetts; 71 acres (now 275). Gen. Henry A. S. Dearborn.
Lexington. Lexington, Kentucky; 40 acres (now 170). Charles S. Bell; John Lutz.
Bonaventure. Savannah, Georgia; 70 acres. Designer unknown.

1849
Elmwood. Detroit, Michigan; 42 acres (now 86). Original designer unknown; Frederick Law Olmsted.
Green Lawn. Columbus, Ohio; 83 acres (now 360). Howard Daniels.
Oak Hill. Georgetown, District of Columbia; 15 acres (now 35). Capt. George F. de la Roche; William W. Corcoran.
Bellefontaine. St. Louis, Missouri; 138 acres (now 333). Almerin Hotchkiss; Frank Hotchkiss.
Mountain Grove. Bridgeport, Connecticut; now 125 acres. Phineas Taylor ("P. T.") Barnum.
Forest Lawn. Buffalo, New York; 80 acres (now 269). Charles E. Clarke; Adolph Strauch.
Holly-Wood. Richmond, Virginia; 45 acres (now 135). John Notman.
South Laurel Hill. Philadelphia, Pennsylvania. James Clarke Sidney; John Jay Smith; James P. W. Neff.
Easton. Easton, Pennsylvania. James Clarke Sidney.
Magnolia. Charleston, South Carolina; now 128 acres. Edward C. Jones.
The Evergreens. Brooklyn-Queens, New York; 184 acres (now 225). Andrew Jackson Downing; Alexander Jackson Davis; Calvert Vaux; Samuel Parsons.

1850
Forest Home. Milwaukee, Wisconsin; 72 acres (now 200). Increase Latham
Mount Feake. Waltham, Massachusetts; now 4 acres. Robert Morris Copeland.
Oakland. Atlanta, Georgia; 6 acres (now 88). Originally City Burial Place; named 1872. Designer unknown.

1851
Cedar Grove. New London, Connecticut; 39 acres (now 55). Dr. Horatio Stone.
Erie. Erie, Pennsylvania. Howard Daniels.
Woodlawn. Chelsea-Everett (Boston), Massachusetts; 100 acres (now 178). H. Weld Fuller.
Ryder. Ossining, New York. Howard Daniels.

1852
Dale. Claremont, New York. Howard Daniels.
Greenwood. New Orleans, Louisiana. Designer unknown.
Elmwood. Memphis, Tennessee; 40 acres (now 80). Designer unknown.

1853
Woodland. Cleveland, Ohio. Howard Daniels.
Spring Forest. Binghamton, New York. Howard Daniels.
Rome. Rome, New York; 25 acres. Howard Daniels.
Brookside. Watertown, New York. Howard Daniels.
Riverside. Waterbury, Connecticut. Howard Daniels.
Rural. Poughkeepsie, New York; 54 acres (now 200). Howard Daniels.
Evergreen. Gettysburg, Pennsylvania. David McConaughy.

1854
Oak Woods. Chicago, Illinois; 180 acres (now 300). No burials until 1860. Adolph Strauch.
Cambridge City. Cambridge, Massachusetts; now 66 acres. Designer unknown.

1855
Sleepy Hollow. Concord, Massachusetts. H. W. S. Cleveland and Robert Morris Copeland; John Shepard Keyes.
Newton. Newton, Massachusetts; now 100 acres. Designer unknown.
Mount Wollaston. Quincy, Massachusetts; 25 acres (now 57). Daniel Brims; Dr. William Pattee; Luther Briggs; Daniel Briggs.
Oak Grove. Gloucester, Massachusetts. H. W. S. Cleveland and Robert Morris Copeland.
Chippiannock. Rock Island, Illinois; 62 acres (now 85). Almerin Hotchkiss.
Green Mount. Montpelier, Vermont; now 35 acres. Designer unknown.
Evergreen. Portland, Maine; now 239 acres. Designer unknown.
Fairmount. Newark, New Jersey; 60 acres (now 150). Designer unknown.
Spring Hill. Lynchburg, Virginia. John Notman.

1856
Laurel Grove. Port Jervis, New York; 35 acres. Howard Daniels with B. F. Hattaway.

1857
Woodlands. Cambridge, New York. James C. Sidney.
Holyhood. Brookline, Massachusetts; 31 acres (now 36.2). Patrick Charles Keeley.
Lake Forest. Lake Forest, Illinois; 32 acres. Almerin Hotchkiss; William LeBaron Jenny; Ossian Cole Simonds.
Wyoming. Melrose, Massachusetts; 49 acres. H. W. S. Cleveland and Robert Morris Copeland.

1858
Calvary. St. Louis, Missouri; 323 acres (now 477). Archbishop Peter Richard Kenrick.
Mount Olivet. District of Columbia. Designer unknown.

1859
Oakwood. Syracuse, New York; 92 acres (now 147). Howard Daniels with Elias B. Leavenworth and Hamilton White; Olmsted & Vaux.
Lindenwood. Fort Wayne, Indiana; 152 acres (now 175). John Chislett; John Doswell; Henry Doswell.
Rosehill. Chicago, Illinois; now 350 acres. William Saunders.

1860
Oak Ridge. Springfield, Illinois; 29 acres (now 300). William Saunders; parts by Adolph Strauch after President Lincoln's death.
Graceland. Chicago, Illinois; 86 acres (now 119). Swain Nelson with

William Saunders; H. W. S. Cleveland and William M. R. French; William Le Baron Jenney; Ossian Cole Simonds.

1861
Hillside. Middletown, New York. Calvert Vaux.
Evergreen. Rutland, Vermont. Designer unknown.

1863
Cedar Hill. Hartford, Connecticut; 250 acres (now 270). Jacob Weidenmann; William Salway.
Woodlawn. Bronx, New York; 313 acres (now 400). James C. Sidney; John Jay Smith.
Mountain View. Oakland, California; now 226 acres. Frederick Law Olmsted.
Soldiers' National. Gettysburg, Pennsylvania. William Saunders; David Wills; David McConaughy.

1864
Crown Hill. Indianapolis, Indiana; 265 acres (now 555). John Chislett; Frederick Chislett; Adolph Strauch; George Kessler.
Arlington National. Arlington, Virginia; now 612 acres. Gen. Montgomery Meigs.

1867
Cedar Lawn. Paterson, New Jersey. Gen. Egbert L. Viele.
West Laurel Hill. Philadelphia (Bala Cynwyd), Pennsylvania; now 187 acres. John Jay Smith.

1869
Woodmere. Detroit, Michigan. Adolph Strauch.
Lake View. Cleveland, Ohio; 200 acres (now 285). Adolph Strauch; John Boddy; Olmsted Brothers; A. D. Taylor.
Highland. Covington, Kentucky; 104 acres (now 300). Adolph Strauch.
Oak Hill. Cedar Rapids, Iowa. H. W. S. Cleveland with William M. R. French.

1870
Highland. Junction City, Kansas. H. W. S. Cleveland with William M. R. French.
Cedar Hill. Newburgh, New York. Charles Downing.

1871
Lakewood. Minneapolis, Minnesota; 130 acres (now 250). Col. William S. King; Charles W. Folsom; A. B. Barton.
Rock Creek. District of Columbia; now 86 acres. First burials in 1719. Designer unknown.

1872
Metairie. New Orleans, Louisiana; 80 acres. Benjamin Morgan Harrod.

1873
Eastwood. Lancaster, Massachusetts. H. W. S. Cleveland.

1876
Riverside. Cleveland, Ohio; 102.5 acres. Edward O. Schwagerl.
Woodlawn. Toledo, Ohio; now 160 acres. Frank Eurich; Frank Jessup Scott; Edward O. Schwagerl.

1878
Homewood. Pittsburg, Pennsylvania; 178 acres (now 200). Designer unknown.
Oak Lawn. Dwight, Illinois. H. W. S. Cleveland with William M. R. French.

1880
New Union. Lincoln, Illinois. H. W. S. Cleveland with William M. R. French.
Forest Hills. Chattanooga, Tennessee; now 100 acres. Col. Abraham Malone Johnson.

1881
Trinity. New York City. Originally founded 1842. Calvert Vaux & Co. with George K. Radford.

1883
Evergreens. Brooklyn, New York. Calvert Vaux & Co. with George K. Radford.
Walnut Grove. Little Rock, Arkansas. George Edward Kessler.

1884
Highland Lawn. Terre Haute, Indiana; 139 acres. Joseph Earnshaw.

1885
Harleigh. Camden, New Jersey. George E. Rhedemeyer.
Riverside. Ashville, North Carolina; now 87 acres. Designer unknown.

1887
Riverside. Macon, Georgia; now 125 acres. Calvert Vaux & Co. with George K. Radford.

1888
Riverside. Trenton, New Jersey. Calvert Vaux & Co. with George K. Radford.
Maple Grove. Wichita, Kansas; now 60 acres. A. A. Hyde; Albert Ellis.

1891
Mount Washington. Kansas City, Missouri; 400 acres (now 200). George Edward Kessler.

1892
Fairlawn. Oklahoma City, Oklahoma. George Edward Kessler.
Cypress Lawn. Colmar, California; 60 acres. Hamden Holms Noble; Alexander Davidson.

1895
Hope. Barre, Vermont; 53 acres (now 65). Edward P. Adams.

1897
Elmwood. Kansas City, Missouri; now 50 acres. Founded 1872. George Edward Kessler.

1902
Oaklawn. Kansas City, Missouri. George Edward Kessler.

NOTES

Abbreviations

AAS	American Antiquarian Society, Worcester, Mass.
AR	*Annual Report*, MAC
BPL	Boston Public Library
BPLRB	Boston Public Library Rare Books Room
HNE	Historic New England, Boston (formerly Society for the Preservation of New England Antiquities)
HUA	Harvard University archives, Houghton Library, Cambridge
HUCLM	Harvard University Countway Library of Medicine, Boston
MHIS	Massachusetts Historical Society, Boston
MHORT	Massachusetts Horticultural Society, Wellesley, Mass.
MAC	Mount Auburn Cemetery Archives, Cambridge
NYPL	New York Public Library
TM	Trustees' Minutes, MAC

Introduction

1. Alexis de Tocqueville met members of the Boston elite, many of whom were founders of Mount Auburn, at a dinner hosted by Alexander Everett.
2. In Britain, the Whigs defended traditional liberties they considered natural, tracing them to the Saxons, holding that they checked the power of the monarchy through Parliamentary power while maintaining the Protestant succession to the throne after the deposition of the Stuarts and the accession of the German House of Hanover with George I in 1714. Their Tory opponents supported the Stuarts, with their tendency toward Roman Catholicism.
3. The term "culture" is used in its nineteenth-century sense, often closely associated with art and literature and hence akin to meanings of "high culture" or "civilization" but also frequently associated with "the idea of care . . . or superintendence of the landscape." Both uses implied spiritual purpose. See *Edgar Allen Poe: Selected Prose, Poetry, and "Eureka,"* ed. W. H. Auden (New York: Holt, Rinehart & Winston, 1950), 401–2. For discussion of voluntary civil associates as a product of individualism in free institutions, see Tocqueville, *Democracy in America*, ed. J. P. Mayer (Garden City, N.Y.: Doubleday, 1969), 513–24.
4. Whiggism in different national contexts shared an opposition to a strong central authority (in England epitomized by the Tories) and an ideology that celebrated "natural law" and "heroes" who defended basic constitutional rights. The historicism it informed long predated the writing of histories such as the tomes (1848–55) by Thomas Macauley so criticized by the British historian Herbert Butterfield (1900–1979) in *The Whig Interpretation of History* (1931; reprint, New York: W. W. Norton, 1965). As my book argues, the first manifestations of Whig historicism are to be found in designed landscapes and monuments.
5. Malcolm MacColl, *Lawlessness, Sacerdotalism, and Ritualism Discussed in Six Letters Addressed . . . to the Right Hon. Lord Selborne* (London: J. T. Hayes, 1875), 418–19.
6. [John Calvin], *The Forme of Prayers and Ministrations of the Sacraments, etc., Used in the English Congregation at Geneva; and Approved by the Famous and Godly Learned Man, Iohn Caluyn* (1556), reprinted in *The Liturgical Portions of the Genevan Service Book* (Edinburg and London, 1931), 161. Also see Horton Davies, *The Worship of the English Puritans* (Westminster: Dacre Press, 1948), 121–22. When Calvinists used the term "church," it referred to congregants accepted for membership, not the structure where they met or some larger hierarchy dictating to individual congregations. In this book, "Church," capitalized, refers to a hierarchy, whether Roman Catholic or Anglican.
7. See Allan Ludwig, *Graven Images: New England Stonecarving and Its Symbols, 1650–1815* (Middletown, Conn.: Wesleyan Univer-

sity Press, 1966); Edward Young, *Night Thoughts on Life, Death, and Immortality*, vol. 1 (Philadelphia: Benjamin Johnson, 1805), 143.

8. Henry St. John Bolingbroke, *The Craftsman* (July 5, 1735), quoted in Michael Leslie, "History and Historiography in the English Landscape Garden," in *Perspectives on Garden Histories*, ed. Michael Conan (Washington, D.C.: Dumbarton Oaks, 1999), 100–102. See the history of usage of the term "revolution" in the *Oxford English Dictionary*.
9. Nature is capitalized here, as it frequently was in the eighteenth and early nineteenth centuries, when meant to epitomize a sacred force, as in "God and Nature" or "Nature and Art." When referring to the nature of a place, indigenous terrain and flora, or a state of being, it remains lower case.
10. John Bunyan, *Pilgirm's Progress from This World to That Which is to Come Delivered under the Similitude of a Dream Wherein Is Discovered the Manner of His Setting Out, His Dangerous Journey, and Safe Arrival at the Desired Country* (1678), ed. Roger Sharrock (New York: Viking Penguin, 1985). This is considered the standard edition. Bunyan's reference to the Celestial City "upon a mighty hill" may have drawn upon John Winthrop's 1630 lay sermon to Puritan settlers aboard the *Arbella* headed to found the Massachusetts Bay Colony. It led to his election as its first governor: "Wee must Consider that wee shall be as a Citty vpon a Hill." John Winthrop, "A Modell of Christian Charity," in *The Puritans: A Sourcebook of Their Writings*, ed. Perry Miller and Thomas H. Johnson, rev. ed., vol. 1 (New York: Harper & Row, 1963), 195.
11. Jacques Delille, "Preface by the Translator," in René Luis Marquis de Girardin, *An Essay on Landscape; or, On the Means of Improving and Embellishing the Country Around Our Habitations* (London: J. Dodsley, 1793), xxxvi. The term "tourism" developed at the end of the eighteenth century in reference to making the principal stops on the Grand Tour. By that time, however, the itinerary had become far more extensive, bringing international travelers into contact with one another, escalating the rate of cross-cultural borrowing. The painter Washington Allston from Boston met Coleridge in Rome in 1806. In 1826 Harvard's president, John Thornton Kirkland, and his wife visited the pyramids in Egypt. Mary Bigelow to [her mother], (June 20, 1826), Bigelow Papers, MHIS.
12. Allegory and historicism were intimately related, as French architectural critic Antoine-Chrysostome Quatramère de Quincy recognized: "By means of allegory, the art of architecture is made *historian* and *narrator*: It explores for us the general and particular subject which it treats, and it informs us of the moral aim as well as the physical use of the building. Allegorical decoration takes the place of inscriptions; and it speaks better." Quatramère de Quincy, "Décoration," in *Encyclopédie Méthodique*, 2, pt. 1, 179, quoted in Anthony Vidler, *The Writing on the Walls* (Princeton: Princeton Architectural Press, 1987), 161–62. Vidler also argues for major Masonic influence on English gardens and their use, factors which may carry over in aesthetic influence on the landscape style of "rural" cemeteries but which I have not attempted to add to this study. I use the term "English garden" (*le jardin anglais* in French) as shorthand for the eighteenth-century "Whig idea of landscape," which contrasted dramatically in style with the artificial linear formality of gardens favored by Tories. For more discussion of the contrasts, see Nigel Everett, *The Tory View of Landscape* (New Haven: Yale University Press, 1994). My study deliberately avoids the landscape reform of the "beautiful" by Lancelot "Capability" Brown because it contained few of the allegorical or historic references of other landscape gardeners in the "picturesque" style and because it had little influence on other landscapes of memory or "rural" cemeteries during the period under consideration in this book. Brown's landscapes of expansive lawns were meant for viewing from a distance or in transit in a carriage rather than on a pensive promenade. A variation of the taste for the "beautiful" began to appear in American landscape design from the 1860s on.
13. Horace Walpole, *The History of the Modern Taste in Gardening* (Strawberry Hill: [by the author], 1780); Rev. William Mason, "The English Garden: A Poem," *The Gentleman's Magazine* 42 (1772): 78–80, quoted in Edward Malins, *English Landscaping and Literature, 1660–1840* (London: Oxford University Press, 1966), 87.
14. Arthur O. Lovejoy, *Essays in the History of Ideas* (Baltimore: Johns Hopkins University Press, 1948), 134; A. A. Tait, *The Landscape Garden in Scotland, 1735–1835* (Edinburgh: Edinburgh University Press, 1980), 7; Christopher Hussey, *English Gardens and Landscapes, 1700–1750* (New York: Funk & Wagnalls, 1967), 112, 89, 100–101. This definition of "fantasy" comes from *The American Heritage Dictionary of the English Language*, ed. William Morris (Boston: Houghton Mifflin, 1976).
15. Lawrence Stone, *The Family, Sex, and Marriage in England, 1500–1800* (New York: Harper & Row, 1977), 3–4; Stone, "Death and Its History," *New York Review of Books* 25.15 (October 12, 1978): 22. David Hume used the word "sentiment" to mean both feeling and thought, thus giving a different interpretation to "sentimentality" in his era than it would acquire in the nineteenth century. David Daiches, Peter Jones, and Jean Jones, eds., *A Hotbed of Genius: The Scottish Enlightenment, 1730–1790* (Edinburgh: Edinburgh University Press, 1986), 18. For ref erences to Twickenham, developed by Pope from 1719 into the 1740s, see http://www.victorianweb.org/previctorian/pope/twickenham.html.
16. Delille, "Preface," iv.
17. William Wordsworth, quoted in F. R. Cowell, *The Garden as Fine Art* (Boston: Houghton Mifflin, 1978), 185. Mortuary themes used in English gardens were drawn from Virgil, Seneca, Lucretius, and Ovid.
18. Much neoclassical symbolism also had distinctly Masonic meaning internationally, a factor too complex for consideration in this book, although many of the men involved in creating the gardens and the monuments, let alone the new political and cultural order on both sides of the Atlantic, had Masonic affiliation. Whiggism involved Masons and non-Masons alike.
19. Gordon S. Wood, *The Creation of the American Republic, 1776–1787* (Chapel Hill: University of North Carolina Press, 1969), 33; Wordsworth, *The Prelude; or, Growth of a Poet's Mind: An Autobiographical Poem*, bk. 11 (composed ca. February 1804) (New York: Appleton, 1850); Edward Everett, "An Oration Pronounced at Cambridge before the Phi Beta Kappa Society, Aug. 27, 1824," *North American Review* 20.11 (1825): 422–23.
20. Justin Winsor, ed., *The Memorial History of Boston, 1630–1800*, vol. 4 (Boston: James R. Osgood, 1881), 86.
21. Harrison Gray Otis to George Harrison, March 2, 1823, in *The*

Life and Letters of Harrison Otis, ed. Samuel Eliot Morison, vol. 1 (Boston: Houghton Mifflin, 1946), 449; Odell Shepard, ed., *The Journals of Bronson Alcott* (Boston: Little, Brown, 1938), 15; [Thomas Green Fessenden], *New England Farmer* 9.7 (September 3, 1830): 53.

22. [Henry A. S. Dearborn], "Mount Auburn Cemetery: Report of the Massachusetts Horticultural Society upon the Establishment of an Experimental Garden and Rural Cemetery, Boston, 1831," *North American Review* 33 (October 1831): 403.
23. Alain Corbin, *The Foul and the Fragrant: Odor and the French Social Imagination* (Cambridge: Harvard University Press, 1986).
24. Ronald Story, *The Forging of an Aristocracy: Harvard and the Boston Upper Class, 1800–1870* (Middletown, Conn.: Wesleyan University Press, 1980).
25. Alexander H. Everett, *An Address Delivered before the Massachusetts Horticultural Society at Their 5th Annual Festival, Sept. 18, 1833* (Boston: J. T. Buckingham, 1833), 19.
26. "Mount Auburn," *New-England Magazine* 1.3 (September 1831): 236–39.
27. H. A. S. Dearborn, "Mount Auburn Cemetery," *North American Review* 33 (October 1831): 397–98; Wilson Flagg, *Mount Auburn: Its Scenes, Its Beauties, and Its Lessons* (Boston: James Munroe, 1861), 272. See Wood, *The Creation of the American Republic*, 33; also excerpted as "The Whig Science of Politics," in *Interpreting Colonial America: Selected Readings*, ed. James Kirby Martin (New York: Harper & Row, 1978), 340.
28. Andrew Jackson Downing, "Improving the Public Ground in the City of Washington," letter to President Millard Fillmore, Winterthur Document (n.d. [1851?]), no. 4836, 6–7, quoted in Walter L. Creese, *The Crowning of the American Landscape* (Princeton: Princeton University Press, 1985), 207. For a chronology of major "rural" and "garden" cemeteries, see Appendix II. The influence can be seen in the design of the suburbs of Clifton (beginning in 1852) just north of Cincinnati, Llewellyn Park (1853) in New Jersey, and Lake Forest (1857) north of Chicago.
29. Garry Wills, *Lincoln at Gettysburg: The Words That Remade America* (New York: Simon & Schuster, 1992), 63, 212, and passim.
30. Edward Bellamy, *Looking Backward* (1888; New York: Viking Penguin, 1982), 44.

1. Common Pits and Grim Graveyards

1. Institutionalization of burials emerged at different times in different areas following conversion to Christianity. The Saxons were not converted until the eighth century, the Danes not until the tenth.
2. *Monumenta Germaniae Historica* (Hanover, 1875–89), quoted in Philippe Ariès, *The Hour of Our Death*, trans. Helen Weaver (New York: Knopf, 1981), 38, 50–51; Ariès, *Images de l'homme devant la mort* (Paris: Seuil, 1983), 20–21.
3. Michel Ragon, *The Space of Death: A Study in Funerary Architecture, Decoration, and Urbanism*, trans. Alan Sheridan (Charlottesville: University of Virginia Press, 1983), 51. In 1783, the French considered introducing wolves surreptitiously into England to weaken British power. Fernand Braudel, *Capitalism and Material Life, 1400–1800*, trans. Miriam Kochan (New York: Harper & Row, 1973), 34. For a depiction of wolves lurking outside cemetery walls, see the mid-nineteenth-century painting *Les Lupens* by Maurice Sand (1828–89) in the Musée Goya, Castres, France.
4. See Maud de Leigh Hodges, *Crossroads on the Charles: A History of Watertown, Massachusetts* (Canaan, N.H.: Phoenix, for the Watertown Free Public Library, 1980), 31; Howard S. Russell, *A Long, Deep Furrow: Three Centuries of Farming in New England* (Hanover, N.H.: University Press of New England, 1976), 23, 83; Edward Doubleday Harris, introduction to Thaddeus William Harris, *Epitaphs from the Old Burying Ground in Watertown* (Boston 1869), ii. By the mid-nineteenth century in New England, wolves had long been exterminated. That permitted Yankees to consider founding new burial grounds on the periphery of urban development.
5. Betty Willsher and Doreen Hunter, *Stones: A Guide to Some Remarkable Eighteenth-Century Scottish Gravestones* (New York: Taplinger, 1979), 60; Henry A. S. Dearborn, "Report," in "Proceedings of the Massachusetts Horticultural Society . . . 1831," *New England Farmer* 9.49 (June 22, 1831), 385. On the French cypress, see C.-P. Arnaud, *Recueil de tombeaux des quatres cimetières de Paris* (Paris: Arnaud & Germain Mathiot, 1824), 1:42.
6. The yew, *Taxus baccata Linnaei*, was called *Iw* in Saxon and *Yw* in Welsh. F. E. Warren, *The Liturgy and Ritual of the Celtic Church* (Oxford: Clarendon Press, 1883), 94; James Stevens Curl, *The Victorian Celebration of Death* (London: Trowbridge, 1972), 45; John Potenger, "Pastoral Reflections on Death" (1691), quoted in John Draper, *The Funeral Elegy and the Rise of English Romanticism* (New York: New York University Press, 1929), 66–69; T. T. W., "Botanical History of the Yew Tree," *Gentleman's Magazine* 56, pt. 2, no. 5 (November 1786): 941. The popularity of planting yews in Scottish graveyards has been attributed to the order by Edward IV that every man must have a bow. The strong but flexible yew branches were perfect for making bows. Yew wood was so precious for long bows that Venetians shipped it to England from Turkey until the sixteenth century, when that supply ran out and the Turks had to import it for themselves from Germany. Fernand Braudel, *The Mediterranean and the Mediterranean World in the Age of Philip II*, trans. Sian Reynolds, 2 vols. (New York: Harper & Row, 1973), 2:800–801; T. J. Pettigrew, *The Chronicles of Tombs*, cited in Willsher and Hunter, *Stones*, 60. The blooming yew produces a hallucinogenic chemical. Also see Vaughan Cornish, *The Churchyard Yew and Immortality* (London: F. Muller, 1946).
7. The name *Druid*, for instance, meaning "knowing the oak tree," applies to an elite Celtic class charged with guarding sacred oak groves and other holy sites (*loci consecrati*), according to Caesar. Carlo Borromeo, *Instructiones Fabricae et Suppellectilis Ecclesiasticae* (Milan, 1577), cited in Richard A. Etlin, *The Architecture of Death: The Transformation of the Cemetery in Eighteenth-Century Paris* (Cambridge: MIT Press, 1984), 90, 380. Borromeo, *Arte Sacra: De Fabrica Ecclesiae* (Milan: Typografia sociale, 1952), capo 27, "Sepolcreti e Cimiteri," 88: "Non vi si devono piantare viti, alberi, arbusti, sterpi di alcun genere, no solo di quelli da frutta, ma nemmanco di quelli che producano bacche d'alcun genere. Anzi non vi si lasci neppure crescere erba o fieno che serva per pascolo angli animali." M. [Henri] Bourde de la Rogerie, *Le Parlement de Bretagne, l'éveque de Rennes et les ifs dans les cimetières, 1636–7* (Rennes, 1931), quoted in Ragon, *Space of Death*, 115; and in John McManners, *Death and the Enlightenment: Changing Attitudes to Death among Christians and Unbelievers in Eighteenth-Century France*

(Oxford: Clarendon Press of Oxford University Press, 1981), 305.

8. Ariès, *The Hour*, 39–41.
9. Léon Vafflard, *Notice sur les champs de sépulture anciens et modernes de la ville de Paris* (Paris: Charles de Mougues Frères, 1867), 22–23, 34. Robert Hertz observes the prevalence in many societies of a second burial of remains after decomposition, attributing the practice to social and psychological as well as practical motivations. In seventeenth- and eighteenth-century French and Italian cemeteries, it was a functional necessity to free grave space for reuse. Robert Hertz, *Death and the Right Hand*, trans. Rodney and Claudia Needham (Glencoe, Ill.: Free Press, 1960), chap. 6. Reinterments persisted even into the mid-nineteenth century in Boston, the records of Mount Auburn Cemetery reveal, but they were voluntary rather than mandatory.
10. Ariès, *Images*, 24–29.
11. P. Lorrain to Pierre Muret, *Rites of Funeral, Ancient and Modern* (London, 1683), quoted in David E. Stannard, *The Puritan Way of Death: A Study in Religion, Culture, and Social Change* (New York: Oxford University Press, 1977), 106; Philippe Habert, *The Temple of Death: A Poem*, trans. John Sheffield Buckingham (London: Daniel Brown, 1701); Louis-Sébastien Mercier, *Le Tableau de Paris, nouvelle édition, corrigée et augmentée*, 12 vols. (Amsterdam, 1782–88), 3:178, quoted in French in McManners, *Death and the Enlightenment*, 63.
12. Stone, *Family*, 3–4.
13. Pierre Patte, quoted in Richard A. Etlin, "Landscapes of Eternity: Funerary Architecture and the Cemetery, 1793–1881," *Oppositions* 8 (Spring 1977): 18; Nicher-Cérisy, *Des Tombeaux* (Paris, [ca. 1796], 20–21; François-Marie Marchant de Beaumont, *Manuel et itinéraire du curieux dans le cimetière du Père la Chaise*, (1820), 3rd ed. (Paris: Emler Frères, 1828), v–vi, 244.
14. Leon Bernard, *The Emerging City: Paris in the Age of Louis XIV* (Durham N.C.: Duke University Press, 1970), 188–89. For a discussion of the new sensitivity to smells, see Corbin, *The Foul and the Fragrant*.
15. Félix Vicq-d'Azyr, *Essai sur les lieux et les dangers de sépultures* (Paris, 1778).
16. Henry Martyn Dexter, *The Congregationalism of the Last Three Hundred Years* (New York: Harper & Brothers, 1880), 11, 26.
17. [Bishop] Henri de Sponde, *Les Cimetières sacrez* (Bordeaux, 1598), quoted in Ariès, *The Hour*, 315–17.
18. Jean Calvin, *Institutes*, trans. T. Norton (London, 1611), 4:10:29; Dexter, *Congregationalism*, 46, 73.
19. *A Directory for the Publique Worship of God, Throughout the Three Kingdomes of England, Scotland, and Ireland. Together with an Ordinance of Parliament for the Taking Away of the Book of Common-Prayer; and for Establishing and Observing of This Present Directory Throughout the Kingdom of England, and the Dominion of Wales. Die jovis 13 martii, 1644* (London: Evan Tyler et al., 1644).
20. City Lands Committee of the Corporation of London, *History of Bunhill Fields Burying Ground, with Some of the Principal Inscriptions* (London: Charles Skipper & East, 1902). *Bunhill Fields Burial Ground: Proceedings in Reference to Its Preservation with Inscriptions on the Tombs* (London: Hamilton, Adams, 1867).
21. "The Cemeteries and Catacombs of Paris," *Quarterly Review* 21.42 (April 1819): 381.
22. In 1777, John Wesley presided at ceremonies laying the cornerstone of the Methodist chapel just across the City Road. The small graveyard behind it contains the tombs of Wesley and other leading Methodist ministers. By the late eighteenth century many newer Protestant sects were more accepting of burial near their churches than their Dissenting ancestors had been. T. D. Woolsey, "Cemeteries and Monuments," *New Englander* 28 (November 1849): 493.
23. *The Diary of John Evelyn*, ed. E. S. DeBeer (London: Oxford University Press, 1959), 563 (October 17, 1671); *Webb's Collection of Epitaphs* (London, 1775), quoted in Curl, *Celebration*, 40.
24. "Cemeteries and Catacombs," 380; Joseph Stevens Buckminster Thacher, "Address at the Commencement . . . 1832," manuscript in "Exhibition and Commencement Performances" (1831–32), Harvard University Archives (hereafter HUA); Mrs. [Isabella] Basil Holmes, *The London Burial Grounds* (London: Fisher Unwin, 1896,) 3.
25. John Hitchcock, "Victorian London Cemeteries," *GenDocs: Genealogical Research in England & Wales* (1996–2003), http://www.gendocs.demon.co.uk/cem.html; A Looker-On [John Ross Dix], *Local Loiterings and Visits in the Vicinity of Boston* (1845), reprinted as "An Englishman's Opinion of Mount Auburn," *Mount Auburn Memorial* 2.3 (July 18, 1860): 19.
26. Burial reform came late to Britain. In the 1810s, Parliament considered banning iron coffins from London burial grounds in land granted for a limited term of years but not in space purchased in fee simple. An act of 1823 allowed burial of suicides in churchyards, albeit at night and without Church rites, ending the practice of interring their bodies in a public highway with a stake driven through them. Compulsory dissection of murderers' bodies did not end until 1832. Official registration of deaths in England did not begin until 1837. The National Society for the Abolition of Burial in Towns (1845) lobbied for the Metropolitan Burial Act of 1852, which ended new burials in old urban churchyards. It stipulated suburban sites to be determined by the General Board of Health with the Commissioners of Sewers and appointed the Burial Board for parishes of the City of London and its liberties. The City of London Cemetery on ninety acres of farmland at Little Ilford, designed by engineer and surveyor Colonel William Haywood with landscape by Robert Davidson, was finally consecrated in 1857. The impulse for documentation and preservation did not arise until the 1880s. After extensive research on graveyards for the London County Council and Metropolitan Gardens Association, Mrs. Holmes placed her "Notes on Their History from the Earliest Times to the Present Day" in the London Metropolitan Archives and the Guildhall Library Manuscript Section. See http://www.londoncemeteries.co.uk/holmes.html.
27. Lady Andros died January 22, 1687/8, and was buried on February 10. Henry Wilder Foote, *Annals of King's Chapel from the Puritan Age of New England to the Present Day*, vol. 1 (Boston: Little, Brown, 1882), 74–76.
28. Increase Mather, *Meditations on Death* (Boston: Timothy Green, 1707); William Cooper, *A Sermon Concerning the Laying of Deaths of Others to Heart* . . . (Boston: B. Green for B. Eliot, 1720), 27. The Mather dynasty of Puritan divines built a family tomb in Copp's Hill Burying Ground near the North Church where Increase was pastor. The Mathers were staunch defenders of the old Puritan theocracy. After the revolt against Andros, Increase successfully obtained a new charter in 1691 from the Protestant sovereigns

William and Mary, which united Plymouth Colony with the Massachusetts Bay Colony.

29. *Historical Sketch and Matters Appertaining to the Granary Burial-Ground* (Boston: Municipal Printing Office, 1902), 8; *Historical Sketch of King's Chapel Burying-Ground* (Boston: Municipal Printing Office, 1903), 41, 52; *Historical Sketch of the First Burying Place in Roxbury* (Boston: Municipal Printing Office, 1904), 41–45. The practice of erecting fences around burials in these graveyards arose to protect graves and stones from browsing cattle more than from the desire to stake out posthumous property. When the grazing of cattle in burial grounds ceased in the Boston area following complaints by physicians in the 1790s, no attempt was made to introduce ornamental plantings or to provide maintenance to keep down weeds. As late as 1841, during the first campaign to add plantings to Dorchester's first burial ground, Samuel Downer found that he had to clear the stubborn growth of "Suckery, Brambles and Full grass" before the ground could be sodded. *Historical Sketch of the First Burying Ground in Dorchester* (Boston: Municipal Printing Office, 1903), 56.
30. The earliest surviving grave marker in Massachusetts is the rough-hewn boulder marked simply "E.L." and dated 1647 in the common burying ground of Ipswich. What would become the region's conventional slab gravestone did not appear in quantity until the 1660s and 1670s. Ludwig, *Graven Images*, 283–87. Peter Benes notes that in Plymouth, the graves of only about half the population received a stone although the town had a resident stonecarver. Peter Benes, *The Masks of Orthodoxy: Folk Gravestone Carving in Plymouth County, Massachusetts, 1689–1805* (Amherst: University of Massachusetts Press, 1977), 12, 41.
31. William Wordsworth, "Essay upon Epitaphs," in *The Excursion: A Poem* (New York: C. S. Francis, 1850), 329–40.

2. The English Garden

1. Philippe Ariès, *The Hour*, 198 and passim; Lawrence Stone, "Death and Its History," *New York Review of Books* 25.15 (October 12, 1978): 22. The old notion was expressed in Robert Burton's *The Anatomy of Melancholy, What It Is, With All the Kinds, Causes, Symptomes, Prognostickes and Severall Cures of It* (1621), which went through five editions before the author's death in 1640.
2. John Milton, *Il Penseroso* (Oxford: Clarendon Press, 1883).
3. Sir Thomas Browne, *Hydriotaphia: Urne-Buriall; or, A Discourse of the Sepulchrall Urnes Lately Found in Norfolk* (London: Henry Browne, 1658).
4. John Evelyn, *Silva; or, A Discourse of Forest-Trees, and the Propagation of Timber in His Majesty's Dominions . . . together with an Historical Account of the Sacredness and Use of Standing Groves, with Notes by A. Hunter, M.D.* 2 vols. (1664; reprint, York, England: Longman, Hurst, Rees, Orme & Brown, 1812), 1:268, 275, 300. A group of "natural philosophers" won a second charter from King Charles II in 1663 as the Royal Society of London for Improving Natural Knowledge, but it is known internationally simply as The Royal Society.
5. Ibid., 1:319, 322. See Therese O'Malley and Joachim Wolschke-Bulmahn, eds. *John Evelyn's "Elysium Britannicum" and European Gardening* (Washington, D.C.: Dumbarton Oaks Colloquium on the History of Landscape Architecture, 1998). Until the Age of Revolutions, the remaining forests had been either natural enclaves suspected of being places of lawlessness and rebellion, as in the Robin Hood legends, or preserved under the control of royalty for hunting as sport. They were not considered useful as timber reserves until Britain had become largely denuded of its forests.
6. Evelyn, *Silva*, 1:341–42.
7. Evelyn, quoted in "Cemeteries and Catacombs," 381.
8. James Stevens Curl, *A Celebration of Death: An Introduction to Some of the Buildings, Monuments, and Settings of Funerary Architecture in the Western European Tradition* (New York: Charles Scribner's Sons, 1980), 102.
9. Cokayne and Clarke in John W. Draper, *The Funeral Elegy*, 190; Isaac Watts, "The Church-Yard," in *Reliquiae Iuveniles: Miscellaneous Thoughts in Prose and Verse, on Natural, Moral and Divine Subjects* (London: James Brackstone, 1742), 107.
10. Draper, *Funeral Elegy*, 21.
11. Louis Cazamian, "Modern Times (1600–1914)," in Emile Légois and Louis Cazamian, *A History of English Literature*, trans. W. D. MacInnes and Louis Cazamian (New York: Macmillan, 1929), 853. For this reason, the best-known poems of the eighteenth century were Young's *Night Thoughts*, Pope's *Essay on Man*, and Thomson's *The Seasons*, published and republished in full and in excerpts into the mid-nineteenth century in America as well as in England. Bostonian Nathan Appleton owned copies of Thomson, now in Harvard's Widener Library.
12. I would argue that the "Puritan spirit" was not solely synonymous with Calvinism but with other offshoots of Protestantism whose adherents were labeled "Dissenters" or "Nonconformists," ever evolving and proliferating to result in the liberal spiritual strains typical of the Deists, who eschewed any ministry, or of the Unitarians, who formed a denomination. It has been argued that the rise of English Freemasonry "possibly" played a central role, since Batty Langley, Robert Walpole, Joseph Addison, Alexander Pope, William Kent, Sir John Vanbrugh, Richard Steele, the Earl of Shaftesbury, James Thomson, Lord Burlington, Lord Cobham, and others reputedly belonged to the secret society, which promoted many ideals associated with the Enlightenment and had a taste for architectural symbolism characteristic of new picturesque gardens. Evidence, however, remains fragmentary and circumstantial. Patrizia Granziera, "Freemasonic Symbolism and Georgian Gardens," *Esoterica* 5 (2003): 41–72. http://www.esoteric.msu.edu/VolumeV/Freemasonill.html.
13. The personification and sacrilization of Nature as a spiritual force, a prime mover, a source of life and morality in the context of which death lost its horror in fact reflects a new belief system.
14. *Diary of John Evelyn*; Robert Burton, *The Anatomy of Melancholy* (1621), quoted in John Dixon Hunt, *The Figure in the Landscape: Poetry, Painting, and Gardening during the Eighteenth Century* (Baltimore: Johns Hopkins University Press, 1976), 65.
15. Erwin Panofsky, "*Et in Arcadia Ego*: Poussin and the Elegiac Tradition," in *Meaning in the Visual Arts* (Garden City, N.Y.: Doubleday, 1955), 312.
16. *Et in Arcadia Ego* is now in the Louvre and *Landscape with the Body of Phocion* is on loan from a private collection to the National Museum of Wales, Cardiff.
17. Edmund Arwaker, J.H. Esq., and Sir F.F., Knight of Bath, quoted in Draper, *Funeral Elegy*, 148–49. In contrast with the imagery of

these verses was the fate of Oliver Cromwell's remains. After the Restoration, Charles II ordered that the Lord Protector's embalmed corpse be removed from its Westminster Abbey tomb and publicly hung at Tyburn, site of criminal executions. When Cromwell's body was finally buried beneath the gallows, his head remained impaled atop Westminster Hall throughout the remainder of Charles II's reign. It is remarkable that Cromwell had been embalmed, a very rare practice in that era.

18. Shaftesbury, quoted in Basil Willey, *The Eighteenth-Century Background: Studies of the Idea of Nature in the Thought of the Period* (London: Chatto & Windus, 1949), 63.
19. Anthony Ashley Cooper, Third Earl of Shaftesbury, *Characteristics of Men, Manners, Opinions, Times* (1711), 2nd ed., 2 vols. (London, 1714), 2:388–95.
20. For definitions of "elysium," see Joseph Addison, *Tatler* no. 123 (January 21, 1710) and *Spectator* no. 417 (June 28, 1712). The translator of Virgil's *Georgics* derived the term from the Elysian Fields, where dead heroes lived according to Greek myth.
21. Sir William Chambers, *A Dissertation on Oriental Gardening* (London: W. Griffin, printer to the Royal Academy, 1772), 37–38; also quoted in Lovejoy, *Essays*, 130–31.
22. See Alexander Pope, *An Essay on Man* (London, 1734); A. Lynn Altenbernd, "On Pope's 'Horticultural Romanticism,'" *Journal of English and Germanic Philosophy* 54 (October 1955): 470–77.
23. Pope, "Epistle IV to Richard Boyle, Earl of Burlington: Argument of the Use of Riches," in *Alexander Pope's Epistles to Several Persons (Moral Essays)*, ed. James E. Willington (Coral Gables: University of Miami Press, 1976), 130–31, lines 47–58. Pope has often been misquoted by zealous landscape gardeners intent on accentuating the prescriptive message for those who would impose Art on Nature, by substituting the imperative voice Pope did not use (eliminating the "s" from "calls," "catches," "joins," "varies," "breaks," "paints," and "designs"), taking away control from the Genius of Place and assigning it to the hand of man.
24. [Anon.], *The Rise and Progress of the Present Taste in Planting Parks, Pleasure Grounds, Gardens, etc. . . . in a Poetic Epistle to the Right Honourable Charles Lord Viscount Irwin* (London: for C. Moran, 1767), 17.
25. Ibid., 17, 20, 23, passim.
26. Kent, quoted in Edward Malins, *English Landscaping and Literature, 1660–1840* (London: Oxford University Press, 1966); James Boutwood, "Poet's Essay in the Picturesque, Alexander Pope's Garden at Twickenham," *Country Life* 143 (March 7, 1968): 512–14; John Dixon Hunt, "Pope's Twickenham Revisited," *Eighteenth-Century Life* 8, n.s. 2 (January 1983): 29–30.
27. Graevius's *Thesaurus* encompassed twelve volumes, published 1694–1699, followed by *Thesaurus Antiquitatum et Historiarum Italiae*, published posthumously, 1704–1725.
28. Peter Gay, *The Enlightenment: The Rise of Modern Paganism* (New York: W. W. Norton, 1966), 59.
29. Batty Langley, advertisement in *Daily Advertiser* no. 138 (1731), quoted in Bernard Denvir, *The Eighteenth Century: Art, Design, and Society, 1689–1789* (London: Longman, 1983), 253. The 1729 publication of Palladio's *Five Orders of Architecture* in London by the architect Colin Campbell made engravings accessible.
30. James Thomson, "Autumn," lines 964 and 1031, in *The Seasons* (1st American ed. Newburyport, Mass.: John Mycall for the Boston Book-Store, 1790).
31. For Switzer, "Art" implied artifice by the "hand of man," not limited to sculpture and architecture. Stephen Switzer, *Ichnographia Rustica; or, The Nobleman, Gentleman, and Gardener's Recreation* (London: D. Brown et al., 1718), iii, xi.
32. Ibid.
33. Batty Langley, *New Principles of Gardening* (London: Bettesworth, Batley et al., 1728). Speculation on the location of the site that inspired Sweet Auburn has varied. Many literary scholars consider it Goldsmith's native Lissoy in Ireland. Others point to English sites such as the village of Nuneham, moved in 1760 a mile from the place where Horace Walpole, first Lord Harcourt, intended to develop his pleasure gardens, Nuneham Courtenay. Or it might be the village of Stowe, displaced two miles from its original site in 1730 by Lord Cobham for the same reason. David Jarrett, *The English Landscape Garden* (New York: Rizzoli, 1978), 8, 130.
34. In addition to examples in France discussed in chapter 3, see Géza Hajós, *Romantische Gärten der Aufklärung: Englische Landschaftskultur des 18. Jahrhunderts in und um Wien* (Vienna: Böhlau Verlag Wien, 1989).
35. Bridgeman, who designed the gardens of Claremont, was the first professional gardener to reject the rigid formality of landscape design imported from France, although his work remained more geometric than "picturesque." Peter Willis, *Charles Bridgeman and the English Landscape Garden* (London: A. Zwemmer, 1977), 121–22. Pope, "Epistle IV," lines 69–70. Two rich Web sites are http://nationaltrust.org.uk/places/stowegardens/elysian_fields/html and John D. Tatter's http://panther.bsc.edu/-jtatter/html, (accessed June 2006).
36. William Gilpin, *A Dialogue Upon the Gardens of the Right Honourable the Lord Viscount Cobham at Stowe in Buckinghamshire* (1748; reprint, Los Angeles: University of California Press, 1976), 28–30. Willis notes that the design of the Elysian Fields recreates a dream allegory of Virtue, Honour, and (Modern) Vanity described by Addison in *Tatler* no. 123 (January 21, 1710) and expanded upon in other writings.
37. See "Stowe: *Templa Quam Dilecta*: How Beautiful Are Thy Temples," http://www.stoweschool.org/history/gardens_park/index.html. Perhaps it was the recurring element of hermitages and the sentiment of retreat to seclusion in English gardens that inspired Andrew Jackson to dub his Tennessee estate "The Hermitage."
38. John M. Robinson, *Temples of Delight: Stowe Landscape Gardens* (London: National Trust, 1990), quoted in Tatter, http://panther.bsc.edu/-jtatter/gothic.html, 2.
39. Sarah Bridgeman, *Stowe Gardens* (London: John Bowles & Son, 1746). [Benton Seeley], *A Description of the Magnificent House and Gardens of the Right Honourable Richard Grenville Temple, Earl Temple, Viscount and Baron Cobham at Stowe in Buckinghamshire* (London: B. Seeley, 1744); George Bickham, *The Beauties of Stowe* (London: John Bowles & Son, 1750); Gilpin, *Dialogue upon the Gardens*, 48. Bickham, the engraver, included sixteen illustrations. Other major guides to Stowe and other picturesque gardens include Samuel Boyse, "The Triumphs of Nature: A Poem," *Gentlemen's Magazine* 12 (August 1742): 324; Daniel Defoe, appendix to *Tour Thro' the Whole Island of Great Britain*; Seeley, *Description*; Bickham the Younger, *The Beauties of Stowe, the Gardens of the Right Honourable Lord Viscount Cobham, Addressed to Mr. Pope* (London: George L. Gilliver, 1732; John Bowles & Son,

1750, 1753, and 1756); Thomas Whately, *Observations on Modern Gardening Illustrated by Descriptions* (Dublin: John Exshaw, 1770).

40. Duchess of Portland, quoted in B. Sprague Allen, *Tides in English Taste (1619–1800): A Background for the Study of Literature*, vol. 2 (Cambridge: Harvard University Press, 1937), 175. Madame Fiquet du Boccage [née Anne Marie Fiquet Le Page], *Lettres sur l'Angleterre* (1762), quoted in Dora Wiebenson, *The Picturesque Garden in France* (Princeton: Princeton University Press, 1978), 25–27. Laurence Whistler, Michael Gibbon, and George Clarke, *Stowe: A Guide to the Gardens* (London: E. N. Hillier & Sons, 1974), 22–23.
41. Aislabie received minimal professional advice from the Palladian architect Colin Campbell, with most of the work done by the estate gardener William Fisher with local labor.
42. Kenneth Woodbridge, *Landscape and Antiquity: Aspects of English Culture at Stourhead, 1718–1838* (Oxford: Clarendon Press, 1970), and *The Stourhead Landscape* (London: National Trust, 1982), 25.
43. William Shenstone, *Unconnected Thoughts on Gardening*, in *The Works in Verse and Prose of William Shenstone, Esq.*, 2nd ed., 2 vols. (London: J. Dodsley, 1765–66), 2:111–31. *The Letters of William Shenstone*, ed. Marjorie Williams (Oxford: Basil Blackwell, 1939).
44. Shenstone, *Unconnected Thoughts*. Shenstone himself chose to be buried in the churchyard at Halesowen rather than at The Leasowes.
45. Shenstone, *Letters*, 204. Richard Graves, *The Spiritual Quixote; or, The Summer's Ramble of Mr. Geoffrey Wildgood: A Comic Romance* (London: J. Dodsley, 1774), 23–25. Joseph Spence, *Observations, Anecdotes, and Characters of Books and Men, Collected from the Conversation of Mr. Pope and Other Eminent Persons of His Time* (1820), 2 vols., ed. James M. Osborn (Oxford: Clarendon Press, 1966), 1:250, 422. Arthur Young, *A Six Months' Tour Through the North of England, Containing an Account of the Present State of Agriculture, Manufactures and Population, in Several Counties of This Kingdom*, 2nd ed., 4 vols. (London: W. Strahan, 1771), 3:280–81. G. G. J. and J. Robinson, *A Companion to The Leasowes, Hagley, and Enville* (London: M. Swinney; Birmingham: J. Holl, 1789).
46. Mrs. Elizabeth Singer Rowe, quoted in Draper, *Funeral Elegy*, 254.
47. Thomas Warton the Younger, *The Pleasures of Melancholy* (London: R. Dodsley, 1747), lines 28–29, 34–39.
48. Thomas Gray, *An Elegy Written in a Country Church-Yard* (London: R. Dodsley, 1751).
49. Michael Symes, "Nature as the Bride of Art: The Design and Structure of Painshill," in *Eighteenth-Century Life* 8, n.s. 2, ed. Robert P. Maccubbin and Peter Martin (January 1983): 63–73.
50. Lady Irwin, quoted in Christopher Hussey, *English Gardens and Landscapes, 1700–1750* (New York: Funk & Wagnalls, 1967), 115; and in Etlin, *The Architecture of Death*, 172.
51. *The Rise and Progress of the Present Taste in Planting Parks, Pleasure Grounds, Gardening, etc. . . . in a Poetic Epistle to the Right Honourable Charles Lord Viscount Irwin* (London: For C. Moran, 1767), 115.
52. Walpole, "On Modern Gardening," written between 1750 and 1770, originally appeared in his *Anecdotes of Painting in England*, vol. 4 (London 1780), 117–51, and described his friend's aversion to baroque French gardens.
53. Nicholas Penny, *Church Monuments in Romantic England* (New Haven: Yale University Press, 1977), 44.
54. John Adams, ambassador to the Court of St. James's, and Thomas Jefferson, ambassador to France, visited several English gardens together in the spring of 1786 using Whately's *Observations*, Seeley's *Description . . . of Stowe*, Seeley's *Guide to Hagley and The Leasowes*, and a volume by Shenstone.
55. *Connoisseur* (March 1756), quoted in Gay, *The Enlightenment*, 41; and/or *Connoisseur* (1755), quoted in Denvir, *The Eighteenth Century*, 152–53.
56. Edmund Burke, *A Philosophical Inquiry into the Origin of Our Ideas of the Sublime and the Beautiful* (Philadelphia: D. Johnson, 1806), 35, 40, 103.
57. James T. Boulton, ed., *Edmund Burke's Philosophical Enquiry into the Origin of Our Ideas of the Sublime and the Beautiful* (South Bend: University of Notre Dame Press, 1968), pt. 1, sec. xiii, 44; pt. 2, iii.
58. One exception was the rustic grotto Brown added beside a man-made lake in Croome Park, Worcestershire, in the mid-1760s, his first independent commission.
59. See Sir Uvedale Price, *An Essay on the Picturesque, as Compared with the Sublime and the Beautiful; and, On the Use of Studying Pictures, for the Purpose of Improving Real Landscape*, 3 vols. (London: J. Mawman, 1810), 1:68–70. Richard Payne Knight, *The Landscape: A Didactic Poem in Three Books, Addressed to Uvedale Price, Esq.* (London, 1794). "The Chinese Origin of a Romanticism," in Lovejoy, *Essays*, 129. For the debate on the picturesque, see Gavin Budge, ed., *Aesthetics and the Picturesque, 1795–1840*, 6 vols. (Bristol: Thoemmes Press, 2001). Knight's poem is reprinted in vol. 1, Price's essays in vols. 3–5.
60. Chambers, *Dissertation*, 37–38.
61. Archibald Alison, *Essays on the Nature and the Principles of Taste* (1790; reprint, Boston: Cummings & Hilliard, 1812), 179–80.
62. A. A. Tait, *The Landscape Garden in Scotland, 1735–1835* (Edinburgh: Edinburgh University Press, 1980), 203, 207. See Sir H[erbert] J[ohn] C[lifford] Grierson, ed., *The Letters of Sir Walter Scott*, 12 vols. (London: Constable, 1932–37).
63. William Wordsworth, "Essay upon Epitaphs," 408.
64. See, for instance, Hajós, *Romantische Gärten der Aufklärung*.
65. Sir Horace Walpole to Rev. William Mason, November 17, 1775, in Walpole, *Letters*, ed. Mrs. P. Toynbee (Oxford: Oxford University Press, 1925); Thomas Whately, *Observations on Modern Gardening*. See Isabel W. U. Chase, ed., *Horace Walpole, Gardenist: An Edition of Walpole's "The History of Modern Taste in Gardening"* (1780; reprint, Princeton: Princeton University Press, 1943).
66. Daniel Webster, "An Address Delivered at the Laying of the Cornerstone of the Bunker Hill Monument" (1825), in *The Writings and Speeches of Daniel Webster*, 18 vols. (Boston: Little, Brown, 1903), 1:180.

3. The French Cult of Ancestors and the Birth of Père Lachaise

1. Horace Walpole, *Essai sur l'art des jardins modernes*, trans. M. le Duc de Nivernois (Strawberry Hill, England: T. Kirgate, 1785).
2. The Yuan Ming Yuan (Garden of Perfect Brightness, or Garden of Gardens) was destroyed, ironically by Anglo-French forces, during the Boxer Rebellion in 1860. The Jesuit Jean-Denis Attiret (1702–1768) describes it in *Lettres édifiantes et curieuses écrites des mission étrangères par quelques missionnaires de la compagnie de Jésus* (Paris: Guérin, 1743), 7–10. It was translated by Joseph Spence

[alias Sir Harry Beaumont] in *A Particular Account of the Emperor of China's Gardens near Pekin* (London: R. Dodsley, 1752). (Unless otherwise noted, translations from the French are my own.)

3. Georges-Louis LeRouge, *Cahiers des jardins anglo-chinois à la mode* (Paris: LeRouge, 1776–1785).
4. Salomon Gessner, *Idyllen* (1756); in French, *Idylles at poèmes champêtres*, trans. Michel Huber (Lyon: J. M. Buryset, 1762).
5. Jean de Cayeux, *Hubert Robert et les jardins* (Paris: Herscher, 1987).
6. Whately, *Observations*; Claude-Henri Watelet, *Essai sur les jardins* (Paris: Chez Perault, 1774); C. C. L. Hirschfeld, *Théorie de l'art des jardins, Traduit de l'allemand*, 5 vols. (Leipzig: Weidmann Erben & Reigh, 1779–1785); in English, *Theory of Garden Art*, ed. and trans. Linda B. Parshall (Philadelphia: University of Philadelphia, 2001).
7. Delille, *Les Jardins; ou, l'art d'embellir les paysages* (1782), quoted in Ariès, *The Hour*, 520–51. Delille, "Preface by the Translator," in René-Louis, marquis de Girardin, *An Essay on Landscape; or, on the Means of Improving and Embellishing the Country Around Our Habitations*, trans. R.-L. Girardin, vicomte d'Ermenonville (London: J. Dodsley, 1793), iv, vi.
8. Jean-Jacques Rousseau, *Les Rêveries du promeneur solitaire* (Paris: Garnier, 1960).
9. Girardin, *De la composition des paysages*.
10. Also, burial of Rousseau there solved a problem. Girardin knew that Voltaire, who had died days before, had been officially "damned" as an atheist and denied Church burial by the Paris clergy. Voltaire was quietly but defiantly entombed at a small Cistercian abbey near Romilly-sur-Seine.
11. René Mathieu, *Ermenonville* (Paris: Nouvelles Editions Latines, 1985).
12. Louis-Stanislas-Cécile-Xavier, comte de Girardin, *Promenade ou itinéraire des jardins d'Ermenonville* (Paris: Chez Mérigot, 1788). The brother of the marquis affixed his name as author to a book by that title published with the marquis's *Promenade ou itinéraire des jardins de Chantilly* (Paris: Desenne, Gattey, Guyot, et Hédouin, 1791).
13. The Touring Club of France purchased most of the estate's gardens in the 1920s, preserving them today along with about thirty of the original *fabriques*.
14. The term *désert*, meaning "wilderness," signified a forest, totally contrary to the notion of a desert as an arid sand waste. Racine de Monville was a close friend of the duc d'Orléans, who developed the Parc Monceau, as well as of Benjamin Franklin during his stay in France from 1776 to 1785. Olivier Choppin de Janvry, *Réponses a 101 questions sur le Désert de Retz* (Croissey-sur-Seine: Société Civile du Désert de Retz, 1988). Although Racine de Monville escaped the guillotine only because the Terror came to an end, the finances of the "playboy" had been devastated by the time of his death in 1797; and the domaine itself passed into other hands. Although visitors still came, other proprietors let the estate fall into ruin. Finally, it was declared a Historical Monument in 1941. Restoration did not begin until 1981.
15. Useful works on the English garden style in France are Alexandre L.-J. Comte de Laborde, *Déscription des nouveaux jardins de la France et de ses anciens châteaux* (Paris: Delance, 1808); J[ean] C[harles] Krafft, *Plans des plus beaux jardins pittoresque de France, d'Angleterre, et d'Allemagne* 2 vols. (Paris: Levrault 1809 and 1810); Wiebenson, *The Picturesque Garden in France*; and Vidler, *The Writing on the Walls*.
16. Cayeux, *Hubert Robert*, 118–19.
17. See [Louis Carrogis de] Carmontelle, *Le Jardin de Monceau, près de Paris* (Paris: Delafosse, 1779); David L. Hays, "Carmontelle's Design for the Jardin de Monceau: A Freemasonic Garden in Late-Eighteenth-Century France," *Eighteenth-Century Studies* 34.4 (Summer 1999): 446–62; Hays, "'This is not a '*Jardin anglais*': Carmontelle, the Jardin de Monceau, and Irregular Garden Design in Eighteenth-Century France," in *Villas and Gardens in Early Modern Italy and France*, ed. Mirka Benes and Dianne Harris (New York: Cambridge University Press), 294–326, 408–19.
18. There was already a cenotaph to Captain Cook in the famed gardens of Stowe. Many of the *fabriques* were moved to the Parc de Jeurre in Morigny-Champigny in 1895.
19. See Prince Charles-Joseph de Ligne (1735–1814), *Coup d'Oeil at Beloeil and a Great Number of European Gardens*, trans. Basil Guy (1795; reprint, Berkeley: University of California Press, 1991). The prince lost his Belgian estates owing to the French Revolution, then accepted diminished exile in Vienna.
20. Laborde, *Déscription*, 109.
21. François-Marie Arouet de Voltaire, "La Considération due aux gens de lettres," in *Lettres Philosophiques*, vol. 12 (Paris, 1878), in *XVIIIe Siècle: Les grands auteurs français du programme*, ed. André Lagarde and Laurent Michard, vol. 4 (Paris: Bordas, 1965), 124.
22. Lucretius and Voltaire quoted in Gay, *The Enlightenment*, 102–4.
23. Voltaire, "Enterrement," in *Oeuvres complètes: Dictionnaire philosophique portatif, ou la raison par alphabet*, vol. 2 (Paris: Garnier Frères, 1878), 550–51.
24. Jean Le Rond d'Alembert, *Preliminary Discourse to the Encyclopedia of Diderot*, trans. Richard N. Schwab (Indianapolis: Bobbs-Merrill, 1963), 53–54, 100; George Armstrong Kelly, "Mortal Politics in Eighteenth-Century France," *Historical Reflections* 13.1 (Spring 1986): 49–50. Plutarch's *Parallel Lives* (ca. 100 AD), comparing the lives of Greek and Roman heroes, was equally popular in the new American republic.
25. McManners, *Death*, 170–71. Claude-Adrien Helvétius, *De l'esprit; or, Essays on the Mind and Its Several Faculties* (London: J. Dodsley, 1759); Abbé Rémi, *Les Jours, pour servir de correctif et supplement aux Nuits de Young* (Paris, 1770).
26. Jan Ingenhousz, *Experiments in Vegetables, Discovering Their Great Power of Purifying the Common Air in Sunshine, and of Injuring It in Shade and at Night, to Which is Joined a New Method of Examining the Accurate Degree of the Salubrity of the Atmosphere* (London: P. Elmsley & H. Payne, 1779); Girardin, *An Essay*, 121–22.
27. Bernardin de Saint-Pierre, *Études de la nature*, quoted in Duval, *Des Sépultures*, 76–81. The new Revolutionary or Republican calendar was instituted on October 24, 1793, and lasted until January 1, 1806. As a rejection of the Gregorian calendar along with Catholicism and its holy days, it had twelve months named after seasonal characteristics. Each month was divided into three décades of ten days, thus eliminating the concept of Sunday. Six days between Fructidor and Vendémiaire were secular feast days.
28. Bernardin de Saint-Pierre, quoted in Duval, *Des Sépultures*, 76–81. See Leo Marx, *The Machine in the Garden*; Mircea Eliade, *The Sacred and the Profane*.
29. Bernardin de Saint-Pierre, *Études*, 5:405. Bernardin's essay "On

the Pleasure of Tombs" was first made available to Americans in the translation of Henry Hunter, *Studies from Nature* (Worcester, Mass.: J. Nancrede, 1797).

30. P. A. Vieillard, "Fouché," *Nouvelle Biographie Générale*, ed. Ferdinand Hoefer, vol. 18 (Paris: Firmin Didot Frères, 1870), 262; Norman Hampson, *The Life and Opinions of Maximilien Robespierre* (London: Penguin, 1974), 181.
31. Pierre-Gaspard Chaumette, *Arrêtés du Conseil-Général de la Commune de Paris rélatif aux différents cultes et aux prêtres* (Paris: le 17 vendémiare, year II [October 8, 1793]), 106–7; Vieillard, "Fouché," 262. Four days later Chaumette decreed the destruction of all "barbarian monuments" from the old regime and publicly staged the mock funeral of an aristocrat.
32. Chaumette, *Arretés*, 106–7; [Avril], *Rapport de l'administraton des travaux publics sur les cimetières, lu au Conseil-Général par le citoyen Avril* (Paris, n.d [1793?]), 7.
33. Abbé Henri Grégoire, *Second rapport sur le vandalisme* (Paris, 1794), 6. Also see Vidler, *The Writing on the Walls*, 168–69.
34. [Abbé] F[rançois]-V[alentin] M[ulot], *Vues d'un citoyen, ancien Deputé de Paria à l'Assemblé Législative sur les sépultures* (Paris, n.d. [1796?]), 5; Delille, "L'Imagination," song 7 (1794), in *Oeuvres*, vol. 9 (Paris: Michaud, 1824), 146.
35. M[ulot], *Vues*, 15–19.
36. Nicher-Cérisy, *Des Tombeaux*, 23–24, 26.
37. [Pierre-Louis] Roederer, *Des Institutions funéraires convenables a une république qui permet tous les cultes et n'en adopte aucun* (Paris: Mathey & Desenne, year II [1793]), cover; C. Guillon, *Sur le respect du aux tombeaux; et l'indécence des inhumations actuelles* (Paris, year VIII [1800]), 1; Doliver, *Essai sur les funérailles* (Versailles: Jacob, year IX [1801]), i; Général F[rancois]-R[éné]-J[ean] de Pommereul, *Mémoire sur les funérailles et les sépultures, Question . . . jugée par l'Institut* (Paris: Onfroy; Tours: Billault, year IX [1801]), cover and v.
38. Duval, *Des Sépultures*, 37, 82–88.
39. Ibid., 20.
40. Ibid., 45–46, 71–73, 85–86.
41. F.-V. Mulot, *Discours sur les funérailles et le respect du aux morts, lu le 15 thermidor, an IV au Lycée des Arts* (Paris, 1796), 15–19. Also see Mulot, *Discours . . . sur cette question: Quelles sont le cérémonies a faire pour les funérailles et le reglement à adopter pour le lieu de la sépulture?* (Paris, year IV [1801]). For an extended appeal for support for the prize-winning proposals by Duval and Mulot, as well as for the runner-up Girard, see A. Gauthier-Lachapelle, *Des Sépultures* (Paris: DuPont, year IX [1801]).
42. Mulot, *Discours sur les funérailles*, 13, 16, 23. M[ulot], *Vues*, 6.
43. Pommereul, *Mémoire*, 4-5, 7, 32, and 37. Pommereul had published *Recherches sur l'origine de l'esclavage religieux et politique du peuple en France* (1783), arguing against the privileged status of priests and urging a government "to rule men emancipated by common sense and equal rights."
44. Athanase-Charles Détournelle, *Mémoire sur les funérailles et les sépultures* (Paris, year IX [1801]), 3–4, 7, 25.
45. J.-M. Coupé, *De la mortalité des sépultures, et de leur police* (Paris: Chez Calixte Vollant, year IX [1801]), 22, 25, 27.
46. [J.-B. Leclerc], Corps Législatif, Conseil des Cinq-Cents, *Motion d'Ordre par J.-B. Leclerc sur l'existence et l'utilité d'une religion civile en France* (Paris, 9 Fructidor, Year V [August 25, 1797]); J.-B. Leclerc, *Rapport . . . sur les institutions rélatives à l'état civil des citoyens, Corps Législatif, le 16 brumaire, an VI* (Paris, 1798), 2–4, 21–41.
47. J[acques] C[ambry], *Rapport sur les sépultures, presenté à l'Administration Centrale du Départment de la Seine* (Paris, year VII [1799]), 13. The proposal for cremation was unprecedented in Western cultures at that time.
48. [Quatremère de Quincy], Département de la Seine, *Rapport fait au Conseil-Général sur l'instruction publique, le rétablissement des Bourses, le scandale des inhumations actuelles, l'érection de cimetières, la restitution des tombeaux, mausolées, etc.* (Paris: Imprimerie nationale, n.d. [ca. 1800]), 25–32. Still, the neoplatonist Quatremère criticized the "irregular style" of gardening, urging "imitation" of primary geometrical forms in landscape design in his 1823 essay "On the Nature, the End, and the Means of Imitation in the Fine Arts." See Sylvia Lavin, *Quatremère de Quincy and the Invention of a Modern Language of Architecture* (Cambridge: MIT Press, 1992). During the Napoleonic era, Quatremère promoted the taste for the Egyptian.
49. Doliver, *Essai*, 1:4–7.
50. J[oseph] de Girard, *Des Tombeaux, ou de l'influence des institutions funèbres sur les moeurs* (Paris, year IX [1801]), quoted in Ariès, *The Hour*, 506–11.
51. Jules Michelet, *Ma Jeunesse*, 6th ed. (Paris: C. Lévy, 1884), 45. See discussion of Lenoir's museum and its historiographic significance in Vidler, *The Writing on the Walls*, 168–87. Mme. Roye de la Rochefoucault sponsored construction of the tomb of Abélard and Héloise to provide "a richer monument to models of love and constance." See F.-G.-T. Jolimont, *Les Mausolées français, recueil des tombeaux les plus rémarquables par leur structure, leurs épitaphes, ou les cendres qu'ils renferment, érigés dan les nouveaux cimetières de Paris* (Paris: Firmin Didot, 1821).
52. On 22 Floréal, year XIII (May 11, 1804), Napoleon banned all burials in churches, temples, and synagogues and inside the boundaries of cities and towns.
53. Two other cemeteries were established north and south of Paris at Montmartre and Montparnasse, although they could not compare with Père Lachaise in terms of either landscape design or social prestige. No cemetery was placed west of the city, initially, as had been suggested, probably because prevailing winds would blow any noxious effluvia from burials into and over Paris.
54. Jolimont, *Mausolées*, 5–6. Jolimont bore the title of *Ingenieur employé au cadastre.*
55. Molière had been buried at night, as befitted one active in the theater, in a common grave in the cemetery of Saint-Eustache in 1673. La Fontaine was interred in a common pit in Saint-Josephe's cemetery in 1792. Alexandre Lenoir's antiquarian repository was officially closed in 1817, and many of his holdings were moved to Père Lachaise. With the monument to Abélard and Héloise, Lenoir kept only a few of the bones that he did not distribute to friends and patrons as souvenirs. Vidler, *The Writing on the Walls*, 223 n. 55. From exile on the island of Saint Helena, Napoleon wrote of his wish to be buried at Père Lachaise, his grave to be marked by a plain, classical stele. Brown, *Père Lachaise*, 18.
56. Marchant de Beaumont, *Manuel et itinéraire*, 42–44. Another leading guidebook that went through numerous editions was Richard, *Le Véritable conducteur aux cimetières du Père La Chaise, Montmartre, Montparnasse et Vaugirard; ou, Guide le plus complet, le plus nouveau et le plus exact, de l'étranger, du curieux, et du promeneur*

dans ces cimetières (Paris: Chez Roy-Terry, 1830). Also see Marchant de Beaumont, *Le Nouveau conducteur de l'étranger à Paris en 1826*, 13th ed. (Paris: Moroval, 1826). (The 6th edition appeared in 1818.) During the siege of Paris on March 30, 1814, students of several military schools unsuccessfully tried to defend the city from the strategic vantage point of the cemetery; but the Russians overtook the site, setting up camp among the graves and cutting down many trees for firewood and to clear lines of fire for cannon batteries. Still, only two decades later the English visitor Mrs. Frances Trollope observed, "The thickly-planted trees and shrubs have grown so rapidly, as in many places to make it difficult to pass through them." "Letter 22: Père Lachaise," in *Paris and the Parisians in 1835* (New York: Harper & Brothers, 1836), 116.

57. Delille, "Preface," v; [anon.], "The Cemeteries and Catacombs of Paris," *Quarterly Review* 21.42 (April 1819): 391.
58. Delille, "Preface," v; Augustus Charles Pugin and C. Heath, *Paris and Its Environs Displayed in a Series of Picturesque Views*, vol. 2 (London: Robert Jennings, 1829), 129.
59. Marchant de Beaumont, *Manuel et itinéraire*, 34, 270.
60. *Atlantic Souvenir*, quoted in Hans Huth, *Nature and the American: Three Centuries of Changing Attitudes* (Lincoln: University of Nebraska Press, 1957), 66–67.
61. Marchant de Beaumont, *Manuel et itinéraire*, 35, 173, and 182.
62. Ibid., v–vi, 244.

4. An American Sensibility to Melancholy

1. Increase Mather and Leonard Hoar, quoted in Stannard, *The Puritan Way of Death*, 80.
2. Lovejoy, *Essays*, 134.
3. Henry S. Randall, *The Life of Thomas Jefferson*, vol. 1 (New York: Derby and Jackson, 1858), 60–61; Edwin M Betts, *Thomas Jefferson's Garden Book* (Philadelphia: American Philosophical Society, 1944), 25–27; Robert H. Kean, *History of the Graveyard at Monticello* (Charlottesville, Va.: Thomas Jefferson Memorial Foundation, 1971), 4. Jefferson's plans predated by fifteen years his visit to several major English gardens in the company of John Adams. Also see Edith Philips, *Louis Hué Girardin and Nicholas Gouin Dufief and Their Relations with Thomas Jefferson* (Baltimore: Johns Hopkins University Press, 1926).
4. Henry F. May, *The Enlightenment in America* (New York: Oxford University Press, 1976), 243.
5. Philip Freneau, "The House of Night" (1796), quoted in Edwin H. Cady, *Literature of the Early Republic* (New York: Holt, Rinehart & Winston, 1967), 349.
6. Fred Lewis Pattee, *The First Century of American Literature, 1770–1870* (New York: D. Appleton-Century, 1935), 33–34.
7. The use of marble markers in New England was not possible until the opening of the first quarries in Dorset and Proctor, Vermont, in 1785.
8. "The Weeping Willow," *New England Farmer* 5.43 (May 18, 1827): 338.
9. "Ornamental Trees," *New England Farmer* 7.6 (August 29, 1828): 42.
10. Archibald Alison published his *Essays on the Nature and Principles of Taste* in 1790 and in a revised edition in 1811. William Prince, *A Short Treatise on Horticulture* (New York: T. & J. Swords, 1828), 216. The author was head of the Linnaean Botanical Gardens in Flushing, New York.
11. See Jane C. Nylander, "Some Print Sources of New England Schoolgirl Art," *Antiques* (August 1976): 292–301; Anita Schorsch, "A Key to the Kingdom: The Iconography of the Mourning Picture," *Winterthur Portfolio* 16 (Spring 1979): 41–47; and Schorsch, *Mourning Becomes America: Mourning Art of the New Nation* (Clinton, N.J.: Main Street Press, 1975). The Litchfield Female Academy (1792–1833) considered the creation of a crewelwork mourning picture the highest test of a student's talents and "delicate sensibilities." The best were of silk thread on silk cloth, sometimes embellished with painting.
12. One model was the engraving by James Akin and William Farrison Jr., "America Lamenting Her Loss at the Tomb of George Washington." The earliest known version of the song appeared in a 1583 music book for the lute. It must be noted that the willow could not have been *Salix babylonica*, the weeping variety, which was not imported from China until the eighteenth century.
13. In the illustrations of Roman antiquities by Giambattista Piranesi (1720–1784), which popularized a taste for ruins in eighteenth-century English gardens, the monument shape that the English termed an urn was called *vaso* or vase, with or without a top, while the form of the *urna cineraria*, translated as "sarcophagus" and sometimes "cinerary urn," was horizontally or vertically rectangular. Both were highly embellished with low-relief sculpture. The latter usually also had an inscription. Sometimes the vase was set atop the sarcophagus, using it as a pedestal.
14. Philippe Ariès, *Western Attitudes toward Death from the Middle Ages to the Present*, trans. by Patricia M. Ranum (Baltimore: Johns Hopkins University Press, 1974), 80.
15. *Report of the Committee Appointed to Inquire into the Condition of the New-Haven Burying Ground and to Propose a Plan for Its Improvement* (New Haven: B. L. Hamlen, 1839), 4.
16. Timothy Dwight, *Travels in New-England and New York*, vol. 1 (New Haven: T. Dwight, 1821), 253.
17. Alison, *Essays*, 144.
18. Dwight, *Travels*, 191.
19. *Report*, 9.
20. Ibid., 254–56.
21. Dwight, *Travels*, 192–93.
22. *Report*, 9.
23. Quotations in the remainder of this section are from Dwight, *Travels*, 192–93.
24. Washington Irving, *The Sketch Book of Geoffrey Crayon, Gent.* (1819–20; reprint, New York: Dutton, 1963), 55, 60.
25. Ibid., 134–35, 161–68, 171–72. The parallels between Irving's criticism of Westminster Abbey and Voltaire's a century earlier are remarkable. See the discussion of Voltaire's critique in chapter 3.
26. Ibid., 90, 96, and 130–36.
27. Ibid., 137.
28. Lewis Pattee, *The First Century of American Literature*, 301–2.
29. Ibid., 269, 273.
30. F. W. P. Greenwood, "The Miscellaneous Poems of William Wordsworth," *North American Review* 9 (April 1824): 356–70. Van Wyck Brooks, *The Flowering of New England, 1815–1865* (New York: E. P. Dutton, 1940), 112.

31. William Cullen Bryant, *Poems* (Philadelphia: A. Hart, 1851), 53–55.
32. Jacob Bigelow to Elizabeth B[igelow] Wheeler, June 16, 1820, in Bigelow Papers, Countway Library of Medicine, Harvard University (hereafter HUCLM); John Quincy Adams, "Death of Children," *Mount Auburn Memorial* 1.39 (March 7, 1860): 310. Also see Joseph Story, "Lines Written on the Death of a Daughter in May 1831," in *The Miscellaneous Writings, Literary, Critical, Juridical, and Political* (Boston: James Munroe, 1835), 167–69.
33. [William Ellery Channing], "Remarks on National Literature," *Christian Examiner* 7 (1830): 269. Edward T. and William Ellery Channing were brothers.
34. "Review of William Wordsworth," *North American Review* 9 (1824): 367.
35. "The Grave of a Mother," *Boston Patriot and Daily Mercantile Advertiser* 1720 (January 9, 1823): 2.
36. [William Tudor], "On Certain Funeral Ceremonies," in *Letters on the Eastern States* (New York: Kirk & Mercein, 1820), 17.
37. Ibid.
38. *Report*, 4. Dearborn and Dr. John Collins Warren were major contributors to the Franklin monument. Dearborn had broached the idea in 1826 to the Bunker Hill Monument Association.
39. Le Capitaine Basil-Hall, *Voyage dans les États-Unis de l'Amérique du Nord*, vol. 2 (Paris: Arthus Bertrand, 1834), 9–11.
40. George Richard Minot wrote a history of Shay's Rebellion (1788); a *Eulogy on the Death of Washington* (1800), delivered to the city of Boston; and two volumes of his *Continuation of the History of the Province of Massachusetts Bay, from the Year 1748* (1798 and 1803).

5. The Necessity for Monuments

1. John Winthrop (1588–1649) coined the term "Citty vpon a Hill" in his lay-sermon, "A Modell of Christian Charity," delivered to those aboard the *Arbella* en route to found the Massachusetts Bay Colony. Early narratives of the founding decades include Edward Johnson, *A History of New England from the English Planting in the Yeare 1628 untill the Yeare 1652* (London: Brooke, 1654); and Nathaniel Morton's *New England's Memoriall*, published in 1669. Puritan histories reprinted in the early nineteenth century include Cotton Mather, *Magnalia Christi Americana; or, The Ecclesiastical History of New England from Tts First Planting in the Year 1620 unto the Year of Our Lord 1698* (New Haven: S. Converse, 1820). An example of New England's commemorative celebration of the founding decades was Thomas Bridgman, *The Pilgrims of Boston and Their Descendants, with Introduction by Edward Everett, also Inscriptions from the Monuments in the Granary Burial Ground* (New York: D. Appleton, 1856). Also see William Hubbard, *General History of New England from the Discovery to MDCLXXX* (Cambridge: Massachusetts Historical Society, 1815).
2. Only late in the nineteenth century, after the cleaning and planting of King's Chapel Burial Ground, did Bostonians erect a funerary monument to Winthrop (though the spot that may not be the Puritan leader's precise resting place) with a table stone of traditional form but distinctly Victorian iconography. For an overview dispelling some misconceptions and assessing the dimensions of the iconophobia of American Puritans, see Dickran Tashjian, "Puritan Attitudes toward Iconoclasm," in *Puritan Gravestone Art II: Annual Proceedings of the Dublin Seminar for New England Folklife* (June 24–25, 1978), 4–5.
3. Samuel Willard, "The High Esteem Which God Hath of the Death of His Saints" (1685), *The Puritans: A Sourcebook of Their Writings*, ed. Perry Miller and Thomas E. Johnson (New York: Harper & Row, 1963), 371–74.
4. Willard quoted in David Stannard, *The Puritan Way of Death*, 130.
5. Warren quoted extensively from Montesquieu and Voltaire. John Warren, *An Oration, Delivered July 4th, 1793, at the Request of the Inhabitants of Boston in Celebration of the Anniversary of American Independence* (Boston: John Gill, 1783), 55–67.
6. Perez Morton, quoted in George Washington Warren, *The History of the Bunker Hill Monument Association* (Boston: James R. Osgood, 1877), 13.
7. John Soley quoted in Warren, *The History*, 10–12.
8. The Massachusetts General Court authorized reconstruction of the Bulfinch monument in stone in 1865, but it was not rebuilt until 1898, when the Bunker Hill Monument Association hired the architectural firm of Little and Browne to do so.
9. Riqueti quoted in Neil Harris, *The Artist in American Society: The Formative Years, 1790–1860* (New York: Simon & Schuster, 1966), 18.
10. Robert McCloskey, ed., *The Works of James Wilson*, vol. 1 (Cambridge: Harvard University Press, 1967), 72; Jeremy Belknap, *American Biography; or, An Historical Account of Those Persons Who Have Been Distinguished in America, as Adventurers, Statesmen, Philosophers, Divines, Warrior, Authors, and Other Remarkable Characters, Comprehending a Recital of the Events Connected with Their Lives and Actions* (Boston: Isaiah Thomas & Ebenezer T. Andrews, 1794–98). Belknap was buried in the Old Granary Burial Ground but was moved to Mount Auburn Cemetery after its 1831 founding.
11. Rev. Peter Whitney, *Weeping and Mourning at the Death of Eminent Persons a National Duty: A Sermon Delivered at Northborough, Feb. 22, 1800, Observed as a Day of National Mourning on Account of the Death of General George Washington* (Brookfield, Mass.: E. Merriam, 1800).
12. "Mount Vernon," *New-England Galaxy* 6.276 (January 24, 1823): 1. "The Apotheosis of Washington," a folk-art reverse painting on glass by an unknown artist (ca. 1800) is in the museum of the Morristown National Historical Park. David Edwin's engraving of the same name (ca. 1800) depicts Washington clad in Roman toga sitting in clouds while cherubs crown him with a laurel wreath of triumph. It is in the Smithsonian National Portrait Gallery.
13. I. Finch, *Travels in the United States of America and Canada, Containing Some Account of their Scientific Institutions, and . . . An Essay on the Natural Boundaries of Empires* (London: Longman, Rees, Orme, Brown, Green & Longman, 1833), 218.
14. E[dward] T[homas] Coke, *A Subaltern's Furlough: Descriptive of Scenes in Various Parts of the United States . . . during the Summer and Autumn of 1832*, vol. 1 (New York: J. & J. Harper, 1833), 99.
15. Ibid, 99; J[ames] S[ilk] Buckingham, *America: Historical, Statistic, and Descriptive*, vol. 3 (London: Fisher, Son, & Co., n.d. [ca. 1840]), 569.
16. Caroline Gilman and Rev. S. Gilman, *The Poetry of Traveling in the United States* (New York: S. Colman, 1838), 7, 19.
17. Rev. Hosea Ballou, "Address on the Re-Burial of Rev. John Murray," (June 8, 1827) in *The Life of Rev. Hosea Ballou: With Accounts*

of His Writings, ed. Thomas Whittemore, vol. 3 (Boston: James M. Usher, 1855), 245.

18. Theodore Dwight, *Summer Tours; or, Notes of a Traveler through Some of the Middle and Northern States* (New York: Harper & Brothers, 1847), 14.
19. Henry Tudor, *Narrative of a Tour in North America* (London: James Duncan, 1834), 68–69; J. S. Buckingham, *The Slave States of America*, vol. 1 (London: Fisher, Son, & Co., 1842), 568–69. Washington's remains were removed from the original wooden coffin, shards of which were distributed around the country like relics. The Philadelphia architect William Strickland assembled a pamphlet on the new sarcophagus in order to spur public demand for such funerary monuments and thus earn commissions: *Tomb of Washington at Mount Vernon* (Philadelphia: Carey & Hart, 1840). Restoration of the estate did not begin until 1858, and then under auspices not of the federal government but of the Mount Vernon Ladies' Association of the Union, chartered by the Commonwealth of Virginia.
20. B[enjamin] Henry Latrobe, "Anniversary Oration Pronounced before the Society of Artists of the United States, by Appointment of the Society, on the Eighth of May, 1811," in *First Annual Exhibition of the Society of Artists of the United States* (Philadelphia, 1811), bound with *The Port-folio* n.s. 5.6 (June 1811).
21. Biddle, quoted in Harris, *Artist in American Society*, 43. For one comprehensive definition of the arts of this period, see [Dr.] Jacob Bigelow, *Elements of Technology, Taken Chiefly from a Course of Lectures Delivered at Cambridge, on the Application of the Sciences to the Useful Arts* (Boston: Hilliard, Gray, Little & Wilkins, 1829).
22. Harris, *Artist in American Society*, 28; John Adams to Thomas Jefferson (December 16, 1816), in *The Adams-Jefferson Letters*, ed. Leslie J. Cappon, vol. 2 (Chapel Hill: University of North Carolina Press, 1959), 507; Adams to Jefferson, January 1, 1817, quoted in *The Autobiography of Colonel John Trumbull, Patriot-Artist, 1756–1843*, ed. Theodore Sizer (New Haven: Yale University Press, 1953), 311.
23. Harris, *Artist in American Society*, 35.
24. Jefferson quoted ibid., 42; Jefferson to Madison, fall 1785, quoted in Wayne Andrews, *Architecture, Ambition, and Americans: A Social History of American Architecture* (New York: Free Press, 1964), 64. I have found no correspondence in which Jefferson reminds Adams of the symbolic, commemorative use of the architecture and landscape they discovered together on their visit to Stowe in 1786.
25. John Adams to Benjamin Waterhouse, February 26, 1817, quoted in *Selected Writings of John and John Quincy Adams*, ed. Adrienne Koch and William Peder (New York: Knopf, 1964), 199–200. The nuances of their debate on the uses of art aside, Henry A. S. Dearborn wanted to publish the Jefferson–Adams correspondence to give "to all future generations an important lesson amidst periods of civil discord." Dearborn called the correspondence an "everlasting monument to the holyness of friendship and the sacredness of confidential intercourse." Dearborn to Jefferson, November 24, 1823, Houghton Library, Harvard University (hereafter HUHL).
26. The name of the library was drawn not from the later reference to Boston as the "Athens of America," but from the Athenaeum and Lyceum of Liverpool, on which it was modeled. By 1851, it was one of the five largest libraries in the nation, with particular strengths in regional history and culture. See Josiah Quincy, *The History of the Boston Athenaeum, with Biographical Notices of Its Deceased Founders* (Cambridge: Metcalf, 1851).
27. David B. Tyack, *George Ticknor and the Boston Brahmins* (Cambridge: Harvard University Press, 1967), 20; [William Tudor], "Instruction for the Fine Arts," *North American Review* 2 (January 1816): 161; *Monthly Anthology* 4 (May 1807): 230. William Tudor Jr. died in Rio de Janeiro of a fever while U.S. chargé d'affaires.
28. Winslow quoted in Harris, *Artist in American Society*, 195. See Marshall Foletta, *Coming to Terms with Democracy: Federalist Intellectuals and the Shaping of an American Culture* (Charlottesville: University Press of Virginia, 2001).
29. Henry Bigelow (Baltimore) to Jacob Bigelow, July 2, 1815, Bigelow Papers, HUCLM.
30. Coke, *Subaltern*, 72. The term "professional" belongs to a later period when it referred to a practitioner who made his living from that career. Credentialing came from accumulation of a portfolio of work. Training generally involved extensive, guided reading and/or apprenticeship in a related trade, as with a stonemason in the case of architects or with horticulturists and gardeners in the case of landscape designers. Schools in those fields did not exist. Benjamin Henry Latrobe (1764–1820) has been called as "America's first professional architect and engineer," although he was born in England, studied in the offices of Samuel Pepys Cockerell and John Smeaton in London, and received commissions for projects before he came to America in 1795 to continue his career. Mills won the privately organized competition in 1836 for the Washington Monument in the national capital, proposing a 600-foot-tall obelisk, barely tapered and with a shallow top, rising from a circular Greco-Roman peristyle, a colonnade of thirty-two Doric columns. Construction of that monument, 55 feet wide and 555 feet high, simplified without the peristyle, progressed slowly from 1848 to 1885.
31. Godefroy had designed the First Unitarian Church of Baltimore in 1817. Coke, *Subaltern*, 71.
32. Jacob Bigelow, *Inaugural Address, Delivered in the Chapel at Cambridge, Dec. 11, 1816* (Boston: Wells & Lilly, 1817), 11–13; reprinted in *North American Review* 4 (January 1817): 271–72.
33. Ibid., 17–18, 23–26.
34. Adams, quoted in George E. Ellis, *Memoir of Dr. Jacob Bigelow* (Cambridge: John Wilson & Son, 1880), 46
35. William Ellery Channing, "War: Discourses before the Congregatonal Ministers of Massachusetts" (1816), in *The Works of William E. Channing, D.D.*, vol. 3 (Boston: American Unitarian Association, 1848), 40–41. A similar opinion was expressed in the same year by Francis C. Gray, in "An Address Before the Society of Phi Beta Kappa on Thurs., the 29th of Aug., 1816," *North American Review* 3 (September 1816): 289.
36. Frederic Cople Jaher, *The Urban Establishment: Upper Strata in Boston, New York, Charleston, Chicago, and Los Angeles* (Urbana: University of Illinois Press, 1982), 64; William Lawrence, *The Life of Amos A. Lawrence* (Boston: Houghton Mifflin, 1888); George Warren, 256.
37. James Fenimore Cooper, *The Crater* (Cambridge: Belknap Press of Harvard University Press, 1962), 444.
38. Daniel Webster, "First Settlement of New England" (December 22, 1820), in *The Writings and Speeches of Daniel Webster*, Vol. 1:

Memoir and Speeches on Various Occasions (Boston: Little, Brown, 1903), 182–99.

39. Daniel Webster, "Adams and Jefferson" (1826), ibid., 322.
40. Edward Everett, *An Address Delivered at Charlestown, Aug. 1, 1826, in Commemoration of John Adams and Thomas Jefferson* (Boston: William L. Lewis, 1826), 35–36.
41. Emerson, quoted in John Burchard and Albert Bush-Brown, *The Architecture of America: A Social and Cultural History* (Boston: Little, Brown, 1961), 24.
42. William Tudor to Harrison Gray Otis (September 2, 1815), in Samuel Eliot Morison, *Harrison Gray Otis, 1765–1848: The Urbane Federalist* (Boston: Houghton Mifflin, 1969), 235.
43. Smith in the *Edinburgh Review* (January 1820), quoted in Daniel J. Boorstin, *The Image; or, What Happened to the American Dream* (New York: Athenaeum, 1962), 47. Edward Everett particularly attacked "our transatlantic critics" in Harvard's Phi Beta Kappa address, "Oration Pronounced at Cambridge . . . Aug. 27, 1824," *North American Review* 20.11 (1825): 422–23.
44. Josiah Quincy, "Speech on the Invasion of Canada" (January 5, 1813), in *Speeches Delivered in the Congress of the United States, 1805–1813* (Boston: Little, Brown, 1874), 396.
45. [Nathan Hale], *Selections from the Chronicle of Boston and the Book of Retrospections and Anticipations, Compiled in the Last Month of the Last Year of the Town, and the First Month of the First Year of the City* (Boston: J. H. Eastburn, 1830), 9–10.
46. William Ellery Channing, "The True End of Life," quoted in Albert Fein, "The American City: The Ideal and the Real," in *The Rise of American Architecture*, ed. Edward Kaufman Jr. (New York: Praeger, 1970), 54.
47. The stone monument erected by the town of Lexington in 1799 on its Common was of modest scale, a stocky obelisk on a pedestal that resembled those gaining funerary use. It bore the names of the patriots killed or wounded there in the first battle of the Revolution on April 19, 1775. Their remains were moved from the town's Old Burying Ground nearby to a vault behind it on April 20, 1835. [William Tudor], "Monument to Washington," *North American Review* 2.6 (1816): 329–40. The bronze equestrian statue of Washington by Thomas Ball would not be erected until 1869, after creation of the Public Garden next to the Common.
48. See Robert E. Cray Jr., "Bunker Hill Refought: Memory Wars and Partisan Conflicts, 1775–1825," *Historical Journal of Massachusetts* 4 (Winter 2001). http://www.findarticles.com/p/articles/mi_qu3837/is_20010/ai_n8933837.
49. Henry A. S. Dearborn, "Bunker Hill," *Boston Patriot* (April 1823). The elder Henry Dearborn had left for Portugal in 1822 to serve as U.S. ambassador.
50. George Warren, 31–35. On the plain of Marathon in 490 BC defenders of Athens repulsed an invasion from a vast fleet of Persian ships. Athenians erected a huge mound over the bodies of the heroic fallen and treated the site as sacred.
51. Ibid., 38. By 1823, the Federalist Party of Massachusetts was essentially defunct, and many of its partisans joined the 1824 campaign to elect the Republican John Quincy Adams president. After Andrew Jackson's 1828 election, they formed the Whig Party. See Shaw Livermore Jr., *The Twilight of Federalism: The Disintegration of the Federalist Party, 1815–1830* (Princeton: Princeton University Press, 1962).
52. George Putnam, *An Address Delivered before the City Government and Citizens of Roxbury on the Life and Character of the Late Henry A. S. Dearborn, Mayor of the City, Sept. 3rd, 1851* (Roxbury: Norfolk County Journal Press, 1851), 6. Dearborn was elected fellow of the American Academy of Arts and Sciences in 1823 and two years later led a state survey of western Massachusetts in a quixotic search for a canal route to link Boston to the new Erie Canal. His historical consciousness was evident when, two days after visiting John Adams, he wrote Jefferson urging publication of the correspondence between the two former presidents. Dearborn to Jefferson, November 24, 1823, HUHL.
53. Putnam, *Address*, 41–43.
54. George Warren, *History*, 47, 115–56.
55. Ibid, 171–72, 176–77.
56. S[amuel] Swett, *Original Planning and Construction of the Bunker Hill Monument* (Albany: J. Munsell, 1863), 8.
57. Ibid., 8–9. George Warren, *History*, 157–59. The Wellington Monument, a 175-foot obelisk with an interior winding staircase to the top, may have inspired the form. It was erected in 1817 in Somerset, England, by local gentry to perpetuate the memory of the Iron Duke. John C[ollins] Warren, "Bunker Hill Monument Association," *Boston News-Letter and City Record*, 15 July 1826: 13–15. These were obelisks in shape alone since a true obelisk is a monolith.
58. John Pierpont, "Ode Written for the Laying of the Corner Stone of the Bunker Hill Monument, June 17, 1825," in *Airs of Palestine and Other Poems* (Boston: James Munroe, 1840); Daniel Webster, *An Address Delivered at the Laying of the Corner Stone of the Bunker Hill Monument* (Boston: Cummings and Hilliard, 1825), 8, 9.
59. John C. Warren, *Oration*, 14–15. *A History of the Origin and Development of the Granite Railway at Quincy, Massachusetts: In Commemoration of the One Hundredth Anniversary* (Quincy: The Granite Railway Co., 1926). The history notes that "Quincy granite or syenite is composed of quartz, feldspar, and hornblende, the [last] taking the place of mica in granite proper" giving "to Quincy syenite the hardness for which it is noted and its power of resistance to the action of the weather. Its crushing test is 17,000 pounds to the square inch." Famed Egyptian structures were built of a similar syenite.
60. George Warren, 253–54.
61. Alexander H. Everett, "June 7, 1836 Celebration," in *A Memorial of the American Patriots Who Fell at the Battle of Bunker Hill, with an Account of the Dedication of the Memorial Tablets* (Boston: By Order of the City Council, 1889), 274.
62. As at the inception of the monument project, Daniel Webster delivered the address at the ceremonies marking its completion. President John Tyler and his cabinet attended. See Sarah J. Purcell, "Commemoration, Public Art, and the Changing Meaning of the Bunker Hill Monument," *The Public Historian* 25.2 (Spring 2003): 55–71. Many Bostonians contributed to the subscription campaign begun in 1836 to build a monument to Washington in the nation's capital. Robert Mills designed a 555-foot obelisk surrounded by a circular colonaded temple, a structure far more ambitious than the Bunker Hill Monument. Work did not begin until 1843 but stopped in 1854 when funds ran out. The monument was finally finished, albeit much simplified, without the temple base, in 1885, after the federal government assumed control, assigning the project to the Army Corps of Engineers.

63. Josiah Quincy, quoted in Frederic Cople Jaher, "The Boston Brahmins in the Age of Industrial Capitalism," in *The Age of Industrialism in America: Essays in Social Structure and Cultural Values* (New York: Free Press, 1968), 82. The retrospective spirit was also evident in the renaming of Cambridge streets, with historical names such as Dunster and Holyoke replacing the generic Wood, Crooked, Creek, Water, and Marsh.
64. T[haddeus] W[illiam] Harris, *A Discourse Delivered before the Massachusetts Horticultural Society in Celebration of its Fourth Anniversary, Oct. 3, 1832* (Cambridge: E. W. Metcalf, 1932), 71–73.
65. [Dearborn], "Mount Auburn Cemetery: Report of the Massachusetts Horticultural Society upon the Establishment of an Experimental Garden and Rural Cemetery, Boston, 1831," *North American Review* 33 (October 1831): 397–98, 406.
66. Ibid., 399, 401–5.
67. Ibid., 401–5.
68. Alexander Everett, *Address*, 18.
69. Gustave de Beaumont, *Lettres d'Amérique, 1831–2*, ed. by André Jardin and George W. Pierson (Paris: Presses Universitaires de France, 1973), 146.
70. Alexander Everett, *Address*, 22–23.
71. Ralph Waldo Emerson, *Nature* (1836) in *Ralph Waldo Emerson: Essays and Lectures* (New York: Library of America, 1983), 7. Cf. Josiah Quincy, *An Address to the Citizens of Boston on the XVIIth of Sept., MDCCCXXX, The Close of the Second Century from the First Settlement of the City* (Boston: J. H. Eastburn, 1830), 9–10.
72. Alexander Everett, *Address*, 22–23.

6 Grave Problems

1. Boston Board of Health (1799), quoted in John Ballard Blake, *Public Health in the Town of Boston, 1630–1822* (Cambridge: Harvard University Press, 1952), 167–70.
2. See *Boston Patriot and Daily Mercantile Advertiser*, December 17, 1821, quoted in Blake, *Public Health*, 213.
3. Ibid., 51, 167–70, 192, and 200.
4. Edward H. Savage, comp., *Boston Events: A Brief Mention and the Date of More Than 5000 Events That Transpired in Boston from 1630 to 1880* (Boston: Tolman & White, 1884), 21; *Boston Intelligencer and Evening Gazette* 11 (March 8, 1823); *Columbian Centinel* 4049 (January 29, 1825), 2; *Boston Patriot and Daily Mercantile Advertiser* 1843 (June 3, 1823); Thomas Bridgman, *Epitaphs from Copp's Hill Burying Ground, Boston, with Notes* (Boston: James Munroe, 1851), xx–xxi. Dr. John Collins Warren successfully appealed for the 1831 repeal of the 1815 Act to Protect the Sepulchres of the Dead by the Massachusetts legislature. Massachusetts General Court, House of Representatives, *Report of the Select Committee of the House of Representatives . . . Legalizing the Study of Anatomy* (Boston: Dutton & Wentworth, 1831). That ended the illicit trade in cadavers.
5. Bridgman, *Epitaphs*, xx–xxi; Samuel Adams Drake, *Old Landmarks and Historic Personages of Boston* (Boston: Little, Brown, 1872), 196. When the last of the Bellingham family died, the family tomb in the Old Granary was given to the family of Governor James Sullivan.
6. [Francis D. Allen, comp.], *Documents and Facts, Showing the Fatal Effects of Interments in Populous Cities* (New York: F. D. Allen, 1822), 14–15. This report included a letter from Dr. Samuel Akerly to F. D. Allen dated October 12, 1822. See also John Duffy, *A History of Public Health in New York City, 1625–1866*, vol. 1 (New York: Russell Sage Foundation, 1968), 98.
7. "The Desolate City," *Columbian Centinel* 4011 (September 18, 1822): 2. One medical historian notes that in 1793 in Philadelphia, "local Republican civic leaders like editor Andrew Brown and merchants John Swanick and Stephen Girard supported Dr. Deveze's explanation that burying the dead inside the city had produced the disease." Martin S. Pernick, "Politics, Parties, and Pestilence: Epidemic Yellow Fever in Philadelphia and the Rise of the First Party System," *William and Mary Quarterly* 29 (1972): 559–86.
8. [Allen], *Documents*, iii. Nicholas Penny notes that in England, "it is only in the middle of the nineteenth century that burial in the earth was at all favoured by the upper classes . . . only then that the soil was likely to remain undisturbed." N[icholas] B. Penny, "The Commercial Garden Necropolis of the Early Nineteenth Century and Its Critics," *Garden History* 2 (Summer 1974): 61.
9. [Allen], *Documents*, iv.
10. Ibid., 7. Dr. Akerly considered vault burials preferable to earthen graves, since bodies decompose there three to four times faster, or in about a year's time. Still, he noted the incidents of offensive effluvia in New York City vaults, perhaps for that reason.
11. Letters to the editor, *Columbian Centinel*, September 10, 17, 24, 28, and November 16, 1796, quoted in Blake, *Public Health*, 159–60; Erwin H. Ackerknecht, "Anticontagionism between 1821 and 1867," *Bulletin of the History of Medicine* 22 (1948): 567. In 1824, Boston merchants persuaded the Board of Health to shorten the summer quarantine season by two months. Caleb H. Snow, *A History of Boston: The Metropolis of Massachusetts* (Boston: Abel Bowen, 1825), 406.
12. [Allen], *Documents*, iv.
13. "City Council," *Columbian Centinel* 4037 (December 18, 1822): 2; [Joseph T. Buckingham], "Tombs Under St. Paul's," *New-England Galaxy* 6.273 (January 3, 1823): 2; *Boston Patriot and Daily Mercantile Advertiser* 12.1714 (January 2, 1823). The physicians were John Collins Warren; James Jackson, Warren's close friend and senior partner in practice with Jacob Bigelow; Aaron Dexter, Warren's brother-in-law; John Dixwell; William Ingalls; John Randall; John Gorham; and Enoch Hale Jr. Bostonians did not overlook the fact that both Warren and Hale were wardens of Saint Paul's. *Columbian Centinel* 4037; *New-England Galaxy* 273. The term applied at that time to the place of burial in a church crypt or cellar was "cemetery," meaning dormitory or sleeping room, in contrast to the words "graveyard" or "burial ground," generally applied to existing outdoor places of interment. An additional definition of "cemetery" developed in early-nineteenth-century Boston, following the example of the French, to distinguish the old burial places from the "cemeteries . . . all situated in the outskirts of the city." The change in terminology signaled not only new usage and form but also, as in France, a shift in notions about death itself.
14. *New-England Galaxy*, March 12, 1824.
15. William Lawrence, *A Sermon on the 75th Anniversary of Saint Paul's Church, Boston* (Boston: By the Parish, 1895), 12–13. Some Bostonians criticized that elite faction as forming the "Aristocratical Party," a group said to show a political, social, and religious attachment to England. See "The Boston Aristocracy," *Boston Pa-*

triot and Daily Mercantile Advertiser 12.1814 (April 30, 1823). The rejection of Episcopalianism in Boston runs counter to the pattern observed in Philadelphia, according to E. Digby Baltzell, *Puritan Boston and Quaker Philadelphia: Two Protestant Ethics and the Spirit of Class Authority and Leadership* (New York: Macmillan, 1979). See also Ann Douglas, *The Feminization of American Culture* (New York, Knopf, 1977), 25; Phillips Brooks, "The Episcopal Church," in Winsor, *Memorial History of Boston*, 3:455; Snow, *History*, 356; Lawrence, *Sermon*, 13–15; *Bacon's Dictionary of Boston* (Boston: Houghton Mifflin, 1886), 355. Samuel Appleton also provided the largest initial contribution for creation of Mount Auburn.

16. Snow, *History*, 356, 347; Savage, *Boston Events*, 32; "St. Paul's Church," *Boston Intelligencer and Evening Gazette* 6 (October 23, 1819), 1. See subscription papers in The Papers of Dr. John Collins Warren, vol. 12, MHIS.
17. Robert A. McCaughey, *Josiah Quincy, 1772–1865: The Last Federalist* (Cambridge: Harvard University Press, 1974), 99; Lawrence, *Sermon*, 15–16; James M. Bugbee, "Boston Under the Mayors, 1822–1880," in Winsor, *Memorial History*, 225.
18. Dr. John Collins Warren's diary, quoted in Lawrence, *Sermon*, 18; Samuel Farrar Jarvas, *A Narrative of Events Connected with the Acceptance and Resignation of the Rectorship of St. Paul's Church, Boston* (Boston, November 1825). One exception is John and Abigail Adams, who were laid to rest beneath the First Church Unitarian (formerly Congregationalist) in Quincy, Massachusetts.
19. "City Council," *Columbian Centinel* 4041 (January 1, 1823): 2. Also see *New-England Galaxy*, January 3, 1823; "The Church-Yard," *Boston Patriot and Daily Mercantile Advertiser* 11.1703 (December 20, 1822).
20. "Church Cemeteries," *Boston Patriot and Daily Mercantile Advertiser* 11.1708 (December 26, 1822).
21. *New-England Galaxy*, January 3, 1823. J. T. Buckingham, born in rural Connecticut in 1779, was an outspoken proponent of freedom of the press who garnered many foes and even libel suits for his journalistic vehemence but had powerful friends like Daniel Webster. But as editor of the *Boston Courier* and the *New England Magazine* as well as the *Galaxy*, he established sufficient public confidence to win several terms in both houses of the Massachusetts legislature and positions of influence in many civic associations. *New-England Galaxy*, March 12, 1824.
22. "Squam Poet," "Inscribed to S.C.," *New-England Galaxy* 6.275 (January 17, 1823): 3.
23. "'Death' from Mr. Croly's *Illustrations of Gems*," *New-England Galaxy* 6.282 (March 7, 1823).
24. Oliver Smith, a philanthropist who helped found the Boston Dispensary, had just planted trees on the Mall along Boston Common to replace those destroyed in the Revolutionary War. Gravel walks crisscrossed the area, making it suitable for ladies strolling in long dresses. John Gorham Coffin, *An Address Delivered before the Contributors of the Boston Dispensary at the Seventeenth Anniversary, October 21, 1813* (Boston: John Eliot, 1813), 9; "City Council," *Columbian Centinel* 4049 (January 29, 1823): 2. Perhaps the charge of bribery was valid. A month after the City Council ruling, David Sears, wealthy warden of Saint Paul's, donated an estate called City Market to Boston.
25. [Joseph T. Buckingham], "Sacred Ground," *New-England Galaxy* 6.277 (January 31, 1823): 2.
26. Ibid.
27. H. Crosby Englizian, *Brimstone Corner: Park Street Church, Boston* (Chicago: Moody Press, 1968), 76–77.
28. The church was called "brimstone corner" in reference to the hellfire and brimstone preaching there by the Reverend Edward Beecher from 1826 to 1830. Some folklorists, however, attribute the name to the gunpowder stored in the cellar during the War of 1812. The Park Street Church was a relatively new congregation, formed in 1809 with a core of twenty-six members, twenty-one from other Congregational churches recently divided by the Unitarian controversy. Until the building of the Somerset Street Church, it boasted the tallest steeple in town, with capitals designed by Solomon Willard. At the Park Street Church, as at Saint Paul's, we see the pride and status attached to membership in a congregation housed in an architecturally prominent edifice at the foot of Beacon Hill, Boston's elite new residential area. *Bacon's Dictionary*, 162; "City Council," *Boston Evening Gazette* 9 (January 18, 1822): 2; "City Council," *Columbian Centinel* 4049 (January 29, 1823): 2; Englizian, *Brimstone Corner*, 77. The Park Street Church built thirty crypt tombs. [Joseph T. Buckingham], "Another Cemetery," *New-England Galaxy* 6.275 (January 17, 1823): 2. Buckingham also suggested that Saint Paul's tombs would remain a curse on the city which "nothing but their final conflagration" would be able to remove. *New-England Galaxy* 6.293 (March 16, 1823). Such was the caustic journalistic style that brought Buckingham a landmark libel suit from Methodist minister J. Maffitt, a case challenging freedom of the press before the bench of Judge Josiah Quincy in 1822. Because of Quincy's decision in favor of Buckingham, the editor became a vocal proponent of Quincy as mayor.
29. "The Vaults of St. Michan's," *New-England Galaxy* 6.275 (January 17, 1823). I vividly recall a similarly grisly tour of the crypts of the fourteenth-century basilica of St.-Michel in Bordeaux in 1956, led by a lantern-bearing sexton jokingly poking the leathered remains of a line of skeletal "mummies" hung up on the walls.
30. McCaughey, *Josiah Quincy*, 92; Josiah Quincy, *A Municipal History of the Town and City of Boston during Two Centuries* (Boston: Little, Brown, 1852), 62, 65–66; *New-England Galaxy* 8.290 (May 2, 1825): 2. Josiah Quincy was a religious liberal. Although he sat in the congregation of Rev. William Ellery Channing at the Federal Street Church, he refused to call himself a Unitarian or to participate in denominational discussions. He greatly disliked sectarianism and was thus representative of many religious liberals in Boston. Edmund Quincy, *The Life of Josiah Quincy of Massachusetts* (Boston: Ticknor & Fields, 1868), 532–33. Quincy was also anti-aristocratic by disposition. He formed many political coalitions and considered himself a champion of the common man as well as a member of the city's cultural and intellectual elite. But few enforcement mechanisms existed to aid Quincy in implementing his resolutions. The mayor was able to name himself chairman of all committees of the Board of Aldermen. Other than that, his promise of "internal police"—maintenance of cleanliness and order, abatement of nuisances, suppression of vice and crime, and protection of public health—was well intentioned but fairly ineffectual.
31. Blake, *Public Health*, 202–4; Tudor quoted, 210. See William Tudor, "On Certain Funeral Ceremonies," in *Letters*, 5–17.
32. *Columbian Centinel* 4094; Boston City Records, *City Council Pro-*

ceedings, June 25, 1823, 271, microfilm reel 18, Boston Public Library (hereafter BPL).

33. *New-England Galaxy* 6.299 (July 4, 1823), and 6.300 (July 11, 1823); [John Gorham Coffin], A Fellow of the Massachusetts Medical Society, *Remarks on the Dangers and Duties of Sepulture; or, Security for the Living, with Respect and Repose for the Dead* (Boston: Phelps & Farnham, 1823). This pamphlet has been erroneously and repeatedly attributed to Dr. Jacob Bigelow in the Harvard Union catalogues, Harvard's Countway Medical Library, and other references. A close reading of the work, however, puts that authorship in question. Whereas Bigelow was a Fellow of the Massachusetts Medical Society in 1823 and did propose a "rural" cemetery to Bostonians two years after publication of the pamphlet, he had not yet left Sudbury, Massachusetts, for Harvard College in early 1801, when the pamphlet's author recounts a visit to Nice: "In 1801, I visited this place as a commissioner of public health, during the prevalence of a bad fever," *Remarks*, 2. Documentation of Coffin's authorship appears in Buckingham's reviews in the *New-England Galaxy*. Also, neither Bigelow's papers nor his biographer makes reference to the younger physician's authorship of such a pamphlet, and Bigelow was careful to claim all his publications. See Ellis, *Memoir of Bigelow*; [Coffin], Remarks, 3–4. Coffin championed preventive medicine as editor of the *Medical Intelligencer* in 1826. From 1818 to 1820, he lectured and wrote on the dangers to health of bathing "longer than two or three minutes at a time or more often than once every other day." Blake, *Public Health*, 240. Perhaps the confusion over authorship stemmed from Bigelow's subsequent theories on "self-limiting" diseases and approaches to preventive medicine similar to Coffin's.
34. [Coffin], *Remarks*, 45, 5.
35. Ibid., 33–34, 57, 61, 64–65.
36. Ibid., 64–65.
37. Ibid., 71.
38. Ibid.
39. "City Council," *Columbian Centinel* 4041 (January 1, 1823): 2. Also see *New-England Galaxy* 6 (January 3, 1823); "The Church-Yard," *Boston Patriot and Daily Mercantile Advertiser* 11.1703 (December 20, 1822).
40. [Tudor], "On Certain Funeral Ceremonies," 17.
41. The ban of 1823 was rescinded to permit construction of a double row of tombs in the Common Burying Ground in 1836.
42. Boston City Records, "Quincy Commission Report," *City Council Proceedings*, August 4, 1823, 311–20.
43. Ibid., 330–36. Quincy's egalitarianism was also evident in his complaint about crypt burials that "the great mass of citizens cannot afford the right, nor could it be extended to all, if they could afford it." He asserted, "Why a minority of the population of any city should be permitted to have the exclusive privilege of poisoning the atmosphere of the majority of all the citizens, is a question not easily answered." Ibid., 326.
44. John Collins Warren to Josiah Quincy, draft of "Letter on Interments, July 1823 Answer," Warren Papers 10.82, MHIS.
45. Nathaniel B. Shurtleff, *A Topographical and Historical Description of Boston* (Boston: Rockwell & Churchill, 1891), 359; Drake, 324–25; Walter Muir Whitehill, *Boston: A Topographical History* (Cambridge: Belknap Press of Harvard University Press, 1959), 55, 98, 144.
46. Warren, "Letter on Interments."
47. Recycling of grave space in colonial times was practiced, if poorly documented. A large vault in the corner of King's Chapel Burying Ground functioned as a charnel house, indicating the need for a place to deposit bones after removal from the grave and reuse of the space. The last recorded burial at King's Chapel occurred in 1796. *Bacon's Dictionary*, 278; *The Charter of the City of Boston, and Ordinances Made and Established by the Mayor, Aldermen, and Common Council, with Such Acts of the Legislature of Massachusetts as Relate to the Government of Said City* (Boston: True & Greene, 1827), 183–85; Savage, *Brief Mention*, 21, 44. Also see "An Ordinance to Regulate the Interment of the Dead" (passed September 26, 1822), in *The Charter and Ordinances of the City of Boston together with the Acts of the Legislature Relating to the City*, ed. Thomas Wetmore and Edward G. Prescott (Boston: J. H. Eastburn, 1834), 186–92; *Columbian Centinel* 4103.
48. Josiah Quincy, *An Address to the Board of Aldermen, Members of the Common Council of Boston, on the Organization of the City Government at Faneuil Hall, January 1, 1828* (Boston: Commercial Gazette Office, 1828); also quoted in *Boston Medical Intelligencer* 5.36 (January 22, 1828), 578, a new journal dedicated to preventive medicine edited by Dr. Coffin. In 1836, Mayor Samuel Armstrong's administration finally succeeded in cutting a swath off the corner of the Common Burial Ground, eliminating a row of tombs, to extend Boylston Street to connect with Tremont Street. One member of the Massachusetts Society for Promoting Good Citizenship later credited Quincy as the catalyst for the creation of Mount Auburn. Mellen Chamberlain, *Josiah Quincy: The Great Mayor* (Boston: By the [Massachusetts] Society [for Promoting Good Citizenship], 1889), 18.
49. Savage, *Boston Events*, 44; McCaughey, *Josiah Quincy*, 90–100; "Burial in Cities," *Boston News-Letter and City Record*, March 4, 1826: 126; "Extract of an Address of the Mayor of Boston to the City Council," *Boston Medical Intelligencer* 5.36 (January 22, 1828): 577–78. From 1813 to 1823, there was one death for every forty-two Bostonians annually. The average for 1824 to 1827 was one in forty-eight, and annual figures continually improved to one in fifty-five for 1826–27 or one in sixty-three for 1827 alone.
50. Quincy, *Municipal History*, 100. In fact, an 1849 ordinance authorized the city of Boston "to purchase and hold land, for a public cemetery, in any town in this commonwealth" and to establish rules and regulations similar to those existing for intramural burials. Peleg W. Chandler, *The Charter and Ordinances of the City of Boston together with the Acts of the Legislature relating to the City* (Boston: John H. Eastburn, 1850), 201.
51. Despite subsequent purchase of a family lot at Forest Hills, Boston's second "rural" cemetery, which opened in 1848, Dr. John Collins Warren ordered that after his death his skeleton should be properly prepared and presented to the Massachusetts General Hospital to become part of the anatomical specimen collection he had donated in 1847 when he resigned his professorship. Dr. John B. S. Jackson initially curated the expanding Warren Anatomical Museum as it acquired the Johann Gaspar Spurzheim Phrenological Collection and medical artifacts. Edward Warren, *The Life of John Collins Warren* (Boston: Ticknor & Fields, 1860), 1:374–75. J. B. S. Jackson, *Descriptive Catalogue of the Warren Anatomical Museum* (Boston: A. Williams & Co, 1870), iii–viii. Jackson, "Autopsy of Dr. John Collins Warren,

May 8, 1856," HUCLM. http://www.countway.med.harvard.edu/rarebooks /exhibits/warrens/warren2.html

7. The Cemetery Idea and the Founding of Mount Auburn

1. [Joseph T. Buckingham], *New-England Galaxy* 8.290 (May 2, 1825): 2.
2. Abel Bowen, "Burial in Cities," *Boston News-Letter and City Record*, March 4, 1826: 126–29.
3. Thomas Green Fessenden, *The American Gardener: Containing Practical Directions on the Culture of Fruits and Vegetables* (Boston: J. B. Russell, 1828), 187.
4. Jacob Bigelow, *A History of the Cemetery of Mount Auburn* (Boston: James Munroe, 1860), 2–3.
5. Ellis, *Memoir of Dr. Bigelow*, 33.
6. Both of Bigelow's parents died in 1816, a year after his brother. Bigelow considered himself a self-made man, recalling in old age, "It is enough for me that I have led a long and happy life, beginning at the bottom of the ladder and ending with the esteem and good opinion of many." Bigelow to an unidentified friend, January 17, 1871, Bigelow Papers, HUCLM.
7. George Ticknor (1791–1871), three years younger than Bigelow and his colleague at Harvard and in many Boston cultural institutions, became Bigelow's lifelong friend. See Tyack, *George Ticknor and the Boston Brahmins*.
8. Bigelow's *Florula Bostoniensis* (Boston: Cumming & Hilliard, 1814) preceded Sir Joseph Dalton Hooker's *Flora Scotica* (1821) and John Claudius Loudon's *Arboretum et Fruticetum Britannicum* (1821) as pioneering works on regional botany. William B. Annin and George Girdler Smith produced most of the illustrations after Bigelow's sketches. See Dirk Struik, *Yankee Science in the Making* (Boston: Little, Brown, 1948), for an assessment of Bigelow's importance.
9. Bigelow, *History*, 2. This Nathan Hale (1784–1863) was the publisher, along with his wife Sarah Preston Everett Hale, of the *Boston Daily Advertiser*, not the heroic Revolutionary War captain. He was the son of the Reverend Enoch Hale, brother of the patriot. He moved to Boston in 1808 from rural Westhampton, Massachusetts. One of his children was the noted Unitarian minister and social reformer Edward Everett Hale; another, Charles, took over the newspaper, along with Edward, while serving as a state legislator.
10. Bigelow, *Inaugural Address*.
11. Several decades later, William Aspinwall's heirs sold his Brighton estate for the creation of Evergreen Cemetery. The Brookline Hospital Church occupies part of the nearby Aspinwall property. Ibid., 137.
12. Bigelow quoted in Cornelia W. Walter, *The Rural Cemeteries of America: Mount Auburn Illustrated in a Series of Views from Drawings Taken on the Spot . . . with Descriptive Notices* (New York: R. Martin, 1847), 29–30.
13. Ibid., 33–34; Jacob Bigelow, "On the Burial of the Dead, and Mount Auburn Cemetery," in *Nature in Disease, Illustrated in Various Discourses and Essays. To Which are Added Miscellaneous Writings, Chiefly on Medical Subjects* (Boston: Ticknor & Fields, 1854), 16; Bigelow, *Modern Inquiries: Classical, Professional, and Miscellaneous* (Boston: Little, Brown, 1867), 119–36; Bigelow, "Extract from 'Nature in Disease,'" *Mount Auburn Memorial* 1.2 (August 31, 1859): 90; Review of Sir Henry Halford, Bart., M.D., *Miscellaneous Works* (London, 1831), in Bigelow, "Disinterment of the Relics of Several Kings," *North American Review* 38.83 (April 1834): 464.
14. H. A. S. Dearborn, "Mount Auburn Cemetery: Report of the Massachusetts Horticultural Society," *North American Review* 33 (October 1831): 397–406.
15. William Cullen Bryant, "A Forest Hymn" (1829), in *Poems*, 130–34; [Bryant], "Thanatopsis," *North American Review* 5.15 (September 1817): 338–40.
16. Bigelow, quoted in Walter, *Rural Cemeteries*, 30.
17. Bigelow, "On Burial," 133. Also see Bigelow, "Disinterment of the Relics," 462–64.
18. May quoted in Walter, *Rural Cemeteries*, 33–34; *Historical Sketch and Matters Appertaining to the Granary Burial-Ground*, 19. Colonel May was the maternal grandfather of the writer Louisa May Alcott.
19. Channing, "Self-Culture" (1828), 456; Channing, "Botany" (1818), in *Works*, 3:45.
20. See Kelly Olds, "Privatizing the Church: Disestablishment in Connecticut and Massachusetts," *Journal of Political Economy* 102 (1994): 277–97.
21. Channing, "Unitarian Christianity: Delivered at the Ordination of Rev. Jared Sparks in The First Independent Church of Baltimore on May 5, 1819," http://xroads.virginia.edu/~HYPER/DETOC/religion/unitarian.html.
22. Alexis de Tocqueville [from New York] to Louis de Kergolay [his cousin in France], June 29, 1831, quoted as "Essay on American Government and Religion," in George Wilson Pierson, *Tocqueville and Beaumont in America* (New York: Oxford University Press, 1938), 421–23; Channing, "Unitarian Christianity." For an overview of the significance of Unitarianism and Universalism, see, in his chapter "The Expanding Enlightenment," Merle Curti, *The Growth of American Thought* (New York: Harper & Row, 1964), 155–57.
23. Channing, "Unitarian Christianity." See J. D. Cushing, "Notes on Disestablishment in Massachusetts, 1780–1833," *William and Mary Quarterly* 26.2 (1964): 169–90.
24. William Ware, "Unitarian Belief," *Unitarian* 1 (November 1827): 19. Maturin M. Ballou, *Biography of Rev. Hosea Ballou* (Boston: Abel Tompkins, 1852), 331.
25. [Robert Manning, ed.], *History of the Massachusetts Horticultural Society, 1829–1878* (Boston: Rand, Avery, for the Society, 1880), 74; Walter, *Rural Cemeteries*, 33–35. Also see Bigelow, "Extract," quoted in "Mount Auburn," *Gleason's Pictorial Drawing Room Companion*, August 13, 1853, 104–5; Edward Everett, "The Proposed Rural Cemetery" (1832), reprinted in Bigelow, *History*, 133–34. The term "friends" often referred to relatives in addition to close acquaintances.
26. T. W. Harris, *Discourse*, 76–78.
27. Vernon Louis Parrington, *Main Currents in American Thought*, vol. 2, *1800: The Romantic Revolution in America* (New York: Harcourt, Brace & World, 1927), 314.
28. Bigelow, "A Discourse on the Burial of the Dead" (1831), reprinted in Bigelow, *History*, 195. He originally delivered the address before the Boston Society for the Promotion of Useful Knowledge at the Masonic Temple. See Wordsworth, "Essay upon Epitaphs," 239–40.

29. H. A. S. Dearborn, *Address Delivered before the Massachusetts Horticultural Society on the Celebration of Their First Anniversary, Sept. 19, 1829*, 3rd ed., vol. 1 (Boston: William D. Ticknor, 1847), 5; Zebedee Cook Jr., *An Address Pronounced before the Massachusetts Horticultural Society in Commemoration of Its Second Annual Festival, the 10th of Sept. 1830* (Boston: Isaac R. Baits, 1830), 10. Published orations and other proceedings are bound together as *Transactions*, Massachusetts Horticultural Society, Boston, now Wellesley, Mass. (hereafter MHORT).
30. Henry A. S. Dearborn, "General Dearborn's Address: Delivered before the Massachusetts Horticultural Society on the Celebration of Their First Anniversary, Sept. 19, 1829," *New England Farmer* 8.26 (January 15, 1830): 203.
31. Z. Cook, *Address*, 17. The Horticultural Society of Paris elected Dearborn, Cook, John C. Gray, Enoch Bartlett (breeder of the pear), and Bigelow honorary members in February 1830. The Caledonian Horticultural Society was founded in Edinburgh in 1809.
32. In 1824 Captain Jonathan Winship and his brother Francis established a nursery in Brighton specializing in ornamental trees and shrubs, one of the first such ventures in the Boston metropolitan area. [Manning], *History*, 52, 57, 60. Dearborn, *New England Farmer* 8.31 (February 9, 1830): 243.
33. Beaumont, *Lettres d'Amérique, 1831–1832*, 144.
34. See Charles E. Randall and Henry Clepper, *Famous and Historic Trees* (Washington, D.C.: American Forestry Association, 1976).
35. See Henry C. Binford, *The First Suburbs: Residential Communities on the Boston Periphery, 1815–1860* (Chicago: University of Chicago Press, 1985).
36. Simon Stone held an Indian deed for the property. Colonel George Sullivan and Charles W. Green first dubbed the old estate Sweet Auburn. Debate remains among literary scholars over whether Goldsmith was referring to his Irish hometown of Lissoy, County Westmeath, or to Nuneham Courtenay, the Oxfordshire town destroyed in 1761 by Lord Harcourt for construction of his landscaped garden.
37. "George W. Brimmer" [from *Boston Daily Advertiser*, September 1838], *Mount Auburn Memorial* 1.44 (April 11, 1860): 345; Caroline F. Orne, *Sweet Auburn and Mount Auburn with Other Poems* (Cambridge: John Owen, 1844), 1–16, 19; C. F. Orne, "Mount Auburn," *Mount Auburn Memorial* 1.29 (December 28, 1859): 228; James Russell Lowell, "Cambridge Thirty Years Ago," intro. to the *Biglow Papers*; and Lowell to George B. Loring (1837), in *Letters of James Russell Lowell*, ed. Charles Eliot Norton, vol. 1 (New York: Harper & Brothers, 1894), 19.
38. *Mount Auburn Memorial* 1.1: 2; T. W. Harris, *Discourse*, 76–78.
39. Benjamin A. Gould, a friend of both Bigelow and Brimmer, visited Père Lachaise. Gould to Bigelow, January 11, 1829, *Bigelow Papers*, MHIS; David B. Chase, "The Beginnings of the Landscape Tradition in America," *Historic Preservation* 25 (January–March 1973): 41.
40. David J. Rothman, *The Discovery of the Asylum: Social Order and Disorder in the New Republic* (Boston: Little, Brown, 1971), 137–38; Nathan Hale, "Mount Auburn," *Boston Daily Advertiser* (1831), in Boston Athenaeum. It is only coincidental that an eighteenth-century ferry across the Charles River was located between Brighton and the current site of Mount Auburn, close to the old center of Watertown. No cemetery founder referred to the latent symbolism of a ferry, suggestive of the mythical route to the netherworld across the river Styx.
41. Bigelow, *History*, 16; Dearborn, "Mount Auburn Cemetery: Report of the Massachusetts Horticultural Society, upon the Establishment of an Experimental Garden and Rural Cemetery, Boston, 1831," *North American Review* 33.77 (October 1831): 405.
42. Longinus, *An Essay on the Sublime*, trans. Nicholas Boileau-Despreaux (1674; Oxford: Leon Lichfield, 1698); Isaac Newton, *Mathematical Principles of Natural Philosophy*, ed. Florian Cajori (Berkeley: University of California Press, 1934), 544–45. Joseph Addison, "Panoramas," *Spectator*, no. 412, quoted in Walter Jackson Bate, *From Classic to Romantic: Premises of Taste in Eighteenth-Century England* (Cambridge: Harvard University Press, 1946), 99.
43. Many dioramas presented romantic landscapes. A major example was Louis-Jacques-Mandé Daguerre's "Holyrood Chapel," exhibited in Paris and London between 1823 and 1825, an elaborate mourning scene depicting a Gothic ruin by moonlight and a white-robed woman praying in front of a funerary monument. Daguerre's "View of Paris from Montmartre" (1831) presented a panorama similar to that seen from Père Lachaise. In 1830 Daguerre also painted dioramas of "The Tomb of Napoleon at St. Helena" and the "Campo Santo at Pisa," a famous Italian cemetery. A diorama, "Transparent Panoramic View of West Point and Adjacent Scenery," attracted almost as much attention in Washington in 1829 as President Jackson's inauguration. Also see Edgar Allan Poe, "The Domain of Arnheim," in *Selected Prose, Poetry, and "Eureka,"* ed. W. H. Auden (New York: Holt, Rinehart & Winston), 1950), 403.
44. Ronald Rees, "The Scenery Cult: Changing Landscape Taste over Three Centuries," *Landscape* 19.3 (May 1975): 42; Marx, *Machine in the Garden*, 246.
45. Z. Cook, *Address*, 10, 27–28.
46. Ibid., 27–28. Another reference to the precedent set by Père Lachaise appears in Alexander Everett, *Address*, 18, 37–46.
47. Brimmer took a $1,000 loss on the property. Martin Brimmer to Bigelow, n.d. [1856?], in Bigelow Papers, box 3 (1854–69), MHIS.
48. T. W. Harris, *Discourse*, 70; Bigelow, *History*, 5–6.
49. Henry A. S. Dearborn, "Historical Sketch," *Transactions of the Massachusetts Horticultural Society, 1829–1838* (hereafter *Transactions*), 1:68–70.
50. H. A. S. Dearborn, "Report," in "Proceedings of the Massachusetts Horticultural Society . . . the 18th of June 1831," *New England Farmer* 9.49 (June 22, 1831): 385.
51. H. A. S. Dearborn, "The Cemetery of Père Lachaise," *New England Farmer* 11 (September 12, 1832): 66–67.
52. Ibid.; H. A. S. Dearborn, "Proceedings of the Massachusetts Horticultural Society . . . Sept. 8, 1832," *Transactions*, 1:35–36; Albert Emerson Benson, *History of the Massachusetts Horticultural Society* (Norwood, Mass.: Plimpton Press, for the Society, 1929). The books Dearborn ordered and relied on included Jolimont, *Les Mausolées français*; Arnaud, *Recueil de tombeaux des quatre cimetières de Paris*; Marchant de Beaumont, *Manuel et itinéraire*; Evelyn, *Silva*; Maliphant, *Designs for Sepulchral Monuments*; and various works by Sir Humphrey Repton. Dearborn and his associates may also have been familiar with Augustus Charles Pugin's *Paris and Its Environs*, containing ten engravings of Père

Lachaise, including detailed descriptions of landscape and monuments. Bigelow also regularly ordered books to be imported by the Boston firm of Cummings & Hilliard.

53. H. A. S. Dearborn, *Address . . . 1829*, 7. Dearborn recognized and reinterpreted Repton, a major English garden theorist, a decade before John Claudius Loudon did, although Loudon is often credited with assembling Repton's writings and propounding the importance of his taste in garden design.
54. H. A. S. Dearborn, "Proceedings . . . Sept. 8, 1832," *Transactions* 1:35–36.
55. H. A. S. Dearborn, "Address," *New England Farmer* 8.27 (January 22, 1831): 211; Bigelow, *History*, 7–8. The act of the General Court, chap. 69, sec. 1 (June 23, 1831), did not mention the experimental garden. The Committee of Twenty formed in June 1831 to determine how to proceed included Story, Webster, Dearborn, Bigelow, Brimmer, Charles Lowell, Samuel Appleton, Edward Everett, Alexander H. Everett, George Bond, Abbott Lawrence, James T. Austin, Franklin Dexter, Joseph P. Bradlee, Charles Tappan, Charles P. Curtis, Zebedee Cook, John Pierpont, L. M. Sargent, and George W. Pratt.
56. Edward Everett to Bigelow, June 20, 1831, quoted in Ellis, *Memoir*, 73. Lake Avernus in Italy was also famous among travelers on the Grand Tour as the site of the grotto of the Cumaean sibyl, where Aeneas began his descent into the underworld. Designers of English gardens and landscape painters, such as Richard Wilson in 1760 and Joseph Mallord William Turner (1775–1851) in 1798, often reinterpreted views of the lake.
57. Bunyan's *The Pilgrim's Progress* (1678) sold over 100,000 copies to every Christian sect in the decade before the Dissenter Bunyan (1628–1688) died. It continued to be a best-seller second only to the Bible throughout the nineteenth century.
58. H. A. S. Dearborn, "An Account of the Proceedings, in Relation to the Experimental Garden and the Cemetery" (June 11, 1831), 65, MAC; Dearborn, "Historical Sketch," 68–70; Peabody, "Mount Auburn Cemetery," 405.
59. H. A. S. Dearborn, "Second Annual Report," 105.
60. Dearborn, "Mount Auburn Cemetery," 406. This assertion that Mount Auburn was the product of "manly sentiment" belies the more recent interpretation by Ann Douglas of the cemetery as evidence of the "feminization of American culture" in her book by that name.
61. The committee planning the consecration included Story, Dearborn, Cook, J. T. Buckingham, Brimmer, George W. Pratt, Z. B. Adams, Charles P. Curtis, and the Reverend Charles Lowell.
62. With the goal of nationalizing the law based on the example of Massachusetts, the Beverly attorney Nathan Dane (1752–1835) funded the innovative chair with $10,000 in proceeds from his nine-volume *Prospectus, or Concise View of a General Abridgment and Digest of American Law with Occasional Notes and Comments* (1822), to which his friend Joseph Story contributed an addendum attesting to the importance and usefulness of the compilation. Story composed the inscription on Dane's gravestone in Beverly: "His fame belongs to his country. Let the gratitude of future ages cherish it."
63. Joseph Story, *Commentaries on the Constitution of the United States; with a Preliminary Review of the Constitutional History of the Colonies and States, before the Adoption of the Constitution. Abridged by the Author, for the Use of Colleges and High Schools* (Boston: Hilliard, Gray, & Co.; Cambridge: Brown, Shuttuck, & Co., 1833). It went through many editions in the nineteenth century, some with annotations by Thomas M. Cooley. The latest reprint is Durham: Carolina Academic Press, 1995. See also Simon Greenleaf, *A Discourse Commemorative of the Life and Character of the Hon. Joseph Story, LL.D., an Associate Justice of the Supreme Court of the United States, and Dane Professor of Law in Harvard University; Pronounced on the Eighteenth Day of September, AD 1845, at the Request of the Corporation of the University, and the Members of the Law School* (Boston: C. C. Little & J. Brown, 1845); William Newell, *A Discourse Occasioned by the Death of the Hon. Joseph Story, LL.D., Delivered in the Church of the First Parish in Cambridge, On Sunday, Sept. 14, 1845* (Cambridge: Metcalf & Co., 1845); George Stillman Hillard, *Memoir of Joseph Story, LL.D.* (Boston: John Wilson, 1868); Gerald T. Dunne, *Justice Joseph Story and the Rise of the Supreme Court* (New York: Simon & Schuster, 1970); James McClellan, *Joseph Story and the American Constitution* (Norman: University of Oklahoma Press, 1971); and R. Kent Newmyer, *Supreme Court Justice Joseph Story* (Chapel Hill: University of North Carolina Press, 1985).
64. Arthur Schlesinger Jr., *The Age of Jackson* (Boston: Little, Brown, 1945), 144–45, 322–26.
65. Story, *Commentaries*, 593; Story, *A Familiar Exposition of the Constitution of the United States* (1840; reprint, Lake Bluff, Ill.: Regnery Gateway Bicentennial Edition, 1986; Story, "The Value and Importance of Legal Studies," lecture delivered August 25, 1829, at his inauguration as Dane Professor of Law at Harvard University, cited in McClellan, *Joseph Story*, 66.
66. William Wetmore Story, ed., *Life and Letters of Joseph Story, Associate Justice of the Supreme Court of the United States, and Dane Professor of Law at Harvard University*, 2 vols. (Boston: C. C. Little & J. Brown, 1851), 1:2 and 2:60–61. Also see "Sketch of the Life of Judge Story," *Mount Auburn Memorial* 1.1 (August 24, 1859): 81. Story suffered what might be considered a nervous breakdown when his first wife's death was almost immediately followed by that of his father in 1815.
67. W. W. Story, *Life and Letters*, 2:60–61.
68. See the chapter "The Domestication of Death" in Douglas, *Feminization*.
69. Bigelow wrote sentimental verse on the deaths of his children. Also see John Quincy Adams, "Death of Children," *Mount Auburn Memorial* 1.39 (March 7, 1860): 310.
70. W. W. Story, *Life and Letters*, 2:62–65; H. A. S. Dearborn, "Historical Sketch," *Transactions* 1:71 and 76; [Manning], *History*, 82; Bigelow, *History*, 11. The Horticultural Society expended $50.82 on putting up seats for the crowd.
71. W. W. Story, *Life and Letters*, 2:63; David Brion Davis, *Antebellum American Culture* (Lexington, Mass.: D.C. Heath, 1979), 146. It was Ware who invited Josiah Quincy to accept the Harvard presidency. Ware's election to the Harvard chair of theology in 1805 was a major event in the Unitarian controversy. Ware's son by the same name was a colleague of Ralph Waldo Emerson's at Boston's Second Church until 1832.
72. W. W. Story, *Life and Letters*, 2:67.
73. Ibid., 2:64–65.
74. See "An Address Delivered on the Dedication of the Cemetery at Mount Auburn, September 24, 1831, by Joseph Story, To Which is Added an Appendix, Containing a Historical Notice

and Description of the Place with a List of the Present Subscribers, and a Map of the Grounds," *New-England Magazine* 1.6
75. (Dec. 1831): 539–41; "Judge Story's Address," in *The Picturesque Pocket Companion and Visitor's Guide through Mount Auburn*
76. (Boston: Otis, Broaders, 1839), 74–75; W. W. Story, *Life and Letters*, 2:64–65.

W. W. Story, *Life and Letters*, 2:64–65; *Picturesque Pocket Companion*, 79.

W. W. Story, *Life and Letters*, 2:67; J. S. Buckingham, *America*, 3:146; "Cemetery at Mount Auburn" [reprint of article from the *Boston Courier*], *New England Farmer* 10.11 (September 28, 1831): 82.

8. Cemetery or Garden?

1. Bigelow, *History*, 134; Edward Everett, "The Proposed Rural Cemetery," in T. W. Harris, *Discourse*, 70.
2. Dearborn, "Proceedings . . . 1831," 1.
3. H. A. S. Dearborn, "An Account of the Proceedings in Relation to the Experimental Garden and the Cemetery of Mount Auburn," *Transactions* 1:68 MHORT; [Dearborn], "Proceedings . . . Oct. 1st, 1832," *New England Farmer* 10.12 (October 5, 1831): 90–91.
4. The members of the Garden and Cemetery Committee were Story, Dearborn, Bigelow, Brimmer, Edward Everett, Benjamin A. Gould, Charles Wells, George W. Pratt, and George Bond. Zebedee Cook Jr., vice president of the Horticultural Society, also participated.
5. *New England Farmer* 3 (1824): 77, 22.
6. Dearborn, "A Treatise on Grecian Architecture" (1828), 2 vols., BPLRB.
7. Manuscript letter from H. A. S. Dearborn, January 18, 1842, included in "Constitution, Reports, Addresses, and Other Publications in Relation to the Massachusetts Horticultural Society and the Cemetery at Mount Auburn from 1829 to 1837," MHORT; Dearborn, "Plan of the Avenues of Mount Auburn and Plan of the Cottage of the Gardener of Mount Auburn and Report of the Garden and Cemetery Committee of the Massachusetts Horticultural Society, September 17, 1834," signed Joseph Story, Chairman, manuscript, New York Public Library (hereafter NYPL). Also see Robin Carver, *History of Boston* (Boston: Lilly, Watt, Colman & Holden, 1832), 148.
8. William Mason, "The English Garden," in *The Oxford Book of Garden Verse*, ed. John Dixon Hunt (Oxford: Oxford University Press, 1993), 131. The picturesque avenues and paths giving access to all parts of the grounds responded to a criticism of English gardens Dearborn gleaned from his readings of Humphrey Repton in "The 'Red Book' from Blaise Castle" (1795–96), excerpt reprinted in *The Genius of Place: The England Landscape Garden, 1620–1820*, ed. John Dixon Hunt and Peter Willis (New York: Harper & Row, 1975), 363–64. Repton, however, was castigating the impersonal mid-eighteenth-century style of Capability Brown's designs, not the seminal work of Pope, Kent, and their generation.
9. John B. Russell quoted in [Manning], *History*, 86–91.
10. The exterior road near Pomeroy's mill cost $200 for right of way, $700 for land, and $250 for materials to surface it. [Mount Auburn Cemetery], "Records of Committees" (November 3, 1831, and January 23, 1835), manuscript book (hereafter "Records"), 15, Mount Auburn Cemetery Archives (hereafter MAC). The roads were "smoothly gravelled" from the start, according to Carver, *History of Boston*, 148. Also see Dearborn, "Historical Sketch," 77–79.
11. Additional evidence appears in Dearborn to George W. Brimmer, "On the Work to Be Done at Mount Auburn during the Winter of 1831–2 and the Spring of 1832," November 20, 1831, from Brimley Place, Roxbury, NYPL. Also see Dearborn, "Plan of the Avenues," NYPL. Copies of some of this correspondence were located in 2006 in the archives, MHORT.
12. H. A. S. Dearborn, "The Proposed Rural Cemetery," in "An Account," 84; Dearborn to Brimmer, "On the Work to Be Done," NYPL. By 1833, Dearborn counted over 1,300 forest, ornamental, and fruit trees at Mount Auburn. [Henry M. Parker], *Notes on Mount Auburn, Edited by an Officer of the Corporation; Intended to Serve as a Stranger's Guide Book* (Boston: James Munroe, 1849), 16; Dearborn, "English Gardens," in "Writings on Horticulture and Other Branches of Rural Industry," vol. 2, 117–19, Rare Books Room, NYPL; [Manning], *History*, 94–95.
13. Bigelow to his family in Boston from the Hotel des Princes, rue Richelieu, Paris, May 2–4, 1833, Bigelow Papers, MHIS.
14. Dearborn to Bigelow, October 25, 1831, MAC. Still, considerable confusion exists in historical accounts as to who deserves credit for creating Mount Auburn—confusion largely produced by competitive claims originating with Dearborn and Bigelow and reinterpreted and perpetuated by their eulogists, then misunderstood by historians relying only on secondary sources. Attribution of credit is further complicated because the cemetery began as a voluntary association, was developed under the auspices of another institution, and finally was incorporated independently. Through these phases, committees made many organizational and design decisions, misinterpreted even by contemporaries. One observer from Baltimore listed Joseph Story, Daniel Webster, Governor Levi Lincoln, Abbott Lawrence, Samuel Appleton, the Everett brothers, Brimmer, and Dearborn as instrumental in creating Mount Auburn, omitting mention of Bigelow entirely. Although Bigelow did not design the landscape initially, he remained a constant proponent of the cemetery through the founding phases and was active for decades after Dearborn dissociated himself from Mount Auburn. The physician became president of the cemetery in 1845. [Stephen Duncan Walker], *Rural Cemetery and Public Walk* (Baltimore: Sands & Neilson, 1835), 4.
15. Dearborn, "Historical Sketch," 68–70; Dearborn, "Mount Auburn Cemetery," 405. John Claudius Loudon closely paraphrased Dearborn in speculating that cemeteries might double as educational institutions for architecture and landscape gardening in his essay "On the Laying Out, Planting, and Managing of Cemeteries," *Gardener's Magazine* (1843): 104–5, 354–67, 589ff; *On the Laying Out, Planting, and Managing of Cemeteries; and on the Improvement of Churchyards* (London: A. Spottiswoode for the Author, 1843).
16. The professional title "landscape gardener" retained currency on both sides of the Atlantic throughout the nineteenth century. Andrew Jackson Downing was the first to coin the title "landscape architect," which began to catch on later in the century through the firm of Frederick Law Olmsted, staffed by many professional landscape designers. One wonders whether Dearborn's school, if

created, might have become affiliated with Harvard, precisely when the college was adding new professional curricula, to become the nation's first professional landscape design school, as influential as the systematic course of study of the law established in 1845 by Story, which was within a decade the model for proliferating law schools, making obsolete the informal practice of an aspiring attorney "reading the law" with a practitioner.

17. Z. Cook in *Transactions* 1:75, MHORT. Cook also called for protection and preservation of useful birds at Mount Auburn, a secondary function that would have made the place America's first bird sanctuary. Dearborn, "Historical Sketch," 68.
18. Dearborn, *Transactions* 1:75; Dearborn, "Historical Sketch," 68.
19. Dearborn, "Historical Sketch," 69–70, 73, 78; Dearborn, "Garden and Cemetery Committee Report," *Transactions* (1831), 1:48. Dearborn to Brimmer, November 20, 1831 MHORT; S. P. Hildreth to the Massachusetts Horticultural Society, February 25, 1833, quoted in "Plants Grown," *New England Farmer* 11 (April 3, 1833): 299.
20. David Porter, quoted in *New England Farmer* 11 (May 22, 1833): 354–55. Other periodic reports of plants and seeds received by the Horticultural Society for Mount Auburn appeared in the *New England Farmer* 10–13 (1832–34). Eastern Orthodox Christians in the Ottoman Empire did not have the same ban on cemetery plantings as Roman Catholics after the Counter-Reformation.
21. Dearborn to George Bond, September 10, 1832, BPLRB. Samuel Appleton loaned $1,000, the largest single amount.
22. Bigelow, *History*, 6.
23. Brimmer to Dearborn, December 9, 1830, *New England Farmer* 11 (May 22, 1833): 354–55. David Haggerston exhibited produce grown at Mount Auburn at the Horticultural Society in June 1834.
24. Bigelow, *History*, 138. Joseph P. Bradlee sold the last twenty-five subscriptions. Although Mount Auburn did not initially levy additional charges, the city of Boston charged for burials in public grounds: "For the use of one horse and car and leader, $1.50; for each additional horse, 75¢. For carrying the corpse from the house to the car and from the car to the grave, tomb, or vault, and placing the same therein and closing the same, including the assistance of the funeral porters, $3." The bereaved were charged "$1 per mile for any distance that a funeral car may be sent out of the City." Charges did not include extra services such as special permission for the tolling of bells, notification of friends, services in the home, placing the corpse in a coffin, carrying it down stairs, and so on. A single funeral in "proper" style with burial at Mount Auburn could cost as much as the family lot itself. Note that the dead were laid out at home; there were as yet no morticians with separate facilities. Few funeral services were held in meetinghouses or churches with the body present. See sec. 11, "An Ordinance to Regulate the Interment of the Dead [Passed Sept. 26, 1833]," in Wetmore and Prescott, *Charter and Ordinances*, 191.
25. Dearborn, *Transactions* 1:75; Henry Blake McLellan quoted in "Sweet Auburn," *Mount Auburn Memorial* 1.2 (June 22, 1859): 12. McLellan is buried in his family's tomb, not on Harvard Hill.
26. Bigelow, *History*, 138.
27. Ellis, *Memoir*, 74.
28. Advertisements appeared in the *Boston Evening Gazette* in the late summer of 1832. Rev. Henry Ware to George Bond, July 4, 1832, BPLRB. A measure of income differentials is that when Joseph Story became an associate justice of the U.S. Supreme Court in 1811, his annual salary was $3,500, less than he was earning in his private practice, combined with his appointment to the faculty at Harvard.
29. Malthus A. Ward, *An Address Pronounced before the Massachusetts Horticultural Society in Commemoration of its Third Annual Festival, Sept. 21, 1831* (Boston: J. T. & E. Buckingham, 1831), 47. The lot was named Saint James in 1848, and a second "public" lot, named Saint John, was opened later. The names were perhaps chosen to win favor for the cemetery among Episcopalians, a growing denomination.
30. Dearborn, "Proceedings . . . Oct. 1st, 1831," *New England Farmer* 10.12 (October 5, 1831): 90–91.
31. Joseph Story, "Report of the Garden and Cemetery Committee of the Massachusetts Horticultural Society . . . September 17, 1834," in Bigelow, *History*, 196–203; Dearborn "The Cemetery of Père La Chaise," in "Proceedings . . . Sept. 8, 1832," reprinted in *New England Farmer* 11 (September 12, 1832): 66–67 and quoted in Alexander H. Everett, *An Address . . . Sept. 18, 1833*, 36–46.
32. John Pierpont, "The Garden of Graves," in *The Token*, ed. S. G. Goodrich (Boston: Gray & Bowen,1832), reprinted (Dedham, Mass.: H. Mann, 1841) for the benefit of the Ladies' Charity Fair, held at Dedham May 26, 1841.
33. John Pierpont, "To My Grave," in *Airs of Palestine and Other Poems* (Boston: James Munroe, 1840), 65–72. Pierpont relinquished the cherished gravesite in 1845, returning the unused plot to the corporation when he accepted a new pulpit in Troy, New York. In 1849 he returned to Medford. On another lot on Lavender Path, Pierpont's red granite marker by architect George Keller, said to represent the Ark of the Covenant, memorializes the "Poet, Preacher, Philosopher, Philanthropist." His grandson John Pierpont Morgan (1837–1913), one of the wealthiest men in the nation, had a larger version of the monument erected at Cedar Hill Cemetery in Hartford.
34. Mary Tyler Peabody letter in the Mount Auburn Archives, quoted in "'No Place Will Possess Stronger Attractions to the Visitor,'" *Sweet Auburn: The Newsletter of the Friends of Mount Auburn Cemetery* (Fall 1992); Mary Tyler Peabody to Miss Rawlins Pickman, Salem, October 8, 1935, Horace Mann II Papers, MHIS.
35. G[eorge] T[icknor] Curtis, "Mount Auburn," *New England Magazine* 7 (October 1834): 316.
36. Ralph Waldo Emerson, April 11, 1834, in *Journals of Ralph Waldo Emerson with Annotations*, ed. Edward Waldo Emerson and Waldo Forbes Emerson, vol. 3 (Boston: Houghton Mifflin, 1910), 270–71; Bliss Perry, ed., *The Heart of Emerson's Journals* (Boston: Houghton Mifflin, 1926), 82–83. See Robert D. Richardson Jr., *Emerson: The Mind on Fire* (Berkeley: University of California Press, 1995).
37. *Essays and Poems, By Jones Very* (Boston: C. C. Little & James Brown, 1839). See Edwin Gittleman, *Jones Very: The Effective Years, 1833–1840* (New York: Columbia University Press, 1967). Fragment from Fuller's journal (Thursday, May 23, 1844) in Bell Gale Chevigny, *The Woman and the Myth: Margaret Fuller's Life and Writings* (Boston: Northeastern University Press, 1994), 535. Emerson later persuaded the town of Concord to dedicate Sleepy Hollow as a "rural" cemetery in 1855 and delivered the consecration address.

38. Dearborn, "Historical Sketch," 77–79; "Trustees' Minutes" (manuscript books, hereafter TM), 1:15, MAC; [Fanny Kemble], *The Journal of Frances Anne Butler, Better Known as Fanny Kemble* (1835; reprint, New York: B. Blom, 1970), 175–76.
39. "Proceedings of the Massachusetts Horticultural Society," *Transactions* 1:106–7; J[oseph] Story, "Report" (September 1832), *Transactions* 1:47; [Joseph T. Buckingham], "Good Advice, But Bitter," *New-England Magazine* 5.5 (November 1833): 401–2.
40. J[oseph] Story, "Report" (September 1832), *Transactions* 1:47; William Kenrick to Dearborn, June 11, 1833, in the Dearborn Papers, BPLRB; George Bond to Dearborn, September 10, 1832, Dearborn Papers, NYPL; Benson, *History*, 40–41; Oakes I[ngalls] Ames, "Mount Auburn's Sixscore Years," *Publications of the Cambridge Historical Society* 34 (1951–52): 80. By September 1833, 259 of 400 lots laid out had been sold, producing revenue of $17,229.72. Lack of corporate records of use of mortsafes does not mean they were not placed on lots. There are no records of proprietors' other temporary additions such as iron benches and urns.
41. Z. Cook to Dearborn, December 30, 1834, in Josiah Little Papers, MHIS. Dearborn had hoped to establish "seminaries of trees and shrubs" as late as that fall. Dearborn to Z. Cook, September 10, 1834, in John C. Gray, *An Address Delivered before the Massachusetts Horticultural Society at the 6th Anniversary*, Sept. 17, 1834 (Boston: J. T. Buckingham, 1834), 29.
42. "Records," April 29, 1833, 14; Dearborn, "Report," *Transactions* 1:104.
43. *Transactions* 1:104.
44. Ibid.
45. Records," 15; H. Dearborn, "Historical Sketch," 73–74.
46. "Records," July 19, 1834, 22; and October 17, 1834, 24; "Report of the Garden and Cemetery Committee," September 17, 1837, "Records," 27; Alexander H. Everett, *Address*. Everett gave a large dinner for Alexis de Tocqueville when the Frenchman and his traveling companion Beaumont visited America in the fall of 1831 in order to introduce them to many of the Bostonians active in the Bunker Hill Monument Association, the Massachusetts Horticulture Society, and the founding of Mount Auburn.
47. "Records," 27; "Report of the Garden and Cemetery Committee," September 17, 1837, in "Records," 27.
48. Dearborn left for upstate New York, then in its frontier stage, serving in 1838–39 as superintendent for the sale of Seneca Indian lands in the Buffalo area before returning to settle on his rural estate in Roxbury.
49. Johann N. Neem, "Politics and the Origins of the Nonprofit Corporation in Massachusetts and New Hampshire, 1780–1820," *Nonprofit and Voluntary Sector Quarterly* 32.3 (September 2003): 344–65.
50. An act in addition to the original charter by the legislature on May 3, 1850, expanded the powers of the corporation to "purchase and hold in fee simple or otherwise, any real estate, or any interest in any real estate, situated and lying in the towns of Cambridge and Watertown . . . provided always, that such real estate by the said corporation so purchased, holden, and possessed . . . shall not at any one time exceed 100 acres in extent, in addition to whatever real estate the said corporation now holds, or is entitled to hold." That authorized subsequent purchases of peripheral land even if not immediately developed for burials. TM 1 (February 12, 1851), 213–14.
51. Leverett Saltonstall quoted in Flagg, *Mount Auburn*, 33.
52. Exceptions to the family-only rule were occasionally made for a beloved family servant or a friend if the proprietor permitted burial without charge. Commonwealth of Massachusetts, "An Act to Incorporate the Proprietors of the Cemetery of Mount Auburn" (1835), in *A Catalogue of Proprietors of the Cemetery of Mount Auburn* (Boston: James Munroe, 1846), xvii–xviii.
53. For instance, after founding and designing Forest Hills Cemetery across town in Roxbury in 1848, General Henry A. S. Dearborn sold his Mount Auburn lot and again reinterred there his mother and his father, General Henry Dearborn, a Revolutionary War hero.
54. "Report of the Garden and Cemetery Committee," September 17, 1837.
55. Attempts to move older remains, if located, may have been impeded by the new Boston code providing "that no person shall remove any bodies, or the remains of any bodies from any of the graves or tombs in this city, or shall disturb, break up, or remove any body in any tomb or graves without the special permission of the Superintendent of Burials." "An Ordinance to Regulate Interment of the Dead," [86], sec. 23, in chap. 24, "Health," in [City of Boston], *The Charter and Ordinances of the City of Boston*, ed. by Thomas Wetmore and Edward G. Prescott (Boston: J. H. Eastburn, 1834), 192.
56. TM (April 12, 1838), 45; (March 9, 1841), 71; (July 14, 1842), 84.
57. TM (September 29, 1843), 101–3; Bigelow, History, 74–75.
58. Walter, *Rural Cemeteries*, 10, 30.
59. Samuel Walker, "Horticultural Societies," *The Horticulturist and Journal of Rural Art and Rural Taste* 6.2 (February 1851): 92.
60. Rev. George Putnam, *Address*, 12–24. Versions of the eulogy were printed in newspapers: "Putnam's Address," *Boston Courier*, September 4, 1851; Putnam, "Address," *Boston Daily Advertiser*, September 9, 1851. Subsequently Robert Manning became a Dearborn partisan in the debate when he edited his *History of the Massachusetts Horticultural Society, 1829–1878* (Boston: Rand, Avery, for the Society, 1880).
61. In 1850 Bigelow "instructed" the superintendent on "how to remove underbrush and trimming of trees . . . for improvement of the grounds" but let trustee Mace Tisdale advise the superintendent on how three of the principal avenues were "to be finished off in the most approved manner." TM 1 (October 18, 1850), 210.
62. Bigelow, *History*, 6, 19, 96.
63. "Gen. H. A. S. Dearborn," *Mount Auburn Memorial* 2.14 (October 3, 1860): 105.
64. Bigelow to Massachusetts Horticultural Society, September 1866, quoted in [Manning], *History*, 115–17.
65. Ellis, *History*, 34, 61–62. Ellis, a minister who graduated in the Harvard class of 1834, was a close friend of Francis Parkman, Bigelow's son-in-law. As president of the Massachusetts Historical Society, Ellis omitted to mention in the eulogy that subsequently, in the 1850s and 1860s, Bigelow was responsible for altering the original "rural" aesthetics of the landscape, making the place more "beautiful" than "picturesque" by eliminating half of the original tree canopy in order to plant ornamentals. That era of landscape change will be discussed in chapter 12.
66. Bainbridge Bunting and Robert H. Nylander, *Survey of Architectural History in Cambridge: Report Four: Old Cambridge* (Cam-

bridge: Cambridge Historical Commission and MIT Press, 1969), 70; TM 1 (March 3, 1848), 169; TM 3 (April 2, 1860), 132. If the debate over cemetery design was not confused enough by partisans of Dearborn and Bigelow, more recent writers have added to the confusion. One article even attributed the design to Nathaniel Dearborn, the prominent Boston printer and author of a series of guidebooks to the cemetery. Jules Zanger, "Mount Auburn Cemetery: The Silent Suburb," *Landscape* 24.2 (1980): 23–28, is perhaps more erroneous and full of misinterpretations than any other source. By the 1860s Wadsworth was taking on small projects in laying out estates and subdivisions, occasionally working as a surveyor on other regional cemeteries.

67. Burton J. Bledstein, *The Culture of Professionalism: The Middle Class and the Development of Higher Education in America* (New York: Norton, 1976), 20.

9. Art and Nature Balanced

1. [Enoch Cobb Wines], A Philadelphian, *A Trip to Boston in a Series of Letters to the Editor of the United States Gazette* (Boston: Little, Brown, 1838), 45. [John Ross Dix], A Looker-On, *Local Loiterings and Visits in the Vicinity of Boston* (Boston: Redding, 1845), 17; excerpt reprinted as "An Englishman's Opinion of Mount Auburn," *Mount Auburn Memorial* 2:3 (July 18, 1860): 19. Henry David Thoreau, *Walden* (1854; New York: Thomas Y. Crowell, 1961), 173.
2. "Mount Auburn," in *Cyclopedia of Useful Knowledge* (1835), 9, an anonymous clipping in the archive of the Mount Auburn Cemetery (hereafter MAC).
3. Trustees' Minutes [hereafter TM], 1 (June 7, 1838), 46.
4. Ibid., 1 (March 9, 1841), 71.
5. Joseph T. Buckingham, "Mount Auburn," *Boston Courier* (September 18, 1838), reprinted in *Mount Auburn Memorial* 2.1 (July 4, 1860): 10; J[ames] S[ilk] Buckingham, *America*, 191–92.
6. Jacob Bigelow, "Mount Auburn!" manuscript poem (n.d.) in the Bigelow Family Papers, MHIS.
7. Walter, *Mount Auburn Illustrated*, 5, 8–9, 15.
8. J. S. Buckingham, *America*, 391–92.
9. Charles Lyell, *A Second Visit to the United States of North America*, vol. 1 (London: John Murray, 1849), 171.
10. TM 1 (July 14, 1843), 83.
11. Peabody, "Mount Auburn Cemetery," 406; Henry A. S. Dearborn, "An Account of the Work Done at Mount Auburn during the Year 1832," *Transactions*; "Records," October 1833, 17, and November 3, 1831, 2. Mount Auburn finally permitted slate stones during the vogue for the Colonial Revival style at the turn of the twentieth century.
12. Hunt, "Pope's Twickenham Revisited," 32. Work orders for erection of monuments are now organized in the archives, MAC.
13. *The Picturesque Pocket Companion and Visitor's Guide through Mount Auburn* (Boston: Otis, Broaders, 1839), 12–13.
14. Jacob Bigelow, "On the Limits of Education," in *Modern Inquiries: Classical, Professional, and Miscellaneous* (Boston: Little, Brown, 1867), 32.
15. Henry Russell Cleveland, "American Architecture," *North American Review* 43.93 (October 1836): 378–80; Joseph Story, "An Address Delivered at the Consecration," in Bigelow, *History*, 157.
16. "A Conservative Unitarian" to the Senior Warden of King's Chapel, November 1841, in Foote, *Annals*, 2:470–71. As members of other Protestant sects became proprietors, crosses began to appear on or as monuments.
17. See Cross, *True Masonic Chart*.
18. Willard intially received $14 for his designs. William Kenrick to Henry A. S. Dearborn, in Dearborn Papers, BPL. On Robert Gould Shaw's order for monuments, see Bigelow to Dearborn, January 13, 1833, BPL. In 1837 the cemetery paid $100 for monument plans. TM 1 (March 22, 1837), 39. Shaw is not to be confused with the young colonel, the Civil War hero (1837–1863), commemorated by a monument on Boston Common by Augustus Saint-Gaudens, dedicated in 1897. Colonel Shaw was the son of abolitionist Francis George Shaw and the grandson of the man who imported the monuments. Architect Hammett Billings designed the neoclassical brownstone enclosure by Alpheus Cary that shelters Shaw's imported low-relief marble plaque at Mount Auburn. Later a bronze plaque was added in memory of his namesake, the colonel, who is buried with his troops in South Carolina. It is difficult to determine which architect, sculptor, or monument dealer was responsible for many of the monuments at Mount Auburn, except for the few that are signed. A meticulous inventory of the funerary art and architecture of the cemetery remains to be done.
19. H. A. S. Dearborn, "Mount Auburn Cemetery," 406.
20. J. S. Buckingham, *America*, 3. [Anon.], "Mount Auburn," *American Magazine* 10 (n.d.), clipping, MAC.
21. See Eliade, *The Sacred and the Profane*, esp. chap. 1, "Sacred Space and Making the World Sacred."
22. Scully, *The Earth, the Temple, and the Gods*, 42–43.
23. *Picturesque Pocket Companion*, 193–94.
24. Josiah Quincy, Harvard's president, acknowledged the elder Shattuck's donation of the lots in April 1833.
25. George Shattuck Jr. to George Bond, n.d., Shattuck Papers 33:4, MHIS.
26. *Picturesque Pocket Companion*, 75.
27. The precedent for excluding any monument or effigy deemed offensive had been set at Père Lachaise, where all inscriptions had to be approved by the superintendent. The provision granting the trustees veto power was included as the seventh "condition" or "limitation" on the "Form for Conveyance of Lots" issued to each proprietor, reprinted in *Catalogue of the Lots at Mount Auburn Cemetery* (Boston: Rand & Avery, 1857), 29. At Père Lachaise such censorship was seldom exercised, as huge mausoleums and elaborate sculptural monuments rapidly crowded out evidence of the picturesque even by the 1830s. The restrained taste in monuments, tombs, and mausoleums at Mount Auburn throughout the antebellum decades contrasts dramatically with that at other major "rural" cemeteries modeled after it, such as Philadelphia's Laurel Hill (1836) and New York's Green-Wood (1838).
28. "Strictures on Mount Auburn," *Boston Evening Transcript*, August 17, 1839: 2.
29. Bigelow, *History*, 142.
30. "Thomas Dowse," *Lowell Citizen*, December 6, 1856, reprinted in *The Living Age* 52.662 (January 31, 1857): 320. Franklin is buried in Philadelphia's Christ Church burial ground.
31. *Picturesque Pocket Companion*, 206, 195.

32. Ibid., 89; George Combe, *Notes on the United States of North America during a Phrenological Visit in 1838–9–40*, vol. 1 (Philadelphia: Carey & Hart, 1841), 135.
33. Harriet Martineau, *Retrospect of Western Travel*, vol. 2 (London: Saunders & Otley, 1838), 232–33. The tomb of L. Cornelius Scipio Barbatus, a consul in 298 BC, was excavated from Rome's Appian Way by 1782, when it was placed in the Vatican Museum to provide a model for copies. Spurzheim's embalmed body (embalming was then very rare) was buried at Mount Auburn after being temporarily deposited in the cemetery's receiving tomb under Boston's Park Street Church. The Boston Phrenological Society was founded on Spurzheim's birthday, December 31, 1832, to carry out the doctor's wishes to have his skull available for study and his brain preserved, the latter "floating in alcohol and hermetically sealed" in the society's iron safe. These were deemed "a very interesting addition to their collection of casts and skulls" begun by Dr. John Collins Warren. When the Phrenological Society disbanded in 1850, Dr. Warren purchased the collection to add to the Warren Anatomical Museum at the Harvard Medical School. See "Death of Dr. Spurzheim," *Boston Medical and Surgical Journal* 11 (November 14, 1832): 225–27; "Remains of Dr. Spurzheim," *Boston Medical and Surgical Journal* 11 (November 21, 1832): 229; and other documents in http://www.countway.med.harvard.edu/rarebooks/exhibits/talking_heads/heads4.html.
34. Lafayette is buried under a modest tombstone, once topped with a tall, crude cross, in the tiny Cimetière de Picpus in northern Paris. I thank Jean-Jacques Faugeron for granting me access to the cemetery, not then open to the public, in 1991.
35. See Joseph Story, *A Discourse Pronounced at the Funeral Obsequies of John Hooker Ashmun, Esq., Royall Professor of Law at Harvard University, Before the President, Fellows, and Faculty, in the Chapel of the University* (Cambridge: Brown, Shattuck & Co., 1833).
36. Mrs. E. C. Kirkland to the Committee of the Alumni of Harvard University Who Propose Erecting a Monument to the Memory of Dr. Kirkland (n.d.), Bigelow Family Papers, MHIS.
37. *Picturesque Pocket Companion*, 189.
38. Thomas Whittemore ed., *The Life of Rev. Hosea Ballou: With Accounts of His Writings*, vol. 4 (Boston: James M. Usher, 1855), 242–47.
39. The trustees had declined the request of the "Society in Brattle Square," his congregation, for donation of a lot. TM 1 (December 22, 1838), 50. Buckminster had introduced Channing, his literary friends, and his congregation to German biblical scholarship, thus promoting the rise of Unitarianism.
40. TM 1 (December 13, 1838), 48–49.
41. Charles Wilkes, *Narrative of the U.S. Exploring Expedition during the Years 1838, 1839, 1840, 1841, 1842*, vol. 2 (Philadelphia: Lea & Blanchard, 1848), 310–11; "A Cruise After and Among the Cannibals," *Harper's New Monthly Magazine* 7.40 (September 1853): 462. Wilkes retaliated for the deaths by killing eighty-seven "Feejee" (Fiji) villagers. Less than three months after the tragedy, a committee aboard ship, still in the South Seas, decided to erect the monument at Mount Auburn. Perhaps it was the monument that stimulated Thoreau's rancor against the "parade and expense" of the expedition. Thoreau, *Walden*, 424.
42. Reverend Alexander Young, *A Discourse on the Life and Character of the Hon. Nathaniel Bowditch, LL.D., F.R.S., Delivered in the Church on Church Green, Mar. 25, 1838* (Boston: Little, Brown, 1838), 98–99. As news of Bowditch's death spread nationally, flags flew at half-mast on vessels out of Baltimore and midshipmen at the Naval Academy donned black crepe armbands for thirty days. No evidence remains of how many of them contributed to the monument, which was far more elaborate and innovative than that proposed by the Reverend Young. Controversy remains over who cast the bronze—Hughes's own studio, the Boston foundries of Gooding & Gavette, Goding & Gorell, Henry N. Hooper & Company, or the Ames firm in nearby Chicopee. Young proposed a "four-sided figure": On one face, "a few geometrical figures, a circle, a triangle, &c around a ship in the center full sail with the American flag flying at the mizzen-peak" and the motto "DIRIGO—I guide." On another face he proposed a relief of two books inscribed "THE PRACTICAL NAVIGATOR" and "MECANIQUE CELESTE" along with a sextant and compass, the ringed planet Saturn, and the constellation Ursa Minor with polestar. Inscriptions on the two remaining sides would proclaim Bowditch "The American Pilot and Mathematician . . . The Expounder of the Mechanism of the Heavens" and acknowledge the contributions for the monument to "their Guide and Benefactor" from "the Seamen of the United States." The remains of Bowditch and his wife were reinterred on Tulip Path in 1864 under a simple sandstone sarcophagus. As if competing on behalf of their local notable Thomas Godfrey, inventor of the marine quadrant, who died in 1749, the Mercantile Library Company of Philadelphia and citizens of Germantown, Pennsylvania, erected an obelisk in Laurel Hill Cemetery over the remains of Godfrey and his parents, recently moved there from the old colonial family burial ground.
43. "Rural Cemeteries," *North American Review* 53.113 (October 1841): 398.
44. A stele marker, a cenotaph, in Bennington, Vermont, notes Channing's death there. It is adorned with bending oaks, shedding leaves, a setting sun, and a lamp of wisdom.
45. Lauretta Dimmick, "Thomas Crawford's Monument for Amos Binney in Mount Auburn Cemetery: 'A Work of Rare Merit,'" *Markers: The Journal of the Association for Gravestone Studies* 9 (1992): 159–95.
46. Mary E. Hewitt, ed., *The Memorial: Written by the Friends of the Late Mrs. Osgood* (New York: G. P. Putnam, 1851); "The Memorial," *Harper's New Monthly Magazine* 2.8 (January 1851): 282. Contributors included George H. Boker, Nathaniel Hawthorne, George Lunt, John Neal, Mrs. Lydia Huntley Sigourney, William Gilmore Simms, Mrs. Oakes Smith, A. B. Street, R. H. Stoddard, Bayard Taylor, a Mrs. Whitman, N. P. Willis, and Bishops Doan and Spencer. [Sarah Payson Willis], Fanny Fern, *Fern Leaves from Fanny's Port-Folio*, ser. 2 (Buffalo: Miller, Orton & Mulligan, 1854), 157–60; Samuel Osgood, "The Monument to Frances S. Osgood—A Reply to the Imputations of Fanny Fern," *New York Evening Post*, October 7, 1854; "Letter from Fanny Fern—Mrs. Osgood's Monument," *New York Evening Post*, October 20, 1854.
47. Damrell V. Moore and George Coolidge, eds., *The Boston Almanac for the Year 1857*, no. 22 (Boston: John P. Jewett, 1857), 59. Amos Adams Lawrence donated the lot. A decade before, the industrialist had also donated lots near his own at Mount Auburn to the Reverends Joseph Stevens Buckminster and Samuel K. Lothrop to ensure their nearness to him in death. Although Lawrence ac-

cepted the secularized cemetery, he seems to have felt that being buried near those saintly men of God was the best alternative to a churchyard or church crypt. Amos Lawrence had had his son Amos Adams Lawrence confirmed as an Episcopalian at Saint Paul's in 1842. The event signaled the shift of many Unitarian families in Boston to acceptance of High Church forms. Perhaps this accounts for the industrialist's desire to surround his family lots with the graves of ministers, albeit of many denominations. It may even suggest his influence in locating the cemetery's first chapel across one avenue from the Lawrence family lot. William R. Lawrence, ed., *Extracts from the Diary and Correspondence of the Late Amos Lawrence* (Boston: Gould & Lawrence, 1855), 176.

48. Whittemore, *The Life*, 304–5, 317, 341. Ballou's body was first placed in a tomb in the Boston Common Burying Ground; but "it was the intention to regard this merely as a temporary burial" and to move the body to a more fitting, permanent site. Ernest Rohdenburg III, "Bracketting Mount Auburn," *Sweet Auburn* (Summer 1998).
49. *Boston Transcript*, October 5, 1866; Janet Heywood, "The Harnden Monument," *Sweet Auburn* (Summer 1998).
50. Bigelow, *History*, 531; Bigelow, *Boston Daily Advertiser*, quoted ibid., 96; "Mount Auburn Cemetery," *New England Farmer* 10.5 (August 17, 1831): 38.
51. *Transactions*, 81–82. There is also a striking, if only superficial and visual, similarity between Mount Auburn's hillside tombs and Hindu temples in the form of single-chamber tombs in caves, the *garbhagrhas*, or "womb tombs," built into rock under moundlike hillsides having only plain stone facades. The same elite Bostonians whom Oliver Wendell Holmes later dubbed "Brahmins," conscious of parallels based on learning and lineage between themselves and the Indian ruling caste, may well have drawn stylistic inspiration from those temple structures, seen during trade with India. Bostonians may have adapted the structural form to an entirely new cultural use—burial—unprecedented in the parent culture, which used cremation. Thanks are due to Barbara Ramusak for showing me the engraved view of "The Temple of Mandeswara near Chaynpore, Bahar" by Thomas Daniell (1808).
52. H. A. S. Deaborn, "An Account of the Work Done at Mount Auburn during the Year 1832," in T. W. Harris, *Discourse*, 81–82. For example, one historian notes that Ralph Waldo Emerson "dug up his son's body, after its decay, to contemplate it," after having done likewise when exhuming his wife. Garry Wills, *Lincoln at Gettysburg*, 72, 276.
53. Gilman subsequently laid out Boston's Back Bay and designed the Arlington Street Church (1861) and Boston's Old City Hall (1863–1865).
54. Steven J. Bennett, "Chinese Topographical Thinking," *Boston University Journal* (January 1978): 14–27. The term and concept of "geomancy" (*feng shui*) were known to Bigelow and appeared in his correspondence in 1854. Bigelow Family Papers, box 3 (1854–69), MHIS. Also see Sarah Rossback, *Feng Shui: The Chinese Art of Placement* (New York: E. P. Dutton, 1983), 51–55.
55. TM 1 (June 5, 1840), 72; L[ucius] M. Sargent, *Dealings with the Dead, By a Sexton of the Old School*, 2 vols. (Boston: Dutton & Wentworth, 1856), 1:46. The 160 articles in the two volumes originally appeared in the *Boston Evening Transcript*.
56. Bigelow, *History*, 129. In 1885 trustees instructed Lovering to remove single-chamber tombs at the request of proprietors and regrade the lots free of charge. Henceforth, no single-chamber tomb would be accepted under perpetual care. TM 1 (September 4, 1854), 280; 6 (October 12, 1885), 371.
57. J. T. Buckingham, *Mount Auburn*, 10.
58. "The Tomb of Spurzheim at Mount Auburn," *Family Magazine* (1853): 404.

10. Embellishing the Picturesque

1. Alison, *Essays*, 180.
2. Henry A. S. Dearborn, "Report," in *Picturesque Pocket Companion*, 46. The Abney Park Cemetery Company opened its first commercial cemetery for Nonconformists (non-Anglicans) on a thirty-two-acre wooded estate near London in 1840, adding an Egyptian Revival gateway. It was a tourist attraction from its inception. Extramural cemeteries became "big business" around London after Parliament passed an 1832 bill "For Establishing a General Cemetery for the Interment of the Dead in the Neighborhood of the Metropolis," followed by the founding of Kensall Green north of Paddington in 1838, Highgate by the London Cemetery Company in 1839, and other competitors at Brompton and Nunhead in 1841, as well as Towers Hamlets in 1841. See Felix Barker, *Highgate Cemetery: Victorian Valhalla* (London: John Murray, 1984), 14–15.
3. Thomas Cole, "Essay on American Scenery," *American Monthly Magazine*, n.s. 1 (January 1836): 1–12, quoted in John Lunsford, *The Romantic Vision in America* (Dallas: Dallas Museum of Fine Arts, 1971). Also see John Conron, ed., *The American Landscape: A Critical Anthology of Prose and Poetry* (New York: Oxford University Press, 1974).
4. H. A. S. Dearborn, "Report," in "Proceedings . . . 1831," 90.
5. Walter Muir Whitehill, foreword to Douglass Shand-Tucci, *Built in Boston: City and Suburb, 1800–1950* (Boston: New York Graphic Society, 1978), viii.
6. Davis was referred to Bigelow by the architect Ithiel Town. Bigelow's study contained a "beautiful array of classical and artistic adornments—the arch of Constantine, models of ancient columns, temples, and amphitheatres, bas reliefs and bronzes. Apollo and the Muses, the busts of the Caesars, the models of York Minster made by his own hand." Andrews, *Architecture*, 112; Charles Bulfinch to Bigelow, November 20, 1828, Bigelow Papers, MHIS; Ellis, *Memoir*, 88; H. A. S. Dearborn, "Report: The Annual Meeting of the Horticultural Society, October 1, 1831, The Committee on Laying Out the Grounds and Forming the Plan of the Experimental Garden and Cemetery at Mount Auburn," *Transactions* 1:77.
7. Bigelow to Deaborn in Congress, Washington, D.C., January 13, 1833, BPL.
8. Edward Everett, "The Zodiac of Denderah," *North American Review* 17.41 (1823): 233–42; Everett, "Hieroglyphics," *North American Review* 32.70 (January 1831): 95–126; John T. Irwin, *American Hieroglyphics: The Symbol of the Egyptian Hieroglyphics in the American Renaissance* (Baltimore: Johns Hopkins University Press, 1980), 8. Everett's 1831 piece was reviewed by J. G. H. Greppo, *Essay on the Hieroglyphic System of M. Champollion, Jr., on the Advantages Which It Offers to Sacred Criticism*, trans. Isaac Stuart (Boston: Perkins & Marvin, 1830). Also see Henry Wheaton,

"Egyptian Antiquities," *North American Review* 30.65 (October 1829): 361–88, on books about Champollion from England, France, and Denmark.

9. See Richard G. Carrott, *The Egyptian Revival: Its Sources, Monuments, and Meaning, 1808–1858* (Berkeley: University of California Press, 1978), 87–88. William Dunlap called the Athenaeum the "only respectable library of the Fine Arts" in the nation in his *History of the Rise and Progress of the Arts of Design in the United States*, vol. 2 (New York: Scott, 1834), 409.
10. Jolimont, *Mausolées*, 5–6. An even more encyclopedic study was *Déscription de l'Egypte; ou, Recueil des observations et des recherches qui ont été faites en Egypte pendant l'expédition de l'armée francaise, publié par les ordres de Sa Majesté, l'empéreur Napoléon le Grand*, from Dominique-Vivant Denon's Commission on Egyptian Monuments, issued in twenty-one volumes between 1809 and 1823. Harvard received copies in 1822, the gift of W. H. Eliot.
11. Alexander Jackson Davis quoted in Carrott, *Egyptian Revival*, 53. Bigelow, *Elements of Technology*, 131.
12. [Dix], *Local Loiterings*, 18.
13. John Frazee, "The Statue and Monument to Washington," *North American Review* 5 (March 1835): 350–52; Henry Russell Cleveland, "American Architecture," *North American Review* 43.93 (October 1836): 379, 381. The trustees failed to heed Cleveland's advice that a permanent gate take the form of a Gothic "wall pierced by three pointed arches, the middle one very lofty and broad for the admission of carriages." After all, as Cleveland acknowledged, the Gothic was more expensive to build than the Egyptian. The suggestion of such an entry, "surmounted by a battlement of open-work, or machicolated . . . supported by buttresses or by octagon towers terminating in light pinnacles," may have inspired Richard Upjohn's design for the gates at Green-Wood Cemetery (1838) in Brooklyn.
14. H. A. S. Dearborn, *An Address Delivered before the Massachusetts Society for Promoting Agriculture Oct. 14, 1835* (Boston: George C. Barrett, 1835), 7; Dearborn, "General Dearborn's Address: Delivered before the Massachusetts Horticultural Society on the Celebration of their First Anniversary, Sept. 19, 1829," *New England Farmer* 8.26 (January 15, 1830): 203.
15. Dearborn, "Mount Auburn Cemetery," 397–406.
16. Walter, *Mount Auburn Illustrated*, 17–20. The intellectual defense of the style might have drawn on "sacred" historians such as the seventeenth-century Jesuit Athanasius Kircher and Bishop Jacques-Bénigne Bossuet, who praised Egyptian civilization as the origin of orderly govenment, law, and philosophy. Gay, *The Enlightenment*, 77–78.
17. Walter, 17–20.
18. Ibid.
19. [Wines], *Trip to Boston*, 44.
20. Stephen Geary, cemetery entrepreneur and architect, built an Egyptian entrance of stone at London's new Highgate Cemetery in 1838. Through the 1840s, Egyptian gates appeared at Rochester's Forest Hills and Philadelphia's Odd Fellows Cemeteries. Others were proposed but rejected for Philadelphia's Laurel Hill (1836) and Baltimore's Green Mount (1838) Cemeteries. The architect Henry Austin designed an Egyptian Revival gateway for New Haven's Grove Street Cemetery (formerly the New Burying Ground) in 1845. Deaborn initially created an Egyptian gateway for Forest Hills Cemetery in Roxbury, but when it came time to replace the wooden structure in stone, another design was chosen. Solomon Willard sometimes receives credit for the Egyptian Revival design of the Old Granary gateway.
21. TM 1 (July 14, 1842), 82–83; (September 29, 1843), 99–100; (April 13, 1844); (May 21, 1844), 114.
22. TM 1 (June 1, 1852), 231.
23. *Picturesque Pocket Companion*, 35; TM 1 (July 14, 1842), 83; (September 29, 1843), 93–101; (May 21, 1844), 114. Joseph Story articulated the initial plan to build a wall around the cemetery in "Report" (September 1832), *Transactions* 1:47.
24. Isaac Smith Homans, *Sketches of Boston, Past and Present; And of Some Few Places in Its Vicinity* (Boston: Phillips, Sampson & Co., 1851), 106.
25. J. S. Buckingham, *America*, 3:392.
26. TM 1 (July 14, 1842), 83.
27. Henry Russell Cleveland decried Harvard's Federal-style buildings as "vast brick barns, destitute alike of symmetry, ornament, and taste." See Augustus Welby Northmore Pugin's *Contrasts* (London, 1836; rev. ed., 1841) and the influential review of it by John Claudius Loudon in *Architectural Magazine* 4 (March 1837): 132–43. Gilman and Gridley J. Fox Bryant designed many of the brownstone townhouses in Boston's new Back Bay neighborhood in the early 1860s. Andrew Jackson Downing, quoted in Wayne Andrews, *Architecture*, 108. George Templeton Strong, *Diary*, ed. Allan Nevins and Milton Halsey Thomas, vol. 1 (New York: Macmillan, 1952), 229; Hammat Billings, "Sketches of Mount Auburn," in Damrell V. Moore and George Coolidge, eds., *The Boston Almanac for the Year 1857*, no. 22 (Boston: John P. Jewett, 1857), 52.
28. Arthur O. Lovejoy, "The First Gothic Revolution and the Return to Nature," in *Essays*, 136, 142, 150–55, excerpts from *The First Gothic Revival and the Return to Nature* (Baltimore: Johns Hopkins University Press, 1932).
29. Batty Langley, *Ancient Architecture Restored and Improved by a Great Variety of Usefull Designs, Entirely New, in the Gothic Mode for the Ornamenting of Buildings and Gardens* (London, 1742); Augustus Welby Pugin and Augustus Charles Pugin, *Examples of Gothic Architecture* (London: H. G. Bohn, 1850), and Augustus Welby Pugin, *The True Principals of Pointed or Christian Architecture* (London: H. G. Bohn, 1853). Edward Everett, the first American to earn a Ph.D. at the University of Göttingen in 1817, knew of Schlegel's notions of the organic principles of form. Schlegel influenced Samuel Taylor Coleridge's "intuitional inspirationalism" and transcendental notions about the organic relationship of Art and Nature, shared by Coleridge's friend the Boston poet and painter Washington Allston.
30. S. Williams, "Notes on Bigelow's Rumford Lectures," manuscript, 13th lecture, Harvard University Archives (hereafter HUA); Bigelow, *Elements of Technology*, 1:293–94.
31. "Architecture in the United States," *American Journal of Sciences and Arts* 18.2 (July 1830): 220–29; Wayne Andrews, *Architecture*, 120. See John Britton's various works on the architectural antiquities of Great Britain (1807–26) and the history of cathedrals (1814–35). Bigelow also read Britton.
32. Hawthorne, *English Note-Books*, quoted in Harris, *Artist in American Society*, 148.
33. Appropriately, America's greatest Gothic architect, Richard Upjohn, was in training in Boston from 1834 to 1835, working for

Alexander Parris. Alexander Jackson Davis had recently designed a Gothic hall for New York University.

34. Cleveland, "American Architecture," 380.
35. American Ecclesiologists favored architects such as John Notman and Richard Upjohn, noted for their work on cemeteries (particularly Philadelphia's Laurel Hill, New York's Green-Wood, and Richmond's Holly-Wood).
36. Walter, *Mount Auburn Illustrated*, 36.
37. TM 1 (September 29, 1843), 99–100, 102.
38. See Shand-Tucci, *Built in Boston*, 18. Many of the chapel competition drawings are now at the Society for the Preservation of New England Antiquities, Boston (renamed Historic New England). Bigelow, Charles P. Curtis, and James Read formed the Building Committee, with power to sign contracts for the chapel. Martin Brimmer and Joseph Story joined Bigelow as a committee to solicit subscription funds.
39. TM 1 (November 15, 1845), 130.
40. Homans, *Sketches of Boston*, 108.
41. Hay initially recommended use of his own works, "scrolls for the walls with illuminated mottos . . . in oil painting and gilding upon a cloth or paper medium . . . easily permanently fixed to the wall . . . by any common painter." D. R. Hay to Bigelow, February 28, 1845, MAC; TM 1 (June 13, 1845), 127; Bigelow to Ballantine & Allan, April 21 and June 14, 1845, MAC.
42. Flagg, *Mount Auburn*, 16. Walter, Ballantine, and Allan charged £150 for the nave and £20 each for the four aisle windows.
43. [Parker], *Notes on Mount Auburn*, 21; TM 1 (April 18, 1848), 170.
44. TM 2 (September 4, 1854), 4. At the beginning of 1850, Mount Auburn was worth $121,529. The figure had soared to $190,040 four years later. The initial construction cost $27,123 and the rebuilding $16,900.
45. Walter, *Mount Auburn Illustrated*, 37; Lyell, *Second Visit*, 1:171; TM 2 (September 4, 1854), 1–4.
46. TM 2 (September 4, 1854), 1–4.
47. Subscribers to the Story statue included Bigelow, Samuel A. Eliot, Nathan and William Appleton, William Sturgis, C. G. and F. C. Loring, Ignatius Sargent, Charles P. Curtis, Richard Fletcher, N. J. Bowditch, J. C. Gray, C. T. Bigelow, William Gray, and J. A. Lowell. TM 1 (January 16, 1846).
48. By the end of 1847, interest on the $2,630 in invested funds came to $130. By the end of 1854, the fund totaled $6,326.68. TM 1 (February 1, 1847), 154; (February 7, 1848), 166; (February 15, 1851), 216; (April 11, 1851), 218.
49. TM 1 (August 7, 1854), 279; 2 (June 1, 1855), 37.
50. Henry James, *William Wetmore Story and His Friends: From Letters, Diaries, and Recollections*. (Boston: Houghton Mifflin, 1903). Other American sculptors in Italy included Edward A. Brackett, Edmonia Lewis, and Harriet Hosmer.
51. [Mount Auburn Cemetery], *Annual Report of the Trustees of the Cemetery of Mount Auburn* (Boston: By the Corporation, 1853). *Annual Report . . . January 1843* (Boston, 1843) (hereafter *AR*). TM 1 (January 3, 1854), 253; (August 7, 1854), 279; (September 4, 1854), 281; 2 (April 21, 1856), 5; Ellis, *Memoir*, 74.
52. TM 2 (October 4, 1854), 1–7; (Apr. 14, 1856), 78; (Apr. 21, 1856), 81–89. Perhaps some trustees questioned off the record whether a potential donor of art or artifacts or the person honored would have to be a proprietor, because that could have been another matter of controversy. Would the person thus commemorated be buried at Mount Auburn or might the artifacts function as cenotaphs?
53. TM 1 (August 7, 1854), 276. Emerson had considered the "Uses of Great Men" in his 1850 essay "Representative Men."
54. Bigelow to John Gorham Palfrey (Oct. 20, 1854), HUA; Ellis, *Memoir*, 74.
55. TM 2 (Apr. 21, 1856), 81–87.
56. [W.F.] B[rown], "Crawford's Statue of James Otis," *Boston Daily Courier*, June 17, 1856.
57. [J. M.] W[ightman], "For the *Atlas*: Mount Auburn Cemetery, letter to the Editor," *Atlas*, June 20, 1856.
58. H., "Mount Auburn," *Christian Examiner*, June 21, 1856.
59. H., A Proprietor, "Mount Auburn Cemetery," *Boston Daily Courier*, June 22, 1856.
60. "A Proprietor since 1831," "Letter to the Editor, Mount Auburn Cemetery," *Boston Daily Courier*, June 24, 1856.
61. W[ightman], "To the Editor: Mount Auburn Cemetery," *Atlas*, June 30, 1856.
62. TM 2 (April 21, 1856), 86–87.
63. TM 2 (August 4, 1856), 97.
64. Millard F. Rogers, Jr., *Randolph Rogers: American Sculptor in Rome* (Amherst: University of Massachusetts Press, 1971), 25–32.
65. Ibid. Because of additional work, Rogers received $8,000 instead of the original $5,000. Thomas Crawford wrote to his wife that his commission "pays very well." Mount Auburn donated the four statues to Harvard in 1935, specifying that they must remain on public display. Now the Winthrop, Otis, and Adams statues are in Memorial Hall and the Story at the Harvard Law School.
66. "Hiram Powers the Sculptor—Inauguration of Powers' Statue of Webster," *Mount Auburn Memorial* 1.15 (Sept. 21, 1859): 117. A Bostonian, "To the Editors," ibid., 116.
67. Justitia, "John Hancock," *Mount Auburn Memorial* 1:17 (October 6, 1859): 134.
68. "Hiram Powers," 117.
69. TM 6 (Mar. 13, 1886), 381.
70. *Proceedings of the Association of Citizens to Erect a Monument in Honour of Gen. George Washington* (Boston: Greenough & Stebbins, 1811). [William Tudor], "Monument to Washington," 329–34. The bronze equestrian statue of Washington by Thomas Ball (1819–1911) was not put in place until 1869, funded by the City and friends of the sculptor.
71. [Henry A. S. Dearborn], "Proceedings . . . 1831," 90; [H. Dearborn], "Garden and Cemetery Committee Report" (1831), and "Report: The Annual Meeting of the Horticultural Society, Oct. 1, 1831," in *Transactions* 46 and 77; TM 1 (June 23, 1832), 9.
72. Bigelow, *History*, 16.
73. John Milton depicts towers in his poems *Il Penseroso* and *L'Allegro*. In the former, the melancholy thinker meditates inside one. In the latter, the happy man views a tower from afar. The funerary associations of towers dated from the Middle Ages, when many were used as "limbos," places for entombment of unbaptized infants, who were not permitted burial by the Church in hallowed ground. Ragon, *Space of Death*, 77.
74. Barbara Jones, *Follies & Grottoes* (London: Constable, 1979), 33; *Essays*, 37–38.
75. "Mount Auburn Cemetery," *Cambridge Chronicle* 7:37 (September 11, 1852): 2.
76. Loose invoices (1852) in The Business Papers, MAC. Henry

Adams, *Mont-Saint-Michel and Chartres* (New York: American Institute of Architects, 1913), chap. 1.

77. "A Stranger's View of Mount Auburn," *Mount Auburn Memorial* 1:46 (April 25, 1860): 362.
78. TM 3 (November 4, 1861), 236.
79. TM 3 (November 3, 1862), 273; (May 2, 1864), 341; (June 6, 1864), 345. These should not be confused with the bodies from family tombs under the Park Street Church moved to Mount Auburn after the church bought a 1,225-square-foot lot on Walnut Avenue in 1862 for sixty bodies and a "bag of bones."
80. TM 4 (Mar. 6, 1865), 10. For a description of Spring Grove's Civil War section and monument, see Blanche M. G. Linden, *Spring Grove: Celebrating 150 Years* (Cincinnati: Cincinnati Historical Society, 1995), 74–79.
81. TM 4 (April 3, 1865), 14–15. Only about thirty bodies of the Civil War dead were shipped home for burial at Mount Auburn by private initiative, representing some of the early experiments in embalming of that era. *AR* (1872).
82. *Boston Evening Transcript*, October 23, 1872.
83. Ragon, *Space of Death*, 111.
84. Bigelow, *An Account of the Sphinx of Mount Auburn* (Boston: Brown and Company, 1872). Bigelow's sphinx is also similar to that illustrated in Johann Bernhard Fischer von Erlach, *Entwurff einer Historischen Architectur* (Vienna, 1721), or in Van Laar, *Magazijn*.
85. A view of the sphinx in the English garden of Prince Beneventi at Valence appeared in Jean Charles Krafft's 1809–10 *Plan des plus beaux jardins pittoresques*, vol. 1, plate 10. Burke, *Philosophical Inquiry*, 64.
86. Ellis, *Memoir*, 71–73.
87. Bigelow, *Account of the Sphinx*.
88. TM 5 (July 10, 1872), 162.
89. TM 5 (December 15, 1872), 193.
90. Andrews, *Architecture*, 112; Bigelow to Otis Norcross, April 17, 1871, HUA. I have never found any primary accounts similar to that which Andrews presents without documentation.
91. TM 5 (February 23, 1971), 65; (Mar. 13, 1872), 143.
92. Mrs. E. A. Dwight, Brookline, to Bigelow (December 19, 1872), box 4, Bigelow Papers, MHIS; Ellis, *Memoir*, 99.

11. The Rage for Mount Auburn

1. "American Forest Trees," *North American Review* 44.95 (April 1837): 358.
2. Thomas Wentworth Higginson, "Cheerful Yesterdays," *Atlantic Monthly* 78.469 (November 1896): 596, 592. Julia Ward Howe, "Reminiscences of Julia Ward Howe," *Atlantic Monthly* 83.497 (March 1899): 339.
3. Lawrence, *Extracts*, 129, 175–76. The story about Franklin Pierce is repeated in John Francis Marion, *Famous and Curious Cemeteries* (New York: Crown, 1977), 57. Sumner lay in state in the Rotunda of the U.S. Capitol in 1874 before interment at Mount Auburn under a simple sarcophagus.
4. Joseph Story, "Consecration Address," in *Picturesque Pocket Companion*, 74; Wilson Flagg, "The Moral Influence of Graves," in *Mount Auburn: Its Scenes, Its Beauties, and Its Lessons* (Boston: James Munroe, 1862), 36–38.
5. Douglas, *Feminization of American Culture*, 253.
6. John Greenleaf Adams, *Christian Victor; or, Morality and Immorality, Including Happy Death Scenes* (Boston: A. Tompkins, 1851). Putnam, *An Address*, 14. Also see Rev. John A. Clark, ed., *Christian Keepsake and Missionary Annual* (Philadelphia: William Marshall, 1839). John Pierpont, "The Garden of Graves," in *The Token: A Christmas and New Year's Present*, ed. S. G. Goodrich (Boston: S. G. Goodrich, 1832), 374–87; Flagg, *Mount Auburn*, 38.
7. Joseph T. Buckingham, "Mount Auburn," *Mount Auburn Memorial* 2.1 (July 4, 1860): 3, reprinted from the *Boston Courier*, September 28, 1838.
8. Walter, *Mount Auburn Illustrated* 5–7, 67, 95, and 113.
9. Ibid., 39.
10. Lydia Maria Child, *The Mother's Book* (Boston: Carter and Hendee, 1831), 81.
11. Channing quoted in William Charvat, *The Origins of American Critical Thought, 1810–1835* (Philadelphia: University of Pennsylvania Press), 78–79.
12. Henry Tuckerman, "The Law of Burial and the Sentiment of Death," *Christian Examiner* 26 (1836), 338. Also see J. Brayer, "The Burial of the Dead," *Christian Examiner* 31 (1842), 137–64, 281–307.
13. Zillah, "Mount Auburn," *Lowell Offering* 1.1 (1840): 13–14. Also see E.E.T., "Burial and Burial Places," *Lowell Offering* 1, ser. 1 (1840), 154–57.
14. "Consecration Dell," *Ladies' Repository*, reprinted in *Mount Auburn Memorial* 1.27 (December 14, 1859), 213. Also see Mary S. B. Dana, "Mount Auburn," in *The Parted Family and Other Poems* (New York: Dayton & Saxton, 1842), 214–16. Caroline H. Gilman, "Sweet Auburn: Now Mount Auburn Cemetery," in *Verses of a Life Time* (Boston: James Munroe, 1849), 154–56; Sarah Payson Willis, "Incident at Mount Auburn," in *Fern Leaves from Fanny's Port-Folio* (Auburn, N.Y.: Derby & Miller, 1853), 260–62. Mrs. F[rances] E[lizabeth] Browne, "Mount Auburn," in *Ruth: A Sacred Drama* (New York: Wynkoop & Hallenbeck, 1871), 34–35. For a longer discussion and extensive excerpts of sentimental verse about Mount Auburn, see Michael McEachern McDowell, *American Attitudes toward Death, 1825–1865*, (Ann Arbor: University Microfilms, 1978), 363–408.
15. Mrs. S[arah] J[osepha] Hale, "Mount Auburn Cemetery," *Godey's Magazine and Ladies' Book* (1844).
16. Orne, *Sweet Auburn and Mount Auburn*, iii–v, 33, 43.
17. Nathaniel Hawthorne, "The Lily's Quest," in *Picturesque Pocket Companion*, 235–38. The "romance" is a genre of fiction not to be confused with the "novel." "Romances" were highly symbolic rather than straightforward in imagination with plausible characters set in real life settings without allegorical meaning. Hawthorne used the term "romance." See Paul Lauter, gen. ed., *The Tenth Anthology of American Literature* (2nd ed., Lexington, Mass.: D.C. Heath, 1994) 1:2110, 2112.
18. Nathaniel Hawthorne, "The New Adam and Eve," in *Mosses from an Old Manse* (New York: Wiley and Putnam, 1846), ed. Roy Harvey Pearce (New York: Library of America, 1982), 746–63. This undoubtedly refers to the effigy of Emily Binney sculpted in 1842 and placed at Mount Auburn that year, to be discussed in chapter 12.
19. Sylvester Judd, *Margaret: A Tale of the Real and the Ideal, Blight and Bloom; Including Sketches of a Place Not Before Described, Called Mons Christi* (Boston: Jordan & Wiley, 1845). A revised edition in two illustrated volumes appeared in 1851. William B. O. Peabody, "Margaret," *North American Review* 62.130 (January

1846): 102–40. "Sylvester Judd," in Evert A. Duyckinck and George L. Duyckinck, *The Cyclopedia of American Literature: Embracing Personal and Critical Notices of Authors* (New York: Charles Scribner, 1856).

20. Edgar Allen Poe, "The Domain of Arnheim," in *Edgar Allen Poe: Poetry and Tales*, ed. Patrick F. Quinn (New York: Library of America, 1984), 859–70.
21. Nehemiah Adams, "Mount Auburn," *American Quarterly Observer* 3 (July 1834): 156–61.
22. *Picturesque Pocket Companion*, 208.
23. Nathaniel S. Dearborn, *Dearborn's Guide through Mount Auburn Cemetery . . . for the Benefit of Strangers Desirous of Seeing the Clusters of Monuments with the Least Trouble*, 6th rev. ed. (Boston: N. Dearborn, 1852), 15–16 (the 12th rev. ed. appeared in 1858); Browne, "Mount Auburn," 34–35. One English visitor attempted to grasp the experience of melancholy on his visit to Mount Auburn by reading "Thanatopsis" and other poems by William Cullen Bryant. See "An Englishman's Opinion of Mount Auburn" (1845), *Mount Auburn Memorial* 2.3 (July 18, 1860): 19.
24. [Levi Merriam Stevens], *Guide through Mount Auburn: A Handbook for Passengers over the Cambridge Railroad* (Boston: Bricher & Russell, 1860), 26, 29.
25. "Mount Auburn," *Gleason's Pictorial Drawing-Room Companion* 5 (Aug. 13, 1853): 104–5.
26. That fanciful view of picturesque Mount Auburn appeared repeatedly in the many editions of [C. F.] *Meyer's Universum, oder Abbildung und Beschreibung des Schenswerthesten und Merkweuerdigsten der Natur und Kunst auf der ganzen Erde* [*Meyer's Universe, or Depiction and Description of the Most Noteworthy in Nature and Art in the Whole World*] published repeatedly and variously from 1833 until 1860 in Hildburghausen (Germany), Amsterdam, New York, and Philadelphia.
27. Flagg, *Mount Auburn* 34–37, 9.
28. Ibid., 11, 37–38; Bernardin de Saint-Pierre and Johann Georg von Zimmerman, quoted in ibid., 28–32.
29. "Introductory," *Mount Auburn Memorial* 1.1 (June 15, 1859): 6. See also "Letters to the Editor," 1.4 (July 6, 1859): 29; "Notices to the Press," l.21 (November 2, 1859); "Our Sheet," 1.24 (November 23, 1959): 188.
30. "Our Sheet," 188.
31. Deforest Safford, "Explanation," *Mount Auburn Memorial* 2.39 (March 27, 1861): 308. A content analysis of the mass-circulation *Godey's Ladies' Book*, which reached a readership of about 150,000, reveals that in the period from 1830 to 1834 about one third of the fiction and poetry concerned themes of death, dying, and the hereafter. From 1850 to 1854, the proportion rose to 81 percent; but between 1875 and 1879, it fell to 30 percent. Richard Meckel, "Consolation in American Periodical Literature, 1830–1880," paper delivered at the conference "A Time to Mourn" at the State University of New York at Stony Brook, October 25, 1980.
32. Caroline Gilman and Rev. S. Gilman, *The Poetry of Traveling*, 158.
33. Mrs. C. H. Putnam, "Letters from Home: Mount Auburn Cemetery," *Young Lady's and Gentleman's Parlor Album* (New York, ca. 1843), 309–12.
34. Hammat Billings, "Sketches at Mount Auburn," *Boston Almanac*, 51; "Mount Auburn," *American Cyclopaedia of Useful Knowledge* (1835), 9, clippings in the Archives, MAC; Andrew Jackson Downing, *Rural Essays*, ed. George William Curtis (New York, 1854), 144.
35. Edward S. Abdy, *Journal of a Residence and Tour of the United States of North America*, 3 vols. (London: John Murray 1835), 1:120.
36. *Picturesque Pocket Companion*, 14; D. Ramon de la Sagra, *Cinco Meses en los Estados-Unidos de la America del Norte desde el 20 de abril al 23 de setiembre de 1835* (Paris: Pablo Renouard, 1836), 333.
37. Carl David Arfwedson, *The United States and Canada in 1832*, vol. 1 (1834; reprint, New York: Johnson Reprint, 1961), 211–13.
38. [Wines], *A Trip to Boston*, 45–46.
39. *Boston Transcript* (1840), clipping in the Archives, MAC.
40. Combe, *Notes on the United States*, 135. Also see C. A. Goodrich, *The Family Tourist: A Visit to the Principal Cities of the Western Continent* (Hartford: Case, Tiffany, 1848), 60–61.
41. [Dix], *Local Loiterings*, 17–19.
42. Lyell, *Second Visit*, 14–16, 171–72. Darwin drew upon Lyell's studies written during expeditions to Europe and North America.
43. Emily Dickinson to Abiah Root, September 8, 1846, *Emily Dickinson: Selected Letters*, vol. 1, ed. Thomas H. Johnson and Theodora Ward (Cambridge: Harvard University Press, 1971), 36.
44. Lady Emmeline Wortley, *Travels in the United States . . . during 1849–50* (New York: Harper Brothers, 1851), 47–48. Also see Mrs. C. H. Putnam, "Letters from Home." Edward Everett, the major American scholar of Greek culture, mentor to Emerson at Harvard and to his other professional friends in Boston, became a U.S. senator and delivered the chief oration at the dedication of the Civil War cemetery at Gettysburg in 1863. The most important and latest assessment of Everett's credentials and rhetoric in shaping and echoing the "culture of death" of his era appears in Wills, *Lincoln at Gettysburg*.
45. "The Diary of Arozina Perkins," in Polly Welts Kaufman, *Women Teachers on the Frontier* (New Haven: Yale University Press, 1984), 69. The New England Museum, simply called the Museum, was opened in 1846, combining several older, eclectic collections from Boston, New Haven, and New York.
46. Anne Henry Ehrenpreis, ed., *Happy Country This America: The Travel Diary of Henry Arthur Bright* (Columbus: Ohio State University Press, 1979), 118; "Extract of a Letter from an English Clergyman," *Mount Auburn Memorial* 1.26 (December 7, 1859): 204; "Mount Auburn," from the *Cambridge Chronicle*, reprint in *Mount Auburn Memorial* 1.45 (April 18, 1860): 357.
47. [Andrew Jackson Downing], *The Horticulturist* 4.1 (July 1849): 9–10.
48. Isabella Lucy Bird, *The Englishwoman in America* (1856; reprint, Madison: University of Wisconsin Press, 1966), 396–97.
49. [Marie T. Courcelles], "Silent Cities," *Cincinnati Daily Enquirer*, February 25, 1877. Bostonians preferred the prince's full title: His Royal Highness Albert Edward Prince of Wales, Duke of Saxony, Prince of Saxe-Coburg-Gotha, Duke of Cornwall and Rothsay, Earl of Chester, Carrick and Dublin, Baron Renfrew, and Lord of the Isles, K. G., and Heir-Apparent to the throne of England. Later King Edward VII (1841–1910); he was the first member of the royal family to visit the United States before he assumed the throne from 1901 to 1910. Some records call the second tree a Yellowwood, a spreading tree with light green leaves that turn yellow in the fall and with pendant, wisteria-like flowers in the late spring; but it did not survive. *Mount*

Auburn Memorial 2.5 (August 1, 1860): 33; 2.17 (October 24, 1860): 132. The old purple European beech survives to the present day thanks to recent dramatic intervention by the horticultural experts on staff.

50. Martineau was born a French Huguenot, her family having resettled in England. Harriet Martineau, *Society in America* vol. 2 (New York: Saunders & Otley, 1837), 227–33; E. P. Powell, "Harriet Martineau in New England," *New England Magazine* 21.3 (November 1896): 289.
51. Martineau, *Society in America*, 231–33.
52. TM 3 (July 11, 1859), 68–69.
53. Bird, *Englishwoman in America*, 396. The board stipulated in 1854 that the gatekeeper be at his post "from sunrise to sunset every day of the week personally except Sabbath forenoon he may substitute another person at his own expense." His salary was paid quarterly. TM 1 (July 14, 1842), 85; (March 12, 1854), 264; 2 (April 7, 1856), 74.
54. TM 3 (May 4, 1859), 57; (July 11, 1859), 69.
55. TM 3 (August 5, 1861), 212.
56. TM 2 (July 5, 1853), 250; 3 (June 6, 1859), 63; (July 11, 1859), 64.
57. Cambridge was not chartered as a city until 1846.
58. TM 4 (January 7, 1867), 120. The founders of the Cambridge Horse Railroad were Gardner G. Hubbard, Isaac Livermore, and Charles C. Little. Livermore branched out from the wool business to land speculation, railroad development, and Democratic politics. Little became a cemetery trustee in 1852, Livermore in 1866. By the 1880s the Union Railway Company had more lines ending at the Mount Auburn terminus than at any other site. The horse railroad, initially located to improve access to the cemetery, eventually helped turn Cambridge into a suburb from which businessmen could commute in half an hour to Boston offices. Passengers could catch cars in either Bowdoin or Scollay Square in Boston. Electrification of the system dated from the 1890s, and the last horsecar ran until 1900.
59. TM 1 (December 26, 1846), 149; (May 3, 1853), 247; 2 (July 7, 1856), 96; 5 (April 12, 1871), 74; (April 24, 1871), 78; (September 13, 1871), 97.
60. TM 1 (July 14, 1842), 84–86.
61. TM 2 (June 18, 1855), 44; (September 4, 1855), 46.
62. TM 2 (August 3, 1857), 209–10; (April 5, 1858), 244; 3 (November 4, 1861), 247; "Records of Committees" (1832), 8; TM 4 (June 20, 1866), 77.
63. [Thomas H. Safford], "Moonlight," *Mount Auburn Memorial* 1.13 (September 7, 1859): 101; Caroline F. Orne, "A Midnight Adventure in Mount Auburn," *Mount Auburn Memorial* 2.19 (November 7, 1860): 151–52.
64. A Trustee to the Editor, "Mount Auburn Cemetery," *Evening Transcript*, November 4, 1856; "Introductory," *Mount Auburn Memorial* 1.1 (June 15, 1859): 6; Billings, "Sketches," 52; "Well-House for Visitors," *Sweet Auburn* (Fall–Winter 2003).
65. TM 4 (September 7, 1870), 295; (April 12, 1870), 323; 5 (October 12, 1870), 30.
66. "Skating," *Mount Auburn Memorial* 1.25 (November 30, 1859): 197.
67. TM 3 (March 4, 1861), 171–75; (August 5, 1861), 212.
68. Edward Waldo Emerson, *The Early Years of the Saturday Club, 1855–70* (Freeport, N.Y.: Books for Libraries Press, 1967), 3.
69. Andrew Jackson Downing, "Public Cemeteries and Public Gardens," *Horticulturist* 4.1 (July 1849): 9–12. See Appendix II for a chronology of the founding of these "rural" cemeteries.
70. Andrew Jackson Downing, "A Talk about Public Parks and Gardens," *Horticulturist*, 3 (October 1848): 157; Downing, "The New York Park," *Horticulturist* 6 (1851): 345–49.
71. Clarence [Chatum] Cook, *A Description of the New York Central Park* (1869; reprint, New York: Benjamin Blom, 1972), 15. So significant is Mount Auburn's landscape design in the development of public parks that the misconception is often repeated that Frederick Law Olmsted laid it out. Yet Olmsted was only three when Bigelow proposed the cemetery in 1825, and only nine in 1831, when Dearborn worked out the initial design from English and French books. By the time Olmsted began his design career in 1857, shifting from writing to supervising construction of Central Park, Mount Auburn was a mature landscape over a quarter century old.
72. Van Wyck Brooks, *New England: Indian Summer* (New York: E. P. Dutton, 1965), 144.

12. Transformation to the "Garden" or "Sculptured" Cemetery

1. Ronald Story, *The Forging of an Aristocracy*, 167.
2. TM 3 (March 4, 1861), 171–75; (August 5, 1861), 212; 4 (February 6, 1869), 219–20.
3. Henry A. S. Dearborn, "General Dearborn's Address," *New England Farmer* (January 15, 1830): 203. See Blanche Linden-Ward, "'The Fencing Mania': The Rise and Fall of Nineteenth-Century Funerary Enclosures," *Markers: Journal of the Association for Gravestone Studies* 7 (1990): 35–58. Ann Douglas uses the term "domestication of death" in *The Feminization of American Culture*. The superintendent reported that several proprietors annually enclosed their lots with hedges, especially arborvitae.
4. Statistics on fences and curbs constructed and removed were recorded regularly from 1842 on in the *AR*, copies of which were published as pamphlets in Boston by the corporation, MAC. *Mount Auburn Memorial* 1.21 (November 2, 1859) 165–66.
5. TM 2 (September 1, 1856), 101; (December 1, 1856), 110; Kathy Fahey, "Decorative Urns at Mount Auburn," *Sweet Auburn* (Winter 2002/2003).
6. Walter, *Mount Auburn Illustrated*.
7. Janet Heywood, "Family Lot Enclosures," *Sweet Auburn* (January 1999).
8. *Mount Auburn Memorial* 1.27 (December 14, 1859): 213; 1.44 (April 11, 1860): 349; 2.6 (August 8, 1860): 44; 2.14 (October 3, 1960): 108.
9. Francis and Theresa Pulszky, *White, Red, Black: Sketches of Society in America* vol. 2 (New York: 1868), 98–99.
10. Andrew Jackson Downing, "Review: *Greenwood Illustrated*," *Horticulturist* 1.5 (November 1846): 230.
11. Downing, "Public Cemeteries and Public Gardens," *Horticulturist* (July 1849), quoted in *Landscape Gardening: Andrew Jackson Downing*, ed. Frank A. Waugh (New York: 1921), 373.
12. William H. Scott, *Horticulturist* 6 (1855).
13. Adolph Strauch, *Spring Grove Cemetery: Its History and Improvements* (Cincinnati: Robert Clarke, 1869), 12, 66.
14. John Jay Smith, "Rural Cemeteries," *Horticulturist* 6 (August 1856): 345–56.
15. Meticulous corporate records show that 37 new fences were

erected in 1858 in contrast to 93 in 1856 and 87 in 1857. Contrary to lore, few if any fences were removed to provide war matériel during the Civil War, although the Federal Arsenal that produced most of the Union ammunition was less than a mile away. Nor does there seem to be rationing of cast iron for civilian uses; a few new fences appeared annually through the war years and until 1873. Some may have been voluntarily removed during the First World War in response to the U.S. War Production Board's appeal "To All Cemeteries" for metal as "a valuable contribution to the war effort." Only very wealthy proprietors set up special funds and entered into expensive perpetual care contracts with Mount Auburn's trustees, who promised to administer the endowment and take over preservation efforts. The fence around the Lawrence lots is a case in point, standing well maintained to the present day.

16. Trustees increased the superintendent's salary to $800 a year in 1854 in consideration of costs he incurred in boarding his workers in the house the cemetery provided for him.
17. TM 1 (August 3, 1852), 234; (May 3, 1853), 247; (March 7, 1854), 263; Bigelow, *History*, 75.
18. TM 3 (November 7, 1859), 88; (July 7, 1862), 265; (March 3, 1863), 290; 4 (February 1, 1869), 208; 5 (February 5, 1872), 121; "Culvert Avenue," *Mount Auburn Memorial* 2.8 (August 22, 1860): 60.
19. TM 1 (September 4, 1854), 280; 2 (February 9, 1857), 168; (March 1, 1858); "Auburn Lake," *Mount Auburn Memorial* 1.18 (October 12, 1859): 141. Loring paid $1,000 for the land.
20. TM 2 (August 3, 1857), 204–5; Bigelow, "The Ponds of the Cemetery," *History*, 74–75.
21. Bigelow, *AR* (1861); TM 3 (February 13, 1860), 118; (March 5, 1860), 120–21; (March 12, 1860), 129; (April 2, 1860), 130–31; (May 7, 1860), 133; (July 2, 1860), 139; (April 17, 1861), 187; (May 6, 1861), 188; (May 13, 1861), 190–91; (May 15, 1861), 192; (September 2, 1861), 226; (September 12, 1861), 227; "Fountains in the Cemetery," *Mount Auburn Memorial* 2.30 (January 23, 1861): 236.
22. Mann resigned in 1861 under a cloud. Bigelow complained that he was not performing necessary work as instructed, that his accounts contained discrepancies of thousands of dollars, and that he had received kickbacks from a painter. The suit the cemetery filed against Mann continued until 1864. The court found the $18,233.92 deficit in his accounts "unfavorable to Mann's integrity"; yet the trustees finally discontinued the suit as a waste of time since the monies could not be retrieved. TM 3 (March 7, 1864), 331–37. Still, Mann chose to be buried at Mount Auburn. TM 4 (October 12, 1869), 251–52. Mount Auburn allocated $8,000 for the waterworks project, provided that the Massachusetts Horticultural Society contribute a quarter of that amount.
23. *AR* (1863). TM 3 (December 1, 1862), 275.
24. Bigelow, *History*, 74, 90–91.
25. TM 1 (July 3, 1854), 275.
26. Bigelow quoted in Jean L. Rosenberg, "The Vistas of Mount Auburn," *Sweet Auburn* (Fall–Winter 1987).
27. Flagg, *Mount Auburn*:, 238; Reverend A. D. Gridley, "Cemeteries," *The New Englander and Yale Review* 22.85 (October 1863): 611.
28. Flagg, "Funereal Character of Trees," *Mount Auburn Memorial* 2.10 (September 5, 1860): 73–74. The *Memorial* regularly described proprietors' lot plantings in a feature article called "The Tour" from July 13, 1859, until March 13, 1861.
29. TM 3 (July 3, 1864), 346; 4 (October 13, 1868), 183–84; *AR* (1864).
30. TM 4 (October 13, 1868), 183–84; (February 1, 1869), 209; (September 14, 1869), 249; (March 7, 1870), 294–95. Sale of wood generated considerable revenue, almost as much as the sale of hay. *AR* (1868); Bigelow, *History*, 121–22.
31. TM 6 (January 14, 1880), 236.
32. TM 4 (January 29, 1866), 38; (January 7, 1867), 90. A flight of steps cost from $375 to $440.
33. TM 3 (December 1, 1862), 275–76; (December 8, 1862), 277–78; (January 26, 1863), 281–83; (December 7, 1863), 309–11.
34. TM 1 (October 4, 1858), 260; 3 (July 7, 1862), 265; (August 4, 1862), 267; (December 1, 1862), 275–76; (November 7, 1864), 352.
35. TM 1 (October 2, 1854), 284; 4 (April 2, 1866), 58–64; 5 (July 21, 1870), 19.
36. "Improvements at Mount Auburn," *Mount Auburn Memorial* 1.2 (June 22, 1859): 133; 1.44 (April 11, 1860): 349. Stevens managed the New England, Revere, and Tremont Houses, hotels in Boston, the Fifth Avenue Hotel in New York, and many others.
37. A[ustin] J. Coolidge, Secretary, to (Superintendent) Captain D[aniel] L. Winsor (March 11, 1862), Letter Book, 1:49; Coolidge to Treasurer of Harvard College, March 18, 1862, 1.52–53; Coolidge to Rev. Burroughs (January 30, 1865), 1:282–83. Beginning in 1861, cemetery officials kept copies of correspondence made by letter press on onionskin paper bound in "Letter Books" rather than loose copies, folded and stacked together in brick-sized parcels wrapped in brown paper and tied with red string, MAC. The board leased land to Alexander McDonald "for the purpose of manufacturing, exhibiting, and selling statuary, monumental and other marble or stone work, for Cemetery purposes." TM 4 (January 7, 1867), 110. Until trustees put an end to the practice, the superintendent occasionally acted "as an agent for individual proprietors presenting plans to stone dealers for estimates," receiving no remuneration. TM 5 (December 13, 1871), 113.
38. Wilson Flagg, "Funereal Character of Trees," *Mount Auburn Memorial* 2.10 (September 5, 1860):, 73–74; TM 1 (September 2, 1854), 284; 2 (November 6, 1854), 9–10; (December 4, 1854), 11; (March 19, 1855), 29; 3 (April 4, 1859), 54; (May 4, 1859), 56; (May 7, 1860), 133. The British garden theorist John Claudius Loudon had championed the "gardenesque" in 1832 as a reaction against the wilder "picturesque."
39. TM 2 (January 7, 1856), 57; (August 3, 1857), 210; (June 7, 1858), 253; (July 6, 1858), 255; 3 (June 2, 1862), 262; "Botanical," *Mount Auburn Memorial* 1.13 (September 7, 1859): 101, and passim in other issues into 1861. The taste for exotic plants grew due to varieties shipped from Asia and other distant places after invention of the Wardian case. Shary Page Berg and Mount Auburn Cemetery, *Master Plan*, vol. 2, *Historic Landscape Report* (Cambridge: By the Cemetery, 1993), 24.
40. TM 3 (January 7, 1861), 152–53; (June 3, 1861), 193; (July 5, 1861), 196–97; (August 5, 1861), 216–17; (September 1, 1861), 222; (October 7, 1861), 229; (November 4, 1861), 235–36; (September 8, 1862), 269; (October 6, 1862), 271; (November 3, 1862), 274.
41. TM 2 (January 5, 1857), 142; (March 2, 1857), 172; (April 6, 1857), 176–78; (February 1, 1858), 228; (February 7, 1859), 269.

The fund was to be invested in the "public debts" of a number of surrounding towns, the state, and the United States, or in real estate mortgages.

42. TM 3 (November 5, 1860), 147; (September 2, 1861), 221–22; (November 4, 1861), 232–34.
43. *Mount Auburn Memorial* 1.22 (November 9, 1859): 173; TM 3 (October 3, 1859), 81. The cost of the granite fronts rose from $3,000 to $4,000 each between 1859 and 1860.
44. *Mount Auburn Memorial* 1.48 (May 9, 1860): 381.
45. "Preservation of the Lodge Tomb," *Sweet Auburn* (Winter 2004–2005). Freeland hired the architects Ware & Van Brunt for their "catacomb tomb" on lots 699–700. TM 5 (March 13, 1872), 144.
46. *Mount Auburn Memorial* 1.28 (February 29, 1860): 301. Douglas, *Feminization of American Culture*, chap. 6, "The Domestication of Death."
47. Appropriately, the great French historian of *mentalités*, Philippe Ariès, elucidated the advent of notions of affective individualism and valuation of children as individuals in *Centuries of Childhood* (New York: Vintage Books, 1962), before he tackled the history of changing deathways in *L'Homme devant la mort* (1978) translated into English by Helen Weaver as *The Hour of Our Death* (New York: Knopf, 1981).
48. Ernest Rohdenburg III, "Henry Dexter—Mount Auburn Sculptor," *Sweet Auburn* (Fall–Winter 1994). The deteriorating, porous marble was given a glass enclosure in 1860. Eventually the Binney family had it removed and replaced by a plain granite marker in 1934.
49. Ball, married to a member of the Chickering family, also produced the bronze equestrian statue of George Washington in 1869 for the Boston Public Garden as well as portraits of Daniel Webster and Edward Everett. Lewis, of African American and Native American ancestry, studied at Oberlin College before taking up a sculptural apprenticeship with Edward Brackett in Boston. She sold a hundred copies of her bust of Colonel Robert Gould Shaw to finance her trip to Rome, where she set up a studio. Dr. Samuel Osgood, "American Artists in Italy," *Harper's New Monthly Magazine* 41.243 (August 1870): 421.
50. "Mount Auburn's Monuments Inventoried," *Sweet Auburn* (Spring 1989). Also see Frances Sargent Osgood, ed., *Poetry of Flowers and Flowers of Poetry, to Which Is Added a Simple Treatise on Botany, with Familiar Examples, and a Copious Floral Dictionary* (Philadelphia: J. B. Lippincott, 1863). For reference to the symbolism of sheaves of wheat over "two aged people," see "Sarcophagus to the Memory of Thomas Wigglesworth, Esq., Mount Auburn," *Mount Auburn Memorial* 1.8 (August 3, 1859): 61.
51. TM 5 (February 26, 1872), 142; (May 8, 1872), 148. See the weekly newspaper *Mount Auburn Memorial* published from June 1859 to March 1861; Linden-Ward, "'The Fencing Mania,'" 35–58.
52. Henry James, "The Ghostly Rental," *Scribner's Monthly* 12.5 (September 1876): 668.

Epilogue

1. See Linden, *Spring Grove;* Frank J. Scott, *The Art of Beautifying Suburban Home Grounds*, 15–16. New editions of Scott's book appeared in 1872, 1873, 1881, and 1886.
2. Israel M. Spelman, "Report," *AR* (1875), 4–5; *AR* (1879).
3. Sidney J. Hare, "The Cemetery Beautiful," *American Association of Cemetery Superintendents* 24 (1910): 40; James C. Scorgie, "Perpetual Care of Monuments and Mausoleums," *American Association of Cemetery Superintendents* 30 (1916): 27; Scorgie, "The Control of Stonework in Cemeteries," ibid. 34 (1920): 54–56.
4. *AR* (1939), 3. The post-hurricane planting included ten species and six varieties of elm, seventeen species of oak, twenty of pine, and fifteen of spruce. Another 850 mountain laurels, a species favored by Bigelow, were added in 1940. Dennis Collins, "The Hurricane of 1938: A Lasting Impact on Horticulture at Mount Auburn," *Sweet Auburn* (Summer 2001). Also see Laurence S. Caldwell, "Modern Cemetery Design and Development," *The American City* (March 1935).
5. Roger T. Peterson, "In Memoriam: Ludlow Griscom," *The Auk* 82 (October 1965): 598–605; Norman P. Hill, M.D., "Ludlow Griscom and Mount Auburn Cemetery," *Sweet Auburn* (Spring 1988).
6. *AR* (1944), 5; TM 10 (September 29, 1949), 202. The papers of Arthur and Sidney Shurcliff are in the Massachusetts Historical Society.
7. TM 12 (September 18, 1966); (July 26, 1967); (October 25, 1972); (March 27, 1973); (April 24, 1973); (June 25, 1974); (July 30, 1974).
8. Jean L. Rosenberg, "The Vistas of Mount Auburn," *Sweet Auburn* (Fall–Winter 1987); Roger S. Kindred, "Mount Auburn: A Living Entity," ibid. (Winter 1989), excerpted from his article in *Cemetery Management* (April 1982).
9. *AR* (1979); TM 13 (May 29, 1979); (September 25, 1979); (May 20, 1980); (October 21, 1980); (January 20, 1981); (February 17, 1981); (November 17, 1981).
10. *AR* (1987); TM 14 (June 16, 1987); (October 17, 1989).
11. "Mission Statement" (1988), in The Halvorson Company, *Mount Auburn Cemetery Master Plan* (Boston: By the Cemetery, 1993).
12. "William C. Clendaniel, the New President of Mount Auburn Cemetery, Introduces Himself and Shares Some Initial Thoughts," *Sweet Auburn* (Summer 1988); Clendaniel, December 1989, in Halvorson, *Master Plan*, 32. The term "museum without walls" seems to have been coined by André Malreaux in his three-volume *Le Musée imaginaire* (1953–54) to describe illustrated books on the arts. It gained currency and redefinition in the late 1960s in the United States as the National Endowment for the Arts began to sponsor Art in Public Places programs to place contemporary sculpture and murals in cities, funded by one-percent-for-art subsidies from public construction projects; and at about the same time, a few major art museums inaugurated sculpture gardens, a trend that has escalated since. Yet, it occurred to me that the original "museums without walls" or sculpture gardens were "rural" cemeteries copied after Mount Auburn's example. When I began a series of public history projects, lectures, and publications on them in 1985, I began to apply that term to the cemeteries; and it elicited a shock of recognition. Of course, Mount Auburn and its progeny were "museums without walls," decades before the invention of the art museum as a public, urban institution.
13. TM 14 (June 17, 1986); (October 21, 1986); (November 18, 1986); (December 16, 1986); (January 17, 1989); Clendaniel, "President's Report," in *AR* (1988), 5–6; "Mount Auburn's New

Trustees," *Sweet Auburn* (Fall 1989); "Changes in Management Structure" and "Retirement of Superintendent Duncan W. Munro," *Sweet Auburn* (Winter 1990)

14. TM (April 18, 1989); (February 20, 1990); (April 17, 1990); (June 25, 1990); (July 24, 1990). See Shary Page Berg, "The Nation's Oldest Rural Cemetery: Mount Auburn Cemetery," *CRM [Cultural Resources Management]* 16.4 (1993): 17–19.
15. *AR* (1990); *Master Plan*, 2, 4, 6; Clendaniel, "Mount Auburn's Master Plan and Its Implementation," *Sweet Auburn* (Winter 1993–94).
16. Clendaniel, "Mount Auburn's Master Plan"; *AR* (1991) and (1992). Recent Consultants in landscape design included Wellington "Duke" Reiter, Julie Moir Messervy, the firm of [Douglas] Read & [Gary] Hilderbrand Associates, and that of Craig Halvorson.
17. National Register of Historic Places Nomination (1975) quoted in Allen Freeman, "The Silent Edge: Gertrude Jekyll's 'Wide Wood Path' Informs a New Burial Ground at Historic Mount Auburn Cemetery," *Landscape Architecture* 94.6 (June 2004): 96–101. The Cambridge Historical Commission nominated Mount Auburn to the Massachusetts Historical Commission for inclusion in the National Register of Historic Places. TM 12 (February 25, 1975), 306.
18. Ralph Waldo Emerson, "Nature" (1836), in Joel Porte, ed., *Essays and Lectures* (New York: Library of America, 1983), 7. Emerson was instrumental in the 1855 founding of Concord's Sleepy Hollow Cemetery, delivered its consecration address, and is buried on "Author's Ridge" there along with Hawthorne, Thoreau, the Alcotts, and other notables.
19. *Picturesque Pocket Companion*, 208.
20. Halvorson Company, *Master Plan*, 6.

BIBLIOGRAPHY

Abdy, Edward Strutt. *Journal of a Residence and Tour in the United States of America from April, 1833, to October, 1834*. 3 vols. London: John Murray, 1835.

Abrams, Meyer Howard. *Natural Supernaturalism: Tradition and Revolution in Romantic Literature*. New York: W. W. Norton, 1971.

An Account of the Proceedings of the Corporation of the City of New York in Regard to the Existence of Cemeteries in the City. New York: New York Evening Post, 1823.

Ackerknecht, Erwin H. "Anticontagionism between 1821 and 1867." *Bulletin of the History of Medicine* 22 (1948): 567.

Adams, Henry. *Mont-Saint-Michel and Chartres*. New York: American Institute of Architects, 1913.

Adams, John Greenleaf. *Christian Victor; or, Morality and Immorality, Including Happy Death Scenes*. Boston: A. Tompkins, 1851.

Adams, John Quincy. "Death of Children." *Mount Auburn Memorial* 1.39 (March 7, 1860): 310.

Adams, Nehemiah. "Mount Auburn." *American Quarterly Observer* 3 (July 1834): 156–61.

Addison, Agnes. "Early American Gothic." In *Romanticism in America: Papers Contributed to a Symposium at the Baltimore Museum of Art* (May 13–15, 1940), edited by George Boas. Baltimore: Johns Hopkins University Press, 1940.

Addison, Joseph. *Tatler* 161 (April 20, 1709); 123 (January 21, 1710).

———. *Works*. London, 1721. Reprint, edited by D. Bond, Oxford: Oxford University Press, 1965.

Albro, John Adams. *An Address Delivered at the Consecration of the Cambridge Cemetery*. Cambridge: Metcalf, 1854.

Alcott, Bronson. *The Journals of Bronson Alcott*. Edited by Odell Shepard. Boston: Little, Brown, 1938.

Alembert, Jean Le Rond d'. *Preliminary Discourse to the Encyclopedia of Diderot*. Translated by Richard N. Schwab. Indianapolis: Bobbs-Merrill, 1963.

Alison, Archibald. *Essays on the Nature and the Principles of Taste*. 1790. Reprint, Boston: Cummings & Hilliard, 1812.

Allen, B. Sprague. *Tides in English Taste (1619–1800): A Background for the Study of Literature*. Cambridge: Harvard University Press, 1937. Reprint, New York: Pageant, 1958.

[Allen, Francis D., comp.]. *Documents and Facts, Showing the Fatal Effects of Interments in Populous Cities*. New York: F. D. Allen, 1822.

Altenbernd, A. Lynn. "On Pope's 'Horticultural Romanticism.'" *Journal of English and Germanic Philology* 54 (October 1955): 470–77.

"American Forest Trees." *North American Review* 44.95 (April 1837): 334–61.

Ames, Oakes I[ngalls]. "Mount Auburn's Sixscore Years." *Publications of the Cambridge Horticultural Society* 34 (1951–52): 77–95.

Amory, Cleveland. *The Proper Bostonians*. New York: E. P. Putnam, 1947.

Andrews, Malcolm. *The Search for the Picturesque: Landscape Aesthetics and Tourism in Britain, 1760–1800*. Stanford: Stanford University Press, 1989.

Andrews, Malcolm, ed. *The Picturesque*. Vols. 1–3. East Sussex: Helm Information, 1994.

Andrews, Wayne. *Architecture, Ambition, and Americans: A Social History of American Architecture*. New York: Free Press, 1964.

Andrieux, C. "Sépulture." *La Décade Philosophique* 18, year VIII [1800]. Paris, 1800.

"Architecture in the United States." *American Journal of Sciences and Arts* 18.2 (July 1830): 220–29.

Arfwedson, Carl David. *The United States and Canada in 1832*. 1834. Reprint, New York: Johnson Reprint, 1961.

Ariès, Philippe. *Centuries of Childhood*. New York: Vintage Books, 1962.

———. *Essais sur l'histoire de la mort en Occident du Moyen-Age à nos jours*. Paris: Seuil, 1975.

———. *The Hour of Our Death*. Translated by Helen Weaver. New York: Knopf, 1981. Originally published as *L'Homme devant la mort*. Paris, 1978.

———. *Images de l'homme devant la mort*. Paris: Seuil, 1983.

———. "The Reversal of Death: Changes in Attitudes toward Death in Western Societies." *American Quarterly* 26.5 (December 1974): 536–60.

———. *Western Attitudes toward Death from the Middle Ages to the Present.* Translated by Patricia M. Ranum. Baltimore: Johns Hopkins University Press, 1974.

Arnaud, C.-P. *Recueil de tombeaux des quatres cimetières de Paris.* 2 vols. Paris: Arnaud & Germain Mathiot, 1824.

[Attiret, Jean-Denis]. *Lettres èdifiantes et curieuses ècrites des missions ètrangéres par quelque missionaires de la compagnie de Jésus.* Paris: Guérin, 1743. Translated by Joseph Spence [Sir Harry Beaumont] as *A Particular Account of the Emperor of China's Gardens near Pekin.* London: R. Dodsley, 1752.

Auzelle, Robert. *Dernières demeures: conception, composition, réalisation du cimetière contemporain.* Paris: Picard, 2001.

[Avril]. *Rapport de l'Administration de travaux publics sur les cimetières, lu au Conseil-Général par le citoyen Avril.* Paris: n.d. [1793?].

Bacon's Dictionary of Boston. Boston: Houghton Mifflin, 1886.

Baedeker, Karl. *Paris et ses environs suivis d'excursions diverses: manuel du voyageur.* 3rd ed. Leipzig: Karl Baedeker, 1872.

Balard, M. *Les Mystères des pompes funébres de la ville de Paris.* Paris: Émile Allard, 1856.

Ballantyne, Andrew. *Architecture, Landscape and Liberty: Richard Payne Knight and the Picturesque.* Cambridge: Cambridge University Press, 1997.

Ballou, Rev. Hosea. "Address on the Re-burial of Rev. John Murray." June 8, 1837. In *The Life of Rev. Hosea Ballou: With Accounts of His Writings,* edited by Thomas Whittemore. Vol. 3. Boston: James M. Usher, 1855.

Ballou, Maturin M. *Biography of Rev. Hosea Ballou.* Boston: Abel Tompkins, 1852.

Baltzell, E. Digby. *Puritan Boston and Quaker Philadelphia: Two Protestant Ethics and the Spirit of Class Authority and Leadership.* New York: Macmillan, 1979.

Bancroft, George. "The Last Moments of Eminent Men." January 1834. In *Essays from the North American Review,* edited by Allen Thorndike Rice. New York: D. Appleton, 1879.

Baridon, Michel. *Les Jardins: Paysagistes–Jardiniers–Poètes.* Paris: Robert Laffont, 1998.

———. "Jardins et paysages: Existe-t-il un style anglais?" *Dix-huitième Siècle* 18 (1986): 438–45.

———. "Ruins as a Mental Construct." *Journal of Garden History* 5 (1985): 89–94.

Barker, Felix. *Highgate Cemetery: Victorian Valhalla.* London: John Murray, 1984.

Barrier, Janine, Monique Mosser, and Che Bing Chiu, eds. *Aux jardins de Cathay: L'Imaginaire anglo-chinois en Occident, William Chambers.* Paris: Éditions de l'Imprimeur, 2004.

Basil-Hall, Le Capitaine. *Voyage dans les États-Unis de l'Amérique du Nord.* Paris: Arthur Bertrand, 1834.

Bate, Walter Jackson. *From Classic to Romantic: Premises of Taste in Eighteenth-Century England.* Cambridge: Harvard University Press, 1946.

[Baudin, Pierre-Charles Louis]. Ministre de l'Intérieur. *Sépultures publiques et particulières.* Paris: Adrien Marèchal, year IX [1801].

Beaumont, Gustave de. *Lettres d'Amérique, 1831–32.* Edited by André Jardin and George W. Pierson. Paris: Presses Universitaires de France, 1973.

Belknap, Jeremy. *American Biography; or, An Historical Account of Those Persons Who Have Been Distinguished in America, as Adventurers, Statesmen, Philosophers, Divines, Warriors, Authors, and Other Remarkable Characters, Comprehending a Recital of the Events Connected with Their Lives and Actions.* Boston: Isaiah Thomas & Ebenezer T. Andrews, 1794–98.

Bell, Edward L. *Vestiges of Mortality and Remembrance: A Bibliography on the Historical Archaeology of Cemeteries.* Metuchen, N.J.: Scarecrow Press, 1994.

Bellamy, Edward. *Looking Backward.* 1888. New York: Viking Penguin, 1982.

Bender, Thomas. "The Rural Cemetery Movement: Urban Travail and the Appeal of Nature." *New England Quarterly* 47 (June 1974): 196–211.

———. *Toward an Urban Vision: Ideas and Institutions in Nineteenth-Century America.* Lexington: University Press of Kentucky, 1975.

Benes, Peter. *The Masks of Orthodoxy: Folk Gravestone Carving in Plymouth County, Massachusetts, 1689–1805.* Amherst: University of Massachusetts Press, 1977.

Bennett, Steven J. "Chinese Topographical Thinking." *Boston University Journal* 26.1 (January 1978): 14–27.

Benson, Albert Emerson. *History of the Massachusetts Horticultural Society.* Norwood, Mass.: Plimpton Press, for the Society, 1929.

Berg, Shary Page. "Mount Auburn Cemetery: An Evolving Legacy of Public Horticulture." *Journal of the New England Garden History Society* 5 (Fall 1997): 9–16.

———. "The Nation's Oldest Rural Cemetery: Mount Auburn, Cambridge." *CRM [Cultural Resources Management, National Park Service]* 16.4 (1993): 17–19.

Berg, Shary Page, and Mount Auburn Cemetery. *Master Plan.* Vol 2. *Historic Landscape Report.* Cambridge: By the Cemetery, 1993.

Bermingham, Ann. *Landscape and Ideology: The English Rustic Tradition, 1740–1860.* Berkeley: University of California Press, 1987.

Bernard, Leon. *The Emerging City: Paris in the Age of Louis XIV.* Durham: Duke University Press, 1970.

Bernardin de Saint-Pierre, Jacques-Henri. *Études de la nature.* Vol. 5. Paris: Didot jeune, 1792.

———. "Of the Sentiment of Melancholy" and "On the Pleasure of Tombs." In *Studies from Nature,* translated by Henry Hunter. Worcester, Mass.: J. Nancrede, 1797.

Betts, Edwin M. *Thomas Jefferson's Garden Book.* Philadelphia: American Philosophical Society, 1944.

Bevington, Michael. *Stowe: The Garden and the Park.* Stowe, England: Capability Books, 1996.

[Bickham, George]. *The Beauties of Stowe, the Gardens of the Right Honourable Richard Lord Viscount Cobham, Addressed to Mr Pope.* London: L. Gilliver, 1732. Reprint, London: John Bowles & Son, 1750, 1753, and 1756.

Bigelow, Jacob. *An Account of the Sphinx of Mount Auburn.* Boston: Brown and Company, 1872.

———. "Disinterment of the Relics of Several Kings." *North American Review* 38.83 (April 1834): 460–65.

———. *Elements of Technology, Taken Chiefly from a Course of Lectures Delivered at Cambridge, on the Application of the Sciences to the Useful Arts.* Boston: Hilliard, Gray, Little & Wilkins, 1829.

———. "Extract from *Nature in Disease.*" *Mount Auburn Memorial* 1.2 (August 31, 1859): 90.

———. *Florula Bostoniensis.* Boston: Cummings & Hilliard, 1814. 2nd ed., enlarged: *Florula Bostoniensis: A Collection of Plants of*

Boston and Its Vicinity, with Their Generic and Specific Characters, Principal Synonyms, Descriptions, Places of Growth, and Time of Flowering; and Occasional Remarks. 8 vols. Boston: Cummings, Hilliard & Co., 1824.

———. *A History of the Cemetery of Mount Auburn*. Boston and Cambridge: James Munroe, 1860. Reprint, Cambridge: Applewood Books, 1988.

———. *Inaugural Address, Delivered in the Chapel at Cambridge, Dec. 11, 1816*. Boston: Wells & Lilly, 1817. Reprint, *North American Review* 4 (January 1817): 271–83.

———. *Nature in Disease: Illustrated in Various Discourses and Essays*. Boston: Ticknor & Fields, 1854.

———. *Modern Inquiries: Classical, Professional, and Miscellaneous*. Boston: Little, Brown, 1867.

———. "On the Burial of the Dead, and Mount Auburn Cemetery." In *Nature in Disease, Illustrated in Various Discourses and Essays. To Which Are Added Miscellaneous Writing, Chiefly on Medical Subjects*. Boston: Ticknor & Fields, 1854. Also in *Modern Inquiries*.

———. "On the Limits of Education." In *Modern Inquiries*.

———. *The Useful Arts Considered in Connexion with the Application of Science*. Boston: Marsh, Capen, Lyon & Webb, 1840.

Billings, Hammatt. "Sketches at Mount Auburn." In *The Boston Almanac for the Year 1857*, edited by Damrell V. Moore and George Coolidge. No. 22. Boston: John P. Jewett, 1857. 51–52.

Binford, Henry C. *The First Suburbs: Residential Communities on the Boston Periphery, 1815–1860*. Chicago: University of Chicago Press, 1985.

Bird, Isabella Lucy. *The Englishwoman in America*. London: John Murray, 1856. Reprint, Madison: University of Wisconsin Press, 1966.

Birnbaum, Charles A., and Robin Karson, eds. *Pioneers of American Landscape Design*. New York: McGraw-Hill, 2000.

Blaikie, Thomas. *Sur les terres d'un jardinier: Journal des voyages, 1775–1792*. Translated by Janine Barrier. Paris: Éditions de L'Imprimeur, 1997.

Blair, Robert. *The Grave: A Poem*. 1808. Reprint, London: Methuen, 1903.

Blake, John Ballard. *Public Health in the Town of Boston, 1630–1822*. Cambridge: Harvard University Press, 1953.

Bledstein, Burton K. *The Culture of Professionalism: The Middle Class and the Development of Higher Education in America*. New York: W. W. Norton, 1976.

Boas, George, ed. *Romanticism in America*. Baltimore: Johns Hopkins University Press, 1940.

Bolton, Robert. *Mr. Bolton's Last and Learned Works of the Foure Last Things, Death, Iudgement, Hell, and Heaven*. London: George Miller, 1633.

Boorstin, Daniel J. *The Image; or, What Happened to the American Dream*. New York: Athenaeum, 1962.

Borromeo, Carlo. *Arte Sacra: De Fabrica Ecclesiae*. Milan: Typografia sociale, 1952.

———. *Instructiones Fabricae et Suppellectilis Ecclesiasticae*. Milan, 1577.

"The Boston Aristocracy." *Boston Patriot and Daily Mercantile Advertiser* 12.1814 (April 30, 1832).

Boston City Records. "Quincy Commission Report." *City Council Proceedings* (August 4, 1823): 311–20.

Boulton, James T., ed. *Edmund Burke's Philosophical Enquiry into the Origin of Our Ideas of the Sublime and the Beautiful*. South Bend: University of Notre Dame Press, 1968.

Bourde de la Rogerie, M. [Henri]. *Le Parlement de Bretagne, l'évêque de Rennes et les ifs dans les cimetières, 1636–7*. Rennes: 1931.

Boutwood, James. "Poet's Essay in the Picturesque, Alexander Pope's Garden at Twickenham." *Country Life* 143 (March 7, 1968): 512–14.

Bowen, Abel. "Burial in Cities." *Boston News-Letter and City Record*, March 4, 1826, 126–29.

Boyse, Samuel. "The Triumphs of Nature: A Poem." *Gentleman's Magazine* 12 (August 1742).

Braudel, Fernand. *Capitalism and Material Life, 1400–1800*. Translated by Miriam Kochan. New York: Harper & Row, 1973.

———. *The Mediterranean and the Mediterranean World in the Age of Philip II*. Translated by Sian Reynolds. 2 vols. New York: Harper & Row, 1973.

Brayer, J. "The Burial of the Dead." *Christian Examiner* 31 (1842): 137–64, 281–307.

Bridgeman, Sarah. *Stowe Gardens*. London: John Bowles & Son, 1746.

Bridgman, Thomas. *Epitaphs from Copp's Hill Burying Ground, Boston, with Notes*. Boston: James Munroe, 1851.

———. *The Pilgrims of Boston and Their Descendants, with Introduction by Edward Everett, also Inscriptions from the Monuments in the Granary Burial Ground*. New York: D. Appleton, 1856.

Bright, Timothy. *A Treatise on Melancholie, containing the Causes thereof, and Reasons of the Strange Effects It Worketh in Our Minds and Bodies: With the Physicke Cure, and Spiritual Consolation of Such as Have Hereto Adjoined as Afflicted Conscience*. London: Thomas Vautrollier, 1586.

Brooks, Phillips. "The Episcopal Church." In *The Memorial History of Boston, Including Suffolk County, Massachusetts, 1630–1880*, edited by Justin Winsor. Boston: James R. Osgood, 1881.

Brooks, Van Wyck. *The Flowering of New England, 1815–1865*. New York: E. P. Dutton, 1940.

———. *New England: Indian Summer*. New York: E. P. Dutton, 1965.

Brown, Jane. *The Art and Architecture of English Gardens*. New York: Rizzoli, 1989.

Brown, Frederick. *Père Lachaise: Elysium and Real Estate*. New York: Viking, 1973.

B[rown, W. F.]. "Crawford's Statue of James Otis." *Boston Daily Courier*, June 17, 1856.

Browne, Mrs. Frances Elizabeth. "Mount Auburn." In *Ruth: A Sacred Drama and Original Lyrical Poems*. New York: Wynkoop & Hallenbeck, 1871.

Browne, Sir Thomas. *Hydriotaphia: Urne-Buriall; or, A Discource of the Sepulchrall Urnes Lately Found in Norfolk*. London: Henry Browne, 1658.

Brownell, Morris R. *Alexander Pope and the Arts of Georgian England*. Oxford: Clarendon Press, 1978.

Bryant, William Cullen. *Poems*. Philadelphia: A. Hart, 1851.

———. "Thanatopsis." *North American Review* 5.15 (September 1817): 338–40.

Bucke, Charles. *On the Beauties, Harmonies, and Sublimities of Nature: With Occasional Remarks on the Laws, Customs, Manners, and Opinions of Various Nations*. Vol. 1. London: G. & W. B. Whittaker, 1823.

Buckingham, James Silk. *America: Historical, Statistic, and Descriptive*. Vol. 3. London: Fisher, Son & Co., n. d. [ca. 1840].

———. *The Slave States of America*. Vol. 1. London: Fisher, Son & Co., 1842. Reprint, New York: Negro University Presses, 1968.

Buckingham, Joseph T. "Another Cemetery." *New-England Galaxy* 6.275 (January 17, 1823): 2.

———. "Good Advice, But Bitter." *New England Magazine* 5.5 (November 1833): 401–2.

———. "Mount Auburn." *Mount Auburn Memorial* 2.1 (July 4, 1860). Originally in *Boston Courier*, September 28, 1838.

———. "Sacred Ground." *New-England Galaxy* 6.277 (January 31, 1823): 2.

———. "Tombs under St. Paul's." *New-England Galaxy* 6.273 (January 3, 1823): 2.

Budge, Galvin, ed. *Aesthetics and the Picturesque, 1795–1840*. 6 vols. London: Thoemmes Press, 2001.

Bugbee, James M. "Boston under the Mayors, 1822–1880." In *The Memorial History of Boston, Including Suffolk County, Massachusetts, 1630–1880*, edited by Justin Winsor. Boston: James R. Osgood, 1881.

Bunhill Fields Burial Ground: Proceedings in Reference to Its Preservation with Inscriptions on the Tombs. London: Hamilton, Adams, 1867.

Bunting, Bainbridge, and Robert H. Nylander. *Survey of Architectural History in Cambridge: Report Four: Old Cambridge*. Cambridge: Cambridge Historical Commision & MIT Press, 1973.

Bunyan, John. *The Pilgrim's Progress from This World to That Which Is to Come Delivered under the Similitude of a Dream Wherein Is Discovered the Manner of His Setting Out, His Dangerous Journey, and Safe Arrival at the Desired Country*. 1678. Facsimile edition, edited by Roger Sharrock, New York: Viking Penguin, 1985.

Burchard, John, and Albert Bush-Brown. *The Architecture of America: A Social and Cultural History*. Boston: Little, Brown, 1961.

Burford, Robert. *Description of a View of the Cemetery of Père la Chaise, Including a Distant View of Paris and the Surrounding Country: Now Exhibiting at the Panorama, Leicester Square, Painted by the Proprietor Robert Burford from Drawings Taken by Him in the Summer of 1834*. London: G. Nichols, 1834.

"Burial." *North American Review* 93.192 (July 1861): 109–36.

"Burials in Cities." *Boston News-Letter and City Record*, March 4, 1826: 126.

Burke, Edmund. *On Taste: On the Sublime and the Beautiful*. New York: P. F. Collier, 1909.

———. *A Philosophical Inquiry into the Origin of Our Ideas of the Sublime and the Beautiful*. 1756. Reprint, Philadelphia: D. Johnson, 1806. Reprint, edited by James T. Boulton, South Bend: University of Notre Dame Press, 1968.

Burton, Robert. *The Anatomy of Melancholy, What It Is, With All the Kindes, Causes, Symptomes, Prognostickes, and Severall Cures of It*. Oxford: Iohn Lichfield & Iames Short, 1621.

Bushnell, Horace. *The Moral Use of Dark Things*. New York: Scribner, 1868.

Butterfield, Herbert. *The Whig Interpretation of History*. 1931. Reprint, New York: W. W. Norton, 1965.

Cady, Edwin H. *Literature of the Early Republic*. New York: Holt, Rinehart & Winston, 1967.

Caillot, Antoine. *Voyage réligieux et sentimental aux quatre cimetières de Paris: ouvrage renfermant un grand nombre d'inscriptions funéraires, suivis de réflexions réligieuses et morales*. Paris: L. Haussmann, 1809.

Caldwell, Laurence S. "Modern Cemetery Design and Development." *The American City* (March 1935).

[Calvin, John]. *The Forme of Prayers and Ministrations of the Sacraments, etc., Used in the English Congregation at Geneva; and Approved by the Famous and Godly Learned Man, Iohn Caluyn*. 1556. Reprinted in *The Liturgical Portions of the Genevan Service Book*. Edinburgh and London, 1931.

———. [Calvin, Jean.] *Institutes*. Translated by T. Norton. London, 1611.

C[ambry,] J[acques]. *Rapport sur les sèpultures, presentè à l'Administration Centrale du Départment de la Seine*. Paris, year VII [1799].

Cappon, Leslie J., ed. *The Adams-Jefferson Letters*. Chapel Hill: University of North Carolina Press, 1959.

Carmontelle, Louis Carrogis de. *Le Jardin de Monceau, près de Paris*. Paris: Delafosse, 1779.

Carrott, Richard G. *The Egyptian Revival: Its Sources, Monuments, and Meaning, 1808–1858*. Berkeley: University of California Press, 1978.

Carver, Robin. *History of Boston*. Boston: Lilly, Wait, Colman & Holden, 1832.

Cayeux, Jean de. *Hubert Robert et les jardins*. Paris: Herscher, 1987.

Cazamian, Louis. "Modern Times (1600–1914)." In Emile Légouis and Louis Cazamian, *A History of English Literature*. Translated by W. D. MacInnes and Louis Cazamian. New York: Macmillan, 1929.

"The Cemeteries and Catacombs of Paris." *Quarterly Review* 21.42 (April 1819): 350–97.

"Cemeteries and Churchyards." *Eclectic Magazine of Foreign Literature, Science, and Art* (August 1844): 449–71.

"Cemetery at Mount Auburn." *New England Farmer* 10:11 (September 28, 1831): 82. Originally in *The Boston Courier*.

The Cemetery Hand-Book: A Manual of Useful Information on Cemetery Development and Management. Chicago: Allied Arts Publishing, [1921].

"The Cemetery of Père-la-Chaise." *New England Farmer* 11.9 (September 12, 1832): 66–68.

Cendres, Julien, and Chloé Radiquet. *Le Désert de Retz: Paysage choisi*. Paris: Éditions Stock, 1997.

Chamberlain, Mellen. *Josiah Quincy: The Great Mayor*. Boston: By the [Massachusetts] Society [for Promoting Good Citizenship], 1889.

Chambers, Douglas. *The Planters of the English Landscape Garden: Botany, Trees, and the Georgics*. New Haven: Yale University Press, 1993.

Chambers, Sir William. *A Dissertation on Oriental Gardening*. London: W. Griffin, Printer to the Royal Academy, 1772.

Chandler, Peleg W. *The Charter and Ordinances of the City of Boston together with the Acts of the Legislature relating to the City*. Boston: John H. Eastburn, 1850.

"Changes in Management Structure." *Sweet Auburn*, Winter 1990.

[Channing, William Ellery]. "Remarks on National Literature." *Christian Examiner* 7 (1830): 269.

Channing, William Ellery. "Unitarian Christianity: Delivered at the Ordination of Rev. Jared Sparks in The First Independent Church of Baltimore on May 5, 1819." http://xroads.virginia.edu/~HYPER/DETOC/religion/unitarian.html.

———. "War: Discourses before the Congregational Ministers of Massachusetts." 1816. "Botany." 1818. "Self-Culture." 1828. In *The Works of William Ellery Channing, D.D.* Vol. 3. Boston and New York: American Unitarian Association, 1848.

The Charter of the City of Boston, and Ordinances Made and Established by the Mayor, Aldermen, and Common Council, with Such Acts of the Legislature of Massachusetts as Relate to the Government of Said City. Boston: True & Greene, 1827.

Charvat, William. *The Origins of American Critical Thought, 1810–35.* Philadelphia: University of Pennsylvania Press, 1936.

Chase, David B. "The Beginnings of the Landscape Tradition in America." *Historic Preservation* 25 (January–March 1973): 41.

Chase, Isabel W. U., ed. *Horace Walpole: Gardenist. An Edition of Walpole's "The History of Modern Taste in Gardening" with an Estimate of Walpole's Contribution to Landscape Architecture.* Princeton: Princeton University Press, 1943.

Chaumette, Pierre-Gaspard. *Arrêtés du Conseil-Général de la Commune de Paris rélatif aux differents cultes et aux prêtres.* Paris, le 17 vendémiaire, year II [October 8, 1793].

Chevigny, Bell Gale. *The Woman and the Myth: Margaret Fuller's Life and Writings.* Boston: Northeastern University Press, 1994.

Cheever, D. W. "Burial Customs." *North American Review* 93 (July 1861): 108–36.

Child, Lydia Maria. *The Mother's Book.* Boston: Carter & Hendee, 1831.

Chinard, Gilbert. *Volney et l'Amérique d'après des documents et sa correspondance avec Jefferson.* Baltimore: Johns Hopkins University Press, 1923.

"Church Cemeteries." *Boston Patriot and Daily Mercantile Advertiser* 11.1708 (December 26, 1822).

"The Church Yard." *Boston Patriot and Daily Mercantile Advertiser* 11.1703 (December 20, 1822).

Ciregna, Elise Madeline. "Museum in the Garden: Mount Auburn Cemetery and American Sculpture, 1840–1860." *Markers: Journal of the Association for Gravestone Studies* 21 (2004): 100–147.

City Lands Committee on the Corporation of London. *History of the Bunhill Fields Burying Ground, with Some of the Principal Inscriptions.* London: Charles Skipper & East, 1902.

"City Council." *Boston Evening Gazette* 9 (January 18, 1822): 2.

"City Council." *Columbian Centinel* 4049 (January 29, 1823): 2.

[City of Boston]. *The Charter of the City of Boston and Ordinances Made and Established by the Mayor, Aldermen, and Common Council, with Such Acts of the Legislature of Massachusetts as Relate to the Government of Said City.* Boston: True & Greene, 1827.

———. "An Ordinance to Regulate Interment of the Dead" and "Health." In Wetmore and Prescott, *The Charter and Ordinances of the City of Boston.*

Clark, H. F. *The English Landscape Garden.* 2nd ed. Gloucester, England: A. Sutton, 1980.

Clark, Rev. John A., ed. *Christian Keepsake and Missionary Annual.* Philadelphia: William Marshall, 1839.

Clarke, G. B., ed. *Descripions of Lord Cobham's Gardens at Stowe, 1700–1750.* Stowe, England: Buckinghamshire Record Society, 1990.

Clemens, S[amuel] L. *The Adventures of Huckleberry Finn.* 1884. Facsimile edition. San Francisco: Chandler, 1962.

Clendaniel, William C. "America's Urban Historic Cemeteries: An Endangered Species." *Historic Preservation Forum: The Journal of the National Trust for Historic Preservation* 1.4 (1977): 7–14.

———. "Mount Auburn's Master Plan and Its Implementation." *Sweet Auburn,* Winter 1993–94.

———. "The New President of Mount Auburn Cemetery Introduces Himself." *Sweet Auburn,* Summer 1988.

Cleveland, Henry Russell. "American Architecture." *North American Review* 43.93 (October 1836): 356–84.

Coffin, David R. *The English Garden: Meditation and Memorial.* Princeton: Princeton University Press, 1994.

Coffin, John Gorham. *An Address Delivered before the Contributors of the Boston Dispensary at the Seventeenth Anniversary, October 21, 1813.* Boston: John Eliot, 1813.

———. A Fellow of the Massachusetts Medical Society. *Remarks on the Dangers and Duties of Sepulture; or, Security for the Living, with Respect and Repose for the Dead.* Boston: Phelps & Farnham, 1823.

Coke, Edward Thomas. *A Subaltern's Furlough: Descriptive Scenes in Various Parts of the United States . . . during the Summer and Autumn of 1832.* 2 vols. New York: J. & J. Harper, 1833.

Cole, Thomas. "Essay on American Scenery." *American Monthly Magazine* 1 (January 1836): 1–2.

Collins, Dennis. "The Hurricane of 1938: A Lasting Impact on Horticulture at Mount Auburn." *Sweet Auburn,* Summer 2001.

Combe, George. *Notes on the United States of North America during a Phrenological Visit in 1838–9–40.* Philadelphia: Carey & Hart, 1841.

Comité de Salut Public de la Convention Nationale. *Rapport du Conseil de Santé sur la fouille des terres des ci-devant églises.* Paris, n.d. [1793?].

Conan, Michel, ed. *Perspectives on Garden Histories.* Washington, D.C.: Dumbarton Oaks, 1999.

Conron, John, ed. *The American Landscape: A Critical Anthology of Prose and Poetry.* New York: Oxford University Press, 1974.

Conron, John Joseph. *American Picturesque.* College Station: Pennsylvania State University Press, 2000.

Cook, Clarence Chatham. *A Description of the New York Central Park.* New York: Huntington, 1869. Facsimile ed., New York: Benjamin Blom, 1972.

Cook, Zebedee, Jr. *An Address Pronounced before the Massachusetts Horticultural Society in Commemoration of Its Second Annual Festival, the 10th of Sept. 1830.* Boston: Isaac R. Butts, 1830.

Cooper, Anthony Ashley, Third Earl of Shaftesbury. *Characteristics of Men, Manners, Opinions, Times.* 2 vols. London, 1711. 5th ed., Birmingham: John Baskerville, 1773. Reprint, London: Grand Richards, 1900.

Cooper, James Fenimore. *The Crater.* Cambridge: Belknap Press of Harvard University Press, 1962.

Cooper, William. *A Sermon Concerning the Laying of Deaths of Others to Heart, Occasion'd by the Lamented Death of the Ingenious and Religious Gentleman John Gore, Who Died Nov. 7, 1720.* Boston: B. Green for B. Eliot, 1720.

Corbin, Alain. *The Foul and the Fragrant: Odor and the French Social Imagination.* Cambridge: Harvard University Press, 1986.

Cornish, Vaughan. *The Churchyard Yew and Immortality.* London: F. Muller, 1946.

Coupé, J.-M. *De la moralité des sépultures, et de leur police.* Paris: Chez Calixte Vollant, year IX [1801].

Courcelles, Marie T. "Silent Cities." *Cincinnati Daily Enquirer,* February 25, 1877.

Cowell, F. R. *The Garden as Fine Art.* Boston: Houghton Mifflin, 1978.

Cray, Robert E., Jr. "Bunker Hill Refought: Memory Wars and Partisan Conflicts, 1775–1825." *Historical Journal of Massachusetts* 4 (Winter 2001). http://www.findarticles.com/p/articles/miqa3837/is-200101/al_n893387.

Creese, Walter L. *The Crowning of the American Landscape*. Princeton: Princeton University Press, 1985.

Crocker, Matthew H. *The Magic of the Many: Josiah Quincy and the Rise of Mass Politics in Boston, 1800–1830*. Amherst: University of Massachusetts Press, 1999.

Cronon, John, ed. *The American Landscape: A Critical Anthology of Prose and Poetry*. New York: Oxford University Press, 1974

Cross, Jeremy. *True Masonic Chart or Hieroglyphic Monitor*. New Haven: J. C. Gray, 1819.

"A Cruise After and Among the Cannibals." *Harper's New Monthly Magazine* 7.40 (September 1853): 455–75.

"Cultivation of the Willow." *New England Farmer* 11.29 (January 30, 1833): 229.

Curl, James Stevens. *A Celebration of Death: An Introduction to Some of the Buildings, Monuments, and Settings of Funerary Architecture in the Western European Tradition*. New York: Charles Scribner's Sons, 1980.

———. *The Victorian Celebration of Death*. London: Trowbridge, 1972.

Curti, Merle. *The Growth of American Thought*. New York: Harper & Row, 1964.

Curtis, G[eorge] T[icknor]. "Mount Auburn." *New England Magazine* 7 (October 1834): 316.

Cushing, J. D. "Notes on Disestablishment in Massachusetts, 1780–1833." *William and Mary Quarterly* 26.2 (1964): 169–90.

Daiches, David, Peter Jones, and Jean Jones, eds. *A Hotbed of Genius: The Scottish Enlightenment, 1730–1790*. Edinburgh: Edinburgh University Press, 1986.

Daly, César. *Architecture funéraire contemporaine: Specimen de tombeaux, chapelles funéraires, mausolées*. Paris: Ducher, 1871.

Dana, Mary S. B. "Mount Auburn." In *The Parted Family and Other Poems*. New York: Dayton & Saxton, 1842.

Dansel, Michel. *Au Père Lachaise: Son histoire, ses secrets, ses promenades*. Paris: Librairie Arthème Fayard, 1973.

Darnton, Robert. "The Art of Dying." *New York Review of Books*, May 13, 1982: 8–12.

Daubermesnil, François-Antoine. *Rapport fait au nom d'une Commission Spéciale, sur les inhumations*. Corps Législatif, Conseil de Cinq-Cents. Séance du 21 brumaire, year V [1797]. Paris: Imprimerie nationale, 1797.

Davies, Horton. *The Worship of English Puritans*. Westminster: Dacre Press, 1948.

Davis, David Brion. *Antebellum American Culture*. Lexington, Mass.: D. C. Heath, 1979.

Dearborn, Henry A. S. *Address Delivered before the Massachusetts Horticultural Society on the Celebration of Their First Anniversary, Sept. 19, 1829*. Boston: Isaac R. Butts, 1829. 2nd ed., Boston: J. T. Buckingham, 1833. 3rd ed., Boston: William D. Ticknor, 1847. Also in *New England Farmer* 8.26 (January 15, 1830): 203.

———. *An Address Delivered before the Massachusetts Society for Promoting Agriculture in Brighton, Oct. 14, 1835*. Boston: George C. Barrett, 1835.

———. "Bunker Hill." *Boston Patriot*, April 1823.

———. "The Cemetery of Père Lachaise." *New England Farmer* 11 (September 12, 183): 66–67.

———. "English Gardens." In "Writings on Horticulture and Other Branches of Rural Industry." Manuscript vol. 2. Rare Books Room, New York Public Library.

———. "Historical Sketch." *Transactions of the Massachusetts Historical Society, 1829–38*. Boston: William D. Ticknor, 1847

———. "Mount Auburn Cemetery: Report of the Massachusetts Horticultural Society upon the Establishment of an Experimental Garden and Rural Cemetery, Boston, 1831." *North American Review* 33.77 (October 1831): 397–406.

———. "Proceedings of the Massachusetts Horticultural Society . . . 1831." *New England Farmer* 9.49 (June 22, 1831): 385.

———. "Proceedings of the Massachusetts Horticultural Society . . . Sept. 8, 1832." *Transactions* 1:35–36.

———. "Report." In "Proceedings of the Massachusetts Historical Society . . . the 18th of June 1831." *New England Farmer* 9.49 (June 22, 1831).

———. "A Treatise on Grecian Architecture." 1828. 2 vols. Manuscript. Rare Books Room, Boston Public Library.

Dearborn, Nathaniel S. *Dearborn's Guide through Mount Auburn Cemetery . . . for the Benefit of Strangers Desirous of Seeing the Clusters of Monuments with the Least Trouble*. Boston: N. Dearborn, 1847. Revised editions published annually until 1858.

"'Death' from Mr. Croly's *Illustration of Gems*." *New-England Galaxy* 6.282 (March 7, 1823).

Defoe, Daniel. *A Tour Thro' the Whole Island of Great Britain, Divided into Circuits or Journies*. 4th ed. London: J. Osborn, 1742.

Delille, Abbé Jacques. "L'Imagination." Song 7. 1794. In *Oeuvres*, vol. 9. Paris: Michaud, 1824.

———. *Les Jardins: ou, l'art d'embellir les paysages: Poème*. Paris: Imprimerie de Philippe-Denys Pierres, ca. 1782. Republished as *The Gardens: A Poem*. Translated by Mrs. Montolieu. 2d ed. London: T. Bensley, 1805.

———. "Preface by the Translator." In René-Louis Marquis de Girardin, *An Essay on Landscape; or, On the Means of Improving and Embellishing the Country around Our Habitations*. Translated by the author. London: J. Dodsley, 1793.

Denon, Dominique-Vivant. *Déscription de l'Egypte: ou, Recueil des observations et des recherches qui ont été faites en Egypte pendant l'expédition de l'armée française, publié par les ordres de Sa Majesté, l'empereur Napoléon le Grand*. 21 vols. Paris: Imprimerie Nationale, 1809–23.

———. *Voyage dans la Basse et la Haute Egypte pendant les campagnes du général Bonaparte*. 3 vols. Paris: Didot, 1802. Reprint, New York: I. N. Longman & O. Reese, 1803; New York: Arno, 1973.

Denvir, Bernard. *The Eighteenth Century: Art, Design, and Society, 1689–1789*. London: Longman, 1983.

Département de la Seine. *Rapport fait au Conseil-Général sur l'instruction publique, le rétablissement des Bourses, le scandale des inhumations actuelles, l'érection de cimetières, la restitution des tombeaux, mausolées, etc*. Paris: Imprimerie Nationale, n.d. [ca. 1800].

"The Desolate City." *Columbia Centinel* (Boston) 4001 (September 18, 1822): 2.

Dethlefsen, Edwin, and James Deetz. "Death's Heads, Cherubs, and Willow Trees: Experimental Archaeology in Colonial Cemeteries." *American Antiquity* 31.4 (1966): 502–10.

Detournelle, Athanase-C[harles]. *Mémoire sur les funérailles et les sépultures*. Paris, year IX [1801].

Dexter, Henry Martyn. *The Congregationalism of the Last Three Hundred Years*. New York: Harper & Brothers, 1880.

Dickinson, Emily. *Selected Letters*. Edited by Thomas H. Johnson and Theodora Ward. Cambridge: Belknap Press of Harvard University Press, 1958.

Dimmick, Lauretta. "Thomas Crawford's Monument for Amos Binney in Mount Auburn Cemetery, 'A Work of Rare Merit.'" *Markers: Journal of the Association for Gravestone Studies* 9 (1992): 159–95.

A Directory for the Publique Worship of God, Throughout the Three Kingdomes of England, Scotland, and Ireland. Together with an Ordinance of Parliament for the Taking Away of the Book of Common-Prayer; and for Establishing and Observing of This Present Directory Throughout the Kingdom of England, and the Dominion of Wales, Die jovis 13, martii, 1644. London: Evan Taylor et al., 1644.

[Dix, John Ross]. A Looker-On. *Local Loiterings, and Visits in the Vicinity of Boston*. Boston: Redding, 1845. Excerpt reprinted as "An Englishman's Opinion of Mount Auburn." *Mount Auburn Memorial* 2.3 (July 18, 1860): 19.

Doliver, Pierre. *Essai sur les funérailles*. Versailles: Jacob, year IX [1801].

Donnet, Alexis. *Déscription des environs de Paris*. Paris: Treuttel et Wurtz, 1824.

Douglas, Ann. *The Feminization of American Culture*. New York: Knopf, 1977.

Downing, Andrew Jackson. "Domestic Notices." *The Horticulturist and Journal of Rural Art and Rural Taste* 1 (January 1847): 328–30; 3 (October 1848): 153–58; 4 (September 1849): 139.

———. "English and American Landscape Gardening." *Horticulturist* 2 (December 1847): 261–63.

———. "Foreign Notices: Père le Chaise Cemetery." *Horticulturist* 1 (October 1846): 189.

———. *Landscape Gardening*. Revised and edited by Frank A. Waugh. New York: John Wiley & Sons, 1921.

———. "Improving the Public Ground in the City of Washington." Letter to President Millard Fillmore. Winterthur Document, n.d. [1851?], no. 4836, Winterthur Archives, Winterthur, Delaware.

———. "The New York Park." *Horticulturist* 6 (August 1851): 345–49.

———. "Public Cemeteries and Public Gardens." *Horticulturist* 4.1 (July 1849): 9–12.

———. "Review: *Greenwood Illustrated*." *Horticulturist* 1 (November 1846): 230.

———. *Rural Essays*. Edited, with a Memoir of the Author, by George William Curtis; and a Letter to His Friends, by Frederika Bremer. New York: George P. Putnam, 1853. Reprint, edited with a new introduction by George B. Tatum, New York: Da Capo Press, 1974.

———. "A Talk about Public Parks and Gardens." *Horticulturist* 3 (October 1848): 157–58.

Drake, Francis S. *The Town of Roxbury: Its Memorable Persons and Places*. Boston: Municipal Printing Office, 1905.

Drake, Samuel Adams. *Old Landmarks and Historic Personages of Boston*. Boston: Little, Brown, 1872.

Draper, John W. *The Funeral Elegy and the Rise of English Romanticism*. New York: New York University Press, 1929.

Duffy, John. *A History of Public Health in New York City, 1625–1866*. New York: Russell Sage Foundation, 1968.

Duncan, Mary G. Lundie. *America as I Found It*. London: James Nisbet, 1852.

Dunlap, William. *History of the Rise and Progress of the Arts of Design in the United States*. Vol. 2. New York: Scott, 1834.

Dunne, Gerald T. *Justice Joseph Story and the Rise of the Supreme Court*. New York: Simon & Schuster, 1970.

Durdent, René-Jean. *Promenades de Paris; ou, Collection de vues pittoresques de ses jardins publiques, accompagnée d'un texte historique*. Paris: M. Guerin & Schwartz, 1812.

Duval, Amaury-Pineu. *Des Sépultures chez les anciens et les modernes*. Paris: Panckoucke, year IX [1801].

Dwight, Theodore. *Summer Tours; or, Notes of a Traveler through Some of the Middle and Northern States*. New York: Harper & Brothers, 1847.

Dwight, Timothy. *Travels in New-England and New York*. New Haven: T. Dwight, 1821.

Early, James. *Romanticism and American Architecture*. New York: A. S. Barnes, 1965.

E.E.T. "Burial and Burial Places." *Lowell Offering* 1, ser. 1 (1840): 154–57.

Ehrenpreis, Anne Henry, ed. *Happy Country This America: The Diary of Henry Arthur Bright*. Columbus: Ohio State University Press, 1978.

Eliade, Mircea. *The Sacred and the Profane: The Nature of Religion*. Translated by Willard R. Trask. New York: Harcourt, Brace & World, 1957.

Ellis, George E. *Memoir of Dr. Jacob Bigelow*. Cambridge: John Wilson & Son, 1880.

Emerson, Edward Waldo. *The Early Years of the Saturday Club, 1855–70*. Freeport, N.Y.: Books for Libraries Press, 1967.

Emerson, Ralph Waldo. *The Heart of Emerson's Journals*. Edited by Bliss Perry. Boston: Houghton Mifflin, 1926.

———. *Journals of Ralph Waldo Emerson with Annotations*. 3 vols. Edited by Edward Waldo Emerson and Waldo Forbes Emerson. Boston: Houghton Mifflin, 1910.

———. *Nature*. 1836. In *Ralph Waldo Emerson: Essays and Lectures*, edited by Joel Porte. New York: Library of America, 1983.

"An Englishman's Opinion of Mount Auburn." 1845. *Mount Auburn Memorial* 2.3 (July 18, 1860): 19.

Englizian, H. Crosby. *Brimstone Corner: Park Street Church, Boston*. Chicago: Moody Press, 1968.

Etlin, Richard A. *The Architecture of Death: The Transformation of the Cemetery in Eighteenth-Century Paris*. Cambridge: MIT Press, 1984.

———. "Landscapes of Eternity: Funerary Architecture and the Cemetery, 1793–1881." *Oppositions* 8 (Spring 1977): 14–31.

———. "Père Lachaise and the Garden Cemetery." *Journal of Garden History* 4.3 (1984): 222.

Evelyn, John. *The Diary of John Evelyn*. Edited by E. S. DeBeer. London: Oxford University Press, 1959.

———. *Silva; or, A Discourse of Forest-Trees, and the Propagation of Timber in His Majesty's Dominions . . . together with an Historical Account of the Sacredness and Use of Standing Groves, with Notes by A. Hunter, M.D.* 4th ed. 2 vols. York, England: Longman, Hurst, Rees, Orme & Brown, 1812.

Everett, Alexander H. *An Address Delivered before the Massachusetts Horticultural Society at Their 5th Annual Festival, Sept. 18, 1833*. Boston: J. T. Buckingham, 1833.

———. "June 7, 1836 Celebration." In *A Memorial of the American Patriots Who Fell at the Battle of Bunker Hill, with an Account of the Dedication of the Memorial Tablets*. Boston: By Order of the City Council, 1889.

Everett, Edward. *An Address Delivered at Charlestown, Aug. 1, 1826, in*

Commemoration of John Adams and Thomas Jefferson. Boston: William L. Lewis, 1826.

———. "Hieroglyphics." *North American Review* 32.70 (January 1831): 95–126.

———. "An Oration Pronounced at Cambridge before the Phi Beta Kappa Society, Aug. 27, 1824." *North American Review* 20.11 (1825): 422–23.

———. "The Proposed Rural Cemetery." 1832. Reprint in Jacob Bigelow, *A History of the Cemetery of Mount Auburn*. Boston: James Munroe, 1860.

———. "The Zodiac of Denderah." *North American Review* 17.41 (1823): 233–42.

Everett, Nigel. *The Tory View of Landscape*. New Haven: Yale University Press, 1994.

Fahey, Kathy. "Decorative Urns at Mount Auburn." *Sweet Auburn*, Winter 2002–2003.

Falip, Edward. *Guide aux sépultures des personnages célèbres inhumés dans les trois grands cimetières de Paris*. Paris: Lagrange, 1878.

Fein, Albert. "The American City: The Ideal and the Real." In *The Rise of American Architecture*, edited by Edgar Kaufman Jr. New York: Praeger, 1970.

Fessenden, Thomas G. *The American Gardener; Containing Practical Directions on the Culture of Fruits and Vegetables*. Boston: J. B. Russell, 1828.

Field, Peter S. *The Crisis of the Standing Order: Clerical Intellectuals and Cultural Authority in Massachusetts, 1780–1833*. Amherst: University of Massachusetts Press, 1998.

Finch, I. [John]. *Travels in the United States of America and Canada, Containing Some Account of Their Scientific Institutions, and . . . An Essay on the Natural Boundaries of Empires*. London: Longman, Rees, Orme, Brown, Green & Longman, 1833.

Fiquet du Boccage, Madame Marie Ann [LePage]. *Letters sur l'Angleterre*. 1770. Translated as *Letters Concerning England, Holland, and Italy*. London: Dilly, 1770.

Fischer von Erlach, Johann Bernhard. *Entwurff einer Historischen Architectur*. Vienna, 1721.

Flagg, Wilson. "Funereal Character of Trees." *Mount Auburn Memorial* 2.10 (September 5, 1860): 73–74.

———. *Mount Auburn: Its Scenes, Its Beauties, and Its Lessons*. Boston: James Munroe, 1861.

Fleming, Laurence, and Alan Gore. *The English Garden*. London: Michael Joseph, 1979.

Foletta, Marshall. *Coming to Terms with Democracy: Federalist Intellectuals and the Shaping of an American Culture*. Charlottesville: University Press of Virginia, 2001.

Foote, Henry Wilder. *Annals of King's Chapel from the Puritan Age of New England to the Present Day*. Boston: Little, Brown, 1882.

Forbes, Harriette M. "Symbolic Cemetery Gates in New England." *Old Time New England: Bulletin of the Society for the Preservation of New England Antiquities* 24 (October 1933): 46–58.

"Forest Hills Cemetery." *Mount Auburn Memorial* 1.20 (October 26, 1859): 156.

Forest Hills Cemetery: Its Establishment, Progress, Scenery, Monuments, etc. Boston: Damrell Moore & George Coolidge, 1858.

"Fountains in the Cemetery." *Mount Auburn Memorial* 2.30 (January 23, 1861): 236.

Fourcroy. *Notice sur la vie et les travaux de Lavoisier, le le 15 thermidor, an IV au Lycée des Arts*. Paris, 1796.

Foxcroft, Frank. "Mount Auburn Cemetery." *New England Magazine* (1896).

Frazee, John. "The Statue and Monument to Washington." *North American Review* 5 (March 1835): 350–52.

Freeman, Allen. "The Silent Edge: Gertrude Jekyll's 'Wide Wood Path' Informs a New Burial Ground at Historic Mount Auburn Cemetery." *Landscape Architecture* 94.6 (June 2004): 96–101.

French, Stanley. "The Cemetery as Cultural Institution: The Establishment of Mount Auburn and the 'Rural Cemetery' Movement." *American Quarterly* 26 (March 1974): 37–59.

Frothingham, Richard. *History of the Siege of Boston, and of the Battles of Lexington, Concord, and Bunker Hill*. Boston: Little, Brown, 1849.

Galignani's New Paris Guide; or, Stranger's Companion through the French Metropolis. Paris: A. & W. Galignani, 1826.

Gauther-Lachapelle, A. *Des Sépultures*. Paris: DuPont, year IX [1801].

Gay, Peter. *The Enlightenment: The Rise of Modern Paganism*. New York: W. W. Norton, 1966.

"General H. A. S. Dearborn." *Mount Auburn Memorial* 2.14 (October 3, 1860): 105.

"George W. Brimmer." *Boston Daily Advertiser* (September 1838). Also in *Mount Auburn Memorial* 1.44 (April 11, 1860): 345.

Gessner, Salomon. *Idyllen*. 1756. Translated into French by Michael Huber as *Idylles et poèmes champêtres*. Lyon: J. M. Buryset, 1762.

Gilman, Caroline H., and Rev. S. Gilman. *The Poetry of Traveling in the United States*. New York: S. Colman, 1838.

Gilman, Caroline H. "Sweet Auburn: Now Mount Auburn Cemetery." In *Verses of a Life Time*. Boston: James Munroe, 1849.

Gilpin, William. *A Dialogue upon the Gardens of the Right Honourable the Lord Viscount Cobham at Stowe in Buckinghamshire*. London: B. Seeley, 1748, 1749, and 1751. Reprint, Los Angeles: University of California Press, 1976.

———. *Three Essays: On Picturesque Beauty, On Picturesque Travel, On Sketching Landscape*. London, 1782. Also in *British Literature, 1780–1830*, edited by Anne K. Mellor and Richard E. Matlak. Fort Worth, Tex.: Harcourt Brace College Publishers, 1996.

Girard, J[oseph] de. *De Tombeaux, ou de l'influence des institutions funèbres sur les moeurs*. Paris, year IX [1801].

Girardin, Louis-Stanislas-Cécile-Xavier, Comte de. *Promenade ou itinéraire des jardins d'Ermenonville*. Paris: Chez Mérigot, 1788.

Girardin, René-Louis, Marquis de. *De la composition des paysages sur le terrain, ou, des moyens d'embellir la nature autour des habitations, en joignant l'agréable à l'utile*. Geneva: Chez F. M. Delaguette, 1777. Translated by the author (as R.-L. Girardin, Vicomte d'Ermenonville) as *An Essay on Landscape; or, On the Means of Improving and Embellishing the Country Around Our Habitations*. London: J. Dodsley, 1793.

———. *Promenade ou itinéraire des jardins de Chantilly*. Paris: Desenne, Gattey, Guyot, et Hédouin, 1781.

Goodchild, Peter H. "'No Phantasticall Utopia, But a Reall Place': John Evelyn, John Beale and Backbury Hill, Herefordshire." *Garden History* 19 (1991): 106–27.

Goodman, Paul. "Ethics and Enterprise: The Values of a Boston Elite, 1800–1860." *American Quarterly* 18 (Fall 1966): 437–51.

Goodich, C. A. *The Family Tourist: A Visit to the Principal Cities of the Western Continent*. Hartford, Conn.: Case, Tiffany, 1848.

Granziera, Patrizia. "Freemasonic Symbolism and Georgian Gardens." *Esoterica* 5 (2003): 41–72. http://esoteric.msu.edu/VolumeV/Freesonill.html.

"The Grave of a Mother." *Boston Patriot and Daily Mercantile Advertiser* 1720 (January 9, 1823): 2.

Graves, Richard. *The Spiritual Quixote; or, The Summer's Ramble of Mr. Geoffrey Wildgood: A Comic Romance*. London: J. Dodsley, 1774.

Gray, Francis C. "An Address before the Society of Phi Beta Kappa on Thurs., the 29th of Aug. 1816." *North American Review* 3 (September 1816): 289.

———. "Ancient Cemetery in Naples: Memoria sullo scovrimento di un antico sepolcreto Greco-Romano di Lorenzo Justiniana. In Napoli, 1812." *North American Review* 5 (1817): 119–27.

Gray, John C. *An Address Delivered before the Massachusetts Horticultural Society at the 6th Anniversary, Sept. 17, 1834*. Boston: J. T. Buckingham, 1834.

Gray, Thomas. *An Elegy Writtten in a Country Church-Yard*. London: R. Dodsley, 1751.

Green, Martin. *The Problem of Boston: Some Readings in Cultural History*. New York: W. W. Norton, 1966.

Greenleaf, Simon. *A Discourse Commemorative of the Life and Character of the Hon. Joseph Story, LL.D., an Associate Justice of the Supreme Court of the United States, and Dane Professor of Law in Harvard University; Pronounced on the Eighteenth Day of September, A.D. 1845, at the Request of the Corporation of the University, and the Members of the Law School*. Boston: C. C. Little & J. Brown, 1845.

Greenwood, F[rancis] W[illiam] P. *A History of King's Chapel*. Boston: Carter, Hendee & Allen & Ticknor, 1833.

———. "The Miscellaneous Poems of William Wordsworth." *North American Review*, n.s. 9 (April 1824): 356–70.

Grégoire, Abbé Henri. *Second rapport sur le vandalisme*. Paris, 1794.

Greppo, J. G. H. *Essay on the Hieroglyphic System of M. Champollion, Jr., and on the Advantages Which It Offers to Sacred Criticism*. Translated by Isaac Stuart. Boston: Perkins & Marvin, 1830.

Gridley, [Rev.] A. D. "Cemeteries." *New England and Yale Review* 22.85 (October 1863): 597–619.

———. "Rural Cemeteries." *Horticulturist* 5 (1855): 278–82.

Guillon, C. *Sur le respect du aux tombeaux; et l'indécence des inhumations actuelles*. Paris, year VIII (1800).

H. "Mount Auburn." *The Christian Examiner*, June 21, 1856.

Habert, Philippe. *The Temper of Death: A Poem*. Translated by John Sheffield Buckhingham. London: Daniel Brown, 1701.

Hadfield, Miles. *The English Garden*. Haverfordwest, England: Shire Garden History, 1988.

———. *A History of British Gardening*. Middlesex, England: Penguin, 1985.

Hajós, Géza. *Romantische Gärten der Aufklärung: Englische Landschaftskultur des 18. Jahrhunderts in und um Wien*. Vienna: Böhlau Verlag Wien, 1989.

Hale, [Dr. Enoch]. "Contagion." *North American Review* 12 (1821): 174–78.

Hale, Nathan. "Mount Auburn." *Boston Daily Advertiser* (1831).

———. *Selections from the Chronicle of Boston and the Book of Retrospections and Anticipations, Compiled in the Last Month of the Last Year of the Town, and the First Month and the First Year of the City*. Boston: [Nathan Hale], 1822.

Hale, Mrs. S[arah] J[osepha]. "Mount Auburn Cemetery." *Godey's Magazine and Ladies' Book* (1844).

Hall, David. "The Gravestone Image as a Puritan Cultural Code." In *Puritan Gravestone Art: Annual Proceedings of the Dublin Seminar for New England Folklife*. Boston: Boston University, 1977.

The [Craig] Halvorson Company. *Mount Auburn Cemetery: Master Plan*. Vol. 1. *Master Plan Overview and Recommendations*. Cambridge: Mount Auburn Cemetery, 1993.

Hampson, Norman. *The Life and Opinions of Maximilien Robespierre*. London: Penguin, 1974.

Harcourt, François-Henri, duc d'. *Traité de la décoration dehors, des jardins et des parcs*. 1774. Paris: Ernest de Ganay, 1919.

Harding, Vanessa. *The Dead and the Living in Paris and London, 1500–1670*. Cambridge: Cambridge University Press, 2002.

Hare, Sidney J. "The Cemetery Beautiful." *American Association of Cemetery Superintendents* 24 (1910): 40.

Harris, Neil. *The Artist in American Society: The Formative Years, 1790–1860*. New York: Simon & Schuster, 1966.

Harris, Thaddeus William. *A Discourse Delivered before the Massachusetts Horticultural Society in Celebration of Its Fourth Anniversary, Oct. 3, 1832*. Cambridge: E. W. Metcalf, 1832.

———. *Epitaphs from the Old Burying Ground in Watertown*. Boston, 1869.

Hawthorne, Nathaniel. "The Lily's Quest." In *The Picturesque Pocket Companion and Visitor's Guide through Mount Auburn*. Boston: Otis, Broaders, 1839.

———. *Nathaniel Hawthorne*. Edited by Roy Harvey Pearce. New York: Library of America, 1982.

———. "The New Adam and Eve." In *Mosses from an Old Manse*. New York: Wiley and Putnam, 1846. Reprinted in *Nathaniel Hawthorne*, edited by Roy Harvey Pearce (New York: Library of America, 1982).

Hays, David L. "Carmontelle's Design for the Jardin de Monceau: A Freemasonic Garden in Late-Eighteenth-Century France." *Eighteenth-Century Studies* 34.4 (Summer 1999): 446–62.

———. "This is not a '*Jardin Anglais*': Carmontelle, the Jardin de Monceau, and Irregular Garden Design in Eighteenth-Century France." In *Villas and Gardens in Early Modern Italy and France*, edited by Mirka Benes and Dianne Harris. New York: Cambridge University Press. 294–329, 408–19.

Headley, Gwyn, and Wim Meulenkamp. *Follies, Grottoes, and Garden Buildings*. London: Aurum Press, 1999.

Helvétius, Claude-Adrien. *De l'esprit; or, Essays on the Mind and Its Several Faculties*. 1758. Translation. London: J. Dodsley, 1759.

Hertz, Robert. *Death and the Right Hand*. Translated by Rodney and Claudia Needham. Glencoe, Ill.: Free Press, 1960.

Hewett, Mary E., ed. *The Memorial Written by the Friends of the Late Mrs. Osgood*. New York: G. P. Putnam, 1851.

Heywood, Janet. "Well-House for Visitors." *Sweet Auburn*, Fall-Winter 2003.

——— "Family Lot Enclosures." *Sweet Auburn*, January 1999.

Higginson, Thomas Wentworth. "Cheerful Yesterdays." *Atlantic Monthly* 78.469 (November 1896): 586–97.

Hildreth, Richard. *The History of the United States*. 6 vols. New York: Harper & Brothers, 1849–56.

Hill, Norman P., M.D. "Ludlow Griscom and Mount Auburn Cemetery." *Sweet Auburn*, Spring 1988.

Hillard, George Stillman. *Memoir of Joseph Story, LL.D.* Boston: John Wilson, 1868.

Hipple, Walter John, Jr. *The Beautiful, the Sublime, and the Picturesque in Eighteenth-Century British Aesthetic Theory*. Carbondale: Southern Illinois University Press, 1957.

"Hiram Powers the Sculptor—Inauguration of Powers' Statue of Webster." *Mount Auburn Memorial* 1.15 (September 21, 1859).

Hirschfeld, Christian Cayus Lorenz. *Theorie der Gärtenkunst/Théorie de l'art des jardins, Traduit de l'allemand*. 5 vols. Leipzig: Weidmann Erben & Reigh, 1779–85. Reprinted as *Theory of Garden Art*, edited and translated by Linda B. Parshall. Philadelphia: University of Pennsylvania Press, 2001.

Historical Sketch of the First Burying Ground in Dorchester. Boston: Municipal Printing Office, 1903.

Historical Sketch of the First Burying Place in Roxbury. Boston: Municipal Printing Office, 1904.

Historical Sketch of King's Chapel Burying-Ground. Boston: Municipal Printing Office, 1903.

Historical Sketch and Matters Appertaining to the Granary Burial-Ground. Boston: Municipal Printing Office, 1902.

History of the City Burial Ground in New Haven, together with the Names of the Owners of the Lots Therein. New Haven: J. H. Benham, 1863.

A History of the Origin and Development of the Quincy Railway at Quincy, Massachusetts: In Commemoration of the One Hundredth Anniversary. Quincy: Granite Railway Co., 1926.

Hitchcock, Henry-Russell. *Architecture: Nineteenth and Twentieth Centuries*. Baltimore: Penguin, 1971.

Hitchcock, John. "Victorian London Cemeteries." *GenDocs: Genealogical Reserch in England & Wales*. 1996–2003. http://www.gendocs.demon.co.uk/cem.html.

Hodges, Maud de Leigh. *Crossroads on the Charles: A History of Watertown, Massachusetts*. Canaan, N.H.: Phoenix, for the Watertown Free Public Library, 1980.

Holeran, Michael. *Boston's Changeful Times: Origins of Preservation and Planning in America*. Baltimore: Johns Hopkins University Press, 1998.

Holmes, Mrs. [Isabella Basil Holmes]. *The London Burial Grounds*. London: Fisher Unwin, 1896.

———. "Notes on Their History from the Earliest Times to the Present Day." From *The London Burial Grounds*. http://www.londoncemeteries.co.uk/holmes.html.

Homans, Isaac Smith. *Sketches of Boston, Past and Present; And of Some Few Places in Its Vicinity*. Boston: Phillips, Sampson & Co., 1851.

Horstein, Edouard de. *Les Sépultures devant l'histoire, l'archéologie, la liturgie, le droit ecclésiastique et la législation civile*. Paris: J. Albanel, 1868.

"Horticultural Societies." *Horticulturist* 6.2 (February 1851): 92.

Howe, Daniel Walker. *The Unitarian Conscience: Harvard Moral Philosophy, 1805–1860*. Cambridge: Harvard University Press, 1970.

Howe, Julia Ward. "Reminiscences of Julia Ward Howe." *Atlantic Monthly* 83.497 (March 1899): 330–43.

Howells, William Dean. *A Traveller from Altruria: Romance*. New York: Harper, 1894. Reprint, New York: Sagamore Press, 1957.

Hubbard, William. *General History of New England from the Discovery to MDCLXXX*. Cambridge: Massachusetts Historical Society, 1815.

Hunt, John Dixon. *The Figure in the Landscape: Poetry, Painting, and Gardening during the Eighteenth Century*. Baltimore: Johns Hopkins University Press, 1976.

———. "Pope's Twickenham Revisited." *Eighteenth-Century Life* 8, n.s. 2 (January 1983): 29–32.

———. *William Kent*. London: Zwemmer, 1987.

Hunt, John Dixon, ed. *Garden and Grove: The Italian Renaissance Garden in the English Imagination, 1600–1750*. Princeton: Princeton University Press, 1986.

———. *Garden and the Picturesque: Studies in the History of Landscape Architecture*. Cambridge: MIT Press, 1992.

———. *The Oxford Book of Garden Verse*. Oxford: Oxford University Press, 1993.

Hunt, John Dixon, and Peter Willis, eds. *The Genius of Place: The English Landscape Garden, 1620–1820*. New York: Harper & Row, 1975. Reprint, Cambridge: MIT Press, 1988.

Hussey, Christopher. *English Gardens and Landscapes, 1700–1750*. New York: Funk & Wagnalls, 1967.

Huth, Hans. *Nature and the American: Three Centuries of Changing Attitudes*. Lincoln: University of Nebraska Press, 1957.

"Improvements at Mount Auburn." *Mount Auburn Memorial* 1.2 (June 22, 1859): 133.

Ingenhousz, Jan. *Experiments on Vegetables, Discovering Their Great Power of Purifying the Common Air in Sunshine, and of Injuring It in the Shade and at Night, to Which Is Joined a New Method of Examining the Accurate Degree of the Salubrity of the Atmosphere*. London: P. Elmsley & H. Payne, 1779.

An Interesting Account of the Plague, Yellow Fever, etc., as They Have Prevailed in Different Countries. Boston: At the request of the Boston Board of Health, James Loring, 1820.

Irving, Washington. *The Sketch Book of Geoffrey Crayon, Gent*. 1819–20. Reprint, New York: Dutton, 1963.

Irwin, John T. *American Hieroglyphics: The Symbol of the Egyptian Hieroglyphics in the American Renaissance*. Baltimore: Johns Hopkins University Press, 1980.

Jackson, [Dr.] J[ohn] B. S. "Autopsy of Dr. John Collins Warren, May 8, 1856." Countway Library of Medicine, Harvard University. http://www.countway.med.harvard.edu/rarebooks/exhibits/warrens/warren2.html.

———. *Descriptive Catalogue of the Warren Anatomical Museum*. Boston: A. Williams & Co., 1870.

Jacques, David. *Georgian Gardens: The Reign of Nature*. London: B. T. Batsford, 1983.

Jaher, Frederic Cople. "The Boston Brahmins in the Age of Industrial Capitalism." In *The Age of Industrialism in America: Essays in Social Structure and Cultural Values*. New York: Free Press, 1968.

———. *The Urban Establishment: Upper Strata in Boston, New York, Charleston, Chicago, and Los Angeles*. Urbana: University of Illinois Press, 1982.

Jakob, Michael. *Ermenonville*. Paris: Éditions de l'Imprimeur, 2002.

James, Henry. *William Wetmore Story and His Friends, from Letters, Diaries, and Recollections*. Vol. 1. Boston: Houghton Mifflin, 1903.

———. "The Ghostly Rental." *Scribner's Monthly* 12.5 (September 1876): 664–71.

Janvry, Olivier Choppin de. *Résponses à 101 questions sur le Désert de Retz*. Croissy-sur-Seine: Société Civile du Désert de Retz, 1988.

Jarrett, David. *The English Landscape Garden*. New York: Rizzoli, 1978.

Jarvas, Samuel Farrar. *A Narrative of Events Connected with the Acceptance and Resignation of the Rectorship of St. Paul's Church, Boston*. Boston, November 1825.

Johnson, Edward. *A History of New England from the English Planting in the Yeare 1628 untill the Yeare 1652*. London: Brooke, 1654.

Jolimont, François-Gabriel-Théodore de. *Les Mausolées français, recueil des tombeaux les plus remarquables par leur structure, leurs épitaphes, ou les cendres qu'ils referment, ériges dans les nouveaux cimetières de Paris*. Paris: Firmin Didot, 1821.

Jones, Barbara. *Follies & Grottoes*. London: Constable & Co., 1979.

Jones, Howard Mumford. *American and French Culture, 1750–1848*. Chapel Hill: University of North Carolina Press, 1927.

Jones, John Andrews, ed. *Bunhill Memorials: Sacred Reminiscences of 300 Ministers and Other Persons of Note, Who Are Buried in Bunhill Fields, of Every Denomination*. London: J. Paul, 1849.

Judd, Sylvester. *Margaret: A Tale of the Real and the Ideal, Blight and Bloom; Including Sketches of a Place Not Before Described, Called Mons Christi*. Boston: Jordan & Wiley, 1845.

Justitia. "John Hancock." *Mount Auburn Memorial* 1.17 (October 6, 1859): 134.

Kaufman, Polly Welts. *Women Teachers on the Frontier*. New Haven: Yale University Press, 1984.

Kean, Robert H. *History of the Graveyard at Monticello*. Charlottesville, Va.: Thomas Jefferson Memorial Foundation, 1972.

Kelly, George Armstrong. "Mortal Politics in Eighteenth-Century France." *Historical Reflections* (Canada) 13.1 (Spring 1986).

[Kemble, Fanny]. *The Journal of Frances Anne Butler, Better Known as Fanny Kemble*. 1835. Reprint, New York: B. Blom, 1970.

Kendall, Edward Augustus. *Travels through the Northern Parts of the United States in the Years of 1807 and 1808*. Vol. 1. New York: I. Riley, 1809.

Ketcham, Diana. *Le Désert de Retz: A Late-Eighteenth-Century French Folly Garden, the Artful Landscape of Monsieur de Monville*. San Francisco: Arion Press, 1990. Reprint, Cambridge: MIT Press, 1994.

Kindred, Roger S. "Mount Auburn: A Living Entity." *Sweet Auburn*, Winter 1989.

[King, Moses]. *King's Handbook of Boston, Profusely Illustrated*. 4th ed. Cambridge: Moses King, 1883.

———. *Mount Auburn Cemetery, Including Also a Brief History and Description of Cambridge, Harvard University, and the Union Railway Company*. Cambridge: Moses King, 1885.

Knight, Richard Payne. *An Analytic Enquiry into the Principles of Taste*. London, 1805.

———. *The Landscape: A Didactic Poem in Three Books, Addressed to Uvedale Price, Esq*. London, 1794.

Koch, Adrienne, and William Peder, eds. *Selected Writings of John and John Quincy Adams*. New York: Knopf, 1964.

Krafft, J[ean]-C[harles]. *Plan des plus beaux jardins pittoresque de France, d'Angleterre, et d'Allemagne, et des édifices, monuments, fabriques, etc., qui concourrent à leur embellisement dans tous les genres d'architecture*. 2 vols. Paris: Levrault, 1809–10.

Kroeber, Karl, and William Wailing, eds. *Images of Romanticism: Verbal and Visual Affinities*. New Haven: Yale University Press, 1978.

Laborde, Alexandre-Louis-Joseph, Comte de. *Déscription des nouveaux jardins de la France et de ses anciens châteaux, mêlée d'obsérvations sur la vie da las campagne et la composition des jardins, avec dessins par Charles Bourgeois*. Paris: Delance, 1808[–1815?].

Laderman, Gary. *The Sacred Remains: American Attitudes toward Death, 1799–1883*. New Haven: Yale University Press, 1996.

Lafargue. *Motion d'ordre . . . sur la police des cimetières et des inhumations. Corps Législatif, Conseil des Cinq-Cents. Séance du 14 frimaire, an VII*. Paris, [1799].

Lagarde, André, and Laurent Michard, eds. *XVIIIe siècle: Les grands auteurs français du programme*. Paris: Bordas, 1965.

Laird, Mark. *The Flowering of the Landscape Garden: English Pleasure Grounds, 1720–1800*. Philadelphia: University of Pennsylvania Press, 1999.

Langley, Batty. *Ancient Architecture Restored and Improved by a Great Variety of Usefull Designs, Entirely New, in the Gothic Mode for the Ornamenting of Buildings and Gardens*. London, 1742.

———. *New Principles of Gardening*. London: A. Bettesworth, J. Batley, J. Pemberton, T. Bowles, J. Clarke, and J. Bowles, 1728.

Lassalle, C. *Promenades pittoresques aux cimetières du Père Lachaise, de Montmartre, du Montparnasse et autres, ou choix des principaux monuments élevés dans ces champs de repos*. Paris: A. Fourmage, 1844.

Latrobe, B[enjamin] Henry. "Anniversary Oration Pronounced before the Society of Artists of the United States, by Appointment of the Society, on the Eighth of May, 1811." *First Annual Exhibition of the Society of Artists of the United States*. Philadelphia, 1811. Bound with *The Port-folio* n.s. 5.6 (June 1811).

Lavin, Sylvia. *Quatremère de Quincy and the Invention of a Modern Language of Architecture*. Cambridge: MIT Press, 1992.

Lawrence, William. *The Life of Amos A. Lawrence*. Boston: Houghton Mifflin, 1888.

———. *A Sermon on the 75th Anniversary of Saint Paul's Church, Boston*. Boston: By the Parish, 1895.

Lawrence, William R., ed. *Extracts from the Diary and Correspondence of the Late Amos Lawrence*. Boston: Gould & Lawrence, 1855.

Lears, T. Jackson. *No Place of Grace: Antimodernism and the Transformation of American Culture*. New York: Pantheon, 1981.

Leatherbarrow, David. "Character, Geometry, and Perspective: The Third Earl of Shaftesbury's Principles of Garden Desgin." *Journal of Garden History* 4 (1984): 332–58.

Leclerc, J.-B. *Rapport . . . sur les institutions rélatives à l'état civil des citoyens. Corps Législatif, le 16 brumaire, an IV*. [November 6, 1797] Paris, 1798.

———. *Corps Législatif, Conseil des Cinq-Cents: Motion d'Ordre . . . sur l'existence et l'utilité d'une réligion civile en France*. Paris: n.p., 9 fructidor, year V [1797].

LeRouge, Georges-Louis. *Cahiers des jardins anglo-chinois à la mode*. Paris: LeRouge, 1776–1785. Reprint: *Détail des nouveaux jardins à la mode: Jardins anglo-chinois, 21 cahiers en plusieurs livraisions, 1776–1789*. Paris: Jardin de Flore, 1977.

Leslie, Michael. "History and Historiography in the English Garden." In *Perspectives on Garden Histories*, edited by Michael Conan. Washington, D.C.: Dumbarton Oaks, 1999.

Levaillant, Maurice. *Les tombes célèbres*. Paris: Hachette, 1926.

Ligne, Prince Charles-Joseph de. *Coup d'Oeil at Beloeil and a Great Number of European Gardens*. Translated and edited by Basil Guy. Berkeley: University of California Press, 1991.

Lincoln, Levi. *An Address Delivered on the Consecration of the Worcester Rural Cemtery, Sept. 8, 1838*. Boston: Dutton & Wentworth, 1838.

Linden, Blanche M. G. "Adolph Strauch." In *Germany and the Americas*, edited by Thomas Adam. Santa Barbara, Calif.: ABC-CLIO, 2005.

———. "Cemeteries." In *Dictionary of American History*, edited by Stanley I. Kutler. 3rd ed. New York: Scribner's, 2003.

———. "Cemeteries and Burials." In *Encyclopedia of the New American Nation*, edited by Paul Finkelman. New York: Scribner's, 2005.

———. "Death and the Garden: The Cult of the Melancholy and the 'Rural' Cemetery." Ph.D. diss., Harvard University, 1981.

———. "Jacob Bigelow," "Henry A. S. Dearborn," and "John Notman." In *Pioneers of American Landscape Design*, edited by Charles A. Birnbaum and Robin Karson. New York: McGraw-Hill, 2000.

———. *Spring Grove: Celebrating 150 Years*. Cincinnati: Cincinnati Historical Society, 1995. Reprint, *Queen City Heritage: Journal of the Cincinnati Historical Society* 53.1–2 (Spring–Summer 1995) [entire combined issues].

———. "Tel l'Eden avant la chute: Les cimetières de Montréal dans le contexte du mouvement des cimetières 'ruraux' de l'Amérique du Nord." ["As Eden before the Fall: The Cemeteries of Montreal in the Context of the North American 'Rural' Cemetery Movement."] Translated by Anne-Marie Bilodeau. *Frontières: Les vivants et le mort* 7.3 (Université de Montréal, hiver/Winter 1995): 5–12.

———. "The Willow Tree and Urn Motif: Changing Ideas about Death and Nature." *Markers: Journal of the Association for Gravestone Studies* 1 (1979–80): 149–56.

Linden-Ward, Blanche. "'The Fencing Mania': The Rise and Fall of Nineteenth-Century Funerary Enclosures." *Markers: Journal of the Association for Gravestone Studies* 7 (1990): 35–58.

———. "The Greening of Cincinnati: Adolph Strauch's Legacy in Park Design." *Queen City Heritage: Journal of the Cincinnati Historical Society* 51.1 (Spring 1992): 20–39.

———. "Putting the Past Under Grass: History as Death and Cemetery Commemoration." *Prospects: Annual of American Cultural Studies* 10 (1985): 279–314.

———. "Putting the Past in Place: The Making of Mount Auburn Cemetery." *Cambridge Historical Society Proceedings* 44 (1976–79): 171–96.

———. *Silent City on a Hill: Landscapes of Memory and Boston's Mount Auburn Cemetery*. Columbus: Ohio State University Press, 1989.

———. "Strange but Genteel Pleasure Ground: Tourist and Leisure Uses of Nineteenth-Century Rural Cemeteries." In *Cemeteries and Gravemarkers: Voices of American Culture*, edited by Richard E. Meyer. Ann Arbor: UMI Research Press, 1989. Reprint, Logan: Utah State University Press, 1992.

Linden-Ward, Blanche, and David C. Sloane. "Spring Grove: The Founding of Cincinnati's Rural Cemetery, 1845–1855." *Queen City Heritage: Journal of the Cincinnati Historical Society* 43.1 (Spring 1985): 17–32.

Linden-Ward, Blanche, and Alan Ward. "Spring Grove: The Role of the Rural Cemetery in American Landscape Design." *Landscape Architecture* 75.5 (September–October 1985): 126–31, 140.

Livermore, Shaw, Jr. *The Twilight of Federalism: The Disintegration of the Federalist Party, 1815–1830*. Princeton: Princeton University Press, 1962.

London City Lands Committee. *History of the Bunhill Fields Burial Ground with Some of the Principal Inscriptions*. London: Charles Skipper & East, 1887.

Longinus. *An Essay on the Sublime*. Translated by Nicolas Boileau-Despreaux. 1674. Oxford: Leon Lichfield, 1698. Reprinted as *An Essay on the Sublime, with Critical Reflexions, Remarks and Observations*, edited by M. Boileau, M. Dacier, and M. Boivin. London, 1712.

Loudon, John Claudius. *On the Laying Out, Planting, and Managing of Cemeteries; and on the Improvement of Churchyards*. London: A. Spottiswoode for the Author, 1843. Originally published as articles in *Gardener's Magazine* 19 (1843).

———. "Review: Augustus Welby Pugin, *Contrasts*." *Architectural Magazine* 4 (March 1837): 132–43.

Lovejoy, Arthur O. *Essays in the History of Ideas*. Baltimore: Johns Hopkins University Press, 1948.

———. *The First Gothic Revival and the Return to Nature*. Baltimore: Johns Hopkins University Press, 1932.

Lowell, James Russell. *Letters of James Russell Lowell*. Edited by Charles Eliot Norton. Vol. 2. New York: Harper & Brothers, 1894.

Ludwig, Allan I. "Eros and Agape: Classical and Early Christian Survivals in New England Stonecarving." In *Puritan Gravestone Art: Annual Proceedings of the Dublin Seminar for New England Folklife*. 1976. Boston: Boston University, 1977.

———. *Graven Images: New England Stonecarving and Its Symbols, 1650–1815*. Middletown, Conn.: Wesleyan University Press, 1966.

Ludwig, Allan I., and David D. Hall. "Aspects of Music, Poetry, Stonecarving, and Death in Early New England." In *Puritan Gravestone Art II: Annual Proceedings of the Dublin Seminar for New England Folklife*. 1977. Boston: Boston University, 1978.

Lunsford, John. *The Romantic Vision in America*. Dallas: Dallas Museum of Fine Arts, 1971.

Lyell, Sir Charles. *A Second Visit to the United States of North America*. Vol. 1. London: John Murray, 1849.

MacColl, Malcolm. *Lawlessness, Sacerdotalism, and Ritualism Discussed in Six Letters Addressed . . . to the Right Hon. Lord Selbourne*. London: J. T. Hayes, 1875.

MacDonald, Edward. *Old Copp's Hill and Burial Ground with Historical Sketches*. Boston: By the Author, 1894.

MacDougall, Elizabeth, and George B. Tatum, eds. *Prophet with Honor: The Career of Andrew Jackson Downing, 1815–1852*. Washington, D.C.: Dumbarton Oaks, 1989.

Mackay, Alexander. *The Western World; or, Travels in the United States in 1846–7*. Vol. 1. Philadelphia: Lea & Blanchard, 1849.

Malins, Edward. *English Landscaping and Literature, 1660–1840*. London: Oxford University Press, 1966.

Maliphant, George. *Designs for Sepulchral Monuments*. London, n.d. [ca. 1820].

[Manning, Robert, ed.]. *History of the Massachusetts Horticultural Society, 1829–1878*. Boston: Rand, Avery, for the Society, 1880.

Marchant de Beaumont, François-Marie. *Manuel et itinéraire du curieux dans le cimetière du Père la Chaise*. 3rd ed. Paris: Emler Frères, 1828.

———. *Le Nouveau conducteur de l'étranger à Paris en 1826*. Revised 13th ed. Paris: Moroval, 1826. [The 6th edition appeared in 1818; the 19th in 1837.]

———. *Vues pittoresque, historiques, et morales du cimetière du Père la Chaise: Dessinées d'après nature par M. M. Vigneron et Duplat et gravées à l'aqua-tinta par M. Jazet accompagnées de leur déscription topographique, monumentale et morale*. Paris: de Plassan, 1821.

Marion, John Francis. *Famous and Curious Cemeteries*. New York: Crown, 1977.

Martin, James Kirby. *Interpreting Colonial America: Selected Readings*. New York: Harper & Row, 1978.

Martin, Peter. *Pursuing Innocent Pleasures: The Gardening World of Alexander Pope*. Hamden, Conn.: Archon Books, 1984.

Martineau, Harriet. *Retrospect of Western Travel*. 2 Vols. London: Saunders & Otley, 1838.

———. *Society in America*. 2 vols. New York: Saunders & Otley, 1837.

Martinet, Marie Madeleine. *Art et nature en Grande-Bretagne au XVIIe siècle*. Paris: Aubier, 1980.

Marty, Joseph. *Promenades pittoresque au cimetière du Père Lachaise*. Paris: Chaillou, 1835.

Marx, Leo. *The Machine in the Garden: Technology and the Pastoral Ideal in America*. New York: Oxford University Press, 1964.

Massachusetts General Court. House of Representatives. *Report of the Select Committee of the House of Representatives . . . Legalizing the Study of Anatomy*. Boston: Dutton & Wentworth, 1831.

Mason, Rev. William. "The English Garden: A Poem." *The Gentleman's Magazine* 42 (1771): 78–80. Reprinted in *The English Garden in Four Books*. York, England: Ward, 1783.

Mather, Cotton. *Magnalia Christi Americana; or, The Ecclesiastical History of New England from Its First Planting in the Year 1620 unto the Year of Our Lord 1698*. New Haven: S. Converse; Hartford: Silus Andrus, Roberts & Burr, 1820.

Mather, Increase. *Meditations on Death: Delivered in Several Sermons, Wherein Is Shewed: I. That Some True Believers on Christ Are Afraid of Death, but That They Have Not Just Cause to Be So. II. That Good Men as Well as Others May Be Taken Out of the World by a Sudden Death. III. That Not Earth But Heaven Is the Christian's Home*. Boston: Timothy Green, 1707.

Mathieu, René. *Ermenonville*. Paris: Nouvelles Éditions Latines, 1985.

Maxwell, A. M. *A Run through the United States during the Autumn of 1840*. Vol. 1. London: Henry Colburn, 1841.

May, Henry F. *The Enlightenment in America*. New York: Oxford University Press, 1976.

McCaughey, Robert A. *Josiah Quincy, 1772–1865: The Last Federalist*. Cambridge: Harvard University Press, 1974.

McClellan, James. *Joseph Story and the American Constitution*. Norman: University of Oklahoma Press, 1971.

McCloskey, Robert, ed. *The Works of James Wilson*. Vol. 1. Cambridge: Harvard University Press, 1967.

McDowell, Michael McEachern. *American Attitudes toward Death, 1825–1865*. Ann Arbor: University Microfilms, 1978. Ph.D. diss., Brandeis University, December 1977.

McDowell, Peggy, and Richard E. Meyer. *The Revival Styles in American Memorial Arts*. Bowling Green, Ohio: Bowling Green State University Popular Press, 1994.

McManners, John. *Death and the Enlightenment: Changing Attitudes to Death among Christians and Unbelievers in Eighteenth-Century France*. Oxford: Clarendon Press of Oxford University Press, 1981.

"The Memorial." *Harper's New Monthly Magazine* 2.8 (January 1851): 282.

Mercier, Louis-Sébastien. *Le Tableau de Paris, nouvelle édition, corrigée et augmentée*. Vol. 3. Amsterdam, 1782–88.

Michelet, Jules. *Ma Jeunesse*. 6th ed. Paris: C. Lévy, 1884.

Milton, John. *Il Penseroso*. Oxford: Clarendon Press, 1883.

Moiroux, Jules. *Le Cimetière du Père la Chaise*. Paris: Mercadier, 1909.

Moore, Charles W., William J. Mitchell, and William Turnbull Jr. *The Poetics of Gardens*. Cambridge: MIT Press, 1988.

Moore, Damrell V., and George Coolidge, eds. *The Boston Almanac for the Year 1857*. No. 22. Boston: John P. Jewett, 1857.

Morel, Jean-Marie. *Théorie des jardins, ou l'art des jardins de la nature*. 2 vols. Paris: Pissot, 1776. Revised ed., Paris: Panckoucke, year XI [1802].

Morison, Samuel Eliot. *Harrison Gray Otis, 1765–1848: The Urbane Federalist*. Boston: Houghton Mifflin, 1969.

Morison, Samuel Eliot, ed. *The Life and Letters of Harrison Gray Otis*. Boston: Houghton Mifflin, 1946.

Mosser, Monique, and Georges Teyssot. *The Architecture of Western Gardens*. Cambridge: MIT Press, 1946.

Mosser, Monique, and Béatrice de Rochebouet, eds. *Alexandre-Théodore Brongniart, 1739–1813: Architecture et décor*. Paris: Musée Carnavalet, 1986.

[Mount Auburn Cemetery]. *Alphabetical and Numerical Lists of Proprietors of Lots in the Cemetery at Mount Auburn on March 1, 1834*. Boston: J. T. Buckingham, 1834.

———. *Annual Report of the Trustees of the Cemetery of Mount Auburn together with the Reports of the Treasurer and Superintendent*. Published annually for the Corporation from 1836 to the present.

———. *Catalogue of the Lots at Mount Auburn Cemetery*. Boston: Rand & Avery, 1857.

———. *Catalogue of Lots Laid Out in the Cemetery of Mount Auburn*. Boston: Nathaniel Dearborn, 1839.

———. *Catalogue of Proprietors in the Cemetery of Mount Auburn on 1st July 1835 . . . together with the Terms of Subscription, Regulations Concerning Visitors and Interments, and the Act of the Legislature Incorporating the Said Proprietors*. Boston: Nathan Hale, 1835.

———. *A Catalogue of Proprietors of the Cemetery of Mount Auburn*. Boston: James Munroe, 1846.

———. "Proprietors' and Trustees' Records." Bound Manuscript records of proprietors' annual meetings and trustees' monthly meetings. Vol. 1. (April 21, 1835–October 2, 1854); Vol. 2 (October 9, 1854–February 7, 1859); Vol. 3 (February 14, 1859–January 30, 1865); Vol. 4 (February 6, 1865–May 10, 1870); Vol. 5 (June 8, 1870–March 12, 1875); Vol. 6 (April 14, 1875–March 13, 1886). Mount Auburn Cemetery.

———. "Records of Committees." Bound Manuscripts of occasional meetings of the committees. Mount Auburn Cemetery.

"Mount Auburn." *Cyclopoedia of Useful Knowledge* (1835): 9. Mount Auburn Cemetery.

"Mount Auburn." *Gleason's Pictorial Drawing Room Companion* 5 (August 13, 1853): 104–5.

"Mount Auburn Cemetery." *New England Farmer* 10.5 (August 17, 1831): 38.

"Mount Auburn." *New England Magazine*, September 1831: 236–39.

"Mount Auburn's Monuments Inventoried." *Sweet Auburn,* Spring 1989.

"Mount Vernon." *New-England Galaxy* 6.276 (January 24, 1823): 1

Müllenbrock, Heinz-Joachim. "The 'Englishness' of the English Landscape Garden and the Genetic Role of Literature: A Reassessment." *Journal of Garden History* 8.4 (October–December 1988): 97–103.

Mulot, [Abbé] F[rançois]-V[alentin]. *Discours . . . sur cette question: Quelles sont les cérémonies à faire pour les funérailles et le reglement à adopter pour le lieu de la sépulture?* Paris, year IX [1801].

———. *Discours sur les funérailles et le respect du aux morts, lu le 15 thermidor, an IV au Lycée des Arts*. Paris, 1796.

———. *Vues d'un citoyen, ancien Deputé de Paris à l'Assemblé Législative sur les sépultures*. Paris, n.d. [1796?].

Muncey, Raymond Waterville Luke. *A History of the Consecrations of Churches and Churchyards*. Cambridge, England: W. Heffer & Sons, 1930.

Neem, Johann N. "Politics and the Origins of the Nonprofit Corporation in Massachusetts and New Hampshire, 1780–1820." *Nonprofit and Voluntary Sector Quarterly* 32:3 (2003): 344–65.

Newell, William. *A Discourse Occasioned by the Death of the Hon. Joseph*

Story, LL.D., Delivered in the Church of the First Parish in Cambridge, on Sunday, Sept. 14, 1845. Cambridge: Metcalf & Co. 1845.

New Haven. *Proceedings of the City of New Haven in the Removal of Monuments from Its Ancient Burying Grounds and in the Opening of a New Ground for Burial.* New Haven: Gray & Hewit, 1822.

Newmyer, R. Kent. *Supreme Court Justice Joseph Story.* Chapel Hill: University of North Carolina Press, 1985.

Newton, Isaac. *Mathematical Principles of Natural Philosophy.* Edited by Florian Cajori. Berkeley: University of California Press, 1934.

Nicher-Cérisy. *Des Tombeaux.* Paris, n.d. [ca. 1796].

Nylander, Jane C. "Some Print Sources of New England Schoolgirl Art." *Antiques* (August 1976): 292–301.

O'Connor, Thomas H. *Fitzpatrick's Boston, 1846–66: John Bernard Fitzpatrick, Third Bishop of Boston.* Boston: Northeastern University Press, 1984.

O'Gorman, James F. *Accomplished in All Departments of Art: Hammatt Billings of Boston, 1818–1874.* Amherst: University of Massachusetts Press, 1998.

O'Malley, Therese, and Joachim Wolschke-Bulmahn, eds., *John Evelyn's "Elysium Britannicum" and European Gardening.* Washington, D.C.: Dumbarton Oaks, 1998.

Olds, Kelly. "Privatizing the Church: Disestablishment in Connecticut and Massachusetts." *Journal of Political Economy* 102 (1994): 277–97.

Order of Services at the Consecration of Evergreen Cemetery. Boston: Tuttle & Dennett, 1850.

"An Ordinance to Regulate the Interment of the Dead." September 26, 1822. In Wetmore and Prescott, *The Charter and Ordinances of the City of Boston.*

"Ornamental Cemeteries." *Yale Literary Magazine* 21 (November 1855): 45–50.

"Ornamental Trees." *New England Farmer* 7.6 (August 29, 1838): 42.

Orne, Caroline F. *Sweet Auburn and Mount Auburn with Other Poems.* Cambridge: John Owen, 1844.

———. "A Midnight Adventure in Mount Auburn." *Mount Auburn Memorial* 2.19 (November 7, 1860): 151–52.

———. "Mount Auburn." *Mount Auburn Memorial* 1.29 (December 28, 1859): 228.

Osgood, Frances Sargent, ed. *Poetry of Flowers and Flowers of Poetry, to Which Are Added a Simple Treatise on Botany, with Familiar Examples, and a Copious Floral Dictionary.* Philadelphia: J. B. Lippincott, 1863.

Osgood, Samuel. "American Artists in Italy." *Harper's New Monthly Magazine* 41.243 (August 1870): 420–25.

———. "The Monument to Frances S. Osgood—A Reply to the Imputations of Fanny Fern." *New York Evening Post,* October 7, 1854.

Panofsky, Erwin. "*Et in Arcadia Ego*: Poussin and the Elegiac Tradition." In *Meaning in the Visual Arts.* Garden City, N.Y.: Doubleday, 1955.

"Paris from Père la Chaise: Recollections of a Solitary Traveller." In *The Atlantic Souvenir.* Philadelphia: H. C. Carey & I. Lea, 1826.

[Parker, Henry M]. *Notes on Mount Auburn, Edited by an Officer of the Corporation; Intended to Serve as a Stranger's Guide Book.* Boston: James Munroe, 1849.

Parreaux, André, and Michèle Plaisant, eds. *Jardins et paysages: Le style anglais.* Lille: PUL, 1977.

Parrington, Vernon Louis. *Main Currents in American Thought.* Vol. 2. *1800: The Romantic Revolution in America.* New York: Harcourt, Brace & World, 1927.

Pascalis, Felix. *An Exposition of the Dangers of Interment in Cities.* New York, 1823.

Pattee, Fred Lewis. *The First Century of American Literature, 1770–1870.* New York: D. Appleton-Century, 1935.

Paulson, Ronald. *Emblem and Expression: Meaning in English Art of the Eighteenth Century.* Cambridge: Harvard University Press; London: Thames & Hudson, 1975.

Peabody, William B. O. "Margaret." *North American Review* 62.130 (January 1846): 102–40.

Penny, Nicholas B. *Church Monuments in Romantic England.* New Haven: Yale University Press, 1977.

———. "The Commercial Garden Necropolis of the Early Nineteenth Century and Its Critics." *Garden History* 2 (Summer 1974): 61–76.

———. "The Macabre Garden at Denbies and Its Monuments." *Garden History* 3 (Summer 1975): 58–61.

Pernick, Martin S. "Politics, Parties, and Pestilence: Epidemic Yellow Fever in Philadelphia and the Rise of the First Party System." *William and Mary Quarterly* 29 (1972): 559–86.

Persons, Stow. *The Decline of American Gentility.* New York: Columbia University Press, 1973.

Pessen, Edward. *Riches, Class, and Power before the Civil War.* Lexington, Mass.: D. C. Heath, 1973.

Peterson, Roger T. "In Memoriam: Ludlow Griscom." *The Auk* 83 (October 1965): 598–605.

Pettigrew, T. J. *The Chronicles of Tombs.* Edinburgh: H. G. Bohn, 1859.

Pevsner, Nicholas. "The Genesis of the Picturesque." *Architectural Review* 96 (1944): 79–102.

Philips, Edith. *Louis Hué Girardin and Nicholas Gouin Dufief and Their Relations with Thomas Jefferson.* Baltimore: Johns Hopkins University Press, 1926.

The Picturesque Pocket Companion and Visitor's Guide through Mount Auburn. Boston: Otis, Broaders, 1839.

Pierpont, [Rev.] John. "The Garden of Graves." In *The Token: A Christmas and New Year's Present,* edited by S. G. Goodrich. Boston: S. G. Goodrich, 1932. Reprint, Dedham, Mass.: H. Mann, 1841.

———. "Ode Written for the Laying of the Corner Stone of the Bunker Hill Monument, June 17, 1825." In *Airs of Palestine and Other Poems.* Boston: James Munroe, 1840.

———. "To My Grave." In *Airs of Palestine and Other Poems.* Boston: James Munroe, 1840.

Pierson, George Wilson. *Tocqueville and Beaumont in America.* New York: Oxford University Press, 1938.

Pike, Martha V., and Janice G. Armstrong. *A Time to Mourn: Expressions of Grief in Nineteenth-Century America.* Stony Brook, N.Y.: The Museums at Stony Brook, 1980.

Planta, Edward. *A New Picture of Paris; or, The Strangers' Guide to the French Metropolis.* London: Samuel Leigh, 1819.

"Plants Grown." *New England Farmer* 11 (April 3, 1833): 299.

Pleasants, J. Hall. *Four Late Eighteenth-Century Anglo-American Landscape Painters.* Worcester, Mass.: American Antiquarian Society, 1943.

Poe, Edgar Allan. "The Domain of Arnheim." First published in *Columbian Magazine,* March 1847. Reprinted in *Edgar Allan Poe: Selected Prose, Poetry, and "Eureka,"* edited by W. H. Auden (New

York: Holt, Rinehart & Winston, 1950); *Edgar Allen Poe: Poetry and Tales*, edited by Patrick F. Quinn (New York: Library of America, 1984).

Pommereul, Général F[rançois]-R[éné]-J[ean] de. *Mémoire sur les funérailles et les sépultures, Question . . . jugée par l'Institut*. Paris: Onfroy; Tours: Billault, year IX [1801].

Ponte, Alessandra. *Le Paysage des origines: Le voyage en Sicile (1777) de Richard Payne Knight*. Translated by Janine Barrier and Danièle Berdou. Paris: Éditions de l'Imprimeur, 2000.

Pope, Alexander. *Alexander Pope's Epistles to Several Persons (Moral Essays)*. Edited by James E. Willington. Coral Gables: University of Miami Press, 1976.

Poulson, Erastus. "The Grave of Washington." In *Our Country; or, The American Parlor Keepsake*, edited by William H. Ryder. Boston: J. M. Usher, 1854.

Powell, E. P. "Harriet Martineau in New England." *New England Magazine* 21.3 (November 1896): 282–90.

Prescott, Edward G., ed. *The Charter and Ordinances of the City of Boston*. Boston: J. H. Eastburn, 1834.

Price, Sir Uvedale. *An Essay on the Picturesque, as Compared with the Sublime and the Beautiful; and, On the Use of Studying Pictures, for the Purpose of Improving Real Landscape*. 2 vols. London: J. Robson, 1794. Expanded eds. in 3 vols., 1796–98, 1801. Reprint, London: J. Mawman, 1810.

Prince, William. *A Short Treatise on Horticulture*. New York: T. & J. Swords, 1828.

Proceedings of the Association of Citizens to Erect a Monument in Honour of Gen. George Washington. Boston: Greenough & Stebbins, 1811.

Pugin, Augustus Charles, and C. Heath. *Paris and Its Environs Displayed in a Series of Picturesque Views*. 2 vols. London: Robert Jennings, 1829.

Pugin, Augustus Welby Northmore. *Contrasts*. London, 1836. Revised ed., 1841.

———. *The True Principles of Pointed or Christian Architecture*. London: H. G. Bohn, 1853.

Pugin, Augustus Welby, and Augustus Charles Pugin. *Examples of Gothic Architecture*. London: H. G. Bohn, 1850.

Pulszky, Francis, and Theresa Pulszky. *White, Red, Black: Sketches of Society in America*. Vol. 2. New York: 1853.

Purcell, Sarah J. "Commemoration, Public Art, and the Changing Meaning of the Bunker Hill Monument." *The Public Historian* (Spring 2003): 55–71.

Putnam, Mrs. C. H. "Letters from Home: Mount Auburn Cemetery." *Young Lady's and Gentlemen's Parlor Album* (New York, ca. 1843): 309–12.

Putnam, [Rev.] George. *An Address Delivered before the City Government and Citizens of Roxbury on the Life and Character of the Late Henry A. S. Dearborn, Mayor of the City, Sept. 3rd, 1851*. Roxbury: Norfolk County Journal Press, 1851.

Quaglia, Ferdinand. *Les cimetières de Paris: Recueil des plus rémarquables monuments funèbres avec leurs inscriptions*. Paris: Levy, n.d. [ca. 1820].

———. *Le Père la Chaise; ou, Recueil de dessins au trait, et dans leurs justes proportions, des principaux monuments de ce cimetière, dessinés et lithographiés par M. Quaglia*. Paris: Ph. Boudon, 1835.

Quatremère de Quincy, Antoine-Chrysostome. "Décoration." In *Encyclopédie Méthodique*. Vol. 2, pt. 1: 179. Paris, n.d.

———. *Essai sur la nature, le but et les moyens de l'imitation dans les beaux-arts*. Paris: L. Didot, 1823. Translated into English as *On the Nature, the End, and the Means of Imitation in the Fine Arts*. London: Smith, Elder, 1837.

———. *Rapport fait au Conseil-Général le 15 thermidor, an VIII, sur l'instruction publique, le rétablissement des Bourses, le scandale des inhumations actuelles, l'érection de cimetières, la restitution des tombeaux, mausolées, etc.* Paris, year VIII [1800].

Quincy, Edmund. *The Life of Josiah Quincy of Massachusetts*. Boston: Ticknor & Fields, 1868.

Quincy, Josiah. *An Address to the Board of Aldermen, Members of the Common Council of Boston, on the Organization of the City Government at Faneuil Hall, January 1, 1828*. Boston: Commercial Gazette Office, 1828.

———. *An Address to the Citizens of Boston on the XVIIth of Sept. MDCCCXXX. The Close of the Second Century from the First Settlement of the City*. Boston: J. H. Eastburn, 1830.

———. *The History of the Boston Athenaeum, with Biographical Notices of Its Deceased Founders*. Cambridge: Metcalf & Co., 1851.

———. *A Municipal History of the Town and City of Boston during Two Centuries*. Boston: Little, Brown, 1852.

———. "Speech on the Invasion of Canada." January 5, 1813. In *Speeches Delivered in the Congress of the United States, 1805–1813*. Boston: Little, Brown, 1874.

R. "Interment of the Dead." *Monthly Anthology* 5 (July 1808): 348.

Ragon, Michel. *The Space of Death: A Study in Funerary Architecture, Decoration, and Urbanism*. Translated by Alan Sheridan. Charlottesville: University of Virginia Press, 1983.

Randall, Charles E., and Henry Clepper. *Famous and Historic Trees*. Washington D.C.: American Forestry Association, 1976.

Randall, Henry S. *The Life of Thomas Jefferson*. Vol. 1. New York: Derby & Jackson, 1858.

Reed, Amy Louise. *The Background of Gray's Elegy: A Study in the Taste for Melancholy Poetry, 1700–1751*. New York: Russell & Russell, 1926.

Rees, Ronald. "The Scenery Cult: Changing Landscape Taste over Three Centuries." *Landscape* 19.3 (May 1975): 42.

"Remains of Dr. Spurzheim." *Boston Medical and Surgical Journal* 11 (November 21, 1832): 229.

Rémi, Abbé. *Les Jours, pour servir de correctif et de supplement aux Nuits de Young*. Paris, 1770.

Report of the Committee Appointed to Inquire into the Condition of the New-Haven Burying Ground and to Propose a Plan for Its Improvement. New York: B. L. Hamlen, 1839.

Reps, John W. "Cemeteries, Parks, and Suburbs: Picturesque Planning in the Romantic Style." In *The Making of Urban America: A History of City Planning in the United States*. Princeton: Princeton University Press, 1965.

Repton, Sir Humphry. *Fragments on the Theory and Practice of Landscape Gardening*. London: T. Bensley and Son for J. Taylor, 1826.

———. *Observations on the Theory and Practice of Landscape Gardening*. London: T. Bensley for J. Taylor at the Architectural Library, High Holborn,1803.

———. *Sketches and Hints on Landscape Gardening*. London: Shakespeare Printing Office,1795.

"Retirement of Superintendent Duncan W. Munro." *Sweet Auburn*, Winter 1990.

"Review of William Wordsworth." *North American Review* 9 (1824): 367.

Riat, Georges. *L'Art des jardins*. Paris: L.-H. May, n.d. [ca. 1810].

Richard et ***. *Le Véritable conducteur aux cimetières du Père La Chaise, Montmartre, Montparnasse et Vaugirard, ou guide le plus complet, le plus nouveau et le plus exact, de l'étranger, du curieux et du promeneur dans ces cimetières*. Paris: Chez Roy-Terry, 1830.

Richardson, Robert D., Jr. *Emerson: The Mind on Fire*. Berkeley: University of California Press, 1995.

The Rise and Progress of the Present Taste in Planting Parks, Pleasure Grounds, Gardens, etc . . . in a Poetic Epistle to the Right Honourable Charles Lord Viscount Irwin. London: For C. Moran, 1767.

Robinson, G. G. J. and J. *A Companion to the Leasowes, Hagley, and Enville*. London: M. Swinney; Birmingham: J. Holl, 1789.

Robinson, John M. *Temples of Delight: Stowe Landscape Gardens*. London: The National Trust, 1990.

Roederer, [Pierre-Louis]. *Des Institutions funéraires convenable à une république qui permet tous les cultes et n'en adopte aucun*. Paris: Mathey & Desenne, year II [1793].

Roger-Marx, Claude. "Esthetique des cimetières." *Art sacré* (Paris: November–December, 1949): 3–5.

Rogers, Millard F., Jr. *Randolph Rogers: American Sculptor in Rome*. Amherst: University of Massachusetts Press, 1971.

Rohdenberg, Edward III. "Bracketting Mount Auburn." *Sweet Auburn*, Summer 1998.

———. "Henry Dexter: Mount Auburn Sculptor." *Sweet Auburn*, Fall–Winter, 1994.

Ronesse, A.-J. *Projet pour les sépultures*. Paris, year IX [1801].

Rosenberg, Jean L. "The Vistas of Mount Auburn." *Sweet Auburn*, Fall–Winter, 1987.

Rossback, Sarah. *Feng Shui: The Chinese Art of Placement*. New York: E. P. Dutton, 1983.

Rothman, David J. *The Discovery of the Asylum: Social Order and Disorder in the New Republic*. Boston: Little, Brown, 1971.

Rotundo, Barbara. "Mount Auburn Cemetery: A Proper Boston Institution." *Harvard Library Bulletin* 22.3 (July 1974): 268–79.

———. "Mount Auburn: Fortunate Coincidences and an Ideal Solution." *Journal of Garden History* 4.3 (1984): 255–67.

———. "Review: *Silent City on a Hill*." *Journal of the Society of Architectural Historians* (June 1991): 218–19.

Rousseau, Jean-Jacques. *Les Rêveries du promeneur solitaire*. Paris: Garnier, 1960.

"Rural Cemeteries." *North American Review* 53.113 (October 1841): 385–412.

Russell, Foster William. *Mount Auburn Biographies: A Biographical Listing of Distinguished Persons Interred in Mount Auburn Cemetery*. Cambridge: By the Corporation, 1953.

Russell, Howard S. *A Long, Deep Furrow: Three Centuries of Farming in New England*. Hanover, N.H.: University Press of New England, 1976.

Sacy, Jacques-Silvestre de. *Alexandre-Théodore Brongniart, 1739–1813: Sa vie, son oeuvre*. Paris: Librairie Plon, 1940.

Safford, T[ruman] H., and De F[orrest] Safford, eds. *Mount Auburn Memorial*. 2 vols. Cambridgeport, Mass.: January 15, 1859–March 27, 1861.

Sagra, D. Ramon de la. *Cinco meses en los Estados-Unidos de la America del Norte desde el 20 de abril al 23 de setiembre de 1835*. Paris: Pablo Renouard, 1836.

"St. Paul's Church." *Boston Intelligencer and Evening Gazette* 6 (October 23, 1819).

"Sarcophagus to the Memory of Thomas Wigglesworth, Esq., Mount Auburn." *Mount Auburn Memorial* 1.8 (August 3, 1859): 61.

Sargent, L[ucius] M. *Dealings with the Dead, By a Sexton of the Old School*. 2 vols. Boston: Dutton & Wentworth, 1856.

Savage, Edward H., comp. *Boston Events: A Brief Mention and the Date of More Than 5000 Events That Transpired in Boston from 1630 to 1880*. Boston: Tolman & White, 1884.

Schlesinger, Arthur, Jr. *The Age of Jackson*. Boston: Little, Brown, 1945.

Schorsch, Anita. "A Key to the Kingdom: The Iconography of the Mourning Picture." *Winterthur Portfolio* 16 (Spring 1979): 41–71.

———. *Mourning Becomes America: Mourning Art in the New Nation*. Exhibition catalogue. Clinton, N.J.: Main Street Press, 1975.

Scorgie, James C. "The Control of Stonework in Cemeteries." *American Association of Cemetery Superintendents* 38 (1920): 54–56.

———. "Perpetual Care of Monuments and Mausoleums." *American Association of Cemetery Superintendents* 34 (1916): 27.

Scott, Frank J[essup]. *The Art of Beautifying Suburban Home Grounds of Small Extent*. New York: Appleton, 1870.

Scott, Sir Walter. *The Letters of Sir Walter Scott*. Edited by Sir H[erbert] J[ohn] C[lifford] Grierson. 12 vols. London: Constable, 1932–37.

Scully, Vincent. *The Earth, the Temple, and the Gods: Greek Sacred Architecture*. New York: Praeger, 1969.

[Seeley, Benton]. *Description of the Magnificent House and Gardens of the Right Honourable Richard Grenville Temple, Earl Temple, Viscount and Baron Cobham at Stowe in Buckinghamshire*. London: B. Seeley, 1744. 3rd ed. Northampton: W. Dicey, 1746.

"Sépultures." *Annales philosophiques, morales et littéraires, ou suite des Annales catholiques*. Vol. 1. Paris: Le Clère, 1800.

Shaftesbury, Anthony, Earl of. *Characteristics of Men, Manners, Opinions, Times, With a Collection of Letters*. 3 vols. Basel, 1790. Reprint, edited by John M. Roberston (2 vols.), Gloucester, Mass. 1963.

Shand-Tucci, Douglass. *Built in Boston: City and Suburb, 1800–1950*. Boston: New York Graphic Society, 1978.

Shapiro, Henry D. "Putting the Past under Glass: Preservation and the Idea of History in the Mid-Nineteenth Century." *Prospects: Annual of American Cultural Studies* 10 (1985): 243–78.

Sharf, Frederic A. "The Garden Cemetery and American Sculpture: Mount Auburn." *Art Quarterly* 34 (Spring 1961): 80–88.

Shenstone, William. *The Letters of William Shenstone*. Edited by Marjorie Williams. Oxford: Basil Blackwell, 1939.

———. *The Works in Verse and Prose of William Shenstone, Esq*. 2nd ed. 2 vols. London: J. Dodsley, 1765–66.

Shively, Charles Allen. "A History of the Conception of Death in America, 1650–1860." Ph.D. diss., Harvard University, 1968.

Shurtleff, Nathaniel B. *A Topographical and Historical Description of Boston*. Boston: Rockwell & Churchill, 1891.

Sickels, Eleanor M. *The Gloomy Egoist: Moods and Themes of Melancholy from Gray to Keats*. New York: Octagon, 1969.

Siren, Osvald. *China and Gardens of Europe of the Eighteenth Century*. New York: Ronald Press, 1949. Rev. ed., Washington, D.C.: Dumbarton Oaks, 1990.

Sizer, Theodore, ed. *The Autobiography of Colonel John Trumbull, Patriot-Artist, 1756–1843*. New Haven: Yale University Press, 1953.

"Skating." *Mount Auburn Memorial* 1.25 (November 30, 1859): 197.

"Sketch of the Life of Judge Story." *Mount Auburn Memorial* 1.1 (August 24, 1859): 81.

Skinner, Aaron N. *History of the City Burial Ground of New Haven, to-*

gether with the Names of the Owners of the Lots Therein. New Haven: N. Green & J. S. Benham, 1863.
Slater, Peter Gregg. *Children in the New England Mind in Death and in Life*. Hamden, Conn.: Archon, 1977.
Sloane, David Charles. *The Last Great Necessity: Cemeteries in American History*. Baltimore: Johns Hopkins University Press, 1991.
Smith, Bradford. *Bradford of Plymouth*. Philadelphia: J. B. Lippincott, 1951.
Smith, John Jay. "Rural Cemeteries." *Horticulturist* 10 (August 1856): 345–56.
Snow, Caleb H. *A History of Boston: The Metropolis of Massachusetts*. Boston: Abel Bowen, 1825.
Spence, Joseph. *Anecdotes, Observations, and Characters of Books and Men, Collected from Conversation of Mr. Pope and Other Eminent Persons of His Time*. London, 1820. Reprint, edited by James M. Osborn (2 vols.), Oxford: Clarendon Press, 1966.
Sponde, [Bishop] Henri de. *Les cimetières sacrez*. Bordeaux, 1598.
Squam Poet. "Inscribed to S.C." *New-England Galaxy* 6.275 (January 17, 1823): 3.
Stannard, David E. "Death and Dying in Puritan New England." *American Historical Review* 78 (1973): 1305–30.
———. *The Puritan Way of Death: A Study in Religion, Culture, and Social Change*. New York: Oxford University Press, 1977.
[Stevens, Levi Merriam]. *Guide through Mount Auburn: A Handbook for Passengers over the Cambridge Railroad*. Boston: Bricher & Russell, 1860.
———. *A Handbook for Passengers over the Cambridge Railroad with a Description of Mount Auburn Cemetery*. Boston: William V. Spencer, 1858.
Stone, Lawrence. "Death and Its History" *New York Review of Books* 25.15 (October 12, 1978): 22.
———. "Death in New England." *New York Review of Books* 25.16 (October 26, 1978).
———. *The Family, Sex, and Marriage in England, 1500–1800*. New York: Harper & Row, 1977.
Story, Joseph. "An Address Delivered on the Dedication of the Cemetery at Mount Auburn, September 23, 1831, by Joseph Story, To Which Is Added an Appendix Containing Historical Notice and Description of the Place with a List of the Present Subscribers, and a Map of the Grounds." *New-England Magazine* 1.6 (December 1831): 539–41. Reprinted as "Judge Story's Address" in *The Picturesque Pocket Companion and Visitor's Guide through Mount Auburn* (Boston: Otis, Broaders, 1839). Reprinted in Jacob Bigelow, *A History of the Cemetery of Mount Auburn* (Boston and Cambridge: James Munroe, 1860).
———. *Commentaries on the Constitution of the United States; with a Preliminary Review of the Constitutional History of the Colonies and States, before the Adoption of the Constitution, Abridged by the Author for the Use of Colleges and High Schools*. Boston: Hilliard, Gray & Co. and Cambridge: Brown, Shattuck & Co., 1833. Reprint, edited by Thomas M. Cooley, Durham N.C.: Carolina Academic Press, 1995.
———. *A Discourse Pronounced at the Funeral Obsequies of John Hooker Ashmun, Esq., Royall Professor of Law at Harvard University, before the President, Fellows, and Faculty in the Chapel of the University*. Cambridge: Brown, Shattuck & Co., 1833.
———. *A Familiar Exposition of the Constitution of the United States*. 1840. Reprint, Lake Bluff, Ill.: Regnery Gateway Bicentennial Editions, 1986.
———. "Lines Written on the Death of a Daughter in May, 1831." In *Miscellaneous Writings, Literary, Critical, Juridical, and Political*. Boston: James Munroe, 1835.
Story, Ronald. *The Forging of an Aristocracy: Harvard and the Boston Upper Class, 1800–1870*. Middletown, Conn.: Wesleyan University Press, 1980.
Story, William W[etmore], ed. *Life and Letters of Joseph Story, Associate Justice of the Supreme Court of the United States, and Dane Professor of Law at Harvard University*. 2 vols. Boston: Little, Brown, 1851.
"Stowe: *Temple Quam Dilecta*: How Beautiful Are Thy Temples." http://www.stoweschool.org/history/gardens_park/index.html.
Strang, John. *Necropolis Glasguensis with Observations on Ancient and Modern Tombs and Sculpture*. Glasgow: Atkinson & Co., 1831.
[Strauch, Adolph]. "Monuments." From *The Report of Spring Grove Cemetery for 1857. Mount Auburn Memorial* 1.28 (December 21, 1859): 218.
———. *Spring Grove Cemetery: Its History and Improvements*. Cincinnati: Robert Clarke, 1869.
Strickland, William. *Tomb of Washington at Mount Vernon*. Philadelphia: Carey & Hart, 1840.
"Strictures on Mount Auburn." *Boston Evening Transcript*, August 17, 1839: 2.
Strong, George Templeton. *Diary*. Vol. 1. Edited by Allan Nevins and Milton Halsey Thomas. New York: Macmillan, 1952.
Struik, Dirk. *Yankee Science in the Making*. Boston: Little, Brown, 1948.
"Sweet Auburn." *Mount Auburn Memorial* 1.2 (June 22, 1859): 12.
Swett, S[amuel]. *Original Planning and Construction of the Bunker Hill Monument*. Albany: J. Munsell, 1863.
Switzer, Stephen. *Ichnographia Rustica; or, The Nobleman, Gentleman, and Gardener's Recreation*. London: D. Brown et al., 1718.
"Sylvester Judd." In *The Cyclopedia of American Literature: Embracing Personal and Critical Notices of Authors*, edited by Evert A. Duyckinck and George L. Duyckinck. New York: Charles Scribner, 1856.
Symes, Michael. "Nature as the Bride of Art: The Design and Structure of Painshill." *Eighteenth-Century Life* 8, n.s. 2 (January 1983): 63–73.
Tait, A. A. *The Landscape Garden in Scotland, 1735–1835*. Edinburgh: Edinburgh University Press, 1980.
Tashjian, Dickran. "Puritan Attitudes toward Iconoclasm." In *Puritan Gravestone Art II: Annual Proceedings of the Dublin Seminar for New England Folklife*. Boston: Boston University, 1978.
Tatter, John D. "Buildings and Monuments: Stowe Landscape Gardens." Birmingham-Southern College. http://panther.bsc.edu/~jtatter/stowe.html.
Tatum, George Bishop. *Andrew Jackson Downing: Arbiter of American Taste, 1815–52*. Ann Arbor: University Microfilms, 1950.
———. "The Beautiful and the Picturesque." *American Quarterly* 3 (1951): 36–51.
———. "The Emergence of an American School of Landscape Design." *Historic Preservation* 25 (April–June 1973).
Taylor, Patricia. *Thomas Blaikie (1751–1838): The Capability Brown of France*. N.p.: Tuckwell Press, 2000.
Taylor, William R. *Cavalier and Yankee: The Old South and American National Character*. Cambridge: Harvard University Press, 1979.
Thacher, Joseph Stevens Buckminster. "Address at the Commencement . . . 1832." In "Exhibition and Commencement Performances." 1831–32. Houghton Library, Harvard University.

"Thomas Dowse." *Lowell Citizen*, December 6, 1856. Reprinted in *The Living Age* 52.662 (January 31, 1857): 320.

T. T. W. "Botanical History of the Yew Tree." *Gentleman's Magazine* 56, pt. 2, no. 5 (November 1786): 941.

Thomson, James. *The Seasons*. First American edition. Newburyport, Mass.: John Mycall, 1790.

Thoreau, Henry David. *Walden*. 1854. Reprint, New York: Thomas Y. Crowell, 1961; New York: Harper & Row, 1966.

Thornton, Tamara Plakins. *Cultivating Gentlemen: The Meaning of Country Life among the Boston Elite, 1785–1860*. New Haven: Yale University Press, 1989.

"Thoughts Connected with Rural Cemeteries." *Christian Review* 13 (March 1848): 22.

Thouret, Michel August. *Rapport sur les exhumations du cimetière de l'église des Saints Innocent: lu dans la séance de la Société Royale de Médicine tenue au Louvre le 3 mars 1789*. Paris: Ph.-Denys Pierres, 1789.

Tocqueville, Alexis de. *Democracy in America*. Edited by Phillips Bradley. 2 vols. New York: Knopf, 1951.

"The Tomb of Spurzheim at Mount Auburn." *Family Magazine* (1853): 404.

"Tombs under Saint Paul's." *New-England Galaxy* 6.273 (January 3, 1823): 2.

Tournebize, Cassilde. *Jardins et paysages en Grande-Bretagne au XVI-IIe siècle*. Paris: Éditions du Temps, 2000.

Townshend, Henry Hotchkiss. *The Grove Street Cemetery*. New Haven: The Society, 1848.

Transaction of the Massachusetts Horticultural Society, 1829–1838. Boston: William D. Ticknor, 1847. Massachusetts Horticultural Society, Boston.

Trollope, Mrs. Frances. "Letter 22: Père Lachaise." In *Paris and the Parisians in 1835*. New York: Harper & Brothers, 1836.

Tuckerman, Henry. "The Law of Burial and the Sentiment of Death." *Christian Examiner* 26 (1836): 338.

Tudor, Henry. *Narrative of a Tour in North America*. London: James Duncan, 1834.

[Tudor, William]. "Instruction for the Fine Arts." *North American Review* 2 (January 1816): 161.

———. *Letters on the Eastern States*. New York: Kirk & Mercein, 1820.

———. "Monument to Washington." *North American Review* 2.6 (1816): 329–40.

———. "On Certain Funeral Ceremonies." In *Letters on the Eastern States*. New York: Kirk & Mercein, 1820.

Tyack, David B. *George Ticknor and the Boston Brahmins*. Cambridge: Harvard University Press, 1967.

Tymeson, Mildred McClary. *Rural Retrospect: A Parallel History of Worcester and Its Rural Cemetery*. Worcester, Mass.: Albert Rice, 1956.

Vafflard, Léon. *Notice sur les champs de sépultures anciens et modernes de la ville de Paris*. Paris: Charles de Mougues Frères, 1867.

Van Laar, G. *Magazijn van Tuin-Sieraden; of Verzameling van Modellen van Aanleg en Sieraad, voor Groote en Kleine Lust-Hoven, Voornamelijk van Dezulke die, met Weinig Kosten, Te Maaken Zijn*. Rotterdam: Johannes Noman en Zoon, 1802.

Van Tassel, David D. *Recording America's Past: An Interpretation of the Development of Historical Studies in America, 1607–1884*. Chicago: University of Chicago Press, 1960.

"The Vaults of St. Michan's." *New-England Galaxy* 6.275 (January 17, 1823).

Very, Jones. *Essays and Poems*. Boston: C. C. Little & James Brown, 1838.

Vicq-d'Azyr, Félix. *Essai sur les lieux et les dangers de sépultures*. Paris, 1778.

Vidler, Alec R. *The Church in the Age of Revolution: 1789 to the Present Day*. New York: Penguin, 1977.

Vidler, Anthony. *The Writing on the Walls: Architectural Theory in the Late Enlightenment*. Princeton: Princeton Architectural Press, 1987.

Viellard, P. S. "Fouché." In *Nouvelle Biographie Générale*, edited by Ferdinand Hoefer. Paris: Firmin Didot Frères, 1870.

Viennet. *Promenade philosophique au cimetière du Père-Lachaise*. Paris: Librairies Ponthieu, 1824.

Vinovskis, Maris A. "Angels' Heads and Weeping Willows: Death in Early America." *Proceedings of the American Antiquarian Society* 86 (1976): 273–302.

Volney, Constantin-François de Chasseboeuf, Comte de. *Les Ruines, ou Méditations sur les révolutions des empires*. 1791. Translated into English as *Ruins; or, A Survey of the Revolution of Empires*. Albany: S. Shaw, 1822.

Voltaire, François Marie Arouet de. "La Considération due aux gens de lettres." In *Lettres Philosophiques*, vol. 12. Paris: Garnier Frères, 1878.

———. "Enterrement." In *Oeuvres complètes: Dictionnaire philosophique portatif, ou la raison par alphabet*. Vol. 2. Paris: Garnier Frères, 1878.

Voss, Frederick S. *John Frazee, 1790–1852: Sculptor*. Washington, D.C.: Smithsonian; and Boston: Athenaeum, 1986.

Vovelle, Michel. *La Mort et l'Occident de 1300 à nos jours*. Paris: Gallimard & Panthéon, 1983.

Walker, G. A. *Gatherings from Grave-yards: Particularly Those of London, with a Concise History of the Modes of Interment among Different Nations from the Earliest Periods*. London: Longman, 1839.

Walker, Samuel. "Horticultural Societies." *The Horticulturist and Journal of Rural Art and Rural Taste* 6.2 (February 1851): 92.

[Walker, Stephen Duncan]. *Rural Cemetery and Public Walk*. Baltimore: Sands & Neilson, 1835.

Walpole, Horace. *Essay on Modern Gardening*. Strawberry Hill, England: By the Author, 1780. *Essai sur l'art des jardins modernes*. Translated by M. le Duc de Nivernois. Strawberry Hill, England: T. Kirgate, 1785. Reprinted as *History of the Modern Taste in Gardening*, edited by John Dixon Hunt. New York: Ursus Press, 1995.

———. *Letters of Horace Walpole, Fourth Earl of Orford*. Edited by Mrs. P. Toynbee. 19 vols. Oxford: Oxford University Press, 1903–1925.

———. *The History of the Modern Taste in Gardening*. Strawberry Hill, England: [by the author], 1780.

———. "On Modern Gardening." In *Anecdotes of Painting in England*. Vol. 4. Strawberry Hill, England: [by the author], 1771: 117–51.

Walter, Cornelia W. *Mount Auburn Illustrated in a Series of Views from Drawings Taken on the Spot . . . with Descriptive Notices*. New York: R. Martin, 1847.

Ward, Malthus. *An Address Pronounced before the Massachusetts Horticultural Society in Commemoration of Its Third Annual Festival, Sept. 21, 1831*. Boston: J. T. & E. Buckingham, 1831.

Ware, William. "Unitarian Belief." *Unitarian* 1 (November 1827): 17–22.

Warren, Edward. *The Life of John Collins Warren*. Boston: Ticknor & Fields, 1860.

Warren, F. E. *The Liturgy and Ritual of the Celtic Church*. Oxford: Clarendon Press, 1883.

Warren, George Washington. *The History of the Bunker Hill Monument Association*. Boston: James R. Osgood, 1877.

Warren, John. *An Oration, Delivered July 4, 1783, at the Request of the Inhabitants of Boston in Celebration of the Anniversary of American Independence*. Boston: John Gill, 1783.

Warren, John C[ollins]. "Bunker Hill Monument Association." *Boston News-Letter and City Record*, July 15, 1826: 13–15.

Warton, Thomas, the Younger. *The Pleasures of Melancholy*. London: R. Dodsley, 1747.

Watelet, Claude-Henri. *Essai sur les jardins*. Paris: Chez Perault, 1764.

Watkin, David. *The English Vision: The Picturesque in Architecture, Landscape, and Garden Design*. London, 1982.

Watts, Isaac. "The Church-Yard." In *Reliquiae Iuveniles: Miscellaneous Thoughts in Prose and Verse, on Natural, Moral, and Divine Subjects*. London: James Brackstone, 1742.

Webb's Collection of Epitaphs. London, 1775.

Webster, Daniel. *An Address Delivered at the Laying of the Cornerstone of the Bunker Hill Monument*. Boston: Cummings & Hilliard, 1825.

———. *The Writings and Speeches of Daniel Webster in 18 Volumes*. Vol. 1. *Memoir and Speeches of Various Occasions*. Boston: Little, Brown, 1903.

"The Weeping Willow." *New England Farmer* 5.43 (May 18, 1827): 338.

Welter, Rush. *The Mind of America: 1820–60*. New York: Columbia University Press, 1975.

Wetmore, Thomas, and Edward G. Prescott, eds. *The Charter and Ordinances of the City of Boston together with the Acts of the Legislature Relating to the City*. Boston: J. H. Eastburn, 1834.

Whately, Thomas. *Observations on Modern Gardening: Illustrated by Descriptions*. Dublin: John Exshaw, 1770. Reprint, London: Garland, 1982.

Wheaton, Henry. "Egyptian Antiquities." *North American Review* 30.65 (October 1829): 361–88.

Whistler, Laurence, Michael Gibbon, and George Clarke. *Stowe: A Guide to the Gardens*. 3rd ed. London: E. N. Hillier & Sons. 1974.

Whitehill, Walter Muir. *A Topographical History of Boston*. Rev. ed. Cambridge: Belknap Press of Harvard University Press, 1968.

Whitmore, William H. *The Graveyards of Boston*. Vol. 1. *Copp's Hill Epitaphs*. Albany, N.Y.: Joel Munsell, 1878.

Whitney, Rev. Peter. *Weeping and Mourning at the Death of Eminent Persons a National Duty: A Sermon Delivered at Northborough, Feb. 22, 1800, Observed as a Day a National Mourning on Account of the Death of General George Washington*. Brookfield, Mass.: E. Merriam, 1800.

Whittemore, Thomas, ed. *The Life of Rev. Hosea Ballou; with Accounts of His Writings*. 3 vols. Boston: James M. Usher, 1855.

Wiebenson, Dora. *The Picturesque Garden in France*. Princeton: Princeton University Press, 1978.

Wilkes, Charles. *Narrative of the U.S. Exploring Expedition during the Years 1838, 1839, 1840, 1841, 1842*. Vol. 2. Philadelphia: Lea & Blanchard, 1848.

Willard, Samuel. "The High Esteem Which God Hath of the Death of His Saints." 1685. In *The Puritans: A Sourcebook of Their Writings*, edited by Perry Miller and Thomas E. Johnson. New York: Harper & Row, 1963.

Willey, Basil. *The Eighteenth-Century Background: Studies on the Idea of Nature in the Thought of the Period*. London: Chatto & Windus, 1949.

Willis, Peter. *Charles Bridgeman and the English Landscape Garden*. London: A. Zwemmer, 1977.

Willis, Sarah Payson. "Incident at Mount Auburn." In *Fern Leaves from Fanny's Port-Folio*. Auburn. N.Y.: Derby & Miller, 1853. Ser. 2., Auburn, N.Y.: Miller, Orton & Mulligan, 1854.

———. "Letter from Fanny Fern—Mrs. Osgood's Monument." *New York Evening Post*, October 20, 1854.

Wills, Garry. *Lincoln at Gettysburg: The Words That Remade America*. New York: Simon & Schuster, 1992.

Willsher, Betty, and Doreen Hunter. *Stones: A Guide to Some Remarkable Eighteenth-Century Scottish Gravestones*. New York: Taplinger, 1979.

[Wines, Enoch Cobb]. A Philadelphian. *A Trip to Boston in a Series of Letters to the Editor of the "United States Gazette."* Boston: Little, Brown, 1838.

Winsor, Justin, ed. *The Memorial History of Boston, Including Suffolk County, Massachusetts, 1639–1880*. Vol. 4. Boston: James R. Osgood, 1881.

Winthrop, John. "A Modell of Christian Charity." In *The Puritans: A Sourcebook of Their Writings*, edited by Perry Miller and Thomas H. Johnson. Rev. ed. Vol. 1. New York: Harper & Row, 1963.

Wood, Gordon S. *The Creation of the American Republic, 1776–1787*. Chapel Hill: University of North Carolina Press, 1969.

Woodbridge, Kenneth. *Landscape and Antiquity: Aspects of English Culture at Stourhead, 1718–1838*. Oxford: Clarendon, 1970.

———. *The Stourhead Landscape*. London: National Trust, 1982.

Wooley, M. E. "The Development of the Love of Romantic Scenery in America." *American Historical Review* 3 (October 1897): 56–66.

Woolsey, T. D. "Cemeteries and Monuments." *New Englander* 28 (November 1849): 489–501.

Wordsworth, William. "Essay upon Epitaphs." *Friend* 25 (February 1810): 408. Reprinted in *The Excursion: A Poem*. New York: C. S. Francis, 1850.

———. *The Prelude; or, Growth of a Poet's Mind: An Autobiographical Poem*. Book 11 [ca. February 1804]. New York: Appleton, 1850.

Wortley, Lady Emmeline. *Travel in the United States . . . during 1849–50*. New York: Harper Brothers, 1851.

Wright, C. Conrad. *The Beginnings of Unitarianism in America*. Boston: Beacon Press, 1955.

Wrighte, William. *Grotesque Architecture; or, Rural Architecture, Consisting of Plans, Elevations, and Sections for Huts, Retreats, Summer and Winter Hermitages, Terminaries, Chinese, Gothic, and Natural Grottos, Cascades, Baths, Mosques, Moresque Pavilions, Grotesque and Rustic Seats, Green Houses, Etc., Many of Which May Be Executed with Flints, Irregular Stones, Rude Branches, and Roots of Trees*. London: Henry Webley, 1767.

Young, Rev. Alexander. *A Discourse on the Life and Character of the Hon. Nathaniel Bowditch, LL.D, F.R.S., Delivered in the Church on Church Green, Mar. 25, 1838*. Boston: Little, Brown, 1838.

Young, Arthur. *A Six Months' Tour through the North of England, Con-*

taining an Account of the Present State of Agriculture, Manufactures and Population, in Several Counties of This Kingdom. 2nd ed. 4 vols. London: W. Strahan, 1771.

Young, Edward. *The Complaint; or Night Thoughts*. London. 1742–45. Reprinted in *Night Thoughts on Life, Death, and Immortality*, vol. 1. Philadelphia: Benjamin Johnson, 1805.

Zanger, Jules. "Mount Auburn Cemetery: The Silent Suburb." *Landscape* 24.2 (1980): 23–28.

Zillah. "Mount Auburn." *Lowell Offering* 1.1 (1840): 13–14.

ACKNOWLEDGMENTS

The evolution of this revised edition goes back to 1977, my second year in the doctoral History of American Civilization Program at Harvard. It drew upon the foundation set under mentors Henry D. Shapiro and Zane Miller at the University of Cincinnati where I earned my masters in history in 1976. Daniel Aaron, chair of my Harvard doctoral program, then encouraged me to tackle the subject of the history of landscapes of death reinterpreted in America from English and French precedents precisely because it was so complex and interdisciplinary, involving issues of philosophy, shifting tastes, and *mentalités* expressed in literature, landscapes, art, and architecture as well as problems of urban growth including public health. Saul Benison with whom I had studied in history of medicine at Cincinnati referred me to Richard Wolfe and others at Harvard's Countway History of Medicine archives who aided my research. Albert Fein, then a visiting professor at the Harvard Graduate School of Design and a pioneering Olmsted scholar, helped me refine a paper from his seminar that became the chapter on French precedents.

When I went to the Mount Auburn offices in the fall of 1977, President Alan Chesney and Superintendent Duncan Munro seemed befuddled about why a Harvard graduate student would want to do research in their chaotic records, then only organized in terms of early bound manuscript trustees' minutes and annual reports; but they welcomingly gave me free reign. Correspondence and visuals then had to be ferreted out from cardboard and tin boxes in what was then the Administration Building basement. Research grants in 1978 and 1979 from the Radcliffe Institute for Advanced Study supported travel for research at other "rural" cemeteries, archives, and libraries in New York, Philadelphia, Baltimore, Cincinnati, and Louisville.

That initially resulted in my 1981 doctoral dissertation, "Death and the Garden: The Cult of the Melancholy and the 'Rural' Cemetery," and then my 1989 Ohio State University Press book, *Silent City on a Hill: Landscapes of Memory and Boston's Mount Auburn Cemetery*, in the Urban Life and Urban Landscape Series edited by Miller and Shapiro. Thanks are due to historian Sam Bass Warner, Jr., for his close reading of that manuscript and his insistence on use of many illustrations as documents. Mount Auburn's book committee of trustees Gordon Abbott, Frank Hatch, and James Storey supported the project at that stage. The Hubbard Educational Trust provided a grant that helped produce and acquire illustrations. The American Society of Landscape Architects bestowed a 1990 merit award on the book that also won a Historic Preservation Book award.

I repeat acknowledgments from that first edition for the assistance of Barbara Puorro Galasso of the George Eastman House International Museum of Photography;

Ellie Reichlin and Lorna Condon at the Archives of the Society for the Preservation of New England Antiquities (now Historic New England); Mary Grenci, Roberta Zonghi, Eugene Zepp, and Dr. Laura V. Monti in the Rare Books Room of the Boston Public Library; Georgia Barnhill at the American Antiquarian Society, Worcester; and Walter Punch of the Massachusetts Horticultural Society. Other critical readers of parts of the manuscript at that stage included Saul Benison, Albert Fein, Barbara Rosenkrantz, Jack Salzman, Howard Segal, Anne Whiston Spirn, and Morris Vogel.

Since the first edition of *Silent City*, my research, publications, lectures, and consulting on historic preservation and public interpretation of "rural" or "garden" cemeteries have continued to expand. Over the next several years, Roger Kindred, Philip Sands, Robert Keller, Newell "Penny" Penniman, and so many others offered hospitality, conviviality, and help at Mount Auburn. Munro took me for an 1983 interview with Herbert Philpott, his predecessor. Some of their insights about twentieth-century developments will appear in this revised book while others await yet another volume.

Miller and Shapiro at University of Cincinnati organized a series of grant-funded public history projects I pursued on Spring Grove Cemetery in 1985 and 1987, with funding from the Joint Program of the Ohio Humanities and Arts Councils for Human Values in the Built Environment. That grew into my book for Spring Grove's 1995 sesquicentennial published by the Cincinnati Historical Society.

More research on picturesque landscapes in France included examples not discussed in the first edition. In 1990, Olivier Choppin de Janvry graciously gave me a personal tour of the Désert de Retz, not open to the public, and gave me information about the preservation efforts there. In 1991 Jean-Jacques Faugeron showed me the tomb of Lafayette in the Paris Cimetière de Picpus, also closed to the public, and supplied me with related publications.

Working as a historical consultant with Elizabeth Vizza of the Craig Halvorson firm of landscape architects of Boston on the 1993 Master Plan for Mount Auburn's historic preservation helped me to clarify and expand my thinking further as did the opportunity Gary Hildebrand, then Chair of the Department of Landscape Architecture in Harvard's Graduate School of Design, gave me in 1994 to teach an expanded version of this book's contents in my seminar "Nature and the City: Nineteenth-Century Urbanism and Landscape Design." Liz Vizza, now in her own landscape preservation practice, continues to offer her valuable insights and friendship as I have been reworking this book. Invaluable in all she knows, she is one of the few dear friends with whom I can discussed minute historic details and broader concepts.

The process of revising and expanding *Silent City* has been greatly aided by Mount Auburn President William Clendaniel since 1988. Janet Heywood, Vice President of Interpretative Programs, my friend since she jointed the Mount Auburn staff in 1988, was daily there for me with her encyclopedic knowledge of the Cemetery and all therein since I began this revision in 2004 to answer the most minute queries and to provide her meticulous reading of manuscript drafts until her retirement in May of 2006. Margaret "Meg" Winslow, now Mount Auburn's Curator of Historical Collections, has been able to respond promptly to any questions, however minute, and to provide quality scans of illustrations from the Archives she has expanded and professionalized. I feel great affection for all at Mount Auburn for their common purpose, expertise, and camaraderie. Now, given the constant, collegial help I have received from Linda Fisher, Jennifer Johnston, and so many others on the staff, the Friends of Mount Auburn Cemetery has far more personal meaning for me than the name of the non-profit corporation supporting the historic institution and its mission. It has been a joy to work with everyone there today.

For this edition, special help came from Nancy Burkett and Jaclyn Donovan of the American Antiquarian Society; Leone Cole of the Watertown Free Public Library; Jack Eckert, Reference Librarian in the Center for the History of Medicine of the Francis A. Countway Library of Medicine; Barbara Puorro Galasso of the George Eastman House; Maureen Horn, Librarian of the Massachusetts Horticultural Society; Jeffrey Mifflin of the Massachusetts General Hospital Archives and Special Collections; Nathan Pendlebury of the Walker Art Gallery of the National Museums of Liverpool; and Nancy L. Swallow of the Corcoran Gallery of Art.

Charles Birnbaum, Coordinator of the Historic Landscape Initiative of the National Park Service Heritage

Preservation Services Program, had suggested that I contact Robin Karson, founding Executive Director of the Library of American Landscape History (LALH), about publishing a second edition; but Robin contacted me first through my old friend Paul Wright of University of Massachusetts Press who located me in exile in Fort Lauderdale via our mutual friend Carol Hurd Green, co-author of another book with me. My thanks are due to Robin Karson and Jane Roy Brown of LALH and to Carol Betsch of University of Massachusetts Press for engineering the production of this book and their championing of appreciation and preservation of historic landscapes.

My former colleagues and constantly stalwart friends Joan Brigham, Flora Gonzalez, and Carol Hurd Green have provided moral support, great conversation, and accommodations in Cambridge through the years, especially after I moved from Boston in 1995. All along, my children Julia Lentini and Marc Lindow grew to maturity with successful careers and families—the pride of my life. Most recently and importantly, Neil Perrone has been more than my anchor. He is my *consigliere*, running interference when hurricanes and other daily traumas disrupt life and the process of writing. Having heard or read the whole manuscript, he has constantly raised insightful questions that have informed my expanded explanations and reorganization. Also, he has made me laugh through the process, a gift beyond measure.

First and last, my mentor and dear friend Henry D. Shapiro (1937-2003) offered his encouragement and intellectual insights about my career and this book from their inception. I have used his valuable marginalia on old manuscripts in my revisions, still feeling his presence; and I only regret he is no longer with us to continue to inspire with his jovial spirit and intellect. I dedicate this revised edition to him and regret that he could not see it in his living years. He cared. He mattered. I can still hear his voice.

Blanche M. G. Linden
Fort Lauderdale, Florida

INDEX